MARTIN BUBER'S
LIFE AND WORK

MARTIN BUBER'S

LIFE AND WORK

The Later Years, 1945-1965

Maurice Friedman

Wayne State University Press   Detroit   1988

92   91   90   89   88   5   4   3   2   1

Library of Congress Cataloging-in-Publication Data

Friedman, Maurice S.
    Martin Buber's life and work.

    Originally published: New York: Dutton, c1981–c1983.
    Includes bibliographies and indexes.
    Contents: [1] The early years, 1878–1923 — [2] The middle years, 1923–1945 — [3] The later years, 1945–1965.
        1. Buber, Martin, 1878–1965.   2. Philosophers, Jewish—Germany—Biography.   3. Philosophers—Germany—Biography.   4. Zionists—Germany—Biography.   5. Jews—Germany—Biography.   6. Jews, German—Israel—Biography.
    I. Title.
B3213.B84F727   1988   296.3′092′4   87–25415
ISBN 0–8143–1946–7 (pbk. : v. 3 : alk. paper)

Erratum

The pages from the original printing by E. P. Dutton, Inc. were used in producing this reprint. Miscellaneous errors were corrected with the exception of a repeated spelling error. Dag Hammarskjöld is spelled consistently as Hammarskjøld.

For Eugenia

who shared in my
meetings with
Martin Buber

"*In hours of clarity man has come to understand that what he likes to call the progress of the human race does not proceed along the highroad at all. Rather we must set out ever again making our way precariously along a narrow ridge between abysses.*"

—MARTIN BUBER, "In the Crisis,"
Paths in Utopia

Contents

CONTENTS

NOTES AND SOURCES

Preface

Martin Buber's Life and Work was originally titled *Encounter on the Narrow Ridge*. This encounter began with the personal events of Buber's life and took place on an ever-wider stage until the second and still more the third volume of *Martin Buber's Life and Work* might properly be named "A Dialogue with the World." *The Early Years* shows the stages through which Buber reached personal wholeness—a ground on which to stand. *The Middle Years* and *The Later Years* show how, standing on that ground, Buber responded to the claims of the world in which he lived. Before I came to Israel in 1966 to do research for this book on a grant that Martin Buber, Hugo Bergmann, and Ernst Simon had helped me to obtain, I received a letter from Hugo Bergmann in which he suggested that one of my main tasks while in Israel would be to find out why Buber was so isolated. After I had been in Israel for two months, I went to see Hugo Bergmann and said to him, "That is the wrong question. The real question is 'Why is Buber so controversial?'" "It is very simple," Bergmann replied. "He was for Zionism and the state of Israel in general, but in many particulars he opposed the dominant policy."

It was not only in connection with the state of Israel that Buber was controversial. Although a greater worker for peace, controversy seemed to surround him his whole life: his opposition to Theodore Herzl, the founder of the Zionist movement, in the name of a democratic and cultural Zionism; his marriage at that time to a non-Jew who converted to Judaism; his espousal of a decentralized, federal socialism; his more than forty years of fighting for Jewish-Arab understanding; his leadership of the spiritual resistance to the Nazis in Hitler Germany; his ceaseless efforts for adult education and the Danish-model folk school; his support of the Halutziuth (Jewish pioneer) movement and the kibbutzim in Israel; his acceptance of the Peace Prize of the German Book Trade after the Second World War; his refusal to take sides in the "cold war"; his advocacy of nuclear disarmament; his championing of the cause of the Soviet Jews; his attack on Heidegger, Sartre, and Jung for contributing to the "eclipse of God"; his opposition to Ben-Gurion on the subjects of Arab refugees, military government in Israel, the "Lavon Affair," the "spy" trial of Aharon Cohen, and the execution of Eichmann.

I have had to make do with a paucity of details about Martin's wife Paula, undoubtedly the most important person in his life. Even reading her German works in their entirety did little to enable me to expand my narration of this "Ruth amid the alien corn." On the other hand, one of my chief sources of knowledge of Buber's life during its last fifteen years was my personal relationship with him: meetings with him (during his three visits to America and my first visit to Jerusalem) and the almost three hundred letters he wrote me. For this reason in the last chapters of *The Later Years* I have allowed my dialogue with Buber itself to show and not just the *product* of that dialogue, as in my earlier book *Martin Buber: The Life of Dialogue*. Along with Buber's numerous other significant relationships, my friendship with him forms an integral part of this "dialography" that traces the movements of Buber's life and thought primarily through its events and meetings and not as an evolution or development, as in conventional biographies.

Neither Hugo Bergmann nor Ernst Simon have shared with us the full story of their friendships with Buber, still less Paula who was a very private person. A seven-month stay at the Buber Archives of the Jewish and National University Library in Jerusalem in 1966 only netted me a dozen out of 45,000 letters to and from Buber ("I should rather that Professor Friedman not have access to a single letter before they are organized according to our philosophy of archiving," the director of the library said in my presence). As a result of all this I have been keenly aware of the lack of concrete personal material for my dialography. I have wanted for this reason to make full use of my own personal contacts and correspondence with Martin Buber. Later biographers will have access to the Buber correspondence as I did not, beyond the selection of 1,500 letters published in the *Briefwechsel*. But they would not otherwise have available to them my own story of my relation to Buber, which I wish to preserve in this fashion for posterity.

There is another reason still for the inclusion of my dialogue with Buber in *The Later Years*. When people ask me, as they often do, "What was Buber like as a person?" I often see behind that question another, unasked one: "Was he really a man of dialogue?" How he related over time to one disciple, who certainly does not claim to be one of the most important persons in Buber's life, affords a glimpse into the way in which he lived "the life of dialogue." This is especially so because I include in my narration the times when I found myself overburdened by his unremitting pressure to see to the finishing up of publishing in which we were coinvolved. At such times he seemed lacking in precisely that "inclusion," or "imagining the real" that forms the cornerstone of his philosophy of dialogue.

I wrote and made a first major cut on *The Early Years* between 1966 and 1969. I did not begin work on *The Middle Years* until 1972, while my most concentrated work on *The Later Years* took place during the years 1977 through 1980. In this third volume, as in the first two, I have myself translated all the material from the German except that already existing in reliable published translation (which did *not* include the exchange of letters between Buber and others edited in three volumes by Grete Schaeder and, as of this writing, still intended to appear in English translation). In this volume, too, I have almost entirely avoided footnotes while referring to notes inserted into the Sources for particular chapters at the back, or to longer Notes also set in the back. I have placed in a long Note to Chapter 14 the material connected with the writing and publishing of Buber's "Mystery Play" *Elijah*.

MAURICE FRIEDMAN

Solana Beach, California
Spring 1983

Acknowledgments

I AM INDEBTED to my former wife, Eugenia Friedman, who shared much of my interchange with Martin Buber, for counsel as to which references to my dialogue with Buber really contribute to an understanding of Buber's life and thought. I am also indebted to my friend Virginia Shabatay who has spent untold hours in helping me to edit and where possible cut both the second volume and the third. I also wish to express my gratitude to my friend and longtime editor Richard Huett for his invaluable assistance in making the second and third volumes accessible to a wider audience. He brought to my attention countless places that needed clarification or retranslation. "In twenty years of editing I cannot recall a book that occupied me as intensively," Huett wrote me. I am also grateful to my friend and former student Judith Stoup (now Laurel Mannen), who accomplished the difficult task of bringing the manuscript of the second and third volumes into finished form.

Once again I must acknowledge my special and unusual indebtedness to Dr. Grete Schaeder of Göttingen, Germany. In *The Later Years,* as in the two earlier volumes of this work, I used her selection and edition of the exchange of letters in the three volumes of the *Buber*

Briefwechsel and did so in such a thorough fashion that, to some extent, *The Later Years,* too, may be looked at as a cooperative endeavor for which she laid much of the groundwork. In addition, in *The Later Years* as in *The Middle Years* she made painstaking criticisms and suggestions that helped me improve the text in numerous ways. Over and above this, Dr. Schaeder performed a special service for *The Later Years* by suggesting a number of specific omissions that would serve the double purpose of cutting down overly long chapters and moderating my own presence in the volume, which she rightly felt might prove irritating to some readers. Even when I could not follow her prompting (as in the case of the advice that Buber gave me about writing a novel, which I retained because I felt it showed something unique and characteristic about his way of approaching work), I am grateful to her for bringing me to reconsider the grounds for my action. Her active help and generous confirmation of my "dialography" have been most heartening as I come to the end of seventeen years of work on these three volumes.

PART I

The End of the Mandate and the Beginning of the State

(1945–1951)

CHAPTER 1

Jewish-Arab Rapprochement and Conflict

DURING THE YEARS of the Second World War, fighting never actually reached Palestine, and the Arabs, though sympathetic to the Nazis as enemies of the Jews, let their revolt against the British Mandate and the Yishuv become relatively inactive during the war. As a result, the war provided a background for Jewish-Arab cooperation, short-lived as that was, and in this movement Buber was fully active, for all his great productivity during this period.

Buber early found himself compelled to take sides in the conflict between the more "political" Zionists and the more "practical" ones, between those who wanted to begin by acquiring political concessions and then build the settlements and those who felt that the factual work of settlement must precede the aspiration to legal rights. His identification with the latter stemmed, he said in 1958, "from the insight that the tremendous double work of completing the rebirth of the Jewish people and its becoming a member of the world of the

Near East cannot be accomplished through a sudden, insufficiently prepared mass settlement, but only through the preparing activity of generations in the land." This meant a pioneering of work and peace, a selective, organic principle of development which would produce a core of Jewish community that could serve as the base for the rebirth of the people. It also meant practical economic and social cooperation with the Arabs, a solidarity founded on trust and working together.

From this standpoint Buber did not hesitate to attack some of the political factions of the Yishuv for wishing to oppose Hitler yet adopt his ways of acting in the name of a Jewish national egotism seen as an end in itself. In "They and We" (November 1939), an essay commemorating the first anniversary of *Kristallnacht,* Buber said that he knew of no view so degrading to the Jews as this one in which the Nazi caricature of injustice, "the grimace of ice-cold baseness, of a cruelty that functions like a machine, a golem on whose brow the name of Satan is inscribed," is taken as a model by some Jews at the very time that Hitler is desecrating and destroying their communities one after the other. Those who say that they want to be strong in order to prosper on the soil of the land want to serve Hitler's god after a Hebrew name has been conferred upon him. "And whoever acts like Hitler will meet his downfall along with him. . . . We must combat the realm of sacrilege by combating the sacrilege." This motif was repeated by Buber in his retrospective address "Israel and the Command of the Spirit" in 1958, and neither his early nor his later statement served to make him popular among his fellow Jews.

Buber, of course, was not simply name-calling. He knew that the Jewish settlement was *not* a henchman of British imperalism, but he lamented that the way in which the Jews came to Palestine made it possible and in many cases inevitable that the Arabs would think this. We have handed over the flag of Zion to the British, who used it for their own purposes, Buber wrote in an essay, "On Our Policy" (1939), and now that they no longer need it, interpret the contract in accordance with their own profits rather than from fixed political principles. British interests lay in a decentralization exactly opposite to the Jewish settlement's need for concentration. Even after the British Empire was replaced by a Commonwealth, the Yishuv was still falsely considered the agent of British imperialism. Instead there should have been a comprehensive plan that could make the Jewish settlement the organic center not only of the Jewish people but also of the rising Near East, a great plan that would have made the Arabs of Palestine partners in the work of building the land. This could have led to a cooperation between the two nations in which the question of numerical proportions would no longer be of decisive importance.

Recalling that he had expressed all these thoughts twenty years before in committees of the Zionist Congress and in the councils of Zionist groups, Buber blamed himself for that prejudice against saying things in public which was dominant in his group. If he and his friends had not placed Zionist discipline above the dictates of their own political understanding, they could have been of greater influence. To those who said that it was now too late to reach any agreement other than total withdrawal from the settlement project, Buber said that while the task had become more difficult, cooperation was still possible on the basis of real trust. Although a thousand buds of Arab trust that were beginning to grow had been destroyed, it was still possible to move in the direction of an alliance and a comprehensive bond between two brother nations.

Buber took up the same criticism from a historical standpoint in "The Gods of the Nations and God" (1941), in which, contrasting the princes of all the nations with the command to Israel to reveal the one, true God, he pointed out that the revelation of God is always a commandment, that the only sphere in which Israel can point out the absolute is in and through its own life. "Though something of righteousness may become evident in the life of the individual, righteousness itself can only become visibly embodied in the structures of the life of a people. . . . Only life can demonstrate the absolute, and it must be the life of the people as a whole." This task was undertaken by generations of pioneers who set the tablets of social justice over their undreamed-of capacity for productiveness. "But the islands they created are swept by the waves of a life that knows no tablets, a life without a common spirit, without a common order." The hope that the settlement would become the center of the Jewish people is meaningless if this center does not have some center other than itself. This motif Buber expanded at great length, more affirmatively in his 1943 essay, "The Regeneration of a People," in which he pointed out that what bound the comrades together was the common binding with the center, that is with the salvation and future of the settlement and with the greater ideal represented in it. There he discussed at length the origin of the type of the Halutz, or pioneer, and the organic selective process which built up the generations of the land until the Hitler years flooded it with people who did not come because of belief in a social and national movement but out of sheer necessity for survival.

In another essay written in these years, Buber set up "Hebrew Humanism" in opposition to that Jewish nationalism which regards Israel as a nation like unto other nations recognizing no task for Israel beyond that of preserving and asserting itself. Buber found the basis for this Hebrew humanism in the humanism of the Bible. This was not for Buber a matter of the ideal versus the practical but of the whole versus the part. "The men in the Bible are sinners like ourselves, but there is one sin they do not commit, our arch-sin: they do not dare confine God to a circumscribed space or division of life, to 'religion. . . .' To divide life into a private life of morality and a public one in which any means can be used to the end is to invite destruction of the people's existence." This is not a matter of absolute pacifism or some impossible total justice but of drawing the demarcation line anew in every situation.

> It is true that we are not able to live in perfect justice, and in order to preserve the community of man, we are often compelled to accept wrongs in decisions concerning the community. But what matters is that in every hour of decision we are aware of our responsibility and summon our conscience to weigh exactly how much is necessary to preserve the community, and accept just so much and no more.

Buber saw this as a choice placed before Zionism in that hour. An Israel that has only a hollow self-assertion as its goal will pass away like all other small nations that tomorrow will be weighed in the balance and found wanting! Only the covenant, the wholeness and uniqueness of an Israel dedicated to the task of righteousness, will bring with it strength and survival.

The prophetic note that sounded forth from "Hebrew Humanism" reverberated also in "False Prophets." The "false prophets," in Hezekiah's time and in ours, pursue an illusion-politics that promises unconditional success and security. They adore what F. Scott Fitzgerald called "the bitch goddess Success" and achieve it by promising it to the people. They honestly want success for the people; they do not deceive intentionally, they are self-deceived, by "the deceit of their own heart." The true prophets, in contrast, "know that ten successes that are nothing but successes can lead to defeat, while on the contrary ten failures can add up to a victory, provided the spirit stands firm." The link with the "suffering servant" becomes clear here when Buber speaks of the moment the true prophet is thrown into the pit, like Jeremiah. Then the spirit that is still alive in Israel "bursts into flame, and the turning begins in secret which, in the midst of the deepest distress, will lead to renewal." The connection with Buber's own life in Israel is equally clear, if not explicit, when Buber speaks of the true prophet as having to endure having the true word he hears "treated as though it only held true for some 'ideological' sphere, 'morals' or 'religion,' but not for the real life of the people." Buber did not claim that he or anyone else was a Jeremiah or a Micaiah. But at every street corner one could still run into the false prophet with "empty air issuing from his mouth." Look him straight in the eye, and perhaps the next time he tells his dream as if it were the word of God, he will trip over a phrase and pause.

Buber's later statements became, if anything, stronger. "Never in the course of our history were spirit and life so far from each other as in this era of 'rebirth,'" Buber commented in 1948, unless, he added, one wants to call collective self-seeking "spirit." The two tendencies in Zionism go back to the early times of Israel, Buber asserted. One is toward "normalization," really a form of *national* assimilation in which, in contrast to individual assimilation, the nation is still identified as Jewish but has lost any meaningful Jewish identity in its concern to be like all the other nations. It was this concern which blinded leaders of the Yishuv to the necessity of founding a comprehensive solidarity with the Arabs. In 1958, Buber stressed the necessity of reaching a genuine understanding so that Israel should not have to exist as an enclave of the Western world in the midst of the already existing peoples of the Near East. The first postulate of the Zionism Buber represented, that of the creation of the core of a community, had been substantially realized even if not completed. But the awakening of a Jewish-Arab consciousness of solidarity had been realized only in sporadic, locally limited undertakings of good neighborliness and never as an organized effort or as a practical program of comprehensive cooperation.

Buber's activity on behalf of Jewish-Arab cooperation was by no means limited to essays and speeches. He was intensely involved in practical politics, although now, in contrast to 1921 and 1929, it was minority politics rather than the mainstream of the Zionist movement. In 1939 a loose working community of those concerned about bettering Jewish-Arab relations was formed under the name of the League for Jewish-Arab Rapprochement and Cooperation. At the request of the League a meeting took place with the Jewish Agency on October 25, 1939, in which Buber, R'Binyamin, and Chaim Kalvarisky, all of Brit Shalom, represented the League and Ben-Gurion and others represented the Agency. In 1940 the League proposed a scheme in which the British Mandate over Palestine would come to an end in ten years, during which period Jewish immigration would be permitted up to the attainment of numerical equality of the Jews and the Arabs. After ten years a binational independent state would be set up on the basis of parity in government and legislative bodies. The scheme also envisaged this state's joining an Arab confederation as an autonomous unit and a practical program for wide economic cooperation between the Jews and the Arabs.

During this same period majority Zionist politics moved in the opposite direction, and in 1942 at the Hotel Biltmore in New York City, the proponents of the creation of a Jewish state won official Zionist policy to their side, including the cooperation of Chaim Weizmann, with whom Buber tried to talk as late as 1944, but who was, reluctantly or otherwise, in the tow of the majority. This call for the creation of a Jewish state with an eventual Jewish majority resulted in the consolidation of all the binationalist groups, left, right, and center. The leftist Hashomer Hatzaïr joined the League for Jewish-Arab Rapprochement and Cooperation, and on June 23, 1942, the organization issued a comprehensive counterproposal, signed by Buber, Kalvarisky, Ernst Simon, Gavriel Stern, David Senator, and others. While reaffirming the principle of building up Palestine as the common homeland of the Jewish people, this statement also called for a "mutual, comprehensive, and permanent understanding and agreement between the two peoples." It recognized the right of the Jews to immigrate to Palestine up to its full economic absorptive capacity and of the Yishuv to become a complete and autonomous economic, cultural, social, and political entity. But it also recognized the right of the Arabs of Palestine to a national autonomous life and to relations with other sections of the Arab people and it affirmed nondomination of one people over the other, regardless of the numerical relationship, and a binational regime that would participate in a federation with the neighboring Arab countries when conditions permitted.

This was a time of growing polarization and politicization, and the activities of the League were subject to sharp and hostile attacks by the dominant Zionist factions both in Palestine and abroad. Those who espoused a Jewish state with a Jewish majority dubbed their program "defeatism," a label which Buber vigorously refuted in a 1941 article by that name. Because he had said that to truly serve an idea meant to pay attention to the changing situations and strive to realize the kernel of one's idea in the form at present possible, Buber was charged with being a political defeatist. In a written response, since no oral response was then possible, Buber said, "It is not at all true that I and my friends expect a 'defeat' of our people." What they really feared was the setback arising from illusionary politics and self-deceptions. Not the abstract idea but the concrete present situation must be the touchstone of preparation and planning. Facing the actual contradictions on this earth is the true enemy of defeatism.

The signing of the League program contributed to the setting up of a new group called Ihud (Union), most of the members of whom belonged to the League but preferred to do so as a bloc rather than be referred to as "the intellectuals." Judah Magnes, who had never belonged to any binationalist organization before, was finally induced to participate in Ihud, which thereafter recognized him as its founder even though he insisted that there simply be an executive committee and that he not be its head. This committee was composed of Buber, Kalvarisky, Magnes, Smilansky, Henrietta Szold (the founder of Hadassah), and Justice Valero, and its first meeting took place on August 11, 1942. It called for a revival of the whole Semitic world through Jewish-Arab social, economic, cultural, and political cooperation: a binational government, participation in a larger Near Eastern federation, and a covenant with the Anglo-American union made up the other planks of its platform, though it was never in fact a party and never sent a single representative to the Knesset once the State of Israel was established.

In September 1943 the Swiss theologian and Old Testament scholar Bruno Balscheit wrote Buber telling him that the Swiss were particularly interested in his ideas concerning a Near East Federation as a solution to the problem of the coexistence of the Jews and Arabs in Palestine. He pointed out that in Switzerland federation had evolved organically and that in general it could not be made but must rise from a common life-feeling of the peoples involved—perhaps in the fight against a common enemy or liberation from some disorder suffered in common. But if such a common life-feeling is found, then linguistic and religious oppositions can exist freely alongside each other within the political order. "Those among us with vision hope from our hearts that you will succeed in finding Palestine such a way in the future." The response from within Palestine was not so encouraging. The new teaching of the youth, wrote Gideon Freudenberg, administrator of the cultural commission of Nahalal, the oldest moshav (cooperative settlement), as proclaimed in the official Youth Day in September 1943, was that three factors are necessary for the realization of Zionism: the political, economic, and *military*. "The youth shall establish an army with all its splendid modern weapons: hand grenades, bombs, light and heavy machine guns, etc., etc."

Buber recognized, in a 1944 essay, that the unique relation of people that constitutes the heart of the idea of Zion and without which Israel could not even achieve the lesser goal of becoming a nation is made more difficult by having "to reckon with the coexistence of another people in the same country, of cognate origin and language but mainly foreign in tradition, structure and outlook." But he saw a high purpose and significance behind the increasing difficulty of the task. "Such is the hard but not ungracious way of life itself."

In 1944 a failing journal of Robert Weltsch's, *Problems of the Day*, was taken over by Ihud and called simply *Problems (Ba'ayot)* with Buber as the editor in chief and Ernst Simon as the editor. In the first issue Buber published an editorial titled "We Establish a Platform" in which he set forth as the goal of *Ba'ayot* the reality that underlay the problems of the Yishuv. To meet the stern demands of the hour of crisis and decision that were upon them Buber proposed to confront the reality of the Yishuv with the idea of Zion whose three essential ingredients were: more equitable relations between individuals and between groups, an independent nation participating in the development and ordering of the Near East, and an alliance of peoples placing the mutual contact of nations on the basis of freedom and justice. As Ernst Simon has pointed out, this editorial contrasts with the editorial with which he opened *Der Jude* more than a quarter of a century before in that it was more concrete and that it did not purport to speak for the Zionist movement as a whole.

Although Ihud included members of the left wing of the Labor Federation, members of the Third Aliyah, the new immigrants from Germany, members of the former Brit Shalom and of the League for Arab-Jewish Rapprochement and Cooperation, religious Halutzim, as well as Buber, Simon, Hugo Bergmann, and Magnes, still it was not able to fulfill Magnes's goal of undertaking practical projects in social and cultural work and in personal relations. It remained a limited circle without strong impact on public life, making its appeal to the people more by the written than the spoken word. Ihud was also fatally divided on the question of immigration, the Marxist "Young Guard" demanding free and unlimited immigration of Jews and Magnes and Buber advocating immigration up to numerical parity but not to a majority. Both Arab and Jewish publicists claimed that Ihud was opposed to Zionism and that it weakened Jewish unity. A storm of protests and demands that Magnes should resign from the presidency of the Hebrew University came from America, and the American Hadassah at its national convention went out of its way to disavow the binationalism of Henrietta Szold, its founder. To the students of the Hebrew University, the overwhelming majority of whom radically rejected Ihud, Buber was more and more regarded as the spiritual head of the Ihud movement. As a result his image became politicized, which often led them to reject Buber as a teacher and as a person as well. Although Buber sought again and again to make an impact on politics in his way, it remained his unlucky love. Surrounded by a small circle of significant men who shared his position, he remained politically isolated. At the same time Nahum Goldmann, Gerson, Ben-Chorin, and many, many others have testified how they were constantly astonished by how this man, who seemingly lived withdrawn in his study, was closely informed and bound up with all the questions and demands of his day and remained so to the end of his life.

In the past, Buber had long spoken for and believed in unlimited immigration for the Jews and had held that an understanding with the Arabs could be reached on this basis. But four years in Palestine were enough to convince him of his error. "The sixty-four-year-old was still thoroughly able and ready to allow himself to be taught by reality," writes Simon. The leadership of the leftist Hashomer Hatzaïr, in contrast, would not subscribe to this limitation of immigration, and expressly separated itself from this aspect of the League's program, as the Marxist Young Guard did from that of Ihud. Thus the front of the binationalists was by no means a solid one. Nonetheless, the lines were clearly drawn. The Zionist majority was ready to renounce the unity of Palestine in order to get a Jewish state. The binationalists, on the other hand, were ready to renounce the Jewish state in order to preserve the unity of Palestine.

In 1945, Ihud published in English a collection of essays on Jewish-Arab cooperation, *Towards Union in Palestine*, edited by Buber, Magnes, and Simon. Buber's contribution to this book was "Our Reply" to those sincere young critics who saw Ihud as a group of "still, pure, admonitory" voices from the height of the "moral Olympus" who urged compromise as a matter of principle. Buber began by rejecting the notion that the members of Ihud were detached intellectuals who did not suffer, and he did so in a deeply personal manner. "Those who suffer most deeply have ceased crying. . . .Those who have been in hell, and have returned to the light of day again, have learned to speak quietly and clearly. . . . no matter whether a whole people is listening or only a few individuals." For the sake of the absolute, it is permissible and defensible to act within the sphere of the relative as the situation demands: "The way of claims and declarations, the way of losing control and lashing out, cannot save us, but only the hard way that leads through compromise to real service of this country." Real service, as Buber saw it, was working toward a great peace with the neighboring peoples "which alone can render possible a common development of this plot of land as the vanguard of the progressing Near East," as opposed to a fictitious, short-lived peace that is no more than a feeble intermission. In isolation, surrounded by hate and distrust, the great creative task that awaits the people of Israel, decimated and violated though they are, cannot even be imagined. Another, equally prophetic, statement that Puber made in "Our Reply" was that sooner or later even those favorably disposed would confront the Yishuv with the question: What proposals have you to make for the peaceful development of the Near East? "Everything will depend on whether another answer, a genuine one, will have matured in us by then."

In a Hebrew essay in 1944, Buber had had one of his first direct confrontations with David Ben-Gurion, the leader of the Zionist majority and later the first prime minister of the State of Israel. Ben-Gurion, in a speech, demanded a numerical majority in the country, in contrast to Joseph Sprinzak, who years before had offered the formula "not a majority but many." In taking the side of Sprinzak against Ben-Gurion, Buber set the tone for all his future encounters with this superb politician. "Many is a concept from the very reality of life; whereas majority is a purely political concept." "We strive towards having as many Jews as possible immigrate to Israel, whereas he strives towards their attaining a majority in the country." The Jews in Palestine could not expect the Arabs to accept Ben-Gurion's assurances that the idea of a Jewish state based on national justice and national equality would be binding on future generations; for the history of relations between majority and minority nations gives no grounds for optimism on this point. "It is natural," said Buber, "that the trust of the Arabs in this respect is no greater than our trust in them." Ben-Gurion's demand for a political majority "will bring only the division of the country, that is, the formation of a tiny Jewish state with complete militarization which will not endure long." Immigration above numerical equality could be attained under binationalism if the Jews succeeded in dispelling the misgivings of the Arabs against a Jewish majority. "Instead of separate national economic systems, there should be a common, nationwide economic system in the success of which both peoples are interested and whose common cherishing of it may bring about mutual trust which in its turn may lead to far-reaching understanding."

In 1944, Buber also published in Hebrew an ironic dialogue about "Biltmore" between a "Loyal One" and a "Traitor." The "Traitor," Buber himself, asks the "Loyal One" why there is so much talk in the streets about the Gibeonites, the non-Jewish people who were allowed to live by Joshua in biblical times but were forced to live only as hewers of wood and drawers of water. The "Loyal One" denies that the Biltmore plan intends to degrade part of the population of the country to the status of second-class citizens, but the "Traitor" points out that if a people is deprived of political, collective equality, then it naturally follows that it will soon assume second-class status. This prophecy is one that even Ernst Simon objected to in the editorial meeting of *Ba'ayot* at which Buber proposed to publish this article. "Surely we who have been so terribly used by others would never treat our minorities in the same way?" Simon protested. But Buber refused to yield, and seventeen years later in his Introduction to the collection of Hebrew essays by Buber *People and World* in which this essay was reprinted, Simon acknowledged, with bitterness, that Buber had been right. Through military and employment restrictions the Arabs in Israel had been reduced, in fact even though not legally, to the status of second-class citizens.

A glimpse of Buber's day-by-day life during this period is provided us by Heinz Politzer, the well-known Kafka scholar who was Buber's neighbor in Dir Abu Tor from the time the Germans marched against El Alamein and threatened the Jewish community in Palestine with destruction, up to the time when the British prepared to depart, leaving the country in a state of utter confusion.

> For more than four years I had the opportunity of observing Buber in his conversations with members of his family, with his Arab servant Jalil, with Jewish students and Arab neighbors, with notables, scholars and clergymen from many nations and of many creeds, and even and especially with children, and I cannot recall one instance when Buber would have withheld himself, when he would not have tried to include in his conversations the silence beneath the words of the other. . . . I very seldom missed the quality of a genuine dialogue.

Gavriel Stern, one-time secretary to Judah Magnes, leftist journalist, and assistant to Buber and Simon in editing *Ba'ayot,* tells that he once brought an Arab teacher to visit Buber. The conversation went rather heavily until the Arab teacher chanced to speak of a "Freudian slip." At that Buber delivered a brilliant lecture on Freud and his own views of him and the whole conversation became much more animated! Isaac Malho, a French-speaking Palestinian Jew, has characterized the Buber of that period as a man who saw humanity as naked from its very genesis, who was not afraid to touch the forbidden fruit of reality, and who wanted to learn to distinguish good from evil. Before the "War of Liberation" Malho, accompanied by several friends, went to see Buber in his house in Dir Abu Tor. After an hour of conversation between Buber and his political antagonists who held that violence was justifiable for a worthy objective, his adversaries found themselves charmed by his sparkling wit and his logic emanating from "a real Jewish heart." "Who knows?" one of them asked on the way home, "perhaps one day it will be necessary to make use of his contacts, his politics of rapprochement on behalf of this nation for which he has always fought courageously."

Buber's relation with Judah Leib Magnes was in itself one of the remarkable dialogues of this period of Buber's life, even apart from the political activities that they shared. This dialogue was founded on a great deal of mutual respect despite the differences in the men's personalities. While both men were eminently practical, Buber's interests were almost universal in their scope, whereas Magnes had restricted himself in his concerns. Buber was much more flexible in tactics than Magnes, who, even in his personal life, remained the president with the personality of a president. As a result, few persons were able to enter into the sort of give and take with him in which they might offer advice. But Magnes was able to accept advice from Buber on many things, even though there was much about which they did not agree. Magnes had something of the austerity of the Quaker in his personality, whereas Buber had a great deal of warmth and humor. Buber often came to the Magnes house for discussions with Magnes alone and with others. The Arab maid who pronounced *b*'s like *p*'s, would say, "Pooper is on the phone." As a result the Magnes family, to itself, called him "Pooper." Once during the time when sugar was scarce, the maid came to Mrs. Magnes greatly agitated and said, "What shall we do? Pooper wants three pieces of sugar in his tea!" "Let him have it and we shall do without it," replied Mrs. Magnes, ready to indulge Buber's inveterate love of sugar. Once some friends in Switzerland sent Buber and his family a package of necessities that were no longer available in Palestine during the war years. At that time only fixed "utility-wares" were to be had, which led Buber to remark to Ben-Chorin, "Soon there will only be utility-people."

A paralysis which seemed to affect not only his soul but to cleave to the world around him made it impossible for a long while for Buber to write a personal letter to anyone outside of Palestine. Only on September 16, 1945, months after the cessation of the war in Europe and a month after the surrender of the Japanese to the United States, did that sense of paralysis lift. The first letter that he wrote was to Hermann Hesse, and the time was the evening after the "long day," as the Jews call the Day of Atonement. "I have not had to become reconciled with anyone," Buber wrote Hesse, "only with all, at times even myself." "I have never ceased to stand in inner communication with you," he added. "You were so present to me the whole time that I have to keep reminding myself that you knew nothing of it." Hesse's last novel, *The Glass Bead Game* (or *Magister Ludi* as it is sometimes called in English translation), had been during that time like a personal message to him and to Paula, a rare "triumph of the spirit," a witness, of the spirit in chains, for that which is not in chains.

In October 1945, Leonhard Ragaz wrote Buber how precious it was to hear from him again and to be in contact with the Holy Land. "That the swastika succeeded in reaching Acropolis but not Zion belongs, for me, to the greatest miracles of the hand of God in these days. And the trust that this hand rules rested strongly on the fact that *you* are in Jerusalem, on Zion or *to* Zion, literally and spiritually." Ragaz could not believe then any more than before in the "Jewish state," "But I believe unshakably that God wills to erect Zion anew in Eretz Israel." Ragaz also believed that one day the two "confessions"— Judaism and Christianity—would meet, and he regarded Buber as the essential contribution to this goal from the side of Judaism and the sure guarantee that this meeting would be total.

Buber's first letter to Hans Trüb after a long break crossed with one from Trüb to him, which Buber took as a sign of the ontic connection between the two of them. That Trüb had composed himself so that he was now really able to write for the first time and leave nothing essential unsaid revealed to Buber "something of the human being in this time, and has confirmed and strengthened my rewon openness to humanity." Trüb told Buber how Rudolf Pannwitz, who had gone with his wife to Switzerland in the summer of 1939, had broken with him when Trüb was no longer able to help Pannwitz financially.

Buber was very struck by this and wrote Trüb that he no longer had access in general to the autocrats of the spirit, who had grown even stranger to him than the others. "They will have to learn humility before one can again undertake something with them." These years had been for him ones of unforeseen productivity and a productivity ever again surprising to him, Buber related, so that some of the plans that had extended over decades had finally been executed. "It is the real epoch of *work* in my life."

Buber gave Trüb a full picture of his life at that time. His university work had been satisfying, but he had rejected the position of rector that had been offered to him because he did not wish to interrupt his own work. Although the housework in wartime had absorbed Paula's energies in a way hardly to be imagined, she had also been able to do important work. They had gone on their first two-week holiday to the sea since 1939 and that had done them, especially Paula, good. "Bärbel," their granddaughter Barbara, who had gone to a trade school, had married a colleague of hers and lived in Haifa as a teacher of drawing. Judith, the younger granddaughter, was living with Martin and Paula and studying at the university. "She too wants to become a teacher." (She became a professor of political science.) "Eva lives with her husband [Ludwig Strauss] and younger son in the great children and youth village Ben Shemen, where Ludwig teaches. . . . Rafael has already for a long time left the kibbutz where he had lived, bought himself a last auto and drives it since then (mostly military transports) with great virtuosity and discretion." Buber asked Trüb in turn for news of his old friends from Germany—Alfons Paquet, Ernst Michel, Wilhelm Michel, Viktor von Weizsäcker, Joseph Wittig. "We have no possibility at all of any connection with Germany."

In December, however, Buber received a report about Germany from Robert Weltsch, who had gone to attend the Nuremberg trials. "Germany is dismally destroyed," Weltsch reported, "and the people have no orientation at all, neither intellectual nor political." The Nuremberg trials Weltsch found to be a showpiece that could have no kindling effect and were wholly uninteresting. "The real cares and problems of mankind lie entirely elsewhere today." But Weltsch did not regret that he was there *or* that he was not at that point in Palestine. "I have written for twenty-five years in vain," he said in a trenchant comment on the direction the official Zionist majority had taken.

Buber's failure to complete *The Place of Faith*, which he was writing during this whole period of surprisingly great productivity, remains intriguing. This was the book in connection with which he had written to Hans Trüb and Ludwig Binswanger while he was still in Germany, asking for information concerning madness and the special world of the schizophrenic and paranoiac that takes the place of the common world that so-called normal people share. In March 1942, Buber read to Walter Goldstein from his notes which he told him were a sketch for a whole book, *The Place of Faith.* "God is only in the real situation," Buber read. Science and knowledge must be without God. That is perhaps cruel but true. "I hope that I shall never become so old or senile that I shall become less toughminded in this matter," Buber said to Goldstein. In December 1945, Buber wrote to Hans Trüb, "For my book about what I call the coexistent chaos, I would ask not merely for literary reference but a deeper participation and cooperation from you. I can get literary references from others, but what I need essentially, it seems to me, I can get only from you: because of our common view. But perhaps I must first explain to you personally what it concerns. It is a work that has been germinating for many years and very slowly; that belongs to its essence." In June 1946, Buber wrote to Ludwig Binswanger of his concern with "the problem of the disintegration of the world-image in certain abnormal states"— dreams, intoxications, psychoses—states that are qualitatively different from what ordinary people experience as regards the coherence and order of the outer world. Expressing the same concern in an August 1946 letter to Trüb, Buber added, "It is not a question of experience, it is a question—as important as it is uncanny—of being itself. Everything psychological can be only an aid here, but an indispensable one. I need it for this second and apparently last part of my philosophy far more than I needed it for the first."

Despite all this, *The Place of Faith* was never published and no manuscript or notes for it are to be found in the Martin Buber Archives in the Hebrew University Library. Whether Buber actually destroyed his notes or simply converted them into the philosophical anthropology that is set forth in *The Knowledge of Man,* such as, "What Is Common to All," we cannot know. My notes on Buber's seminars on "The Unconscious" that he gave to members of the Washington School of Psychiatry and published in his "Gleanings" are the only other glimpse we can get into this unfinished "second part" of Buber's philosophy.

During this period, as always, Buber kept in contact with his friends abroad and with the developing situation in Palestine. At the end of January 1946 Eduard Strauss wrote Buber a birthday letter from New York in which he said, "I feel myself altogether driven out of my home by every word that I hear from the Land. The little strength that I still have I use, when the possibility is afforded me, to attack criminal superficiality and the cynicism of the all too complacent."

At the very same time Albert Einstein wrote Buber from America reporting on his testimony in Washington before the Anglo-American Committee of Enquiry regarding the problems of European Jewry and Palestine. With remarkable frankness Einstein spoke to the Committee, composed of six Englishmen and six Americans, of how the British Mandate Government had from the beginning sought to sabotage the realization of the Balfour Declaration by making immigration difficult, limiting the landholding Jews, and by systematic incitement of the Arab masses, along with arranging for riots in which the Mandate government systematically cooperated. Einstein proposed, like Magnes, a binational government directly under United Nations' supervision, since there was no hope for betterment of conditions as long as the British retained the Mandate, and the erection of a Jewish state with division of the existing populations seemed to him impracticable. This was hard for the British half of the Committee to take, as Einstein himself reported, though he gave his testimony quietly and amiably without any passion. "I almost forgot that I shared with them my conviction," wrote Einstein, "that from the standpoint of the British government the Commission was a sort of 'smoke-screen' and that they did not have the slightest intention of letting themselves be influenced by its recommendations and proposals." At this some of the British members of the Committee became heated, and Einstein responded, "I would be delighted if I am proved to be wrong."

From Washington the Anglo-American Committee proceeded to Palestine. The Jewish Agency wanted the Jewish case to be presented by a single front of those favoring a Jewish state, but Ihud insisted on giving its independent testimony for a binational state. This took the form of a written statement asking for the immediate admission of 100,000 Jews, whether or not the Arabs consented, a Swiss model federation, two national communities with powers of taxation for cultural purposes, a gradual plan leading to binational independence and an eventual Middle East federation, and an attack on the discredited notion of self-determination by tiny nationalist sovereign units, such as Woodrow Wilson had hoped for at the end of the First World War. On March 14, 1946, in the hall of the Young Men's Christian Association in Jerusalem, Magnes, Buber, and Moses Smilansky presented oral testimony on behalf of Ihud. Buber and

Magnes made it clear that they "were not speaking in the name of the Hebrew University, where various opinions were held, but as residents of the country, and as Jews who thought it their duty to give voice to a view which, though different from the official Zionist program, was shared by large numbers of the population." Buber explained Ihud's concept of Zionism, and Magnes spoke of how binationalism was envisaged, including the concepts of political and numerical parity between the two nations. Buber declared that Israel's ability to form ties of cooperation and partnership with the Arabs, who were also struggling for national liberation and spiritual renaissance, was the test of the dream of Zion. But he also pointed out that what was at stake went beyond the boundaries of Zionism and even of the Near East. If a successful solution could be found to the Palestine problem, then a first, pioneer step "will have been taken toward a more just form of life between people and people." Magnes claimed that "a large part of the inarticulate section of the population believes more or less as we do."

Magnes's biographer, Norman Bentwich, describes this occasion as Magnes's "finest hour" politically. Richard Grossman, an English M.P. on the Commission, stated that, listening to Magnes, he undestood why he had been told that he "was the only reasonable Jew in Palestine." Judge Joseph C. Hutcheson, Jr., American chairman of the Committee, stated just before the closing of the hearing: "Dr. Magnes, I am not ready to assess your proposals, but I am a fairly old man, and I recognize moral power when I see it. If other leaders of opinion could show similar courage, sincerity, and wisdom, a solution of the problems of Palestine would soon be found."

The report of the Committee in May, after it had retired to Palestine to ponder the evidence, represented something of a victory for Ihud. It recommended the immediate immigration of 100,000 Jews, repeal of discriminatory legislation about land transfer, which kept Jews and Arabs separate, and the establishment of a Trust Administration of the United Nations which should take the form of neither a Jewish nor an Arab State but a binational country moving toward binational independence. This report was unanimous, but the British government, as Einstein had predicted, paid no attention to it and instead put forward a plan of its own that was immediately rejected both by Jews and Arabs.

After the Anglo-American Commission's report, Magnes went to America for a half year in order to plead his cause before the American public and to remove delusions and false accusations concerning binationalism. During his absence Buber and Moshe Smilansky wrote to General Sir Evelyn Barker, Commander in Chief of the British Army in Palestine, pleading with him to commute the death sentence for Joseph Simhon and Michael Ashbel, two Jewish youths who had taken part in the terrorist activities of the revisionist Irgun Zvai Le'umi, a national military organization outside of Haganah that had made an armed attack on the military airfield at Kastina. Buber and Smilansky pointed out that they had taken the same position in the case of Arabs sentenced to death during the riots and that, as persons who had worked tirelessly for peace in Palestine, they were obliged to point out that carrying out death sentences could only heighten the tension and make the attainment of peace more difficult. The two youths were subsequently pardoned. Buber's intervention on behalf of these terrorists, whose own position and activities he opposed with all of his being, is important for understanding Buber's encounter on the narrow ridge. Those who are themselves polarized tend to see others in the same way. There have been Jewish groups in and out-side of Palestine who have mistakenly maintained that Buber pled for the lives of Arab terrorists sentenced to death but refused to plead for the lives of Jewish terrorists. One such case was that of the Jewish terrorist Dov Gurner. Here too the persistent rumor that Buber did not intervene for him is mistaken. Gavriel Stern, editor at that time of *Ba'ayot,* assures us that Buber and Henrietta Szold wrote a letter in common, which is reported in *Ba'ayot.*

The high point of cooperation between Jews and Arabs in Palestine at this time also turned out to be the most poignant and tragic. The League for Jewish-Arab Rapprochement and Cooperation in Pales-tine found an Arab counterpart in the Arab body known as Falastin el-Jedida (The New Palestine). The founder and leader of this organi-zation was Fauzi Darwish El-Husseini, a cousin of the bitterly anti-Zionist Mufti of Jerusalem and himself an active Arab nationalist who had been jailed for his part in anti-Jewish riots. At a public meeting in Haifa on June 22, 1946, Fauzi had endorsed the essential Ihud posi-tion of a binational state supervised by the United Nations with the problem of immigration to be worked out within the framework of a general agreement and on the basis of the economic absorptive capac-ity of the country. At the end of August 1946, Fauzi spoke at the home of Chaim Kalvarisky, urging an active Arab counterforce against the "Arab party" led by his cousin the Mufti, attacking the official policy of both Arabs and Jews as producing only damage and suffering, and calling on Arabs and Jews to unite and work hand in hand against the imperialist policy which played them off against each other.

On November 11, 1946, five members of Falastin el-Jedida signed an agreement with the League of Jewish-Arab Rapprochement and Cooperation, calling for cooperation, political equality, Jewish immigration according to the country's economic absorptive capacity, and a future Near Eastern federation. This agreement had been prepared by an active campaign on the part of Fauzi and his supporters which reached out to Muslim and Christian teachers, journalists, businessmen, and workers among the Arabs. Their activities extended to publishing an Arab organ, *El-Akha* (Brotherhood), and acquiring a clubroom. These activities were not unaccompanied by Arab warnings and threats, but Fauzi, undeterred, replied, "History will judge which of us followed the right path." On November 23, less than two weeks after this agreement was signed with the promise of the League to support the activities of Falastin el-Jedida, Fauzi was murdered by unknown Arab extremists. A few days after his murder his cousin Jamal Husseini, co-leader of the Arab party with the Mufti, said: "My cousin had stumbled and received his proper punishment." No Palestinian Arab politician had ever before openly negotiated with the Jews and signed an agreement with them. Fauzi's friends came to see Buber and other leaders of the League for Jewish-Arab Rapprochement and Cooperation declaring that they were not afraid to carry on and asking advice as to what they should do now that Fauzi was dead. "Go home in peace," Buber and his friends told them. "They will kill you as they killed Fauzi." The Arab and the Jewish men of peace parted in sadness, and no similar counterthrust of Arab moderates against the extremists arose to deflect the onrush of events toward war.

In April 1947, Hugo Bergmann went to India to attend the Conference on Asian Relations in Delhi at which thirty-four nations were represented. From the Middle East were present only Egypt, the Arab League through a single representative, and Turkey, through an observer. As head of his delegation Bergmann represented the standpoint of the Jews in Palestine. The president of the conference censured Bergmann on account of the "political" character of his speech. Bergmann and his delegation forthwith left the hall. Called back by the Indians, Bergmann spontaneously held out his hand to the representative of the Arab League. Writing to Buber from Bombay, Bergmann characterized the conference as "a great event and a great organizational activity." The conference had a Middle and East

Asian character and the Palestine Jewish delegation of nine persons were barely noticed until the incident in the second opening session took place. Bergmann's action, which he described to Buber as sudden and unpremeditated, and somehow *"put into my mind,"* brought his delegation a storm of applause from the conference so that they were for a time "in the limelight" and their situation was at once noticed by their colleagues from Ceylon, Burma, and other Far Eastern countries. Nehru, through whose error the whole situation had arisen, according to Bergmann, invited the delegation to his house for dinner the next evening. Bergmann knew that all this did not change the political situation, which was still like a wall of opposition, but the attention of the conference was drawn to their work in national economy, and demands came to them from all sides for agronomists, technicians, chemists. Expeditions planned to go to Palestine to visit them, and in the council of the newly founded Inter-Asian Relations Organization, Bergmann, along with the representative of the Arab League, was one of thirty members. This gain later proved insubstantial, since the committee was never convened.

In June 1947, there began what R. M. Graves, the mayor of Jerusalem, described in a book as an "experiment in anarchy": a war of all against all in which three peoples—the British, the Arabs, and the Jews—raged against one another. In June 1947, David Werner Senator wrote Buber after his return from a trip to America telling him how important Buber's successes in his European lecture tour of various universities and cities was for the Hebrew University and for the whole of Jewish Palestine in creating spiritual, cultural, and personal ties with prominent intellectual leaders in many countries. At the same time he told him of the worsening situation in Palestine after the carrying out of new death sentences for members of the Irgun Zvai Le'umi. "The Zionist leadership is as usual tragicomic. They do not mean what they say and they do not say what they mean, and they clearly hold that to be the apex of political wisdom." Through Ben-Gurion's personal intervention the overwhelming majority of Hadassah in America delivered a stinging rebuff to their founder Henrietta Szold, a staunch leader of Ihud, and voted for the partition of Palestine, leaving only the League and Hashomer Hatzaïr in favor of a binational state. Meanwhile the terror mounted, often in small acts which seemed to Senator even more characteristic and important for the psychology of the Yishuv and the youth than those which made the headlines. Finally Senator informed Buber that Magnes was seriously ill with a strained heart and told him how much it would mean to Magnes if he were to receive a letter from on the occasion of his seventieth birthday (July 8, 1947).

Buber wrote Magnes a letter which was at once intensely personal— "It [*Magnes's seventieth birthday*] touches the depths of my soul"—and at the same time a public tribute published in the summer issue of *Ba'ayot*. In it he recounted for the first time the traumatic experience which he had at the Zionist Congress of 1921 when his resolution for Jewish-Arab cooperation was whittled down in the name of compromise until there was nothing left of its substance. "I could not undertake any new action whereby I should again be placed before the choice between truth and realization," Buber declared. From then on he had to renounce "resolutions" and content himself with "personal talks." But when he came to Palestine, where Magnes sought to further the same radical striving for Jewish-Arab cooperation that finally took the form of "our Ihud," Buber received from Magnes a great gift: the possibility of again being politically active within the framework and in the name of a political group without sacrificing the truth in so doing. "I am not concerned about the purity and salvation of my soul," Buber explained. "If the situation should arise—which by the nature of things is impossible—that I had to choose between the salvation of my soul and the welfare of my people—then I know I would not hesitate." Buber, rather, identified Magnes and himself as persons who recognized that there could be no opposition between the truth of God and the welfare of Israel. What was in question, therefore, in the gift that Magnes had made to Buber was the latter's conviction, which had become ever clearer to him as he grew older, "that since I came to the recognition that the truth is the seal of God while we represent the wax in which this seal is to be imprinted, I may not injure the truth."

The British government, realizing that it was impotent to deal with the situation in Palestine, had turned to the United Nations, which sent its own Special Commission in the early summer of 1947. Since Buber was still lecturing in Europe and Smilansky was ill, the testimony of Ihud in July was made by the ailing Magnes accompanied by Marcus Reiner of the Haifa Technion and Gavriel Stern, who was then the editor of *Ba'ayot*. The warm welcome of the Anglo-American Commission was missing, and in the report which the Special Commission made to the United Nations Assembly in the fall of 1947, the majority went on record for partition of Palestine into a Jewish and an Arab state with Jerusalem under an international trusteeship. The minority were for a binational, independent federal state, but with political power exercised by the Arab majority. Both majority and minority agreed that the Mandate should be ended as soon as possible. In the debates at the United Nations leading up to the two-thirds vote for partition on November 29, binationalism was not even mentioned as an alternative to partition. "One after the other get up and declare that they would like to vote for a federal plan, but that unfortunately no such plan exists," Magnes wrote Hugo Bergmann the day before the vote.

On November 8, 1947, Buber sent a letter to his old friend Arnold Zweig on the occasion of his sixtieth birthday in which he suggested that, despite all differences, they had in common their concern about how "this wretched little people are led there where no 'way' leads." But Zweig responded from Haifa, where he now lived, that what divided them was the deep and difficult question as to what is real and necessary. "I am so much wholly with you and Magnes," he wrote, "but through living my life I have learned that it is not the spirit that builds the bodies—as I still thought in 1931." "Social structures determine consciousness—this I have experienced here at every turn," Zweig paraphrased Marx, foreshadowing his immigration to East Berlin in 1948.

On November 29 the United Nations Assembly decided by a two-thirds vote in favor of the partition of Palestine. The next day a party of Jews, driving in Palestine, was ambushed and killed. A day later serious rioting occurred in Jerusalem, and the war that Buber and Magnes had consistently warned would accompany partition broke out. Summing up the situation ten years later, Buber wrote: "Since a Jewish-Arab solidarity had not been instituted, . . . the Arab peoples received the mass immigration as a threat and the Zionist movement as a 'hireling of imperialism'—both wrongly, of course. Our *historical* reentry into our land took place through a false gateway." Of the outbreak of war, he said: "The unhappy partition of Palestine took place, the cleft between the two peoples was split wide asunder, the war raged. Everything proceeded with frightening logical consistency and at the same time with frightening meaninglessness." A personal remark Buber added at this point again showed the utter concreteness and realism of his encounter on the narrow ridge: "I am no radical pacifist: I do not believe that one must always answer violence with nonviolence. I know what tragedy implies; when there is war, it must be fought." This remark in no way means that Buber gave up his concern for doing whatever possible *in each situation* for Jewish-Arab relations. In January 1948, Buber, Magnes, and Senator sent a letter to the Hebrew and English press appealing to public opinion and to the Jewish leadership to take steps to prevent vicious mob attacks by Jews: "Let recent regrettable incidents serve as a warning not to let the mob rule us, not to destroy with our own hands the moral foundations of our life and of our future."

On January 27, in a letter to Ernst Simon, who was lecturing in New York, Buber pointed out that, despite being blessed with some gift for imagining the real, he had failed to grasp "how we here in this city (particularly in this city) live. Next to surrender of the soul to the irreconcilable contradiction, everything that I have experienced before, for example in Hitler Germany, was a gentle idyll." The former was organized terror, which had by no means reached its height; the latter was simple anarchy. What was and was not happening and what threatened to happen in the Old City of Jerusalem, the actions of the mob that seemed to be particularly ferocious in Jerusalem and that matched "ever more successfully" those of the Arab counterpart, and the decisions and nondecisions of "our current [local] 'leadership,' " which in any case more and more resemble those of the opposition"— all these added up to that totally absorbing claim on Buber's attention exercised by the city of Jerusalem in which he continued to live throughout the war. Simon wrote Buber from New York that he had read in the *New York Times* the report of the open letter that Buber had sent to the Yishuv along with Magnes and Senator (Buber had doubted that it would even be published), and he congratulated him on his courage. "Once again I am proud that I belong to your circle and may call myself one of your disciples." That very afternoon (January 30) Simon learned of Gandhi's assassination.

When the battle over Jerusalem could no longer be avoided and the United Arab armies' invasion practically cut the city off from the rest of the country and besieged it, Buber remained in the threatened city, although the possibility had been offered him of saving himself and Paula by going to Tel Aviv. Once, during the worst days of the siege, Buber encountered Schalom Ben-Chorin on Ben-Yehuda Street in the center of the city and said to him: "Even if they were to send an airplane to my doorstep, I would not leave this Jerusalem in which what I wanted to avoid is happening." In February 1948, when the English in response to Jewish acts of terrorism indulged in their own terrorist act by destroying Ben-Yehuda Street, Buber was extremely depressed. A distinguished Arabic family, that of Jussuf Wahab Dajani, tried in vain to protect Buber and his family in their Arabic quarter. Before the war many of the Arabs in Dir Abu Tor had great respect for Buber and called him "the old saint" and "the old man." After the Jewish-Arab war broke out, the Arabs in the neighborhood divided, according to Buber's own testimony, into one faction that was for the Bubers and one that wanted to kill them. The Haganah made use of Buber's house, even using his books as a protection against Arab bullets, so that many of his books bear bullet marks. Finally it became too difficult for the Bubers to stay on, and they moved with such of their belongings as they could take to the Grete Ascher Pension in Rehavia, a modern quarter of Jerusalem bordering on the new campus of the Hebrew University, established after Mount Scopus became inaccessible. Buber went out in the car of Dr. Graham Brown, an Anglican archdeacon.

After the Bubers left, Dajani closed off the room in which Buber's library was housed. A few days later Iraqi troops came to the house. "Where are the Jews who lived here?" they asked. "They are no longer here," Dajani replied. A house search followed. "What is this closed room?" an Iraqi soldier asked. "Stop!" said Dajani. "Behind this door there is the great library of Professor Buber on the history of religions. You will have to kill me if you want to get into this room." "Now, what do you take us for?" asked the Iraqi captain. "Do you think we are barbarians?" At which he withdrew. In a speech about Buber over a West German radio station in 1962, Albrecht Goes said that in the light of what the Nazis did during the *Kristallnacht* in November 1938, no German could hear this story except with shame!

In the Arabic village they had decided not to kill Buber, but the ways out were dangerous because of the "unofficial war" that began in December and lasted until May 15. Gavriel Stern, who took responsibility for Buber's house after Buber left, along with the Dajanis who protected it from plundering, went on one of many trips to the Buber's house to bring out their furniture and equipment, there was a terrorist incident against the Arabs. As a result the Arabs surrounded Stern's car, and he and his companions thought they were lost. But the Arab officials said, "We know who you are and who your friends are," meaning the Bubers. The place was without any police, and so it was an act of courage on Stern's part. This moving of books and furniture lasted six weeks, but they were never harmed. The Arabs plundered and destroyed everything in the house of Buber's neighbor, but the Bubers' house was excellently looked after and its possessions remained completely untouched during the whole Arab occupation. There was even a saying among the Arabs that Buber was still living there, writing and thinking. Even among his "enemies" Buber was a living legend.

In February 1948, Magnes wrote Buber a long letter on the occasion of his seventieth birthday which, in contrast to the hopeful ending of Buber's own birthday letter to Magnes, was pessimistic and almost bitter concerning the common cause for which the two men fought:

> The tragedy of these days does not lie in the fact that after the dancing and jubilation over the U.N. resolution, confusion and trouble now reigns—the injury of dear, irreplaceable human life, fighting and again fighting the end of which is not in sight. The tragedy lies in the fact that today, as in the days of the prophet Micah (3:9–10), "the heads of the house of Jacob and the masters of the House of Israel," as it says, "build Zion with blood. . . ."
>
> The fearful suffering that our people had to endure was so great that it robbed us of the capacity for patience. We were not in the condition . . . to content ourselves with everyday creative work, and we fell prey to the *fata morgana* of the state, as if it were a shield that could protect us against the enmity of the peoples.
>
> Now you witness the wreck of almost all the things that were dear to you. In the land of Israel the House of Israel has become a people like all other peoples, and it has no faith in the election, or in the religious and moral mission of the people of Israel. . . . You see how all your efforts to instill into the people the spirit of mutual understanding with the neighboring peoples are come to naught.
>
> You, the man of spirit *par excellence,* must endure torments of the spirit when it becomes clear to you that within the people of Israel, your own people, the spirit exercises no actual effect, but only the fist and force.

In the light of Magnes's death eight months later, of which he must have been well aware when he wrote this letter, his conclusion is particularly touching:

> Do you look into the future with the most extreme pessimism? I fear so; for that is the actual reality. God grant that it is not come to a new destruction! In any case my birthday wish for you today is that you do not allow your courage to sink; that it may be granted to you to continue as ever your contending with the actual reality despite all; that a long life be allotted you until you may behold HIS return to Zion in truth.

In March 1948, Buber wrote to Salman Schocken thanking him for his seventieth birthday letter and commenting, "It was strange enough to celebrate this day in the unimaginable confusion of today's Jerusalem. Of the highly different atmosphere into which Palestine has split asunder, that here is by far the most absurd. When a week ago during my course (in the Rehavia Gymnasium where the lectures now take place) an English bullet passed over my head and into the wall, I and the students remaining to me experienced that barely as a disturbance, rather as a natural event and accepted it with the requisite humor. But just therein lies the absurdity of our present situation." Buber added that he was happy that Schocken wished seriously to consider the publication of his translation of the Book of Job, which he had completed during the past years. But he could not make the necessary revisions in it; for he had no access either to the university library on Mount Scopus or to his own, which he had to leave behind in Dir Abu Tor, where it was from time to time shot through by English bullets defending Jemin Mosche, a quarter of Jerusalem.

Two weeks later Buber wrote Heinz Politzer that there existed no more communication between Abu Tor and Jewish Jerusalem, but that he had heard that amid the utterly chaotic shooting thirteen English cannonballs had penetrated his house and had among other things bored through the oil portrait of Buber painted by Emil Rudolf Weiss. "For the rest what takes place here, especially in this city—this raging of all against all—is simply indescribable. I suspect that nothing like it has ever yet taken place in an already quite variegated human history." To Ernst Simon, Buber wrote that the hourly reaction to the unimaginably cruel and senseless events there placed a great inner and outer demand on everyone and especially on "so routineless and disoriented a man, abandoned without defense to every situation, as I still always am and clearly must also remain." Although there was no real celebration of his seventieth birthday, the great response from all over the world, revealing thereby that there are still human beings, was comforting: "I confess that I was in need of some comfort."

Buber also reported to Simon that they were working intensively in Ihud and that "a not insignificant number of the much afflicted people of Jerusalem openly profess our cause, in contrast to which, of course, *those who are at ease in Tel Aviv* [a play on Amos 6:1] want to know nothing further of us." In April, Buber wrote that the local situation was more problematic than ever: "The few persons among us who have preserved a vision of the reality are in an incredibly difficult position because they must fight on three fronts—two outside and one within. Of the real happenings barely anything is published.

'Public opinion' is almost exclusively dominated by the phraseology of *ressentiment.*"

To Hugo Bergmann, Buber confided that in those hours or quarter-hours of philosophizing that were, despite all, still afforded him, he was occupying himself more intensively than ever "with the category of the human (I really mean category), with its possibility, and all that I have learned about the human in the months of disorder, flows into it." Thus "Distance and Relation," which is Buber's most abstract piece of philosophical writing and the cornerstone of his most mature philosophical work, *The Knowledge of Man,* had its origin not in the serenity and contemplation traditionally associated with philosophers but in the midst of what Buber later called the most dreadful year of his life. Similarly Paula, no less a titan than her husband, wrote what Buber considered her most important work, the epic novel *Am lebendigen Wasser* (By Living Waters) during the siege of Jerusalem when she was under the strain of caring for the whole household, including Buber himself, several grandchildren, and nine cats, with very little resources of any kind. From that time on until Buber's death seventeen years later there emerged a note that one was to hear again and again in the years to come: his need to expedite his publishing affairs in a way that he had not done until then.

On April 13 a convoy, carrying doctors and nurses to the Hadassah Hospital and professors and workers of the university to Mount Scopus, was ambushed by Arab bands and for hours left a helpless victim of savage onslaughts, while British forces were stationed within a mile, and Magnes and others vainly besought their aid. Ten of the university staff and the director of Hadassah Hospital were among the seventy killed. On May 14, the Executive of the Jewish Agency and the Jewish National Council proclaimed in Tel Aviv the independence of Israel, which was immediately recognized by Harry Truman for the United States and shortly afterward by the Soviet Union. That marked the end of the "unofficial war" and the beginning of the official one. In the Foreword to *Two Types of Faith,* which he wrote "in Jerusalem during the days of its so-called siege, or rather in the chaos of destruction which broke out within it," Buber confessed that the work involved had helped him "to endure in faith this war, for me the most grievous of the three." On May 28 the Old City was surrendered to the Arabs and remained in their hands until two years after Buber's death.

That Magnes was not wrong about the pessimistic light in which Buber would see the future is shown by the essay on "Two Kinds of

Zionism" that Buber wrote in May 1948, the very time in which the State of Israel was declared and the official war began. One kind of Zionism was concerned with the covenantal task of Israel, the realization of true community on the land. The other was concerned with becoming like all the other peoples. This opposition was no different from that in biblical times except that then the second tendency failed whereas now it seemed to be succeeding to a dreadful degree. "Never in the course of our history were spirit and life so far from each other as now in this epoch of 'rebirth.' Or will one name the collective selfseeking that recognizes no higher criterion and obeys no higher command, 'spirit'?" The "Zionism" that had won out in Palestine "desecrates the name Zion; it is nothing more than one of the crassest nationalisms of our time that recognizes no higher authority than the—supposed!—interest of the nation." Buber saw in this a form of national assimilation much more dangerous than the individual; for it destroys the essential core of Israel. When the illusion that the Arab majority would consent to become a minority was shattered, official Zionism consented to split the very land it was to "redeem" in order that it might be a majority and substituted for true independence the watchword of "sovereignty" "in a time in which the sovereignty of the small states is disappearing with ever increasing speed!" "Instead of striving to become the community of initiative within the framework of a Near Eastern federation," Buber added in truly prophetic words, "one set as one's goal a little state that runs the danger of living in constant antagonism to its natural, geopolitical surroundings and to have to devote its best forces to military instead of social and cultural values."

Buber concluded "Two Kinds of Zionism" with a sad personal confession:

> Fifty years ago when I joined the Zionist movement for the sake of the rebirth of Israel, I did so with a whole heart. Today my heart is torn. A war concerning political structure always threatens, in fact, to degenerate into a war concerning the national existence. Therefore, I can do nothing other than to take part in it with my own existence, and my heart trembles today like the heart of every Jew. But I cannot rejoice even at a victory; for I fear that a victory of the Jews means a defeat of Zionism.

By July, with enormous expenditure of effort and money, the Bubers had rescued most of their belongings, with the books lying in sacks in various places. Buber had to give up the lecture he had planned to give for the plenary session of the International Philosophy Congress in Amsterdam in August 1948. In late summer of 1948 Count Folke Bernadotte, president of the Swedish Red Cross, came to Palestine as mediator in the Arab-Jewish war and as the director of the U.N. Armistice Commission. On September 17 this highly revered figure was assassinated by Jewish terrorists. Werner Kraft brought the news to Buber, who had not yet heard it. Buber was speechless with shock. Many years later when a concerted effort was made to raise support from influential world thinkers for a Nobel Prize in Literature for Buber, Ernst Simon said that the Swedish ambassador in Israel had told him that because of the murder of Count Bernadotte, it was still impossible for an Israeli—even one like Buber who had steadfastly opposed all acts of terrorism—to receive the Nobel Prize.

In October 1948, Buber published in *Ba'ayot* an article titled "Let Us Make an End to Falsities!" in which he characterized the feelings of both sides concerning the Arab-Jewish war in terms of the "mass psychology" and "hypnosis" that made each feel that *it* was the injured party—the very terms that he rejected so bitterly when Frederik Van Eeden used them of Germany at the beginning of the First World War! In opposition to the simplistic statement that the Arabs started the war by attacking the Jews, Buber added a historical *aperçu,* asserting, "When we started our infiltration into the country we began an attack 'by peaceful means.'" Everything then depended on convincing the other people that was already there—the Arabs—that the attack was not an attack at all, by awakening in them the belief in "our community of interest." On the positive side, this meant developing a *genuine* community of interests by including the Arabs in their economic activity. On the negative side, it meant holding back all proclamations and political actions of a unilateral nature, i.e., postponing all political decisions until that community of interests had found its true practical expression. It was so evident that neither of these things had been done that Buber did not need to draw the conclusion but could leave it to the reader: "on the basis of these plain facts, and not of any empty slogans, let all who know the meaning of responsiblity search their own hearts as to what we have done, and what we have left undone." The impact of such a statement in wartime can be only scarcely imagined.

In January 1949, Buber confided to Walter Goldstein something more of the toll that the Arab-Jewish war, which had finally come to a halt, had taken of him. The confusion of this most dreadful year of his life had deprived him, he felt, of his power to counsel people.

Before that, whenever he saw a person, he saw the person's whole life at once. "Now that is no longer so." The depth of Buber's feeling about the war is reflected in a poem which he wrote in 1948 and dedicated to Ludwig Strauss but which he did not publish until he included it in "Gleanings" which he selected for preservation just before his death. In this poem, "November," the association between the violence that the Nazis perpetrated on the Jews and that which the Jews were now taking part in in the name of Zionism is gently but unmistakably made:

> The scrolls burned slowly and long.
> I saw from the distance the sparks scatter,
> I saw how the parchment burst open,
> And when I forced my glance to continue,
> I saw: the ashes sank.
> Only the Word is left.
>
> The destroyers are now long since disposed of,
> A vile band of hangmen and thieves.
> With them went the rage and the madness
> And the cold greed for the plan of plunder.
> I saw: the path has become empty.
> Our Word has remained.
>
> But we, are we speakers of the word?
> Are we able to proclaim it and to love it?
> I see us struggling—for the sake of what hoard?
> Powerful the arm—and the heart withered?
> O homeless Voice
> In which the Word remained!

CHAPTER 2

Biblical Judaism and Hasidic Tales

BUBER'S PRODUCTIVITY during this period of anarchy, confusion, and war was no less astonishing than that during his five years in Nazi Germany. In addition to continuing the translation of the Hebrew Bible, he wrote three important books of biblical commentary, a book on the historical relationship of Israel and Palestine, a book on the history of utopian socialism, and a book of interpretations of Hasidism, and he revised and rewrote his whole corpus of Hasidic tales. In 1949 Buber wrote to his translator Ronald Gregor Smith:

> You are right in saying that I am "writing so much." But do you want to know why? Because I am copying here, so to say, from my mind the books I have composed but not written in the course of many years before coming to Palestine, and here I simply have to write them. As you know, all of them deal with one subject, only in different ways.

BIBLICAL JUDAISM

The starting point for all this activity was a public lecture which

Buber gave in Tel Aviv in 1939 and repeated in London in 1946, "The Spirit of Israel and the World of Today." In this lecture Buber suggested that the Marcionism of the liberal Protestant theologian Adolf von Harnack had been put into practice not by the church but by Hitler, who by means of violence and terror brought to the highest pitch in history that longstanding anti-Semitism which had its origin in the desire of the nations to reject the demand placed upon them by the Hebrew Bible. Harnack wished to reject the Old Testament as a canonical document on liberal grounds, but the practical result of his and Marcion's teaching was the absolution of the nations of the world from any demand placed upon them by means of an extreme dualism between the life of the redeemed soul on the one hand and that of existing society on the other. "In the former there is not justice but there is lovingkindness, while in the latter there is not even true justice," Buber contended. The effect of Marcionism, the extrusion of the Jewish element from Christianity, "means an extrusion of the divine demand and concrete messianism; its separation from the divine truth calling for fulfillment." At the same time Buber demanded of the Jews that they not use "the spirit of Israel" merely as a metaphorical mask for national egoism. "The true spirit of Israel is the divine demand implanted in our hearts," and this demand means building real community composed of real families, real neighborhoods, and real settlements, and a real nation which develops relationships of a fruitful and creative peace with its neighbors. Only the realization of the kingship of God in the evolving pattern of a true people could entitle the Jews of Palestine to set up the spirit of Israel against the overt and covert Marcionism of the other nations and to oppose, to the dualism of action without responsibility, a responsible life in the service of unity. Some of Buber's Christian friends reproached him for stressing the Marcionite element in Christianity while the majority of his Jewish fellow-citizens of Palestine, as we have seen, did not heed his admonition. Nonetheless, in *Moses* and *The Prophetic Faith* Buber continued his documentation begun in *The Kingship of God* of the messianic demand of biblical Judaism for justice, righteousness, community, and peace. In his 1942 essay "The Gods of the Nations and God" Buber declared that there is no revelation without commandment; for we can point out God only in and through this life of ours. The distinction between righteousness and unrighteousness can be converted into the fullness of life only in and through the nation; for only the life of the people as a whole can demonstrate the absolute. "Though something of righteousness may become evident in the life of the individual, righteousness itself can only become visibly embodied in the structures of the life of a people. . . ." After centuries of exile and historical constraint, a Jewish settlement was once again established on the soil of Palestine. In the first decades of this settlement "generations who discovered within themselves an undreamed-of working power and efficiency set the tablets of social justice up over their work." But in recent years the work of those generations has been inundated by a life that knows no tablets of social justice. The Yishuv was to be the center of the Jewish people, but what is the spiritual center of this center? Buber's biblical work over a forty-year span can be looked upon as an untiring effort, despite the increasingly deteriorating political situation, to try to restore the covenant to the heart of this center.

In *Moses* Buber wrote the book against Freud which Lou Salomé wisely dissuaded him from writing when he was a young man—only now it was on Buber's ground and not on Freud's. In a footnote to the Preface, Buber wrote: "That a scholar of so much importance in his own field as Sigmund Freud could permit himself to issue so unscientific a work, based on a groundless hypothesis, as his 'Moses and Monotheism' (1939), is astonishing and regrettable." Toward the end of this Preface, Buber rejected as a fundamental error Freud's (and Leo Baeck's) description of biblical Judaism as "Monotheism." What is important, Buber wrote, is not the numerical oneness of God, "but the way in which this Unity is viewed and experienced and whether one stands to it in an exclusive relationship which shapes all other relations and thereby the whole order of life." Within this context Buber then explicitly rejected Freud's thesis, though not naming him in so doing: "The universal sun-god of the imperialist 'Monotheism' of Amenhotep IV is incomparably closer in nature to the national sun-god of the ancient Egyptian Pantheon than to the God of early Israel, which some have endeavoured to derive from him." Buber, whom Else Lasker-Schüler described as having a "Moses mouth," saw Moses as one who was summoned to have the Word burst forth in him and thus he became God's "mouth." "That Moses experiences Him in this fashion and serves Him accordingly is what has set that man apart as a living and effective force at all times; and that is what places him thus afresh in our own day, which possibly needs him more than any earlier time."

In *Moses* Buber again held steadfast to the narrow ridge: that between the traditionalist's insistence on the literal truth of the biblical narrative and the modern critic's tendency to regard this narrative as of merely literary or symbolic significance. The traditionalist tends to regard the events of the Bible as supernatural miracles, and the attempt to equate them to our own experiences as illicit. The modernist sees them as impressive fantasies or fictions, interesting from a purely immanent and human point of view. Between these two approaches Buber set down a third:

> We must adopt the critical approach and seek reality, here as well, by asking ourselves what human relation to real events this could have been which led gradually, along many bypaths and by way of many metamorphoses, from mouth to ear, from one memory to another, and from dream to dream, until it grew into the written account we have read.

Here Buber called his treatment of biblical history "tradition criticism" as distinct from "source criticism." This tradition criticism seeks to penetrate beneath the layers of different redactions of tradition to a central unity already present in the first and developed, restored, or distorted in the later ones.

> Tradition is by its nature an uninterrupted change in form; change and preservation function in the identical current. Even while the hand makes its alterations, the ear hearkens to the deeps of the past; not only for the reader but also for the writer himself does the old serve to legitimize the new.

The Bible as "literal truth" and the Bible as "living literature" are thus supplanted in *Moses* by the Bible as a record of the concrete meetings in the course of history between a group of people and the divine. The Bible is not primarily devotional literature, nor is it a symbolic theology which tells us of the nature of God as he is in himself. It is the historical account of God's relation to man seen through man's eyes. "Miracle," to Buber, such as the parting of the Red Sea that enabled the Israelites to escape from the pursuing Egyptians, is neither an objective event which suspends the laws of nature and history nor a subjective act of the imagination. It is neither "supernatural" nor "natural" but a third alternative: an event which is experienced by an individual or a group of people as an abiding astonishment which no knowledge of causes can weaken, as wonder at something which intervenes fatefully in the life of this individual and this group. Thus it is an event of dialogue, an event of the *between*.

The real miracle means that in the astonishing experience of the event the current system of cause and effect becomes, as it were, transparent and permits a glimpse of the sphere in which a sole power, not restricted by any other, is at work. To live with the miracle means to recognize this power on every given occasion as the effecting one. That is the religion of Moses, the man who experienced the futility of magic, who learned to recognize the demonic as one of the forms by which the divine functions, . . . and that is religion generally, as far as it is reality.

Buber saw the tragedy of Moses as the tragedy inherent in revelation. "It is laid upon the stammering to bring the voice of Heaven to Earth." But he also saw Moses as the person who withstood evil not because he recognized it as Satan but precisely because he recognized it as God. What the Second Isaiah later said of God, "Who makes peace and creates evil," Moses already understood when he was attacked at night by a stranger who tries to kill him and whom he kills instead. This is the perilous encounter with the God who has promised to be with him but not in any form that he can conjure—"I shall be there *as* I shall be there." No matter how nocturnally dread and cruel the power may be, it is proper to recognize YHVH in or behind it and "to withstand Him, since after all He does not require anything else of me than myself." Even Hitler and the Nazis that Buber had to endure he did not attribute to a devil utterly sundered from God!

Perhaps the most powerful example of what the "narrow ridge" meant for Buber's approach to the Bible is the autobiographical fragment that he told concerning "Samuel and Agag." Once when he was riding in a train in Germany, Buber met a pious and observant Orthodox Jew and they fell to discussing the Bible and in particular that passage where the prophet Samuel tells Saul that he has lost the succession to the kingdom because, after conquering the Amalekites and killing them and their animals, he spared the life of Agag, the prince of the Amalekites. The Amalekites were the people who swooped down upon the Israelites in the rear as they marched forty years through the wilderness. The Amalekites wantonly killed all they could, as a result of which Moses declared eternal war between Israel and Amalek, and Amalek became a symbol in Jewish history from Hamann to Hitler. According to the story in First Samuel 15, Samuel then called before him Agag, who said, "Surely the bitterness of death is over." "As you have made other mothers childless, so I shall make your mother childless," responded Samuel "and hewed him into pieces before the Lord in Gilgal."

When he first read this story as a boy, it profoundly troubled him, Buber confessed to his traveling companion, and even now he could not believe that it was the will of God. His companion's brow darkened and his eyes flamed. "So you do not believe it?" he said. "No, I do not believe it," Buber replied. Then, his eyes still more threatening and his brow still darker, the man pressed, "So, you do not believe it!" "No," Buber maintained, "I do not believe it." Then, pushing the words out one in front of the other, the man said, "What, what then do you believe?" "I believe," Buber answered without thinking, "that Samuel misunderstood God." Then something extraordinary happened: the angry brow cleared, the eyes became positively gentle and radiant. Then the man said, "I think so too."

In the end it is not surprising, Buber reported, that if a really pious Jew of this sort has to choose between God and the Bible, he chooses God. But in the years since that happened, Buber asked himself again and again if he had given the right response and again and again came up with a Yes and a No. Yes, insofar as this particular dialogue was concerned "so that the dialogue might not come to naught." But No insofar as one might think that he meant that only this one interpretation of God's will had been a misunderstanding.

> God does not abandon the created man to his needs and anxieties; He provides him with the assistance of his word; He speaks to him, He comforts him with His word. But man does not listen with faithful ears to what is spoken to him. Already in hearing he blends together command of heaven and statute of earth, revelation to the existing being and the orientations that he arranges himself. Even the holy scriptures of man are not excluded, not even the Bible.

We have no objective criterion for distinguishing between the manufactured and the received from the voices and pens out of which the text of the Hebrew Bible has arisen. We have only faith—when we have it.

> Nothing can make me believe in a God who punishes Saul because he has not murdered his enemy. And yet even today I still cannot read the passage that tells this except with fear and trembling. But not it alone. Always when I have to translate or to interpret a biblical text, I do so with fear and trembling, in an inescapable tension between the word of God and the words of man.

The orthodox and the fundamentalist escape this tension through a bibliolatry that tries to freeze the word of the Bible into an objective statement handed down by heaven—as if words meant something in themselves without their being spoken and heard! The liberals try to escape it by approaching the Bible with the touchstone of the "progressive" and the "universal," accepting what they feel fits the most "modern" morality and rejecting what does not. Buber preserved the tension and with it the encounter on the narrow ridge.

The first answer that Moses receives to the question, "Who shall I say sent me?" is the God of your fathers, the God whom you *recognize*. The second is "I shall be as I shall be": "He who promises his steady presence, his steady assistance, refuses to restrict himself to definite forms of manifestation." This God does not need to be conjured, for he is always with you, but this God also cannot be conjured. If Buber thus disdained magic, the attempt to get in touch with the divine in order to use it for one's own purpose, he, by the same token, disdained success. "Always and everywhere in the history of religion the fact that God is identified with success is the greatest obstacle to a steadfast religious life." Moses had to engage in an uninterrupted, never-despairing struggle against the "stiff-neckedness" of Israel, that is, against this permanent passion for success, and this is the identical struggle that Buber had to engage in with the modern Israel that sought security in the Land. Yet Buber saw in this something positive: the audacity which enabled the people to perform their deeds of faith as a people. But he pointed out that the unfamiliar and excessive privations of the journey which cause great suffering to the people had to be accepted too; for a "historical deed always means the surmounting of suffering, the suffering inherent in being human."

The importance of Moses for our time Buber also found in the Ten Commandments, the soul of which he saw in *Moses* as the word *Thou*. This Thou means the preservation of the Divine Voice. "At all times, . . . only those persons really grasped the Decalogue who literally felt it as having been addressed to them themselves." How autobiographical this statement is we already know from "The Education of Character," in which the lightning flash of "Thou shalt not" strikes the heart of a "man," Buber himself, so that he does the exact opposite of what he was going to do with all the passion which he was going to bring into that action. Of equally modern relevance in Buber's *Moses* because it goes against the universalist approach to comparative religion, is his insistence on the atypical and the unique as having a central place in the history of the spirit just because it is *history,* not timeless truth, and his related insistence that the "firm letter" ought not be broken down by any general hypothesis based on the comparative history of culture as long as what is said in that text is historically possible. Those who reject Moses' God as a patriarch will find a modern, if unwelcome, relevance in Buber's insistence that the unity and imagelessness of God places God above sex. To preserve its true character, the anthropomorphic metaphor must not transgress the bounds of spirituality and affect the essence of God. Any representation of God in any specifically human or animal form, even symbolically, would of necessity draw God down into the sphere of sexuality. "A sexually determined God is an incomplete one, one who requires completion; it cannot be the one and only God."

Perhaps most remarkable, given Buber's earlier statements about his relationship to the *mitzvot* or commandments, of Jewish Law, is Buber's discussion in *Moses* of the rebellion of Korah against Moses. Korah, claiming that everything is already holy and does not need to be hallowed, leads his band of followers against the leadership of Moses and the "law" which Moses is imposing upon the people. Moses' humility, which is one with his fundamental faith in spontaneity and in freedom, is precisely what provokes Korah's reaction, and since the whole work of the Covenant between God and people is threatened, Moses must now doom the rebels to destruction. "There is certainly something sinister," asserted Buber, again without subscribing to any literal "miracle," "underlying the legend of the earth which opened its mouth and swallowed up the rebels." Buber here comes down on the side of "law" against lawlessness, although he still means by "law" the Torah, or instruction of God in the dialogue with him, rather than any fixed universal that can be detached from God's address and man's response:

> Without law, that is, without any clear-cut and transmissible line of demarcation between that which is pleasing to God and that which is displeasing to Him, there can be no historical continuity of divine rule upon earth.
>
> The *true* argument of the rebellion is that in the world of the law what has been inspired always becomes emptied of the spirit, but that in this state it continues to maintain its claim of full inspiration. . . .And the *true* conclusion is that the law must again and again immerse itself in the consuming and purifying fire of the spirit, in order to renew itself and, anew, refine the genuine substance out of the dross of what has become false. . . . As against this comes the false argument of the rebels that the law as such displaces the spirit and the freedom, and the false conclusion that it ought to be replaced by them.

The false would become true as soon as the presence of God comes to be fulfilled in all creatures, but those eschatologies, like the pseudo-messianism of the followers of Sabbatai Zvi (the seventeenth-century Kabbalist and "mystical messiah" of Palestine) and Jacob Frank, that proclaim that to be already the case cannot withstand the realities of history. "The 'Mosaic' attitude facing this is to believe in the future of a 'holy people'; and to prepare for it within history."

"You have simply *read* without adding anything to the text," Eduard Strauss wrote Buber in 1947 about *Moses*. "You have the eyes that allows one to penetrate through the palimpsest." Whoever calls this book a poet's work does it wrong, Strauss added. It is a book that speaks, that teaches one to *read* until suddenly one *hears* the Voice. In 1949 Max Brod wrote Buber that what he said in *Moses* "is simply *the* right, *the* true—equally far from skepticism, from literal belief, and from pseudocriticism." A few years later in his contribution to the Buber volume of the Library of Living Philosophers, Brod characterized *Moses* as "the most penetratingly expressive" of Buber's books, the one "which of all his exegetical works is most clearly illumined by the radiance of poetry," a quality which unfortunately does not come through in the translation. In the same year Rudolf Pannwitz told Buber that *Moses* was an excellent example showing that analysis does not need to destroy but can spiritually re-create what has been illuminated. In 1958 the American philosopher Walter Kaufmann wrote Buber that the original title of a review-article that he wrote on several of Buber's books for *Commentary* was "Martin Buber Points a Way Back to Moses," to which Buber responded that what he said of *Moses* was "very close to my heart."

The Prophetic Faith completes and crowns Buber's years of concern for the origin of messianism in the Bible, and in many ways it is his most impressive book of biblical exegesis. In it he resumes the thesis of *The Kingship of God* that there can be no split between the "religious" and the "social," that Israel cannot become the people of YHVH without just faith between men. To recognize YHVH as Lord of the world means that man cannot establish in earthly life his own regime and satisfy the power above by cult. "The God of the universe is the God of history." He is the deity Who walks with his creature and with his people along the hard way of history. Our path in the history of faith is not a path from one kind of deity to another but from the "God Who hides Himself" (Isaiah 45:15) to the God of history that reveals Himself.

The prophet of Israel is a partner in this revelation. Contrary to the popular conception, he hardly ever foretells an inevitable future but speaks to an actual and definite situation in the present. Even his message of disaster is meant to awaken man's real power of decision so that he may turn back to the covenant—the fulfillment of the kingship of God. Human and divine turning correspond, not as if man's turning brings about God's, but God responds to man's turning back, even as he responds to man's turning away. The Israelite prophet "knows" God not as a subject knows an object but in the intimate contact of the two partners of a two-sided occurrence. He does not seek God in order to hear future things but for the sake of this contact which, like that of Adam knowing Eve, is fully mutual and fully real. Thus the name YHVH, which was disclosed at the revelation to Moses in the thornbush, is unfolded in the "righteousness" of Amos, the "lovingkindness" of Hosea, and the "holiness" of Isaiah. "Only all together could express what is meant by the being present of the ONE Who is present to Israel, Who is 'with it.'" This revelation of God's presence is also a demand placed on man; for there is something essential that must come from him. This prophetic situation of reciprocal dialogue carries over to the messianic; for the messianic prophecy, too, conceals a demand and an alternative. It is not prediction, but a conditional offer. "The righteous one, whom God 'has,' must rise out of this historic loam of man."

The Messiah of Isaiah is not a divine figure who takes the place of man's turning or brings about a redemption which man has merely to accept and enter into. The belief in the coming of a messianic leader is the belief that at last man shall, with his whole being, speak the word that answers God's word. Through the nucleus of Israel that does not betray the covenant and the election (Isaiah's "holy remnant"), the living connection between God and the people is upheld, and from their midst will arise "the perfected one." Through his word and life, Israel will turn to God and serve as the beginning of his kingdom.

> The Messiah—whether he is regarded more as the man whom God has found, or as the man whom God has sent . . . is anointed to set up with human forces and human responsibility the divine order of human community. . . . The Messiah of Isaiah is godlike, as is the man in whom the likeness has unfolded, no more and no less. He is not nearer to God than what is appointed to man as man; nor does he pass over to the divine side; he too stands before God in indestructible dialogue.

When Isaiah's hope for the true king is disappointed, the hopes of his successor, the anonymous prophet known as Deutero-Isaiah, turns to the prophet, the *nabi,* and here, not as a success story, but out of the depths of history and of the suffering of the "servant," the messianic task is continued. The word is spoken to the prophet as between person and person, and it is left to him to translate it into a human language and to answer, lamenting, complaining to God, disputing with God about justice, praying. In Jeremiah the dialogue of Israel's faith has reached its pure form. If only man truly speaks to God, there is nothing he may not say to him. And to man, to Israel, Jeremiah places God's demand not for religion, but for community, in order that God's kingdom shall come. "Therefore here, where He blames a people for not having become a community, man's claim upon man takes precedence of God's claim." God leaves to man the choice of opening his heart to the hard truth or of accepting the easy lie as truth. "This God makes it burdensome for the believer and easy for the unbeliever; and His revelation is nothing but a different form of hiding His face." All that can help man here is the force of extreme despair, a despair so elemental that it saps the last will of life or renews the soul by prompting it to turn with its whole being. The faith relationship has to stand the test of an utterly changed situation and be renewed, if at all, in a different form.

The God against whose remoteness Job struggles, the deity who rages and *is silent,* who "hides his face," brings Job and Deutero-Isaiah to the despair arising from the eclipse of the divine light. Only when God draws near Job again, when he *sees* God, is this despair lifted. In the midst of precisely *this* eclipse of God, Buber made one of his most remarkable statements of faith: "The creation itself already means communication between Creator and creature. The just Creator gives to all His creatures His boundary, so that each may become fully itself." The meaning of this faith can be understood only in terms of the succession of God's "servants": Job the faithful rebel, Abraham, Moses, David, and Isaiah, a succession that leads to Deutero-Isaiah's servant of the Lord, whose sufferings especially link him with Job. Only in the depths of suffering does the servant discover the mystery of "the God of the sufferers" in which the communion with God becomes more real and more powerful than death. The "servant" is not concerned with the "immortality of the soul" but the eternity of God. If man lives in communion with God, he knows that God is eternal and that God is his "portion."

"The *zaddik,* the man justified by God, suffers for the sake of God and of His work of salvation, and God is with him in his suffering." Deutero-Isaiah's "suffering servant of the Lord" voluntarily takes on himself all the griefs and sicknesses of the people's iniquities in order to bring them back to YHVH. The "servant" cannot be identified either with Israel or with Christ, as is traditionally done. According to *The Prophetic Faith* the servant is not a corporate but a personal being that takes shape through the generations in many likenesses and paths of life. In suffering for the sake of God, the servant comes to recognize that God suffers with him and that he is working together with God for the redemption of the world. The servant thus completes the work of the judges and the prophets, the work of making real God's kingship over the people. Although he is a prophet, he is no longer a powerless opposition to the powerful; for it is laid on him to inaugurate God's new order of peace and justice for the world. This kingdom now signifies in reality all the human world. Yet there remains a special tie between the personal servant and the servant Israel. Through his word and life, Israel will turn to God and become God's people. When the suffering servant is allowed to go up and be a light for the nations, the servant Israel, redeemed and cleansed, will establish God's sovereignty upon itself and serve as the beginning of his kingdom.

There are three stages on the servant's way: first, the futile labor of the Israelite prophet in Israel, the arrow decreed to remain in its quiver though promised a great work in the future; second, the *acting* of the affliction when the servant not only endures but accomplishes it by suffering willingly; and third, the work born out of affliction in which the anointed servant upon whom God's spirit has descended becomes the sharp arrow expelled from the quiver, the light sent to the nations to proclaim a message. These three stages cannot be accomplished in the life of any one servant, nor can the servant draw himself out of the quiver and reveal himself. The third stage is that of fulfilled messianism, the stage which to Buber was clearly unthinkable in an unredeemed world. The stage in which Israel and mankind persistently live is the second one, that of the work of suffering, and here the unity between personal servant and the servant Israel passes over to their unity in suffering. "The great scattering, which followed the splitting up of the state and became the essential form of the people, is endowed with the mystery of suffering as with the promise of the God of sufferers." Living and writing in a time just after the greatest suffering that the diaspora, the *galut,* had ever known, Buber undoubtedly had the extermination of the Jews in the Nazi Holocaust in mind when he spoke of this unity of the personal servant and the servant Israel in the willing acceptance of suffering:

As far as the great suffering of Israel's dispersion was not compulsory suffering only, but suffering in truth willingly borne, not passive but active, it is interpreted in the image of the servant. Whosoever accomplishes in Israel the active suffering of Israel, he is the servant, and he is Israel, in whom YHVH "glorifies Himself." The mystery of history is the mystery of a representation which at bottom is identity. The arrow, which is still concealed in the quiver, is people and man as one.

"Only a viewpoint that is Biblical in a very profound sense," writes the eminent Old Testament scholar J. Coert Rylaarsdam in a discussion of *The Prophetic Faith,* "could so consistently illuminate every part of the Bible it touches." "Professor Buber," says Rylaarsdam, "is in a unique way the agent through whom, in our day, Judaism and Christianity have met and enriched one another." James Muilenburg, another distinguished biblical scholar, points in particular to Buber's statement in *Prophetic Faith* that the literary and religious development of a tradition "need not in any way parallel one another, as it is very possible that a primitive religious element is only found in a late literary form." "If these wise words had been heeded in the past," writes Muilenburg, "the course of Biblical criticism would have been quite different from what it has been." Muilenburg finds *The Prophetic Faith* one of the best expositions of the prophets of Israel. Particularly the chapter on "The Great Tensions" (Elijah, Amos, Hosea, Isaiah) "is not only filled with keen insight and warm appreciation, to which few parallels can be found in contemporary treatment of the prophets, but also with a deep understanding of the fateful issues involved in the ministry of these prophets." Muilenburg also singles out as of great consequence what Buber has to say about the nature of Baal worship in *The Prophetic Faith:*

> Nowhere, so far as the writer is aware, has anyone succeeded in portraying the inner mysteries of nature worship and of the sexual drives associated with them with such power, lucidity, and interior grasp. Only through such an appreciation of the hold which nature religion exerts on its devotees is one able to sense the momentousness of the conflict between Yahweh and Baal or its significance in the history of world religion.

As if anticipating the "eclipse of God" which was more and more to become a central theme in Buber's thought in that year and those that followed, Ewald Wasmuth wrote him in 1951 that after all the noise about the death of God, he could imagine people losing touch with the Bible for some centuries and then someone's reading Buber's *The Prophetic Faith* and finding in it such power that his heart would beat and he would seek again the sources, and the breath of God would return into a godless world.

JEWISH-CHRISTIAN DIALOGUE

Buber's personal Jewish-Christian dialogue during the 1940s was as much one of contending as it was of mutual understanding. In 1940 he agreed to take part in a Jewish-Christian dialogue in Jerusalem organized by Schalom Ben-Chorin. However, sometime after he read the essay that Ben-Chorin sent him and the other participants on "The Question of Christ for the Jews," he reconsidered and abruptly withdrew, much to Ben-Chorin's dismay. Buber called this way of conducting a dialogue between Jews and Christians in Jerusalem basically false. He added a note of personal warning to Ben-Chorin that his dialectical gifts had often led him to misjudge the seriousness of a situation and the weight of the responsibility. "In a Jewish sphere in which utterances about religious topics are almost always accepted and treated purely intellectually, that might have no serious consequences. But in the meeting between Judaism and Christianity everything is unforeseeably binding and momentous, or can become so in an instant."

Ben-Chorin responded that he was greatly disappointed and claimed that he was fully aware of the seriousness of the situation. "In the hour of uttermost threat, Jews and Christians in the city which is holy to both of them should enter honorably and without reservation into a common dialogue of faith." After talking with Buber about this event and reflecting on it, Ben-Chorin later attributed Buber's refusal to a desire on Buber's part not to start from a controversial question but from a common ground which the two religions shared, such as the prophetic message of the Old Testament. For his own part, he held that one could begin the dialogue from either side, the Old Testament or the New, and should if one did not want the dialogue to degenerate into fine phrases.

That even at this period Buber did not wish to avoid confrontation with Christians on the question of Christ is shown by the fact that in 1942 and 1943 he held a series of lectures at Rabbi Kurt Wilhelm's synagogue in Jerusalem that formed the core of *Two Types of Faith*, his book on Jesus and Paul. In 1943 Buber wrote to Lina Lewy, the

Jewish disciple of Leonhard Ragaz, in response to her essay "Do We Need Jesus?" that he could not affirm, as she did, the "Union of the Old and New Testament" "because Jesus, to whom I feel close and united in many things, is for me just not what he is for you, the Messiah; because in general I may not believe in a Messiah who has already come, so and so many years ago; because I sense the unre-deemedness of the world all too deeply to be able to agree with the conception of a completed redemption—even if it be only of the 'soul' (I *will* not live with a 'redeemed' soul in an unredeemed world)." "*God* is our help in all need and none outside of him. But this was also—of this I am certain—the faith of Jesus himself. I do not believe in Jesus, but I believe *with* him."

Buber, to be sure, believed with Ragaz, as the latter wrote him, in the superiority of Israel to both Judaism and Christianity. When he learned of the death of Ragaz in December 1945, he was shattered in his innermost heart, as he told Lina Lewy. "To the cause of the reality of faith, which is common to all genuine Jews and Christians, it is a great, irreparable blow; especially for those of us who strive for the renewal of Israel which nowhere in the world had such a friend as Ragaz, who, although himself a Christian, was a true 'Israelite' accord-ing to his image of Israel." It was in a memorial address for Ragaz in Kurt Wilhelm's synagogue in Jerusalem that Buber made his most concise and impassioned statement on the place of Jesus in the Jewish community, a statement which shows at once the sympathy and the "otherness" which have marked his dialogue with his Christian friends. It also shows, as does the letter to Lina Lewy, the indelible impact of the Holocaust on Buber:

> I firmly believe that the Jewish community in the course of its renais-sance, will recognize Jesus; and not merely as a great figure in its reli-gious history, but also in the organic context of a Messianic development extending over millennia, whose final goal is the Redemp-tion of Israel and of the world. But I believe equally firmly that we will never recognize Jesus as the Messiah Come, for this would contradict the deepest meaning of our Messianic passion. . . . In our view redemp-tion occurs forever, and none has yet occurred. Standing, bound and shackled, in the pillory of mankind, we demonstrate with the bloody body of our people the unredeemedness of the world. For us there is no cause of Jesus; only the cause of God exists for us.

Buber began his memorial address on Ragaz with the statement, "In this darkest hour of our history only a few call themselves our friends." Some did so because the Jews were persecuted, others out of a respect for the Jews, as the bodily continuation of that horde that once stood about the burning mountain, still others out of horror because since the days of the shambles and gas chambers even the most secure among us appear to them as the living dead, an only seemingly living generation. In contrast to these, Ragaz was a true friend of the Jews; for, recognizing all the fragmentation of their inner existence, he nonetheless saw in them the chrysalis in which Israel awaits its renewal. He saw Israel as called upon to live a certain life, the life of a righteous people. "The way to this life leads," said Buber, "over the mass graves of the gas chambers. It is the way that a dreadful and merciful God, our Lord and the Lord of the world, 'whose plans are not our plans,' leads us to ourselves, to what he intends for us." Although we understand him today even less than ever; yet from his cruel signs we can read in blood and fire that we are still chosen—not as individuals but as a people. "Conscience is no 'Jewish invention,' as that subman Hitler is supposed to have said; but in this our weak, obstinate, unfaithful Jewish existence it has become flesh." Ragaz was a genuine friend because he saw this and because, in opposition to those who hold that the election of Israel has passed over to Christianity, he held that Judaism and Christianity are the two living streams of Israel and that each must become itself in order to be able to come to the other. Ragaz foresaw an acceptance by the Jews of the person of Jesus but not of the Christian Christ, and it was to this expectation that Buber spoke in his impassioned statement on "the cause of Jesus."

Buber's "meeting" with Archbishop Hakim of Jerusalem, in contrast, was an encounter which was in no sense a genuine dialogue. Representing the Arab Christian churches, Hakim attacked Zionism on the grounds that it is based on biblical promises in the Old Testament which were abrogated by the New. "All promises given to the people of Israel in the Old Testament have been annulled by the advent of Chirst." Buber replied in a letter to the *Palestine Post* that "instead of paving the way for the Peace of God by revealing that, in spite of everything, religion as an authority immediately responsible to God stands above the atrocious battles raging between the peoples of this miserable mankind, representatives of religious communities had added fuel to hatred and hostility. Hakim used as a political argument the declaration that God has abrogated and annulled his Covenant with Israel, and he did this in the very city where once, in the hour of the first catastrophe, the word was spoken of Israel: 'I will bring them back to this place' and then, 'I will make with them an eternal covenant'—two pronouncements that, in this connection, cannot be understood as meaning any other community but this people of the Jews."

According to Ben-Chorin, Buber finally could not tolerate hearing the Bible spoken of as the Old and New Testaments. "God does not make any testaments," he once ironically remarked, "no Old and no New." He knew, of course, that the word *testament* in this connection means the old and new covenant, but theologically the word "testament" has often taken on the character of a last-will disposition of God for all those orthodox Jews and Christians who will not admit any further development. In Ben-Chorin's first conversations with Buber about Jesus, the church, and theology, Buber radically rejected systematic and dogmatic theology. "I speak as a scholar of religion and know religions of which you have perhaps no inkling," he said to Ben-Chorin. He was particularly skeptical of modern religion, since in his view religions could arise only out of an unquestioned binding with transcendence, not out of intellectual speculations or romantic enthusiasms. He saw the Mormons and the Christian Scientists in America as caricatures of religion in the nineteenth century, and their widespread dissemination made no impression on him. On the other hand, he followed with great sympathy the fight of the worker priests in France around 1950, who went into the proletarian quarters in order to live with the workers and assist them. Decades before, Leonhard Ragaz had given up his professorship and settled in the workers' quarter of Zurich in order to carry the message of the kingdom of God for this earth out of the cathedral and into the houses of the weary and heavy-laden.

Even when he conducted his Open Forum "experiments in dialogue" in the Jerusalem synagogue of Rabbi Kurt Wilhelm, Buber refused to take part in the service beforehand. Most religious people, and not only the Orthodox, could not understand Buber's "religious abstinence." Buber's living faith was an unmediated and thereby a primal Jewish one, Ben-Chorin explains, adding that it is often overlooked that the Jewish Law has taken on the function of a mediator between God and the people of Israel. Buber's total rejection of mediation, his direct dialogical knowledge of God, caused him also to renounce for himself all covert Jewish forms of mediation. More radically than the Hasidim, Buber rejected every division of life into holy and profane spheres. Buber forsook the rituals that designated set days and hours, circumstances and spheres, as holy in order to bring into the light of God those wide stretches of everyday life that the Jewish rituals leave in the darkness of profanity.

PHILOSOPHY AND PSYCHOLOGY

In December 1947, Hugo Bergmann wrote Buber from Stockholm, where he was giving some lectures on Buber, raising the questions of reciprocity in the I-Thou relationship when the partner is an animal, a plant, or a stone; and whether *every* genuine I-Thou relationship is at the same time a revelation of God. In responding to the first problem, which Buber conceded was not sufficiently clarified in *I and Thou,* Buber made an important stride in the development of his own philosophy. In contrast to those who see nature as dead and inanimate, Buber held that every genuine perception (*Wahrnehmen,* literally "true taking" in the German)—in the sense of the full readiness of the perceiving being—is at the same time a genuine receiving (*Wahrgeben,* literally "true giving" in the German) from the side of the "object." "The so-called passivity of nature is not its innermost reality. The more genuine the beholding, the more it is a real meeting between the actual human person and the reality of nature, which is in itself unknown and unknowable yet can be beheld." The participation of nature in the meeting is totally different from that of the human person and can even totally escape our observation. Yet we ought not for that reason to degrade it to mere metaphor, as when we say, "This *works* on me." The totality of this experience Buber later designated as the threshold of mutality—within which there are gradations. There can be no question here of a *dialogue,* only of a kind of mutuality. Therefore in "Dialogue" Buber did not speak of this world. In the Postscript to the second edition of *I and Thou* in 1958 Buber spelled out this new understanding explicitly and at length.

To Bergmann's second question Buber replied that he meant nothing other than the Hasidic teaching that every relationship to any thing or being can be "raised" to a relationship to the divine. But this is only a statement about our side of the relationship, not an "objective" revelation. "The danger of activism is greater in the Hasidic conception than in my own more restrained one," Buber wrote Bergmann, and added: "In no way do I mean that God speaks to us only through the I-Thou relationship to a finite Thou; rather he speaks to us in every manner, both through every medium and without any other medium than our own nature." The acoustical voices of which the Bible speaks Buber saw not as an experience coming from the outside but as a voice surging up "in the ears" of the person himself, which nonetheless is altogether transcendent.

In response to an article that Walter Kaufmann sent him in 1949 on "Nietzsche's Admiration for Socrates," Buber made a statement to Kaufmann that showed his own thoroughly dialogical approach to the "eternal values." Remarking that Kaufmann might have done more to answer the question—"Why this ambivalence?"—Buber suggested that one could, for example, show that Nietzsche wanted to be a Socratic man and that he did not succeed because he was lacking in the immediacy of human relationships and that Nietzsche increasingly doubted his own capacity to grasp eternal values until he finally denied those that were at hand and in their place proclaimed "new" values that were no values at all. "Both motives could, in my opinion, even be demonstrated to be finally one; for the living reality of eternal values is only given to human beings in the immediacy of relationship." To a correspondent concerned with the concept of personality in recent German literature, Buber averred that the stress should not be laid on "love," which is a peak and a grace, but on immediacy and wholeness in general in the relationship to the other, to the adequate making present of his existence, including the unreserved "entering-into-him." To Ernst Michel, who had married again (his first wife died just after the war), Buber wrote in 1950 that "the person who as a whole . . . enters into marriage with the other and forms a bond with him may sense in a special manner that only discloses itself thus, the aeonian character of human existence."

In the short statement "On the Situation of Philosophy" that he wrote for the International Congress of Philosophy in Amsterdam in 1948, Buber presented a remarkably concise and cogent critique of the later writings of Heidegger on truth. "Heidegger rightly postulates that we must not proceed from the notion of truth as an 'agreement of a representation with the object that is represented,' but from truth as an inherent property of Being, its 'unconcealment.'" But Heidegger tries to relate this unconcealment simply to man and his essence, as though Being sent man forth in order to attain to adequate openness through him. In doing so Heidegger is ignoring three ground-breaking discoveries in the critical self-knowledge of man: the way in which our knowledge is bound to the historical nature of our existence (Vico), to the forms of our perception (Kant), and to the sociologically and psychologically determined diversity of the knowing individual (Marx and Freud). "It is a hopeless illusion to wish to set in opposition to the dogma of man's conditionedness the simple assertion that he is unconditioned. The light of the truth inherent in Being breaks up in the human spirit and becomes manifest to the world in such brokenness." Our task is to apprehend a *human* truth: "The future competence of the philosophizing person depends upon his knowing his thinking as *both* conditioned *and* unconditioned *in one . . .*"

Despite his failure to complete *The Place of Faith,* Buber's interest in psychology continued during these years and with it the development of his philosophical anthropology. In 1946 in reply to a question of Hans Trüb's, Buber declared that the world is clearly, first of all, that against which the soul "pushes." For the infant, the world is not the mother's breast, which belongs to him, but the table corner which causes him pain. Thus world is first of all what presents itself emphatically as "other than I," which I do not include in my soul and cannot enter into. The perception of world *as world* takes place ever again through vexation, resistance, contradiction, absurdity—which must be overcome before one can come to an understanding or even to a friendship with or love for the world. This conception of the world led Buber to a critique of the modern misuse of the concept of the "unconscious."

The world is not mine, Buber wrote Trüb, but it can "become" mine again and again in genuine meetings, not mine as *in* me, but mine as *with* me. This fact has become obscured by the modern conception of the "unconscious." The unconscious is to be acknowledged as a psychological auxiliary—to be treated with foresight and restraint, to be confronted ever again with reality, always to be grasped dynamically and not statically, as process and not as something that can be fixed as an object. But it pretends to be immensely more. Through the fiction of the "world in the soul," therefore of a world that is mine in me, it wants to conceal the possibility of the "life of the soul with the world." This was one of Buber's clearest statements on the danger of "psychologism," to which he had pointed at length a quarter of a century before in his address to Jung's and Trüb's Psychological Club in Zurich on "The Psychologizing of the World."

Buber counseled both Hans Trüb and Ernst Michel in the strongest terms against employing theological terms in their psychological writings, advice which the former accepted and the latter rejected. Buber pointed out to Michel in 1949 that his essay on hysteria was intended for nonbelievers as well as believers and questioned in any case whether a theological category such as Transcendence could properly be included in an essentially anthropological-psychological presentation. Michel replied that for him being addressed as Thou by Transcendence was the enduring central reality of human existence. We try to escape this reality in "unbelief," but it remains in effect through *negative* symptoms, such as hysteria. This is an excellent example of the difference between Buber's *anthropological* approach to the philosophy of dialogue and the *theological* approach of so many of the Christian thinkers who adopted it.

In the same letter Michel spoke to Buber of the "painful event of the departure of our beloved friend Hans Trüb," whose posthumous book *Healing through Meeting* he and Arie Sborowitz edited and Buber introduced. This book was an *Auseinandersetzung,* or discussion, of the dialectical psychology of Jung against which Trüb developed his own dialogical-anthropological approach to psychotherapy. In this introduction to *Healing through Meeting* Buber did not mention Jung, but in a letter to Trüb in 1946 Buber anticipated his own famous controversy with Jung five years later. Commenting on the *Introduction to Mythology* by Jung and Karl Kerényi, which he found "very instructive to the unprejudiced reader," Buber said that seemingly the two authors deal with the same subject from different sides. But in truth Kerényi means by myth something that arises *out of contact with the world,* as the disclosure and shaping of the mysteries of this reality; Jung, in contrast, understands by myth what arises of its own *in the soul* and what ultimately cannot express or mean anything else than the mysteries of the soul itself.

PERSONAL AND LITERARY

In 1947, Buber went to Europe, where he gave more than sixty lectures at universities in Holland, Belgium, Sweden, Denmark, France, and England. The enthusiastic reception that he received in England and Holland surprised him and made clear to him that he was more in touch with the intellectual, cultural, and spiritual life of Europe than he had thought. This was true in France, too, though there it was more an intellectual receptivity that met him than a personal one. He was also told of a "Buber renaissance" in Germany, although at this time he would not consider visiting Germany, much less lecturing there. On the same trip he renewed contact with his old friend Lambert Schneider, who became again his main publisher in

Germany in the years to come. Another form of renewal of ties was the exchange of letters that Buber had with the Welsh scholar Benjamin Morse, who sent Buber two essays he had written on Buber's influence on Rilke, particularly *The Legend of the Baal-Shem* on the Ninth "Duino Elegy." Eduard Strauss wrote Buber from New York of a lasting feeling of alienation which he described as "America sickness." Although he claimed that Buber could not understand what he was feeling, he reminded Buber of an hour years before in Frankfurt when in response to Strauss's complaints Buber sprang up suddenly with the spontaneity characteristic of him and said, "What would you have really? There is still Mozart!" Kurt Singer, writing Buber from Sydney, Australia, in 1948, reminded him of the time in Hamburg when the two of them sat in the Chinese junk and watched the masts of the sailboats rise and fall on the lightly moving water: "I remember no hour more still, absorbed in its nearness and presentness."

In 1948, for Buber's seventieth birthday, Nahum Glatzer wrote Buber from New York that he was "the greatest Jewish spokesman of our day." Glatzer also reminded Buber that he had said to him that he wanted to live to be very old. At the same time Hugo Bergmann reported to Buber from Stockholm the response of Nelly Sachs (the Jewish poetess who was later to win the Nobel Prize for Literature at the same time as Buber's friend Shai Agnon) to his lecture on Buber. Nelly Sachs, whose book of poems *In the Dwellings of Death* was shortly to appear, wrote Bergmann of how greatly enriched she had been by, and of how very, very close she felt to, Buber. "It seems to me to be not only the truest, but also really the only way that a deepened Judaism, that again is concerned with hallowing the everyday and the whole human being, can go. I have often had the remarkable experience with my Swedish poet friends, whom I have sought to bring close to Buber and to whom I have lent the Hasidic tales, that even those who are averse to every fixed dogma can easily relate Judaism's conception of a world that is not yet redeemed but waiting to be redeemed, with their own conception, so often close to existentialism."

In 1949, Buber wrote Bernard Rang, the son of his late friend Florens Christian Rang, reproving him for the liberties he had taken in recasting his father's writings on Goethe into the form of a "dialogue" between his father and himself. The real reader is not seized by a content, but by a living form, a living unity of content and form. "As with a genuine poem, so with a genuine exposition, nothing can be rewritten without injuring an artery of life." At the same time Buber told Max Brod that Brod's novel on Galileo had achieved the rare feat of really conveying the earthly destiny of the spirit through narrating the spiritual struggles in the depths of the person between one spiritual urge and another. One novelist after another in our time has failed to make visible the way in which the destiny of life and the destiny of the spirit are united.

Probably the most unlikely of Buber's writings during these years of war and crisis is a delightful little piece titled "Advice to Frequenters of Libraries," published by the *Branch Library Book News* of the New York Public Library. A real book, Buber suggested, is "not a mere congeries of reflections, descriptions, emotional outpourings," but one that deals with a single theme and expresses its author in a unified fashion. To read a book truly means to enter its realm without preconceived notions and let it astonish you, no matter how unusual its manner. Genuine reading requires time, not racing through the pages but allowing for breathing, reflection, deliberation, looking at the author, savoring your pleasure, reconcentrating your thoughts.

> Pauses are as important in our relations with books as in our relations with human beings; pauses are the touchstone of all relationships, the test of the genuineness of both parties; if the relationship is a true one, it will only be enhanced by pauses.

After you have visited the library ten times to read books, you should go there once to look at them; for more than any other product of the human race, books should arouse our sense of wonder. "The man who wrote the book you now hold in your hand cast his bread upon the waters—so that it might ultimately come to you." Allow the objective form to dissolve and you will find yourself in the presence of a great soul: "Marvel of marvels!" In transmission and reception the spirit is preserved. Then after going ten times to look at the books, go once to look at the readers and feel how each of them, like yourself, wants to make contact with the spirit that has been sent forth and is waiting to be received. They all share in a common desire, a common thirst to live in touch with the spirit. If you look at the features, gestures, and postures of each you will learn something you will not be able to learn as well anywhere else—that books are great but man is greater.

> I know men whose relationship to books is perfect, but who have no direct contact with other men. . . . He who does not truly concern himself with mortals is not permitted to come into the presence of the immortals. If you cannot turn wholeheartedly to your neighbor in the

reading room when he asks you to interpret a passage from Plato, you will realize, sooner or later, that your own contact with Plato was a contact with a ghost.

The eternal spirit that reveals itself to us in books will escape us if we do not bear witness to it in our communication with other persons.

"Advice to the Frequenters of Libraries" is very close in spirit to the beautiful little essay "Books and Men," which Buber wrote in 1947 and privately printed and distributed to his friends. "Books and Men" is a personal confession that crowns Buber's development from the "easy word" to the "hard word" and from the spiritual and cultural preoccupations of his youth to his later unwavering commitment to the "lived concrete."

> If I had been asked in my early youth whether I preferred to have dealings only with men or only with books, my answer would certainly have been in favour of books. In later years this has become less and less the case. Not that I have had so much better experiences with men than with books; on the contrary, purely delightful books even now come my way more often than purely delightful men. But the many bad experiences with men have nourished the meadow of my life as the noblest book could not do, and the good experiences have made the earth into a garden for me. On the other hand, no book does more than remove me into a paradise of great spirits, where my innermost heart never forgets, I cannot dwell long, nor even wish that I could do so. For (I must say this straight out in order to be understood) my innermost heart loves the world more than it loves the spirit. I have not, indeed, cleaved to life in the world as I might have; . . . again and again I remain guilty towards it for falling short of what it expects of me, and this is partly, to be sure, because I belong so to the spirit.

The manna of books cannot equal the brown bread of men on whose crust I break my teeth, a bread of which I can never have enough. In the most venerable of living men I always find more to love than to revere: I find in him something of this world, that is simply there as the spirit never can be. All the prattle of men yields no word such as sounds forth out of books; yet out of the human silence behind the prattle whispers to you the spirit *as soul.* "She is the beloved."

> I knew nothing of books when I came forth from the womb of my mother, and I shall die without books, with another human hand in my own. I do, indeed, close my door at times and surrender myself to a book, but only because I can open the door again and see a human face looking at me.

This is the testimony welling up from the soul of the man who knew early that he was destined to love the world!

TALES OF THE HASIDIM
AND *THE WAY OF MAN*

The two volumes of *The Tales of the Hasidim (The Early Masters* and *The Later Masters)* which Buber published originally in Hebrew under the title *Or Hagganuz* and later in German, English, and French, among other languages, crown Buber's lifetime of retelling Hasidic legends and stories. In them, two earlier German works written since Buber rejected his original overly free poetic re-creations for ones that remain closely faithful to the simple rough originals, are included, and even these were totally reworked. By far the greater part of them were written after Buber's arrival in Palestine in 1938. In his Preface written in the summer of 1946 Buber credited "the air of this land" with the urge to this new and more comprehensive composition. The Jewish sages of old said that it makes one wise, but to Buber it granted a different gift: the strength to make a new beginning even after he had regarded his work on Hasidic legends as completed. The form that Buber found for these tales was that of the "legendary anecdotes" which reconstruct the events that lie at the heart of the tales. "They are called anecdotes because each one of them communicates an event complete in itself, and legendary because at the base of them lies the stammering of inspired witnesses who witnessed to what befell them." The Hasidim believed that telling stories about the *zaddikim* was in itself a real event that carried to future generations the power that once was active by propagating it in the living word. This quality of story as event is beautifully captured by a story within a story that Buber told in the Preface:

A rabbi, whose grandfather had been a disciple of the Baal-Shem, was asked to tell a story. "A story," he said, "must be told in such a way that it constitutes help in itself." And he told: "My grandfather was lame. Once they asked him to tell a story about his teacher. And he related how the holy Baal-Shem used to hop and dance while he prayed. My grandfather rose as he spoke, and he was so swept away by his story that he himself began to hop and dance to show how the master had done. From that hour on he was cured of his lameness. That's the way to tell a story!

In the Preface, Buber attributed the preponderance of anecdotes to the general tendency of the Jewish Diaspora spirit to express the events of history and of the present in such a way that they are cleanly culled from the mass of the irrelevant and culminate in a significant saying. In Hasidism, the *zaddik* expresses his teachings in actions that are symbolic and, frequently, in utterances which supplement or help to interpret those actions. Although Buber saw parallels in *The Little Flowers of Saint Francis,* he contended that in the literature of the world he knew of no other group of legendary anecdotes which illustrates to such a degree the way in which a single incident conveys the meaning of life "so homogeneously and yet with such variety, as the Hasidic anecdotes." When an Israeli scholar visited the distinguished Greek writer Nikos Kazantzakis in a hospital in Copenhagen, he asked the latter concerning some stories in his life of Saint Francis that he did not recognize from the Latin sources. "You ought to know," said Kazantzakis. "I took them from Buber's *Tales of the Hasidim!*"

Psychology and adornment had to be eschewed in favor of the "naked" anecdote. Moreover, of the material Buber had collected these two volumes represented only one-tenth. Many anecdotes were set aside because they were not sufficiently significant in themselves or for the understanding of Hasidic life. But even more had to be set aside because they did not serve to characterize one of the *zaddikim* on which the book centers. In contrast to various "Hasidic anthologies" which organize their tales by topic, Buber retained the organic unity of tales grouped about a *zaddik,* thereby revealing a uniqueness in the teaching of each Hasidic rabbi and a subtle interconnection between one tale and another that no topical arrangement could capture.

To the Hasid the concrete is itself the bearer of spiritual truth. "'You can learn something from everything,'" including what man has made, said the rabbi of Sadagora.

> "What can we learn from a train?" one Hasid asked dubiously.
> "That because of one second one can miss everything."
> "And from the telegraph?"
> "That every word is counted and charged."
> "And the telephone?"
> "That what we say here is heard there."

The Hasidic exegesis of the Bible takes place with a freedom that manages to remain close to the spirit of biblical Judaism while adding a unique twist of its own. Although the *zaddik* explains the verse within him, he also asks that you become an ear listening to the universe of the word. Another characteristic of *The Tales of the Hasidim* is their humor. When the disciples of Rabbi Pinhas told him how afraid they were that the Evil Urge would pursue them, he replied, "Don't worry. You have not gotten high enough for it to pursue you. For the time being, you are still pursuing it!"

"The great crime of man is not the sins that he commits," said Rabbi Bunam, but "that he can turn at every moment, and does not do so." "In this day and age," said Rabbi Moshe of Kobryn to a disciple who complained that his wretched circumstances were an obstacle to learning and prayer, "the greatest devotion, greater than learning and prayer, consists in accepting the world exactly as it happens to be." If a Hasid starts to pray in one place and moves to another, the first place cries out mournfully, "If you met with obstacles here, it was a sign that it was up to you to redeem me." Man was not created to perfect his soul, said Menahem Mendel of Kotzk, but "so that he might lift up the Heavens."

In later generations the fervent love for the *zaddik* often degenerated into "a coarsened form of reverence on the part of those who regard him as a great magician, as one who is an intimate of heaven and can right all that is wrong, who relieves his Hasidim of straining their own souls and secures them a desirable place in the hereafter." One of the signal contributions that Buber makes in *The Tales of the Hasidim* is his subtle delineation of this decline in his discussion of particular *zaddikim* in the long introduction that precedes each volume. "The wise Rabbi Bunam's profound table talk and crystalline parables bear powerful witness to the religious truth," Buber expounded, "but he cannot be regarded as the body and voice of the religious spirit." The brilliant aphorisms of the later *zaddikim* "are not parts of a unified thinking life." "Many great men of the later generations are characterized by the fact that they have everything except the basic unity of everything. The great *zaddik* of the earlier generations, in contrast, was himself an image of the teachings. His every action 'was the stature and the word of the Torah.' His truth was possessed only when it was lived."

The most effective single portrait in *The Tales of the Hasidim* is the sixty-five pages devoted to the Baal-Shem. "Worry and gloom are the roots of all the power of evil," the Baal-Shem warned. "Alas, the world is full of enormous lights and mysteries," he exclaimed, "and man shuts them from himself with one small hand!" Like Jesus, the Baal-Shem preferred sinners who were humble to scholars and the self-righteous who were proud. The "service of men in the world to the very hour of their death," said the Baal-Shem, is "to struggle with the extraneous and time after time to uplift and fit it into the nature of the Divine Name." What matters is not mystical exercises *(kavanot)* but the wholehearted turning to God *(kavana).* "What are all special mystical intentions compared to one really heartfelt grief!"

Although himself a great scholar, Dov Baer, the Maggid, or preacher of Mezritch, followed the Baal-Shem in emphasizing fervor rather than intellectual subtlety: "Every mystery of the world can be unriddled by the particular kind of meditation fitted to it. But God loves the thief who breaks the lock open: I mean the man who breaks his heart for God." The biblical dialogue between God and man is bodied forth, with characteristic humor, in Rabbi Bunam's answer to his own question, Why is it written, "I am the Lord thy God, who brought thee out of the Land of Egypt," rather than "who created heaven and earth"? "Heaven and earth," exclaimed Bunam; "then man might have said: 'Heaven—that is too much for me.' So God said to man: 'I am the one who fished you out of the mud. Now you come here and listen to me!'" To Hasidism the love of one's neighbor is just another side of one's love for God. "Pray for your enemies that all may be well with them," Rabbi Mikhal commanded his sons. "And rest assured that more than all prayers, this is, indeed, the service of God." Rabbi Moshe Leib of Sasov could not turn away a drunken peasant who demanded admission to his house in the middle of the night; for "if God gets along with him, can I reject him?" Moshe Leib learned to love men from listening to two drunken peasants one of whom said to the other, "How can you say you love me when you do not know what I need?"

"Everyone must have two pockets," said Rabbi Bunam. "In his right pocket are to be the words: 'For my sake was the world created,' and in his left: 'I am earth and ashes.'" "There is no rung of human life on which we cannot find the holiness of God everywhere and at all times," for there is no place which is not a ground of hallowing. The direction of man's passions means the hallowing of his urges, but it does not mean a superhuman perfection that overcomes them entirely. "Ye shall be holy unto me, but as men," expounded the rabbi of Kotzk, "ye shall be humanly holy unto me." We should not be preoccupied with our own sins but with our share in the redemption of the world. "Have I sinned or have I not sinned—what does Heaven get out of it?" asked the rabbi of Ger. "In the time I am brooding over it I could be stringing pearls for the delight of Heaven."

Buber's *Tales of the Hasidim* offers us a deeply impressive image of the person whose piety meant joy in the world rather than turning away from it—a joy compounded of ecstasy and suffering. "We pray that God may accept our call for help," said Rabbi Uri of Strelisk, "but also that he, who knows that which is hidden, may hear the silent cry of the soul."

In 1949 when Martin Buber presented Paula with a copy of the German edition of *The Tales of the Hasidim,* he wrote in it an inscription in the form of a poem that recalled their earlier work together creating the legends of the Baal-Shem. This was one of the poems that Buber himself selected for preservation in "Gleanings" just before his death.

> *Do you still know, how we in our young years*
> *Traveled together on this sea?*
> *Visions came, great and wonderful,*
> *We beheld them together, you and I.*
> *How image joined itself with images in our hearts!*
> *How a mutual animated describing*
> *Arose out of it and lived between you and me!*
> *We were there and were yet wholly here*
> *And wholly together, roaming and grounded.*
> *Thus the voice awoke that since then proclaims*
> *And witnesses to old majesty as new,*
> *True to itself and you and to both together.*
> *Take then this witness in your hands,*
> *It is an end and yet has no end,*
> *For something eternal listens to it and listens to us,*
> *How we resound out of it, I and Thou.*

In 1949 Hermann Hesse wrote to Buber thanking him for the new volume in the Library of World Literature:

> It has for a long time been my wish to see the tales of the Hasidim collected thus. I am happy to have experienced that, and for you it must be a no less great joy. Seemingly it was a long way from the scattered anecdotal legends of that epoch of Eastern Jewry to this book of world literature. But where a light burns, its beams do not get lost, and if the stories of the ancient Chinese about the lives and sayings of their wise men could wait two thousand years for their entrance into the pantheon of the nations, without losing anything of their force, then the two centuries from the blooming of Hasidism to this classic collection is a short time.

Hesse, who had himself received the Nobel Prize for Literature the previous year, nominated Buber for this same prize. In his letter to the Swedish Academy, Hesse spoke of Buber as "the great teacher and leader of the spiritual elite among the Jews." "As translator of the Bible, as rediscoverer and interpreter of Hasidic wisdom, as scholar, as great writer, and finally as a wise man, as teacher and representative of a high ethic and humanity, he is, in the opinion of those who know his work, one of the leading and most valuable personalities in the present day literature of the world." In a letter that Hesse wrote to a friend explaining his nomination of Buber for the Nobel Prize in Literature, it was to *The Tales of the Hasidim* in particular that he pointed:

> Martin Buber is in my judgment not only one of the few wise men who live on the earth at the present time, he is also a writer of a very high order, and, more than that, he has enriched world literature with a genuine treasure as has no other living author—*The Tales of the Hasidim*. . . . Martin Buber . . . is the worthiest spiritual representative of Israel, the people that has had to suffer the most of all people in our time.

These letters, Buber confided to me later, were written with "a sympathy that I know is deep." Writing to Hesse himself after he had received from friends in Stockholm the wording of Hesse's letter of nomination, Buber said, "I have once again felt, and with a forcefulness as never before, how unimportant 'fame' is and how important is confirmation by those to whom our trust belongs. We mortals need to be confirmed by our mortal brothers." This theme of confirmation was to be central to the philosophical anthropology that Buber set forth in *The Knowledge of Man* in the years immediately following and particularly in "Distance and Relation," which concludes with the sentence: "It is from one man to another that the heavenly bread of self-being is passed."

In December 1949, Buber's old friend Rudolf Pannwitz informed Buber that, aside from the enrichment, he found in *The Tales of the Hasidim* "something conclusive: the canon of a religion." Of *For the Sake of Heaven* ("the second part of the canon, a religious tragedy and secretly a genuine drama") and *The Tales of the Hasidim* taken together, Pannwitz wrote: "Both books point thus as a perfect crystallization into infinite and chaotic backgrounds which join wonderfully with the meaningful teaching of the books."

In his contribution to *The Philosophy of Martin Buber,* Walter Kaufmann says of Buber's *Tales of the Hasidim* that they are definitive in their simplicity. "It was Buber who cut these diamonds. . . . he achieved perfection by cutting." Kaufmann contrasts Buber's courage in daring to end a story at the right point with Luke, who sets the sayings that are found in Matthew in inferior settings. In *The Tales of the Hasidim* "Buber presents gem upon gem without mounting each in a setting of inferior quality. Buber's stories cannot be improved by cutting. That is more than one can say of the art of any of the four evangelists." Kaufmann is aware that many might regard what he is saying as blasphemous, but he holds to his positions, even dismissing the criticism that Buber is not an impartial historian because of the religious significance of what Buber has given us:

> What saves Buber's work is its perfection. He has given us one of the great religious books of all time, a work that invites comparison with the great Scriptures of mankind. . . . The rank of these works does not depend on their positivistic accuracy but on their profundity. And that is true also of *The Tales of the Hasidim.*

Like the great religious scriptures, Buber's Hasidic tales draw on a living religious tradition, selected and given form. "Buber's collection has grown out of his own long dialogue with a tradition, and it loses none of its original impressiveness after one has lived with it for a generation. . . . Here is religion that stands up to philosophic questions as the sophisticated discourses of theologians don't." Kaufmann agrees with Hermann Hesse that Buber, with his *Tales of the Hasidim,* has enriched world literature with a genuine treasure as has no other living author. "These stories will surely be remembered widely when the theologians of our time have gone the way of Harnack and Schleiermacher, not to mention lesser names that have long been forgotten by all but specialists."

In the Author's Foreword written in the spring of 1959, Buber said that in the two volumes of *Hasidism and the Way of Man (Hasidism and Modern Man* and *The Origins and Meaning of Hasidism),* in contrast to *The Tales of the Hasidim* and *For the Sake of Heaven,* he directly and explicitly expressed "the message to the human world that Hasidism did not want to be, but that it was and is." Buber saw the truth of Hasidism as vitally important for persons of *all* faiths; "for now is the hour when we are in danger of forgetting for what purpose we are on earth, and I know of no other teaching that reminds us of this so forcibly." "Hasidism has never set foot in the world of man as Christianity has done," Buber concluded, but "because of its truth and because of the great need of the hour, I carry it into the world against its will." Just how much this was against the will of Hasidism was illustrated all too clearly in June 1965 when the young men of the Hasidic

Bratslaver Seminary in the Mea She'arim in Jerusalem spoke of Buber's death with the Yiddish phrase that one uses for the death of an animal!

Rivka Schatz-Uffenheimer, a disciple of Gershom Scholem and a former student of Buber at the Hebrew University, has pointed out that the Orthodox have misunderstood Buber's relation to Hasidism. Buber never wanted to propagate Hasidism as such, but Hasidism was for him an impressive example of a kind of piety that is tied to life and that has overcome the unholy division into sacred and profane spheres by the hallowing of the whole of life. Nowhere is this clearer than in the little book *The Way of Man* according to the teachings of the Hasidim, which was originally given by Buber as a series of lectures in Holland. In 1948, Hermann Hesse wrote Buber that *The Way of Man* "is probably the most beautiful of your works that I have read." *The Way of Man,* writes Gershom Scholem, "is not only a gem of literature but also an extraordinary lesson in religious anthropology, presented in the language of Hasidism and inspired by a large number of authentic Hasidic sayings."

The Way of Man is an entirely different kind of work from any of Buber's other Hasidic writings. It consists of six sections, each in the form of a commentary on a Hasidic tale, supplemented by other tales and sayings. Yet it is far more than a mere interpretation or summary of Hasidic teaching. No other of Buber's works gives us so much of his own simple wisdom as this remarkable distillation. It ranks with *I and Thou, For the Sake of Heaven,* and *The Tales of the Hasidim* as one of the great and enduring classics. Even more than between the separate tales in each section of *The Tales of the Hasidim,* the sections of *The Way of Man* are organically linked so that it is, in itself, a way of wisdom, which no philosophical statement, however profound, can be. No timeless truth can tell us when we must be concerned about "heart-searching" and when about not being preoccupied with ourselves.

"Heart-Searching," the first section, does not mean introspection or self-analysis but listening to the address of the signs that speak to your life. Only if this is done can life become a way, and only when it becomes a way can we discover our particular way, the unique direction to which we are called. But this can be done only if we listen to those repressed forces that seem to wish to lead us astray but may contain the residue of our "I," our inmost passion. Thus the "Particular Way" leads in its turn to "Resolution," which itself leads back on our lives in such a way as to give us greater personal wholeness. It is lack of wholeness, in turn, which leads us to allow others to expect from us what we are not in fact prepared to give. For this reason "Resolution" must lead in its turn to "Beginning with oneself." "The root of all conflict between me and my fellow-man is that I do not say what I mean and I do not do what I say." If we begin with ourselves, we do not expel conflict and tragedy from the world, but we take responsibility for our presence and for our address to others who respond to us. This wisdom ought not lead us, however, to be preoccupied with ourselves or to regard ourselves as our end. Our goal, our concern, is our work on the world, and our "self-realization," while important, even indispensable, is nonetheless only a by-product of this concern. In that contest we can attain the wisdom of living a true life—here where we stand.

There is a false heart-searching which makes one say, "I shall never get out of where I am; there is nothing I can do about myself." Seeing oneself in this way, one loses one's resources for change. But this is precisely what makes it false: that one focuses on one's image of oneself rather than on responding to what draws one and evokes one's inmost passion. In the "Particular Way" Buber talks about what each person must do to find his inmost wish, what draws his heart most strongly. But sometimes what stirs most deeply within us we know only in the form of the "evil urge," our undirected passion. We have so suppressed our contact with ourselves that only the seemingly "extraneous" is left of what is really us. By no means is it our task to extirpate this evil urge; rather we must give it direction by our response to what calls to us in our uniqueness. At first glance, this resembles Freudian sublimation, as Buber himself pointed out. But the difference is that for Freud the relation to the other is the *means* to the sublimation of the libidinal energy, whereas here it is the other way around. The essential relation to others is the end in itself, and the way to it is the directing of the evil urge.

At rare moments most of us realize that our lives do not participate in a true, fulfilled existence, that it has passed us by. We look every place for it, but there is only one place where we can find it—here where we stand. "If we had power over the ends of the earth, it would not give us that fulfillment of existence which a quiet, devoted relationship to nearby life can give us. If we knew the secrets of the upper world, they would not allow us so much actual participation in true existence as we can achieve by performing with holy intent the task belonging to our daily duties." If we think only in terms of short-term goals, we shall never achieve any true existence. "God dwells where man lets him in." This is our task—to hallow the world by letting God in.

CHAPTER 3

•————————————————————————————•

Kibbutz Socialism
and Adult Education in Israel

•————————————————————————————•

PATHS IN UTOPIA AND KIBBUTZ SOCIALISM

ALONG WITH *What Is Man?* two other expressions of Buber's activity as professor of social philosophy and later as chairman of the Department of Sociology at the Hebrew University were his important theoretical essay "Society and the State" (1951) and his book *Paths in Utopia,* published in Hebrew in 1947 and in English translation in 1949. While the former represents a far-reaching distinction between the "political principle" and the "social principle," the latter is a history of decentralistic socialism, including separate chapters on Proudhon, Kropotkin, Landauer, Marx, and Lenin, as well as one on the kibbutzim of Palestine. Writing to Lambert Schneider, to whom he wished to entrust the German edition of *Paths in Utopia,* Buber said: "The book has had a strong success in England; in the Sunday Times it was characterized as the most important book of the year. I believe that it has a special task to fulfill in Germany—as an intellectual-historical presentation of 'utopian socialism' and criticism of the teachings of Marx and Lenin."

What sets Buber apart from men like Reinhold Niebuhr, Bertrand Russell, and other contemporary political thinkers, and what brings him into fellowship with men like A. D. Gordon, Albert Camus, Carlo Levi, and Ignazio Silone, is the basic distinction that Buber makes between the "social principle" and the "political principle." The "social principle" is the concrete principle of real fellowship and real community. It refers to the amount of social reality that is in existence or being created at any time, and it finds its expression in various social and communal groupings and interrelations. The "political principle," on the other hand, is a basically abstract principle which sacrifices the social reality of fellowship to the domination of government and the surplus power which the state claims for its ever-impending battle with other states and which it uses to increase still further the ascendancy of the political principle. The latent crisis that exists between nation and nation makes the political surplus above what is necessary for order inevitable, but a social restructuring toward maximum decentralization compatible with given social conditions is possible and necessary if mankind is not to be swallowed by the political principle. The social vitality of a nation, its cultural unity and independence, depends on the social spontaneity to be found in it. Social education and a concern for real social change are necessary if this spontaneity is to be preserved and enhanced.

To create new fellowship and social spontaneity in a world in which capitalism has left man lacking in organic social structure and in which communism has lost sight of social regeneration in favor of a rigid political centralism, Buber proposed a federalistic communal socialism. Buber distinguished his socialism from theoretical utopian socialism, which he characterized as a schematic fiction that contrives systems of absolute validity on the basis of an abstract notion of human nature. Topical socialism begins with the diversity and contrariety of the trends of the age and grows out of the needs of a given situation. At the same time this local and topical realization must be nothing but a point of departure for the higher goal of an organic society. This social restructuring can find its progressively comprehensive embodiment, in Buber's opinion, in full cooperatives of ownership and work, village communes, and relations between communes which lead to a *communitas communitatum*—a community of communities eventually broadening to a world confederation of commonwealths, a grouping of nations which, like the individual commune, will preserve the maximum social spontaneity compatible with the situation and the given time.

> The essential point is to decide on the fundamentals: a restructuring of society as a League of Leagues, and a reduction of the State to its proper function, which is to maintain unity; *or* a devouring of an amorphous society by the omnipotent State. . . . The right proportion, tested anew every day according to changing conditions, between group-freedom and collective order; *or* absolute order imposed indefinitely for the sake of an era of freedom alleged to follow "of its own accord."

In 1950 the Oxford University economist S. H. Frankel wrote Buber concerning the very great importance that he saw in *Paths in Utopia* for economic thinking, "and in particular . . . how far it will be possible to break down the over-centralization of our modern societies into those smaller communal units which can alone protect the soul of man, and give him a new ideology of common service in close contact with his fellow men, and in joint endeavour in a group whose meaning he understands." Your letter "arrived while I was ill and somewhat depressed and it did me good," Buber replied, and went on to propose common talks and cooperation in working on the question as to how far decentralization can be effected in the face of the tremendous national centralizing economic forces of our time.

> The acknowledgement of my books as a literary and intellectual performance does not satisfy me at all: they are intended to influence human life and actions. I was glad, therefore, when, two weeks ago, I was told by some Indian scholars and politicians that they are organizing a group which is "to work on the idea of a decentralized state." I consider your letter of no less importance, as such ideas cannot be realized without the support of economic thinking.

It is too bad that Buber could not have lived to witness the impact of the economist E. F. Schumacher's book *Small Is Beautiful!*

In 1953 the German educator Heinz-Joachim Heydorn published an essay, "Martin Buber and Socialism," which began with a moving testimonial to Buber as a person, whom Heydorn, like Heschel, saw as more important even than Buber's books. What makes Buber's life great, Heydorn wrote, cannot be discovered merely through what he has written in his books or through any sum of his sayings.

> Outside of Albert Schweitzer I know no one who has realized in himself a similar great and genuine deep identity of truth and life. . . .

> This little, old man with the penetrating, incorruptible eyes has already today begun to stand out in the brokenness of our time like a legendary figure; he is a living proof of what this life is capable of when it wills to fulfill itself fearlessly and only in responsibility.

That a genuine social revolution can take place only from below, declared Heydorn, will first become convincingly clear when we are able to free ourselves from the predominance of a purely political thought that does not understand the long-term problems of our modern life:

> Buber's inquiries represent, in my opinion, the most important contribution that has been made in many years to the question of socialism. Here the basic question of all renewal is posed once again: the question about man. But this question remains closely bound to reality; it is concerned with man in his present-day form, with man in our time. The reality in which this man lives, the reality of his technical greatness, has barred him in growing measure from the true road to himself. We shall not be able to reopen this road for him if we wish to redeem him through purely political means without restoring to him the immediacy of his existence.

The most important vehicles for social restructuring, Buber announced in *Paths in Utopia,* are the full cooperatives, or village communes, which combine production and consumption, industry and agriculture, in a cooperative community revolving around commonly held land. The most promising experiment in the village commune, in Buber's opinion, has been that of the Jewish collective settlements in Palestine. These have been based on the needs of given local situations combined with socialistic and biblical teachings on social justice. The members of these communes have combined a rare willingness to experiment and unusual critical self-awareness with an "amazingly positive relationship—amounting to a regular faith— . . . to the inmost being of their Commune." The communes themselves, moreover, have worked together in close cooperation and at the same time have left complete freedom for the constant branching off of new forms and different types of social structure, the most famous of which are the kvutza and the kibbutz. The rapid influx of Jewish refugees from the Nazis into Palestine during the years of the Third Aliyah resulted in many cases in the rise of a quasi-elite who were not able to provide true leadership for the communes and came into conflict with the genuine *halutzim.* Despite this fact and the politicization which in recent years split kibbutzim along party lines, Buber felt that the Jewish communes were of central significance in the struggle for a structurally new society in which individual groups would be given the greatest possible autonomy and yet would enjoy the greatest possible interrelationship with one another. In 1952 in America, Buber reaffirmed his conviction that the most important decision of the next generations is that between a socialism of power and a spontaneous socialism springing up from below, between the "political principle" and the "social principle." "The coming state of humanity in the great crisis depends very much on whether another type of socialism can be set up against Moscow, and I venture even today to call it Jerusalem."

In 1944, Buber contrasted the early Jewish settlements in Palestine, which were merely groups of small private farmsteads, with those newer ones created by the communal will of human beings working in cooperation, and he characterized these newer settlements as "the passage from a decaying conception of communal living to a new and organic one."

> Those early settlements with their frail rows of cottages remind one of the street of some small Moldavian town, of which one was surprised to learn that it had a name. The ingenious and harmonious layout of the living quarters of the new colonies around a functional center is reminiscent of those noble suburbs of Amsterdam where groups of like-minded workers established the external structure of their lives around the fixed center of a cultural meeting place or people's hall.

The communal experiments in Palestine differed from the many remarkable, short-lived experiments of communists or anarchists in the nineteenth century, especially in North America, in that the latter were based on some religious doctrine or secularist dogma which rigidified them from the beginning. The kibbutzim and kvutzoth, in contrast, remained flexible, both in their response to the cruelly severe demands of the environment and to their desire for a life of mutual trust, help, and responsibility. Moreover, the Jewish village communes did not remain isolated, as the earlier experiments did, but regarded themselves as part of the general process of rebirth. Thus they formed that very community of communities for which Buber called: "From the beginning there has been a powerful tendency among the various groups to confer, to exchange experiences, and to act in the unison of a common path." "Nowhere, as far as I see, in the history of the Socialist movement," wrote Buber in *Paths in Utopia*, "were men so deeply involved in the process of differentiation and yet so intent on preserving the principle of integration." The failure of the quasi-*halutzim* did not lie in their relationship to the idea, the community, or their work, but to their fellows. This is not a question of intimacy, such as exists in the small *kvutza* and is lost in the big, but of openness. "A real community need not consist of people who are perpetually together; but it must consist of people who, precisely because they are comrades, have mutual access to one another and are ready for one another."

Buber saw his image of the socialist restructuring of society as based on an eternal human need: "The need of man to feel his own house as a room in some greater, all-embracing structure in which he is at home, to feel that the other inhabitants of it with whom he lives and works are all acknowledging and confirming his individual existence." In a Foreword that he wrote for the English architect E. A. Gutkind's book *Community and Environment: A Discourse on Social Ecology* (1953), Buber characterized a man's own house as "the winning throw of the dice which man has wrested from the uncanniness of the universe; . . . his defense against the chaos that threatens to invade him," but also as standing between the houses of his neighbors. "If the world of man is to become a human world, then immediacy must rule . . . between human house and human house." The principle of mutual confirmation which Buber expanded in much more abstract terms in "Distance and Relation" (1951) was stated with clarity, concreteness, and conciseness in pointing to the significance of the attempt of architects to build surroundings that invite meeting and centers that shape meeting:

> The unavowed secret of man is that he wants to be confirmed in his being and his existence by his fellow men and he wishes them to make it possible for him to confirm them, and, to be sure, the former and the latter not merely in the family, in the party assembly or in the public house, but also in the course of neighborly encounters, perhaps when he or the other steps out of the door of his house or to the window of his house and the greeting with which they greet each other will be accompanied by a glance of well-wishing, a glance in which curiosity, mistrust, and routine will have been overcome by a mutual sympathy: the one gives the other to understand that he affirms his presence. This is the indispensable minimum of humanity.

Hermann, or as he now calls himself Menachem, Gerson later testified as to how right Buber had been in *Paths in Utopia* in his understanding of the problems of the kibbutzim, the central importance of the human relations among its members and the importance of not becoming "happy islands," as in America, but remaining connected with other kibbutzim and with the broad movement of social regeneration. Buber was able to do this because he remained in touch with the life of the kibbutzim, not only with those persons he already knew (like Gerson, who came back into contact with him after a twenty-year separation) but with many of the new younger generation of kibbutznikim who, especially in the last years of his life, came in increasing numbers to see him.

ADULT EDUCATION IN ISRAEL

In 1940, in a long essay, "National and Pioneer Training," Buber pointed to three things the halutz type lacked as it had developed in Palestine: a healthy organic relation to tradition, freedom from prejudices against the world of faith, and reverence for all the secrets of nature, human life, and spirit. All three of these deficiencies were manifest in the contact Buber had with the young people in Ramat Jochanan, a *kvutza* in the western part of the Plain of Jezreel where Buber went in 1943 to take part in a Passover seder. The older members of the commune were deeply moved by the way in which Buber read a passage from the Hasidic rebbe Israel of Rishin, and many of them regarded it as the high point of the seder. "I have never before heard such a manner of speaking," one of them wrote Buber. "It was as though the letters floated before me. Not only every word, but every letter had, so to speak, a particular meaning." But the young people, whom the writer characterized as "Hebrew-speaking *goyim*" (gentiles), found what was so dear to their elders absolutely alien. "Your talk found no echo in the young. Since the psychological presuppositions were lacking, they disappeared early. Possibly we in our generation are the last who will possess these treasures and take nourishment from their riches." In October 1943, Buber visited Nahalal, the oldest Moshav and one of the first settlements in the Emek Valley. Gideon Freudenberg warned Buber in advance that the young people had no vital relationship to the Bible, being far more concerned with political, economic, and military matters. Yet Freudenberg later wrote Ernst Simon that, although the young people, due to their lack of education, left Buber's talk dissatisfied, Buber nonetheless exercised an enormous influence, and most of all with his sharpest opponents. But it was not until the last five years of his life, as we shall see, that the youth of the kibbutzim once again sought out Buber, and the educational movement of the kibbutzim drank deep from the well of his writings, his teachings, and his presence. In the intervening years, Buber had a deep impact on general adult education in Israel, a cause which had been dear to his heart since he had first proposed that there be a university in Jerusalem in 1903.

When Buber came to Palestine in 1938 he continued the demand that adult education be placed in the center of the activities of the Hebrew University, and he belonged to its Committee on Adult Education, which drew up a countrywide program of lectures and courses on a great variety of intellectual and practical subjects. These activities extended to elementary and secondary schoolteachers, workers' villages, a Workers' College in Tel Aviv, and single lectures and/or courses offered in 136 cities, villages, and kibbutzim. These activities in themselves did not satisfy Buber, however. In 1947, Buber wrote to David Werner Senator proposing the erection of a house for adult education on the land belonging to the university. He reminded Senator that in 1924 in London he had submitted a detailed plan for the establishment of a central institution for education of the people, which had been accepted with the promise of a speedy execution but which had never materialized. Then in 1944 several spontaneous partial efforts had come into being which he felt should now be integrated and established on a broad base. Without injuring the uniqueness of these educational movements that had arisen out of kibbutzim and Youth Aliyah, Buber proposed a central initiative, designing of programs, selection of teachings, training of teachers, technical and administrative direction, all of which could be done only through a great central institution on Mount Scopus. Buber envisaged that such a folk school center would arouse enthusiasm and could perform a great and enduring educational task for all the growing youth of the Yishuv and would enrich and form its inner life and help to build up the new type of Jewish human being that would be required for the great tasks of the hour. Eight months later (in October 1948) Nathan Rotenstreich, a professor of philosophy at the Hebrew University and later the dean, replied at length to this plan with his own suggestions of how it could be applied among the soldiers of the Israel defense army (the Haganah), the volunteers who had come from different countries of the Diaspora to fight in the war against the Arab states, and the young people who had come with the Youth Aliyah.

Rotenstreich did not touch, except in passing, on the special problem of the education of the "Oriental students," as the new immigrants from the various countries of the Near East were called. After the war, however, the Jews in Morocco, Algeria, Egypt, Lebanon, Syria, Yemen, Saudi Arabia, and elsewhere were dispossessed of their property and forced to leave homes where their ancestors had lived in many cases for two thousand years. It was this mass immigration of Oriental Jews into the new State of Israel that occasioned the great, unforeseen problem of education and finally brought into being the institution that Buber envisaged, the Beth Midrash l'Morei Am, the School for the Education of Teachers of the People. Buber was invited by the Hebrew University Adult Education Center, the government, and the Jewish Agency to set up a center that would train teachers who would themselves go to live in the camps and hostels for immigrants as well as in settlements established by the newcomers.

On the advice of Ernst Simon, Buber recommended that Dr. Gideon Freudenberg be summoned from the Moshav Nahalal, where he was chairman of the cultural council, to take over the day-to-day practical administration of the institute which Buber would direct. Zalman Shazar, then minister of culture and education and later president of Israel, brought Freudenberg to Tel Aviv and suggested that they go together to Buber. Freudenberg, who had seen Arabs come to Nahalal at night to murder the inhabitants, had written a strong reply to Buber's article in *Ba'ayot* which suggested, as it seemed to Freudenberg, that it was really the Jews who were the attackers. As a result, he said to Shazar that Buber would not accept him. When they went to see Buber, Freudenberg realized, as he later told me, that Buber was a great man. "I read your article," Buber said to Freudenberg. "It was very good. Of course, I am not convinced, but we shall have time to talk about it."

Freudenberg became the director of action or principal, Buber the director of ideas and president of the school in daily contact with the students. The people in the provisory camps were 50 percent Oriental Jews and 50 percent from European detention camps and, before that, Nazi concentration camps. It was agreed that the teachers to be trained should themselves be new immigrants. At first, the institute was established for a year and then extended because of its great success.

Writing about this "new venture in adult education" in 1950, Buber pointed out that while there was probably more activity in the sphere of adult education in Israel than in any other country of comparable size, the teachers tended to look upon it as a hobby and the students as something supplementary, not as an education toward life. The mass immigration had shown the need of teachers for the people whose main preoccupation was the teaching of adults, people capable of realizing that this was a calling of primary importance more exacting than other professions, for it claims the person's entire being. The new school was to train a small group every year, the number to be kept limited so that the teacher might get to know the students individually and establish contact with every one of them. Contact, the meeting between persons, is the root and basis of education. This means that the teacher should not be on a higher plane than the student; for a truly reciprocal dialogue in which both sides are full partners means the genuine interchange of experiences between the matured mind and the mind still in formation. The teacher should ask genuine questions, and the student should answer from the depths of his own personal experience. Yet it is not question and answer, Buber pointed out, but the dialogue between person and person that lies at the heart of education.

> Teaching itself does not educate; it is the teacher that educates. A good teacher educates when silent as well as when speaking, during recess, during an occasional conversation, and through his own behavior, provided he really exists and is really present. He is an educator by touch. The people's school is based upon the encouragement of contact between teacher and students—upon the principle of dialogue; dialogue of questions from both sides, and answers from both sides, dialogue of joint observation of a certain reality in nature, or in art, or in society, dialogue of joint penetration into one of the problems of life, dialogue of true fellowship, in which the breaks in conversation are no less of a dialogue than speech itself.

University education *may* concern itself with character; adult education *must*. A part of this concern is the recognition that "the maturing person usually acquires his interior shape and form in a hurry," with the result that the essential process of spiritual formation is often ended prematurely and an insecure and imaginary self-confidence and control over life-situations takes its place. "Adult education must see as its first duty the shaking up of this false confidence and the confronting of the prematurely established shape and form with the reality of a world and of man that has not been truly absorbed nor formed yet." Only thus can the disastrous contradiction between existence and appearance be overcome and a real spirit of independence formed which can learn to serve the public in the midst of which it exists.

Buber saw as the first object of study the clarification of concepts, a sort of Socratic workshop or experimental laboratory which would try to counteract the inordinate confusion, misunderstanding, and empty talk of public life by a constant testing of concepts which would inculcate in the teachers of the people a sense of responsibility with regard to speech. The curriculum, Hebrew and other subjects, should be determined by the social, cultural, and political reality at this historic juncture and should be taught in such a way that the students should draw their own conclusions with regard to this reality. Subjects such as Jewish history, contemporary Jewish affairs, Hebrew language and literature, Jewish sociology, and the geography of Palestine should not be taught in a vacuum but in the spirit of prophetic universalism that alone could establish a true bond between the masses of newcomers and the national rebirth. "Living Judaism can only be taught in such a manner as to restore faith in the meaning of the world and of life to those who have lost it."

It was decided not to admit to the school former teachers; for they would for the most part have been teachers of children. Freudenberg also insisted on a residential community in which the students from fifty countries could speak Hebrew together with him and his wife. Thus the school became also an *ulpan*, a place for intensive learning of Hebrew where they were in contact from morning to night and talked over things they had heard during the day. In this way it was possible to influence not only the minds but also the hearts of the students. No money was supplied by the Ministry. The students had to pay through loans from the Jewish Agency. Forty to fifty teachers of the people were thus trained every term and received diplomas as adult educators. In Jabotinsky Street in Jerusalem there was a pension the whole of which was rented for this purpose for the four years the school lasted.

The ages of the students ranged from seventeen to fifty, their education from below high school to university graduates with many years of teaching experience abroad, their understanding of Judaism ranging from shallow to profound. Because of the pressing need, the course had to be limited to one year and students had to work at least fourteen hours daily. "In the course of my life, I have not seen such intensity of learning from morning until midnight," Buber reported. The six hours of daily lessons took the form not of lectures but of seminars in which all the students took as active a part as possible. This allowed for individual attention to the student, since the classes were of thirty or fewer. The teachers, who were brought from the Hebrew University and elsewhere, had to be ready to give the students whatever assistance was necessary, advising them and, in many cases, even consoling them because they had suffered so much. Those who came from the detention camps brought with them a stress that the teachers and the directors had to help them overcome. But Buber and Freudenberg also felt responsible for their future existence and advised them as to how they could solve their financial problems and how they could marry and build a family. Freudenberg, who lived with them, told them his office was always open, and Buber himself was always ready to receive them when they wanted to speak with him.

By now Buber had been living for some time in his third and last home in Jerusalem, the beautiful Arab-style house in Talbiyeh on 3 Chovevei Zion (most appropriately, "Lovers of Zion" Street). The hostel on Jabotinsky Street was around the corner. Buber gave Freudenberg a call at ten every evening, and they sat together until very late hours to speak on the problems of the day and on the whole philosophy of mankind. When a prospective teacher of the people came, Buber and Freudenberg sat together in the office of the school and talked with the candidate about his or her interests and intentions. In this way they gained impressions about the personality of the candidate and his or her qualifications for this type of demanding work. "Buber knew if this man or this woman was apt for the work," Freudenberg has said. "We had very, very few disappointments."

Buber himself taught a course on the Bible, one time spending three months on the meaning of the Hebrew word *re'ah* in *Ahavta l're'ah cmocha,* usually translated as "Love your neighbor as yourself." When Buber taught, he did not read from notes but would just speak. He gave every pupil an opportunity to interrupt and ask questions, after which he would continue his talk. Buber's influence on the students was very great, according to Freudenberg, not because of the content of his teaching but because of his personality. "When he read from the Bible and the prophets, it was as if the prophets themselves came into the room." Thus Buber himself embodied the aim of the school, which was, primarily, addressing the wholeness of the person, since "only whole persons can influence others." What he had spoken of ten years before in his address to the teachers of Tel Aviv he now was able to make a reality—the conjunction of situation and person in the education of character. "Character is not above situation," Buber stated in his discussion of the school in America in 1951, "but is attached to the cruel, hard demand of this hour."

The school was faced with periodic financial crises, which reflected those of Israel itself at this time. Once when the Jewish Agency did not proffer its share and Freudenberg had to pay out of his own pocket, Buber went to the Agency and refused to leave their office until they gave him one thousand pounds! In the third year, the Ministry of Education requested that the number of students be doubled, which necessitated setting up two separate classes, each having the same curriculum. At the end of each year of the course, Freudenberg went with all of the fifty pupils for four or five weeks to one of the great camps to live with them in the tents in order to give them confidence and help them begin their work. Every student of the institution formed a class and began to teach Hebrew. Freudenberg invited the chief teachers to come, and Buber also came to watch his former students working under these primitive conditions. By the end of the second year there were approximately 800 teachers working among 250,000 new immigrants. These teachers included the 67 graduates of Buber's school, but 85 percent of the teachers had no training whatsoever and no qualifications other than a slight knowledge of Hebrew. In the third year the camps were replaced by settlements of *Machbarot,* crude little houses, or shacks, sometimes built of tin, where the immigrants had to live and work. During this year the school also went to Beer Sheva, which was at that time a city of immigrants. There was no *ulpan* there, so the mayor let Freudenberg use children's schools in the evenings for his classes.

The directors of the *ulpanim,* the intensive, five-month institutions for learning Hebrew, sent their very best students to Buber's school, and after only one year they returned to their *ulpan* as teachers. A particularly close link existed with the Ulpan Akiba in Natanya, north of Tel Aviv, directed by the remarkable Israeli Shulamit Katz-Nelson. This *ulpan* more than all the others retained a special international character with pupils from as many as thirty different countries at one time. As many as ten of its teachers came from the School for the Teachers of the People. Shulamit herself came from a famous Israeli family and had been a terrorist during the Arab-Jewish war. After the war she was a teacher of eight-year-olds, giving them music and painting as well as regular instruction. Sudenly she felt she had to develop and therefore must work with adults. Her uncle, Zalman Shazar, then minister of education, opposed it, but she got herself released in the middle of the year, even though another teacher had to teach ten hours a day until they could find a replacement for her. She came without any adult teaching experience to be the director of the *ulpan* in Nahariya. She had never spoken freely to adults before. Now she found her text in the legends and dialogues of Rabbi Akiba, who learned the Hebrew alphabet at forty. The institution that she created there, both internally and in its relations with the Arabs, was so much in the spirit of Buber that after a visit there, Hugo Bergmann said he had received a whole course in human relations and wrote an article declaring that Ulpan Akiba embodied Buber's dialogue in Israel!

After Buber's death in 1965 the Hebrew University announced plans for the establishment of an ambitious and extensive "Martin Buber Center for Adult Education and Continuing Education" in a large building to be constructed for this purpose "in grateful recognition of Buber's pioneering work." The Martin Buber Center for Adult Education was opened in 1972 on the new-old Mount Scopus Campus overlooking Jerusalem in an impressive building which includes a Martin Buber room in which Buber's study is preserved exactly as it was in his house in Talbiyeh, with his desk, the picture of Paula, the pictures of Florence and Rome, the art history books in the old bookcase, his magnifying glass and pen. The director of the Martin Buber Center is Dr. Kalman Yoran, a graduate of the Beth Midrash I'Morei Am. Dr. Yoran hopes to revive Buber's and Freudenberg's School for Educating Teachers of the People in order to train adult education teachers to work in all the communities of Israel. At the same time the Center does impressive work in continuing education and is in touch with the local developments in adult education throughout Israel in exactly the way that Buber proposed.

PART II

Postwar Germany and Jewish-Christian Dialogue

(1945–1961)

CHAPTER 4

Two Types of Faith:
Jesus and Paul

THE RESUMPTION OF Buber's interrupted dialogue with German thinkers and friends in Germany after the defeat of Hitler and the end of the Second World War was an important part of a whole new phase of his involvement in Jewish-Christian dialogue. It centered on *Two Types of Faith,* the book on Jesus and Paul that Buber wrote during the siege of Jerusalem and published in Germany, England, and America in the early 1950s. In its paperback edition *Two Types of Faith* is subtitled "A Study of the Interpenetration of Judaism and Christianity," but it is also a study of their fundamental divergence and, in particular, of the messianism of biblical Judaism that Buber felt was continued and reinforced by Jesus as opposed to the altogether different messianism of Paul and John which revolved around the belief in the risen Christ rather than around the biblical *emunah,* or trust, that Jesus preached.

Even before the publication of *Two Types of Faith,* Buber was already discussing this theme with the Roman Catholic Karl Thieme, one of the editors of the *Freiburger Rundbrief* "for the Furthering of the Friendship between the Old and the New People of God—in the Spirit of Both Testaments." In March 1949, Buber wrote Thieme that he too held that only through looking at Judaism and Christianity as realities that actually *mean* God and as such are *meant* by God may one do justice to their mutual relation. In June, however, Buber wrote Thieme that he read with astonishment in the *Rundbrief* the latter's words, "as a temptation to consider the Jews irremediably 'spiritually dead,' i.e., unconvertible." "Until now I was convinced that you were concerned for a genuine understanding with those believing Jews who have understood and accepted the fact of a believing Christianity. But how is such an understanding possible if you identify spiritual life for the Jews with convertibility? I live my spiritual life in the immediacy between God and me, and my corporeal life as well. I can no more believe that God allows a Christian to put this in question, than that I could do the like vis à vis a Christian. Judaism and Christianity stand with each other in the mystery of our Father and Judge: so the Jew may speak of the Christian and the Christian of the Jew not otherwise than in fear and trembling before the mystery of God. On this foundation alone can genuine understanding exist between Jew and Christian."

This letter is important not only in itself but also as indicating, along with the earlier one, the spirit in which *Two Types of Faith* was written. It was not, as many Christians imagined, merely a judgment of a believing Jew against Christianity. Thieme responded by telling Buber of that insight which it had cost him half a human life of intensive occupation with the word of the people of God and the people of God's word to acquire: his relative acknowledgment of Judaism had as its other pole the absolute certainty of its ultimate fulfillment in the grace of the returning Jesus. "Does not the believing Jew hope that the Christian *in the end* will see Jesus only as a human prophet who had also led him to *a* personal God?" he asked Buber.

"After you have spoken to me out of the substantial depths of your person and your experience, it is neither desirable nor permissible for me to continue the discussion," Buber answered. "Only I do want still to say that at any rate I—who am in no way a believing Jew in the representative sense—do *not* hope for a final time when Christians will see Jesus 'only' as a prophet. I am convinced in ultimate seriousness that as the Jews are not destined to become Christians, so the Christians are not destined to become Jews." Expanding on this theme in October, Buber declared that God's truth does not allow itself to be trapped in the human dialectic of such an either/or. On the question of unique sonship Buber confessed that he *heard* both a Yes and a No when he read the New Testament. "I *hear* in Mark 10:18 another voice than in John 14:6, and I hold to the former speaker and not to the latter. I believe I have reason to trust my hearing ears 'bored' by God (Psalm 40:7) and by him 'opened' (Isaiah 50:5)—how can I do otherwise! At any rate, I am certain, as you probably are too, that God, when he wants to redeem, can redeem through whom he will. I do not see redemption as completed, and again it is my eyes that do not see this." "That the mystery will be fully revealed in the end, I believe as you do: only I anticipate that *all* human articles of faith will be resolved in it. . . ." Thieme in his response said that he too saw this world as being more and more unredeemed.

This correspondence was published at Thieme's request in his *Rundbrief.*

When Thieme reviewed *Two Types of Faith* in the *Rundbrief* in 1951, he failed to note, as his own disciples later pointed out after his death, that Buber had explicitly declared in the Foreword that he did not mean to imply that Jews and Christians *in general* have believed thus, "but only that the one faith [*emunah*] found its most typical representation among Jews and the other [*pistis*] among Christians." Buber was well aware of the interpenetration of the two types of faith in both religions, including a Hellenistic religiosity which seeped into Judaism before it helped to found Christianity. Thieme, in any case, found Buber's image of Jesus incomprehensible and his image of Paul a downright caricature!

Although Buber rejected the "demythologizing" for which the great New Testament scholar and theologian Rudolf Bultmann is famous, he wrote him in 1949 that he was one of the theologians of our time from whom, for more than three decades, he had been able to learn most in understanding of the New Testament, and he also acknowledged him in his Foreword to *Two Types of Faith*. To Albert Schweitzer he acknowledged, in the Foreword, a debt for "his renewed emphatic reference to the meaning of the servant of God in Deutero-Isaiah for Jesus" while confessing that the "Jewish roots" which Schweitzer found in Paul seemed to him connected "only with a peripheral Judaism, which was actually 'Hellenistic.'" Schweitzer was also important to Buber in his insight into the imminent expectation of the Kingdom on Jesus' part. But above all as a person:

> I thank Albert Schweitzer for that which he gave me to know di-
> rectly—through his person and his life, the openness towards the world
> and through this the peculiar nearness to Israel . . . I still treasure in my
> heart, never to be forgotten, the hours of a walk we took together
> through the scenery of Koenigsfeld and through that of the Spirit, and
> not less the day when we, so to speak hand in hand, opened the session
> of a philosophical society in Frankfurt-am-Main with two rather un-
> philosophical lectures on religious reality.

Buber thanked the theologian Rudolf Otto "for his profound understanding of the divine majesty in the Hebrew Bible. . . ; but even more for the noble frankness with which he opened to me his believing heart in our peripatetic conversations." The first of those conversations was particularly impressive to Buber because he had to drive a wedge through the wall of psychologizing which Otto had erected around himself, "and then not merely an important religious individuality was revealed but, in the meeting between two men, the Presence." The fourth theologian whom Buber thanked was, of course, Leonhard Ragaz, who looked forward to a future understanding between the nuclear community of Israel and a true community of Jesus on the basis of the common message of Jesus and the prophets of the turning of man and of the Kingship of God. Ragaz, in fact, saw his dialogue with Buber as the preparation for this understanding.

In the essay with which he introduced his collection of Hasidic books in 1927, Buber has said that the meaning of Jesus' appearance for the Gentiles "remains for me the real seriousness of Western history." But from the standpoint of Judaism, Jesus is the first of those men who stepped out of the hiddenness of the quiver in which God has left the Servant and have acknowledged their Messiahship in their souls and in their words. "That this first one in the series was incomparably the purest, the most legitimate, the most endowed with real Messianic power—*as I experience ever again when those personal words that ring true to me merge for me into a unity whose speaker becomes visible to me*—alters nothing in the fact that he was the first in this series; indeed it undoubtedly belongs . . . to the fearfully penetrating reality that has characterized the whole series of those who proclaimed themselves the Messiah" (italics added). If we put this together with what Buber wrote to Thieme about hearing, we can grasp the astonishing fact that for Buber the dialogue with Jesus (as with Plato and a few others whom he read) was not a metaphorical but an actual dialogue with the person of Jesus who became present to him in the merging of various of his sayings. In *Two Types of Faith* Buber seriously questioned the implication that Jesus saw himself as the Messiah. But he retained the dialogue with the person who reached him through the voice:

> From my youth onwards I have found in Jesus my great brother. That Christianity has regarded and does regard him as God and Saviour has always appeared to me a fact of the highest importance which, for his sake and my own, I must endeavour to understand. . . . My own fraternally open relationship to him has grown ever stronger and clearer, and today I see him more strongly and clearly than ever before.

Curiously enough, this confession of Buber's has aroused great antagonism both among Christians and Jews. Some Jews have taken it as proof that Buber was really more in touch with Christianity than Judaism. Others, like Buber's friend Max Brod, who had himself written a great book, *Judaism, Christianity, and Paganism,* found it presumptuous. Eugen Rosenstock-Huessy in his *Sociology* claimed that Buber had spoken disparagingly of Jesus as his "elder brother" whose greatness lay simply in the fact that he belonged to the family of Jews. Others read "great brother" to mean "big brother" and resented the familiarity that this implied. Buber himself reported to Ben-Chorin that a friend had said that he very much regretted not having warned Buber against using this expression. Buber was well aware that it was held against him and explained in print that he had already said something like it in "Dialogue" twenty years before when he said that the Jew knows Jesus from within the stirrings of his Jewish being. But he did not at all wish to avoid the unpleasantness that it caused him because it concerned something close to his heart. He did not claim to know much about the historical Jesus because, as he said to Ben-Chorin, the writers of the four Gospels were not biographers. But individual sayings of Jesus had entered so deeply into his heart that he sensed unmistakably the genuineness of the speaking man, whose powerful speech stirred him.

Two Types of Faith is the last in that series of biblical studies in which Buber dealt with the origin of messianism, and in that sense represents the completion of the foundation Buber laid seventeen years before in *The Kingship of God*. In *Two Types of Faith* Buber identified faith as trust *(emunah)* with biblical and Pharisaic Judaism and with the teachings of Jesus; faith in the truth of a proposition *(pistis)* he identified with Greek thought and Paulinism. Jesus stood in the shadow of the Deutero-Isaianic suffering servant of the Lord, but he stepped out of the real hiddenness which is essential to the servant's work of suffering. Even then, however, Buber did not believe that Jesus held himself divine in the sense in which he was later held. Furthermore, whatever was the case with his "messianic conscious-ness," Jesus, insofar as we know him from the Synoptic tradition, did not summon his disciples to have faith in Christ but in God. The faith which he preached was the Jewish *emunah*—"that unconditional trust in the grace which makes a person no longer afraid even of death because death is also of grace." Paul and John, in contrast, made faith in Christ *(pistis)* the one door to salvation. This meant the abolition of the immediacy between God and man which had been the essence of the Covenant and the kingship of God. "'I am the door' it now runs (John 10:9): it avails nothing, as Jesus taught, to knock where one stands (before the 'narrow door'), it avails nothing, as the Pharisees thought, to step into the open door; entrance is only for those who believe in 'the door.'"

Buber saw Jesus as demanding that the person go beyond what would ordinarily be his full capacity in order to be ready to enter the Kingdom of God which draws near. But Jesus follows biblical Judaism in holding that God has given man the Torah as instruction to teach him to direct his heart to him. The Torah is not an objective law independent of man's actual relationship to God, Buber declared here. It bestows life only on those who receive it for the sake of God so that something of hearing still clings to the divine command. "Fulfillment of the Torah means to extend the hearing of the Word to the whole dimension of human existence."

Paul, in contrast to Jesus, posits a dualism between faith and action based on a belief in the impossibility of the fulfillment of the law, which he conceived as an independent objective set of rules that made all men sinners before God and their salvation dependent upon ac-cepting the proposition that God suffered, died, and ascended in Christ. Trust in the immediacy between man and God is further destroyed through Paul's strong tendency to split off God's wrath and his mercy into two separate powers, with the world given over to the power of judgment until the crucifixion and resurrection of Christ bring mercy and redemption. He sees man as vile by nature and incapable of receiving pardon from God until the advent of Christ. Paul's God has no regard for the people to whom he speaks but uses them up for the higher ends of his divine plan. God alone makes man unfree and deserving of wrath, while in the work of deliverance God almost disappears behind Christ. As compared to Paul, the Christian

Paulinism of our time does not emphasize the demonocracy of the world, but it too sees existence as divided into an unrestricted rule of wrath and a sphere of reconciliation. ". . . De facto the redeemed Christian soul stands over against an unredeemed world of men in lofty impotence." In this connection Buber cited the statement of his old friend Emil Brunner in his book *The Mediator* in which Buber says that "the law itself demands from God the reaction"; "God would cease to be God if He allowed His honour to be impugned." Buber's response to these statements is as impassioned a declaration as can be found anywhere in his writings:

> If the whole world should tear the garment of His honour into rags nothing would be done to Him. Which law could presume to demand anything from Him? . . . And that He would cease to be God—'God' is a stammering of the world, the world of men, He himself is immeasurably more than 'God' only, and if the world should cease to stammer or cease to exist, He would remain. In the immediacy we experience His anger and His tenderness in one; no assertion can detach one from the other and make Him into a God of wrath Who requires a mediator.

Buber contrasted the modern Paulinism of Emil Brunner* and the Protestant crisis theologians with Franz Kafka's "Paulinism of the unredeemed." Kafka knew from within that "eclipse of God" which, in the years immediately following, Buber himself was to put forward as the character of this hour of human history. Kafka's "unexpressed, ever-present theme is the remoteness of the judge, the remoteness of the lord of the castle, the hiddenness, the eclipse, the darkness." He describes most exactly, from inner awareness, "the rule of the foul devilry which fills the foreground." But Kafka, the Jew, also knows that God's hiding himself does not diminish the immediacy: in the immediacy God remains the redeemer and the contradiction of existence becomes for us a theophany.

> Kafka depicts the course of the world in gloomier colours than ever before, and yet he proclaims Emunah anew, with a still deepened "in spite of all this," quite soft and shy, but unambiguous. . . . In all its reserve, the late-born man, wandering around in the darkened world, confesses in face of the suffering peoples of the world with those messengers of Deutero-Isaiah (45:15): "Truly Thou art a God Who hides Himself, O God of Israel, Saviour!" So must Emunah change in a time of God's eclipse in order to preserve steadfast to God, without disowning reality.

---

*See Note to Chapter 4.

If Buber concluded that Paulinism cannot overcome Marcionite dualism, he also anticipated for Christianity "a way which leads from rigid Paulinism to another form of *Pistis* nearer to *Emunah*." Judaism and Christianity will remain different until mankind is gathered in from the exiles of the religions into the Kingship of God. "But an Israel striving after the renewal of its faith through the rebirth of the person and a Christianity striving for the renewal of its faith through the rebirth of nations would have something as yet unsaid to say to each other and a help to give to one another—hardly to be conceived at the present time."

In May 1949, after he had read the manuscript of *Two Types of Faith,* Hugo Bergmann wrote Buber that he found it an unconvincing apologetic which did injustice to Christianity and to Paul, whom Buber treated with unsympathetic sharpness. Bergmann agreed with the Anglican theologian James Parkes who holds that Paul did not attack the Law as such but the Law as an alternative for salvation. The attempt to link Jesus *with* Judaism *against* Christianity must fail, Bergmann wrote, because the "founder" of Christianity is not the living, but the dead and risen Jesus, and if Jesus really did rise from the dead, then Paul is right in seeing this new beginning of mankind as of decisive importance. "And is there not the possibility of a *pistis* which is permeated by the security of *emunah* so that the conceptual separation, which is certainly correct, is dissolved in a higher synthesis?" Bergmann also criticized Buber's reliance on the demythologizing theologian Bultmann, since it seemed to Bergmann presumptuous for man with his total lack of knowledge about the nature of the world to decide what is against nature.

In contrast to the criticisms of his Jewish friend, Bergmann, Buber received a highly appreciative letter from Albert Schweitzer in 1951. Schweitzer was deeply touched by Buber's memories of their conversations together and his acknowledgment of Schweitzer's influence, and he was astonished that Buber wrote *Two Types of Faith* during the siege of Jerusalem. "During those difficult days my thoughts went often to this city." Schweitzer, even more radical than Buber, asserted that he could not find any genuine tradition contained in the Gospel of John, which he saw as representing Greek Christianity and bearing the message of the Logos rather than of the Jewish Messiah. There is no longer any place in it for the historical. For Paul, said Schweitzer, the love of God was no longer a question because he was so assured of his security in God that he no longer had any need to mention the love of God. "Statements such as Brunner's . . . I cannot comprehend.

He speaks of God as if he knew him through and through, including his concept of honor! That is all so childish. . . . His compassion, in the Old Testament too, is so great that he knows nothing of injured honor—God is not the lieutenant of the guards that these people make him into."

Eugen Rosenstock-Huessy, who saw himself as standing much nearer to Catholicism, informed Buber that in actuality there is a third type of faith which is incognito and which bears the other two. "Your Christian crown witnesses are, to be sure, Christian according to their souls but in thought merely Greek, above all Schweitzer and Bultmann. The anti-Paulinian coloration condemns their whole theology to remain theology of the law, i.e., . . . too late for the life of faith. If Jesus had not lived forty years before the fall of Jerusalem and Moses had not had to die before entering Canaan, then the law and Paul would not have been necessary. In both faiths is neither *pistis* nor *emunah*, but creative sacrifice, a spiritual rebirth through the love of the next one." Nonetheless, Rosenstock-Huessy saw *Two Types of Faith* as a landmark. "It places the Christians before the decision whether they may and will persist . . . in their Greek, cosmological, second type of faith [faith in the truth of a proposition]."

In a monograph on "Buber and Judaism" that he wrote in 1958, Ernst Simon took a highly critical attitude toward *Two Types of Faith*, questioning whether faith in the Sinai event and the giving of the Torah might not be seen as *pistis* and faith in Christ as a person as *emunah*. For Simon, Buber's own failure to embrace the Jewish Law largely invalidated the distinction he tried to make between Jewish and Christian faith. "Buber bases Jewish faith on the dialogue with God, which reaches its highest point with the prophet and not on the breadth of the patriarchal, popular, Halakhah tradition." Christianity dispensed with Halakhah because it believed that the Messiah had come. But since Buber did not see the Messiah as come, by what right did he reject the law? "We today are sons of the nay-sayers of the time of Christ and Paul, who did not throw off the yoke of Torah and *mitzvot*. As far as I see, Buber does not consider at all this messianic aspect of Halakhah."

Yet Buber in no way attacked the Jewish Law in *Two Types of Faith*. Simon himself quotes Buber as expressing the attitude of Jewish faith by saying, "The observance of God's command is of a religious validity if it is kept with the individual's whole being and with the whole intention of faith *(kavanah)*." Yet he concludes: "Since Buber lacks the belief in the revelatory basis of the Torah as a law, he cannot keep its commands as the commands of the Lord, while every other way of keeping them is just keeping a custom or habit." But Buber saw Torah as instruction, not law, and as instruction grounded in the dialogue with God, and *this* faith in the revelatory basis of Torah he did not lack; for this is *emunah.* What he did lack was the Orthodox faith in the proposition that the Law is divine and required because God gave it on Sinai, and this Buber understood even more clearly than Simon to be the faith of *pistis.*

Buber's own openness to *both* types of faith as found in the New Testament is witnessed by his statement in *Two Types of Faith:* "Not merely new symbols but actually new images of God grow up from human biography and precisely from its most unpremeditated moments." The Protestant theologian Franz von Hammerstein complained that whereas as a Jew Buber approached the "Old Testament" as a unity and as a revelation of God, he dismembered the New Testament into separate parts which he set in opposition to one another in the manner of an exegetical-critical historian of religion. Therefore, he cannot read the New Testament correctly or understand Paul, much less recognize the new community to which the Christians belong, which has called into question the absolute claim of the old people, Israel. In July 1955, Buber wrote to Karl Heinrich Rengstorf, director of the institute for Jewish studies in which Hammerstein later published his book, saying that from a chapter he had read of it in a periodical he received the distinct impression that Hammerstein ascribed to him a religious particularism "of which I know myself free." "I have never believed in a special salvation for the Jews and have given expression to that explicitly and clearly enough. . . . It is painful to me to be, nonetheless, so misunderstood."

Max Brod in his essay on "Judaism and Christianity in Buber's Work" had a very different judgment from Hammerstein:

> In his book *Two Types of Faith* . . . he read the Greek text of the Gospels and the Epistles with the same critical dedication to the sound of the words and their meanings, to style, rhythms, and repetitions, and with the same contemporary and direct understanding for the particular situation involved, which has unfailingly characterized his exposition of great religious texts. In short, methodologically he read the New Testament with the same dedication of a person resolved to experience concretely the unique full meaning of the text as he had interpreted the Hebrew sentence structure of Israel's Bible. . . . In his perspicacious presentation Buber does full justice to a great faith that is not his own (and in his judgment is not the belief of Jesus either).

Brod was particularly gratified by Buber's insight into the affirmation that lies at the heart of his friend Franz Kafka's supposed "nihilism." Brod too saw Kafka's message as emerging from the very heart of Israel and paraphrased approvingly Buber's statement about Kafka: "The unredeemed soul refuses to give up, for its own salvation, the existence of the unredeemed world, for which it suffers. It can make such a refusal because it is secure." This, wrote Brod, is the anti-Pauline Paulinism of the unredeemed "that has infiltrated into Judaism in this age of the deepest concealment of God."

Another Jewish response to *Two Types of Faith* is that of Nahum Glatzer, who, in his contribution to *The Philosophy of Martin Buber,* states that if "elsewhere in his Bible work, Buber opens himself to the critical suggestion, right or wrong, that 'basically his interpretation of the Old Testament is a documentation of his own views' [J. Coert Rylaarsdam], in his defense of the prophetic idea of Creation . . . Buber appears as a genuinely Jewish Biblical exegete. . . ." And this, Glatzer added, "is the ground on which Buber, representing the faith of Israel, faces Pauline Christianity and the Marcionite impulse everywhere, an understanding critic, a brotherly helper." Glatzer recognized, as Simon did not, that Buber knowingly dissociated "himself from Sinai the mount of the Law while adhering to Sinai the mount of revelation" and that he became thereby the grand expounder of the prophetic meaning of the Voice speaking in Revelation and of the prophetic criticism of the distortion of the Law in ritualism and legalism. Glatzer is like Simon in seeing the Torah, "mastering day-to-day life between early Revelation and late decline," as the central concern of both biblical and postbiblical Israel, which remains outside the main province of Buber's work. Yet his conclusion in regard to Buber's critique of Paul's attitude toward the Torah is the opposite of Simon's:

> Yet, in a decisive moment, the Law does enter Buber's vision: in his valiant debate—this term suggests itself because of the pronounced personal, immediate nature of the controversy—with Paul's concept of the Law. It is as if only Buber, who, as no Jew before him, has gained freedom from the yoke of the Law (while all the more carrying the "yoke of the Kingdom of God"), could call for an understanding of Israel, free in the Law, in the presence of the Jew of Tarsus whose unfreedom under the Law had such far-reaching consequences in the history of faith.

The Protestant biblical scholar James Muilenburg makes a surprisingly similar and even more affirmative assessment of Buber's contribution to the Jewish-Christian dialogue in his essay "Buber as Interpreter of the Bible." He not only sees Buber as "the greatest Jewish thinker of our generation" and a "profoundly authentic exponent and representative of the Hebrew way of thinking, speaking, and acting," but also as "the foremost Jewish speaker to the Christian community."

> He, more than any other Jewish writer, tells the Christian what is to be heard in the Old Testament, what the Old Testament is really saying and what it certainly is not saying. . . . What is more, he has a deep interest in and sure grasp of much of the New Testament, a warm appreciation of the historical Jesus, and a recognition of the place where Jew and Christian go different ways. More than any other Jewish thinker of our time, he stands at the frontier which separates Christianity from Judaism. He is the best contemporary corrective to the persistent Marcionism of large segments of the Christian Church. He gives Jewish answers to Christian questions, the kind of answers Christians must have if they are to understand themselves. . . . He, more than any other Jewish scholar of our time, has opened the Scriptures of the Old Covenant for the Christian community . . . Without an understanding and appreciation of the Old Covenant, the Scriptures of the New Covenant must remain forever closed.

The German theologian Willehad Paul Eckert expressed a closely similar judgment in 1964 in a book dedicated to the memory of Karl Thieme. In contrast to Thieme, Eckert declared that "the meeting of the absolute claim in Jewish as in Christian faith is the presupposition for a dialogue that does not do violence to the other because it accepts the other in his otherness." *Two Types of Faith,* in particular, Eckert saw as one of the most important invitations to dialogue "which it is our duty as Christians to accept and to consider."

More serious than Thieme's response to *Two Types of Faith* is that of another Catholic, the Swiss theologian Hans Urs von Balthasar. Von Balthasar expanded his essay on "Buber and Christianity" in *The Philosophy of Martin Buber* into a whole little book, which constituted a sort of "lonely dialogue," "lonely" because he knew that Buber would not come over to Christianity, a note which Buber himself found highly distasteful. Von Balthasar opened his book with a left-handed compliment that seems to imply that Jews are still such newcomers to the German language that it is a rarity when one turns up who uses it well: He has expounded his reflections "in a classical German untainted by those fatal lapses of taste which mark the work of some

Jewish writers, and its form no less than its content disarmed the equally fatal prejudices against the Jews." Then von Balthasar contrasted Buber with Franz Rosenzweig, Leo Baeck, and Marc Chagall, each of whom also "sought to present an unweakened, undistorted picture of Judaism in a language intelligible and palatable to the contemporary Western mind."

> It is precisely in those circles that Buber's originality stands out so clearly. It is then that one can appreciate his architectonic and strategic sense, his capacity for combining delicate feeling for what is just and right with an innate sense for what is proper and fitting at the time—his grasp of the specific weight of ideas, their relations and their situation and the constellations they form and of the system of co-ordinates in which to insert the structure of thought created by his own genius. His is a carefully reckoned, if ultimately very simple, monumental structure.

On the other hand, von Balthasar accuses Buber of lacking what can only be seen as the specifically Christian form of *pistis*—the "transcendent element implied by the fulfillment" of the prophets in Christ which gave it "a lasting basis" and "an outlet in the inner mystery of the divine," i.e., the Trinity, which "is latent and presupposed in all that is most unique in Judaism." In abysmal contrast to Ragaz and even to Thieme's relative acceptance of Judaism, von Balthasar argues:

> Israel can only really become conscious of its role in the Kingdom of God to the extent to which it is prepared to moderate its absolutist attitude, and allows itself to be saved in Christ; then it can receive the mission towards which it has always been drawn, the role which it abandons when it denies the transcendent character of the resurrection and the ascension.

On this basis, von Balthasar attacked Buber's "Zionist notion of the sacramental principle of Israel" and "the absolute correspondence between the people of Israel and the Land of Palestine." From the standpoint of the "prophetic dynamism" which issues into the New Testament, von Balthasar claimed that "Jerusalem in the post-Christian era cannot be looked upon even as a secondary centre of genuine significance. . . . Once the centre, the sanctuary has ceased to exist, the Land can no longer have any biblical significance. The old cult cannot be restored, and even from an Old Testament point of view it is superannuated: it no longer corresponds to the present phase of religious consciousness." If the mystery of Christ is not visible in the background, von Balthasar concluded, then Buber's "dialogue moves relentlessly forward to Job's question to God . . . eating down deeper and deeper with the passage of time, like a cancer."

What von Balthasar meant by this last statement was that Buber's biblical dialogue with God must founder on the problem of evil if it does not have the transcendent solution to this problem offered by the advent of Christ. Buber, in his response, claimed Job (his father) squarely as his own in that combination of trusting and contending that marked the biblical figure and that marks the "Modern Job," that second type of modern rebel which I designate in *Problematic Rebel* and *The Hidden Human Image*. In so doing, Buber reaffirmed the biblical *emunah* against the *pistis* which lies at the heart of von Balthasar's Christianity:

> Without Christianity, so von Balthasar says to me, the dialogical leads inevitably to Job's question to God. Yes, that it does, and God praises "His servant" (Job 42:7). My God will not allow to become silent in the mouth of His creature the complaint against the great injustice in the world, and when in an unchanged world His creature nonetheless finds peace, it is only because God has again granted him His nearness and confirms him. Peace I say; but that is a peace compatible with the fight for justice in the world.

By the same token Buber rejected von Balthasar's censure of his religious socialism as offering man only a social future, a shallow utopia, a false hope. Like the prophets, Buber held that while justice cannot *make* the earth into the kingdom of God, our success in living *with one another* is our human share in the preparation of the divine kingdom. "And they may have even agreed, these old messengers, that true institutions belong to true relations as the skeleton to the flesh." In contrast to Carl Mennicke, who led the union of religious socialists to which Paul Tillich belonged in Berlin, Buber believed in both the future perfection of society *and* a future transformation of the world:

> Only in the building of the foundation of the former I myself may take a hand, but the latter may already be there in all stillness when I awake some morning, or its storm may tear me from sleep. And both belong together, the "turning" and the "redemption," both belong together, God knows how, I do not need to know it. That I call hope.

Finally, in contrast to von Balthasar's assertions that Buber's position was "the absolute identity of nature and supernature," Buber passionately affirmed that above nature there is no supernature, only God.

> He is above nature, and bears it and permeates it, as He is above the spirit and bears it and permeates it. Both are grounded in Him, and He is as little bound to them as to all the other realities, unknown and unknowable to us, that are grounded in Him. He pours out His grace right through all chains of causation, He alone and no supernature.

Buber did not mean that *emunah* exclusively belongs to the Jews. He declared that in the course of his life he had come to know a succession of Christians who had an ideal relationship of trust in God that could not be injured through any failure or misfortune and this trust did not originate in *faith that* God was made man in Christ. The latter was only an aid to comprehension.

> I experienced this most strongly several years ago in conversation with the leading personality of an important Christian sect. It was one of those conversations that is conducted between two persons without reservation. We spoke of the readiness, common to both of us, to be overtaken by "eschatological happenings," in an entirely unexpected manner contradicting all previous conceptions. Suddenly I heard my partner say the words: "If God should then demand it of me, I am ready, even to give up . . ." Where I have here placed three periods, the center of the Christian dogma was stated. Even now, while I write this, I feel the emotion of that moment.

The person Buber referred to was the English Quaker Joan Fry. To understand the importance of this testimony we must bear in mind that English Quakers, in contrast to many American members of the Society of Friends, *do* believe in the divinity of Christ.

For many Christians, Christ is not the "I" of the I-Thou relationship with God, but the "Thou." In *Two Types of Faith* Buber declared that insofar as Christianity fixes God in the image of Christ, it prevents God from hiding and therefore from revealing himself ever anew, and he pointed out that what was explicitly said by the theologian Nathan Söderbloom, and by Shatov in Dostoevsky's novel *The Devils* or *The Possessed*, is true for many Christians—that Christ remains real for them even when God becomes uncertain or unreal. "Without Christ I would have to think that God was the devil," the American Quaker economist Kenneth Boulding once said.

Emil Brunner's fear that a Christian might be tempted by *Two Types of Faith* to come over to Buber's view was justified in at least one significant case, that of the Evangelical theologian Hermann Maas. Maas had been a pastor in Heidelberg since 1914. In 1933 he committed himself fully to helping the persecuted Jews and repeatedly placed his life in jeopardy by so doing. In 1950 he was the first German invited to visit Israel and in 1970 was one of the "thirty-six righteous" persons who were commemorated by a tree being planted in their name in Jerusalem. In February 1953, Maas wrote Buber that *Two Types of Faith* had wholly and conclusively drawn him over into Buber's spiritual world and his faith. "I have read the book and thought through it again and again, and each time I penetrate more deeply into its world of faith, which is also mine." "I not only thank you for all you have given me," Maas concluded, "but I thank the eternal God for giving you to us as a wise and holy man. When I say 'holy' I mean a man for whose sake it is easier to believe in God in days of need, doubt, and anxiety."

Buber's old friend Rudolf Pannwitz attacked *Two Types of Faith* from the standpoint of a defense of *gnosis* as the true perennial philosophy that runs through the history of man, far older than any forms of belief or faith. In contrast to "the Jewish Christ" Pannwitz put forward a "founder Christ" who could in no way be seen within the context of biblical Judaism, a Christ who has "absorbed much gnosis." This Christ *produced* his own sacrificial death "as a unique and conclusive embodiment of the Near Eastern sacred Easter drama." Buber responded to Pannwitz's attack by coining another set of polar types, resembling but by no means equivalent to I-Thou and I-It, or *emunah* and *pistis: devotio* and *gnosis,* the former a Latin word and the latter Greek. *Devotio* Buber saw as a serving and sharing which does not concern itself with the mysteries and whose highest trial of strength is martyrdom ("*Devotio,* in fact, is what the Romans called the self-sacrifice of generals for the sake of victory"). *Devotio* does not presume intimacy, as Pannwitz assumed, but standing in committed service to the divine made present in facing partnership. "His Lord may be on all sides of him—in that this man serves Him He is over against him." The real sacrifice of self, which Jesus embodied, is the embodiment of this *devotio,* or *emunah.* Wholly turned toward God in the everyday, one says Thou, that is, dares to stand toward him in free and serving partnership. In all service the man of *devotio* "regards his bodily death, his faithful mortality, as the most human of all presences and with just this attitude, time after time, comes to meet the Eternal."

Buber, like Pannwitz, held myth to be indispensable though not central and, contrary to what Pannwitz thought, did not see himself as making a negative valuation of Christianity even there wherein its myth threatens to swallow man. Through faith in Christ the Gentiles "found a God," Buber stated in *Two Types of Faith,* "Who did not fail in times when their world collapsed, and further, One Who in times when they found themselves sunk under guilt granted atonement." What was evil to Buber was "not expressing reality in the form of myth and thereby bringing the inexpressible to speech but turning myth into universal gnosis and tearing it out of the historical-biographical ground in which it took root." Myth is still compatible with existential reality because it is bound to faith: gnosis is not. In this connection Buber summed up concisely his own approach to the content and manner of faith of Jesus: not to cling to any image ("even memory mythicizes, particularly memory that wishes to hand itself down"), but to the one voice, "recognizable ever anew, that speaks to my ear out of a series of undoubtedly genuine sayings." "The image of the speaker may be indistinct," Buber added, "but the voice is distinct enough," and so too is the central significance to Jesus of persevering in immediacy with God, the great *devotio.*

Pannwitz's long essay on Buber's Hasidism in which his critique of *Two Types of Faith* was contained appeared in the distinguished German periodical *Merkur* in September 1954, and Buber's reply followed in October. In November, Pannwitz issued a still-sharper attack on what he saw as Buber's claim to *judge* Christianity from the standpoint of Judaism, on the "arch Jew" speaking of Jesus as his "great brother" as he would never have spoken of Moses, and on Buber's "subjectivist theology": "mystical orthodoxy, orthodox mysticism, existential piety." In the light of the earlier closeness between Buber and Pannwitz, this can only seem a "lonely dialogue" on both sides. There was another rift between Buber and Pannwitz aside from their disagreement about Christianity. Ernst Michel and Arie Sborowitz worked together to edit Hans Trüb's posthumous book *Healing Through Meeting;* Pannwitz, who received great personal help from Trüb during the years when he was a refugee, refused to take part in this task. "He does not know the meaning of gratitude!" Buber commented.

"Without the constant meeting with Judaism, Christianity evaporates into mere idea or mere ideology," wrote Willehad Paul Eckert in 1964 in an essay on "Missed Chances for Christian-Jewish Meeting in German History." Through Buber's extensive lecture trips in Germany from 1953 to 1963 and through what might fairly be described as German-Christian pilgrimages of guilt to Jerusalem—that meeting took place for some parts of the German segment of Christianity. When Buber was in Tübingen, a delegation of Protestant theologians visited him to discuss the problem of revelation. The starting point of these theologians was Luther's statement that revelation takes place only in shame and self-abasement, a view to which they were all the more inclined because of the guilt of their own people which, they felt, made them ready for revelation. Buber rejected Luther's view and declared that revelation was tied to only one thing—the dialogical readiness of man. Revelation can take place in shame, but not *only* in it. Even this apparent humility is hubris, since it limits the grace of God. The Protestant theologians accepted Buber's view against Luther's and struck out the "only" from their own explanation!

In Buber's lecture trip in 1958 his meetings with Catholics, especially the groups surrounding Karl Thieme and Hans Urs von Balthasar, were more important than those with Protestants. In 1961 Buber took part in a Church Day in Berlin devoted to creating a working community of Jews and Christians that might create a new relation between the German Evangelical Church and Judaism. In his address to this group Buber declared that such Jewish-Christian dialogue was possible only if the church would give up its claim to superiority. Some Evangelical theologians were, in fact, ready to give up this claim, but the church would not. Buber realized the task to be a difficult one because, even where the church does recognize Israel, it is with considerable reservation. The church, in Buber's view, would need to give up its missionary posture toward Israel and to substitute genuine love for "tolerance." Buber was deeply moved when the spiritual founder of the Reconciliation Action (Aktion Sühnezeichen) in Berlin wholly spontaneously offered to build a synagogue for the Reform Jewish community in Jerusalem, a project which did not materialize because of the Jerusalem community and not through the fault of the Reconciliation Action, which was free of every vestige of missionary intent.

Once while Buber and Ben-Chorin were speaking in Buber's home, Buber's great grandchildren were building a booth, or tabernacle, for the Jewish feast of Succoth in front of Buber's study. Ben-Chorin mentioned the vision of the prophet Zechariah (14:16–18) in which the Feast of Booths would be extended to include all peoples and asked Buber why just this national festival of Israel, which reminds the Jewish people of the forty years of wandering in the wilderness, should become a festival for all peoples. "Because the peoples of the

'Cross' must take upon themselves the homelessness of Israel," Buber remarked.

The eminent Swiss theologian Karl Barth modified his teaching of God as the "Wholly Other" by adopting an I-Thou philosophy of his own. Although he was clearly under Buber's influence in doing so, Barth suggested that the main difference between *his* I-Thou philosophy and that of Buber is that Barth makes "freedom of the heart between man and man the root and crown of the concept of humanity." Responding to Barth in 1954, Buber pointed out that among the Hasidim "the freedom of the heart is . . . the innermost presupposition, the ground of grounds." In a rare, if not unique, positive concession to *contemporary* Hasidism, which he mostly ignored as "degenerate," Buber concluded: "But I would, I could, show Karl Barth here, in Jerusalem, how the Hasidim dance the freedom of the heart to their fellowman."

CHAPTER 5

Postwar Germany
and the Peace Prize

IN JUNE 1946, Adolf Sindler, a German-Jewish doctor who had immigrated to Palestine in 1937, wrote Buber from a camp in Egypt where he was in charge of the education of twenty thousand German prisoners of war. He saw it as his cardinal task to confront these German prisoners with the crime of Germany against the Jews and with the "Jewish question" through educating them in German-Jewish history, poetry, and other forms of Judaica. To this end he wrote Buber asking him for material that could be used by the several hundred academicians working with him, including many theologians. "Certainly 'education' is necessary in this case—the most sinister of its kind in world history," Buber replied. "But how is such education possible in the deeper sense, hence as influence not upon the attitudes and customs of men, but on the substance of the soul itself and the conviction growing out of it?" The high call to the "turning" is always accompanied by the promise of a new life, and this, Buber said, was lacking in the current situation to a frightening degree. "One does not banish demons by admonishing them to do better, especially when what is concerned is not individuals but a nation in whose soul the sickness of the human soul has broken out into dreadful abscesses." But, above all, Buber questioned whether the Jews, the passive partner of the monstrosities, the sacrificial object, were in a position to understand this guilt at its innermost roots. "The essential today must be said by Germans to Germans. And if it must remain unsaid, we cannot step into the place of the legitimate speakers that the hour demands." At the same time Buber declared himself ready to supply information, material, and help if the Germans themselves asked for it.

In July 1946, Ernst Michel wrote Buber from Frankfurt to give him a "sign of life," reporting that his son had fallen in the war, that his wife had died in March from an operation, that his home with everything in it had been burned in 1944, and that he lived in a furnished room near his daughter, who was looking after him while her husband was still in a Russian prison camp. In September, Michel wrote that he stood entirely within Buber's way of thinking, as his new book *The Partner of God: Indications for Christian Self-Understanding* would show. "Be assured that in Germany you will find a community that has remained faithful to you, which has also persevered in its relation to the Jewish people, even when its action has remained 'underground.'" The Frankfurt Quaker Rudolf Schlosser, who had made it possible for Buber and, through Buber, other Jews to continue to speak to groups when the Nazis had banned public speaking, had distributed hundreds of copies of Buber's last Lehrhaus lecture, "The Election of Israel," before he was killed in an air attack.

About this same time Josef Minn, a director of studies in Bonn, wrote Buber suggesting that he return to Germany. "What is now happening in Germany concerns me directly despite, indeed because of, its chaotic nature," Buber replied, "and in the question that so strongly grips me of what now will become of man this element is an important one." But, he added, he did not feel himself called to return to Germany and give direction. In this connection "something has happened." "But do not misunderstand me, my friend," Buber added; "it is altogether desirable that what I have thought and put into words during the more than a hundred months since I have been gone (far more than in any earlier corresponding time-span of my life) should reach the Germans to whom it is accessible in a near or distant future, if possible in a near one. But collectively I cannot single them out and talk with them, other than to individuals (as just now to you)."

In May 1947, Buber wrote Hans Trüb from Copenhagen that he could not give a talk to the Working Group for Fighting Anti-Semitism because he had always opposed Jews taking part in such organizations. The lecture on "The Spirit of Israel and the World of Today" that he planned to give in Zurich would undertake to deepen the discussion about the meaning of hatred of the Jew. "But I should obscure the purpose of this lecture were I to present it under the banner of 'resistance.' Its primary intent is criticism of the relation of the Jews to Judaism, its secondary a criticism concerning the 'Marcionism' of Christians, but the second also is something altogether different from resistance."

In 1948 at the time of Buber's seventieth birthday there came, after the long break in communication, a pile of letters from Germany, mostly congratulations, from known and unknown, persons and institutions, among which many were quite sympathetic. In December 1949 the Evangelical theologian Karl Heinrich Rengstorf, professor of New Testament and of the history and literature of Judaism in Münster and director of the Institutum Judaicum Delitzschianum, wrote Buber urging him to complete the translation of the Hebrew Bible into German so that they might not be left with a "torso." He predicted, quite rightly, that this piece of work would be greeted with enthusiasm in Germany. Buber replied that this touched on a sore point, since for a long time there had been no publishing house that dared undertake it, and now that there was, he himself was in the midst of another work that he could not interrupt. Yet there remained in Buber's heart a "perhaps" which later flowered into a certainty so that he did, indeed, complete this lifework with the work of his life.

In March 1950, Rengstorf wrote Buber urging him to follow Leo Baeck, who had come to them in 1948, and Alfred Wiener, who had come in 1949, and lecture at the two-day student conference on "Church and Judaism" sponsored by the Evangelical Church in Germany on the subject of "Israel—Our Land." "You will grant that I have some impression of what it would mean for you to come to Germany after you had to leave this land of your decade-long activity under such shameful circumstances," Rengstorf said. "But in view of the intensity of our desire (of how close it is to our heart) and of the importance of our work for the future of our nation and our church, I dare ask, despite all that has happened and despite your age, that you not refuse our request." Rengstorf made it clear that his institute stood ready to honor Buber publicly and pointed out that the new prize essay of the institute was Franz von Hammerstein's "The Problem of the Messiah in Martin Buber." Rengstorf was, in fact, the first renowned Evangelical theologian to try to persuade Buber to give public lectures in Germany because he foresaw the great impact that Buber would have on the German universities.

In April 1950, Buber's old friend the novelist and essayist Alfred Döblin, who had emigrated to France and the United States and then returned to Germany after the war, asked Buber, in the name of the Mainz Academy of Sciences and Literature, to become a corresponding member. Buber replied in a formal letter thanking them for the honor but declining "for all kinds of reasons that have nothing to do with the Academy itself." In a personal letter to Döblin, Buber told him that since the end of the war he had given all kinds of help and advice to a growing number of persons from Germany who had turned to him for his assistance, including denazification proceedings. "I have also proclaimed publicly my undiminished interest in Germans of good will," he averred. "But I cannot bring myself to take part in the activity of German public institutions; for this demands a degree of association of which I do not feel myself capable." "But," he concluded, "I greet all that exists and occurs in Germany that is of genuine spirituality and genuine humanity with a deep and unreserved sympathy." To this letter Döblin sent a moving reply, affirming all of Buber's work in Israel and explaining why, on religious grounds (he had converted to Catholicism), his own concern was no longer with land and state and political home. "I think," Döblin wrote, "that when one has, like you, fought and given his whole life practically and ideally for the Jewish people . . . he can certainly not act and react otherwise than you have done."

In May 1950, Karl Rengstorf repeated his invitation, despite Buber's refusal and because of the very reason that Buber gave: that there were persons there who, because of their participation in the Nazi extermination of the Jews, no longer had faces for him. "I dare do so because I struggle with my whole heart and all my might that the people here shall again have faces. I dare it so much the more because I know that the destruction of their faces is connected with what has been done to you and yours." But, as their experiences with Leo Baeck and Alfred Wiener had shown and as Buber could show even more, "they can only recover their faces or come to a new face if one again meets them." Rengstorf assured Buber that his invitation to come in 1951 to give the Münster lectures was also an invitation of the rector and the Senate of the University of Münster.

In July, Rengstorf wrote Buber that his latest letter of refusal had shamed him. "Naturally I understand you," he added, "but what helps in these matters is not understanding but love. There lie the missed opportunities of the past and there too the roots of German guilt and the basic reasons why we have lost our faces. Without love man cannot live." Now that Buber declared himself ready to talk to a small circle of especially invited persons, Rengstorf no longer dared to ask him to. But he wanted Buber to know how many of his colleagues and students loved him and diligently studied his books and eagerly wanted to see his face and hear his voice and meet him. Buber then informed Rengstorf that he planned to spend December in Germany and would at that time gladly meet with him and those colleagues and students of whom he had spoken.

"At such gatherings instead of lecturing I am ever more inclined to answer without reservation every genuine question." "It is as you say," Buber concluded. "Without love man cannot live—not truly, not as man. But love today more than ever before seems to be grace—felt out of grace, received out of grace. Thank God, I know it when I meet it." After his month in Germany, Buber wrote Rengstorf that he had learned much "and, God willing, something will come of it."

Since Buber did not wish, while he was in Germany, to be asked questions concerning political matters or the religious situation in Israel, in January 1951, Karl Thieme suggested to Buber that he invite Lambert Schneider and Professor Viktor von Weizsäcker to an evening in Frankfurt, commemorating the twenty-fifth anniversary of the founding of *Die Kreatur*. After this event had taken place, von Weizsäcker wrote Buber that his joy in seeing him again had been somewhat marred by the fact that when he came to Heidelberg Buber fell into the company of "old-fashioned people who believed that they could sit around and reflect on what the world really is," people who ended by burdening Buber with "a theological indiscretion." This reminded von Weizsäcker of Friedrich Gundolf's answer to the question, What is sociology? "Sociology is the art of expressing what everyone knows and what no one is interested in in such a way that no one understands it and everyone is interested in it." "But you have given me comfort and encouragement," von Weizsäcker concluded, "and for that I thank you."

At this time another old friend from Germany, Elisabeth Rotten, sent Buber her thanks for his essay on "Books and Men," which had called to her mind a statement of his about which she had very often thought. "Before, you said in a conversation in Heppenheim, work lay in the recesses of life. Now you were concerned to find room for life—the intercourse with men—in the recesses of work." Rotten agreed with Buber that it is better to be with men without books than to be with books without men. "But perhaps that is so only because certain books have awakened and deepened in one what binds human beings to one another in the genuine sense and makes them into fellowmen. And the most fortunate thing is to have to do with books out of which speaks a person whose tone is familiar, a person who is a spiritual source from which one may draw in presence and absence."

In February 1951 the Protestant theologian and professor of New Testament at the University of Göttingen, Alfred Jeremias, thanked Buber for his contribution to the understanding of the Servant in Deutero-Isaiah. "I could not dare to express this word of thanks to you," he concluded, "if I did not add that the monstrous blood-guilt of my people toward Israel weighs on me daily as a heavy burden. That I myself, since 1933 a member of the Confessional Church [with Dietrich Bonhoeffer], only escaped by a miracle the death which because of my attitude threatened me, alters nothing of this."

In 1961, in conversation with Werner Kraft, Buber spoke of Hans Carossa, Oskar Loerke, and Viktor von Weizsäcker as persons who literally died of Hitler. In his essay "Guilt and Guilt Feelings" (1957), Buber spoke of these same three men, but not by name: "I have seen three important and, to me, dear men fall into long illnesses from their failing to stand the test in the days of an acute community guilt." It was certainly Carossa whom Buber had in mind when he spoke of the third of these men as not letting "himself be forgiven by God for the blunder of a moment because he did not forgive himself." Viktor von Weizsäcker and Loerke he characterized, not necessarily in that order, as one who "refused to acknowledge his self-contradiction before the court of his spirit" and as another who "resisted recognizing as serious a slight error he remembered that had very serious consequences." Before 1933, when the direction in which events were moving was already clear, von Weizsäcker once asked Paula Buber: "And what will you do if the discrimination comes?" Paula Buber looked at him with her large eyes open wide and asked, "What will *you* do, Professor?" Although von Weizsäcker did nothing terrible, his pride stood in the way of recognizing what he did do and its consequences. Von Weizsäcker died in 1957, the very year in which Buber wrote "Guilt and Guilt Feelings."

The German doctor, poet, and novelist Hans Carossa made a remarkable confession of guilt to Buber personally and to the world at large through his autobiographical novel *Unequal Worlds* published in 1951. Carossa was a friend of Ludwig Strauss, Buber's son-in-law, and was tied to Paula Buber through their common Bavarian descent. Carossa was elected against his will to membership in the Prussian Academy of Writers and later, under pressure, elected to the Nazi-dominated European Association of Writers, of which he became president in 1942. Afterward he grieved for many years, right up to his death, over this and over his failure to offer resistance early enough. Speaking about the twilight into which he had fallen, Paula Buber remarked to Martin and to Albrecht Goes, "I am from Bavaria, and I know Carossa's inner character. With us it's like this: One looks on for a while, and does nothing, and then one finds oneself already in the soup." Goes pointed out that Carossa was able to prevent a great deal of trouble and finally laid his whole life on the line. "It was hanging on a thread—on one afternoon." "A man who wrote *A Child-hood*," Buber joined in, "one must somehow hold dear regardless of the circumstances." Buber also remarked to Werner Kraft in 1961 that Ludwig Strauss and he had forgiven Carossa. When Kraft said that Carossa was not immoral but stupid, Buber replied with great earnestness: "No, he was smart, only at times stupid, limited."

In July 1951, after Buber had read Carossa's self-accounting, *Unequal Worlds,* Buber thanked him for sending it: he had read it not only with that attentive enjoyment with which he read all his books "in order to become aware each time what that is and what it means when life really (rare enough!) is narrated, but also with that special attentiveness with which one receives a disclosure that directly concerns one. None of my German friends have given it to me, and with two of them I cannot rid myself of the feeling that their silence contributed to their death." One of these, as we have seen, was Oskar Loerke, poet, novelist, essayist, and a member of the Berlin Thursday Society to which Buber belonged before the First World War. Loerke died in 1941, but he remained very much alive to Buber, who sent a letter of gratitude to Hermann Kasack for his essay on Loerke's life that had not only enriched the image in Buber's memory but made it truly an image for the first time. "For the image of a dear departed is not, indeed, a fixed one but rather a shape that changes through real time. . . ."

What moved Buber in Carossa's novel was not just the inner history of the Nazi years alone, but also what he saw as an important contribution to the understanding of the destiny of the spirit in our time. Buber saw this destiny as a succumbing and not as a "shipwreck," as the philosophers (Karl Jaspers for one) say "with somewhat too much pathos." "The might of the vile does not come from below alone," Buber wrote Carossa. "The good works in it as well as the evil—only it is not a passionate good. Is the passion of the good . . . only to be found outside of public life, which is, therefore, abandoned to the other passion, the one without grace?" Buber asked. "Your book does not speak of all that, it only indicates, it only narrates—but genuine narrating is already almost a redeeming."

When Carossa's wife died in 1956, Buber told him that they were more than ever with him. "May I ask you to think of us as your friends?" Buber provided Carossa with invaluable help during the last years of the latter's life. Some time before Carossa's own death in 1956, when they were taking leave of each other after spending some time together, Carossa seized Buber's arm and said, in an unforgettable tone of voice, "Is it not true that one cannot do evil with the whole soul?" Buber had stated in his book *Good and Evil,* which Carossa had recently read, that while good can be done only with the whole soul, evil is never done with the whole soul. Carossa was not asking a theoretical question but the most essential personal question of his life. Buber looked at Carossa and confirmed both his statement and that of Carossa himself by saying, as answer and farewell, "Yes."

In December 1951, Dr. Bruno Snell wrote to Buber informing him that he had been awarded the Goethe Prize of the University of Hamburg for the year 1951. The annual prize, established the preceding year, had been awarded then to Professor Carl Burckhardt, Swiss historian, writer, and diplomat, and president of the International Red Cross. In awarding the Goethe Prize to Buber they wished to honor his great scholarly activities but before all his working for genuine humanity which serves the mutual understanding of men and the preservation and continuation of a great spiritual tradition. Snell invited Buber to come to the University of Hamburg in February to receive the prize and to lecture to the academic youth of the university. Buber was fully aware that in accepting a prize from a German university, no matter how humane and noble its purpose, he would be deeply offending Jews throughout the world, and particularly in Israel, who felt that no Jew should have anything to do with Germany in a public capacity. Nonetheless, Buber accepted it "as one of the first few signs of a new humanity arising out of the antihuman chaos of our time." He saw it, moreover, not, as in old times, in the great vision of individuals, at times scholars and philosophers, but in the fight of every people with itself, and as such he regarded and accepted it as a more than personal confession, an institutional one. He could not come to Hamburg in 1952, however, because of his commitments in America which would occupy him until his return to Israel.

On December 30, 1951, Karl Rengstorf wrote Buber that if, as Buber said in his book on "The Hasidic Message" and as he too believed, Hasidism has a special mission to our time, then it has one above all to the Germans who find it difficult to find their way back to being human because they had fallen in love with a marionette (Hitler). And again he awaited and hoped that Buber would sometime publicly show his face on German soil in order to help those who could recover their human face only in a meeting with a human being. On January 5, 1952, Rengstorf told Buber that he had read in the *Jewish Chronicle,* an important Jewish weekly published in London since 1851, the reasons why Buber had accepted the Goethe Prize, and he thanked him in the name of his friends and co-workers. The reasons you gave "shame me, make me happy, and encourage me all at the same time!" Rengstorf saw Buber's action as serving peace and even more than that. Buber responded that this letter was of especial value to him as a sign from Germany and as an important confirmation of the position he had taken, and he sent a copy of it to his friends in Israel who had advised him against accepting the prize.

There was, as anticipated, a hostile reaction in the Israeli press to Buber's accepting the Goethe Prize. On December 31, 1951, Buber published in the Israeli press the explanation that he had accepted the prize in order to strengthen the prohuman circle in Germany in its fight against the antihuman. A rejection of the prize would have strengthened that circle's enemies, he believed. Both the University of Hamburg and Buber were accused, in letters published by *Ha-aretz* (Tel Aviv), the most important liberal Hebrew daily in Israel, of impure motives. This led Rabbi Benjamin to write defending Buber, as a result of which the attack broadened to include *Brit Shalom,* charging them with wanting to conclude an unworthy peace with the Germans, as it did before with the Arabs. Gershom Scholem then wrote to *Ha-aretz* saying that the time for an act of reconciliation with Germany had not yet come but demanding an honorable recognition of the will toward reparation and signed himself a member of Brit Shalom. David Werner Senator wrote Buber in January that he too had thought Buber unwise in accepting the prize because the wounds were still too fresh, but after he read the attacks published in *Ha-aretz* he concluded that Buber clearly had had the right instinct and that "the fight against the narrow-minded and aggressive nationalism of this time must perhaps be carried out through just such provocative acts."

Buber donated the money from the Goethe Prize to *Ner* (Light), the monthly journal which after the establishment of the State of Israel had replaced *Ba'ayot* as the official organ of Ihud. On January 25, 1952, Buber advised Bruno Snell from New York that he could not fulfill Snell's renewed invitation that he give a lecture at a celebration, not only because of technical difficulties but also for more essential reasons which he did not want to withhold from Snell personally:

> As much as it has been granted me in every genuine meeting with a German to accept him without reservation as a person and to communicate with each circle made up of such persons, it has still not been possible for me up to this time to overcome the facelessness of the German public, which has persisted for me since the events of 1938 and after. A public that is not made up of persons each of whom has been selected, as is the case with the student body of a school of higher education, cannot fulfill the indispensable presupposition for my speaking publicly: being able to regard every face that I turn toward as my legitimate partner. Among the burdens which the history of this age has laid on me, I experience this as one of the most difficult.

In March 1952, Lambert Schneider wrote Buber of his plans to publish Paula Buber's novel *Storm of Gnats* although he knew that the book would have to overcome great resistance. "My involvement since the war in anti-Nazi writings and books friendly to Jews—a cause close to my heart—has created for me no public. People here do not want to read what happened; people do not want to think about guilt and reparation, and I am coming to sense that clearly. . . . One lives more comfortably as Catholic, Protestant, or any other type of publisher. . . . But if one has once published the *Kreatur,* then one has a hard time fitting into any acceptable category."

In December 1952, Buber wrote to Romano Guardini, the distinguished German Catholic theologian whom he had known since 1918, thanking him for sending him a printed copy of his lecture at the University of Munich on "Responsibility: Thoughts on the Jewish Question." "While reading it, I noticed that something had changed for me," Buber said. "It was again possible for me to speak publicly in Germany." This letter marked a turning point for Buber that had important consequences, since the following year he was awarded and accepted the Peace Prize of the German Book Trade that had been awarded to Romano Guardini himself in 1952. It also opened the way for Buber to come to Hamburg in June 1953, where he received the

Goethe Prize and gave a lecture on "The Limits and Validity of the Political Principle."

In the midst of these deeply moving events, the correspondence between Buber and Hans Blüher forms something of a tragicomic episode, but one, nonetheless, which affords us a deeper insight into what it meant for Buber to walk the narrow ridge in his encounter with Germans during the postwar years. Hans Blüher was a German philosopher of culture and writer, influenced by Nietzsche, who had worked in the Wandervogel part of the Youth Movement and written many books and articles about it. He was already personally acquainted with Buber before 1916, during the time when Buber lived in Berlin. In the 1920s Buber intervened to protect Blüher from committing suicide, an intervention which Blüher himself wished for. Blüher lived to write in his old age a metaphysics of nature and religion, but in 1931 he published a book titled "The Revolt of Israel against the Virtues of Christianity" which lent arguments to the vulgar anti-Semitism that he did not himself espouse. This book contained the sentence: "That Martin Buber, together with Gustav Landauer and other less pleasing manifestations of Judaism, gave support to that circle that later crippled the nation's power of resistance against the enemy goes without saying. How could he as a Jew do otherwise after the Balfour Declaration on Palestine was put forward?"

In 1949, Blüher sent Buber a copy of his metaphysics, and in 1953 he sent him a letter congratulating him on his seventy-fifth birthday, enclosing a chapter on Gustav Landauer from his autobiography in which Buber himself often figured "seen from the standpoint of an old Prussian." Buber thanked Blüher for his letter and for his earlier book, which he had read with interest. But he also took occasion, in a very long and detailed letter, to bring to his attention, despite all the time that had elapsed since then, that Blüher had done him an injustice in that sentence from his book quoted above. He also pointed out numerous other errors and distortions. "Please note well that I have nothing personal against you; that is not my way," Buber concluded. "But I would gladly know how you stand today in regard to a book composed of such material which you flung to the German readers at the most critical time. What is at stake here is the great and universally significant question of how the speaker of a word that had effect on its readers stands in responsibility for what was spoken."

After a lapse of many months, Blüher wrote Buber complaining that in answer to his purely human letter of congratulations he had, to his astonishment, received an extensive register of sins, peccadilloes from twenty-one years before, whereas what he had expected was a human response corresponding to Buber's own philosophy. "There is the angry Jehovah driving wretched Adam out of the garden . . . unreconcilable, vengeful, ineradicable, an eye for an eye, a tooth for a tooth." "You want to stamp me as a predecessor of Hitler," Blüher added. "That is the usual method today of defaming someone, . . . although you know that fifteen years before Hitler I predicted the Hitler program and warned against it. But you would rather bite off your tongue than admit that something that I did was good and right." Blüher also put forward the remarkable theory that according to "essential history," which needs no documents, it does not matter whether such slanders as the vicious *Protocols of the Elders of Zion* (a spurious nineteenth-century document purportedly by "elders of Zion" revealing their plans to assume domination of the world) are true or not, since they are "essentially" true! As for his own methods of fighting, he had never used unfair means against Buber, he declared, "although you were a deadly enemy of my Fatherland." He also opined that Buber could not have done better than to fall into his hands during the days of the pogrom. "Let us hope that the demeanor of today's Jews does not give cause for a new pogrom that may not take place in harmless Germany but in America." "I write this letter," Blüher concluded, "not because I hope to have even the slightest influence on you but to defend my honor against the false accusation of anti-Semitism and to show where the real falsification lies."

"That is what comes of answering a letter that one no longer remembers precisely as it was," Buber replied. His point-by-point letter did not grow out of wrath, Buber declared, but out of the "composed wish to induce someone with whom one once shared a spiritual experience to a fundamental weighing of inner and outer connections. Instead of which you cut out this 'Jehovah' doll to which—too much honor!—you give my name and vent at him a good German rage. Can you really not at all grasp that this time too I have not fought against you but for you? No, Hans Blüher, I have never held you to be a vulgar anti-Semite, but I meant—since apparently you had not noticed it yourself—that you should become aware that you had made highly erroneous public utterances at a highly critical time that have actually furthered the cause of the most vulgar anti-Semitism." Instead of dealing seriously with the material Buber had set before him, "as in my view a man of the spirit is obliged to do where it concerns a word sent by him into the world and its responsible effect," Blüher had contented himself with sweeping away "the image of the real Buber, which, covered with dust, still lies in some corner, some little chamber of your memory" and replaced it by a doll. Buber pointed out that he had not brought this correction to his attention in a public polemic but in a private letter that he had not even brought to the attention of a third party. "That is just these evil Jewish customs!" And Blüher missed the most important communication: "that and why I do not harbor a grudge against you."

It is remarkable that Buber did not respond at all to Blüher's slanders and distortions when Blüher was only an accuser, but as soon as Blüher stepped back into a relationship with Buber, Buber held him accountable—a poignant illustration of the difference between accepting the other and confirming him that Buber was later to stress in his dialogue with Carl Rogers. In December 1954, Blüher wrote again to Buber saying that he did not want the year to expire without coming to a clear understanding with him. He had heard a rumor to the effect that Israeli S.S. men (sic!) had posted insulting posters against Buber on the walls of Jerusalem and expressed his sympathy at what he took to be Buber's loneliness. "We proceed from different standpoints. You: 'Everything that is good in Christianity is Jewish'; I: 'Everything that is good in Judaism is Christian.'" But they agreed on the all-important, Blüher declared, including that the notion of "race" in which Blüher had once believed somewhat was nonsense. "You can have no idea of the confusion of thought that prevails here," Blüher added. "But this letter is solely concerned with remaining in touch with you, and I hope that here I do not have to expect a refusal."

Buber responded with a long letter in which he said that he could not close himself to an initiative such as his, "even though I have never felt any animosity toward you, and the resumption of contact between us that you propose is most welcome." "Whether it is a question of Jews or Germans," Buber stated, "I shall always fight against identifying a people with its dregs. . . ." Buber's second letter to Blüher must have got through to him; for Blüher clearly cared about resuming the broken dialogue before his death, which occurred only a few months later. Actually he was already fatally ill when he wrote the letter responding to Buber's point-by-point citations from his book. This letter, in fact, produced in Blüher a crisis that was not evident from his own response but does indeed show through in his last letter to Buber. Thus the tragicomic farce ended with pathos and with something of a real meeting.

Although Buber clearly had in mind Nazi Germany when he wrote

What Is Man? (1938), as we have seen, the section of that book which he devoted to a critique of Heidegger in no way alluded to Heidegger's own activities as a Nazi. Because of the wide influence of Heidegger's thought on philosophy, theology, and existential psychiatry and psychology in Europe and America, many influential thinkers have either ignored or soft-pedaled this aspect of his career, which he himself never in any way disowned before his death in 1976. The fact is that from 1933 until around 1936 Heidegger was an active member of the Nazi party who identified himself with Hitler and the Nazi cause and who took part during his time as rector of the University of Freiburg in all the S.A. activities that led to further persecution of the Jews and of dissidents and to the exclusion of Jewish professors, including fellow disciples of his own Jewish teacher Edmund Husserl.

In 1962 a bibliography of Heidegger was put out to honor him, leaving out all of his Nazi utterances, except those that found their way incidentally into such books as his *Introduction to Metaphysics* (1936). The Swiss scholar Guido Schneeberger published a whole book titled "Supplement to Heidegger: Documents of His Life and Thought" containing all Heidegger's speeches and written statements during his Nazi period.* When Buber read Guido Schneeberger's book, he said to Werner Kraft that Heidegger was worse than Ernst Jünger. Both he and Kraft were struck by a photograph of Heidegger with a Hitler mustache, "a Hitler of the intellectual sphere."

In 1951, Buber wrote a critique of Sartre, Heidegger, and Jung, titled "Religion and Modern Thinking," which he later included in his book *Eclipse of God.* In contrast to Sartre, whom he characterized as "a remarkable psychological observer and highly gifted literary man, for whom genuine ontological considerations are always intermingled with entirely different matters," Buber spoke of Heidegger as one "who undoubtedly belongs to the historical rank of philosophers in the proper sense of the term." As an integral part of his discussion of Heidegger's thought on religion, Buber spoke of Heidegger's devotion to Nazism and Hitler. There can be no doubt, Buber said, that it was current history that had led to Heidegger's belief in an entirely new "Coming One," to be distinguished from all previous images of the divine. In Heidegger's Rectoral Address of May 1933, he praised in general terms "the glory and the greatness" of the successful "insurrection." The title of this address, in which Heidegger embraced Nazism, was "Die Selbstbehauptung der deutschen Universität," and

---

*See Note to Chapter 5.

Selbstbehauptung, as Walter Kaufmann has pointed out, is that very term that Buber used in the second part of *I and Thou* to refer to that "false drive for self-affirmation [I should prefer 'self-assertion'] which impels man to flee from the unreliable, unsolid, unlasting, unpredictable, dangerous world of relation into the having of things"! In his manifesto to the students of November 3, 1933, Heidegger proclaimed Hitler (whom Buber described here as "the sinister leading personality of the then current history") as "the present and future German reality and its law." "Here history no longer stands, as in all times of faith, under divine judgment, but it itself, the unappealable, assigns to the Coming One his way." Buber recognized that by history Heidegger did not mean a list of dated events. "History exists," wrote Heidegger, "only when the essence of truth is originally decided." But, commented Buber, "it is just his hour which he believes to be history in this sense, the very same hour whose problematics in its most inhuman manifestation led him astray. He has allied his thought, the thought of being . . . to which he ascribes the power to make ready for the rise of the holy, to that hour [of Hitler's Nazism] which he has affirmed as history. He has bound his thought to his hour as no other philosopher has done. . . ."

Before "Religion and Modern Thinking" was published in *Merkur* in 1952, the editor wrote Buber pleading with him to delete or modify his criticism of Heidegger's Nazism. "The wounds of the post-war era are already great," he declared. "Must we make them worse?" "He is talking about metaphorical wounds," Buber said, "but I am talking about real wounds, millions of them." A few years later, however, Buber agreed to speak with Heidegger on the subject of "Speech" at an event planned by the Bavarian Academy of Fine Arts, and Martin and Paula Buber met with Heidegger and his wife in a castle in Germany in preparation for this event. "I have already said what I have to say against him," Buber said in explanation. The meeting took place the end of May together with Carl Friedrich von Weizsäcker, the noted physicist, in Altreuthe at the Castle of Count Schaumburg-Lippe at the invitation of Count Podewils, general secretary of the Bavarian Academy of Fine Arts. "The meeting with Heidegger (who is more to my taste than his writings) and Weizsäcker was very interesting," Buber wrote me. "The Munich conference will be in June: on the first of the six evenings I shall speak on 'Die Wirklichkeit der Sprache' [The Reality of Speech]. I must write it down before the end of this year—a heavy task." Because of Paula's death, Buber did not take part in the Munich conference in 1958. In November 1964, Hans Fischer-Barnicol wrote Buber a long letter about Heidegger and the Zen Buddhist philosopher and master Keji Nishitani in which he quoted the latter as saying that Heidegger had confessed to him that all he now reads is Heidegger! Fischer-Barnicol concluded with the question of whether it would not be a good idea for Buber to fulfill Heidegger's wish for a dialogue with him. "Perhaps it might help him?"

In June 1953, Erich Lüth, a German journalist who after the war was active in trying to bring about a reconciliation between Germany and Israel and in the work of the Society for Christian-Jewish Cooperation, confessed to Buber, after having visited Israel, that every German, including those who feel themselves shamed by National Socialism, travels in Israel in deep uneasiness and humility. Along with the joy of seeing again old friends whom he had thought dead, "stood the shadow of the others whom we were too weak, too helpless and, in truth, probably also too cowardly, to rescue and to protect. At times we have probably tried to be brave. But it is only a small consolation that it is beyond the strength of most men always to be brave and not to shun death. So we too were destroyed, if in another sense." This is the consciousness that Lüth carried with him throughout his stay in Israel. He had wanted very much to be up to a meeting with Buber but was not able to arrange it. Buber had written him later that he would see and talk with him in Hamburg. "How happy I am," he responded, "and how you have lightened my heart."

In June 1953, Buber wrote to Albrecht Goes that prior to his next trip to Europe he had been going through letters that he had received since 1933, insofar as they were preserved, and he had come across Goes's letter to him of August 1934 in which he asked Buber about the attitude of responsibility. This letter affected him in a special way. "I now felt the inquiring spirit of the then young . . . man more strongly than I did at that time," Buber admitted. "The world today is so constituted that one may not remain silent concerning any experience of genuine closeness," Buber added in explanation of why he was writing. "I do not know to what extent you are still identical with the writer of the letter (I am today more receptive than I was at that time) but you surely still stand in such an intimate relationship to him that you can give him my greeting directly." Goes responded warmly that Buber had always remained with him as one of his two or three most important life masters and that his letter had touched "all the roots of life." This was the beginning of a close relationship that lasted until Buber's death.

On June 17, 1953, Arthur Georgi wrote Buber from Hamburg saying that the Peace Prize of the German Book Trade, which had been awarded in 1951 to Albert Schweitzer and in 1952 to Romano Guardini, was being awarded to him for 1953 and invited him to speak at a ceremony at St. Paul's Church in Frankfurt on September 27. Buber, who was himself in Germany at the time, wrote Georgi accepting the prize and agreeing to lecture in Frankfurt on "Genuine Dialogue and the Possibility of Peace." The 10,000 German marks which Buber received for the prize he donated to the cause of Jewish-Arab understanding.

On Sunday, September 27, 1953, while tens of thousands listened in through loudspeakers, Martin Buber was awarded the Peace Prize of the German Book Trade by Arthur Georgi, who characterized Buber as a "man of truth who proclaims and fashions a humane spirit suffusing all living things; interpreter of his people's destiny in history, philosopher of dialogue, theologian and educator." Albrecht Goes then gave an address titled "Martin Buber: Our Support," in which he told of how he turned to Buber in 1934 and also of Buber's most recent letter to him, written before either Buber or Goes knew that they would be together on this occasion. In spelling out what he meant by "our support" Goes made the indentical distinction between "leader" and "teacher" that Buber had made years before in his essay on Ahad Ha'am: "The truth which is directed at me and to which I owe an answer does not come from a Führer's command to me, no matter what kind it may be. He who lives by fiat does not live as a personality. A bondsman does not listen." Through Buber, in contrast, said Goes, "We were not instructed but shown a direction; life-masters, not school-masters, spoke to us; not finished things came into our hands but the fullness of possibilities, and the reflection of the primal light was over them." The answer to the questions was in the language of our time, but the countenance spoke of many eras of the *zaddik*—majestic but close as a brother, fiery but smiling. The questions were and are the same: "How can a fruitful life unfold . . . when we are abandoned to abysses, to negations, which we discover outside of us *and* within ourselves?" "How can the profound loneliness of our human existence be overcome in truth?" "The trust which Martin Buber radiates is the trust of the true zaddik," including the readiness to be sad with others and to keep silent "because we are united by the insight that it is hard really to love one's fellow men."

By virtue of such service you have become a support for us. Not the dictator who wants to coerce, nor the preceptor whose share is the parts, but one who accompanies us through the endless duration of the moment, who opens our eyes to the immeasurable grace of the moment.

Before an audience which included Theodor Heuss, President of the West German Republic, and many of the most distinguished politicians and thinkers of Germany, Buber gave his own address on "Genuine Dialogue and the Possibilities of Peace." In language stronger than had been used in Germany from such an elevated rostrum, he called those who took part in the Nazi Holocaust to account:

About a decade ago a considerable number of Germans—there must have been many thousands of them—under the indirect command of the German government and the direct command of its representatives, killed millions of my people in a systematically prepared and executed procedure whose organized cruelty cannot be compared with any previous historical event. I, who am one of those who remained alive, have only in a formal sense a common humanity with those who took part in this action. They have so radically removed themselves from the human sphere, so transposed themselves into a sphere of monstrous inhumanity inaccessible to my conception, that not even hatred, much less an overcoming of hatred, was able to arise in me. And what am I that I could here presume to "forgive"!

At the same time Buber clung to his lifelong conviction that a people ought not be judged as a whole, and he distinguished between the different and even contending impulses within the German people:

When I think of the German people of the days of Auschwitz and Treblinka, I behold, first of all, the great many who knew that the monstrous event was taking place and did not oppose it. But my heart, which is acquainted with the weakness of men, refuses to condemn my neighbor for not prevailing upon himself to become a martyr. Next there emerges before me the mass of those who remained ignorant of what was withheld from the German public and who did not try to discover what reality lay behind the rumors which were circulating. When I have these men in mind, I am gripped by the thought of the anxiety, likewise well known to me, of the human creature before a truth which he fears he cannot face. But finally there appears before me, from reliable reports, some who have become as familiar to me by sight, action, and voice as if they were friends, those who refused to carry out the orders and suffered death or put themselves to death, and those who learned what was taking place and opposed it and were put to death, or those who learned what was taking place and because they could do nothing to stop it killed themselves. I see these men very near before me in that especial intimacy which binds us at times to the dead and to them alone. Reverence and love for these Germans now fills my heart.

Buber regarded the youth of Germany who had grown up since these events as probably the essential life of the German people, and he saw them caught in a powerful inner dialectic—a part "of the great inner struggle of all peoples being fought out today . . . in the vital center of each people." He had found in the German youth, despite their being rent asunder, more awareness than elsewhere of "the struggle of the human spirit against the demonry of the subhuman and the antihuman." "The solidarity of all disparate groups in the flaming battle for the rise of a true humanity" laid on Buber, "the surviving Jew chosen as symbol," the obligation to "obey this call of duty even there, indeed, precisely there where the never-to-be-effaced memory of what has happened stands in opposition to it." In giving thanks, Buber expressed his solidarity with the battle of the fighters for humanity among both Germans and Jews against the contrahuman.

On Buber's eightieth birthday in 1958, Theodor Heuss, still President of West Germany, sent him a long letter in which he recalled in detail the occasion of Buber's being awarded the Peace Prize and of the speech that Buber gave. "We were thankful that you were there," wrote Heuss, "and how you, who named yourself an 'arch-Jew,' deeply gripped us all, your hearers, with clear delimitations without any glossing over (impossible in itself), yet with the capacity for distinction of a spiritually free nature, speaking of the fated Jewish tragedy, of destiny, of that subhuman cruelty that remains forever bound with the darkest stretch of German state history." Heuss also told of how four years before in December 1949, a few weeks after he had taken office, he had spoken at a ceremony of the Society for Christian-Jewish Cooperation in Wiesbaden and had opposed to the contemporary propaganda-talk of a "German collective guilt" the much more weighty spiritual burden of a "collective shame," "from which we could not and ought not free ourselves by lightheartedly looking away." In that connection he spoke of Buber as the finest example of the German-Jewish symbiosis and said that his work "could not be simply dismissed from the German cultural history of the last forty years," that through the beauty of his speech he had "been an enricher of the German spirit." "That is one of the weird paradoxes of this bad time," Heuss commented: "while they, who as usurpers of a supposed historical task drove you out of the German cultural arena, did their best to ruin its most beautiful possession, the German language, you were, and remained, its nourisher and a guardian of its values." Heuss concluded with a long reminiscence about Franz Rosenzweig, whom he had met in Florence in 1909, and tied it too to the Nazi past: "Rosenzweig, who with brave superiority went through so much pain and suffering, was spared—and we were spared—that violation of his helpless nobility that would have taken place had he lived to be apprehended and exterminated by the Nazis. Death was still autonomous and tactful."

Buber, in replying to Heuss, said that he was the most visible among those Germans with whom he felt a real connection, sharing most profoundly the world's suffering. In the "Greeting and Welcome" that he expressed to Theodor Heuss when he came to Israel in 1960, Buber reiterated that he saw Heuss as representing the renewed freedom of Germany before the nations of the world, just as at the time of self-debasement of the German people he represented that freedom in the faithful steadiness of his personal existence. At that time Buber recalled how he stood on the platform in Frankfurt in 1953 to receive the Peace Prize of the German Book Trade to express his thanks "to that other Germany that had conferred the Prize on me":

> I saw you sitting before me in the first row, next to my late wife. And my heart still knows how before I began to speak, I first looked at my wife—she who had instilled the lasting presence of a genuine and free Germany into my life. But then I looked at you, in whom was unmistakably manifest to me the German authenticity that had overcome the German self-betrayal.

Two years before, in a discussion of his attitude toward postwar Germany, Buber had quoted a favorite saying of his grandmother: "One never knows in advance how an angel will look." On this occasion, as Buber certainly anticipated, the "angel" bore two quite different aspects. The unique and unprecedented homage of the prohuman element in Germany was accompanied by bitter and often vicious attacks on Buber in the Israeli press and in the Yiddish and the German and English Jewish newspapers in Switzerland, England, and the United States. In June 1953 in the Knesset, the Israeli parliament, Rabbi Mordecai Nurok, representative of the Orthodox Jewish Mizrahi party, protested that "a certain professor has seen fit to lecture to murderers of our people in some towns of that bloodstained country, and even to receive a prize at their hands." Although the

Speaker interrupted several times to say that the matter had no connection with the budget, Rabbi Nurok managed to finish his protest.
In January 1954, a letter posted from Jerusalem and signed by Hanar
Haleumi (National Youth) threatened the lives of the editors of the
Israeli weekly *Haolam Hazeh (This World)* if they published an interview with Buber. "Never mind! I am used to such threats," Buber
responded to my concern. In Jerusalem a group of radical students
passed out handbills attacking Buber as a "false prophet." In
America, Trude Weiss-Rosmarin, editor of the *Jewish Spectator* and
herself a well-known Jewish thinker, published an article accusing
Buber of "creeping to the cross," like Heinrich Heine, the great
nineteenth-century Jewish poet who converted to Christianity—
because Buber gave his talk in St. Paul's Church! Commenting on this
article, Buber said: "I am somewhat astonished at Trude Rosmarin.
The Paulskirche has very long ago ceased to be a church. It has been
chosen for the ceremony because of its historical character: the German revolutionary parliament of 1848 assembled there and since
then it is a kind of universalist and democratic (and antichauvinist)
symbol. The former two prizes, 1951 to Schweitzer and 1952 to Guardini, have also been given there, so it is a kind of tradition."

Meanwhile the Yiddish press in America, which had attacked
Buber before Frankfurt, received a digest of his speech which
prompted *Der Tag* (the leading Yiddish daily in New York) to say that
no Jew had ever spoken so sharply to the Germans about their doings.
"This attitude is not much better than the other one," commented
Buber.

At this time Buber received a letter from a refugee German Jewish
merchant, Albert Dann, who had lived in England since 1938, remarking upon the impact of Buber's speech and his personality, and
declaring that the reason Buber gave for his acceptance of the Goethe
Prize and the Peace Prize was "most convincing and most noble," and
Buber's assertion that he bore no hatred in his heart but strove to
bring about an understanding with the youth "must indeed gladden
everyone who thinks about the last dreadful years." If Albert Dann
had known Buber's thought better, he would have realized that
Buber's statement that he could not hate those who took part in the
Holocaust was a more terrible condemnation than any hatred because
even hatred is an affirmation of the humanity of others, and it was
precisely this that had disappeared in the "facelessness" of the Nazis
of that day! "That it was precisely in St. Paul's Church in Frankfurt
that you spoke such world-uniting words particularly pleased me"

Dann continued, "since in that same place, over a century before, my grandfather, Rabbi Dr. Leopold Stein, as president of the Assembly of Reform Rabbis of Germany, spoke similar words of peace." Buber replied that his letter had given him joy, especially what he said about his grandfather and the rabbinical assembly. "In the Jewish world press, from America to Israel, strong reproaches have been made against me because I spoke in a 'church.'" From Germany itself Buber received many hundreds of letters giving wholehearted approval.

In Israel, Buber was totally isolated in his action. Even his closest friends, such as Hugo Bergmann, advised him against accepting the Peace Prize. When Buber returned to Israel he said to Bergmann, "Ich muss die Reifeprüfung bestehen"—"I must withstand the test of maturity" (literally, matriculation examination). In a speech over the Israeli radio Kol Yisrael (Voice of Israel) a year after Buber's death Bergmann told this whole story, including his own opposition to Buber's action as evidence that Buber was the conscience and sentinel of mankind!

In early 1954, Hans Klee, the editor of the Jewish weekly in Zurich, attacked Buber for accepting the Peace Prize before an audience which statistically must have contained "murderers and comrades, friends, and relatives of murderers." Klee declared that Buber's statements about not expecting people to be martyrs was contrary to Jewish tradition and more blameworthy even than his acceptance of the prize itself. Buber's action was a thoroughly *political* one, Klee claimed, and at the same time he accused him of being closely allied to Christianity. Buber responded at length, and the correspondence between the two was published both in Israel and in the *Freiburger Rundbrief,* in the latter under the title "Eternal Enmity?"

"I cannot condemn a people as a people," Buber said, "as the Christian church has so often done in branding the Jewish people as murderers of the Messiah," for I must distinguish between the actively guilty, the passively guilty, and the not guilty ("I do not say 'innocent' because there is none"). Far from having the German listeners regard Buber's speech as an exoneration of themselves, as Klee assumed, every serious public reference to that speech showed that it had brought about severe self-appraisals. Buber reported that after some of his university lectures, leading German scholars, "at times in a manner without precedent in Western civilization, confessed that their share in the guilt of nonresistance was the greatest burden of their lives and described their complete transformation in the most vivid terms." Buber also pointed to what he said in his widely disseminated address "The Validity and Limits of the Political Principle": "We saw people, who were of the most scrupulous honesty in their private lives, as soon as their party had indicated to them who the (in this case inner) 'enemy' was, day after day, undoubtedly with peaceful consciences, lie, slander, betray, rob, torment, torture, murder." As for Klee's accusation that his actions were "political," Buber said he was ready to take personal responsibility for political action: "In this most dangerous hour of history no politics can help other than the human."

In July 1953, Buber wrote me that he had given his speech "The Validity and Limitations of the Political Principle" in seven German universities (Heidelberg, Frankfurt, Bonn, Münster, Hamburg [in connection with the prize ceremony], Tübingen, and Göttingen) "and was surprised by the strong response. In Göttingen many hundreds of students assembled after the lecture before the University to give me an 'ovation.'"

In December 1953, Viktor von Weizsäcker's wife, Olympia, wrote Buber asking, in veiled terms, whether the feeling of having done wrong with regard to Nazism might not lead to a happier result if one had become really open to change. Buber wondered what her letter really meant and implied in his answer that he was ready to help her if she wrote more personally and concretely. "I believe in human help," he said, "but not 'in general.'" No one can say to his friend wherein he has done wrong, but he can give him information as to wherein in a particular matter and situation he there and at that time acted falsely. "The mystery of spiritual duality seems to me to lie in the fact that two persons come at times to stand on different sides of the same situation. Then, as long as both are still alive, the one can help the other discover the right and wrong in his, the other's, share in the common situation."

In December 1953, Buber also wrote Lambert Schneider supporting the publisher's intention of nominating Carl Burckhardt for the Peace Prize of the German Book Trade for 1954. "Burckhardt is one of the few prominent really genuine Europeans of our time. . . . His relation to the cause of peace is free from all abstract political elements; the peace that he stands for is a wholly vital one." In January 1954, Fritz Kaufmann, a disciple of Husserl's who was dismissed from his position at the University of Freiburg and who found refuge in America, wrote Buber that he believed that it was because Buber was so severe in placing the demand of the spirit upon the Jewish people that his hearers in Heidelberg felt (as Löwith assured Kaufmann) that he had the authority to call them to account when he spoke on "The Validity and Limitations of the Political Principle." "If that is so, then these lectures—despite all attacks—fulfill a function. More than that: they belong to the fulfillment of your own life-task which you regard as the task of man. They fulfill an unconditional duty and carry out, despite all inner and outer resistances, the primordial fact of communication."

Erich Weniger, German professor of education, wrote Buber from Göttingen how profoundly encouraging and heartening his visit there was, including the spontaneous response of the many students. Despite the endless cares that surrounded the university, politics, and the condition of Germany, meetings such as that with Buber showed that there was no ground for despair. Oskar Hammelsbeck, German professor and adult educator, revealed to Buber in October 1954 that for more than a quarter of a century Buber had belonged to those figures who had been companions and helpers to him on his life way. Despite his unconcealed opposition to Nazism, he confessed that he too shared in the guilt for the atrocities carried out against Jews and others from the years 1933 to 1945. Albrecht Goes published in 1954 *The Burnt Offering*, a novella which, like his novel *Unquiet Night*, was an open, honest, and human treatment of the Hitler years. "Your story has deeply moved us," Buber informed Goes. "It is a proclamation of genuine humanity. . . ." Goes replied saying how heartened he was by newspaper reports that Buber had been with Gustav Heinemann, head of the entire German synod of the Evangelical Church and later President of the German Republic, as well as with other leaders. Romano Guardini told Buber how much it gladdened him that so many listeners, above all students, had attended his lecture on "Man and His Image-Work" at the Bavarian Academy for Fine Arts and that they had expressed such heartfelt reverence for Buber.

In 1954, Friedrich Hielscher published a book entitled *Fifty Years among the Germans* in which he told of his renewed contact with Buber, broken off during the Nazi years, and of how, when the Nazis put him in prison, Buber's Hasidic tales had helped him. When he was arrested by the Gestapo in 1944, he felt utterly defenseless, since he did not know how much the enemy knew. When he was being led to his cell, the Gestapo officer told him, trembling with rage, of a serious Bible scholar with whom he had dealt just before him. "Do you know, swine, what he said to me? 'You sausage-end,' he said, 'if Jehovah wills, you will disintegrate this very moment into a thousand pieces. But if he lets you do with me what you want, do you believe then you are anything other than his instrument to test me?' What a piece of shit!" This experience only confirmed for Hielscher what he had already found in Buber's Hasidic tales, such as the tale of Shelomo of Karlin which Buber titled "With the Sword at His Throat":

> Rabbi Shelomo was on a journey in the company of one of his disciples. On the way, they stopped at an inn and sat down at a table. Then the rabbi gave orders to warm mead for him, for he liked his mead warm. In the meantime, soldiers arrived, and when they saw Jews sitting at the table, they told them to get up in loud, angry tones. "Is the mead warm yet?" the rabbi asked the man who served drinks. At that the soldiers struck the table with their fists and shouted: "Off with you, or else. . . !" The rabbi only said: "Isn't it warm yet?" The leader of the soldiers drew his sword from the scabbard and put the blade to the maggid's throat. "Because, you know, it mustn't get really hot!" said Rabbi Shelomo. Then the soldiers left the inn.

"I could not have understood evil as a grace from heaven without their help," testified Hielscher and added, "I told myself daily, 'If these poor fellows, belonging to no military family, have confirmed their faith in the midst of misery and today still confirm it . . . will you then succumb?'"

When Buber spoke at a German university during his visits in the 1950s, reports Goes, he was concerned neither to please nor to shock but, going straight to his subject, engaged in his own patient monologue and dialogue, distributing before thousands "the bread of being together." "I have never known anyone who was less concerned about supplying material with which to ignite the flammable part of an audience." Goes also describes his personal dialogues with Buber or with Martin and Paula together. Buber, over seventy-five, exactly thirty years older than Goes, was in no way impeded by any signs of weakness. "His eyes were clear, his hearing excellent; a soft tone of voice was just as likely as an animated outburst. His stupendous memory never lapsed, and this venerable personage hardly seemed to know what fatigue meant." On one occasion after a more than four-hour conversation, Goes, concerned that he had wearied Buber beyond all propriety, stood up and mumbled an apology. "But what do you expect?" Buber said. "A good conversation must be long, it must be possible for it to be long."

Occasionally Buber would tell a story, as of the time when he left his magnifying glass in a German taxicab. The driver brought it into the hotel and asked for the little gentleman with the big white beard. The bellhop could not locate Buber, and the driver came back three times, evidently wanting to hand Buber the magnifying glass himself. When he finally found Buber and gave him his glass, Buber said, "You went to a lot of trouble." "Well, yes," said the Berlin taxi driver, "people like me would like to do something right, too." When Goes suggested that Buber was a magnet for nice stories, Buber hit the table with his flat palm and said "Good!" meaning, suggests Goes, "One can call to life either evil deeds or deeds of righteousness."

In 1959, Thilo Koch interviewed Buber in Jerusalem for a German television station. Asked about the Holocaust, Buber said: "Although millions of Jews were murdered, for me the historical fact is ultimately a problem of the German people."

> I do not forget for a moment and cannot forget what has happened. But I ask myself ever again from where and how did it happen, and then I do not arrive at any general motive of hatred of the Jews but at a particular historical crisis of the German people that I hardly understand, something that has taken place only once in history: that such a people has succumbed to the subhuman, and by such a people I mean precisely the people of Bach and Hölderlin.

The Holocaust had revealed something more elemental, more momentous even, than the hatred of the Jews: the unprecedented subhuman acts perpetrated by one people upon another.

Koch closed the interview by saying:

> I know it has been difficult for you to give us this interview. It has been difficult for you to say what you have said in the last minutes, and it is difficult for me to have heard it. I am so thankful to you that just for this conversation you did not withhold yourself, and I am moved by it.

In 1960 when German students were asked to name the greatest spiritual figures of our time, Buber was placed third, along with Pope John XXIII. That same year a German-Israel student group from a church college in Berlin came to see Buber in Jerusalem and asked him what hope there was in a superficial, meaningless world. There is hope, Buber answered. The real happening takes place in the stillness, unnoticed by anyone. In response to Buber's request that they be concrete, the students spoke of the guilt of their parents, the crime of the older generation against the people of God. One cannot ask anyone to be a martyr, Buber replied, but where there is sin, there is hate, and where there is hate there must be reconciliation. Yet true reconciliation is possible only where the person who is guilty turns to a better way. "In this, Germany is lacking," said Buber and meant not only the Nuremberg trials, at which every one of the accused answered "Not guilty" but also the whole older generation in Germany. But the younger generation too will be guilty if they do not seek a better way; for, as in a Greek tragedy, they bear the sins of their parents too.

In 1961, Paul Schallück, in an essay in a book edited by Thilo Koch titled *Portraits of German-Jewish Intellectual History,* testified that through meeting Buber and reading his works he had come to understand the German-Jewish symbiosis from Moses Mendelssohn to Buber and the special contribution of the Jews to German culture, developing, sublimating, deepening, and illuminating it, but then the German part of that symbiosis fell into the darkness of romanticism and Hitler. "I hold a new, changed, and to be sure, also deeper and broader symbiosis of the German with the Jewish spirit to be possible, and as far as our German people is concerned, even necessary," wrote Schallück. Fully aware of the difficulties, he nonetheless wished that the future of his people might be linked with the Jewish people in a new symbiosis.

In December 1961, Heinz Kremers asked Buber what he thought concerning the development of the relation of the West German Republic to Israel. Buber replied that he saw it first of all as a relation of the Republic to itself. For centuries it had been burdened by a geographical situation that gave Germany few political successes. This situation led the Germans to accept uncritically successful politics and successful politicians and to surrender themselves to political "charismatics." As a typical example Buber told of how he and Paula, when they first came to Jerusalem from Germany, could find no place to live in the overflowing city. A German Evangelical pastor took the Bubers in with open arms and gave them a beautiful place in which to live. Buber was deeply moved by the love this German showed him, coming as it did just when they had left Germany for good. He was deeply shocked, therefore, when the pastor said, "One may think of Hitler what one will. One thing is for me certain: God has visibly blessed him"!

Kremers understood Buber's remarks as a question addressed to Germans of today—"whether our relation to Israel will not again be burdened by our faith in the success of our politics!" Is the fear of experimenting so great that we will not dare to resume diplomatic relations with Israel? Kremers asked, and stated it as his firm conviction that the Evangelical Church of Germany should demand as quickly as possible a resumption of diplomatic relations with Israel and reparations that would give Israel economic aid. Anyone who studied the history of the Evangelical Church in the days of the Third Reich would be shocked, wrote Kremers, by the fact that only in isolated cases were there protests against the persecution of nonbaptized Jews and attempts to help them. Citing Dietrich Bonhoeffer's statement that the church is a church only when it is a church for others, Kremers declared that the church in this concrete case should dare to be a church for others, a church for the world!

In 1964, in an essay on "Martin Buber's Concept of Responsibility," Paul Rohrig stated that Buber had not only taught what the life of dialogue is but also confirmed the truth of his teaching by his existence. "He even did the utmost in that, after all the dreadful happenings, he soon again began the dialogue with us Germans. . . . We have reason enough to listen with the greatest attention to Buber's words pointing the way, knowing what it means that this voice comes from the midst of that people upon which the Germans inflicted unspeakable suffering."

In 1958, on the occasion of Buber's eightieth birthday, Hans Kohn published an article in an important German journal in which he spoke of the great crowds that attended Buber's lectures in Germany, most of which were comprised of young people.

> Drawing from biblical and Hasidic sources, he was still deeply rooted in that—intellectually so fruitful and existentially so rich in tension, so creative and so fragile and, because of that, wholly unique—German-Jewish dialogue that, like so much else in Germany, came to an end and disappeared with Hitler's rise to power. The changed, post-Hitler Germany rightly greets in Buber a venerable figure that reminds it of the greatness of its own past. To the world Buber signifies one of the essential thinkers and persons of our time. To Germany he means more.

What Buber represented to postwar Germany was precisely the courage and strength with which he walked the narrow ridge and encountered the Germans on it. In July 1960, Buber received a letter from the Society for Christian-Jewish Cooperation of Darmstadt informing him that the administrative head of the county of Bergstrasse wanted to place a plaque on his house in Heppenheim commemorating the long years that Buber lived there and that the society would like to sponsor a ceremony on that occasion at which Buber himself might speak if he planned to be in Germany the following year. Buber responded:

I believe I may say that I have served the cause of the reconciliation of peoples to the best of my abilities. But that is a cause which can only thrive under the sign of truth. It would not do justice to the truth, in my opinion, if a plaque were erected on the house in which my family and I lived during the years 1916–1938 which only commemorated the fact of this dwelling but left unmentioned the fact that it was plundering and expropriation which marked the end of our connection with this dwelling. A commemorative plaque such as you plan would, to be sure, mean a high honor for my person, but it would not thereby show the honor due the historical truth which should serve the coming generations as admonition and warning.

In 1975 this writer sent a letter to the mayor of Heppenheim at the request of a German committee fighting the plans to demolish the "Buber house" in favor of a freeway and received a long but negative reply. However, in March 1978, a letter arrived from Margarete Exler of this same committee saying that Buber's house in Heppenheim had been saved after all:

The government of the Federal State of Hessen will take care of it and it shall in future be the quarters of the International Council of Christians and Jews (ICCJ) connected with a meeting-room for different purposes, not only to keep the memory but also the ideas of Martin Buber alive, so that people may be enabled to practice them in their daily life.

The letter had on it a commemorative stamp with a picture of Buber and the dates of his life, and it was postmarked "Martin Buber 1878–1978/in Heppenheim 1916–1938."

PART III

America

(1951–1960)

CHAPTER 6

First Visit to America:
Eclipse of God

IN NOVEMBER 1948, Louis Finkelstein, chancelor of the Jewish Theological Seminary of America, the institution that trains Conservative rabbis, approached Buber about coming to America to lecture at the seminary. Buber responded warmly that he would like to meet the next Jewish generation in the immediacy of life face to face and not just through his books, for he was more than ever convinced of its significance "for our future." Because of his work in the School for the Teachers of the People, Buber twice had to postpone coming so that his first visit to America did not take place until the academic year 1951–52.

My own contact with Buber's thought began in 1944 at a time when he was almost unknown in America and not a single one of his books had been published in the United States. As an undergraduate at Harvard I had become a socialist and a pacifist. During three and a half years of Civilian Public Service work camps, including a year and a half "detached service" as an attendant in an institution for the feebleminded, I had become a thoroughgoing mystic, spending three hours a day in meditation and such other time as I could, with a twelve-hour work day, devoting myself to "recollection" and reading of mystical and devotional literature. Although my mother came from a distinguished line of Lubavitcher Hasidim in Lithuania, she had never mentioned Hasidism to me nor was it mentioned in the exceptionally diluted Reform Judaism in which I was raised in Tulsa, Oklahoma. During one furlough when I visited Tulsa, my mother became alarmed at how deeply I was immersed in the Hindu Vedanta (I saw Swami Yatiswarananda of the Ramakrishna Order in Philadelphia once a week) and in Christian mysticism and told me of her Hasidic background. A young Conservative rabbi with whom she put me in touch sent me to see his professor at the Jewish Theological Seminary, Dr. Simon Greenberg, who was at that time still the rabbi at Har Zion Synagogue in Philadelphia, and Rabbi Greenberg (whose son Daniel later married the daughter of Ernst Simon) lent me an early British translation of *The Legend of the Baal-Shem* and Ronald Gregor Smith's original translation of *I and Thou. The Legend of the Baal-Shem,* as I have recounted in the autobiographical chapters of *Touchstones of Reality,* "was the first Jewish book that . . . spoke to me as a mature, thinking man." In it "I found an image of an active love and fervent devotion no longer coupled with self-denial or metaphysical theorizing about unity with the divine. After my immersion in the individualistic and world-denying forms of mysticism, . . . Hasidism spoke to me in compelling accents of a wholehearted service to God that did not mean turning away from my fellow men and from the world."

In 1945, Rabbi Greenberg sent me to the seminary in New York to meet Abraham Joshua Heschel, with whom I remained in close friendship until his death in 1972. Heschel told me not to write to Buber because he was a very busy man. By the winter of 1950 I had completed most of a 560-page doctoral dissertation on "Martin Buber: Mystic, Existentialist, Social Prophet—A Study in the Redemption of Evil" for the Committee on the History of Culture at the University of Chicago. My mother visited Israel in the spring of 1950 and I sent with her a long letter to Buber. In it I told him how close I felt to him as a person and a thinker and about the events in my life leading up to my dissertation, which Joachim Wach, my professor in the history of religion at the University of Chicago, had recommended for publication to the University of Chicago Press.

My mother managed to find a time when Buber could see her, and as he later said to her on the telephone, "something came of it." In April 1950, Buber wrote me in English:

> What you write me and even more what your mother told me about you and your life has interested me very much and I want to help you. I suggest you send me your dissertation, I will read it and send you my remarks. Another thing may prove more important yet: I want you to write down your life-experience for me—not thoughts on life, but the tale itself. It must be done of course in utter frankness, but without any self-analysis. It will not be easy but you must overcome the difficulties. I shall read it attentively, I shall not yet tell you about my impression of it, but the knowledge will show me what I may be able to do for you.

In July 1950 after I had completed my dissertation and received my doctorate, I sent Buber a twenty-three-page single-spaced autobiograpy detailing some of the events that I have touched on in *Touchstones of Reality*. In August, Buber responded with a letter which in itself illustrated concretely his important distinction between "acceptance" and "confirmation":

> Your autobiography is just what I wanted it to be. You have acquired a good deal of inner, personal (I mean, not analytical) frankness and yours is a delightful gift of self-expression. What is not yet sufficiently developed is the power of seeing the others instead of feeling their relationship to you. As long as you do not see them more really you will not be able to describe them, to make us see them. What you do say about them is interesting, but for the sake of yourself only, not of them, and it should be for the sake of them too. True narration means coherent events between fully perceptible persons. Of course, I had asked you to tell me about yourself, and so you were not obliged to do more than that. But can you tell, that is to say: do you know by your eyes, who Ellie is? I mentioned Ellie, because your girls are more perceptible than your boys. Your telling the "psychodramas"—and you should tell them indeed—will be a real tale only if we learn to know the actors, and even to know their eyes and the seeing of those eyes and even how those eyes were seeing you.

Later in August, Buber wrote me that he had received and read my dissertation and that he thought it "a really important book" which "deserves indeed to be published and read." The problem of evil and its redemption on which I concentrated my work, he saw as "the central human problem indeed." It was not only "a unifying center," as I had put it, "but the best of all possible centers." He also wrote that, in spite of the many remarkable books and essays written on his thought, my dissertation was the first successful attempt to give a comprehensive and systematic representation of his ideas and to show their essential unity. Its third main merit, as he saw it, was that "by a very careful comparing of earlier and later texts," I had "given a reliable description of a development, not in a biographical form, as [Hans] Kohn has done, but by tracing the way of a peception to its (not yet full) elucidation." A few days later Buber sent me many pages of detailed comments and suggestions plus a long bibliography of books and essays about him that I did not know even existed!

Thus after the completion of my doctoral dissertation, at a time when most young scholars put away their subject in favor of more mature ones, there began many years of intensive work with Buber, translating, editing, and introducing his works, as well as writing *The Life of Dialogue,* which took almost four years after my dissertation. During the fifteen years in which we worked together, I never ceased to be amazed by Buber's faithfulness to even the smallest detail or the endless patience with which he would enter into a dialogue with me about just the right translation of a German word into English. I experienced Buber's response to my dissertation as a turning point in my life, and indeed it was. It was not only a confirmation of my work on him beyond anything I might have dreamed of, but also a confirmation of me as a person that helped give meaning and direction to my life.

In February 1951, Buber wrote me from Glasgow, Scotland, saying that while in London he had spoken to Sir Herbert Read about my book. Sir Herbert Read, poet, critic, man of letters, and a director of Routledge & Kegan Paul publishers in London, was one of the first persons to recognize Buber's significance in England. Because of him Routledge published *Between Man and Man* and *Paths in Utopia,* and he had placed Buber's approach to education at the center of his own book *Education Through Art.* "He seems very inclined to publish it [my book] together with the University of Chicago Press," Buber wrote me, "but he thinks it must be abridged—which of course is the view of one publisher, but of a really understanding one. Now, if you agree to do this harsh work of shortening, I am of course ready to help you." The contact with Sir Herbert Read turned out to be essential, for, despite the highly favorable readers' reports, the Board of Directors of the University of Chicago Press turned down my book because they had not heard of Buber! Routledge's agreement to print the book in England finally made it possible for the University of Chicago Press to co-publish it.

"I had," declared Buber at the end of his letter about Sir Herbert Read, "some glorious hours at the Scottish fiords." Two weeks later he wrote me from London that he did not think it necessary to bring his ideas into connection with all the thinkers I had in mind and concurred with my own idea that it might be a plan for another book. "When shortening the book you should preserve what is essential to the understanding of the ideas themselves." The only exception he made was a chapter comparing *For the Sake of Heaven* and *The Brothers Karamazov,* which he felt to be important, although in the end this chapter too had to be eliminated.

In the fall of 1950 Buber suggested I should translate his essay "On the Suspension of the Ethical" for *Moral Principles of Action,* edited by Ruth Nanda Anshen. I objected that I did not see myself as a translator and had never in fact had a formal course in German. "I can tell," he replied, "you are faithful and you are readable." Thus began a series of almost a dozen books of Buber's that I translated and in most cases also edited and introduced. I sent Buber my translation of his essay and he sent back a detailed commentary wherever he had a question. At the end of his comments on "On the Suspension of the Ethical," a discussion of Kierkegaard's *Fear and Trembling,* he wrote, in response to my letters, "The idea of an '*entirely* impersonal' God has no place in my mind and will, I hope, never find one."

"On the Suspension of the Ethical" is the first of the essays that I translated for *Eclipse of God.* Like all the others, while starting from a scholarly standpoint, it ended with a fervent statement about our time. To Kierkegaard's claim that the "knight of faith" must suspend the ordinary ethical in favor of the "absolute duty to the Absolute," Buber posed the question, "Are you really addressed by the Absolute or by one of his apes?" Although the voice of Moloch prefers a mighty roaring to the "voice of a thin silence," in our age it appears to be extremely difficult to distinguish the one from the other. In the past, images of the Absolute, "partly pallid, partly crude, altogether false and yet true," gave men some help against the apes of the Absolute which bustle about on earth. But now that "God is dead," in Nietzsche's words, and the eye of the spirit "can no longer catch a glimpse of the appearance of the Absolute," false absolutes rule over the soul and the suspension of the ethical fills the world in a caricaturized form. Well-conditioned young souls sacrifice their personal integrity in order that equality or freedom may come (originally Buber also wrote "the kingdom" but deleted it because of the sensitivity of Christian theologians). "In the realm of Moloch honest men lie and compassionate men torture," really and truly believing "that brother-murder will prepare the way for brotherhood!"

In asking me to translate the second essay, "Religion and Reality," Buber wrote that it expounded a thesis concerning the development of modern thought that "I think of particular importance for our time." Tracing a development through Spinoza, Kant, Hegel, Nietzsche, Bergson, and Heidegger, Buber characterized the thinking of our time as aiming to preserve the idea of the divine as the true concern of religion while destroying the reality of the idea of God and of our relation to him. "This is done in many ways, overtly and covertly, apodictically and hypothetically, in the language of metaphysics and of psychology." Specifically modern thought can no longer endure a God who is not confined to man's subjectivity. Whenever man has to interpret encounter with God as self-encounters, his very structure is destroyed. "This is the portent of the present hour." Buber was particularly eloquent in his rejection of Bergson's identification of God with a creative process, "making the concept of God utterly meaningless" and still more with the image of creative energy operating without contradiction.

> The divine force which man actually encounters in life does not hover above the demonic, but penetrates it. To confine God to a producing function is to remove Him from the world in which we live—a world filled with burning contradictions, and with yearning for salvation.

In contrast to the "death of God" Buber set forth the metaphor of the "eclipse of God" as a real happening that does not take place in God or in the human spirit but between us and God. "Eclipse of the light of heaven, eclipse of God—such indeed is the character of the historic hour through which the world is passing." If one insists, like Heidegger, that it is within earthly thought that we discover the power that unveils the mystery, one denies the effective reality of our vis-à-vis and contributes to the human responsibility for the eclipse. We can do away with the name God, which implies a possessive, but "He who is denoted by the name lives in the light of His eternity" while "we, 'the slayers,' remain dwellers in darkness, consigned to death."

The two other essays that Buber sent me in August 1951 were "Religion and Philosophy" and "Religion and Ethics." "Religion and Philosophy," which contrasted philosophy as the bond between the Absolute and the general with religion as the bond between the Absolute and the particular, was the hardest single piece of Buber's that I ever had to translate. In the same mail he wrote me a long letter with thirty-one separate points answering questions I had put to him in connection with what later became my book *The Life of Dialogue.* He confirmed my perception that tragedy in *For the Sake of Heaven,* like the very heart of tragedy in general, consists of two contending persons being each as he is and without sufficient resources to bridge the opposition. He also wrote, in response to my concern about the various Christian theologies that converted the I-Thou to a Thou-I, "I am most decidely opposed to all the theologies putting the emphasis on the Thou as subject. They have not grasped the mystery of creation of man." "Everything that I have written on dialogical existence means ontology—but not ontological analysis," he added. He wished that I would bring out the epistemological consequences of his thought in *The Life of Dialogue,* "but it must not be done by bringing my thought nearer to that of Heidegger to whom I am more opposed than ever although I feel myself as in the days of my youth, and even more, near to Heraclitus whom he treats as his father." "I think Heidegger's Heraclitus interpretation utterly erroneous," he added in parentheses. To my question about his own understanding of himself as a philosopher, he replied, "I have no inclination to systematize but I am of course, and, by necessity, a philosophizing man and when Plato's Socrates speaks on philosophers, my innermost being knows what he means." In opposition to Kierkegaard, who, following the tracks of Hegel, distinguished three qualitatively different "stages in life's way"—the aesthetic, the ethical and the religious—and made the choice between the aesthetic and the ethical an absolute either/or, Buber wrote me:

> Aestheticism is degeneration, the aesthetic attitude is an indispensable part of true life, and the real aesthetic attitude is never autonomous. I had to overcome the aestheticism of my youth, but I do not remember in my life a conflict between the aesthetic and the ethical. (It must be noted, by the way, that Kierkegaard's misunderstanding of the category of the aesthetical . . . has been fatal.)

Buber still held the I-Thou relationship with nature to be real, but not complete, because it lacks effective reciprocity. The process of self-becoming is important, he wrote me, but it is necessary to distinguish it from "psychological egotism," of which he saw Jung as an example. Buber hesitated to publish a new edition of *Ecstatic Confessions,* for, despite all warnings, it could lead to misunderstandings, since it is "too 'mystical.'" He advised me strongly that in writing my book on him I should avoid above all detailed exegesis of separate essays. "If you have to sacrifice, sacrifice 'Buber.'" My friend Arthur Cohen had suggested to me that I ask Buber to write a Foreword to *The Life of Dialogue*. Buber responded by saying, "The question of the preface we must talk over. I do not yet 'see' it and therefore do not feel inclined to write it, but I want you to explain what you mean by it. You must understand the thought is somewhat disturbing. I would have to say: This is Myself. I have not this kind of relationship to myself. Will you know what I mean when I tell you that I am not interested in myself?" I never again raised the question with him.

Buber closed this long letter with more bibliographical suggestions in the course of which he told me that Paul Honigsheim, a German sociologist, a disciple of Max Weber, had written an article in 1948 for Buber's seventieth birthday: "I was ashamed to read on the last page (a comparison with Dostoevsky) that he calls me 'der verwirklichte Aljoscha' ["the realized Alyosha," the saintly young hero of *The Brothers Karamazov*]. I am, alas, very far from it."

On September 10, Buber wrote me that he was on the verge of approaching another translator, not knowing if I would do the essays, but was able to destroy the letter to him in time. "I prefer you decidedly, you being the only possible translator knowing *'everything,'* and so the whole terminology too." "Bringing all this here into tolerable order before leaving for half a year," Buber wrote me later from Jerusalem, "is a formidable task, and there is only my humour to help me." At the end of still another letter, he raised a question concerning the title of my dissertation, "Martin Buber: Mystic, Existentialist, Social Prophet." "What about giving your book a 'quieter' title?" he wrote. "As for myself, I do not feel myself all this. I have simply something to tell or, rather, something to show—and those designations are so big!"

On October 31, Buber flew to New York from Israel. The seminary put him up at the Hotel Marcy on 96th Street and West End Avenue, where he resided throughout his stay in New York. The first time that I went to New York to see him was perhaps the most memorable of our many meetings over nine years. He received me into his apartment room and looked me searchingly in the eyes while taking my hand. My first response was to how totally "other" this man seemed after I had felt such kinship to him through his writings and letters. He was less than five feet. I am five feet ten. His eyes were of a depth, gentleness, and directness that I have never before or since encountered. He asked me to sit down. "You must not think that I am interested in you mostly because you have written a book on me," he said, and he added, speaking of himself, "My books are not what is important to me. They are like snake skins that I shed when I need to." I spoke to him of my wife: "She is very different from me." "All the better!" he responded. We also talked of women in general. "Someday you will learn that one woman is more than twenty." I understood what he meant: into one relationship one may bring one's whole self. Into twenty relationships one brings only fragments of oneself.

Buber told me of his meeting with T. S. Eliot five days before in London. They were brought together by Ronald Gregor Smith, translator of *I and Thou* and *Between Man and Man.* There were only two other persons present. Eliot was very shy but directly frank, which Buber did not usually find with persons who first met him. Having constructed a scale of attitudes toward evil in connection with my doctoral dissertation and having just planned a year course on "Philosophy and Literature" at Sarah Lawrence College which would include Buber's *I and Thou* and T. S. Eliot's *Four Quartets,* I asked Buber whether he did not find his opinions very different from those of Eliot. "When I meet a man I am not concerned with opinions but with the man," said Buber. I took this response as a reproach, and it was. I had turned Buber and Eliot into positions in a dialectic within my own mind and lost the reality of their dialogue as persons meeting each other! Fifteen years later when I wrote T. S. Eliot asking his support for Buber for a Nobel Prize, Eliot confirmed Buber's sense of the rareness of the meeting between them. "I only met Buber once," Eliot wrote me, in agreeing to support Buber's nomination, "but I felt then I was in the presence of greatness."

A few days later I asked my wife Eugenia, who had not yet met Buber, to take to him my translation of a lecture that he needed for an out-of-town appearance, since I was tied up at Sarah Lawrence. "Don't expect him to talk to you," I said to her. "He has only a half hour to leave to make the plane to Cleveland." When Eugenia came in, Buber asked her to sit down. "What work do you do?" he asked. "I was a college teacher," she said, "and I worked two years as a university librarian. Now I am trying to find a job as an editor." "Pardon me," said Buber and laughed, "but I don't see you at all as an editor. I see you rather as working with young children." "But not boys over nine," he added. "Women cannot understand them." Buber's words came at the very moment of decision for Eugenia. She received two offers of editorial positions but turned them down in favor of getting a second M.A. in early childhood education leading to years of highly successful work as a nursery school teacher. More than "successful," Eugenia brought a rare presence to nursery school work which no training or techniques could have given her. When she asked Buber later how he knew with such sureness which path she should follow, he answered, "I do not know." He too related to people not through techniques but through presence.

Buber's first visit to America was also the occasion for his official retirement from the Hebrew University. Now that he had retired, he had been asked to teach a seminar in biblical faith when he got back, something that had been strictly forbidden to him as long as he was serving officially. "I am just the same person as I was before," Buber complained to me. "Why can I do it now when I could not then?" The answer, of course, was that same opposition by the Orthodox that had originally prevented his teaching religion in any official capacity in the university. Actually I doubt if he ever taught a seminar in biblical faith even later. After he got back, he informed me that he had been asked to teach a seminar in comparative religion, and he had accepted.

I never took a note during or even after my many conversations with Buber, so what has remained of them is only what Buber himself called the work of the "organic selective memory." At his public lectures and in seminars and discussion groups I did take notes. One of these was a small group who met with Buber in his hotel suite at the Marcy. Buber did not lecture to us; he simply answered questions. Asked what proof he could offer for his religious attitudes, he answered, "The 'man of faith' (I prefer not to say 'believing man') has decided for faith without objective proof and precisely this is his situation." "What I mean by religion is just one's personal life. One usually does not dream of putting his personal life at stake—of really meeting abyss with abyss. I must by violence of the spirit bring the person I meet to deal with his personal life. I must not show him that his arguments are wrong by their content but that arguments— argumentation as such is wrong. I must break down his security by driving him to confront his self. He puts me in a situation of responsibility for him . . . struggling with him against him—using as allies the forces deep within him. I can venture this only if he comes in utter sincerity without any restraint. It is just a question of personal relationship—nothing else."

One sympathetic but ambivalent young man questioned the relevance of Buber's books to life. "If my books do not speak to you, burn my books!" responded Buber without a trace of anger or irony. Malcolm Diamond of Princeton, who was also doing his dissertation on Buber, raised the question of "subjectivity" in Buber's thought. "Subjectivity always means opinion, reflection," said Buber. "I don't speak of this at all—only about being, existing." But he was also not talking about "objectivity," he explained. "God has to do with every living being but not with ideas. Philosophical thinking is a transposition of reality to another plane altogether." Asked about the Jewish Law, or Halakhah, Buber conceded that his position might be mistaken for antinomianism, or lawlessness, and that it might be misused by an irresponsible person to confirm him in his irresponsibility. But for the responsible person Buber saw the *personal* as the only way. "In three hundred years there may be a new Halakhah. But now this is just the way of modern man. I am only against life becoming rigid. I want to warn man against *anticipated* objectivation." Of course, objectivation will come again and again, and when it does the tradition can only be renewed through the personal way. "On this personal way one may discover things that are not only true for oneself but for others. One cannot live without danger, without risk—the question is to choose between risks."

Perhaps the most important thing Buber said in his discussion concerned his relationship to Judaism. In no sense did he proceed as a theologian who accepts what the tradition says simply because it is the tradition. Only what he could confirm out of his own personal testing and wrestling would he affirm. "There are things in the Jewish tradition I cannot accept at all," Buber said, "and things I hold true that are not expressed in Judaism. But what I hold essential has been expressed more in biblical Judaism than anywhere else—in the biblical dialogue between man and God. In Hasidism this is developed in a communal life. I want to show that Judaism can be lived. It is most important that the Jews today live Judaism."

Some notion of Buber's incredible expenditure of energy during this first trip to America can be gained just from the list that Buber shared with me of the first two months. Between November 8 and December 21 he delivered twenty lectures in New York, Cleveland, Chicago, and Detroit and at such colleges and universities as Dartmouth, Haverford, Brandeis, Yale, Columbia, the University of Chicago, and Wisconsin. In addition to these lectures, Buber received a stream of visitors, met with publishers, carried on an active correspondence with people all over the world, worked with me on the translations of his lectures, and worked with Professor Seymour

Siegel of the seminary on the pronunciation of English (*Thou* was the one word Buber could never master: it always came out "vow"!)

The three seminary lectures had to be moved to the Horace Mann Auditorium at Teachers College, Columbia, because of the huge crowds who wished to hear Buber. At this time he was not yet well known in America, and none of his books had yet been published here. But around New York there were many, many people, like my colleague the composer and professor of music, André Singer, who were eager to see the man who had been of such great help to them during the dark days of Nazi Germany and Nazi Austria. The three lectures that Buber gave for the seminary comprised a new series of "Talks on Judaism" and were later published as a little book, *At the Turning.*

After Buber's death they were published in *On Judaism,* which also included the first translation of the earlier speeches. In the first of these new speeches, "Judaism and Civilization," Buber rejected, as a cheap slogan, the argument that his view amounted to "civilizational optimism." A civilization, like an individual person, can hallow itself and open itself to the holy without curtailing or "primitivizing" its existence. At the heart of Judaism is this concern to use the actual human substance to build the kingship of God rather than replace it with some new divine work, and this is the essence of the prophetic protest against the kings who shirked the task of hallowing the life of the human, with all its various spheres fully developed, into a united whole. But when the Jews stepped out of the ghetto, the foundation of Judaism, the unique unity of people and religion, developed a deep rift which has since become ever deeper. This is true of the Diaspora, where there is nowhere a wholehearted effort to hallow Jewish communal life; and this is also true of the Jewish State:

> A home and the freedom to realize the principle of our being have been granted us anew, but Israel and the principle of its being have come apart. . . . People try to conceal the rift by applying basic religious terms, such as God of Israel, and Messiah, to purely political processes . . . but the holy reality. . . . escapes any speech which does not mean just it, that is, the fulfillment of God's truth and justice on earth. True, it is a difficult, a tremendously difficult undertaking to drive the plowshare of the normative principle into the hard soil of political fact; but the right to lift a historical moment into the light of what is above history can be bought at no cheaper price.

This last statement is the one that made such a deep impression upon my great friend A. J. Muste, the leading American pacifist whose whole life was devoted to the prophetic call for justice and peace, a devotion matched by only a few of the Jews whom Buber designated "the keepers of the roots." During the discussion afterward, a man said to Buber that he ought not to despair so quickly about the state of Israel. "Despair!" Buber exclaimed. "I never despaired even in the darkest days of our people."

In his second seminary lecture, "The Silent Question," Buber presented Judaism via a critique of two modern French Jewish thinkers who turned away from it—Simone Weil and Henri Bergson. Both Bergson and Weil saw Israel as an embodiment of a principle of social life which was either a stage to be surpassed, as for Bergson, or the great obstacle, the "Great Beast" of the Apocalypse, according to Weil. In opposition to the dualism both posited between that spiritual interior in which they found their touchstone of reality and the external, social world, Buber portrayed Judaism as according inwardness its rightful place but contesting the self-sufficiency of the soul: "Inward truth must become real life, otherwise it does not remain truth. A drop of Messianic consummation must be mingled with every hour; otherwise the hour is godless, despite all piety and devoutness." Social humanity built upon real relationships between its members is fundamentally different from any "Great Beast": "Judaism rejects the 'We' of group egotism, of national conceit and party exclusiveness, but it postulates that 'We' which arises from the real relationships of its components and which maintains genuine relations with other groups." He who loves brings God and the world together—this Hasidic teaching is the consummation of Judaism, and in it is realized, if anywhere, that "active mysticism" for which Bergson called. In an impassioned statement Buber characterized the Hasidic message to all as "You yourself must begin":

> Existence will remain meaningless for you if you yourself do not penetrate into it with active love and if you do not in this way discover its meaning for yourself. Everything is waiting to be hallowed by you. . . . For the sake of this your beginning, God created the world. He has drawn it out of Himself so that you may bring it closer to Him. Meet the world with the fullness of your being and you shall meet Him. That He Himself accepts from your hands what you have to give to the world is His mercy. If you wish to learn to believe, love!

The third seminary lecture, "The Dialogue Between Heaven and Earth," reveals the coming together of Buber's interpretation of the Hebrew Bible and his philosophy of dialogue with an explicitness that cannot be found in any of his other writings. "To God's sovereign address, man gives his autonomous answer." Even man's silence is an answer. Lamenting, supplicating, thanks- and praise-giving man experiences himself as heard and understood, accepted and confirmed. "The basic teaching that fills the Hebrew Bible is that our life is a dialogue between the above and the below."

> What happened once happens now and always, and the fact of its happening to us is a guarantee of its having happened. The Bible has, in the form of a glorified remembrance, given vivid, decisive expression to an ever recurrent happening. In the infinite language of events and situations, eternally changing, but plain to the truly attentive, transcendence speaks to our hearts at the essential moment of personal life. And there is a language in which we can answer it . . . our actions and attitudes, our reactions and our abstentions.

This understanding of the totality of our responses as our responsibility in the dialogue with transcendence is almost identical with what Buber wrote in 1957 in the Postscript to the second edition of *I and Thou*, without referring at all to the Bible. Warning that we be careful not to understand the conversation with God as something happening solely outside the everyday, Buber declared that God's speech penetrates everything biographical and historical in our lives "and makes it for you and me into instruction, message, demand." "Happening upon happening, situation upon situation, are enabled and empowered by the personal speech of God to demand of the human person that he take his stand and make his decision."

It is also in "The Dialogue Between Heaven and Earth" that the real heart of Buber's understanding of this hour as one of the "eclipse of God" is laid bare. He does not use this language here but rather the biblical language of God's hiding his face, yet he inserts into it an unmistakable autobiographical confession. When God seems to withdraw himself utterly from the earth and no longer participates in its existence, the space of history is full of noise but empty of the divine breath. "For one who believes in the living God, who knows about Him, and is fated to spend his life in a time of His hiddenness, it is very difficult to live." After this confession, Buber went on to speak about Psalm 82, but he ended the essay with the question of how a Jewish life or, more correctly, a life with God is still possible in a time in which there is an Auschwitz. Elie Wiesel, himself a survivor of the Holocaust, has said, "With the advent of the Nazi regime in Germany, humanity became witness to what Martin Buber would call an eclipse of God." It was above all, in fact, in the name of the "Job of Auschwitz" that Buber called this an age of the "eclipse of God." In language reminiscent of his interpretation of Kafka, Buber said in "The Dialogue Between Heaven and Earth," "The estrangement has become too cruel, the hiddenness too deep," and asked whether we can still speak to God, hear his word, call to him, or, as individuals and as a people enter into dialogue with him. "Dare we recommend to the survivors of Auschwitz, the Job of the gas chambers: 'Give thanks unto the Lord, for He is good; for His mercy endureth forever'?" The only answer that the biblical Job received was God's nearness, that he knew God again. "Nothing is explained, nothing adjusted; wrong has not become right, nor cruelty kindness." And how is it, Buber asked, with "all those who have not got over what happened and will not get over it?" Buber revised his original response to his own question, writing a new and more powerful ending, one that shows, if anything does, the trust and the contending that mark "the Modern Job":

> Do we stand overcome before the hidden face of God like the tragic hero of the Greeks before faceless fate? No, rather even now we contend, we too, with God, even with Him, the Lord of Being, whom we once, we here, chose for our Lord. We do not put up with earthly being; we struggle for its redemption, and struggling we appeal to the help of our Lord, who is again and still a hiding one. . . . Though His coming appearance resemble no earlier one, we shall recognize again our cruel and merciful Lord.

Many of Buber's American audiences had trouble understanding him because of his accent and some because the level of his lectures were pitched to a European university setting not often appropriate for America. For example, when Buber lectured at the Rockefeller Chapel at the University of Chicago, more than two thousand people crowded in. But the questions raised by the works of Sartre and Heidegger, to which Buber was addressing himself, had not yet reached the Middle West, so the people there were unable to appreciate Buber's answers.*

When Buber came out from Rockefeller Chapel, he saw a woman standing there whom he had known in Frankfurt in the 1930s. He went up to her with tears in his eyes and took her hand. Another time, after a lecture at Yale University, Buber spent twenty minutes speaking directly to a woman who had found courage to ask him a question from the audience. Years later she spoke of how much this dialogical immediacy had meant and still meant to her. Buber's immediacy of

---

*See Note to Chapter 6.

dialogue was not always gratifying to others. Once before a dinner at Yale in his honor, when the person in charge said, "Professor Buber will deliver grace," Buber replied shortly, "Don't believe in it."

One of Buber's most memorable lectures in America was the one he gave at the Park Avenue Synagogue in New York City. There he presented one of his interpretations of the Psalms from his small book *Right and Wrong*. At one point he said, in the words of the Psalm, "I shall not die but live." It seemed the most personal declaration conceivable and, at the same time, a statement made for all Israel. After the lecture, Buber answered questions informally. "Professor Buber, why have you had such an influence on the Protestants?" asked one man, clearly implying, in this Jewish setting, that Buber must not really be a good Jew if he could have had great influence on Protestants. "Ask the Protestants!" Buber responded. Another posed a query that made Buber ask, "Have you really lain awake at night thinking about this question?" Unlike the public's ordinary conception of a lecturer, Buber never dealt with general cultural questions. In the most public of settings he would only answer "real questions," questions in which the questioner staked herself or himself. "This is really pilpul," Buber said of another question that night, "pilpul" being the name for the type of hair-splitting that became common when the study of the Talmud had degenerated into sterile casuistry. What was most impressive, however, was that although not being an observant Jew himself, Buber at seventy-three walked miles on a cold winter's night across Central Park coming home from the synagogue rather than ride on the Sabbath and violate thereby a religious law important to the Conservative Jewish seminary which had been his host!

Among the old friends with whom Buber made contact again while he was in America was Eduard Strauss, who was active in adult education at Rabbi Hugo Hahn's Congregation Habonim (the nearest thing to a transplant of the Frankfurt Freie jüdische Lehrhaus) until his death in 1952. Buber again saw Abraham Joshua Heschel, who since 1944 had been Professor of Jewish Ethics and Mysticism at the Jewish Theological Seminary in New York. Another old friend was Albert Einstein, who spent many years at Princeton University before his death in 1955. Einstein and Buber were delighted to discover that they both liked Ellery Queen mystery stories! Later Buber confided to me that Einstein was very depressed over the atomic bomb, which his own researches had helped bring into being, and that as a result he refused an operation that might have saved his life. After the scientist's death Buber wrote Rudolf Kayser, Einstein's son-in-law, "I think of Einstein often and from the depth of my heart. It was at that time [of Einstein's death], despite the rareness of our personal contact, as if a support had been torn away from me." "Father Einstein told me with great enthusiasm of your visit in Princeton," replied Kayser. "He felt such closeness and admiration for you that each new meeting was a great joy for him."

In "Man and His Image-Work" Buber told of a conversation he had had forty years before with Einstein in which he had been pressing him in vain with a concealed question about his faith. Finally Einstein burst forth: "What we [and by this "we" he meant we physicists] strive for is just to draw his lines after *Him.*" Einstein meant by "draw after" what one does in retracing a geometrical figure. At that time Einstein's desire seemed to Buber an innocent hubris. But in the light of the new physics that came to light since then Einstein's strivings began to seem more and more seriously questionable.

> The fundamental impossibility of investigating the electron, the "complementarity" of contradictory explanations—and the lines of being that God has drawn! And nonetheless we must proceed from this unimageable, unrealizable, uncanny, unhomelike world. . . .

Buber was also a friend of Niels Bohr, who said to Buber in a conversation that the complementarity theory of modern physics was valid across the board. In a small circle with whom he met on his seventy-eighth birthday, including Ernst Simon, Buber demanded of his companions what could be said of the single, unambiguous relationship of truth and reality in the light of the complementarity theory. He reiterated with emphasis Niels Bohr's assertion that "even the verbs 'be' and 'know' have lost their simple, unambiguous meaning." How close Buber was in spirit to Bohr is shown by the fact that Bohr, when he was named to the Order of the Elephant in Denmark and had to devise a family shield, chose the Taoist yin and yang symbol with the motto *contraria sunt complementa* (opposites are complementary). For neither Bohr nor Buber was complementarity merely a negative limit to our knowledge. It fit in closely, on the contrary, with that *coincidentia oppositorum* of Nicholas of Cusa that had informed Buber's earliest thought from his doctoral dissertation, with the opposites of Heraclitus and Lao-tzu and the polarities of *Daniel.* Buber could still say to the "x," as Goethe once said to the full-blown rose, "So it is you, so it is really you!" We can enter into direct dialogue with nature, which we

can never know as it is minus our relation to it. In a letter to his friend
Kurt Singer, Buber explained that he in no way equated the small x
with the realm of atomic physics but only with the realm intended by
it. "That goes back especially to a conversation with Niels Bohr but
also to my last conversation with Einstein."

The lecture on "Religion and Philosophy" that Buber gave before a
great audience at Columbia University was an expanded revision and
enlargement of an earlier essay that he had given for the
Schopenhauer Society in German. Contrasting Epicurus and the
Buddha, Buber claimed that the personal manifestation of the divine
is not decisive for the genuineness of religion, but standing in relationship to the divine with one's whole being is. "Even when the
'Unoriginated' is not addressed with voice or soul, religion is still
founded on the duality of I and Thou. Even when the philosophical
act culminates in a vision of unity, philosophy is founded on the
duality of subject and object." The highest certainty in every religion
is "that the meaning of existence is open and accessible in the actual
lived concrete, not above the struggle with reality but in it." At a
luncheon at the Cathedral of St. John the Divine in New York City
with Bishop James Pike, Reinhold Niebuhr, and others, I asked
Buber how he could make this statement about all religion in the face
of the Hindu Vedanta, which, in its nondualistic tradition, rejects the
duality of I and Thou in favor of the One without Second, the identity
of Brahman and Atman. "That is its philosophy," Buber replied, "its
religious reality is still the lived concrete." At the same time Buber
rejected Reinhold Niebuhr's simplistic distinction between Western
religions as historical and Eastern as nonhistorical, pointing out that
Buddhism too, in many of its forms, is a history religion.

The religious must struggle to protect the lived concrete as the
meeting place between the human and the divine against all those
forces that threaten its quality of presentness and uniqueness—
metaphysics, gnosis, magic, politics. It must also reject historicizing
the moment into the merely past or technicizing it into a means to a
future end. But the meaning is not to be won through any type of
analytical, synthetic, or phenomenological investigation of and reflection upon the lived concrete, such as modern existentialist
philosophies are given to, but only in the unreduced immediacy of the
moment.

> Of course, he who aims at the experiencing of the experience will
> necessarily miss the meaning, for he destroys the spontaneity of the

mystery. Only he reaches the meaning who stands firm, without holding back or reservation, before the whole might of reality and answers it in a living way. He is ready to confirm with his life the meaning which he has attained.

In contrast to Alfred North Whitehead, who in *Religion in the Making* contrasted the "fear of God" of the "Old" Testament with the "love of God" of the New, Buber stressed that the *beginning* of wisdom is the fear of God. The person who tries to begin with the love of God "does not love the real God who is, to begin with, dreadful and incomprehensible" but loves an idol which is easily shattered by reality. The person of faith does not settle down in the gate of dread as a home, as some modern theologians suggest, but he goes through it and only then is he directed to the concrete contextual situations of existence. He does not accept the concrete situation as "God-given" in its pure factuality. Rather he may oppose it with all his force, but he will not remove himself from this situation as it actually is. "To him even the sublimest spirituality is an illusion if it is not bound to the situation."

Philosophy, in contrast, begins ever anew with a primary act of abstraction through which one looks away from the concrete situation. It sees the absolute in universals. Philosophy gives us the world as an objective and self-contained connection of all being, natural and spiritual, and it gives us a thought continuum which makes possible "objective" mutual understanding. Religious communication of a content of being in contrast, takes place only in paradox—not as a demonstrable assertion but as a pointing to what is experienced only in the hidden realm of existence of the hearing person. In religious reality the person is concentrated into a whole in which thought is included as an autonomous province. In genuine philosophers there is a totalization without a personal unification. Thinking overruns and overwhelms all the faculties. "In a great act of philosophizing even the finger-tips think—but they no longer feel." None of this is to question that philosophical truth means a cogitative real relation to being—valid documents of voyages of discovery in which genuine thought-relations to being, made possible through abstraction, are manifest as systems of thought.

For man the existent is either face-to-face being or passive object *(Gegenüber oder Gegenstand).* The child that silently speaks to his mother by merely looking into her eyes and the same child that looks at something on the mother as any other object shows these two basic modes of relating to existing being. A few months after Buber's granddaughter Barbara gave birth to Buber's first great-grandchild, Tamar, Buber remarked to me, "When I became a father, I was a mere boy. I saw nothing. When I became a grandfather, I saw a little something. Now that I am a great-grandfather I really see." What Buber saw as already present in embryo in the infant of six months he also traced in its full development to the heights of human existence. I-Thou finds its highest intensity and transfiguration in religious reality, in which unlimited Being becomes, as absolute person, my partner. I-It finds its highest concentration and illumination in philosophical knowledge in which the subject is extracted from the immediate lived togetherness of I and It and the It is detached into contemplated existing beings, or contemplated Being itself. "The religious reality of the meeting with the Meeter, who shines through all forms and is Himself formless, knows no image," yet God suffers that we look at him through all these necessarily untrue symbols until, as happens again and again, they swell up and obstruct the road to God by claiming to be reality themselves. Then comes round the hour of the philosopher, the *atheoi* like Socrates, who destroys the untrue images in his prayer to the again unknown God and by so doing arouses the religious person and impels him to set forth across the God-deprived reality to a new meeting with the nameless Meeter.

In the discussion that followed "Religion and Philosophy" at Columbia University, Buber said that he had been more often criticized for the I-Thou relationship with nature than for any other part of his philosophy. But when he looked at the great tree outside his window, he could not deny the reality of the meeting with it.

In an article in Ragaz's journal *Neue Wege* in 1953, Hugo Bergmann complained that "Religion and Philosophy" had sharpened the duality between I-Thou and I-It into an unbridgeable polarity that had torn asunder the prayer to God and the thinking about God and had depreciated all metaphysics and made vain every philosophical striving to attain to ultimate truth through thought. This meant, he claimed, an impossible spiritual schizophrenia that ignored the emphasis of St. Augustine, St. Anselm, and Maimonides on the cooperation of knowledge and faith, on believing in order to know. If in the face of the central role that science plays in today's intellectual world we do not want to arrive at a faithless philosophy, on the one side, and a faith inimical to knowledge, on the other, then religion and philosophy must work with each other.

Buber responded that in reality it is the factual thinking about God that subjects God to the laws of human logic which tears apart the factual prayer. ("Many people know how to pray to God who do not know how to speak about him," said Buber in *Eclipse of God,* "and many theologians who speak about God do not know how to pray to him.") Every genuine praying person knows that dreadful moment when God, who first inclined Himself to him and lifted him up, like the mother to the helpless child creeping on the ground, unexpectedly departs from Him. In such a moment the thought, "God is good. He will not abandon me in my need," comes unbidden to the mind. But one may not construct this into a theological proposition that God has such and such attributes. In the reality of faith one trusts in God only because "Thou art there."

From classic Greek philosophy we derive knowledge as a distancing "insight" into an objectively disposable subject. There is another knowing of a wholly different kind, which finds its classic expression in the holy scriptures of the people of Israel. This latter kind of knowing does not mean an *insight* but a *direct contact* for which mutuality is essential. As man and wife experience their intercourse as a "knowing," so God experiences his knowing of Israel (Amos 3:2, Hosea 6:6). Philosophy ever again identifies its objectifying perspectives of the Absolute with itself. What Buber questioned was not whether this identification of the Absolute with philosophy originates in experience, but whether it represents the right faithfulness in the face of the experience. What is essential when the philosopher speaks of God is that he be fundamentally aware that in so doing he has reached the limits of his method. "I do not, of course, prohibit him in his system from replacing the name of God by a concept. But he can only do that legitimately when he has placed himself before the face of the living God, has addressed him and opened himself to his claim. Then and then only will the Thou of meeting be tremblingly pointed to and witnessed, like the trembling needle of the magnet, in the 'He' or 'It' that he undertakes to determine."

In 1961, I sent Buber a copy of the baccalaureate address that I gave at the University of Vermont in which I pointed for the first time to that common attitude of Buber and Camus that in *Problematic Rebel* (1963) I was to identify as that of the "Modern Job"—the attitude in which dialogue and rebellion, trust and contending are inseparably coupled. "It need not matter whether this rebellion be expressed in terms of the 'atheism' of a Camus or the 'theism' of a Buber," I said in *Problematic Rebel.* But in my baccalaureate address I referred to Camus as an atheist without quotes. Buber replied, "I would not call Camus an atheist. He was one of the men who are destroying the old images. You know how I feel about them." The reference Buber was making was to the conclusion of "Religion and Philosophy." When symbols tend to become more than signs and pointers to God and claim to be reality itself, then the philosopher comes who rejects both the image and the God which it symbolizes. To it the philosopher opposes the pure idea, which he even at times understands as the negation of all metaphysical ideas. This prayer of the philosopher to the again unknown God Buber identified with true insight, as the attitude of Camus. In 1958 in a panel which we shared on Buber and Literature at a University of Michigan intercollegiate conference, the distinguished American literary critic R. W. B. Lewis told me that at the Salzburg Festival in Austria, Camus had said to him that he did not mind being called religious in Buber's sense of the term. As Lewis later expressed this in *The Picaresque Saint,* "Camus acknowledges a profound respect for Buber. . . . And Camus is even willing to say that, for himself, 'the sacred' is just that presence felt in the silence during a moment of genuine awareness. . . . Only in what Buber calls the condition of being aware is even a transitory moment of communion accomplished."

Buber once referred to Camus as "my friend" in talking with me, from which I assume that they had met on one of Buber's trips to France, perhaps when Buber was given an honorary doctorate at the Sorbonne. In 1952 Buber wrote to Camus that his book *The Rebel (L'Homme révolté)* appeared to him "to be of such importance for human life in this hour" that he would like to recommend it to Mosad Bialik, the national publishing house of Israel, for publication in Hebrew translation. Camus wrote Buber from Paris that he had read *I and Thou* with great admiration and profit and that he had not hoped or, better put, expected Buber to agree with his writings. "I am gladdened and honored." When Camus's book of essays *Resistance, Rebellion, and Death* was published in America, I. F. Stone, the editor of *Dissent,* wrote an article on it which he titled "Albert Camus: The Life of Dialogue," concluding with the statement, "Camus lived the only life worth living—the life of dialogue."

Douglas Steere, the well-known American Quaker philosopher, took Buber to visit Pendle Hill, the Quaker Center for Study at Wallingford, Pennsylvania, where I taught for many years, and he also took him to Haverford College for two days of lectures. In those days, late each Thursday morning, the whole college, faculty and students alike, crossed a little bridge and trooped up a block-long path to the Quaker Meeting House, where they sat together in silent worship. As

Douglas Steere walked with Buber to the meetinghouse, he explained to him the Quaker way of breaking the silence with a brief message if the Spirit moved one to do so. Steere explained that no message was expected from Buber, but that if something came to him that he wanted to share with the four hundred students and staff, he might simply rise and share it. Buber told Steere that he had been in some Quaker meetings in London and knew the procedure, but he also assured him that as a guest, he would never dream of breaking the silence. True to his own philosophy that one cannot know in advance that one will *not* speak, Buber did speak after all.

> The meeting convened and after ten minutes or so Gilbert White, the President of the College, rose and spoke of what a great thing it was that men could meet each other across barriers of race, of nationality, of economic status, of age and could reach out and touch each other. . . . He had barely sat down when Martin Buber rose in his place . . . and after leisurely taking in the whole group with his eyes, he began to speak. He told us that it was a great thing to transcend barriers and to meet another human being, but that *meeting* another across a barrier was not the greatest thing that one man could do for another. . . . The greatest thing . . . that any man could do for another is to *confirm* the deepest thing he has within him.

Douglas Steere was a friend of Alfons Paquet who had belonged to the intimate Frankfurt circle with which Buber met once a week. During Buber's talk with a sizable group of the Haverford faculty one afternoon, Steere sought to draw from Buber the secret of this Frankfurt group's intense and continuing aliveness.

> He thought for a time and then exploded with a single word, *Rücksichtslosigkeit*—that is, to follow the argument ruthlessly wherever it goes, with no holds barred, and with a determination to press through to the full truth involved. This all-out honesty with each other, he felt, kept the way open for experiences of new insight and truth to break through.

Knowing that Buber was leaving for Los Angeles to teach for some months at the seminary's University of Judaism, I felt under great pressure to complete, before he left, some of the new chapters that I was writing for my book on him. The previous summer I had spent in research on the books he had referred me to, and, particularly, on the German and Swiss Christian theologians. Trying to digest all this and work it into my chapters at great speed proved so frustrating that I finally did something I had never done before. I put all the notes away in a drawer and wrote, without referring to my notes, four chapters one after the other, relying solely on my memory and understanding. When I brought these four chapters to Buber, he asked me, "Do you always write like this? In a rapture?" Of these chapters he was particularly struck by the one on "Ethics" and thought that might be a way forward for me. "I am interested in what you will be doing in five years," he said.

For all his understanding and confirmation of me, I often sensed that I struck Buber as decidely different from the young persons he was used to. He was for me at that time, in fact, more the prophet of the It than the Thou. "If you do not bring your life into some sort of order, you will be a really unhappy man by the time you are fifty," he once said to me. With Eugenia, on the other hand, Buber felt "simpatico" from the start, perhaps because she had the sort of whole presence that one also sensed in Paula. "Eugenia has the kind of active intelligence that I like," Buber once said to me; whereas of a brilliant young man whom he and I knew he said to me, "He does not really have the sort of spontaneous intelligence that I like." When Buber agreed to come to our apartment for dinner on my thirtieth birthday, Eugenia was terribly anxious and went to great efforts to make a cake which Buber, who was used to eating his big meals at noon, did not even touch. I told Buber that I was very superstitious about turning thirty, and this seventy-three-year-old man, who was fives times as active as I, promised to help me through this crisis as best he could: "On his brithday a man is entitled to any wish," he said. I asked him again about the "turning" and other matters close to my heart, and he in the course of our conversation told me how he really heard the voice of Jesus and of Plato when he read authentic passages from them. After his visit Eugenia tried to communicate to her best friend, who lived in Ohio, something of what meeting Buber had meant to her:

> Martin Buber is greater than his books. And this, it seems to me, is a very telling statement in itself because his books are very great. Martin Buber is greater than his books because he *lives* what he has written, and the living embodiment of the word is a more marvelous achievement than the writing down of the word.
>
> I have seen him in many different situations and always I have received the same impression of him—*a real human* being interested in just this life we all live and in how to hallow just this very life. I have never understood what it means to be a real human being, but Martin Buber has now shown me. He is, second, a religious man, not a spiritual

man or a mystic. The difference is very important. . . . Finally, I would say about Martin Buber that he is a man to whom one could tell anything about one's life and feel positive that he would not be shocked and that he would not judge.

He is a short man, built stockily. He has a remarkably fine head, very imposing with his white beard that makes him look like a prophet. His brown eyes are the most outstanding physical feature he has. I shall never forget the look he gave me the first time I met him. I would not call his eyes penetrating, but rather *open*. Sometimes when he looks at you, you feel that you are looking right *into* the man and you feel a sudden great, comforting warmth. He confirms the other person. He smiles and laughs often; often when he smiles, his face has a charming, disarmed look. I have seen him several times with a stern look that passed quickly, and he is always serious. This last doesn't bother me at all; in fact, it's a relief to me.

I know that Martin Buber has suffered very much, but his suffering has knit him together into a whole human being. Often a suffering human being is like a sick or crippled human being. But not so with him. He turns to and responds to human encounter with his whole being in an absolute, consistent steadiness. I heard him say that the teacher's function is "to give the student trust, just to be there for him, like a mother is for the child." That is what Martin Buber does, he gives one trust.

That same week I worked with Buber at his hotel suite on the statement he was preparing for the Israeli press about his reasons for accepting the Goethe Prize. He was so terribly fatigued that he had to lie down on the couch in the room, and I felt keenly how here too in America he did not "withhold" himself. Even so, I brought up once again my concern about serving God with the "evil" urge. Buber looked at me and laughed and said, "You don't understand. I really *am* tired!"

Buber remarked to me that people in America were "very polite," by which he did *not* mean "in genuine dialogue." "There are some cities," Buber said to me, "that we call *'nachtschöne,'* beautiful at night. New York is one of them." On the way to Los Angeles, Martin and Paula stopped to see the Grand Canyon, and this made an enormous impression on them both. "Los Angeles is indeed 'as unusual' as New York," Buber wrote me from there, "but not by far as important. Since yesterday we are living on the roof of this hotel and on a night like this we are looking down on all the singularity of the town—utterly unable to see it as a single entity, it is an agglomeration of agglomerations. But of course seeing these mountains and this ocean together was a unique experience."

Once in Los Angles when Buber was traveling some distance in a taxi, the taxi driver suddenly turned toward him and said, "Mister, I've got something to ask you. The other day I read that you don't have to get mad at people right away. What do you think about that?" Buber agreed and asked him where he had read it. "In a magazine," the taxi driver replied. "Don't laugh, but the guy who said that is seven hundred years old." "You mean, he lived seven hundred years ago?" Buber asked. "Yeah, that's what I said. . . . Name of Francis." "Francis?" "Oh, yes, Francis of Assisi." "Oh, then you have read something good," said Buber and told the taxi driver about St. Francis of Assisi. After Buber had paid his fare and left, he missed his eyeglass case and decided that the handsome case must have fallen out of his pocket in the cab. Twenty minutes later when he came out of the building, he encountered the cab driver walking toward him, with the case in his hand. As Buber himself pointed out in telling the story, for such a driver time is money and gasoline is more money. Recognizing that, Buber said to him, "Thank you. That was good of you. You are a nice man." At this, this giant of a man put his arms around the diminutive Buber and declared, "Nobody has ever said that to me!"

In January, Buber wrote me from Los Angeles concerning my statement that the *coincidentia oppositorum*—the paradoxical unity of what are usually considered irreconcilable opposites—lies at the very heart of Buber's philosophy: "I had a deep attachment to this concept—and even the *complexio oppositorum,* as Cusanus aptly says, more concretely indeed—from my youth on." In response to a comment I made about Bach's Magnificat, which I sang with the Harvard Glee Club when I was a student at Harvard, Buber declared: "Bach's Magnificat—one of the very rare examples of the soul saying adequately what is incumbent on it to do: by doing it." Buber also informed me that he had met Robert Maynard Hutchins, who, from letters Hutchins had written him and still more from their personal conversation, showed he knew some of Buber's books quite well. Responding to a statement in one of my proposed chapters, Buber remarked, "I would not go so far as to say that true dialogue is rare in itself (although it is rare, of course, in its perfect form)"—an interesting counterpart to his insistence on the "eclipse of God."

About my own work on my book on him Buber wrote me: "Shortening the book will now be for you a great piece of work, a hard work of composition. Such a work demands from the spirit a particular kind of intensity and continuity. You must devote to it a certain number of hours (not less than two) daily, and never interrupt it, even if it should bore you sometimes." Buber also told me that he had received from an English writer, E. A. Gutkind, the manuscript of his book *Environment and Community.* "He quotes me in it as 'the most human of all modern philosophers.' If there must be a superlative, let it be this indeed!"

In March 1952, Buber wrote me concerning Harper & Brothers' request for more essays to fill out *Eclipse of God.* One essay on the imitation of God he did not think suitable in itself and also because "it is specifically Jewish, and 'Eclipse' is not and should not become such, being meant for every man who is seriously interested in its subject." He was also much concerned about the problem of a concluding chapter—what later became "God and the Spirit of Man." "I have felt many times the need for it," he admitted, "but have not been able to write what I want to be said. I shall try again and hope to succeed, but I cannot yet tell when." "To you personally," he added, "(and what I am saying to you is of course for Eugenia too) I may explain that this chapter is, as it was, inclined to take the shape of a prayer, and I do not want to end this 'philosophical' book by a prayer."

At the request of the Jewish Peace Fellowship to which I belonged, I asked Buber whether he would meet with its members when he returned to New York. Buber wrote me in March 1952 from Los Angeles, "I am no pacifist; for I do not know at all whether in a given situation in which fighting had become necessary, I would not fight. ["One must choose between 'ism' and situation," Buber once said to me, "including pacifism," and he also said, "I could not have been a conscientious objector, like you, in the face of Hitler."] Of course, I am with my whole heart for peace, but not for the usual peace which only continues and prepares for war in a veiled form." Buber said he had nothing at all against discussing this with a small group in unreserved openness and proposed the evening of April 12. We met, accordingly, with a few members and leaders of the Jewish Peace Fellowship. One member asked Buber why Israel did not unilaterally disarm. "Because the first day the Bedouins would look on in amazement," responded Buber, "and the second they would ride in."

Paula Buber impressed me as an amazingly strong person. Joachim Wach had described Martin and Paula, after he had seen them at a European conference on the history of religions, as being like Blake's etchings of Job and his wife, and this proved to be the case. When I attempted to speak to Paula in German (she knew no English), she suggested that we wait until I had learned German better or she had learned English! In 1958 we did converse in German. Miriam Beer-

Hoffman, the daughter of Buber's old friend Richard Beer-Hoffman, told me during the Bubers' first visit to America of how beautiful it was to her as a child to see Martin and Paula reading aloud to each other.

Before Buber left America in April 1952, the seminary had a great celebration in his honor. Reinhold Niebuhr was too ill to speak, but Paul Tillich came. Along with his own personal indebtedness to Buber, Tillich expressed the feeling that he was undoubtedly more Greek than Buber. At Brandeis University a remarkable dialogue between Buber and Tillich took place: it led Tillich, mistakenly, to conclude that Buber was angry at him, as he told me when I asked him to contribute to the "philosophical interrogations" of Buber that I was conducting.

On April 28, after the Bubers had gone, I wrote Buber: "It is hard to believe that you are really gone, that I can no longer enter the Hotel Marcy and find you there at the door of Room 701 where you will invite me in and speak with me. I shall always be deeply grateful that my personal 'direction' so coincided with yours that I was in New York during the year of your visit." "Eugenia and I were often unhappy," I added, "when we saw how hard you had to work and how tired you became. But you have given a great deal to many, many persons while you were here, not merely lectures but wholly personally. You have given of yourself unbelievably, and that will certainly bear fruit in the life and thought of the persons with whom you came in contact, as with Eugenia and me. I only have a bad conscience that I have so often made demands of you when you were tired and that in the anxious knowledge of how short a time you would be here lost the feeling for the present."

In the same letter I wrote Buber about his book *Images of Good and Evil,* which he had sent me in manuscript in his own handwriting in the German and which I had now read again in the English translation. I had eagerly awaited this book because it dealt with the very subject on which I had written my dissertation. ("That is your penalty for writing on a living man!" Joachim Wach said to me.) Eugenia found it Buber's most important book since *I and Thou,* and I was deeply impressed by its depth and simplicity and by the way in which it united the wisdom of the myths with the wisdom of personal experience. "I shall never cease to be astonished," I confessed to Buber, "at how each of your works expresses something really new and yet remains within the unity of your thought. But this work says something new that I could not even have foreseen when I treated your work from the standpoint of this problem."

I shall not attempt to reproduce here anything of my discussion of Buber's new view of evil in *The Life of Dialogue*, only to indicate wherein its newness lies. One new thing is his use of biblical and Zoroastrian myths, which embody what has taken place in countless factual encounters with evil directly without passing through any conceptual form, and the coupling of this primordial mythic intuition with directly experienced reality in such a way as to extend and deepen his philosophical anthropology. Another is the designation of two stages of evil—a first in which evil grows directly out of "decisionlessness," the failure to find the direction to God through responding with one's whole being to the concrete situation, and a second in which evil takes the form of a decision, but not with the whole being. The first stage looks back to Buber's teaching of "Direction" in the first dialogue of *Daniel* (1913). In the first stage, unable to bear the tension of possibility and to go through the difficult path of bringing itself toward unity, the soul clutches at any object past which the vortex happens to carry it and cast its passion upon it, grasping, seizing, devouring, compelling, seducing, exploiting, humiliating, torturing, and destroying. This vision of man as bowled over by possibility as by an infinitude is very similar to Kierkegaard's concept of the origin of sin and the Fall in *The Concept of Dread*. More important, it stands in a direct line with that threat of infinity that brought the fourteen-year-old Buber close to suicide, with the temptation of the creative man to lose himself in the infinity about which Buber wrote when he was twenty-five, with "The Day of Looking Back," in which he recalled at fifty how Paula Buber had set a limit to delusion and madness and helped him make a real decision as a young man, and with the "fiery stuff" of one's possibilities that circles around the person who must give direction to the "evil urge" (*I and Thou*).

In the second stage of evil, the repeated experiences of indecision merge into a fixation which produces a crisis of confirmation. That Yes which others spoke to him and which he could speak to himself "to liberate him from the dread of abandonment, which is a foretaste of death," is no longer spoken. In a pinch one can do without the confirmation of others but not of oneself. Those who do not then make the remarkable turning back to the good or become pathologically fragile in their relationship to themselves extinguish the image of what they are intended to be in favor of an absolute self-affirmation which says that what I say is true because *I* say it and what I do is good because *I* do it. It was undoubtedly Buber's experience with the Nazis and with the war in Palestine that led him to deepen his view of evil to include this second stage.

The great significance of this second stage of evil is its concrete base in human existence which makes understandable such extreme phenomena as Hitler and the Nazis without resorting to the dogma of original sin or agreeing with Sartre's assertion that the events of recent years make it necessary to recognize evil as absolute and unredeemable. Less than ten years later, during the trial of Adolf Eichmann, looking at the pictures and reading the description of Eichmann during his trial, I thought of what Buber had asserted in *Good and Evil* about the product of this crystallized inner division: "They are recognizable, those who dominate their own self-knowledge, by the spastic pressure of the lips, the spastic tension of the muscles of the hand and the spastic tread of the foot."

Writing his friend Kurt Singer in February 1953, Buber told of the more than seventy lectures he had delivered in America in universities and seminars from coast to coast and of the effect of these lectures, surprising even to himself, "most strongly on the young who were in many ways altogether different from what I had imagined them to be." The most important of these lectures were those that were later collected in *Eclipse of God,* and of these the most important were the two that made up "Religion and Modern Thinking." Although in *What Is Man?* Buber had developed his position through a systematic discussion and critique of other thinkers, only in "Religion and Modern Thinking" did Buber adopt an aggressively critical position because of the danger he sensed in contemporary strains of thought. In *I and Thou* Buber wrote, "Of course, God is the Wholly Other, the Mysterium Tremendum that appears and overthrows, but He is also the wholly same, nearer to me than myself." At that time Buber was trying to correct the overemphasis of Karl Barth and Rudolf Otto on the transcendence of God. In *Eclipse of God* his emphasis was the reverse, because meanwhile the situation had reversed: "Those who restrict God to the transcendence limit Him unduly," he wrote, "but those who make God wholly immanent mean something other than God." Since those who deny our relation with transcendence contribute to the human responsibility for the eclipse of God, Buber felt it necessary to attack the highly influential philosophies of Sartre, Heidegger, and Jung in "Religion and Modern Thinking."

In the lecture on Sartre and Heidegger, Buber quoted Sartre as saying that there is no universe other than that of human subjectivity and that man must recognize himself as the being through whose appearance the world exists. This "sounds like the thesis of a resurrected idealism," commented Buber. Sartre's statements about the silence of the transcendence combined with the perseverance of the religious need in modern man may have an entirely different meaning than Sartre imagines, Buber suggested. If God is silent toward man and man toward God, "then something has taken place, not in human subjectivity but in Being itself. It would be worthier not to explain it to oneself in sensational and incompetent sayings, such as that of the 'death' of God, but to endure it as it is and at the same time to move existentially toward a new happening, toward that event in which the word between heaven and earth will again be heard." Sartre's conclusion that it is up to us now to give life meaning and value "is almost exactly what Nietzsche said, and it has not become any truer since then," Buber ironically remarked:

> One can believe in and accept a meaning or value, one can set it as a guiding light over one's life if one has discovered it, not if one has invented it. It can be for me an illuminating meaning, a direction-giving value only if it has been revealed to me in my meeting with Being, not if I have freely chosen it for myself from among the existing possibilities and perhaps have in addition decided with some fellow-creatures: This shall be valid from now on.

In the original German manuscript of "Religion and Modern Thinking" that Buber sent me there was a footnote in which he linked Sartre's statement that "If God is dead all things are allowable" with the peripheral Islamic political-religious sect of the Assassins (from which we also get the word *hashish*, since they were "enjoyers of hashish"), the group that lived on a mountain and murdered passersby and whose secret was that they did not believe in God. Nietzsche took over their teaching from the noted orientalist Joseph von Hammer-Purgstall and Sartre from Nietzsche, Buber wrote me. Since the Assassins were clearly a type of antinomian Gnostic sect, this connection was particularly fascinating. Nonetheless, I wrote Buber saying that he could not connect Sartre with them, since Sartre explicitly quotes Dostoevsky to this effect in his essay "Existentialism Is A Humanism." But where Dostoevsky draws back from the consequences, Sartre accepts them without blinking an eye. Dostoevsky himself attributed a similar gnostic antinomianism to Ivan Karamazov, who held that if there were no God, values were not merely baseless but one was morally bound to do the exact opposite of what had formerly been the moral law. Buber wrote me from Los Angeles agreeing that Sartre undoubtedly did not know Hammer-Purgstall's book *The History of the Assassins* (1818), in which it is written: "That nothing is true and everything is permissible remained the ground of their secret teaching." "He might have heard of the Assassins from another source," Buber added, and he retained a reference to it in the German edition even though he had me eliminate it in the English. "When giving the lecture on the subject at Yale University," Buber added, "one of the professors afterward asked one of the students if he could not ask me for details about that Jewish sect. So the student asked me."

Although Buber criticized Heidegger along with Sartre in the first half of "Religion and Modern Thinking," he by no means lumped the two together. He was well aware that Heidegger is neither "atheist" nor "existentialist" in Sartre's definition of those terms. In his "Letter on Humanism" Heidegger characterizes Sartre's definition of existentialism as existence preceding essence as being merely a reversal of Plato's metaphysical statement which, "like metaphysics itself, remains oblivious of the truth of Being." He also rejects Sartre's use of "humanism" as an unacceptable subjectivity. In place of Sartre's statement that "we are on a plane where there is only man," he declares, "We are on a plane where there is principally Being." To Heidegger, man is the shepherd of Being who lives in proximity to Being. Man's thought cannot *create* the house of Being, but it can lead the humanness of man in history into the realm where what is whole and holy *(das Heile)* arises.

> In such proximity, if at all, it may be decided whether and in what manner God and the gods withhold themselves and night prevails; whether and in what manner the day of holiness dawns; whether and in what manner, in the dawn of holiness, a manifestation of God and the gods may renew itself. The holy, however, which is but the essential habitat of divinity and merely provides the dimensions for the gods and God, begins to shine only when, after much preparation, Being has cleared and illumined itself and has been experienced in Its truth.

Buber pointed out, however, that in Heidegger's view it is precisely in *human* thought about truth that Being becomes illuminated. The prophets of the Judeo-Christian tradition, in contrast, according to Heidegger, do not foretell the word of the Holy but announce "the God upon whom the certainty of salvation in a supernatural blessedness reckons." "I have never in our time encountered on a high philosophical plane such a far-reaching misunderstanding of the prophets of Israel," commented Buber. In fact, the prophets of Israel "have always aimed to shatter all security and to proclaim in the opened abyss of the final insecurity the unwished-for God who demands that His human creatures become real, they become human, and confounds all who imagine that they can take refuge in the certainty that the temple of God is in their midst." Buber also confessed "that for me a concept of being that means anything other than the inherent fact of all existing being, namely, that it exists, remains insurmountably empty." Contrasting Heidegger with Meister Eckhart who places God above Being, Buber remarked that if by the statement, "Being is the nearest thing," Heidegger means something other "than that I myself am, and not indeed as the subject of a *cogito,* but as my total person, then the concept of being loses for me the character of genuine conceivability that obviously it eminently possesses for Heidegger."

Buber's main thrust, however, was against Heidegger's theses concerning the "appearance" of the divine. Heidegger's view is incompatible with the real transcendence of the divine: Being or Beings have always stepped into relation with us *of their own will* and allowed us to enter into relation with them. "Being turned toward us, descended to us, showed itself to us, spoke to us in the immanence. . . . That has always distinguished religion from magic." God wills to need man as an independent partner in dialogue, as comrade in work. "God does not let Himself be conjured, but He also will not compel." Through man's giving or denying himself, "the whole man with the decision of his whole being" may have an immeasurable part in the actual revelation or hiddenness of the divine.

> But there is no place between heaven and earth for an influence of concept-clarifying thought. He whose appearance can be effected or co-effected through such a modern magical influence clearly has only the name in common with Him whom we men, basically in agreement despite all the differences in our religious teachings, address as God.

Sartre has brought Nietzsche's expression of the death of God to a *reductio ad absurdum,* Buber contended, through his postulate of the free invention of meaning and value, whereas Heidegger has created out of it a concept of a rebirth of God out of the thought of truth which falls into the enticing nets of historical time. "The path of this existentialism seems to vanish."

Heidegger never responded directly to Buber's critique. In one of his later writings, however, he dispatched the I-Thou relationship, in passing, on much the same grounds as he had dispatched Sartre: its supposed subjectivity in contrast with his own objective concern with the "unconcealment" of truth through the "disclosure" of Being:

> The much spoken-of I-Thou experience belongs to the metaphysical sphere of subjectivity. . . . The self-glorious I, to be sure, has a limit set in the Thou and its center of gravity is now placed in the relationship, the between, the *inter* of the *subjects*. But the sphere of subjectivity is not thereby left in principle but rather confirmed in principle. The being-in-itself of the subject is broken up in the "between," but this, as the now "real" subjectivity of the subject, directly confirms subjectivity as the realm of human existence.

That Buber himself was no stranger to that waiting for the appearance of the Coming One of which Heidegger spoke is shown by *Eclipse of God* and "The Dialogue Between Heaven and Earth" and by his private correspondence, in particular a remarkable letter that he wrote the Hungarian Ernst Szilagyi in July 1950 in response to his question, "How is a Jewish life still possible after Auschwitz?" But in no way did Buber content himself with the sphere of human subjectivity, as Heidegger implied in his critique of the I-Thou relationship. Buber took the reality of the transcendence seriously in a way that Heidegger himself clearly could not grasp. He insisted on the seriousness not only of the eclipse but also of the hiding of God, which will not cease even when, in whatever form, we know again "our cruel and kind Lord."

In the concluding essay on "God and the Spirit of Man" that Buber wrote for *Eclipse of God,* he pointed to two stages in philosophizing—one in which the human spirit fuses its conception of the Absolute with itself "until, finally, all that is over against us, everything that accosts us and takes possession of us, all partnership of existence, is dissolved in free-floating subjectivity," and one in which the human spirit annihilates conceptually the absoluteness of the Absolute and in so doing destroys its own absoluteness. Now the spirit can no longer exist as an independent essence but only as a product of human individuals "which they contain and secrete like mucus and urine."

Buber also pointed to two pseudoreligious counterparts of the reality of the relation of faith—controlling and unveiling, magic and gnosis. In magic, one celebrates rites without being turned to the Thou and without really meaning its Presence. Magic wishes to control the power that it conjures up. "Instead of understanding events as calls which make demands on me, one wishes oneself to demand without having to hearken." In gnosis the power of the intellect is used to unveil and display the "divine mysteries," the holy It. In many theologies, as well as theosophies, "unveiling gestures are to be discovered behind the interpreting ones."

Genuine prayer, in contrast, asks that the divine Presence become dialogically perceivable. The simplest presupposition for such prayer—"the readiness of the whole man for this Presence, simple turned-towardness, unreserved spontaneity"—is destroyed today by overconsciousness that I am *praying,* that *I* am praying. He who is not present perceives no Presence, and modern man cannot be spontaneously present so long as he holds back a part of his I which does not enter into the action of prayer with the rest of his person, an I to which the prayer is an object—"the subjective knowledge of the person turning-toward God *about* his turning-toward."

What is in question with both modern philosophy and modern religion is not the choice between I-Thou and I-It but whether the I-Thou remains the architect and the I-It the assistant, the helper. If the I-Thou does *not* command, then it is already disappearing. Yet precisely this disappearance of "I-Thou" is the character of this hour:

> In our age the I-It relation, gigantically swollen, has usurped, practically uncontested, the mastery and the rule. The I of this relation, an I that possesses all, makes all, succeeds with all, this I that is *unable* to say Thou, unable to meet being essentially, is the lord of the hour. This selfhood that has become omnipotent, with all the It that surrounds it, can naturally acknowledge neither God nor any genuine Absolute which manifests itself to man as of non-human origin. It steps in between and shuts us off from the light of heaven.

In his essay on "Buber and the Philosophies of Existence" in *The Philosophy of Martin Buber,* the distinguished French philosopher Jean Wahl misunderstood Buber's metaphor of the "eclipse of God" as introducing an "almost gnostic" conception of a strange and hindering element. What Buber was saying was not that God is *hidden*—the *Deus absconditus* of the Gnostics—but that God *is hiding.* "The eclipse of the light of God is no extinction," Buber concluded in "God and the Spirit of Man"; "even to-morrow that which has stepped in between may give way." If the I-Thou relationship has gone into the catacombs today, "who can say with how much greater power it will re-emerge." As Buber had said of the work of the suffering servant hidden in the depths of history, so here he asserted that the most important events in history are the beginnings of new epochs, determined by forces previously invisible or disregarded. "Each age is, of course, a continuation of the preceding one, but a continuation can be confirmation and it can be refutation."

In May, Buber wrote me from Zurich and told me that he had written the German original of "God and the Spirit of Man" on the long boat trip which he desperately needed to recover from the overexertions of his half year in America. Buber finished the final page of "God and the Spirit of Man" the last day on the boat. "Physically, I did not feel well," Buber added, "(nor did my wife—the 'airconditioned' cabin, devoid of windows, was terribly lacking in air and light), but the spirit was with me, faithfully."

Buber's last statement on the "eclipse of God" was his reply to Emil Fackenheim's assertion in *The Philosophy of Martin Buber* that the silence, or eclipse of God, is a "most troubling question":

> One may also call what is meant here a silence of God's or rather, since I cannot conceive of any interruption of the divine revelation, a condition that works on us as if it were a silence of God. . . . These last years in a great searching and questioning, seized ever anew by the shudder of the now, I have arrived no further than that I now distinguish a revelation through the hiding of the face, a speaking through the silence. The eclipse of God can be seen with one's eyes, it will be seen.
>
> He, however, who today knows nothing other to say than, "See there, it grows lighter!" he leads astray.

CHAPTER 7

Devotio *versus* Gnosis: *Buber* versus *Jung*

IN 1934, Buber took part in the Jungian Eranos Conference at Ascona, Switzerland, and he would have done so again in 1935 had it not been for the Nazi restrictions on his lecturing. In addition he had for many years had close relations with many Jungian analysts, the chief of which was Hans Trüb. Yet in 1951, Buber devoted the second half of his sharply critical essay "Religion and Modern Thinking" to Jung, and when he was lecturing on Heidegger and Sartre at City College in New York City, he remarked to me that he held Jung to be even more dangerous than Heidegger. What is in question, simply, is that Jung's gnostic transformation of faith seemed to Buber to contribute far more in actuality to the human responsibility for the "eclipse of God" than Heidegger's thought-magic. That part of Heidegger's thought which deals with the coming appearance of the divine has been less influential, in fact, than that part of Jung's thinking which transmutes faith into *gnosis;* for the latter is central to Jung's highly popular philosophy of individuation. This same issue of *gnosis*—knowing *about* faith—versus *devotion*—*actually living faith* in the dialogue of address-ing and being addressed—lies at the heart of the other famous con-troversy which has lasted beyond the 1950s and beyond Buber's death—that with Gershom Scholem over the interpretation of Hasid-ism, though in this case the controversy was initiated by Scholem and not by Buber.

When the controversy between Buber and Jung came into the open in 1951, many people in Europe, America, and Israel were shocked. The traditional enemy of religion was Freud, while Jung was hailed as its great friend. Many of Jung's followers were close to Buber and vice versa, and not a few considered themselves disciples of both men who, ostensibly, shared a common concern with "modern man in search of a soul." What is more, Jung's "collective unconscious," or "objective psyche," has an unmistakable transpersonal, objective, and numinous, or awe-inspiring, nature that led Jung to identify it with Rudolf Otto's *Mysterium Tremendum.* In "Religion and Modern Thinking" Buber himself called Jung "the leading psychologist of our day" and pointed out that he had made religion, in its historical and biographical forms, the subject of comprehensive observations.

What Buber criticized Jung for is that, for all his disclaimers, "he oversteps with sovereign license the boundaries of psychology" by defining religion as "a living relation to psychical events which. . . . take place . . . in the darkness of the psychical hinterland" and con-ceives of God in general as an "autonomous psychic content." That these are not merely psychological statements, as Jung would claim, but metaphysical ones, Buber showed by quoting Jung's statements that otherwise "God is indeed not real, for then He nowhere impinges upon our lives" and that God is "for our psychology . . . a function of the unconscious" as opposed to the "orthodox conception" according to which God "exists for Himself," which means psychologically "that one is unaware of the fact that the action arises from one's own inner self." Psychology becomes to Jung the only admissible metaphysic while remaining, for Jung, an empirical science. "But it cannot be both at once," commented Buber.

Buber also criticized Jung's understanding of the soul through which alone the collective unconscious, the sphere of the archetypes, can enter into experience. "The real soul has without question pro-ducing powers in which primal energies of the human race have individually concentrated," commented Buber, who was certainly no stranger to these matters in his early concern with myth and with

Jewish peoplehood. But it can never legitimately make an assertion out of its own creative power but only out of a binding real relationship to a truth which it articulates. Modern consciousness, with which Jung clearly identifies himself, "abhors faith and . . . the religions that are founded on it" and turns instead with its "most intimate and intense expectations" to the soul as the only sphere which can be expected by man to harbor the divine. The new psychology thus "proclaims the new religion, the only one which can still be true, the religion of pure psychic immanence." What is more, it turns to the soul, in Jung's own words, "in the Gnostic sense" as the new court which replaces conscience by the unity of good and evil. This union of opposites is, Buber pointed out, the mature expression of a tendency characteristic of Jung from the beginning of his intellectual life: "In a very early writing, which was printed but was not sold to the public, it appears in direct religious language as the profession of an eminent Gnostic god [Abraxas], in whom good and evil are bound together and, so to speak, balance each other." In modern mandala dreams "the place of the deity," Jung explains, "appears to be taken by the wholeness of man," which Jung calls the Self. Although Jung avoids the suggestion of the deification of man in some places, in others the Self, the marriage of good and evil, is elevated by Jung to the highest possible place as the new "Incarnation" whose prospective appearance Jung repeatedly intimates. "If we should like to know," says Jung, "what happens in the case in which the idea of God is no longer projected as an autonomous essence, then this is the answer of the unconscious soul: the unconscious creates the idea of a deified or divine man." "This figure," commented Buber, "is the final form of that Gnostic god, descended to earth as the realization of the 'identity of God and man,' which Jung once professed."

What concerned Buber was not questions of creed or belief or metaphysics but what happened to the relationship of faith itself in actual human existence. "Whatever may be the case concerning God," Buber paraphrased Jung, "the important thing for the 'man of modern consciousness' is to stand in no further relation of faith to God." When one knows oneself called to a work which one has when one has not done or fulfilled a task which one knows to be one's own, one knows what it means to say that one's conscience smites one: for conscience is the voice which compares what one is with what one is called to become. This court of conscience is dispensed with by Jung in favor of the soul which is integrated in the Self as the unification, in an all-encompassing wholeness, of good and evil. Jung sees the Self as including the world, to be sure, but "the others," declared Buber, "are included only as contents of the individual soul that shall, just as an individual soul, attain its perfection through individuation." All beings who are "included" in this way in my self are, in fact, only possessed as an It. "Only then when, having become aware of the unincludable otherness of a being, I renounce all claim to incorporating it in any way within me or making it a part of my soul, does it truly become Thou for me. This holds good for God as for man." Buber characterized the way which he advanced in opposition to Jung's as one that "leads from the soul which places reality in itself to the soul which enters reality."

The German original of "Religion and Modern Thinking" was published in February 1952 in *Merkur.* In the May issue Jung wrote a reply to Buber and to a separate critical essay by the well-known German writer Count Herman von Keyserling. What was most immediately evident in this reply was Jung's annoyance at both Buber and Keyserling for what seemed to him to be their total misunderstanding of his thought and what he was trying to do, a tone which bears out the biblical scholar Benjamin Uffenheimer's statement that Buber was ready to enter into dialogue with Jung but Jung did not want a dialogue with Buber. Jung's references to this controversy between him and Buber in the letters are all in the same tone. "Buber does not understand psychic reality," Jung wrote in one letter and in another, Buber "thinks he can talk of God without saying which, and without proving that this is the only right one. These absurdities have to be cleared up for once." In a letter to Mitchell Bedford, the young man who tried in vain to get Buber to psychoanalyze himself for him for his doctoral dissertation, Jung disclaimed any "slightest personal friction" between him and Buber and said he had no personal opinion of him, having met him only a few times.

In a letter of 1954 to the distinguished Jungian thinker Erich Neumann, Jung not only criticized Buber's "underhand way of doing holy business" but also declared: "It is evident that Buber has a bad conscience, as he publishes only *his* letters and does not represent me fairly, since I am a mere Gnostic, though he hasn't the faintest idea of what the Gnostic was moved by." As a matter of fact, I suggested to Buber that he publish Jung's reply in *Eclipse of God,* but Buber said he had no right to do so. We did, however, give the reader the German and English references for finding Jung's reply (something Gershom Scholem has never done for Buber in the many places he has published his critique of Buber's interpretation of Hasidism).

Jung's fullest discussions of the controversy between Buber and him are to be found in a series of letters he wrote to Bernhard Lang (who later wrote a book on Buber) in June 1957 and in a letter of June 1960 to Robert C. Smith, who wrote his doctoral dissertation on Buber and Jung. To Lang, Jung elaborated at length his distinction between metaphysical and psychological statements, dismissing Buber as someone without "the ghost of an idea" of Kant's epistemological barrier, as "a theologian who naively thinks that what he believes must necessarily be so," and as someone who "blandly assumes that everyone thinks the same as he does when he says 'God.'" He also asserted that Buber completely misunderstood the bits of Jung's writings that he knew "because he has no conception of psychology," that "Buber completely overlooks the existence of the individual psyche," and that Buber "thinks he can override all other ideas of God by assuming that his God-image is *the* God-image." Jung did not deny that our psychic structure projects an image of *something*—"a substrate, an *ousia* about which it is impossible in principle to make any assertion because it would only be yet another conception." He ended, curiously enough, by abscribing to Buber that very conception of faith as *knowledge* that Buber rejected in his contrast between *emunah* and *pistis* in *Two Types of Faith*. Dismissing everything that men assert about God as "twaddle," Jung confessed that he could not "interpret the inner experience in its metaphysical reality, since its essential core is of a transcendental nature and beyond my human grasp." The actual experiences contain a real mystery which cannot be fathomed by man, but the statements about them are merely subjective declarations of faith which contain no mystery and are properly objects of psychological research. Jung's 1960 letter to Smith was in much the same vein, asserting that, like all pioneers, he was necessarily a "monologist" about matters such as the autonomy of the God complex, which Buber, lacking any practical experience in depth psychology, could not possibly understand.

"Jung has sent *Merkur* an answer and *Merkur* asks me for an answer to it," Buber remarked at this time. "I will write a very short one—it is a hopeless matter: two different spheres, I seeing his and he not seeing mine." The strangest thing about Jung's reply was that he ascribed Buber's criticism of him to Buber's "orthodoxy," a statement the irony of which no one could be unaware who knew what Buber had had to live through for fifty years, and particularly in Palestine and Israel, from the constant attacks of the Orthodox Jews on his conceptions of Judaism and Hasidism.

In his reply to Jung, which was published in the same issue of

Merkur and as a supplement to *Eclipse of God,* Buber remarked that as a rule he did not bring his own beliefs into the discussion but held them in check for the sake of human conversation.

> But it must be mentioned here for the sake of full clarity that my own belief in revelation, which is not mixed up with any "orthodoxy," does not mean that I believe that finished statements about God were handed down from heaven to earth. Rather it means that the human substance is melted by the spiritual fire which visits it, and there now breaks forth from it a word, a statement, which is human in its meaning and form, human conception and human speech, and yet witnesses to Him who stimulated it and to His will. We are revealed to ourselves—and cannot express it otherwise than as something revealed.

Jung, who always indignantly rejected any charges of psychologism and clearly saw himself as a fully empirical psychologist, replied to Buber that he was doing no more than saying that all *statements* about God are necessarily psychic statements and hence subject to the realm of psychology. Buber replied that either this is tautology—since all human statements include the psyche—or it is an unwarranted statement that no nonpsychic reality corresponds to this psychic statement. No science qua science has a right to make any judgment concerning the truth of the belief in God, Buber averred. Jung pointed out to Buber that men do in fact have many and different images of God, which they themselves make. Buber responded, with gentle irony, that he was already aware of this and had many times stated and explained it. "But that which is essential is still the fact that they are just images, painted in the intention of faith directed towards the Imageless whom the image 'portrays,' that is, means."

Why Buber saw Jung's modern Gnosticism as more dangerous than Heidegger's modern magic is made unmistakably clear in Buber's final paragraph of his reply to Jung:

> The psychological doctrine which deals with mysteries without knowing the attitude of faith towards mystery is the modern manifestation of Gnosis. Gnosis is not to be understood as only a historical category, but as a universal one. It—and not atheism, which annihilates God because it must reject the hitherto existing images of God—*is the real antagonist of the reality of faith.* Its modern manifestation concerns me specifically not only because of its massive pretensions, but also in particular because of its resumption of the Carpocratian motif. This motif, which it teaches as psychotherapy, is that of mystically deifying the instincts instead of hallowing them in faith. [italics added]

Jung declared his little "Abraxas" opus to be a poem, but Buber countered by saying that every unprejudiced reader will take it to be a confession of the ambivalent Gnostic "God" who balances good and evil in Himself by taking part in evil intelligently. Here again stands the opposition of Moses, who proclaimed the task of hallowing everything, and Korah, who proclaimed everything to be already holy! In several essays Buber made exactly this contrast between Hasidism and the antinomian gnosticism of the radical Sabbatians and the followers of Jacob Frank, two pseudo-messianic movements that directly preceded Hasidism.

The issue Buber put before Jung, at its simplest, was this: Either truth is reduced to the psychic and becomes mere tautology or the psychic is elevated to Truth and becomes a false hypostasizing. For Jung is not a Gnostic, who traditionally believed in a totally transcendent God, but a *modern* Gnostic, whose touchstone of reality is the collective psyche, or Self. For all the numinous, guiding quality of Jung's collective unconscious, it is still an It and not a Thou. It can neither be addressed as Thou nor can one live in real dialogue and contending with it, as could man with the transcendent yet present God of the Hebrew Bible. It certainly has a quality of over-againstness; it can never be identified with the conscious person or even with the personal unconscious. But there is no mutuality, no give and take, no sense that Jung's God needs man for the very purpose for which he created him. Indeed, Jung's God is not the Creator but a demiurge finding his place within a larger order as Zeus did within the Greek cosmos; for Jung's ultimate touchstone of reality is not the autonomous content of the unconscious psyche that he calls Self but the unconscious psyche itself. The placing of the divine in the unconscious, however archetypally and universally conceived, still psychologizes God *and* reality, robbing our meeting with "the things of this world" of any revelatory power other than the mimetic reflection of our forgotten and buried inner truths. If Jung had not asserted the psyche as *the* exclusive touchstone of reality, he could have bestowed great honor upon a realm which undoubtedly has profound meaning, whether that of the shadow, the anima, the animus, the Great Mother, or any of the other life-symbols that slumber in our depths, without hypostasizing that realm into an inverted Platonic universal and elevating this larger-than-life-size sphere to the now empty throne of the Absolute.

In June 1952, Buber brought to my attention the June issue of the

Neue Schweizer Rundschau with the "beautiful article by Kerényi, 'Martin Buber as a Classical Author.'" "It is interesting also as a fine sign of moral independence, Kerényi being one of the teachers in Jung's institute and Jung being the autocrat he is," Buber added. This last remark was not a reference to Jung's thought but to his personality as Buber knew it from the many disciples of Jung with whom he associated in the 1920s and 1930s. It is interesting in this connection to reflect how Hans Trüb's moving toward Buber and away from Jung must have affected Jung, since Trüb had been so close to Jung that Jung had asked Trüb to be the therapist for his own wife, Emma.

In answer to a question of mine about the German existentialist philosopher Karl Jaspers, Buber wrote me in July 1952, "Jaspers is an important thinker, but when reading his book on the 'philosophical faith' [*The Perennial Scope of Philosophy*] I did not feel as I do when reading a religious book, as I feel when reading even the most philosophical of Kierkegaard's. I have Jaspers (and Marcel) in mind in the second sentence of 'Religion and Modern Thinking.'" In this sentence Buber made clear that he did not mean by the relation of modern thought to religion "the attempts to think from the standpoint of the reality of faith, or to create an understanding between it and philosophy based on mutual tolerance." On the other hand, Buber saw his difference from Jung as a philosophical as well as a religious one. Jaspers and Marcel are both "existentialists of dialogue" and, like Buber, they understand thoroughly the epistemological implications of "communication," or the I-Thou philosophy as an alternative to the traditional subject-object approaches. Jung, in contrast, carries forward a specifically modern, post-Kantian idealism in which reality and thought, or in this case a highly dynamic, superpersonal consciousness, are identical. But by "reality" Jung does not mean the external object. Jung's whole epistemology is based on the contrast between inner and outer with a distinct depreciation of the outer as the "persona"—the social role, the ego which must submit to the unconscious, or pay the price of becoming neurotic, or the external world which finds its true meaning only in the depths within. In 1960, Robert Smith, a young American scholar writing a doctoral dissertation on Buber and Jung, shared with Buber his own correspondence with Jung on the issues that he saw in the Buber-Jung controversy. Responding to this correspondence, Buber wrote Smith: As to Jung, "he obviously has not read me at all and so he does not even imagine the existence of another epistemology than the one focused on the subject-object relation."

In September 1954, Rudolf Pannwitz's essay on Buber's Hasidism was published in *Merkur*, and, in October, "Christ, Hasidism, Gnosis," which Buber himself described to be as "a short but poignant reply." To understand the last section of this reply that dealt with Hasidism itself and its connection with Buber's earlier controversy with Jung and his later controversy with Scholem, we must look back at some of Buber's essays on Hasidism originally written in Hebrew in Jerusalem from 1940 to 1943 and published in German as "The Hasidic Message" in 1952 and in English as *The Origin and Meaning of Hasidism* in 1958. In these essays Buber occupied himself with the researches Scholem had made into the pseudo-messianic movement of Sabbatai Zvi and his own research into the pseudo-messianism of Jacob Frank. In each case Buber saw Hasidism as the antidote to this messianic poison precisely because of its message of "hallowing the everyday"— working for a redemption that could not come at all at any fixed hour but only through persevering in an unsentimental life with the concrete reality of everyday. In so doing Buber increasingly sharpened the contrast between Hasidism and the Kabbalistic mysticism on which it was based and laid the groundwork for the ideal types of *gnosis* and *devotio* that he employed in his reply to Pannwitz.

In these essays Hasidism still remains a mysticism, to be sure, but it is a mysticism with a difference. Not only is there no *unio mystica,* but the central significance of ecstasy, which stood as the foundation of "The Life of the Hasidim" in *The Legend of the Baal-Shem,* is now ignored in favor of the hallowing of the everyday. In "God and the Soul" Buber contrasted the mysticism of the great Hindu philosopher Sankara and of Meister Eckhart with that of Hasidism. In Hasidism it is not "God" but the "Godhead," the perfect unity before and after creation, who is the commanding God who sets man in the world in order to love Him and be loved by Him. "Everything follows from this; for man cannot love God in truth without loving the world in which He has set his strength and over which His Shekinah hovers. People who love each other in holy love help each other approach the love with which God loves His world." From this Buber concluded that "in Hasidism—and in it alone, so far as I can see, in the history of the human spirit—mysticism has become *ethos.*" In "The Place of Hasidism in the History of Religion," similarly, Buber suggested that Hasidism is the one mysticism in which history remains important (because revelation takes place in unique moments of time and thus entails history), the one mysticism where the seemingly incompatible spheres of revelation and illumination do meet.

Buber's major comparison and contrast in this essay was between Hasidism and Zen Buddhism. Both are what I have called "mysticisms of the particular." Both stress whatever one happens to be doing at the moment. In Hasidism and Zen, moreover, the teacher is the person who, through immediate contact with the disciple, transmits the message intact. This teaching is usually not some objective knowledge but a personal and unique communication. Truth in both, Buber said, is not found in the content of a teaching, but in human existence itself. And the relation between teacher and disciple is central. "I know of no two religions comparable to Hasidism and Zen in which the transmission from generation to generation is so important," Buber claimed.

But Buber also *contrasted* Hasidism and Zen, suggesting that in Zen the concern for the particular is essentially a way of getting away from intellectualism to understanding the Buddha nature in oneself. Hasidism, in contrast, is concerned with the created task of redemption of those people, animals, and things with which one has to do. Hasidism is concerned with the redemption that takes place *between* us and the things of this world. Hasidism says that God is in our prayers, that God is prayer. But it does not see God as the substance of the soul. Even the most personal mysticism rests in the shadow of the historical revelation. Zen divorces the knowledge of the transcendent from discursive thought. The things themselves do not matter to Zen in their concrete particularity. But their nonconceptual nature is a symbol of the Absolute which is superior to all concepts. In Hasidism, the things themselves *do* matter; for it is a mysticism in which time is hallowed. One of the attacks that Scholem later made on Buber's interpretation of Hasidism was precisely on this point. He claimed that the Hasidim were interested in the particular only to nullify it, that they were really Gnostics and Neo-Platonists concerned with the Transcendent. Buber's response to this, which Scholem did not reply to, was that there were two streams within Hasidism—one, that of the founder, the Baal-Shem Tov, in which the hallowing of the everyday for its own sake is emphasized; the other, that of his great disciple the Maggid of Mezritch, in which the particular is mainly of importance as a stage of a dialectical process in which it is finally nullified in order to reach the Transcendent.

It is in "The Beginnings" and "The Foundation Stone," however, that the issue between the *gnosis* of the Kabbala and the *devotio* of Hasidism is fully joined. In "The Beginnings" Buber asserted that what constitutes the uniqueness and greatness of Hasidism is not a teaching but a mode of life by which a community is shaped. Hasidic life is not the realization of the teaching; for the Baal-Shem's effects on others arose from the fact that he *lived* in such a way that his life worked as a teaching not yet grasped in words. It is not the objective content of what he said that is important but that it pointed to a way of life. As a result, the whole personal attitude of faith that constitutes the essence of Hasidic life works to form community, and there arise as the Baal-Shem's successors a series of men with the same kind of life who have received their inspiration and molding from him. "The 'zaddikim' of these five generations form together a group of religious personalities of a vitality, a spiritual power, and a manifold orignality such as, to my knowledge, have nowhere in the history of religions been concentrated in so short a span." Because Hasidism is in the first instance not a category of teaching, but one of life, our chief source of knowledge of Hasidism, Buber claimed, is its legends and only afterward its theoretical literature. What was handed down was events from individual life transported into the atmosphere of communal living.

To bring out the significance of Hasidism, Buber contrasted it with the pseudo-messianism of Jacob Frank. As already noted, Buber compared Frank to Hitler as a person whose magic power over others grew from his complete lack of self-restraint. All Frank's late-gnostic fantasy was only window dressing, concealing the fact that he was committed to nothing except himself, and he managed this egoism without having any sort of foothold in reality. The delusion that produced this absence of restraint was due to his need to compel others to nourish himself; for the nihilistic belief in himself was threatened by the crisis of self-awareness. The demonic community that surrounded him and that announced the decay of the community of Israel, "at once unfettered yet wholly bound to a leader who leads them into nothing, affords an unsurpassable spectacle of disintegration." Frank wanted to make the alien fire of "sin" so much his own that he could offer it and the "strange actions" that proceed from it to God. He wanted to penetrate into the very depths of the Kingdom of Sin in order to overpower it, to fill the impurity with the strength of holiness until it burst from within.

Buber understood what was at issue in Frank's revolt in thoroughly modern terms. The Frankist doctrine of "strange actions" and the Hasidic doctrine of "alien thoughts" proceed from the same common presuppositions: "the abyss has opened, it is not for any man to live any longer as though evil did not exist. One cannot serve God merely by avoiding evil; one must engage with it." In "The Foundation Stone," Buber claimed that the Sabbatian-Frankist revolt did not bring Judaism to the rim of the abyss, as is usually said, "but caused it already to lift one foot into the yawning gorge." The seeds of disintegration have penetrated into the furthest reaches of the people so that even those who fiercely fought the evil had to withstand its assault in the dark depths of their own soul, in the turmoil of dreams. Buber described this poison as "the lust for overrunning reality."

> Instead of making reality the starting point of life, reality that is full of cruel contradictions but for that very reason calling forth true greatness, namely the quiet work of overcoming the contradictions, one surrenders to illusion, intoxicates oneself in it, subjugates life to it. To the degree that one does this, the core of his existence becomes at once completely agitated and crippled in his power to give direction to its impulses.

When an illusory world is set in place of the actual, "superstition reigns, fraught with deadly peril." The Sabbatian notion that one could redeem evil by doing it without intending it as evil Buber branded as "an illusion, for all that man does reacts on his soul, even when he imagines that his soul floats above the deed." "These are the days in which one still fulfills the commandments, but with a soul that looks away from its own acts, the days of self-temptation in which one imagines behind the demonic mask the countenance of divine freedom waiting to be discovered. One does not let oneself be deluded by the temptations, but one also does not drive them out." As a result, "the realms are overturned, everything encroaches on everything else, and possibility is more powerful than reality."

The Hasidic teaching that Buber opposed to this "lust for overrunning reality" was not new, but it took on a different deepened, fully modern significance. The Baal-Shem must heal not only the people but the broken relation between heaven and earth. His concern is not with final redemption and hastening the end but with that renewal which will make possible the beginning of a real life for the real God in the real world. In contrast to the unconditional devotion of the Frankists to Frank, the Baal-Shem and the *zaddikim* who followed him took responsibility for the souls entrusted to them and yet did not allow the sparks of responsibility to be extinguished in those souls. "These men mediated between God and man, but they pointed men with great seriousness to that immediate relationship to God that no mediation can replace." The Hasidic hallowing of the world is not "an isolated Messianic action, but a deed of the everyday that prepares the Messianic completion."

> The great *kavana* is not joined to any particular selection of the pre-scribed: everything that is done with kavana can be the right, the re-deeming act. Each action can be the one on which all depends; what is decisive is only the strength and concentration of hallowing with which I do it.

In the realm of "alien thoughts" the object of desire must become transparent to set the glance free to turn to God. But in the realm of the natural existence of man—his life with nature, his work, his friendship, his marriage, his understanding with the community, one need not renounce or turn away but hallow all that one does, ex-changing a casual for a genuine relation to them. This is, as Buber said in "The Foundation Stone," a mysticism that makes use of Kab-balistic speculations "only in order to bind them ever again to human existence and the personal task of man."

Speaking of the Baal-Shem, Buber said, "the reality of a man who has lived in intercourse with the reality of a being in its fullness awakens the reality in us and helps us to live in intercourse with the reality of being in its fullness." "We must transform the element that wants to take possession of us into the substance of true life." Buber distinguished this Hasidic teaching from the psychoanalytic theory of "sublimating the libido," pointing out that the latter is limited to psy-chic events alone whereas the former means real contact with other beings. Buber translated the language of the "evil urge" into modern language of fantasy and imagination, but imagination here is "no free play of the soul but a real meeting with real elements of being who are outside of us." "What we suppose we effect merely in our souls, in reality we effect on the destiny of the world."

All temptations come from God, but they are real temptations, Buber wrote, the only difference being that in the age of the Baal-Shem evil and good are no longer sundered like two distinct qualities but resemble, rather, that which is unformed and that which is formed. This is exactly the language of Buber's anthropological treat-ment in *Good and Evil*. In the hands of the Baal-Shem the Lurian Kabbala's teaching of the sparks became an ethical teaching that em-braces the whole of human life. Unlike all ascetic teaching, this does not mean surmounting reality and withdrawing from the world but bringing this very world into dialogue with God. "Only on the path of true intercourse with the things and beings does man attain to true life, but only on this path can he take an active part in the redemption of the world." Nothing is so alien to the holy that it cannot become its vessel. Here, sin, as in Buber's anthropology, is just what by its nature one cannot do with one's *whole* being. In the Sabbatian-Frankist revolt, sin was pronounced holy. In Hasidism what is called for is to hallow the intercourse with all things and beings in the life of the everyday. "Hasidism affirmed the natural reality of the still unmessianic hour as the material to be hallowed."

We are now ready to understand the Hasidic part of Buber's reply to Pannwitz and something of Buber's controversy with Scholem. Pannwitz, like Scholem, tended to see Hasidism as an applied *gnosis* that entered into the life of the people, just as the Kabbala is the great Jewish elaboration of *gnosis*. Buber, in contrast, held that the Kabbala could become ethos, as he wrote in *The Tales of Rabbi Nachman* (1907), only through a true religious revolution that was the work of *devotio*. While Hasidism, like Sabbatianism, based itself on the Kabbala, it took over from the Kabbala only what it needed "for the theological foundation of an enthusiastic but not overexalted life in responsibility" for the piece of world entrusted to one. From being unbinding spirituality, gnostic teachings become an integral part of authentic life. "In the place of esoterically regulated meditations has stepped the task of endowing each action with strength of intention, not according to any prescriptions but in response to the moment." The holy no longer appears in the seclusion of ascetics but in the joy of the Hasidic leaders and their communities, and—what was unthinkable in the circles of the old Kabbala—the "simple man," the man of the original *devotio*, who possesses neither rabbinic nor Kabbalistic learning, is held in honor because he serves God with his whole being. "Where the mystic vortex circled, now stretches the way of man." "In Hasidism *devotio* has absorbed and overcome *gnosis*," Buber concluded. "This must happen ever again if the bridge over the chasm of being is not to fall in."

Buber's last significant statements concerning *devotio* versus *gnosis* appeared in his "Replies to My Critics" section of *The Philosophy of Martin Buber*.

> I am against gnosis because and insofar as it alleges that it can report events and processes within the divinity. I am against it because and insofar as it makes God into an object in whose nature and history one knows one's way about. I am against it because in the place of the personal relation of the human person to God it sets a communion-rich

wandering through an upper world, through a multiplicity of more or less divine spheres.

Gnosis attempts to include God in the structure of knowledge erected on the base of the I-It relation, a structure which from now on passes as complete and "claims the absolute legitimacy of the transmutation in an allegedly finally valid appeal to the 'known' mysterium." The being into which this structure is here transmuted ultimately signifies the annihilation of lived concreteness *and* of creation, Buber claimed. "Thereby it not only offends the transcendent but also human existence."

CHAPTER 8

Dialogues with Americans

ON THE SUBJECT of the personal uniqueness that one is called upon to realize, Buber wrote me in 1952: "The purpose of my uniqueness may be felt more or less dimly, it cannot be sensed; the objective direction to it does not mean a definite aim. It is not as if I first became aware and then took the direction—I become aware in taking the direction. . . . More precisely: in responding to God, in taking the direction to Him I become aware, in some measure, of the person meant for me in Creation."

Direction and personal uniqueness need as corollary and aid the personal "confirmation" we receive from others, a term Buber used in "Distance and Relation" (1951) and later in "Elements of the Interhuman" (1954). This also was an important issue in Buber's dialogue with the American psychologist Carl Rogers in 1957. If man becomes man through the twofold movement of setting at a distance and entering into relation, that means, argued Buber, that men become selves with one another and need to be "made present" by active imagining of what the other is thinking, feeling, and willing in order to exist as men. In the full making present, something of the character of what is imagined is added to the act of imagining: I add my will to the other's. Confirmation occurs when the other knows that he is made present by me in his self and when this knowledge induces the process of his inmost self-becoming. "For the inmost growth of the self is not accomplished, as people like to suppose today, in man's relation to himself, but . . . in the mutuality of acceptance, of affirmation, and confirmation." An animal is what it is unquestionably, but the human person needs confirmation as this unique person that he or she is called to become. "Sent forth from the natural domain of species into the hazard of the solitary category, surrounded by the air of a chaos which came into being with him, secretly and bashfully he watches for a Yes which allows him to be and which can come to him only from one human person to another."

"The child in the womb is already created as a uniqueness to be developed," Buber claimed, "and this fact is decisive: the origin of personality is the origin of the *potential* personality: uniqueness." It is this uniqueness which must be confirmed by others, who must overcome the temptation to impose their own uniqueness and must really *mean* the person they confirm in his or her uniqueness. "By confirming, I mean only: confirming the other as 'this being,' not partially." Particularly important here is that people tend to be "confirmed" in our culture only in terms of their function or social role, and this is less than the whole being. "A man is not function alone; he is also non-functional existence, 'the silent depth of the person.' If I confirm only his function, I have not yet necessarily grasped, not yet necessarily understood him as 'this being.'"

At this time I was thinking of again taking up the novel that I had begun five years before and set aside. A close friend, who had himself been involved in the later stages of the "psychodrama," urged me not to complete the novel on the grounds that no great communication is really personal or autobiographical. "I do not understand what your friend means by saying that," Buber commented. "Some of the greatest are, to begin with Plato's Seventh Epistle and to end with Kierkegaard's *Point of View for My Activity as Author*. . . . You should write the novel indeed." Buber had a special passion against what he himself called the "hinderer," one who prompts another in such a way as to obstruct that person's hearing the direct, personal claim of the situation. Buber knew that what prompted me to write the novel was not so much its autobiographical content as my desire to witness to what I had learned from these events about what Buber himself called "the lust for overrunning reality." In December 1954, Buber wrote me: "As to the novel, my advice is: tell the tale, unceasingly the tale, shun psychology, but give the whole world of the soul in the tale itself. If the tale gets 'breathless,' the better for it. Neither sentiments nor sentences—only events, but events saying *everything*." In the spring of 1957, we talked once more about my novel on the way to Chestnut Lodge, the psychiatric facility of the Washington School of Psychiatry. This time Buber advised me to take off six months and do nothing else than write the novel but to work on it only two or three hours every morning. He suggested that I begin by a sketch of Otto Will, the tall, heavy-browed, intense director of Chestnut Lodge, by whom he had been particularly struck.

In October 1952, Buber received a letter from Mitchell Bedford, a student in the third year of the graduate School of Religion at the University of Southern California, in Los Angeles, saying that he was writing his doctoral dissertation on a comparison of Kierkegaard and Buber and asking Buber to send him a description of his early family life, and in particular of his relation to his mother. In a letter to me Buber commented, "He is obviously a Freudian, as he is writing about 'mothers.' Why those people think infancy more influential on *ideas* than youth I cannot understand." Here Buber was perhaps thinking of his own crises of youth, such as his nearly committing suicide at the age of fourteen because of the infinity of time and his despair a few years later over the death of his uncle. Bedford sent Buber two further letters "asking me very insistently for 'facts' (in the sense of modern psychology) of my life," Buber reported. In December, Buber sent him a letter which is an important document because it reveals not only Buber's fight against the psychologizing of the world but also his attitude toward biography in the ordinary sense of the word. It gives us some insight into why he always said to reporters that his personal life was just that and why he remarked to his American psychologist friend Katherine Whiteside Taylor before his death, "No one will ever write this man's biography!" "I am not in the least offended," Buber wrote Bedford. "I rather like you and your (somewhat blinded) insistence, and your (somewhat simplistic) enthusiasm, and I think I would like them no less if I were not their subject. But I want you to understand (you are able to) what I shall tell you now:

1. I do not like at all to deal with my person as a "subject" and I do not think myself at all obliged to do it. I am not interested in the world

being interested in my person. I want to influence the world, but I do not want it to feel being influenced by "Me." I am, if I may say so, commissioned to show men some Realities, and I try to do it as adequately as possible. To reflect on why I have been commissioned . . . has not only no attraction for me but even no sense. There are men who want to explain themselves to the world; Kierkegaard did; I do not. I do not even want to explain myself to myself.

2. In order to see what a writer (or a "speaker") has to show you there is no need to know more about his personal qualities or his personal life, than what his sayings, his works themselves tell you. It is not true that you would be better endowed to take what Shakespeare is ready to give you if you knew more about his biography, or better endowed to take what Homer is eager to give you if you knew anything about his—or to receive Plato's gift better if he had written you a letter on his private experiences instead of writing the Seventh Epistle about his adventures in expressing and materializing the Spirit.

3. It is true that "the life of a philosopher is always of interest because of the light it throws on the development of his thought." But what is meant here by the "life of a philosopher"? Speaking of Plato: if we knew what in his infancy he felt about his parents would it help us to grasp the development of his thought as much as the fact of his meeting a man called Socrates or even the fact of his meeting a man called Dion helps us to grasp it? More than that: if we knew his father and his mother would it not help us more than if we knew the infant's subconscious attitude to them? "Real life is meeting."

4. You believe in psycho-analysis as the means to detect essential and hidden truth, I do not. You think you obtain by it the revelation of the psychic depths. I think you obtain by it only a certain adaptation of the psychical process taken as a given object (which it never is). You want to react behind lived actuality. I want to seize it itself. And you ask me to serve what I cannot acknowledge!

So let us please close this chapter."

In *The Way of Man* Buber stated, "The root of all conflict between me and my fellowman is that I do not say what I mean and I do not do what I say." He certainly did not err in this respect. In January 1953, Buber wrote, "Of course, most psychoanalysts, knowing me to be an 'adversary,' will deny having learned anything from me." This situation was to change radically by 1957.

In 1952, Buber's old friend and Zionist co-worker Chaim Weizmann died after serving four years as the first President of the State of Israel. "Some people in Government circles wanted me to become President," Buber reported in November, "but the opposition was very strong. Of course, I would not accept even a unanimous vote." In response to a question, he said that he had heard nothing from Robert Hutchins about his idea of bringing together in America spiritual leaders of the world for a real dialogue, at which the public and the press would be present. "I had opposed rather strongly the introducing of an atmosphere of publicity into such talks," Buber averred, "one drop of publicity being sufficient to poison the whole undertaking."

In January 1953, Buber received a critical review of *Eclipse of God* and *At the Turning* written for *Commentary* magazine by Will Herberg, Professor of Judaica and sociology of religion at Drew University. Herberg, a former leader of the Lovestonite communists, had experienced a total conversion in which, under the impact of Reinhold Niebuhr, he almost became a Christian. But Niebuhr himself had urged him to remain Jewish, pointing out to him how important the concern for social justice was in the Hebrew Bible. Herberg's book *Judaism and Modern Man* (1951) had a great impact on American Jewish thought, representing an approach at once informed by the Jewish existentialism of Buber and Rosenzweig and the Neo-Orthodox theology of Niebuhr. But Herberg, like Niebuhr, had remained a resolute enemy of mysticism. When I first met Herberg in his home in New York, this enormously powerful and impassioned man stood over me for two hours inveighing against Hasidism as not really Jewish, and in his anthology, *The Writings of Martin Buber,* not a single page of Buber's Hasidic teachings and interpretations appeared! In contrast, in *To Hallow This Life,* the anthology of Buber's writings by the Unitarian minister Jacob Trapp, Buber's Hasidic writings are fully represented. Although Herberg's approach to Judaism was covenantal, his view that the church's concept of the *corpus Christi* was a continuation of the covenant Buber could not accept. The biblical concept of the *holy people,* in which the word *people* indicates "the people in its corporeal existence, in the generative connexion of its generations, has no romantic character at all," Buber wrote Herberg in response to his criticism. "Rosenzweig was even inclined to translate it by *heiliger Leib* [holy body]. The pretension of the church to be the realization of that concept, a pretension based on the supposition that Israel had been rejected by God, meant, and means, giving up the biblical fullness of the concept, the unity of body and spirit, replacing the body-element by the mystical corpus Christi." On the subject of messianism, Buber cautioned Herberg against confounding the biblical concepts of "the days of the Messiah" with "the end of days." The first he saw as "the accomplishment of history by God's completion of the creation of man with man's cooperation." About the second, "the real 'eschaton,' the *end of time,* we are not allowed to speak, not even allowed to think: According to the Midrash, when Jacob tried to speak about it, the Shekinah left him." The apocalyptic writers are illegitimate, Buber added, because they mean to "unveil" it. To both the supernaturalism of Herberg and the naturalism that Herberg attacked, Buber opposed the attitude of the narrow ridge: "There are, in my opinion, two dangers for Messianic faith: seeing the future prophesied in too human, too humanitarian terms, as Maimonides and [Herman] Cohen did, and seeing it in too divine, too theological terms, as you do, among others." "As for myself," Buber wrote Herberg, "I can believe as occurring *in time* only what, according to my belief, can begin to occur the very next moment."

Herberg replied that he had found traces of a mystical attitude or predisposition in Buber's essays, even though he knew that since *I and Thou* Buber's basic stance had been even antimystical. And since he saw mysticism as opposite to biblical faith, Herberg, like Niebuhr, felt obliged to criticize Buber for any vestiges of mysticism he suspected still remained. Although Herberg recognized the difference between Israel and the Church and rejected the Christian claim that the Church had replaced the "old" Israel, he believed that one had to acknowledge that the Church, according to its own lights, forms an organic community, a "people" in a genuine, if not ethnic or "national" sense. (Herberg denied that Israel is a "nation" in the usual sense of the term.) "Christianity in its structure of faith is every bit as much a community as Judaism; it is no individualistic faith, as is often said and which much in your writings might make us believe." Herberg also accepted Buber's distinction between the "days of the Messiah" and the "end of days," but he saw both of them as beyond the natural, unimagable but nonetheless affirmable in faith. "If we separate the days of the Messiah from the future world-time, the first becomes unquestionably a utopia."

At that time Buber wrote me about Franz Kafka: "I knew Kafka first in Prague in the time of my lectures there, and then he came to see me in Berlin. He was really unhappy and had a most unusual gift of universal and undaunted humor that enabled him to tell a story of his unhappiness in real stories, without any vestige of the charming sentimentality of Werther and René so modern man could use them as a sublime mirror. When occasionally he felt happy he did not allow himself as the teller of the stories to believe in the happiness of the man F. K." Perhaps just to prove that a "prophet" is not entirely "without honor in his own country," on May 6, three months after his seventy-fifth birthday, the Hebrew University conferred on Buber the honorary doctorate, until then conferred only on Albert Einstein, Chaim Weizmann, and Judah Magnes.

In July, Buber spoke of the writer "Georg Munk": "My wife does not like at all that people write about her *person*. Just to avoid it she chose the pseudonym." Buber's old publisher the Insel Verlag accepted for publication Paula's epic novel *By Living Waters,* and she spent the next summer revising it. It is striking that this story of German Catholic families recaptures down to the minutest details what must have been Paula's life in Munich before her marriage and reflects nothing of her forty-five years of life with Martin in Berlin, Heppenheim, and Palestine. The two of them planned to go to Italy after the award of the Peace Prize in Frankfurt on September 27. "We shall not go to the Dolomites," Buber advised me: "in contrast to former times there is now too much noise there in summer time." The first of September, Buber reported from Amsterdam that he had lectured in a circle (in the Oüde Loo, the charming Old Castle) in which the "Queen of Holland was the most interesting person." "The Queen I meant is Juliana," he later explained. "Her mother is a very different person." He added that a new edition of the Buber-Rosenzweig translation of the Hebrew Bible was coming out in four volumes from Jakob Hegner Verlag in Cologne (Köln). He also expressed his pleasure that the University of Chicago Press finally accepted *The Life of Dialogue* for publication in cooperation with Routledge & Kegan Paul. "I am afraid the cutting will cost you a lot of work." To my report that Will Herberg claimed that the decisive change in Buber's philosophy was due to Rosenzweig's essay on "Atheistic Theology," Buber responded, "I have been influenced decisively not by men but by events, particularly in the years 1916–1919," and added, "I am somewhat astonished that H. thinks *such* a change can be effected by other persons instead of life itself."

The day before his speech at Paulskirche in Frankfurt on the occasion of receiving the Peace Prize of the German Book Trade, Buber wrote me from Heidelberg, "The Schwarzwald was very beautiful, but I have been somewhat ill (it is an old chronic affliction of the viscera— I have had it now for forty years—which from time to time takes on an 'acute' form and makes me really suffer); now I am well again." In January 1954, Buber told me that he had written in "these last weeks a Biblical mystery-play." In March he said that the title of his mystery-play was *Elijah.* "I have wrestled with the subject a great part of my life. . . . No plan to publish." He also declared that he could not say *anything* about finishing his anthropology. "It is a question of pure grace."

My simultaneous friendship with both Buber and Heschel placed me under great tension concerning the question of the observance of the Jewish Law, or Halakhah. While Heschel never demanded of me that I become Orthodox, he made it very clear that fulfilling the Law was the way to real participation in Judaism or, as he was to write in *God in Search of Man,* "the holy dimension of existence." When I learned from a disciple of Heschel's that Buber did not observe Jewish Law and ritual (I had assumed he did because of his beard!), I experienced great, but only temporary, relief. In 1954, I wrote to Buber about this problem, and he responded in March from Heidelberg that he could not see such a question independent of personal existence: "For me I know that I try to do what I experience I am ordered to do; but how can I make this into a general rule about ritual being right or wrong?" What he then asserted gives us more insight into his attitude toward the Jewish Law than anything he had written since his correspondence with Rosenzweig on the subject thirty years before:

> I open my heart to the Law to such an extent that if I feel a commandment being addressed to me I feel myself bound to do it as far as I am addressed—for instance, I cannot live on Sabbath as on the other days, but I have no impulse at all to observe the minutiae of the Halakhah about what work is allowed and what not. In certain moments, some of them rather regular, partly on occasion I pray, alone of course, and say what I want to say, sometimes without words at all, and sometimes a remembered verse helps me in an extraordinary situation; but there have been days when I felt myself compelled to enter into the prayer of a community, and so I did it. This is my way of life, and one may call it religious anarchy if he likes. How could I make it into a general rule, valid for instance for you! I cannot say anything but: Put yourself in relation as you can and when you can, do your best to persevere in relation, and do not be afraid.

I was particularly struck by Buber's last remark to me; for I had said nothing about being afraid, yet he had sensed the anxiety that lay beneath my questions as to what was the right course and how I could find it. Years later when I read Albrecht Goes's essay on Buber in which he said that every person has something written on his face and on Buber's it was "Do not be afraid!" I thought of this letter. "Religious anarchy" is exactly what Gershom Scholem later accused Buber of, but when he wrote that Buber had never once set foot in a synagogue during his thirty years in Israel, I judge from this letter that he was mistaken.

In 1955, when I was writing on Buber's exchange with Rosenzweig in connection with the Jewish Law, I asked him whether one could not be open to the Law just as one was to the teachings. "Of course, one may be 'open to all of the Law,'" he responded, "but not by *doing* anything before being 'touched.'* I can learn tentatively, but I cannot act tentatively. I do not need decision in order to perceive but I need decision in order to act." "By opening my heart I cannot find 'historical revelation,' only personal," he added in response to another question. "I do not distinguish between me as a mere individual and as a member of Israel, but I am utterly unable to accept anything as God's commandment that I do not hear as such, and I can hear only through this person that I am. Every historical document is the work of transformation, but the Voice in the dialogue itself is not."

In 1957, Buber received a sharp letter from Emil Marmorstein, an English Jewish educator and writer, who informed him that his sins were "a source of vexation." Buber answered, "I have searched my conscience and it has become clear that you cannot mean anything other than the injury to this and that practical command . . . when you 'demand' that I 'hold to the commands of the Torah.'" Buber's response to Marmorstein was perhaps his last full statement on the Jewish Law, particularly since he never found time to write the book on the Law that he told me he wanted to write:

> You evidently have not in general considered the possibility that I seek to fulfill as best I can what, in my belief, is God's command and that I am not in a position to hold something to be His command that I cannot believe comes from Him. Or shall I accept that you feel yourself justified in demanding that I force myself to exertions in order that I believe in the end what till now I have not been able to believe? Shall I, would you like me to, accept that in *articulo mortis* I learn to believe something, as the Christian priests do when they speak of such things to a man my age? It seems that your warning threatens me with the serpent that does not die. But I stand where I stand and fear Him, into whose hands every night I commend my soul, but no serpent and no fire. He, the Teacher, to whose teachings I listen as best I can, does not demand of me that I force myself to believe what my innermost belief contradicts and to fulfill as His command what my adoring heart says is not His word but only that of the collective being that we know under

---

*See Buber's letter to Rosenzweig of July 13, 1924, *Briefwechsel*, Vol. II, pp. 200f.

the name tradition. He demands of me only to open my heart to His truth, and what my opened heart understands as His truth—whether it be in the *written teaching* or in the *oral teaching* and elsewhere—that I must seek to fulfill with my whole soul. Since I recognized, around forty years ago, that this is my way, I have striven to walk on it, and my whole work was guided by this striving. How far I could complete what I had undertaken neither I nor you can say; it is the business of the One to make the judgment about the work and about the heart, the *intention of the heart* in it.

One fact still must be stated. In all the years no one has ever heard a single critical word from me about the tradition, and when someone tells me that he lives his life according to the Torah in your sense of the term, I answer him: that is your good fortune. To you personally I give this answer.

In 1951, Buber sent me a copy of a letter to him from the German Benedictine monk Father Caesarius Lauer, with which Buber said he was totally in agreement, a letter that warned against the danger of remaining content with dialogical philosophizing in place of lived dialogue:

> The "dialogue" about dialogue is growing on all sides. That should make one glad, but it disquiets me. For—if all the signs do not deceive— the talk about dialogue takes from men the living experience of dialogical life. . . . In dialogue it is the realization that is decisive, since it is working reality, that means—Life. Now, the word certainly belongs to this realization, as Ebner has well shown. But just the word, not talk, logicizing dialectic. . . . It is just the "spiritual" man of today who suffers in a frightful fashion the old temptation of the human spirit, that is to say, that of objectifying the living accomplishment. . . . These "dialogical" dialecticians do not seem to notice that the dialogue is essentially a way. However, "the way is there that one may walk on it," as you once said.

Father Caesarius was quoting in this last sentence from Buber's Preface to his Hasidic collection *Das verborgene Licht* ("The Hidden Light," 1924). This letter so impressed me that I wrote Father Caesarius and obtained his permission to publish it in *The Life of Dialogue*. Later I learned from Buber that he had gone to the Sahara, as a result of this discontent. In March 1954, Buber wrote me that he had had only a card from Father Caesarius from Algiers, without an address, in which he said he would write soon. "I have felt for some time I have brought some disquiet into his life," Buber wrote, "and now I must wait till he tells me more." In April, Buber said that Father Caesarius had written him that he was again in Germany but had conscientious scruples about his order. "I shall advise him to remain and to suffer within," Buber told me. In February 1956, Caesarius Lauer wrote Buber from Oberwesel that he had received the copy of *The Life of Dialogue* that I had sent him. "He came back from the Sahara with a heavy soul," Buber wrote me, "and does not yet know what to do next." Father Caesarius returned to Maria Laach for a year and a half and then left it. Before this took place, Buber responded angrily to a suggestion from Harold Stahmer that he should persuade Lauer to come to a Benedictine monastery founded by monks from Maria Laach in Vermont. "I do not tell people what to do," Buber wrote Stahmer. It seems that in this case he really wanted to dissuade Lauer from leaving and was upset about the part his writings had played in Lauer's decision to leave. Karl Lauer does not wish the considerable correspondence between Buber and him to be published before his death but has agreed that Stahmer, who is a friend of his from the latter's one-year stay in Maria Laach, may eventually publish it.

In "The Validity and Limitation of the Political Principle," which I translated for Buber about this time, Buber resumed in more concrete form what he had said about the distinction between the social and the political principles in "Society and the State." Starting from Jesus' saying, "Give to Caesar that which is Caesar's and give to God that which is God's," he sought to demonstrate that what Jesus meant was not a dualistic division of life between the spiritual and the material, as is commonly thought, but the distinction between the indirect aspects of society, which are the means, and the direct, which give these means meaning. The human person, ontologically regarded, constitutes a union of two spheres—that of wholeness and that of separation or division. "What is legitimately done in the sphere of separation receives its legitimacy from the sphere of wholeness." Giving to the state what is due it in the sphere of separation is authorized by the sphere of wholeness in which we give God what is due him: ourselves. Give to God your immediacy in direct relationship with him, Jesus' saying about the tribute money says to us, and from so doing you will learn ever anew what you shall give to Caesar in the indirect relations of politics, money, and the structure of society.

In the opinion and attitude of a very great part of the modern world, in contrast, it is held that public regimes may legitimately determine human existence, "since the political environment constitutes the essential condition of man, and it does not exist for his sake but he for it." Whether the remainder that is left after the abstraction of the essential part for Caesar can still be booked to the account of "God" is hardly of importance. In the modern world to discuss the validity and limitations of the political principle means to criticize at the decisive point the one absolute that has not been relativized—the political archons of the hour. Proceeding from a discussion of Hegel, Marx, and Heidegger, Buber pointed out that if historical time and history are absolutized, it can easily occur that in the midst of present historical events the time-bound thinker ascribes to the state's current drive to power the character of an absolute. "After that, the goblin called success, convulsively grinning, may occupy for a while the divine seat of authority." Here too Buber was talking about a direction of movement, not an either/or but an ever newly drawn demarcation line, the "*quantum satis*" of "as-much-as-one-can." "If the political organization of existence does not infringe on my wholeness and immediacy, it may demand of me that I do justice to it at any particular time as far as, in a given conflict, I believe I am able to answer for." He was well aware of the cruel conflicts of duties and in no way implied that under *all* circumstances the interest of the group is to be sacrificed to the moral demand. "But the evident absence of this inner conflict, the lack of its wounds and scars, is to me uncanny." "I want to tell you," Buber wrote me at this time, "that I am not on principle opposed to 'security'; what I am opposed to is sacrificing the very meaning of life (not less than that!) to security."

At this time Buber was revising *The Legend of the Baal-Shem* for a new edition in the Manesse Library of World Literature and for the Harper edition in America. Thus the book of Buber's that I first read and that had such a great impact on me became the first of his books that I translated as a whole, two of the essays of *Eclipse of God* having been translated by others. Some of this revision was of content, but many abridgments were made for reasons of style. "I can no longer endure, for instance, so many adjectives," Buber declared. It was at this time too that Buber decided to leave out "The New Year's Sermon,"* my favorite of all the twenty-one legends: "I do not like it any more, it is not real enough; the theme is important, but it is not 'fulfilled.'" In September when he had finished the revision of *The Legend of the Baal-Shem,* Buber confided: "As you have seen, I have revised it very thoroughly, but it was necessary. It has improved very much, more than I had hoped it would. But revising it has been a most difficult piece of work. I was rather shocked by the pathetic

---

*See Volume One, Chapter 6, where I tell this story.

lightheartedness of my youth. And you, perhaps, are shocked now by my merciless cutting! But later on you will understand I have been right."

In the same letter he announced that he had finished his paper on the anthropology of art, which later became the chapter on "Man and His Image-Work" in *The Knowledge of Man.* "It too was a piece of work, but of another kind altogether. I had to 'lunge' into the subjects of cosmology and epistemology which I had thought about very much in the course of many years but without trying to formulate anything. Now I was 'forced' to do it."

About this time Buber began negotiating, largely through me, for a translation of *The Tales of Rabbi Nachman* by Horizon Press. This book, which had not yet been translated, "had been very popular in its time," Buber informed me and was now to be published in German in an enlarged new edition of fifty thousand copies in the Fischer Bücherei (little books) series. He wanted the *Nachman* translation and a new translation of his interpretations of Hasidism which had been published in a very bad translation by Philosophical Library in America—as soon as possible, the one by February 1955, the other by May. "I do not like their slow ways," Buber wrote me about Horizon Press. "If they are not willing to do it, I have in mind to propose the whole corpus to another publisher. . . . You must understand, my dear, that at my age I like to see matters settled," a note which entered increasingly into the correspondence between us from this time on. Another new note was Buber's concern for royalties: "I must in the next few years get some money in order to be able to buy the house we are living in in Jerusalem, because the Government, which owns it, threatens to sell it to someone else. A few days ago I received from the Government department the conditions, and they are very heavy (a sum much larger than we thought, 55% to be paid at once and the rest in the course of three years). I do not like to think about money but I have to now." Eventually an agreement with Horizon Press was reached, and I accepted the task of translating *The Tales of Rabbi Nachman.*

It was at this time that Buber sent me, in response to my own deep concern, the answer to my questions concerning meditation and mysticism that I quoted in Volume One in the chapter on "Encounter with Mysticism." What replaced the spontaneous meditations that occurred in his early days, Buber said, "is something very different, something always bound to a reality, to a situation. I cannot but think all this talk about meditation rather exaggerated." He added that if I would reread attentively the introduction to *Ecstatic Confessions,* I would see that even then, in his "mystical" period, he did not believe in mysticism as a (momentous) 'union' with the Divine or the Absolute, a union occurring . . . in the course of mortal life, i.e., as interruption." "The term 'mysticism' has become more nebulous since the days of my youth," Buber continued, "and therefore I do not like to use it without explaining thoroughly what I mean. Of course, you may call it mysticism if something is 'told' me through a situation; I do not call it that, because this 'being told' is simply the minimum of revelation, the elemental form of universal revelation, and revelation has nothing to do with mysticism. As for 'meditation,' as far as I can see people mean by it absorption in the absolute Self, more or less by the 'inner' way; this is very far from what I mean by a religious attitude." A month later in response to still further questions of mine, Buber wrote: "Of course meditation may be of use for some people, just as a kind of concentration or so. Hasidism is in general not mystical in the sense of *unio mystica,* but it is in the sense of *ekstasis.* As long as *unio mystica* is not meant by it, I have no objection to mysticism; what I do not like are simply ambiguous terms."

In December 1953, the German original of "Prophecy, Apocalyptic, and the Historical Hour" was published in *Merkur.* In this essay Buber set forth one of his last sets of polar opposites, two ideal types held in tension with each other, that characterized his thinking from its earliest to its most mature stages. These polarities give Buber's thought elasticity and subtlety, but for the same reason they are often the occasion of misunderstanding and confusion. "Letting go and deciding," "orienting and realizing," "I-Thou" and "I-It," person and ego,* dialogue and monologue, *emunah* and *pistis, gnosis* and *devotio* are not so much resumed as given historical depth and dimension by this last set of terms: prophecy and apocalyptic. Unfortunately, many readers are not trained to think either dialectically or phenomenologically, and for this reason they want to read Buber's polar terms as incompatible opposites, as either/ors between which one must choose. This has been as great an obstacle to the understanding of his thought, even by scholars, philosophers, and theologians, as any other single factor.

Buber's concern with prophecy and apocalyptic was already fully foreshadowed in *For the Sake of Heaven.* Like *For the Sake of Heaven,*

---

*I use here Walter Kaufmann's rendering of *Eigenwesen.* See *I and Thou,* trans. by Kaufmann, p. 111 and note 7, pp. 111f.

this essay was a response to the current historical situation; it too was a "Word to the Time." Buber began "Prophecy, Apocalyptic, and the Historical Hour" by contrasting two different ways of responding to a crisis: drawing on one's primal resources and contributing to the decision about the next hour or "not letting oneself be fooled," i.e., fatalistically resigning oneself and letting oneself be carried along. The soul's innermost question of trust is: "Do I dare the definitely impossible or do I adapt myself to the unavoidable?" Transposed from biography into history, this is the question that confronts our time, and in order to make that question clear Buber reached into the history of biblical faith, disregarding all that is atypical, to contrast the basic attitude of the classical prophets, such as Jeremiah and Isaiah, with that of the late apocalyptics, such as the Revelation of John and the apocryphal so-called Fourth Book of Ezra. The former, the prophet, affirms man as a unique being, created to be the center of surprise in creation. Only such a being, with the power to choose between ways, is suited to be God's partner in the dialogue of history. "The future is not fixed, for God wants man to come to Him with full freedom, to return to Him even out of a plight of extreme hopelessness and then to be really with Him." The mature apocalyptic, in contrast, no longer knows a historical future in the real sense; for the end of all history is near. Prophecy arises out of a time of strength, apocalyptic out of decadence. The one is *spoken* to the *present*. The other is *written* for the future. "Wherever man shudders before the menace of his own work and longs to flee from the radically demanding historical hour, there he finds himself near to the apocalyptic vision of a process that cannot be arrested."

Marx's vision of an arbitrary leap out of the aeon of necessity into that of freedom is an optimistic apocalyptic. "In its modern shape, too, apocalyptic knows nothing of an inner transformation of man that precedes the transformation of the world and co-operates in it; it knows almost nothing of the prophetic 'turning.'" But today even this apocalyptic is not of real importance, even for the adherents of Marxism. Instead, like the "modern Paulinism" of *Two Types of Faith,* there prevails a completely secularized, thoroughly disenchanted apocalyptic attitude which has no hope for the future but preserves the character of the present as being all-too-late. The irremediable old age of the world is accepted as self-understood. This new apocalyptic no longer says, "One cannot swim against the stream," since the image of the stream, to which an outlet belongs, is already too full of pathos. Rather it says, "An old period must behave like an old period if it does not wish to be laughed at." Its only poetry is one of self-directed irony, its only art is one that atomizes things, and faith has become altogether unseemly. Buber's own personal experience in trying to rebel against this indirectness that has penetrated all human relationships, and in being upbraided as a romantic full of illusions, is clearly mirrored in his description of the present hour:

> If he resists the flagging of the dialogical relationship between men, he is forthwith reproached with failing to recognize the fated solitude of present-day living. . . . If one declares that one of the main reasons why the crisis in the life of the peoples appears hopeless is the fact that the existential mistrust of all against all prevents any meaningful negotiation over the real differences of interest, he is set right by a smile of the shrewd: an "old" world is necessarily shrewd.

Buber *did* rebel in favor of the depths of history which he saw as continually at work to rejuvenate creation and therefore in league with the prophets, in favor of the risk of inner transformation which transfigures the "customary soul" into the "surprise soul." Turning does not mean a return to an earlier, guiltless stage of life, but swinging around to where the wasteful aimlessness becomes walking on a way, and guilt is atoned for in the newly arisen genuineness of existence.

> As in the life of a single person, so also in the life of the human race: what is possible in a certain hour and what is impossible cannot be adequately ascertained by any foreknowledge. . . . One does not learn the measure and limit of what is attainable in a desired direction otherwise than through going in this direction. The forces of the soul allow themselves to be measured only through one's using them. *In the most important moments of our existence neither planning nor surprise rules alone:* in the midst of the faithful execution of a plan we are surprised by secret openings and insertions. *Room must be left for such surprises,* however; *planning as though they were impossible renders them impossible.* One cannot strive for immediacy, but one can hold oneself free and open for it. One cannot produce genuine dialogue, but one can be at its disposal. Existential mistrust cannot be replaced by trust, but it can be replaced by a reborn candour. [Italics added.]

This passage makes incontrovertibly clear what should have been clear all along: that Buber never put forward ideal types in order to affirm one and reject the other but as a part of a lifelong struggle that there should be *room* in the modern world for realization, I-Thou, person, *emunah*, *devotio*, freedom, surprise, dialogical immediacy, and the courage to trust.

In December 1954, Buber wrote an essay in honor of Albert Schweitzer's eightieth birthday. He titled it "A Realist of the Spirit," and he pointed to Schweitzer as the true doctor who has to do with the unity of body *and* soul and who knows he must begin, like Jesus, with the healing of the body, since the soul knows better how to wait. In theology, too, Schweitzer recovered the basic meaning of the spiritualized conception of redemption, that of the actual salvation on earth of the whole human being. Schweitzer's concept of the reverence for human life also is concerned with actively honoring and helping the body-soul totality of the individual living man. "Not only ethical but also political questions will be misunderstood if one thinks that one may deal with them as independent of the awesome reality of human living and dying." Schweitzer's existence manifests and confirms the created togetherness of spirit and life which in our day have been sundered from each other more radically than in any earlier time.

When my book *Martin Buber: The Life of Dialogue* was published, the American Protestant theologian Reinhold Niebuhr sent me a copy of the review that he written of it for the *New York Times Book Review*. He ended his review by quoting Heinz-Joachim Heydorn's statement that, next to Albert Schweitzer, Buber was the greatest symbol of responsibility of our time. Niebuhr took exception to Heydorn's exception; for he thought Schweitzer's reputation as a saint ungrounded in view of his paternalistic treatment of the native Africans with whom he worked. The *New York Times Book Review* did not, of course, print this statement about the person whom the American public revered more than any other person of that time. "What you tell me about the judgment Niebuhr passed on Schweitzer is incomprehensible," Buber wrote me. "I have known Schweitzer for many years and never saw anything 'fake' in him. Of course he is not a 'saint'—who is? But I believe him to be a true man."

In 1955, Niebuhr wrote *The Self and the Dramas of History,* based on Buber's philosophy of dialogue, and Will Herberg sent Buber his review of the book. "I am writing for readers of good will and not for philosophers," Buber responded to a question of Herberg's about *I and Thou.* "I mean: for philosophers too, as far as they have the good will, but I must 'obey' the first class, as far as I can do it." In his Preface to his anthology *The Writings of Martin Buber,* Herberg claimed that *for Buber* God is always I and man always Thou. "Against Herberg's view of man 'being the Thou simply,' the Bible brings two great arguments," Buber rejoined: "the book of Job (who only at the end gets an answer) and the book of Psalms (nearly all of them asking for a dialogue or thanking for an answer)." But Herberg, under Niebuhr's influence, felt so strongly that Buber *should* hold God to be always I and man always Thou that he could not bring himself to change his Preface to what Buber really thought! Buber also questioned Herberg's description of the interrelation of the dialogue between man and man and between man and God as "triadic." "Man can establish a genuine relationship with God only in relationship with men, and he can establish relationship with men only in relationship with God," Herberg explained. To Herberg this showed the interdependency of the two relationships to men and to God. But this is by no means what Buber meant by the "eternal Thou," the meeting with the nameless Meeter who is met in the between and not in some separate relationship interdependent with the human one.

Buber asked me to give Niebuhr his essay "The Validity and Limitation of the Political Principle." "It is obvious he does not know it," Buber commented. "I have never been antipolitical, neither in theory nor in practice, but I think it vitally important to fix the boundaries of politics, at least as long as it is not possible to put the power of decision in the hands of the best men (not the philosophers, as Plato thought, but the best men indeed), a thing that would increase the tragedy in the life of those men but would diminish the tragedy in the life of mankind." "Herberg, like Niebuhr, has not grasped *why* my 'social philosophy' is as it is: because I do not see any salvation, any true help coming from the non-personal. What they think to be 'practical' is nothing but theory of a practice (just as is Marx's philosophy) and never becomes, never became real *praxis,* real act. What is *done* in the social field, is done out of personal relation, out of 'decrowding the crowd.' To show this I have written (to match *Paths in Utopia*) the third part of 'Dialogue' and 'Society and the State,' and I would go on, if I were only asked real questions on the subject." Both Herberg and Niebuhr accepted Buber's I-Thou philosophy on the level of interhuman and divine-human relationships, but in the realm of the social and the political they held him to be "utopian."

"Herberg is a good man indeed," Buber confided, "but I hope for him he will one day liberate himself from a certain theologism." Niebuhr's comments on Buber's social philosophy and Buber's replies I later incorporated in the Buber section of *Philosophical Interrogations.* Buber's summation of the issue between him and Niebuhr is perhaps the most concrete single expression in Buber's social philosophy of his teaching of the "demarcation line":

What he calls the basic structure of society is historically and even pre-historically (this is my opinion against the prevailing opinion of ethnologists) based on personal relations, and where it subdues them it becomes wrong. As to modern technical society, of course it depends upon "artfully constructed equilibria of power," but what depends on them is its order and not its justice. If Niebuhr cannot concede it, then obviously we shall have to distinguish carefully between two very different kinds of "justice," and I for myself am harassed by the thought that the concept of justice must be split in two, bearing even different names. I cannot see the God-willed reality of justice anywhere than in "being just," and this means of course: being just as far as it is possible here and now, under the "artful" conditions of actual society. So in my opinion it is not the justice that depends upon them, but ever again the realisable "how much" of it. *Sometimes, striving to be just, I go on in the dark, till my head meets the wall and aches, and then I know: Here is (now) the wall, and I cannot go further. But I could not know it beforehand, or otherwise.* [Italics added.]

"Niebuhr is interested in society as an institutional reality and I as in a relational one (equals as far as built upon personal human relations)," Buber commented in 1959.

In 1955, Frances Gunther, the wife of the famous American journalist John Gunther, established a scholarship at the Hebrew University for the best essay or book on Buber's thought. That same year a young man named John Olney contacted Buber with ambitious plans to establish an American scholarship based upon reading Buber's *I and Thou,* his purposes being to make the book better known in America, to promote America's side of the "Cold War," and incidentally to make some money for himself. "Does he think I represent the 'Western' view?" Buber exclaimed. "Besides, *I and Thou* cannot—and shall not—become a 'most widely read book.'" "It is a pity for such a lot of activity," Buber added, "but I have an 'objective' aversion against the idealistic extravagances of the business spirit, especially if they try to involve me in their affairs."

In 1954 the Columbia University Department of Religion approached me about a position. Buber said it was time for him to bear witness and wrote a letter for me. In contrast to the usual academic recommendation Buber did not dwell on scholarly promise and achievement but on what really mattered to him: his concern for "inclusion," or "imagining the real":

Friedman had to . . . build up something like a system out of what was never intended to become such a thing. This he could do only by true understanding, his best quality indeed. He understands the ideas he meets, and he understands even the persons who thought them, as persons who thought precisely these ideas and not different ones. . . .

I have the impression I have told you what perhaps no other could tell you about the man.

In 1956–1957 I was Visiting Professor of Religious Philosophy at the Hebrew Union College–Jewish Institute of Religion at Cincinnati, the seminary that trains Reform rabbis. When the question arose of creating a chair for me in contemporary religious thought, Buber advised:

> If you want seriously ("existentially") to act educationally for the poor (very poor!) cause of Judaism, you will decide to go to Cincinnati, taking on yourself a lot of anger, disillusion and conflicts. I would not even advise you to do so . . . if you do not feel in your heart strong enough to meet even the rather important contrarieties of everyday that await you in that ambiance—strong enough and loving enough. It is indeed a question of love, involving love for the "unlovable."

In October 1955, Buber dictated two pages on revelation in reply to questions I asked him. This later became one of the fragments on revelation that he preserved in "Gleanings," thus providing a striking illustration of how his thought at times came into being in response to "real questions." As in his reply to Jung, he here used the simile of "a divine fire seizing a lump of ore, entering it, melting it, transforming it," so that the flame of God dwells in it, never to be distinguished from it. Buber saw himself as speaking for those persons for whom the distinction between the divine and human part in revelation had become a personal problem which they could neither ignore nor overcome: "These cannot go back on their knowledge, which is an organic part of their personal faith. But neither can they renounce the historical tradition that has molded them religiously. What they can and must do, is to listen again and again, in order to learn which of the commandments of tradition can be heard by them as being commanded by God to them, and of course to live accordingly. This can be done only in the stern responsibility of faith."

After I had translated *The Tales of Rabbi Nachman*, Horizon Press postponed its publication of the book in order to ask the painter Marc Chagall whether he would do illustrations for it. Buber was not at all pleased by this: "You must understand, my dear, that I am not as young as you are and so time has for me a somewhat different significance than for you. I want to settle things." In May, Chagall told Buber in Paris that he had been asked to illustrate Nachman, but

Buber did not ask him his decision. "Entre nous," Buber wrote me from Heidelberg, "his daughter wanted me to ask him to make illustrations to the *Tales of the Hasidim,* but I did not want to. He is a very remarkable artist, and his new illustrations to the Bible are beautiful, but I rather prefer the tales to remain unillustrated." In July, Buber added in a letter from Zurich, "I appreciate him highly, but his 'Hasidism' and mine are different and should better not be mixed."

In October 1956, Buber painted a picture of what was, without question, a typical work day, day in and day out, year in and year out until his final illness: "I have to deal now with 1) re-writing the guilt lectures, 2) preparing the dream lecture, 3) reading proofs of the Bible translation, Vol. 3, and 4) comparing the French translation of *Tales of the Hasidim,* Vol. 2. If you add to all this the daily business (editorship of the Pedagogic Encyclopedia, correspondence, serious talks with visitors everyday, Ihud affairs etc.), you will get a nice day's work." The most remarkable thing was that despite this crushing load of work he was *fully* present for every person who came to see him!

CHAPTER 9

Second Visit to America: Encounter with Psychotherapy

IN 1956, Leslie H. Farber, chairman of the faculty of the Washington (D.C.) School of Psychiatry, conceived of the idea of bringing Buber to America to give the Fourth Annual William Alanson White Memorial Lectures, and I acted as a go-between in arranging Buber's visit. In response to my first letter Buber asked me to give him some more details about the school and its members, "particularly what kind of human beings they are." "I do not yet see myself in such an institute. But the fact is that some days before your letter my wife said to me: 'We did not see enough of the grand wild nature of America' (We saw only the Great Canyon that impressed us very much, but the course of the Hudson we saw only from the railway window), and I answered; 'Who knows—we may yet see more of it.'"

Buber listed as the essential points: "1) the atmosphere must be one where such an attempt as mine of a synthetical life can make itself understood. [Since 1921 Buber had identified his own point of view as that of "psychosynthesis" as opposed to "psychoanalysis," though he did not mean by this the approach of his friend the Italian psychiatrist Roberto Assagioli.] 2) the conditions must be such as to enable us to see the scenery more intensely; and I cannot renew the absorbing and tiring experience of an American lecture-tour." The trip would have to be the following winter or spring because of Buber's "work as editor-in-chief of our Encyclopedia of Education (in 5 great volumes, the first of them is going into print just now)." In March, Buber wrote me that the invitation of the Washington School had given him a stimulus "to make my critical attitude to certain terms, such as Libido, the Subconscious, the Archetypes, theoretically clearer than I have done till now. . . . Of course, the main problem is that of the psychical life as such."

In March, Farber sent Buber a formal invitation to give the William Alanson White Memorial Lectures, centering them on his philosophical anthropology and its contributions to psychology. He described the Washington School as an eclectic group open to every criticism and particularly interested in Buber's criticism of Freud's theories of the unconscious and dreams, which I had told Farber about. Farber also described at length Harry Stack Sullivan, the founder of the Washington School, and his theory of interpersonal psychiatry, which Farber rightly thought might be close to Buber's own approach. Sullivan, declared Farber, was "a man of remarkable courage, willing to oppose the Freudians on all public occasions." Philosophically, theologically, and artistically naïve, Sullivan wrote in a pompous and pedantic manner and tried to give his theories "scientific" respectability through borrowing from modern physics. This only broadened the already existing cleavage between what he was in his private life and how he appeared as a public person. "Despite this he was an inspiring teacher with an almost exquisite capacity for relationship."

"I was rather surprised by the great spiritual freedom that underlay your essay," Buber responded to "Martin Buber and Psychiatry," which Farber had given as a public lecture for the Washington School of Psychiatry. "We need now in psychology as elsewhere, a phase of real freedom. I was impressed by what you say in the paper and in the letter about Sullivan; obviously nothing was lacking but just that freedom." In his response, Farber pointed out that his circle differed from other psychiatric or psychoanalytic groups in their continuing concern with the treatment of schizophrenia. "Though most of us have been trained in psychoanalysis, Freud's theories of the narcissistic nature of schizophrenia were of little use to us. We learned early

Martin Buber at seventy.
*Photograph by Alfred Bernheim,
Jerusalem*

Buber and Leslie H. Farber, chairman of the faculty of the Washington School
of Psychiatry, 1957.

Buber and Prime Minister David Ben-Gurion at a celebration in honor of
Buber's eightieth birthday at the Hebrew University,
Jerusalem, Israel, February 1958.

Paula Buber
in her last years.

Photograph of Buber by a
photographer who came to Israel
to take pictures of flowers, with
an inscription to the author.

For Maurice Friedman
MB

Buber reading in his study
in Talbiyeh, Jerusalem.
*Photograph by
W. Braun, Jerusalem*

Buber talking with United Nations Secretary General Dag Hammarskjøld in his study in Talbiyeh, Jerusalem, 1959. *Photograph courtesy United Nations*

Buber in his house in Talbiyeh with his great-granddaughter Tamar Goldschmidt. *Photograph by David Rubinger, Jerusalem*

Buber, Ernst Simon (left), and Hugo Bergmann (center)—his two closest friends and disciples— together on the porch of Buber's home in Jerusalem. *Photograph by David Rubinger, Jerusalem*

Buber at around eighty.

Buber in Switzerland, summer 1962.
Photograph by Naemah Beer-Hofmann

Torchlight parade of Hebrew University students in front of
Buber's home in Talbiyeh on the occasion of Buber's
eighty-fifth birthday, February 8, 1963.
Photograph by David Harris, Jerusalem

Buber delivering his speech "A Believing Humanism" as part of the Erasmus Prize ceremony in Amsterdam, summer 1963. *Photograph by Inez van 't Hoff*

Buber receiving the Erasmus Prize—Queen Wilhelmina *(left)*, Barbara Goldschmidt, Buber's granddaughter who accompanied him on the trip *(immediate left)*, and Prince Bernhard *(right)* giving the Prize. *Photograph by Inez van 't Hoff*

Buber with Princess Beatrix at dinner. *Photograph by Inez van 't Hoff*

Buber, much relaxed, at the sanitarium in Switzerland where he spent the summers, July 30, 1963. Naemah Beer-Hofmann, who took the picture, wrote on the back of it: "He was in very good spirits and said, 'Eine Ewigkeitsstunde überm See dieser Welt' (An eternal hour over the sea of this world)."

that it was often possible to have rather intensive relations with schizophrenics but, these relations . . . were easily fragmented, the consequence being a growing preoccupation with our own failures in sustaining these relations."

Farber also told Buber about Frieda Fromm-Reichmann (the first wife of Erich Fromm), who was the leading clinical psychiatrist at Chestnut Lodge, the private (and highly expensive) sanitarium outside of Washington where most of the members of the school had received some of their training. She too had been interested in the treatment of psychoses in Europe, and next to Sullivan she had had the greatest personal influence on Farber's group. "She has little of Sullivan's chronic exasperation—or his grandiosity, for that matter. On the other hand she is apt to romanticize the schizophrenic, regarding him as a misguided genius." Where Sullivan turned to the theories of physics, Fromm-Reichmann turned to the romanticism of the nineteenth century, falling back on such terms as *empathy* and *spontaneity*. Sullivan was the first chairman of the faculty of the Washington School of Psychiatry, Fromm-Reichmann the second, and Farber the third. Fromm-Reichmann was, in fact, a pioneer in direct work with schizophrenics, like Margaret Sechaheye in Switzerland, and it is she who is the psychiatrist portrayed in the book and movie *I Never Promised You a Rose Garden*, which is set in St. Elizabeth's hospital in Washington, where she also worked.

Farber concluded by expressing his conviction that Buber's lectures and seminars would have an enormously liberating effect on the school—and ultimately on psychiatry in America in general.

In May 1956, Buber wrote me from Paris asking me to make some notes for him on the psychological "open questions" that I thought most important for America. "As for me, you know my conviction that all the main concepts of psychology are 'in crisis.'" In August, Buber complained of his repeatedly unsuccessful attempts to write a lecture for the Washington School on dreams and the unconscious. He could not think about the possible publication of a part of it in a psychoanalytic journal until it was completely done, "and this work is exceptionally hard." "If people ask you to intervene in such affairs," he added, "please tell them I am intractable. My dear Maurice, I want you to know once for all that I really am not a literary man. Writing is not my job but my duty, a terribly severe one, and when I write I do it under a terrible strain."

Later that same month when he was back in Israel, Buber declared that he had not been able to work for nearly two weeks due to the worst *hamsin* (hot desert wind) in many years. With its passing, he began to work again, but only slowly. "As to the subject of dreams," he wrote, "I will think again on it. The practical problem is that I have some rather strong doubts concerning the treating of dreams in all the schools of analytical psychology, i.e., the symbol theory in its usual application." Later he said that he was thinking about giving two lectures on dreams. Margaret Rioch of the Washington School, who came to see him in London, asked Buber if he and Paula would like to stay in a private house, but he said without hesitation that they always preferred to stay in a hotel with a working room and a kitchen ("It is necessary for dietary reasons that my wife should be enabled to prepare meals herself"). Buber had also declined all of the many invitations he had received to lecture outside of Washington, including the University of Chicago. He finally consented to a public lecture in Washington on "What Is Common to All," a seminar on biblical faith for Columbia University "for a small circle of teachers," and a three-day intercollegiate seminar on his thought at the University of Michigan.

The Washington School of Psychiatry originally wanted to publish Buber's lectures in a book, but to this Buber saw an insuperable obstacle, since he wanted to include them, along with others, in his philosophical anthropology (*The Knowledge of Man*). I proposed, as a compromise, returning to what I thought was the original plan: two books, one the essays on anthropology and the other the essays on psychology, including what was finally titled *Guilt and Guilt Feelings,* as well as the lectures on dreams and the unconscious. To this Buber responded with his usual decisiveness: "You suppose the two new ones deal with psychology and the rest with anthropology, but you are mistaken: all these essays and lectures, the old and the new, the written and the unwritten, are anthropological essays, and if I treat 'psychological' subjects, I treat them anthropologically. I show, if I may say so, that their truth is anthropological. . . . You must understand, my dear, that the anthropology book in its entireness and coherence, is for me more important than my lecturing, although I like lecturing as you well know. . . . I would rather renounce the whole lecturing plan than to wrong my book. I hope you understand—as far as it is possible for a young man to understand an old one, old men having entered a sphere totally unknown to the young."

In September, Buber informed Farber that in addition to two already completed lectures, "Distance and Relation" and "Elements of the Interhuman," the latter in somewhat abridged form, he planned two new lectures on "Guilt and Modern Psychology" and "Basic Concepts of Psychology," the second to deal with the unconscious and Freud's theory of dreams. These last two lectures would represent a critical attitude toward what it means to live in the thought world of modern psychology and therefore needed thorough discussion in the closed seminar. This new investigation of prevailing psychological concepts could be accompanied by the explanation of some of the anthropological concepts that Buber himself had introduced, such as acceptance and confirmation. The foundation of the seminar work should be in some measure systematic questions from the participating psychologists. This could be facilitated, Buber suggested, by ordering the problems in advance and communicating that to him beforehand. "It is naturally desirable that psychological cases (in brief) be used as examples. But it must be clear to all that I cannot deal with the psychotherapeutic side of the matter except in so far as questions of principle arise out of it."

In October 1956, Buber wrote me that he thought he could send me "Dreams and the Unconscious" to translate by December. Later that same month he even considered taking "Dreams and the Unconscious," which he saw as two lectures, out of the anthropology book and giving it to the William Alanson White Foundation exclusively along with the essay on guilt, "to make a small book that may be called *Guilt and Dream,* or vice-versa." Later that same month he announced that he had nearly finished rewriting his essay on guilt and hoped to be able to send a copy in about ten days. This, too, came to two full lectures. "As to the other subject," referring to dreams and the unconscious, "I have not yet mastered it entirely; there are too many relations of dreams and too many conflicting theories." In November, Farber came up with an acceptable compromise, the William Alanson White Lectures to be published in the foundation's journal, *Psychiatry,* as they later were, and then by Harper's in the anthropology book. "The 'Unconscious' is the most difficult thing on earth to be dealt with ontologically," Buber stated at that time, and two weeks later he declared that it had become rather difficult to put his thoughts into their final form. This may have had to do with the Sinai invasion by Israel, for in the same letter he wrote that he assumed the slowness of communication was due to this situation and added, "I am overburdened with work more than ever, but I am well and I try to bear faithfully the import of the hour." As a result, he proposed to Farber to preserve the four lectures ("Distance and Relation," "Elements of the Interhuman," and the two in "Guilt and Guilt Feelings"), but to transfer "the highly complicated subject of the Unconscious to the Seminar." This is, in fact, what happened. Even so, at the end of November, Buber said that he still hoped to be able to finish in time the first, general part of the dream chapter and to make it into a lecture. A few days later, he added, "I cannot now work, as I had in mind to, on the Unconscious; I am not yet well enough and not able enough to concentrate. But with God's help I shall do my best in time." The end of December, after overcoming a recurring illness, he had toiled again over the unconscious and made some notes. "But they are too abstract, too heavy for an American lecture, and I am inclined to think I can use them only for the Seminar."

Two days later Farber asked Buber if he had any special wishes concerning the size and makeup of the seminars, especially since persons of all sorts had expressed an interest in taking part. "I commiserate with you in your task of 'analyzing the usual analysis of the unconscious,'" Farber added. "In my own poor efforts in this direction I have usually ended with the sensation that I was foundering in a thick pea-soup." Buber responded that twenty was by no means too many (the actual group was close to thirty) and that his only concern about the makeup of the group was that the participants be persons who think for themselves and are ready to contemplate even the most familiar subject from a new perspective. "The chief aim is the clarification of concepts generally used as if they were thoroughly clear. . . . Each talk should last as long as the problems demand and the technical conditions allow. . . . As far as possible everyone shall participate in all the talks."

In January 1957, in response to a question of mine as to whether I might help him in some way in preparing his lecture on the unconscious, Buber responded:

> My notes on the Unconscious are not understandable to anyone except myself. I have written them in order to expand them later on, but I have not succeeded. The main point, about which I beg you not to speak to any one, is that I have been led by my thoughts deep in the problem of body and soul and that I have not yet found the language necessary to express what I mean. I think to elucidate the questions in the seminar as simply and slowly as possible without giving answers needing a new terminology. If a stenogram will be made, it may be useful to me in furthering formulation.

In February 1957, Farber informed Buber that a private foundation had agreed to provide the money ($25,000) for a documentary film to be taken of the seminar meetings if Buber agreed. In the most tactful manner possible, Farber suggested that although he was aware of the risks, such a record might be of great value to many seminaries and universities around the world that otherwise would never have the opportunity to see and hear Buber. "Too, I believe such a film would have historical significance." Farber had found Willard Van Dyke, maker of the documentary films *The River* and *The City,* who was willing to make it. Buber responded that to his very great regret he would have to say no this time. "My experience is (at any rate my experience with myself) that being filmed injures the spontaneity of the dialogue, and this is what I need most: full spontaneity. This was my motive when some days ago I declined the proposal of Dean Pike that a television film of a dialogue with me be made. I am sure you understand that the rejection of certain modern technical contrivances is necessary *in this connection.*" When Leslie Farber, Eugenia, and I went to the airport to meet Buber in New York, he said that he would not even agree to having the seminars taped and added, "In twenty-five years no one will even know what I am talking about!"

The overall title of the Fourth William Alanson White Memorial Lectures that Buber gave in Washington in March and April 1957 was "What Can Philosophical Anthropology Contribute to Psychiatry?" The first lecture, "Distance and Relation," was all right as Ronald Gregor Smith had translated it. But on the second, "Elements of the Interhuman," Buber and I had to work together more than sixteen hours revising Smith's translation. At one point we reached an impasse on the right punctuation to be used in breaking up one of Buber's overlong German sentences. "Grammar is not a subjective matter," Buber said to me and then, turning to Eugenia, who was present, he said, "Your husband is a very stubborn man." "You call *me* stubborn!" I exclaimed, when I finally realized that he was serious. Buber seemed to me by far the most stubborn person I had ever met. As Theodor Heuss expressed it more kindly a year later, in a letter to Buber on his eightieth birthday, "You have always been an inwardly independent man."

Buber began "Elements of the Interhuman" by distinguishing between the *social* in general and the *interhuman,* the latter term he had used fifty years before for the social psychological. Now, in contrast, he singled out the "interhuman" as the sphere in which persons are really present, or ready to be present, for each other. In pointing to this sphere, Buber rejected those existentialists who assert that the basic factor between men is that one is an object for the other, and he also stressed that the psychological is only the hidden accompaniment to the dialogue whose meaning is found in the "between." The most important new contribution of this lecture was the distinction Buber made between "being" and "seeming," the duality of which he saw as the essential problem of the sphere of the interhuman. These two are ideal types, commonly found mixed together but needing to be distinguished conceptually to recognize their anthropological importance. In both "being" and "seeming" one is concerned with influencing the other, but in "being" one proceeds from *what one really is,* whereas in "seeming" one proceeds from the *impression one wishes to make* on the other person by what one seems to be. It is our "privilege" as human beings to produce a "look" meant to appear like a spontaneous expression of our personal life.

> Where the semblance originates from the lie and is permeated by it, the interhuman is threatened in its very existence. It is not that someone utters a lie, falsifies some account. The lie I mean does not take place in relation to particular facts, but in relation to existence itself, and it attacks interhuman existence as such. There are times when a man, to satisfy some stale conceit, forfeits the great chance of a true happening between I and Thou.

Truth in the interhuman does not depend upon persons letting themselves go before each other or saying everything that comes to mind, but it does depend upon not letting seeming creep in between oneself and the other, upon communicating oneself to the other as what one is. "This is a question of the authenticity of the interhuman, and where this is not to be found, neither is the human element itself authentic." The temptation to seeming originates in our need to be confirmed by one another, our wish that they approve of what we think, what we do, and what we are. To yield to this temptation is our essential cowardice, to resist it our essential courage.

> This is not an inexorable state of affairs. . . . One can struggle to come to oneself—that is, to come to confidence in being. One struggles, now more successfully, now less, but never in vain, even when one thinks he is defeated. One must at times pay dearly for life lived from the being; but it is never too dear.

When we find it more and more repellent to be represented by ghosts, the will is stirred and strengthened in each of us to be confirmed in our being as what we really are and nothing else, "till the semblance vanishes and the depths of personal life call to one another." What

Buber did *not* accept was that anyone is "seeming" by nature, neither the child—"I have never known a young person who seemed to me irretrievably bad"—nor the older person who may have layer upon layer of seeming which can be penetrated only with great difficulty if at all. "Man as man can be redeemed."

That this is no easy optimism is shown by Buber's statement that the greater part of what is today called conversation among men would be more properly described as speechifying, as powerfully illustrated by Chekhov in his play *The Cherry Orchard.* Responding to Sartre's attempt to fix this blind alley as primal fate and to brand every thought of a breakthrough as reactionary romanticism, Buber characterized it as "the clearest expression of the wretched fatalism of modern man." Once again, in the midst of his most systematic philosophy, Buber injected an impassioned personal testimony:

> He who really knows how far our generation has lost the way of true freedom, of free giving between I and Thou, must himself, by virtue of the demand implicit in every great knowledge of this kind, practise directness—even if he were the only man on earth who did it—and not depart from it until scoffers are struck with fear, and hear in his voice the voice of their own suppressed longing.

Since it is only in partnership that a being can be perceived as a whole, the presupposition of genuine dialogue is that awareness in which one perceives the wholeness of the other as a person whose spirit, or dynamic center, stamps a person's every utterance, action, and attitude with the recognizable sign of uniqueness. But this perception of one's fellow as a whole, as a unity, and as unique is opposed by the analytical, reductive, and derivative look that predominates in our time. Modern man tries to take apart not only the so-called unconscious but the psychic stream itself, which can never, in fact, be grasped as object, to reduce the multifaceted person to a manageable equation, and to derive the dynamic central principle from some genetic formula. "An effort is being made today to destroy the mystery between man and man. The personal life, the ever near mystery, once the source of the deepest meanings, is leveled down." Buber was not attacking the analytical method indispensable to the human sciences, but that overstepping of the boundary which impairs the essentially different knowledge of the uniqueness of the human person. These were strong words to address to a school of psychiatry, even a relatively eclectic and open-minded group like the Washington School. The antidote to this modern attitude Buber found in "imagining the real"—"a bold swinging—demanding the most intensive stir-ring of one's being—into the life of the other."

In his discussion of the contrast between the educator (who helps the other unfold) and the propagandist (who, not trusting the truth, wishes to impose his conclusions), Buber made clear that he accepted the Aristotelian image of entelechy and the importance of individua-tion. But he made equally clear that individuation is only the indis-pensable personal stamp of all realization of human existence, a necessary presupposition but not as such ultimately essential. What *is* essential is the turning to the partner that "means" the other, and the highest to which that other is called, to which one brings oneself without reservation. This turning is frustrated when some of those present do not take an active part, as Buber illustrated with an anec-dote about a conversation between himself and two friends: two of the men engaged in the conversation fell into a duel because of the silent, but influential, presence of the three wives. The first man abandoned the usual composure and strength with which a "master of conversa-tion" speaks and instead scintillated, fought, and triumphed while the other friend, a man of noble nature and objective fairness, "lost." The "performance" may have been a success, but the dialogue was de-stroyed.

Although "What Is Common to All" was not one of Buber's memo-rial lectures, he did give it in Washington at that time and it is essential to a proper understanding of the third lecture, "Guilt and Guilt Feel-ings." When Buber first mentioned in November 1955 that he was writing a new chapter for the anthropology book, he identified it only as being "on dreaming and being awake." "What Is Common to All" is indeed the only remnant we possess of Buber's projected book on *The Place of Faith* with its concern for the special worlds of the schizo-phrenic. Only here he related it more basically to dreaming and to drugs. When he had completed it in December, he said that the writ-ing of it was particularly important for him and that he intended to use it in April 1956 for a lecture at the Sorbonne and in May at the University of London. About his experience in London he wrote: "The Heraclitus lecture seemed to impress thinking people in Paris and here very much. Here there was a very vital discussion, only questions and answers but with real immediacy." In July he reported that the lecture had met with an even greater enthusiasm: "The Munich press compared the effect with that of Schelling's Munich lectures." Buber referred to "What Is Common to All" as the "Hera-clitus lecture," because it starts from a fragment of Heraclitus that says, "One must follow that which is common." By this Heraclitus meant the single world that the waking have in common. In "What Is Common to All," Buber elaborated this to an anthropology of the "We" in which men build together a common cosmos through the common *logos*—the speech-with-meaning through which they bring their individual experiences into the common world. Although the dream itself has its rightful place in that withdrawnness inaccessible to the We, Heraclitus, and Buber after him, rejected those who act like sleepwalkers when they are awake—"that dreamlike refusal of the We through whose illusion the common day is broken asunder." In his early thought, Buber often compared Heraclitus's teaching of the swinging opposites to the yin and yang of Taoism, but in "What Is Common to All" Buber *contrasted* the common world of Heraclitus with the special world of Taoism and still more with the dream and deep dreamless sleep of the Hindu Vedanta. The latter's teaching of the identity of the self and the absolute contradicts the arch reality out of which all community stems—human meeting. In contrast to Aldous Huxley, who titled the first chapter of his *Perennial Philosophy* "Tat Twam Asi," Buber maintained that when taken seriously in the factual, waking continuity of intercourse with one another, the ancient Hindu "That art thou" becomes the postulate of an annihilation of the human person, one's own person as well as the other. The person in its uniqueness is essentially other than all that is over against it. Not when, as in the Upanishad, the husband says to the wife, "I am you," but when each says to the other, "I accept you as you are" do we first arrive at uncurtailed human existence.

In contrast to Heidegger, who interprets Heraclitus's *logos* as being the Word through which man brings Being into its unconcealment, Buber saw it as "the sensuous, meaningful word, the human talk which contains the meaning of the true." This means that though the logos cannot be identified with empty talk, it is nonetheless bound to "the word that is spoken" (to use the title of another chapter in *The Knowledge of Man*) and is the expression of the "between." It also means that the common cosmos, which is built up through this common speech-with-meaning, does not arise through people subordinating their personal existence to the collective but through each making his or her contribution to the common out of the uniqueness of person and situation. Therefore, an Amos or a Socrates who stands in tension with society is building the common cosmos far more than the person who merely conforms. The person must actualize in the common logos what is unique to him without curtailing that uniqueness and just through realizing his uniqueness work on the common cosmos. This working together is not like a team hitched to a great wagon but a strenuous tug of war, a battle and strife; yet it is a common battle that helps to build the common cosmos. "Out of the extremest tension, when it takes place in the service of the logos, arises ever anew the harmony of the lyre."

Buber devoted two sections to a critique of Aldous Huxley's counsel to use mescaline in order to get "chemical holidays" and to experience what the artist and mystic experience. Buber pointed out that the mystic does not seek the mystical experience but rather is seized by it. Buber relied heavily on the report of mescaline users that the bodily centers of contact tended to become numb. The world was transfigured in sheer glory of color for Huxley, but he did not want to have contact with his wife (a critique which Huxley himself later put into the mouth of one of the main characters of his novel *Island*). What concerned Buber was the illegitimacy of the arbitrary searching for mystical experience and the inauthenticity of that "situationlessness" which Buber held to be the true name of all the paradises which man creates for himself by chemical or other means. He compared them to the dream state and schizophrenia as in essence uncommunal, in contrast with every situation, even that of those who enter into solitude, which is enclosed in the community of logos and cosmos. "Man may master as he will his situation, to which his surroundings also belong; he may oppose it, he may alter it, he may, when it is necessary, exchange it for another; but the fugitive flight from the claim of the situation into situationlessness is no legitimate affair of man."

Even though Buber could not at that time have anticipated the widespread acceptance of Huxley's counsel that was to take place in the years to come, Huxley was by no means for Buber an isolated example. Though man has always had his experiences and thoughts as I, it is as We that he has constructed and developed a world out of his experiences and raised his ideas into the sphere of the between. The flight from the common cosmos in all its stages is the flight from the existential claim on the person who must verify himself in We and by the same token from the authentic spokenness of speech in whose realm a response is demanded. For the typical person of today, the flight from responsible personal existence has *polarized* into the general collective which takes from the person his responsibility *or* into the attitude of a self which "finds the great general indulgence in the security of being identical with the Self of being." The clearest mark of this kind of person is that he cannot really listen to the voice of another, since the other is only his object. "In our age," said Buber, "in which the true meaning of every word is encompassed by delusion and falsehood, and the original intention of the human glance is stifled by tenacious mistrust, it is of decisive importance to find again the genuineness of speech and existence as We." Without it humanity will not persist in existence.

Buber's distinction between existential guilt and neurotic guilt in his third William Alanson White Lecture was also a division into ideal types of two phenomena which in our everyday life are usually profoundly and even bewilderingly mixed. The latter are identical with the taboos about which Freud and others spoke, whether they be those of a culture or those internalized under the influence of the Oedipus complex. Such "guilt" is repressed into the unconscious, whereas existential guilt is remembered but not as guilt for which one is now responsible. Buber defined existential guilt as the guilt that one takes on oneself as a person in a personal situation and, another way of saying the same thing, as the injury that one inflicts on the common order of existence. This "objective" guilt cannot be understood as long as one thinks in the ordinary terms of individual versus society. Most people in our culture are so recently "freed" from the guilt imposed by social taboos that they tend to resist Buber's existential guilt as just another guise for the old restrictions that they feel they have thrown off. This is why "What Is Common to All" is essential to understanding "Guilt and Guilt Feelings." That objective order which one injures—*the order whose foundation we know and recognize as the foundation of our own and of all common human existence*—is nothing other than that common world built out of the common speech-with-meaning of which Buber speaks in "What Is Common to All." Existential guilt, therefore, is the result of a violation of the common which is also and by the same token an injury to the authenticity of one's own personal existence. That is why it is not a question of any society or religion or Platonic ideals being *imposed* on a person from without but of the very meaning of interhuman personal existence. We know this from the smaller groups to which we belong, such as the family and the community; for we know what it means to injure such a group by what we do or what we fail to do. The interhuman is not Harry Stack Sullivan's "interpersonal," which is as much I-It as I-Thou, as much impersonal social sense as meaningful reciprocity and partnership, but neither is it just the dyad of I and Thou. It is the group whose members are there for one another.

Buber reproved psychotherapy for the negative or indifferent attitude that it had so long taken toward the ontic character of guilt. For Freud, guilt feelings were to be understood as the consequence of dread of punishment, the child's fear of loss of love, or even a masochist's need for punishment. For Jung, guilt in the ontological sense can only be in one's relationship to oneself—one's failure in the process of individuation but not a reality in the relation between the human person and the world entrusted to him.

Existential guilt is not just a borderline case. It exists in some measure wherever authentic guilt feeling burns, "and the authentic guilt feeling is very often inextricably mingled with the problematic, the 'neurotic,' the 'groundless.'" The penetrating insight connected with existential guilt, to Buber, was the impossibility of recovering the original point of departure, the irreparability of what has been done, the irreversibility of lived time, "a fact that shows itself unmistakably in the starkest of all human perspectives, that concerning one's own death." "From no standpoint is time perceived so like a torrent as from the vision of the self in guilt," said this seventy-nine-year-old man who had already spoken five years before of that "dread of abandonment which is the foretaste of death."

Buber then enjoined psychotherapists to be concerned with existential guilt and the concrete situations out of which it arises, as for the most part they had not been until now. "The doctor must lay his hand in the wound of the order and learn: This concerns you." The doctor who becomes aware of a reality of the between that is inaccessible to any of the psychological categories, such as repression and becoming conscious, recognizes that the goal of healing has been transformed because the place and context of sickness has been changed from the within to the between. For such a therapist, all that has to be done becomes much more difficult but also radically real. Buber illustrated this with the story of Melanie, which he had referred to briefly before in "Healing through Meeting," his introductory essay to Hans Trüb's posthumous book of the same name. Melanie broke up an engagement and took over the man involved, only later to be herself supplanted by another woman. To friends who took her in at the time (perhaps the Bubers themselves), Melanie confessed her guilt "without glossing over the fact that it had arisen not out of a passion, but out of a fixed will." But later she went to a well-known psychoanalyst who liberated her from her feelings of disappointment and guilt so that she was able to lead a successful social and professional life. She mistook the social whirl for the world of friendship, and she saw her clients as persons to be seen through and manipulated. Her artificial heart comfortably took the place of her paining and admonishing one. As a result, she lost the chance to become the person that her existential guilt called her to become.

The psychotherapist is no pastor of souls who mediates salvation but only someone who furthers healing, but where a person is sick from existential guilt, like Oscar Loerke, Viktor von Weizsäcker, and Hans Carossa, all three of whom suffered from having given too little resistance to the Nazi regime, the therapist may and should guide the patient to where an essential help of the self can begin. However, when the therapist has guided the person to the watchtower, it is the patient himself who must ascend it and see the way that is the right one for him to walk. "For at this high station all becomes personal in the strictest sense." The therapist must recognize that there exists real guilt, "fundamentally different from all the anxiety-induced bugbears that are generated in the cavern of the unconscious." He must come to this knowledge not out of any religious tradition but must allow it to arise anew from the historical and biographical self-experience of the generation living today, which knows in what measure we have become guilty. "Under the schooling of this knowledge, which is becoming ever more irresistible, we learn anew that guilt exists." It is our objective relationship to others that makes it possible for us to expand our environment into a world. It is our share in the human order of being, the share for which each of us bears responsibility. Injuring our relationship to others means injuring at this place the human order of being. It also means that we remain responsible for this injury; for "no one other than he who inflicted the wound can heal it."

Buber distinguished between three different spheres in which guilt can be atoned: that of the law, that of ethical guilt and conscience, and that of religious guilt. Of these three only the middle sphere, that of conscience, is the proper province of the psychotherapist. Buber held that the psychotherapist, while not able to go the whole way with the patient, must know the three stages of that way—first, the existential illumination of guilt, in which one says that I who am so different from the me of that time am nonetheless the person who is responsible; second, the perseverance in that illumination; and third, the reparation of the injured order-of-being either at the point where one injured it, if the person is still alive, or restoring the order-of-being injured by one through an active devotion to the world. At this point Buber ventured a bold interpretation of Stavrogin's confession—

inauthentic because merely literary—and of Joseph K's refusal to confess. The first, from Dostoevsky's novel *The Devils* (*The Possessed*, 1875), and the second from Kafka's novel *The Trial* (1915), represented to Buber two stages in modern man's flight from real guilt. The first says one is not guilty because one is superior and exempt from the common law, and the second says that there is no real guilt since we are all merely men here and there is no higher court. Reaffirming Pascal's dictum that man's greatness is bound up with his misery, Buber defined man as "the being who is capable of becoming guilty and is capable of illuminating his guilt."

The seminars were held in the Cathedral School next to the Washington (Episcopal) Cathedral. Participating in the group were prominent psychoanalysts from the Washington School as well as from as far away as San Francisco, plus one or two theologians, like Bernard Mollegan of the Virginia Theological Seminary, and some philosophers.* During the intermission in the last of the evenings of seminars, the noted neuropsychiatrist David Rioch said, "Now I'm going to get Buber. I'm going to ask him about God." When the seminar resumed, David Rioch asked, "What can you say about God in healing?" Buber walked over to Rioch, faced him, and said: "In that moment when the name of God is mentioned, most human circles break asunder as persons without knowing it. In that moment the commonness of thinking—the fact of thinking together—is disrupted. The difference between the world with God and without is so enormous that a discussion of God must be divisive except in a group united by a real common faith. People say God without meaning reality, merely as a sublime convention of the cultured person." Of all Buber did and said during his whole stay in Washington, his refusal to speak about God was what impressed David Rioch most!

Buber accepted what modern psychology meant by the unconscious insofar as it is taken literally as a hidden sphere which has real effects. But he rejected the understanding of the unconscious by Freud, Jung, and most other psychoanalysts, namely, that the unconscious is psychic in nature. Instead he put forward the idea that it may be just the wholeness of the person before the separation and elaboration into the physical and the psychic, the "body" and the "soul," the outer senses and the inner sense. This implies that the unconscious is not just a psychic deep freeze in which dreams and ideas dwell in already psychic form ready to float up to the surface when the repression is

---

*See Note A in Sources for Chapter 9.

overcome. A dream is an elaboration by the psyche of an event in the unconscious which we can never know in itself. What is more, its form and meaning are in important part formed by our interpersonal and interhuman relationships, the most important of which, for the patient in therapy, is the relationship with the therapist himself. Buber told a dream in which at one moment he walked forward and a wind was blowing into his face. In his dream he said to himself, "Ah, this is the other time." "I felt not only the one line of time going on from birth to death," he explained, "but also as if there were another line of time coming toward me, striking me. Upon reflection I thought, 'Oh, this is the same thing with space as with time.'" In dreams that we remember, Buber claimed, there is sometimes an interposition of spaces, meaning that here things are going on and here there are other things, without intermingling. Here they are, so to speak, two planes, two space dimensions going on, one in the face of the other. Even more curious are appearances in time. Buber also told of a dream which went on until at one moment he felt in the dream, "It is not as it should be—what now?" It was as if he were writing a story and thought of changing it. "From this moment on the same scene occurred again and again with some variants. Finally, I succeeded in changing the last scene and it continued. This recurred many times." "There was a time in my life when I knew very much of dreams and then less and less," Buber said, "so now it is only remembering."

Buber also spoke of lying awake in a state of unusual lucidity after being asleep. "I remember . . . nights of extraordinary lucidity without sleep." In these nights the sort of problem solving takes place that also occurs in sleep. "It is an extraordinary wakefulness—much more than in the common world. This is not dream or sleep." This may be a hint of what replaced the mystic hours for Buber after he gave them up. David Rioch asked Buber if he knew anyone who had had a night of lucidity without having worked diligently on a problem beforehand. "Yes, myself," Buber responded, "once or twice as a surprise, as a continuous surprise, and it determined the course of my other thought afterward."

Buber told of a schizophrenic friend whose illness he followed for years. The man had a wife with astonishing willpower who wanted to see him recover once for all. She visited him in those catatonic moments when he assumed attitudes, positions, and movements some of which are not possible to a normal person, and she actually succeeded in making the same movements as he. He let her into his particular world, and she left the world that is common to all. To the same degree that he let her in, he came out. Twenty-five years later the man came to visit Buber and told him that he had been normal for a series of years—a professor in the university respected by all—whereas his wife no longer ventured to go out of her house or even leave her bed by day. They talked together for hours, but when Buber left, the professor told Paula that he had been very useful to the British during the war through his connection with the stars which enabled him to tell them when Nazi war planes would come over! His seeming normality was only adjustment and not the healing of the "atrophied personal center." Later he became a professor in the Soviet Union. One thing Buber said then which has always remained with me is that the so-called normal person does not prefer the real world to the world of the schizophrenic because it is a *better* world—the world of the schizophrenic may be better—but because it is real.

Buber looked forward to a new, more musical type of therapist who would not simply follow the theories of his or her school but would practice "obedient listening" and discover the right method and response for each particular person and each particular dream. You would not interpret a poem by the same method as a novel or the poems of Keats by the same method as those of Eliot, Buber observed. "The real master responds to uniqueness."

In the strongest illness manifesting itself in the life of a person, the highest potentiality of this person is manifesting itself in a negative form. If this is so, confirming the person *as he is* is only the first step for the therapist. She must also take the other person in her dynamic existence, her specific potentiality. In the present lies hidden what *can become.* The patient's potentiality makes itself felt to the therapist as that which the therapist would most confirm. Trying to understand the implications of his new approach to the unconscious, I asked Buber whether, if the unconscious is not a psychic sphere *within,* it might not have *more* direct contact with and part in the interhuman than the psychic. If that were so, there would be an immediate relationship between two unconsciouses rather than one filtered through the psyche of each person, as we usually imagine. Buber's response confirmed my insight:

> If the unconscious is that part of the existence of a person in which the realms of body and soul are not dissociated, then the relationship between two persons would mean the relationship between two non-divided existences. The highest moment of relation would be what we call unconscious. The unconscious should have, may have, will have, more influence in the interhuman than the conscious. For example, in

shaking hands, if there is real desire to be in touch, the contact is not bodily or psychic, but a unity of one and the other. The unconscious as such does not enter easily into action. . . . The unconscious sometimes leads to a half-articulated exclamation which all the prepared words cannot, however. The voice becomes the direct instrument of the unconscious in this case.

Buber told Farber that as a young man he wanted to be a therapist, but he found the psychiatric clinics of that time, where the patients were displayed before an audience, abhorrent. Although Buber took a different vocational path, he acquired over the years a deep insight into psychotherapy. Farber himself testifies that he has never read a better description of mania than that "flight into pseudo-decision" of which Buber wrote in *Good and Evil*. Social puberty lasts much longer than people think, Buber remarked to Farber—sometimes into middle and old age. Buber also told Farber that he found Sullivan's approach to guilt superficial. "I have been concerned with guilt all my life while he treats guilt just as a form of anxiety." Freud struck Buber as a person temperamentally given to silence, and this is how Buber struck Farber. Siegfried Bernfeld, whom Farber knew in San Francisco in the last years of Bernfeld's life, belonged to the second circle around Freud and was Buber's secretary for a number of years. Bernfeld had what Buber regarded as "a fetishism for interpretation."

The seminars closed on a poignant note. Margaret Rioch asked Buber whether there is an essential difference between the teacher-pupil relationship and the therapist-patient one. Buber pointed out that both have in common what he later called the "normative limitation of mutuality," namely, that the helper experiences the relationship from her own side *and* that of the person helped. If the pupil or patient could do this, there would be no need of therapy. But Buber also claimed that "there exists a specific, rather problematic but nonetheless legitimate, superiority of the therapist" which the teacher does not have. "The therapist in the most favorable cases can really heal," whereas "the teacher is a rather tragic person because in most cases learning is fragmentary." "The therapist is fragmentary too. There is no complete development of the person," Margaret Rioch rejoined. "The existential element means bringing the patient to self-healing, which is the same task as teaching," Buber conceded.

Buber spoke of Jung as assuming a nonphenomenological yet psychical reality in his treatment of the unconscious. This seemed to Buber illegitimate. We know from continuous life-experience only about being, which embraces the physical and the psychic. "The assumption of a psyche that exists as something exists in space should be either a metaphor or an entirely metaphysical thesis about the nature of being for which we have no basis at all in experience." But if Jung dealt wrongly with the problem of the unconscious, Freud did not deal with it at all. Buber saw Freud, like Marx, as one of the great simplifiers; i.e., "one who places a general concept in place of the ever-renewed investigation of reality." He treated a new aspect of reality as if it were the solution of one of the riddles of being. "Fifty years of psychotherapeutic thought have been based on this danger- ous manner of thinking. Now this period is at an end." When we drove together on the way to Chestnut Lodge, Buber said to me, "If you live long enough, and I hope you will, for I love life, you will see a time when Freud is no longer held to be important." He predicted that by the twenty-first century there might no longer be "psychia- trists" and the separation of mind and body implicit in that designa- tion.

At Chestnut Lodge, Buber met Frieda Fromm-Reichmann, whose illness had prevented her from taking part in the seminars. She asked Buber if she could talk with him alone and when she did so, later, confided in him her great, almost despairing loneliness. Buber ad- vised her to go spend several months in a small town where she was not known so that she might experience ordinary relationships with people. Instead she followed the advice of a colleague who said that she should go somewhere people knew her. A year later she died. When Leslie Farber gave a memorial lecture for her a year or two later he titled it "The Therapeutic Despair."

The main activity at Chestnut Lodge was listening to a long case report given by one of the psychiatrists who was himself of Hasidic ancestry. He had picked for his case a young woman of mystical and poetic leanings, clearly assuming that this was what would interest Buber. But Buber, without commenting on her poetry or mysticism, only said, "I do not see the line of therapy in this case." About her he asked what he asked of his schizophrenic friend: Was it merely an adjustment or did real existential healing, healing through meeting, take place in which not just a certain part of the patient, but the very roots of the patient's being are healed?

Once after I had given a lecture at the Washington School of Psychiatry, which Buber attended, Leslie Farber asked Buber whether he had had such energy when he was my age. "Oh, much more," he said smiling. "Once when I was giving a lecture I noticed that some of my friends who were sitting in front were looking weary. I learned later that I had talked for three hours!"

When Martin and Paula flew to Michigan in mid-April 1957, they had a reunion with their granddaughter Judith, who was now the wife of Professor Joseph Agassi, a philosopher of science under the influence of Karl Popper. (She said of herself, in the language of Jacob Taubes, that she was more critic than disciple of her grandfather, but later as a professor of political science she took an interest in his social philosophy.)

A number of notable scholars took part in the panels surrounding Buber at Michigan, among them Kenneth Boulding, the economist; Ross Snyder and Perry LeFevre of the Divinity School of the University of Chicago; and R. W. B. Lewis, who was then at Rutgers. The most notable event at this conference was the dialogue between Buber and the noted American psychologist Carl R. Rogers, founder of the "nondirective" or "client-centered" approach to psychotherapy. There were a number of striking resemblances between him and Buber, and during the dialogue these resemblances emerged, but along with them some important differences.

The dialogue took place in the Rackham Auditorium at the University of Michigan in front of an audience of four hundred, with the understanding that there would be no question period. Buber consented to its being taped, as a result of which it is preserved verbatim as the Appendix to *The Knowledge of Man*. Rogers's opening question was amusing: "How have you lived so deeply in interpersonal relationships and gained such an understanding of the human individual, without being a psychotherapist?" Buber answered Rogers's question autobiographically by telling about the time he studied psychiatry at the Psychiatrische-Klinik. But what was most important was his inclination to meet each person, to change something in the other, and also to let himself be changed by *him*. In 1918, when he was forty, he realized how the war had influenced him through compelling him to "imagine the real," and he gave as his main illustration of this his response to Landauer's death. From then on, especially in his meetings with young people, he felt that he had to give something more than just his inclination to exchange thoughts and feelings. "I had to give the fruit of an experience."

What emerged most clearly in Buber's dialogue with Rogers was his concern with situation and with limits, even the limits of genuine dialogue. This led to the first issue between them. Rogers insisted that there was a complete mutuality between him and his clients. "I see you *want to* be on the same plane," Buber said. "But there is also a certain situation which may sometimes be tragic and even more terrible than what we call tragic. You *cannot* change this." Buber asked Rogers whether he had ever worked with schizophrenics and paranoiacs and was not surprised when Rogers answered in the negative. To Buber, paranoia set a limit for dialogue.

> I can talk to a schizophrenic as far as he is willing to let me into his particular world that is his own. . . . But the moment he shuts himself in, I cannot go on. And the same, only in a terrible, terrifyingly powerful way, is the case with a paranoiac. . . . He does not open himself and does not shut himself. He *is* shut. . . . And I feel this terrible fate very strongly because in the world of normal men there are analogous cases, when a sane man behaves, not to everyone, but to some people *just* so, as if he had been shut in and the problem is if he can be opened, if he can open himself . . . this is a problem for human beings in general.

"Out of a certain fullness," Buber said to Rogers, "you give him what he wants in order for him to be, just for this moment, so to speak, on the same plane with you." But this is a situation that lasts not even for an hour but for minutes, minutes made possible by the therapist. At one point in this interchange Rogers remarked, "Now I'm wondering who is Martin Buber, you or me," to which Buber responded, "I am not 'Martin Buber' in quotation marks!"

"When you get to what is deepest in the individual, that is the very aspect that can most be trusted to be constructive or to tend toward socialization or toward the development of better interpersonal relationships," said Rogers. "What you say can be trusted . . . stands in polar relation to what can be least trusted in this man," said Buber. "When I grasp him more broadly and more deeply than before, . . . I see how the worst in him and the best in him are dependent on one another . . . I may be able to help him just by helping him to change the relation between the poles. The poles are not good and evil, but yes and no, acceptance and refusal. Perhaps we can even strengthen the force of direction in him because this polarity is very often directionless." All existential relationship begins with accepting the other as he is, said Buber. For that reason it *cannot* be an "unconditional positive affirmation of everything he says, does, and is." But confirming means accepting the whole potentiality of the other and even making a decisive difference in his potentiality. We can recognize in the other the person he has been *created* to become and confirm him in relation to this potentiality that is meant by him so that it can answer the reality of life. "Just by my accepting love, I discover in you what you are meant to become." Buber said that he experienced cases where he had to help the other against himself, help him to find his unique personal direction.

> The first thing of all is that he trusts me. Yes, life has become baseless for him. He cannot tread on firm soil, on firm earth. He is, so to speak, suspended in the air. . . . What he wants is a being not only whom he can trust as a man trusts another, but a being that gives him now the certitude that there *is* a soil, there *is* an existence. The world is not condemned to deprivation, degeneration, destruction. The world *can* be redeemed. *I* can be redeemed because there is this trust. And if this is reached, now I can help this man even in his struggle against himself. And this I can do only if I distinguish between accepting and confirming.

After the dialogue, Buber said to me, "I was very kind to him. I could have been much sharper." But he also said that Rogers had really brought himself as a person and that it was because of this that there had been a real dialogue. In fact as a result, he canceled the last paragraph in the manuscript of "Elements of the Interhuman" in which he had stated that it was impossible to have a public dialogue. This canceled paragraph read:

> In our time when the understanding of the essence of genuine dialogue has become so rare, its presuppositions are so fundamentally misunderstood by the false sense of public life that it is imagined that such a dialogue can be carried on before a public of interested listeners, with the help of the appropriate publicity. But a public debate, no matter how "high level," cannot be spontaneous, or immediate or unreserved; a radio discussion put on to be listened to is separated by a chasm from genuine dialogue.

Buber was very possibly thinking of the proposal by Robert Maynard Hutchins, former president of the University of Chicago, to bring together spiritual leaders for a "dialogue" in public. When he returned from Michigan to New York, he saw Hutchins again at a banquet and commented afterward that he was more like a Roman than a Greek because he stood on his dignity. "A great man does not stand on his dignity."

The last major event in Buber's second visit to the United States was a seminar on biblical faith at Columbia University arranged by Jacob Taubes for May 1957. The seminar was restricted to the faculties from a number of universities and colleges in the area around New York City. Reinhold Niebuhr, James Muilenburg, Joseph Campbell, Walter Kaufmann, Malcolm Diamond, Michael Wyschogrod, and quite a number of other eminent scholars from different fields were present. Buber dealt with the interpretation of a number of verses, particularly from the New Testament. At one point he remarked that the passage in Matthew that came directly after "Since the days of John the Baptist men have tried to take the Kingdom of Heaven by violence" did not seem to him genuine. When asked for his reason, Buber said, "It is merely my own subjective feeling." After several continued to press him, he finally stated, "I do not hear the voice of Jesus in it." At this James Muilenburg became very red in the face and pounded the table, saying "That's pure subjectivity!" "But I told you," said Buber mildly.*

Michael Wyschogrod, an Orthodox Jewish professor of philosophy who was very much concerned with Kierkegaard and Heidegger, suggested a connection between the Holocaust and the spiritual break that arose in Judaism since the Enlightenment and that produced such a terrible falling away. Buber went over to Wyschogrod and said to him, with utter sincerity, emphasizing every word, "I could not believe in a God who would condemn six million people to death because of their sins." At another time during the seminars, Joseph Campbell asked Buber, "Is this God of Israel the same as Shiva?" Buber, who did not know Campbell and his interest in universal mythological motifs, responded that only God can liberate the religions from their exile and melt down all the images of God into the one imageless God. Buber was referring to a stance that he had already adopted more than thirty years earlier when he founded *Die Kreatur,* the only journal in Germany (or anywhere else for that matter) to be coedited by a Jew, a Protestant, and a Catholic:

> Every religion has its origin in a revelation. No religion is absolute truth, none is a piece of heaven that has come down to earth. Each religion is a human truth. That means it represents the relationship of a particular human community as such to the Absolute. Each religion is a house of the human soul longing for God, a house with windows and without a door; I need only open a window and God's light penetrates; but if I make a hole in the wall and break out, then I have not only become houseless but a cold light surrounds me that is not the light of the living God. Each religion is an exile into which man is driven; here he is in exile more clearly than elsewhere because in his relationship to

*See Note B in Sources for Chapter 9.

God he is separated from the men of other communities; and not sooner than in the redemption of the world can we be liberated from the exiles and brought into a common world of God. But the religions that know that are bound together in common expectation; they can call to one another greetings from exile to exile, from house to house through the open windows.

Later I told Buber about Campbell's universalistic approach to religion (He had not yet written *The Masks of God,* but his approach was well known to me from his book *The Hero with a Thousand Faces* and my years of association with him as a colleague at Sarah Lawrence College) and that Campbell had edited some of the books of Heinrich Zimmer, the German scholar on Indian religion. "Ah, I knew it," Buber exclaimed, meaning that he sensed where Campbell was coming from. He and Paula talked warmly of Zimmer, whom they knew and who had married the daughter of Buber's friend Hugo von Hofmannsthal.

After the seminars Malcolm Diamond wrote Buber that the last evening was unforgettable. "I have learned much from the encounters, especially as concerns your manner of dealing with the Bible. You have a unique ability to understand and respond to persons who pose questions about your work out of the most varied inclinations, points of view, and kinds of language. No one who was there can forget it."

At the time of the Columbia seminars Buber met one evening with several prominent theologians and religious philosophers, including Paul Tillich, Reinhold Niebuhr, and Abraham Heschel, and a number of graduate students from Union Theological Seminary and Columbia University. Professor Benjamin Nelson kept interrupting Buber's talk with questions and would not let him proceed. After this had gone on for fifteen minutes, Buber said, "Dr. Nelson. We have a fundamental difference. You wish to create God in your image. I wish Him to create me in His image." Grasping the bottle of citron that he was drinking, Buber thereupon walked out and the students present were deprived of the exchange between great minds that they had been so eagerly looking forward to.

CHAPTER 10

Last Visit to America and Paula's Death

IN JUNE 1957, at a celebration in Stuttgart in honor of Hesse's eightieth birthday, Buber gave a speech titled "Hermann Hesse's Service to the Spirit." This speech not only expressed the warm friendship between the two men that had lasted for over forty years but also Buber's understanding of Hesse's special place in the destiny of the spirit in our time. The true storyteller like Hesse narrates landscape, concepts, and even the happenings of the soul as unbroken event. Buber saw Hesse as entering into the service of the spirit just forty years before, during the First World War. "In the middle of his life the hand of the spirit had torn the poet Hesse out of carefree storytelling and compelled him to report epically wrestlings of the spirit, its dangers and risks, that is as events of the life of man with man." In our age the destiny of the spirit has manifested itself as the crisis of its relation to life. "Overpowered by storming and demanding life, the spirit contested its own office as the finder of truth and the speaker of law; it set life free and wanted now only to be its interpreter." What emancipated life would do with its freedom, Buber laconically remarked, we have fully experienced since then.

Before that took place, Hesse, in the First World War, wrote his inflammatory novel *Demian* in which the creative spirit spoke in the name of the unbound life, rebelled against the tyranny of an absolute morality, and glorified sovereign individuation. It is no accident that in *Demian* Hesse's championing of a sovereign Cain against an obsequious Abel is joined to the proclamation of that gnostic God Abraxas already found in an early writing of Jung's, the being who "has the symbolic task of uniting the divine and the diabolical" and thus possesses in eternal fullness that "integration of the evil" for which Jung calls. Yet it is precisely with this daring breakthrough, preceded by an equally audacious rupture, that Hesse's service of the spirit begins.

This does not mean that Buber's judgment of Abraxas when encountered in Hesse's work was any kinder than when encountered in Jung's. The way of the human spirit always commenced with rupture and breakthrough, but everything depends upon the direction then taken:

> One cannot go back, and one may not remain standing there where one has reached, for he who remains in the rupture forfeits the life of the spirit. In the search for the living God one must now and again destroy the images that have become unworthy in order to create room for a new one. But the Abraxas is no image of God at all but a complex concept . . . of a fusion of good and evil of ultimate validity. One must turn one's back on it if one wants to go forward. For a being that simply represents and legitimizes ourselves, elevated into the unconditional, is not of a divine nature.

And in his next novel, *Siddhartha,* Hesse did turn his back on it. In *Siddhartha* the rebellion of spirit against spirit is not for the mere release of elemental forces repressed by the spirit but for the spirit's sake in order that what it may love in the world and what it must despise should no longer be prescribed. Between the world of *Demian* and that of *Siddhartha* stands the beginning of the cruel lesson of our age: "that life, when it is no longer obedient to the spirit, rages against itself and destroys itself." Siddhartha embraces "sin" as a general essence, but when faced with the exploitation of the weak by the strong, he takes up his stand against evil. "In an age in which the spiritual have in so many different ways made themselves the slaves of the holders of power" (Buber was undoubtedly thinking of Hans

Carossa, among others), Hesse "has fearlessly confirmed the spirit's free holding of its ground."

After *Steppenwolf,* which Buber characterized as an "intermezzo appassionato," an inner biography going back in a strange way to the phase of the rupture, Hesse began his ascent anew with *Narcissus and Goldmund,* which Buber called "a hard and basically melancholy work" but also "a grandly conceived dialogical relationship" "between the spirit which is ever anew at the point of starting out, roving, vehemently grasping" and shaping what is grasped into image "and the ascetic spirit, devoted to thought, answering life with the idea." Narziss is wrong when he says to his antagonist and friend, the sculptor Goldmund, that spirit cannot live in nature, only against it, as its opponent. Only the two taken together, the one who submits to nature and the one who resists it, are the spirit. Only the life of the artist and not that of the monk is really narrated. This is a guilt toward the thinking spirit which Hesse compensated grandly in *Magister Ludi.*

What links Narziss with *The Journey to the East* and *Magister Ludi* is the "law of service," the service of the spirit. The communal reality of *Journey to the East* and the great peace that prevails in *Magister Ludi* could not have been attained otherwise than in striding through the fire of the opposites, which continues to glow, transformed, in the heart of the Journey and the Bead Game. In these two works the category of "We," the communal reality of the spirit which builds worlds out of the word, is included in Hesse's work. In the Bead Game, in which the total contents and values of our culture, music and mathematics, art and science, are perfected through the most extreme high discipline of the spirit, Joseph Knecht works for the spirit "with a great, never-slackening devotion and in a serenity that nothing can trouble." Yet he comes to understand the Bead Game as an avoidance of the responsibility of the spirit for the world of living and suffering men entrusted to it. Giving up his high office, Joseph Knecht leaves the order and, to win the trust of the son of his friend whom he wants to tutor, follows him in a precarious swimming race and drowns. "When I read this conclusion of the splendidly executed book," confessed Buber, without reference to his own role as a spiritual leader of the Jews in an age of Hitler and Arab-Jewish conflict, "I am touched each time in a strange fashion by the conception of the sacrificial death, which, in Knecht's story of an imaginary earlier incarnation, the rain maker of a matriarchal tribe takes on himself because he has not averted a cosmic catastrophe."

Hermann Hesse has not only made more visible the obstacle-ridden path that can lead to a new wholeness and unity but, also as a person, has always interceded for the wholeness and unity of the human being. "The servants of the spirit in all the world together call out a great greeting of love to you," Buber concluded. "Everywhere where one serves the spirit, you are loved." Unfortunately, Hesse himself was not present to hear these stirring words. In November he wrote Buber that neither Buber nor Hesse's friends in Germany had sent Buber's speech to him and only now had he succeeded in obtaining a copy. Hesse refused to believe, he said, that Buber held against him his not having been present. "Beyond the physical hindrances which have not allowed me to travel for years, I have had reasons enough for not having visited my home for a quarter of a century," Hesse explained, referring perhaps to that protest against German militarism that had made him leave Germany for Switzerland in the first place. "Your speech made a strong impression on me," Hesse went on, confessing that he had been too much taken up with artistic problems of form and representation to have been able to recognize what Buber had found in his books. But now that life and work gave him sufficient distance, he agreed with Buber entirely. "The restlessness and the desire that drove me from book to book were, in fact, just as you have seen them. And how much the tenor of your speech, its warmth and friendship, moved and gladdened me I hardly need to say!"

It was about this time, May 1957, that Buber commented on the marble head that the American Jewish sculptress Erna Weill had chiseled of him while he was in New York: "The 'Buber' of Erna Weill is too 'monumental' for my feeling of myself." Today this head of Buber is to be found at the Hebrew University in Jerusalem.

In October, Buber received a letter from Mascha Kaleko, a lyrical and satiric writer of prose and verse who in 1938 left Berlin for New York, where she married the composer and conductor Hemyo Vinaver. She asked Buber for advice as to how to deal with the young persons whom she directed to Hasidism but who invariably returned replying, "Now we have read your Buber and even Scholem—where do we go from here?" Her reply that there are no "directions for use" never satisfied them, for in Zen and Yoga they found something to "do." "Is it so that serious study of the Kabbala is only possible via the traditional way?" she asked. "And doubly denied to women?" "Is there really no 'practical' way of practice and meditation that leads to the world of the Jewish mystic?" she concluded.

"A generally teachable 'way' does not exist," Buber replied to

Kaleko, speaking not for Jewish mysticism in general but for Hasidism, where he pointed her to such little stories as "The Way" and "The Most Important," which emphasize the present and the unique. Buber suggested for the young people about whom she wrote that they each, in the specific situations of their personal life, hallow their relations with the beings and things which they meet. "Any other instructions prove sooner or later—at times all too late—to be illusory. All 'instructions' lead to false security, which is worse than genuine despair." "I have written you as hard and severely as I have," Buber concluded, "because you mentioned your twenty-year-old son."

In October 1957, Buber wrote me, "Again for some time I had no news from you. I think you are overworked, which is not a good thing at all." But in November he said, "You would do me a favor if you could, in spite of your being overworked, send me regularly short reports about what is going on. I have such a tremendous lot of work to finish before going to Princeton [where he had been invited for the spring of 1958 on a research fellowship] that I must divide beforehand my time much more rationally than I am used to," and two days later he added: "For the first time I am not succeeding in coordinating the time *disponible* and the work that must be done before a certain time (in this case, my departure). Of course, much time is taken up by people wanting to talk to me, but I cannot change my way of receiving them all. And all the letters to be answered!"

I wrote Buber before he came about the possibility of the eight "Talks on Judaism" being translated into English and he replied that he had no objection. "The eighth of them I think even of some importance just now for the young American Jew." This was the one on "Herut," or freedom. Buber was actively concerned about the translation of *The Kingship of God* and was ready to give it to another press if Harpers could not do it in the foreseeable future. "The whole matter rests on one point," Buber asserted. "I want to assist with the translation of this book as I did with some other books, and I cannot work as quickly as in former years. I think this book a rather important one." A week later he asked me kindly to settle the "Kingship of God" affair for him. "The publishers cannot understand, but you will, that I want to do something just for this book." The book was finally translated by Richard Scheimann, who met Buber at the home of his and my teacher Joachim Wach, when Buber came to Chicago in 1951 and who, now, years later, repaid his sense of Buber's presence—"slowly and softly, gazing intently into the eyes of each one who addressed him . . . a genuine charismatic"—by undertaking this arduous task.

The book itself was published in 1966, after Buber's death, but Buber set the guidelines for the translation ("as literally as possible") reading and commenting on the translation of the text, though not the notes.

In response to the numerous invitations to Buber to lecture and give seminars while he was in Princeton, he said, in December, "I have to do a tremendous lot of work in Princeton and cannot go away for a week of seminar or the like. Princeton means for me quiet and work with very few and short interruptions." He agreed to give a public lecture for Princeton and one at the Union Theological Seminary in New York, but aside from that, he refused all other invitations. One invitation which he accepted came from me in the name of the American Friends of Ihud, a group which I had chaired since 1956. In 1956, I had been approached by Joseph Ben-David, a young man from Israel who came in the interest of Ihud and proposed that we should start an American group to support it. With indefatigable energy he built up a circle around him, including a number of Jewish leaders of a variety of persuasions—pacifist, socialist, anti-Zionist, Zionist—along with some non-Jewish adherents. In the early stages these included a baron and a society lady who seemed to be the baron's inseparable companion. I wrote Buber expressing my concern about all this, and he responded from London in May 1956:

> Your opinion of Ben-David is correct. He is an honest man, but a radical ideologist, who does not recognize reality and consequently does not know how to deal with it. When he went to America, I warned him he cannot represent Ihud.   Corbett and the Baron came to see me in Paris. I tried to explain things to them, particularly that there is no sense in becoming a political party. I spoke precisely and rather severely, but with Corbett one cannot argue, she is much too "personal." At the end she declared she wants to go to Jerusalem. So I was obliged to write a long letter to Ernst Simon, warning and preparing. I have not heard anything from her since. The Baron seems to be sincere, but she is the very demon of enthusiasm.

In August, I wrote Buber again as well as Simon, this time expressing my anxiety at what seemed to me a predominantly anti-Zionist tone within the Executive Committee of the "American Friends" of Ihud, an Israeli organization all of whose adherents had been and were staunch Zionists. This was of particular concern to me, since from the outset I had been asked to be the chairman of the organization and had accepted this position. The program of the American Friends of Ihud was unexceptionable. But the workings of the organization in practice, including our Executive Committee, at times made me feel as if we were closer in fact to the American Council of Judaism, with its strong anti-Zionist position, than to Ihud, something that was perhaps inevitable due to the politicization and polarization of the issue in America, where it seemed unthinkable, in 1956, that people could be *both* Zionist and concerned with Arab-Jewish rapprochement, as were Magnes, Buber, Smilansky, Simon, Henrietta Szold, and other leaders of Ihud in Israel. Buber's response was unequivocal:

> The problem you put before me has only one possible solution. The Friends of Ihud, as such, cannot differ in their political declarations from those of Ihud. An American society for promoting friendship between Jews and Arabs, or the like, may publicly say what they want to say, but a society using the name of Ihud is particularly bound and particularly responsible. For me at least no discussion is possible on this point. I shall raise it expressly in the next meeting of our board.

In his next letter, after the meeting of the Board of Ihud, Buber wrote me that Ernst Simon would communicate with me when in New York. "What he says will be said in my name too."

The American Friends of Ihud decided to hold a great celebration in memory of the tenth anniversary of the death of Judah Magnes, and in honor of Buber's eightieth birthday, while Buber was in America during the spring of 1958. The purpose of the meeting was to raise money for *Ner*. Buber agreed to speak on this occasion, although he wrote me in January 1958: "I have the impression you think I can give a lecture on the *Ner* meeting. I cannot prepare anything, but I am willing to answer freely what you or anyone may say or ask." This was not possible, because the meeting was held at the Community Church in New York before several thousand people. Roger Baldwin spoke, as did Erich Fromm, both members of our Board of Directors. Before the opening of the meeting, in front of a section of the audience, the vice-chairman of the American Friends of Ihud, Rabbi Isidor Hoffman, Jewish chaplain at Columbia and a leading American pacifist, insisted that Erich Fromm speak last and not Buber; otherwise "the whole work of the American Friends of Ihud would be ruined." Although I greatly admired Erich Fromm, I could not accede to this, since it was Buber who represented the spirit of Ihud, if anyone did, whereas Fromm was known to be anti-Zionist in his views.* Buber's speech lasted for almost an hour and was an ambi-

*See Note in Sources for Chapter 10.

tious attempt to present an overview of the whole Zionist movement with the split between those who wanted to achieve Zion by diplomatic means and those like Buber and his friends, who believed in organic colonization *and* in Jewish-Arab good-neighborliness and cooperation. In the course of this overview Buber suggested that *some* of the Jews in Palestine had chosen to use Hitler's methods—to place their trust in power, rather than in the spirit, in their attempts to build Zion. It was precisely this passage that was picked up by the Jewish press in America and in Israel, and was severely criticized. From Soglio, Italy, on his way back to Jerusalem, Buber informed me in July 1958:

> I have been vehemently attacked by some Israel newspapers because of the Hitler passage in my speech and it has even been misquoted. But I have seen now—too late, this is my own fault—that the text in the Newsletter is somewhat misleading. How could "the majority of the Jewish people" think, even after Hitler's defeat, that he did what he did "with impunity"? It makes no sense. In my notes I find the following sentence: "In the days of Hitler the majority of the Jewish people saw that millions of Jews have been killed with impunity, and a certain part [of the Jewish people] made their own doctrine that history does not go the way of the spirit but the way of power."

Buber sent a "rectifying communication" to the editor of *Ha-aretz,* which had not criticized him, in which he also said: "I must add now that that part of the Jewish people did not change this opinion even after Hitler's defeat. I oppose now as I opposed then, with all my force, those who believe in the doctrine of 'Not by the spirit, but by power' and act upon it."

Later, Buber, on further reflection, felt himself obliged to write down, for the American Jewish press, "a clear and precise exposition of my views on the problems of the evolution of the Zionist movement and especially of its crisis in the days of Hitler and the consequences of this crisis up to the present." He asked me to consult with Heschel, if necessary, about the best place in which to publish it. "I attach particular importance to the matter and am rather satisfied now that I have got a strong motive to do it, as I should have done long ago." Soon after, Buber sent the article, asking me to translate it. Since it was too long to send as a communication to different Jewish newspapers, he asked that one be chosen where it would receive the relatively largest publicity. It was published in *Congress Weekly* and later as an addition to the original text for the paperback edition of *Israel and the World* under the title "Israel and the Command of the Spirit." It was published later in Hebrew in Israel. How deeply Buber felt this mistake about the Hitler reference, and how personally he took it, he expressed in this same letter in which, touchingly, he saw it as the first real failing of old age:

> I am sorry for the confusion I have caused concerning the Hitler passage, I do not exactly understand how I did it. My heart cannot recover from it, because here, as far as I see, is the first negative sign of old age, and I had hoped to be spared. I like to be old, I like the strange experiences of old age, I like even the burden and the difficulties, but I hate causing confusion.

In 1957 the Magnes Foundation approached me about editing a volume of essays on Jewish-Arab cooperation in honor of Judah Magnes. Buber, Marcus Reiner, Ernst Simon, and Simon Shereshevsky undertook to advise me; and they sent essays by Ahad Ha'am, Magnes, Buber, Hans Kohn, Hannah Arendt, and others with a new Preface by Buber. While working with Buber in Princeton, I talked the whole matter over with him. "Why did you think you could edit it?" he asked me. "I thought that I could understand the issues even if I was not an expert on the Middle East," I replied. "That was a mistake!" Buber cried, springing up from his chair and touching me on the shoulder at the same time, as if only through actual physical contact could he communicate what he had to say.

Martin and Paula had been given a house to live in in Princeton, and I spent many, many hours with them there, working together with Buber on his replies to the essays in *The Philosophy of Martin Buber* and the questions for the "Philosophical Interrogations." Often I stayed for lunch or dinner and occasionally spent the night with Malcolm and Barbara Diamond. Paula, Martin, and I conversed in German—about Kafka (who anticipated the concentration camps, according to Paula), about my career, and many other subjects. Once Buber remarked to me in the basement where we did our work, "What did you do to get involved with 'the Buber'?" and his tone was a mixture of wonder and commiseration. Another time when he had gone above and I remained below, he descended the stairs, looking searchingly in my eyes. Although I did not look away, I could not take the full intensity of his gaze and veiled over my own, as if to protect myself from a deeper question than at that moment I could bear. That silent question, to which I never referred by so much as a word, has remained with me and always will.

During 1956 and 1957, I worked with Buber editing and translating *Pointing the Way,* which included most, but not all, of the essays in his German collection *Hinweise* and some others besides. One of the essays which was included was "The Teaching of the Tao" (1911), which we have discussed in Volume One in "Encounter with Mysticism" (Chapter 5). The Foreword to *Hinweise* contained the statement: "I have included only those essays that I can stand behind today." I pointed out to Buber that he could not really say this of "The Teaching of the Tao," since it still stressed a "unity" which was not really compatible with his philosophy of dialogue. I suggested to him that he write an addition to the Foreword to explain why he nonetheless felt he had to include this essay. "The Foreword shall indeed explain what you hint at," Buber wrote me in August 1956. "The 'unity' of which the Tao essay speaks, is not the unity of Being, but that of 'the one thing that is necessary,' but you are right that the essay is too 'mystical.'" Buber did, in fact, write a whole new Foreword in which he explained that he could not affirm all of "The Teaching of the Tao" yet he had included it because it belongs to that "mystical . . . stage that I had to pass through before I could enter into an independent relationship with being." The genuine ecstatic experience which usually underlies the belief in a union of the self with the all-self leads the person who has that belief to regard everyday life either as an obscuring of or a preparation for the true life. Instead of bringing into unity his whole existence as he lives it, from the hours of blissful exaltation unto those of hardship and of sickness, he constantly flees from it into the detached feeling of unity of being, elevated above life. In these "higher hours" the great dialogue between I and Thou is silent; "nothing else exists than his self, which he experiences as *the* self. That is certainly an exalted form of being untrue, but it is still being untrue." Now Buber pointed to the "one thing needful" not as the unified life of the "central man" of "The Teaching of the Tao" but "being true to the being in which and before which I am placed."

Ursula Niebuhr, the wife of Reinhold Niebuhr, told me an amusing sequel to these events. On the very morning in which Reinhold Niebuhr's review of *Pointing the Way* appeared in the *New York Times Book Review* (in the spring of 1958), Martin Buber happened to be coming over to the Niebuhrs' for breakfast (Niebuhr was then at the Institute for Advanced Studies). In the generally favorable review, Niebuhr went out of his way to attack "The Teaching of the Tao" as an evidence of a lingering mysticism that Buber had not been able to overcome. When Martin Buber entered, holding the review in his hand, he turned immediately to Niebuhr, who towered above him. Buber put his index finger against Niebuhr's stomach and said accusingly, "You did not read my Foreword!" "That is right," Niebuhr admitted. "I did not read the Foreword."

When Martin and Paula arrived in New York the beginning of March 1958, Eugenia and I went to meet them in a car driven by my Sarah Lawrence student Kitty McCaw (in those days I did not yet drive). Kitty, who later became one of the leading graduate students in philosophy at Northwestern University, asked Buber whether he would meet with her and some other members of the philosophy seminar which she chaired and for which I was the faculty adviser. "Do you think women can really think?" responded Buber humorously, and agreed. I met regularly over two months with six young women from the philosophy seminar, all of them excellent students whom I had known and worked with in my classes for one, two, or even three years. I tried to impress upon them that Buber would only answer "real questions," and they tried conscientiously to prepare themselves for the meeting. Despite this, they could not really understand just how concrete Buber meant their questions to be until they had been with him for a while. Occasionally, I interpreted a question, since these were students I knew extremely well, and I was fearful lest a misunderstanding get the discussion going on a wrong track. Buber did not particularly want this help, and I learned something totally unexpected about dialogue and dialectic at a deeper level than I could have anticipated. Each of the six, without Buber's in any way asking for it, not only told him the question she had prepared but told him the concrete experience that lay behind the question and gave rise to it. Although I knew them well (many of them were my *donnees,* or advisees, as well as my students) and I knew their thinking, these experiences were totally new to me. One student whose question seemed to me particularly inane impressed Buber so much by the experience she told him of sitting by the bedside of her dying mother when she was sixteen that he referred to it three weeks later when Eugenia and I saw him and Paula off on the boat. Another student told Buber of how she would spend days at a time out of touch, wandering around. He suggested to her that she should find someone to talk with and looked at me in such a way that it suddenly occurred to me that, close as I was to her and the other students, perhaps I had been failing in my responsibility when beyond a certain point I would suggest that a student go to talk with the college psychiatrist! There was no discussion of theology or "sin"; yet one of the things that

Buber said then provided a whole deeper insight into the problem of temptation and guilt. "When one is tempted," he said, "the choice is not between becoming guilty and not becoming guilty but between giving in to the temptation or reaching a whole new stage where one has never been."

When the Bubers left in early June, Eugenia and I took him a copy of Archibald MacLeish's play *J.B.*, thinking it would interest him because of his interest in Job. (Later I became certain that MacLeish's interpretation must have offended Buber.) Paula was not too pleased to see us show up, no doubt thinking that at least on the boat she was entitled to a rest without visitors! Paula was a strong woman, given to an enormous amount of physical and intellectual work. "She was too strong. She was a Viking!" Buber's secretary Margot Cohn said to me. Once when she had injured her shoulder moving a heavy trunk, Buber told me, she had refused to see any doctors because she did not believe in them. When Buber wrote me from Soglio, Italy, in July 1958, about the essay correcting the Hitler passage in his American Friends of Ihud speech, he said that they hoped to be home by August 4, after staying at Zurich and Venice. "When we arrive in Israel, the danger of war may have become imminent," he added. On August 2 he reported from Venice: "My wife took ill here a few days ago (a thrombosis, but seemingly not a very grave one) and we, I and my daughter, who came from a journey to Greece to meet us here, have brought her to a hospital on the Lido. My daughter stays here with her, and I stay in a nearby hotel." He also said that the next ship from Venice to Haifa left on August 30, "and we think to go with it." "I will try as best I can to go on with the work." On August 13 he wrote from Venice:

> My wife died two days ago. Her strong heart resisted at first the new hemorrhaging and then the pulmonitis for days and days, till it could not resist any more. We have buried her, I and my children, in the old cemetery of the Jewish community here on the Lido, full of old trees. Some days before her death she had uttered suddenly: " . . . The grave of Platen [the German poet] in Syracuse. . . ."
> We are returning Friday 15, to Israel.

A year later, Albrecht Goes learned more of the details of Paula's death when he met again with Martin in the same apartment in Tübingen where Martin and Paula had lived the previous summer, only this time Buber was accompanied by his daughter Eva, whose own husband had died in 1953.

Waiting for the boat which was to take them back to Israel, they had stopped over in that city [Venice] for two days, and with a strange impatience—so Martin Buber recalled—his wife had forgone a gondola ride so as to finish correcting a certain manuscript. Then the ship was ready, they occupied their cabin—and she collapsed. The ship's doctor came, examined the patient, and asked about her age. "What? Eighty-one years old? I am sorry, but I cannot let you take the trip." So they took a gondola to the hospital on the Lido, with the patient seeming to be in a deep coma.

"I set up my papers on a table in her room," said Martin Buber. "The room was located on one of the upper floors of the hospital. When she regained consciousness, she would immediately have a view of the open sea, the area before Torcello. And so it was: Early the next day she came to: she recognized me, took a sip of tea, and then spoke one single sentence in a very clear voice. Without anything preceding or following it, she said only this: 'Platen's grave was near Syracuse.' We had hardly mentioned Platen in recent weeks."

Goes recalled that the year before she had quoted lines from two other German poets, Mörike and Hölderlin, and he himself now quoted two lines from Platen: "To view the sea and the marble halls of Venice with yearningly astonished senses." "If it cannot be my new home Jerusalem, that receives me. . . ," Goes speculated, trying to re-create Paula's semiconscious thoughts, "then let it be here, facing the sea, the sea that is the same in Venice and in Syracuse." Soon Paula fell asleep again and did not respond when Martin and Eva talked to her after she had made some moans. But suddenly she said: "I felt quite safe on the boat. And Ludwig is such a good swimmer." The boat would have taken her back to Israel where her late son-in-law Ludwig Strauss, also a German writer but a Hebrew poet too, had swum to the "other shore" five years before her.

On her last day, Paula said: "My brother has a solid house quite near by." Goes thought, without saying it, of the concern of Jews about a good grave ever since the days of Abraham, and Eva said: "My mother could not have known that the Jewish cemetery of Venice is quite close to the hospital. We could only take that 'solid house' to mean a grave." Martin commented that Paula had no brother. "But when some parting sorrow is removed from her, then the one who takes it off her soul presumably is a brother. We shall not unravel this." Goes recalled the verses of Mignon: "I hasten from the beautiful earth / Down to that solid house." Only Mignon's plea for eternal youth is here replaced by "the silence that trusts."

In August 1958, Hugo Bergmann published in the German-speaking magazine of the Jews in Israel from Central Europe an article on Paula Buber in which he spoke of her great influence in helping Buber to escape the overly aesthetic and uncommitted life of his youth. "Paula Buber was other than we are," Bergmann concluded. "But when she, as she often did in her speech, said, as a matter of course, 'we Jews,' then we felt ourselves confirmed. We did not make it easy for her among us. We did not always learn what we had to learn from her great, pure, solid, astringent, critical, but always deeply genuine figure. She walked her separate way unerringly."

In September, Buber wrote thanking Eugenia and me "for your good words that have done me good." "The structure of my life has been broken up so thoroughly that I have given up all plans for lectures abroad, including Munich." The reference to Munich concerned the lectures on speech with Martin Heidegger at the Academy of Fine Arts that had been planned for more than a year. "I have not been able to work till now, but I have in mind to begin again the day after to-morrow," Buber added. "I mean to begin with re-writing the seven chapters of the responses for the *Living Philosophers* I have drafted in Princeton, and I will send you a copy." He also needed to write the last chapters, including the one on the Bible as well as the answers for the *Review of Metaphysics* and, after finishing all the responses, "the Autobiography, a rather brief one." Six more letters followed in the next twelve days, in the last of which he said, "Work is the only earthly help in my present situation." In October, Buber wrote, "My work now is a kind of 'walking against the wind.'"

A week later Buber's friend Ewald Wasmuth informed him of the death of Buber's old friend from Frankfurt the classical philologist Walter Otto. "Human relationships are highly enigmatic," declared Wasmuth, "and in order to judge them rightly one must apparently know a great deal more at times than one may after all know." "It is comforting to know," Buber responded in October, "that in my last talk with him what had remained unspoken precisely that troubled state, from which he suffered, was dissolved before the end. What you have said about human relationships I feel in my soul." "You should not wait for 'signs of life,'" Buber replied to Wasmuth, referring to the impact of Paula's death on him. "That one must continue to live one learns obediently to accept if not to understand."

From New York, the philosopher Hans Jonas wrote Buber after he had learned of Paula's death: "Never have I seen a more perfect community of two who remained what they were while affirming the other. That the choice of youth can so prove itself and become ever more true in the course of time—such success is the highest tribute to the good fortune of the original meeting. . . . It was always beautiful to see you two together. . . . The blessing of that infinite communion which the two of you shared must penetrate your present aloneness."

In February 1959, Buber sent out from Jerusalem to the thousands of people who had written him about Paula's death a printed statement which said that he had been ill and only now was able to follow the longing of his heart and thank all the friends and intimates "who, in this darkest hour of my life, have bestowed on me their comfort, yes their consolation. For it was a comfort to learn how the great presence of the one to whom I have vowed myself forever really wove itself and endured in all the souls. She spoke at times of this earthly immortality and it is indeed the only one that can be grasped by our earthbound imaginations. All of you who have given me news of it receive the thanks of one who is alone but not abandoned!"

In May, Buber wrote that he had in mind to go with his daughter Eva to Switzerland and Germany before the fourth of June. "In the last week of August we shall be in Venice for the erection of the tombstone," something which is customarily done in Jewish ritual practice only a year after the burial. But in August he reported from Switzerland that he had been in bed for twelve days with a heavy attack of acute colitis, "and the doctor here (a good one) expressly forbids my going to Venice. . . . My son will go to Venice alone and I go there with my daughter later on, when my state of health will permit it." In June, Goes had written Buber from Venice that he wanted to send him a yellow flower from Paula's grave in the Lido, where he had been that morning: "Among the great trees of the Lido cemetery, I was happy."

In 1961, Buber wrote, as a Foreword to *Spirits and Men,* his own selection from three of Paula's books of tales, a short essay in which he described her as "'the blessed woman,' who ventured upon the brokenness of the human house." She was a narrating person for whom images become events and who "imparted our human time to the elemental spirits, who know only cosmic, destinyless time. She brought them into that time into which the dark threads of our afterknowledge of our birth are interwoven with the still darker threads of our foreknowledge of our death." In December 1961, Buber received from the Swiss literary and art critic Heinz Helmerking a letter which marvelously confirmed Buber's own insight into the relation between Paula as a person and as a writer. Paula "told her stories with the rare gift of the old story tellers," he wrote. "When she read aloud her thoughtful stories, I heard again the cadence of the story teller."

What spoke to me most strongly is the total absence of any trace of psychologizing and thereby also every attempt at explanation. This world is simply there; seen by the poet and called into the word of the narrative, it is created there in order to do its work. Its working is magically strong because no motive of any sort stands behind it, no tendency. . . . Therefore the enchantment is great, the reader hangs with the inner ear on the lips of the story teller who has magically woven for him a wonderful—in the old sense of the term—world in order to reveal to him all the suffering and rapture of the creature, to shake him up humanly and at the same time to make him happy again. In short what the great story tellers of the Orient wished when they told their hearers something is what takes place in her writings.

CHAPTER 11

Replies to Critics

IN 1956, I RECEIVED a letter from Paul Arthur Schilpp, founder and director of the famous Library of Living Philosophers, asking me if I were ready as "a labor of love" to take on the work of editing a *Philosophy of Martin Buber* volume for the series, something which he could not do himself because he was still occupied with finishing up the volume on the noted symbolic logician Rudolf Carnap. When I talked with Schilpp on the telephone, I expressed astonishment that one of the five members of the board was the well-known philosopher Richard McKeon, who had been taken off my dissertation committee at the University of Chicago after he had stated that Buber was not important enough to devote a dissertation to since he was merely a derivative of Kant. "Your book must have converted him," said Schilpp. "He was one of the most enthusiastic!"

Schilpp himself helped with the formation of the list and did the actualy inviting, but all the work of editing, correspondence, bibliography, and the translation of Buber's autobiographical fragments and his "Replies to Critics" I did myself during the ten years that led up to the American and English edition of the Buber volume (the German was published in 1963, the Japanese abridged edition in 1971).

The Library of Living Philosophers had the format of an intellectual autobiography by the author, essays on every aspect of his work by philosophers from around the world, and replies by the author to the criticisms made of him. The series, which began in 1939, already included volumes on the philosophy of Dewey, Santayana, Whitehead, G. E. Moore, Bertrand Russell, Ernst Cassirer, Albert Einstein, Sarvepalli Radhakrishnan (the philosopher vice-president of India), Karl Jaspers, and C. D. Broad.

At the same time I accepted the task of conducting a "philosophical interrogation" of Buber for a series edited by the philosophers Sydney and Beatrice Rome and destined, originally, for publication in an issue of *The Review of Metaphysics*. The *Review of Metaphysics* series was made up of short questions by a variety of philosophers addressed to the philosopher being interrogated through the conductor, who chose the contributors and edited and forwarded their questions. Happy at what appeared to be a recognition of Buber by philosophers, many of whom had formerly dismissed him as "not technical," I accepted both these tasks and thus took on an intensive decade of work with Buber and with thinkers around the world.

Much of the correspondence between Buber and myself from the fall of 1956 on was devoted to the "LLP" volume, as we called it, and the "Rev. of Met." In July 1956, Buber informed me that Fritz Kaufmann, a phenomenologist from Freiburg who now taught at the University of Buffalo, had approached him on the subject of a volume of Living Philosophers being dedicated to Buber. Although Hugo Bergmann in Israel and Walter Kaufmann in the United States had particularly pressed for such a volume, Fritz Kaufmann was, in fact, my chief adviser in editing the work until his untimely death in 1958.

In April, Fritz Kaufmann had given a beautiful speech in German on "Baeck and Buber" at the Congregation Habonim in New York, which I later translated into English for publication in *Conservative Judaism*. "In the sea of suffering that surrounded Jewry, Baeck and Buber have become and remained, particularly for the German Jews, the firm pillars of a community consecrated in suffering." Kaufmann characterized them as *zaddikim*, each in his way guardians and representatives of the Covenant. Kaufmann recalled how Buber at the first conference of the Mittelstelle for Adult Education at Herrlingen performed *havdalah*, the ceremony at the end of the Sabbath, "and as the school children there crowded around him he reminded us of the image of God the Father in Michelangelo's Sistine Chapel with the young angels clinging to the folds of his garment." And he pictured Baeck, "as a pupil who came out of Theresienstadt described him to me: standing upright in a dark, overcrowded barrack in the middle of the crowd, standing there unmoving for hours, teaching from the abundance of his knowledge and his visions." He also pictured them as he last saw them, both in the fullness of physical and spiritual strength.

> Buber, then seventy-five, was full of praise for "brother body," which, tender and tough, allows him almost incredible productivity as teacher, philosopher, theologian, historian, poet, and translator. The rich modulation of his voice and the well-rounded beauty of his handwriting show the philosopher-artist—in contrast with Baeck's gothic and even clumsy handwriting that looks like a splintery woodcut, the outcome of the author's struggle with resistant material. Now eighty-three, Baeck seemed rejuvenated after living through an accident and two operations, tall and bony, untiringly active as teacher and speaker, at his desk and on trips from land to land, and from continent to continent, as a traveler through the landscapes of nature, of history, and of the human soul.

In November, only a few months after Kaufmann's speech, Baeck died in London. "An era of Jewish humanism has lost thereby its last and noblest representative," Kaufmann wrote Buber in December: "—one in whom human mildness streamed forth even in the readiness for and the severity of martyrdom. I honored him like a holy father."

Fritz also recalled in his speech how in his first conversation with Buber around 1920 he asked Buber whether one can break through and escape the pack of demons who rend us. Buber replied by referring him back to himself: "Have you tried it?" He also recalled a conversation in Berlin in the summer of 1936, a conversation that lasted until the early hours of dawn, in the apartment of Moritz Spitzer. Buber, with a sad shaking of the head, remembered his efforts for Jewish-Arab understanding and cooperation at the Zionist Congress in Karlsbad in 1921 and said, "Now, I fear, it is too late!" "When we descended to the still, empty, echoing streets of the city," reported Kaufmann, "we heard the first newspaper boys calling out, 'Riots in Palestine!'"

Most precious in Kaufmann's speech was the honesty with which he cut through the public image to Buber the man, recognizing that loneliness became his fate, much more than for Baeck. "The silver beard of the sage covers the wounded streak of the mouth. The nocturnal wrestling is taken for a success story. But as far as it is a victory, it is a victory in tension with defeats." In contrast to Baeck, who reported even the tensions and divisions of human existence in the serene tone of an objective statement, Buber had passed through the demons' deluding play of flames and in his own self had fought out the fate of the Jewish person. "In Buber himself there lives something of the 'terrible dismemberment, the limitless despair, the infinite yearning, the pathetic chaos' of many Jews at the turn of the century," reflecting the Jewish movement of Zionism which was born out of the loss of every inner security in the Diaspora. Buber has taught us to endure, forever insecure and uncertain. But Buber himself, Kaufmann implied, is lonelier than those he taught. "He is walking on a narrow ridge, the path illuminated only in unexpected, lightning flashes by meetings with the eternal Thou. . . . This is necessarily a hard, essentially lonely path." In the incorruptible gaze of Buber's searching eyes is the composedness of him who cannot conform to the established law because he wants to be open and obedient to the demand of the hour. "But in it too is the sadness of abandonment felt by one who is resigned to others' being essentially just different—already Rosenzweig was frightened by this feeling of distance—and who is attacked by those close to him with a kind of tragic love-hate, while those far removed are his adherents." We can now, perhaps, better appreciate the sensitivity and compassion of his insight into Buber's own personal tragedy:

> The brilliant appearance of Buber on the firmament of European and Jewish literature has something deceptive about it. He is a master of the word. But the word has also often mastered him. . . . Our deepest admiration should not be just for the noble, often magical ring of his language, nor even for the dark profundity of his thought. It should include the clear-sighted love in which there is always a grain of compassion—love for the man who is endeavoring to convert his life and writing into honest and artless response—and who does not always succeed (he is, indeed, human). But everybody who has ever been addressed by him in a revealing hour of genuine dialogue will honor him—a son of Israel who with a wounded hip still wrestles with God that He may bless him.

When Kaufmann sent a copy of his speech to Buber, Buber responded to a passage with the comment, "Monotheism is indeed nothing else than the ever new re-cognizing." In his December 1956 letter to Buber, Kaufmann proposed to use Buber's place in the history of monotheism as the starting point for his own essay on Buber's philosophy of religion for the Living Philosophers volume. "The preparation of the volume has demanded a great deal of work," Kaufmann wrote Buber, "and does still, although I now leave the continuation for the greater part to Friedman. The beginning stages were disappointing because it is precisely our Jewish friends, on whom I thought I could count, who have left us in the lurch: only Glatzer and Simon have so far accepted. . . . I have appealed anew to Scholem, Heschel, Taubes: they have perhaps not fully understood what is at stake." Rudolf Bultmann's acceptance was, unfortunately, only a gesture; for he was in bad health and in no condition to work.

In August 1957, Buber wrote Fritz Kaufmann that he had not yet been able to read his book *Thomas Mann: The World as Will and Representation,* "which may be caused in part by my ambivalent relation to this extraordinary artist (I have rarely been as pained by reading a story as I was by 'The Law')." "I may perhaps break a lance, not for the Mann book but for Mann himself," Kaufmann replied. "It seems to me that Martin Buber is capable of a greater justice than judging the author of *Joseph and His Brothers* . . . by a novella that is really 'naughty.'" This could not have much appealed to Buber, because he did not care for *Joseph and His Brothers* either! But Kaufmann made a strong case for Mann's illusion-free humanity and movingly pleaded that the fact that Mann's Moses is not ours should not be held against him. "We may not let our relation to so great a phenomenon and, beyond that, to one of the most honest persons in the fight against the nihilism in and around him, be troubled by too great a sensitivity to a half *faux pas.*"

Kaufmann had originally proposed his and my friend Marvin Fox as editor, but Buber wrote him in September that he was "strictly against Fox as the only editor" and explained that I was necessary to assure the proper balance. "I added clearly enough," Buber wrote me, "that Schilpp may leave it if he does not like it." Buber was troubled that Marvin Fox was an Orthodox rabbi whose philosophical thinking was far from his own. "I do not think it fair that the editors' work is unpaid," Buber added, "but this obviously cannot be changed." Although it would be desirable to deal in the volume with his interpretation of religion and revelation, Buber advised that a controversy on the Jewish Law "would be better placed in an especially Jewish context." Fritz Kaufmann proposed, as a compromise, myself as "assistant editor," i.e., Schlipp as editor in name with my doing the actual work (what Ernst Simon later characterized, when I described it to him, as the "German system"!) with Fritz Kaufmann as "jury" and Fox as expert for the Hebrew concepts, passages, and contributions. Although Buber and I both accepted this compromise, in practice Fox did not serve in any other role than that of contributor, since Buber himself was really my chief adviser and aid on matters Hebrew and otherwise.

"I am rather doubtful about *purely* theological subjects being treated here," he wrote me in January 1957; "(this is why I opposed Jewish law); Religion—yes, there is a philosophy of religion, but Revelation? For such subjects as revelation what matters is only the really philosophical treatment." It was appropriate that editors Walter Kegley and Charles Bretall, who had once approached Buber but did not follow through, devoted a volume of their series The Library of Living Theologians to Paul Tillich, whereas Buber appeared in the Schilpp series. Although Tillich's thinking was systematic, as Buber's was not, there is no doubt that Tillich was basically a theologian whereas Buber was a philosopher and philosophical anthropologist.

Ernst Simon's contribution to the Buber volume grew into a book, *Martin Buber: The Educator,* which he cut down for the sake of the volume but unfortunately never published all in one piece. Sarvepalli Radhakrishnan promised us an essay for the volume. In November 1957, Buber wrote suggesting that I remind him. "It is desirable Asia (outside of Israel) should be represented, and he is the best man for this." Unfortunately, this essay, like a number of others that were promised, never materialized. By this time Buber had accepted the invitation from Princeton University to come there for three months in the spring of 1958, and he planned to write most of the "Autobiography" and the "Replies to His Critics" there "where I shall have the leisure for this work, as I have to give the seminar not more than once a week and to go twice to New York." "I do not at all intend to describe my development," he wrote, "only to tell about some 'milestones,' things that *occurred.*"

During this same period Buber also provided me with most helpful suggestions for the *Review of Metaphysics* list, about half of the thirty interrogators coming in the end from him, the other half from my own acquaintance. One of those he suggested was his and Franz Rosezweig's old friend Eugen Rosenstock-Huessy. This suggestion was particularly interesting because in 1955 I had brought to Buber's attention a highly critical article "Dich und Mich" (You and Me) which Rosenstock had published about Buber in the *Neue Schweitzer Rundschau.* Buber, before he had succeeded in obtaining it, had written me: "He did not send me his last book (in German). Maybe he has a grudge against me, as I could not approve wholeheartedly his 'Atem des Geistes,' although I found it a very interesting book." Rosenstock "will certainly put hard questions," Buber acknowledged when he suggested him, "but that is all right."

Early in 1957, Buber began preparation for a new German and English edition of *I and Thou.* Buber asked me to draw up for him a list of the questions that I felt most often occurred to people concerning *I and Thou,* and he wrote what he originally conceived of as a preface and later changed to a postscript, or afterword, on the basis of these questions. "Although I can only answer a part of your questions in this context," he informed me in September 1957, "it will become longer than I first thought, because the questions demand a very precise treatment." The ones which he dealt with were those concerned with the problems of mutuality and its "normative limitation." Buber also made a number of changes in the text and in Ronald Gregor Smith's translation of the Postscript, including adding a very important paragraph about the relation between our relationship to the "absolute Person" and our relationship to one another:

> As a person God gives personal life, he makes us as persons capable of meeting with him and with one another. But no limitation can come upon him as the absolute Person, either from us or from our relations with one another; in fact we can dedicate to him not merely our persons but also our relations to one another. The man who turns to him therefore need not turn away from any other I-Thou relation; but he properly brings them to him, and lets them be fulfilled "in the face of God."

This correction arrived at Heidelberg too late to make the German edition, which was already printed, Buber reported. "So there will be an unavoidable difference between the German and the English edition." I do not now remember whether this was because of my own delay or Buber's, very possibly the former, since Buber wrote me: "Let me give you on this occasion an advice out of my own experience: always arrange the things you have to do according to their urgency. One of the most important problems of human life is this practical one of right and wrong *tempo.*"

In *The Life of Dialogue* and in correspondence with Buber I raised some questions concerning Ronald Gregor Smith's translation of certain key terms in *I and Thou.* I pointed out that in all Buber's writings the German word *Umkehr* was used in the sense of *teshuva,* or turning;

yet Smith had translated it in the first English edition as "reversal." Smith accepted this change and also my urging that *Erlösung* be translated by "redemption" rather than the more Christian "salvation." On one point no solution was reached: in *Ich und Du* Buber speaks of the "Ich-Es Verhältnis" and the "Ich-Du Beziehung." At the beginning of my translating Buber's writings, Buber strictly enjoined me never to translate two different words by the same word and never to translate the same word by two different words. Yet Smith had translated both *Verhältnis* and *Beziehung* by the word "relation." The American philosopher Philip Wheelwright raised a question concerning this in his contribution to the Living Philosophers volume on "Buber's Philosophical Anthropology." I too pressed the same question, and Buber raised it several times with Smith. Smith, however, could see no way out, since "relationship" to him stood only for a family relationship. In 1961, Walter Kaufmann suggested "relation" (say of two balls on the billiard table) for *Verhältnis* and "relationship" (between two persons) for *Beziehung*. This is exactly how I thought they should be translated. Unfortunately, in Walter Kaufmann's own translation of *I and Thou,* he sometimes uses "relationship" for I-Thou and sometimes "relation," the latter particularly in connection with "acts of relation." (It *would* be hard to speak of "acts of relationship"!)

Buber's Postscript to the 1958 edition of *I and Thou* was in itself one of his most important "Replies to Critics": for I did not pose only my own questions but those concerning the I-Thou relationship with nature, fellow humans, art, and God that had most often been advanced by his critics as well as by ordinary readers of the little classic. Although Buber was not willing to give up the I-Thou relationship with nature, he recognized that it was confusing to the reader and even said to me that had he to write *I and Thou* again he would try to find some different vocabulary to make the distinction. In his Postscript he divided the relationship with nature into a liminal, or threshold, relationship with the animals who share with us the quality of spontaneity, and a preliminal or prethreshold sphere stretching from stones to stars to planets. Man wins from tamed animals and occasionally non-tamed ones an often astonishing active response to his addressing them "which in general is stronger and more direct in proportion as his attitude is a genuine saying of *Thou.*" Although plants cannot "respond" in this same sense, there is a reciprocity of being in its course *(seiend)*. "Our habits of thought make it difficult for us to see that here, awakened by our attitude, something lights up and approaches us from the course of being." This is that "bestowing side of things" that Buber spoke of in "With a Monist" and that I referred to as the impact of otherness in my chapter on Buber's "Theory of Knowledge" in *The Life of Dialogue*. We contribute to this manifestation but it is by no means the mere subjectivity of the romantic nature poet or mystic:

> That living wholeness and unity of the tree, which denies itself to the sharpest glance of the mere investigator and discloses itself to the glance of one who says *Thou*, is there when he, the sayer of *Thou*, is there: it is he who vouchsafes to the tree that it manifest this unity and wholeness; and now the tree which is in being manifests them.

Buber also distinguished a "supraliminal" sphere of the spirit, and this too he divided into two fields—what of spirit has already entered the world and can be perceived by our senses and what of spirit has not yet entered the world but is ready to do so and become present to us. The first can be pointed out; the second cannot. Buber illustrated the first realm by the traditional sayings of a master who died thousands of years ago and whose voice we can hear as being identical with the voice that speaks to us in other genuine sayings of the same master. In this indivisible wholeness of something spoken no separation into content and form is possible. But what Buber meant was not limited to the continued influence of a personal life, as he illustrated from his personal experience with a Doric pillar:

> Out of a church wall in Syracuse, in which it had once been immured, it first came to encounter me: mysterious primal mass represented in such simple form that there was nothing individual to look at, nothing individual to enjoy. All that could be done was what I did: took my stand, stood fast, in face of this structure of spirit, this mass penetrated and given body by the mind and hand of man.

Here the concept of mutality is transformed into a concrete content "which coldly declines to assume conceptual form but clearly and reliably points beyond itself through what is."

In the fifth section of his Postscript, Buber discussed the "normative" limitation of mutuality in the relationship between therapist and client, teacher and student, pastor and parishioner, and in so doing brought into still greater clarity what he had said in his essay on "Education" and in his dialogue with Carl Rogers. It appears that "full mutuality is not inherent in men's life together." "It is a grace, for which one must always be ready and of which one never gains an assured possession." But the teacher must practice "inclusion" in a way that the pupil cannot, without bringing the specific educative relationship to an end or changing it into friendship. If the genuine psychotherapist is satisfied merely to "analyze" his client, "i.e., to bring to light unknown factors from his microcosm, and to set to some conscious work in life the energies which have been transformed . . . , he may be successful in some repair work." He may help a diffused and unstructured soul collect and order itself, but he will not achieve the regeneration of an atrophied personal center. "This can only be done by one who grasps the buried latent unity of the suffering soul with the comprehensive glance of the doctor." This is possible in the person-to-person attitude of a partner who experiences the effect of his own action by standing both at his own pole and, "with the strength of his ability to make his partner present," at the other. "But again, the specific 'healing' relation would come to an end the moment the patient" practiced "inclusion" and experienced the event from the doctor's pole as well. This does not mean that the student, client, or parishioner does not glimpse anything of the other as a person. There is mutuality of contact and mutuality of trust and *some* sense on both sides of where the other is coming from. But the responsibility and concern is focused by both partners on the educating or healing of the one who is helped and not on that of the helper. I learn from my students, but I cannot demand that they set *my* learning as their goal. When I met Erich Fromm after sending him an early essay on Buber and therapy that I titled "Healing Through Meeting," he said to me, "I like your title very much. In fact, my patients heal *me*." But he did not mean by that that the *goal* of the therapy was the healing of Dr. Fromm, only that it took place as an unaimed-at and usually unexpected by-product.

The sixth section Buber devoted to the question of how the relationship to the eternal *Thou* can be at once exclusive and inclusive and answered it in the language of *Eclipse of God* that God *is* not a person in His essential being but, nonetheless, is *also* a person in that He "enters into a direct relation with us men in creative, revealing, and redeeming acts, and thus makes it possible for us to enter into a direct relation with him." "This ground and meaning of our existence constitute a mutuality, arising again and again, such as can subsist only between persons." God is not a limited person, however, but the *absolute* Person whose speech to us penetrates what happens in the life of each one of us "and transforms it for you and me into instruction, message, demand." "The existence of mutuality between God and man cannot be proved, just as God's existence cannot be proved,"

Buber concluded, and added, with a clear thought of those readers who would come to *I and Thou* after his own death, "Yet he who dares to speak of it, bears witness and calls to witness him to whom he speaks—whether that witness is now or in the future."

Another type of "Reply to Critics" was the letter Buber sent Malcolm Diamond about the latter's doctoral dissertation on him. When Buber learned from me that Diamond had written this dissertation, titled "Paradox without Anguish," he declared, "It must be critical." It was not only critical but also appreciative, and Diamond retained this combination in his revision of his dissertation for his book *Martin Buber: Jewish Existentialist.* Buber helped Diamond with this revision through his letters and through their personal talks when Buber was at Princeton University, where Diamond is professor of Religion. "You overaccentuate the element of concepts and conceptual presuppositions in my 'teaching,'" Buber told Diamond, "and then you do battle with these conceptual presuppositions of your own making." What Buber then added can stand as an important hint to any reader of his works:

> The reality of the human situation, to which I seek to *point,* cannot be expressed adequately in the language of concepts. But the use of this language is indispensable when the ontic character of a reality, for example that of the dualism of the basic human attitudes, is to be presented. Then there is no other way than to speak in "paradox." But that means in the final analysis to unite with the hearer or reader in three presuppositions: 1. That as hearer or reader he likewise thinks paradoxically; 2. that he repeatedly takes the step from grasping of a concept to the comparison with his own experiences; 3. where a corresponding experience of his own is lacking, he should seek with his own person to have this experience.

"In the final analysis I do not appeal, as you assume, to the historical prototypes (the prophets, etc.)," Buber concluded, "but to the actual and possible life of my reader. The intention of my writing is really a wholly intimate dialogical one."

In Princeton in the spring of 1958, Buber and I went over the contributions to *The Philosophy of Martin Buber* and to what later became the Buber section of *Philosophical Interrogations.* Buber began with the draft of his answers to the LLP, preferring to leave the autobiography for the end, "so I would be able to put into it what has not been said in the answers." "By the way, some of the contributors make answering not a pleasant job at all, as they do not grasp at all the place where I stand." The day before he had been visited by the

Canadian philosopher Emil Fackenheim, who wrote the LLP essay on "Revelation," and he explained to him some points. "This was possible, because he understands my position."

In October 1958, Buber wrote me concerning the death of my chief adviser on the Living Philosophers volume, Fritz Kaufmann. After having had to leave Freiburg at the time of Heidegger's rectorship under the Nazis, Kaufmann had worked in a partially paid position at Northwestern University and then, after being brought to Buffalo University by the phenomenologist Marvin Farber, had reached a miserable situation in which not a single graduate student was allowed by the department to work with him. Finally, a modicum of happiness was in sight. He moved to Switzerland, bought a house near the grave of his beloved Thomas Mann, and was beginning to teach in the College of Jewish Studies that Hermann Levin-Goldschmidt had founded in Zurich. Then his heart, which had already given him much trouble, finally gave out, and he died at the age of sixty-seven. "The death of Fritz Kaufmann has been for me too a great shock," Buber proclaimed. "I felt deeply once more the cruel fate of human planning—and the great Nevertheless."

In October, Buber again mentioned the Autobiography for the LLP volume: "The task of writing an autobiography is a rather heavy one, as I do not have that kind of memory," and in December he added, "I want to tell only of those events or situations that have influenced my thought." In February 1959 he announced that he had gone through "a rather disagreeable form of flu, called the Asiatic one" and was returning to normal life very slowly. Nonetheless, he was willing to put aside the work on the Bible and finish the Autobiography. In March he reported that the Autobiography was "proceeding but slowly, because of inner difficulties." In April the North German Broadcasting Station had asked him when in Germany to read for them some chapters of the Autobiography. These were later rebroadcast and also made into records. Some parts of the Autobiography were culled from anecdotes already written in other contexts, like "The Horse" and "The Conversion" from "Dialogue" and "Report on Two Talks" from *Eclipse of God,* whereas others were composed especially for this volume. In December he declared: "*Till now* I have been utterly unable (I mean: my soul has been) to write another autobiographical chapter. It is a kind of disinterestedness in my past that has overcome me. But the interest may come back, if only for just the time necessary to write the chapter. Indeed I wish it myself." In the seminars at the Washington School and in his dialogue with Rogers, Buber steadfastly objected to speaking of a "dialogue with oneself" because it lacks the otherness and surprise necessary for real dialogue. But in this case at least, one can speak of "A Dialogue of Self and Soul," to use the title of a poem by Yeats!

In December 1960, two years before the publication of the German volume of The Library of Living Philosophers, the "Autobiographical Fragments," finally completed, were published separately for a Christian German publisher's edition under the title *Begegnungen,* or *Meetings,* by which title they are now also separately published in English. They quickly took their place as one of Buber's enduring little classics. In the LLP volume on philosopher Karl Popper, the autobiography ran to some 250 pages of a closely knit personal-intellectual history. Buber's, in contrast, came to less than fifty pages, even with three appendices. "These 'events and meetings' are in the fullest sense of the term 'teaching' and perhaps, in the end, the most real teaching that Martin Buber has left us," I wrote in my Introduction to the English-language edition of *Meetings.* "Some of the most profound of Buber's hard-won insights are contained within them like a vein of gold in marble. They await extraction by those who wrestle and contend with them until they are compelled to divulge their secret." In March 1961, Hermann Hesse notified Buber of "the great participation, joy and excitement" with which he had read and reread *Meetings.* "In your life I found some figures and experiences of the same streaming and convincing power as those in Frankenberg's *Life of Jacob Boehme.*" In September 1963, on the initiative of Hans Fischer-Barnicol, Buber recorded a series of "Autobiographical Fragments" which were broadcast by many German radio stations and later broadcast again after Buber's death. In addition to Germany and America, *Meetings* has also been published as a separate book in Holland, Israel, and Japan.

In October 1958, Buber sent me a number of responses to my own LLP essay on "The Bases of Buber's Ethics." In connection with one passage that I quoted from "The Education of Character," he pointed out that he was speaking "only of the 'great character and not of everyman" and added, "When re-reading the whole of page 12 I have the feeling that you are not thinking enough about Everyman. (I am thinking more and more about him.)" At another place he noted: " 'To be addressed' is not enough: the man addressed must hear, must listen to it, *this* is religion." And later: "We do not respond 'to the present' but to God who is sending it, 'speaking' it." Regarding personal trust, he asserted: "If I 'trust in a person,' I do not primarily mean by it that *I* 'shall find,' that *I* 'shall enter,' etc., but rather that, whatever this person may do, he will remain for me this person I trust in. Of course this is a paradox, but all great trust means a paradox." "Trust means neither the present nor the future Thou, but just the person." And finally: "Emunah indeed is the trust that dialogue is the 'reality' but not necessarily the dialogue with men, rather, in the last instance, the dialogue with God." This is also what, ultimately, Buber understood to be the case with confirmation.

In November 1958, Buber wrote me that my uncertainty about translating his responses to the *Philosophical Interrogations* meant a great difficulty for him:

> Of course, I understand very well about your want of time. But if you could not do it, who could? I have worked on these answers now in the thought that what I write will as agreed be translated at once. You may have felt that I am working now in a different manner, finishing or wanting to finish one job after the other. But the problem's solution does not depend on me alone, and I want help, probably more than at any time before. As you know, I have postponed the two last an-thropological essays in order to fulfill the American obligations. I tell you all this as frankly as I am accustomed to speak to you!—I want you just to *see* what is. The truth at the root or rather the reality at the root is simply this, that the dimension of time has become for me different from what it was.

Of course, I made time to do the translations! In January, Buber wrote me, "It is a kind of alleviation for me that you have done the *Review* translation."

Paul Weiss, the editor of *The Review of Metaphysics*, announced late in 1958 that the "Philosophical Interrogations" could not be pub-lished until four other issues were published first (in fact, *The Review* never published them!). Buber found this to be a serious matter. "I will not wait until he has published the four issues," he declared.

> A great part of my answers are of such a kind, that—if they have to be published first in English—it is highly desirable for me to be able to revise the translation, and my age is a fact. Therefore, I have in mind, if there is no other solution, to take my answers back and to publish the important ones in German (together with the questions, provided the questioners agree). When my original texts will have been published, the *Review* may publish the translation or not. I shall not be any longer interested. . . . I empower you to act in my name according to what I have said. By the way, I have sent Thieme the answers to him and I think to do it with others too, for instance with Rosenstock.

Please do not delay the settling of this affair, as far as it depends on you.

I understand very well that you have taken a lot upon you and I understand your difficulties. But you will, I hope, understand me too. Things must be settled now, in one way or another. Should you not like to write to Weiss, I am ready to do it myself.

Three years later, in 1961, after various promises and procrastinations, Buber again asked me to ascertain finally the situation. "If they are not willing to make a binding decision now, i.e., before the end of September, I shall ask them to return to me my manuscript." The following April he wrote me in the same vein, "How is the unpleasant problem of the *Review of Metaphysics* to be solved definitely?" In June he wrote me:

I have no answer from Sydney Rome [the editor of "Philosophical Interrogations"] and feel utterly unable to write him once more objectively on the subject, but I authorize you to tell him in my name what you suggest should be told. . . . It would not further the cause if I wrote Rome what I think of it. It is the first and certainly the last experience of this kind in my life.

I had myself by that time solved the problem by bringing Sydney Rome into touch with Arthur Cohen, who was then religion editor at Holt, Rinehart and Winston, which published *Philosophical Interrogations* as a book in 1964, much to Buber's satisfaction and my own.

Although Buber did not live to see the English edition of *The Philosophy of Martin Buber* and was unhappy about its postponement, the publication of the German edition took place in 1963 and neither he nor I experienced quite the vexations with that that we did with the *Philosophical Interrogations*. In January 1959, Buber wrote me that my suggestions for additions to his responses for LLP had been important for him. I wrote Buber that Marvin Fox was disturbed by Buber's responses to his essay on ethics—Buber referred to him as "my critic," who is a careful reader but reads under the dictates of his criticism—and had asked me whether I thought Buber would talk with him. "Of course, I would like to talk to Marvin Fox, if he will come before the end of May," Buber wrote me in April. Unfortunately, that did not happen.

I found my position as middleman in both the *Philosophical Interrogations* and the Living Philosophers volume an increasingly unpleasant one, since in both cases I had to bear the brunt, from both Buber and the contributors, of long delays that were totally beyond my control. Sometimes I felt as if Buber were the "old man of the mountain" who was riding my shoulders! Finally I remarked to Buber at his home in Jerusalem in the spring of 1960 that I was almost sorry that I had taken these tasks on. Buber gave me a quick look and asked if I were sorry "about the whole thing," by which I assumed he meant all of my work about and with him. "Of course not," I said, but I got the impression that he was anticipating a repetition of the sort of turning away he had experienced from Gerson and others. I was painfully aware from then on of a distance that I did not have the resources to overcome from my side and that Buber never fully bridged from his.

In May 1961, Buber suggested that the authors of the LLP essays be allowed "to make corrections that have become necessary by the lapse of time since they were written—as for instance about the Bible translation, said to be incomplete." In July 1963, Buber wrote me that he was highly dissatisfied with the latest postponement of The Library of Living Philosophers volume.

> I want to tell you what this situation means for me. Among the Responses I wrote in Princeton as something that would be published at once there is a series of explanations that make my work more understandable. If you had not asked me to write the Responses, I would have written down *these explanations* as such and published them as such. I do not want to let them wait any longer for a publication, in German and in English, because by far most of my readers have read me in one of these two languages. . . . I have in mind to give the German text to *Die neue Rundschau,* and which American review would you suggest for the English? It must be one that would promise to publish what I give them *very soon.* (I will not go through the same experience I had with the *Review of Metaphysics.* . . .)
>
> I want you, Maurice, to understand that all this is a very serious subject—and to help me to overcome it. You have sufficient imagination and energy for both problems.

What held the Buber volume up in America for years was the Carnap volume of the LLP series. Once Buber remarked to me somewhat humorously that if he had a school of followers like Carnap, he would be put out by their delay too. Later all traces of humor on the subject deserted him.

In February 1962, Buber astonished me by his own failure in "imagining the real" when he wrote, "it cannot be very difficult to choose the most important titles out of the bibliography of Catane." I did, indeed, complete the bibliography, but so far from it being a simple matter of selecting from Moshe Catane's bibliography, which only went up to 1958 and was intended for an entirely different purpose, I had to cull over seven hundred items of *philosophical* importance in many languages and from many sources. This proved, indeed, to be one of the most exacting tasks of many such that I have done.

Although Buber appreciated the contributions to the volume, answered them as faithfully as he could, and conscientiously sought to clear up any misunderstandings, he once remarked that the essays in the volume represented the whole range of possible misunderstandings of his thought! One of the saddest "mismeetings" was that between Buber and Charles Hartshorne, the famous American process philosopher. Hartshorne used to say that Buber was no metaphysician, yet he decided that he belonged to the "good guys," i.e., the panentheists,* and put him in that category in his book *Philosophers Speak of God.* Hartshorne followed Whitehead and Plato in holding that if God is absolute, he is not in relation, and if he is in relation, he cannot be absolute. He was invited to write the essay on "Buber's Metaphysics" for the volume, and he did so. Halfway through the essay, he remarked that he liked Buber's metaphysics very much and added, with candor, "I ought to. I have remade it in my own image." But Buber's "absolute Person" stuck in his throat. That he could not swallow. When Buber wrote his reply, he said that he could not acknowledge as his own Hartshorne's interpretation of his metaphysical position, and added:

> Because I say of God, that He enters into a relationship to the human person, Hartshorne says that this makes God relative! He thinks that is proved by the sentence: the relative depends for being what it is upon some relation to another. As if an absolute being had to be without relationship!
>
> I confess that I do not know what to do with Hartshorne's concept of a relative perfection; it affects me on each new examination as equally unacceptable. And when I hear, besides, "the divine essence is nothing else than God's idea of his individuality," I mark once again how difficult it is for me to find a common language with a modern metaphysician.

At the beginning of his essay, Hartshorne modified his former statement to read: "Buber has no metaphysics; Buber is one of the greatest of metaphysicians."

> This, in somewhat paradoxical language, is my feeling about my assigned topic. He does not, formally speaking, have a metaphysics, a

---

*Panentheism is the view that all reality is part of the being of God. It is to be distinguished from pantheism, which identifies God with the total reality.

general system of ultimate categories, carefully defined and defended against rival systems. He is, I imagine, little interested in such things, and I daresay that what I can offer here will not, for the most part, be much to his liking. . . . Yet there are some pages in *Ich und Du* that seem to me among the most inspired ever written on the relations of the creation and the creator. True, they are couched in the language of piety, of existential response, rather than that of theory and rational evidence. It could be called a kind of poetry—and great poetry. Some similar thoughts can be found in Berdyaev, but mixed with philosophical ratiocinations and polemical attacks, and somewhat marred by an element of Manichean "hatred of reality." The thoughts are also in Whitehead, embedded in a maze of philosophical subtleties. In Buber there is an austere simplicity and centrality, with just sufficient polemical indications to mark off the point of view from some of its most important rivals, and there is no distracting assemblage of arguments or evidences. One feels the sheer force of actual experience, from which, in one way or another, all evidence must come.

"You begin, dear Hartshorne, with the sentence, I am no metaphysician and I am one of the greatest metaphysicians," Buber wrote in the conclusion to his short reply. "After attentive reading of your essay, I am far more strongly convinced than I was at the beginning of the reading, that we can make only the first half of your sentence the basis for an understanding."

Hartshorne, who was invariably mild and gentle, was quite angry with Buber because of his reply and said that he must be senile. To an appeal to Buber urging him to change or expand his reply for the English edition, Buber responded that he was "most willing to change the reply . . . but I must first know what it is that he feels offended by. I cannot imagine what he means." That was the end of the matter.

In the Editors' Preface to *The Philosophy of Martin Buber,* I pointed out that the form of Schilpp's Library of Living Philosophers is particularly congenial to Buber's philosophy of dialogue, since it gives other philosophers the opportunity to question and criticize the philosopher while he is still alive, and it gives the philosopher the opportunity to respond to their questions.

Thus it introduces into the critical dialectic that has traditionally constituted philosophical interchange the basic elements of a dialogue in which really different points of view may come into fruitful contact. The philosopher must endeavor to understand the points of view from which he is questioned while at the same time pointing out to his critics those misunderstandings in their criticism that arise from seeing his philosophy from the outside rather than from within.

Needless to say, the result in the case of the Buber volume, as of every other, was at best a mixture of meeting and mismeeting. In my Preface to the Buber section of *Philosophical Interrogations* I added that dialogical "truth" takes the form of question and answer much more readily than of simple statement. "What is more, Professor Buber has indicated that much of his thought remains unexpressed because he has not been asked to develop it." Not only does the Buber section of *Philosophical Interrogations* form an invaluable supplement to the longer essays and *responsa* of *The Philosophy of Martin Buber,* it may be that the short question and direct answer of the interrogations made for much more genuine dialogue than the traditional essay form and systematized *responsa* of the larger volume.

When Ludwig Binswanger was invited to contribute to *Philosophical Interrogations,* he wrote that no questions occurred to him, precisely because he was too close to Buber for them to arise: "I have for decades been in such close personal and scientific contact with him and find his work, as far as it falls within my competence, so conclusive, so clear and consistent, that almost no doubt remains about which I must ask him for fuller particulars." Lewis Mumford, on the other hand, replied that he disagreed with Buber's thought until he met the man!

The "Philosophical Accounting" that Buber placed at the beginning of his "Replies to My Critics" is an important general response and testimony that could not have been invoked by the more specific questions of the *Interrogations.* Rejecting those who wished to see him as a philosopher, a theologian, or in terms of any other traditional category, Buber declared himself "an atypical man" who, since he matured to a life lived on the basis of his own experience during the years 1912–1919, "had the duty to insert the framework of the decisive experiences that I had at that time into the human inheritance of thought, but not as 'my' experiences, rather as an insight valid and important for others and even for other kinds of men." This communication had to be a philosophical one which would relate the unique and particular to the "general," discoverable by every person in his or her own existence. "I had to make an It out of that which was experienced in I-Thou and as I-Thou." Buber was convinced, moreover, "that it happened not otherwise with all the philosophers loved and honored by me. Only that after they had completed the transformation, they devoted themselves to the philosophy more deeply and fully than I was able or it was granted to me to do."

Buber saw reason as included in the great experience of faith which he had, as one of its bearers which can function as a trustworthy elaborator:

> It is incumbent upon reason to apply logic to what is above logic, that for which the law of contradiction does not hold valid; it is incumbent upon reason to avoid inner contradictions; but it may not sacrifice to consistency anything of that reality itself which the experience that has happened commands it to point to. If the thought remains true to its task, a system will not necessarily come out of it, but certainly a connected body of thought more resolved in itself, more transmittable.

This refusal to go along with the autocratic form in which reason usually appears in no wise meant that Buber's communication of faith might properly be called a theological one; for theology is a teaching about God, even if a negative one. "But I am absolutely not capable nor even disposed to teach this or that about God." "I cannot leave out of consideration the fact that man lives over against God," Buber added, "but I cannot include God himself at any point in my explanation, any more than I could detach from history the, to me indubitable, working of God in it, and make of it an object of my contemplation. As I know no theological world history, so I know no theological anthropology in this sense; I know only a philosophical one." His thinking did not derive from anything traditional, as important as the theological element had been in his scholarship and reporting, but from his own experience of faith. His philosophy did not serve a series of revealed propositions but "an experienced, a perceived attitude that it has been established to make communicable." "I am not merely bound to philosophical language, I am bound to the philosophical method, indeed to a dialectic that has become unavoidable with the beginning of philosophical thinking." If he did not replace the name God by a general concept, that was not because he disagreed with Heraclitus, who held it to be inadmissible to say only "Zeus," but because unlike Tillich, he had no doctrine of a primal ground *(Urgrund)* to offer. "I must only witness for that meeting in which all meetings with others are grounded, and you cannot meet the Absolute."

Buber also pointed out in his "Philosophical Accountings" that he had never held that inner life and thinking is exclusively composed of I-Thou and I-It. "Every essential knowledge is in its origin contact with an existing being and, in its completion, possession of an enduring concept." But the continuum between cannot be divided up into one or the other; for it is a noetic movement from a personal meeting to a factual knowledge-structure in which the two primal words cooperate:

> Authentic philosophizing originates ever anew in contacts born of the I-Thou relationship that still affords no "objective" knowledge. Now the transposition into the structured order of It takes place, and, if a real workman is at work, there may stand at the end the freestone structure of a system. . . . The fiery track of the original contacts is inextinguishable. . . . To the penetrating genesis-glance each bold metaphysical setting manifests its origin in a meeting of the knowing person with an element of being that manifests itself through what meets him in a living way.

Buber did not claim for himself, however, "the freestone structure of a system"; for the theme that he had to develop was not suited to being developed into a comprehensive system. He had to make visible a neglected, obscured, primal reality and to restrict his teaching to what would point to it. He could not philosophize about being but only about the human twofold relationship to being. Therefore, his philosophizing had to be essentially an anthropological one, starting with the question of how man is possible. For this a compact structure was suitable but not one that joined everything together. Even Buber's philosophy, therefore, must be subsumed under that pointing which he spoke of in the Foreword to *For the Sake of Heaven*. In this vein Buber stated in his "Replies," "I point to something in reality that had not or had too little been seen. I take him who listens to me by the hand and lead him to the window . . . open the window and point to what is outside. I have no teaching, but I carry on a conversation." Unlike the great systematizers, Buber did not claim that the experience on which he based his philosophy was other than a limited one. But he rejected any attempt to designate that experience as "subjective."

Buber's refusal and incapacity to construct a total philosophical system marked his essential modernity; for it grew out of his recognition of the validity and limitations of his philosophy as a pointer to reality. In both *The Philosophy of Martin Buber* and *Philosophical Interrogations*, Buber acknowledged the continuity between the I that detaches itself from the other and the I that turns to it, but he would not recognize this self-consciousness as "an isolated I that stands over against neither a Thou nor an It." Whereas the distinguished French philosopher Emmanuel Levinas saw this self-identification as the source of "happiness," Buber also saw it as the source of "the deepest suffering of which we are capable" and hinted darkly that this polarity of feelings "points us back to a deep duality of which . . . my philosophy perhaps merely makes manifest the foreground that we can grasp." Buber made a distinction which he regarded as of fundamental importance between the first "lightning flash" of self-consciousness and the second "elaborated" one in which the self becomes an object to itself. He denied the Israeli philosopher Nathan Rotenstreich's claim that the first emerging of the I is the center of existence in favor of regarding it as an aura about the center, and reflection, which Rotenstreich also emphasized, as the play of a searchlight that shines upon the aura. Reflection, like the It, is necessary but not sufficient for full human existence: "Without it the human being known to us would not exist, yet it does not belong to its primal phenomena." Persons must be present for a personal meeting to take place, but developed consciousness of the I and its reflective elaboration is not essential: "I see that Socrates reflects, I do not see that Francis does so; the relation of both men to their disciples is genuinely personal."

In his replies, Buber commented ruefully on "the psychology of misunderstanding" which he illustrated by Rotenstreich's claim that Buber's statement in "Dialogue" that "in real faith the dictionary is put down," means that he advocated an empty, formal dialogue with no real content. "It is for me of the highest importance that the dialogue have a content," Buber responded, only this content does not belong to the isolated word in the dictionary where speech only shows us its general applicability, but rather, to the word in its living context in conversation, poetry, prayer, and philosophy. The more concrete and concretizing the word, the more it does justice to the unique, the coming to be, the formed. Buber did not deny that contents in general allow generally valid and binding propositions to be transmitted; "but in so doing the peculiar, that which by its nature is unique, is lost." These latter contents are not codifiable; even the most universal commands attain unforeseen interpretations which the situation itself furnishes.

In a response to the French Catholic existentialist philosopher Gabriel Marcel, Buber conceded that his use in *I and Thou* of the statement "In the beginning was relation" now seemed to him too ambiguous because of its many overtones. At the same time he did not feel himself empowered to go back and change *I and Thou* to fit his present insight: "At that time I wrote what I wrote in an overpowering inspiration. And what such inspiration delivers to one, one may no longer change, not even for the sake of exactness. For one can only measure what one might acquire, not what is lost."

In an assessment of "Buber's Triumphs and Failures" on the occasion of his centenary year, Walter Kaufmann suggested that this was perhaps because, unlike Kaufmann's own hero Nietzsche, Buber did not have that many inspirations. This is to misunderstand the faithfulness with which Buber stood in relationship to dialogic truth, a faithfulness best expressed in the line Buber himself so often quoted from Nietzsche: "One receives, and one does not know who gives." The form and content of a real philosophic text cannot be separated for the sake of an analytical consistency that loses sight of the fact that existential thinking takes place really in a specific time and in a specific situation and not abstracted from them.

In his essay on "Buber's Religious Significance" in *The Philosophy of Martin Buber*, Kaufmann systematically attacked Kierkegaard, Jaspers, Heidegger, and Sartre—the very figures who occupy the central place in his anthology *Existentialism from Dostoevsky to Sartre**:

> If we find the heart of existentialism in the protest against systems, concepts, and abstractions, coupled with a resolve to remain faithful to concrete experience and above all to the challenge of human existence—should we not find in that case that Kierkegaard and Jaspers, Heidegger and Sartre had all betrayed their own central resolve? That they had all become enmeshed in sticky webs of dialectic that impede communication? that the high abstractness of their idiom and their strange addiction to outlandish concepts far surpassed the same faults in Descartes or Plato? that not one of them was able any more to listen to the challenge of another human reality as it has found expression in a text? and that their writings have, without exception, become monologues?

After this devastating judgment, Kaufmann ended his essay with the remarkable conclusion that "in reality there is only one existentialist, and he is no existentialist, but Martin Buber."

Buber's response to criticisms of his category of "the between" was that it will have to remain for a long while within the unaccustomed; "but I do not believe that the human spirit can do without it in the long run." But this too is only a pointing. Asked how he could speak of love as attesting to the existence of the beloved, Buber could only testify from direct and indirect experience, that the great love for an actually existing being is qualitatively different from the most po-

---

*See Note to Chapter 11.

etically compelling fantasy or image because it accepts the other wholly just as she is, which the latter cannot do.

Eugen Rosenstock-Huessy's contribution to the *Philosophical Interrogations,* which Buber found to be one of the most interesting, criticized Buber's "single-aged" view of man in favor of a "pluri-aged," historical view of man. To Rosenstock, the pronouns stand for names and cannot be basic, therefore: "You are Mr. Friedman and Maurice Friedman long before you are I or Thou," Rosenstock wrote me. Buber characterized Rosenstock's emphasis on names as "an Old Testament manner of thinking to which I cannot adhere" and added: "I myself am deeply opposed to him who claims that at the time of one's own death one should remember the death of the person who gave one his name (who could have been the superintendent of an orphanage). Next to my death there is place for no remembrance other than that of the person with whom I have exchanged the most genuine Thou of my life" (Paula). Rosenstock opposed to Buber's "single-aged socialism," which emphasized the present, a pluri-aged, religionlike communism, which emphasized three or more generations. Against this historicism Buber contended: "My thought is not 'single-aged.' But my faith is."

> I believe in that hour in the life of individuals and of the human race, where the historical bursts open and the present reveals itself. I believe in this hour because I know it. I know that it opens persons to each other and establishes community between them. . . . My innermost heart is indeed with those (in the near or remote future) who, driven into high despair by the pseudo realization of this religionlike world program [communism], by this planetary centralism of power that will quite possibly invert everything, will summon with their last strength the single-aged and all-aged present, the presence between men.

In philosophical interchange as in theological, Buber's witness remained a passionate one.

In response to the reproach often made to him that his concern was a spiritual elite rather than for man as man, Buber made it absolutely clear that what interested him was dialogue ("heart-will and grace in one") even between idiots rather than the loftiest pseudo-interchanges of geniuses: "I have many times perceived how the soul of a so-called idiot extends its arms—and thrusts into emptiness," he claimed; whereas "I have often known of highly spiritual persons whose basic nature it was to withhold themselves from others even if they occasionally let this or that person come near them."

Buber's replies to his critics took on an important historical over-tone when Ernst Simon quoted approvingly Franz Rosenzweig's criti-cism of *I and Thou* as not doing justice to the It; for here Buber gives us in writing the response which he probably made to Rosenzweig orally: "Indeed it does not do justice to it," Buber asserted. "At another time it would perhaps have been granted to me to sound the praises of the It; today not so: because without a turning of man to his Thou no turn in his destiny can come." This in no way meant that Buber did not prize science with its so-called objective knowledge. Science gives us our orienting connection with the space-time sphere in which we live, and without it no handing down of an organized body of knowledge from generation to generation would be possible. Our current world views are built on science's current "position." What is more, Buber recognized a relation—"one that remains ever mysterious to me"—between the basic knowledge of mathematics and being itself, upon which the triumph of inherited knowledge of the human race from Euclid to Einstein is founded. But he refused to see science as exclusively the province of the It. What an original inves-tigator discovers in his contacts with the unique still has the essential structure of the I-Thou relationship: a person and a presence which that person stands over against—not yet object, the contact of the unique with the unique, still prior to all transposition into the general. The investigator must from time to time radically remain standing before concrete reality in order to attain general insights or exact formulae. "But at the beginning of his way he is ever again led by the genius of meetings until that genius can safely deliver him to the reliable spirit of objectification."

Science, however, is only an aid, not a reliable objective technique, in the work of the true therapist or educator. In the hands of a person without a true vocation, psychology or pedagogy will be deceptive and misleading. The methods developed by the different schools of therapy can be used to heal or destroy, depending upon the therapist. "Outside of the responsibility practiced by a responsible person, 'nor-mative' generalizations that are made in the name of science have no real meaning for me."

This qualification in no wise meant that Buber sought some hy-pothetical perfect I-Thou relationship unmixed with I-It. "I am not at all concerned about perfection," Buber replied to a question of Mal-colm Diamond's, but that the I-Thou relationship be realized where it can be and that the life of man be determined and formed by it. "For I believe that it can transform the world . . . into something very much more human . . . than exists today." Real persons can participate in one another's lives not only in space but in time, as when they think of each other at the same time. But they do so only by means of their difference, by means of the uniqueness of each person. This concern for particularity and uniqueness is in no way diluted when Buber joins together our relation to our fellowman and our relation to God; for his rejection of a special sphere of "religion" and of "ethics" was by the same token a rejection of any generalities in favor of the lived concrete.

Even in dealing with the theory of knowledge, Buber managed to remain quite concrete. Thus in denying that we can have a discussion with things, he reported how several times in his youth he wanted to fix an object, to compel it so that it would be "only" his conception; "but it refuted me through the dumb force of its being." Another time Buber used the example of an English sheepdog which a child looked in the eyes, and the child remained standing, . . . laying his hand on the dog's head and calling him by a name he invented on the spot. "When later at home the child sought to recall what had been special about the sheepdog, he managed without ideas or categories; he only needed them when he had to relate the occurrence to his best friend." The "truth" that one attains through such conceptualization and dialectical reasoning is only a preparation and a practice. It attains its authenticity only when it steps out of the realm of concepts into that of meeting. This movement between I-Thou and I-It was lost to the American theologian Edmond Cherbonnier when he raised the question whether Buber's philosophy was open to any criticism and correction at all. Quoting my statement in *The Life of Dialogue* of "the logical impossibility of criticizing I-Thou knowing on the basis of any system of I-It," Cherbonnier suggested Buber had a built-in immunity to criticism which enables him to dismiss a critic not by refuting but by declaring that he has failed to understand. Buber rejected categorically any suspicion of a claim to speak *ex cathedra*:

> Inner contradictions are no less possible here than in a Socratic philosophy, and with him who seriously seeks to point out to me such a contradiction, I go seriously into it. In no way, therefore, do I reject consistency. But where I am compelled to point to "paradoxes," there are none that are meant as being beyond possible experience; rather a silent understanding is again and again established between me and those of my readers who are ready, without holding back, to make their own the experiences that I mean.

The corrective office of reason is incontestable, Buber said at another point, and it can be summoned at any moment to set right the incongruity between my sense perception and what is common to my fellowmen. In the I-It relation what is received in the I-Thou is elaborated and broken up, and here "errors" are possible which can be corrected through "objectively" establishing and comparing what has passed and passes in the minds of others. But in the true I-Thou relationship there is no knowledge of objective facts, hence nothing that can be corrected as an "error" by comparison with the data of the I-It. Reason with its gigantic structure of general concepts, "cannot replace the smallest perception of something particular and unique, cannot by means of it take part in the grasping of what here and now confronts me."

One of my own questions to Buber was whether it would not be helpful to distinguish between that I-It knowledge which points back to I-Thou knowing and that which is so abstract that it does not, such as an operationalist description of interpersonal relationships from the standpoint of a behaviorist observer, as opposed to a poem or a novel. Buber agreed about the distinction, but he did not regard them as types different by nature:

> On the one hand, there exists no abstraction so ethereal that a person who lives greatly could not summon it by its secret primal name and draw it down to the earth of bodily meetings from which it originated. But on the other, precisely in our time the gross absence of relationship has begun to find a consistent "empty" expression in novels and in drama. It may be more difficult to confront this contemporary literature with the genuine might of human relationship than the defective description of the behaviorist psychologist.

A second question that I asked Buber was whether the categories of our thought have some objective logic of their own. In my chapter on theory of knowledge in *The Life of Dialogue* I had characterized them as merely secondary derivatives of I-Thou knowing, products of abstraction and objectification. Buber responded that he could not hold the logical foundations of the "world" that is transmitted from generation to generation to be secondary derivations from either I-Thou or I-It. Nor could he formulate a metaphysical thesis that would lead beyond the duality of these aspects. "But how I-Thou and I-It again and again have co-operated and co-operate in the human construction and reconstruction of a 'world' accessible to human thought, I have attempted to indicate by the category of 'we,' in 'What Is Common to All' [*The Knowledge of Man*]."

In a question under "Education" in the *Philosophical Interrogations* the distinguished Italian psychoanalyst Roberto Assagioli asked Buber how modern youth might be induced to discover and recognize the sacred. Buber, who had once said to me that there could be a saint living today but such a person would not be a modern man, embodying the contradictions of modern existence, replied that he had known no one whom he could call a saint but many whose everyday performances, without being meant to be such, are actually holy acts because one who comes into contact with them feels against his will and his world view: "Those acts are genuine to the roots; they are not a shoot from an alien stem; their roots reach into that sphere which I cannot reach and from whose inaccessibility I suffer in the overlucid hours of midnight." Drawn into connection with that sphere by those genuine actions he has encountered this person experiences not "the holy" but hallowing, the *humanly* holy, and spontaneously does something differently than he was accustomed to. He puts more of himself into it, brings to it more intention and meaning. "Finally he opens himself to the sphere from which the meaning of our existence comes to us."

The interchange between Buber and Robert Hutchins was based on my article "Martin Buber's Concept of Education: A New Approach to College Teaching," in which I set forth a typology using Hutchins as illustrative of what Buber called the "funnel," Dewey as an example of what Buber called the "pump," and the dialogical as the narrow ridge between them. Hutchins agreed that a great teacher like Socrates or Buber can start with anything and move by ordered stages to the most tremendous issues, but "the ordinary teacher who begins with triviality is almost certain to end there." Great books, in contrast, offer the thoughts of great men about great issues which we may apply to the concrete reality of our time. Buber agreed that there is a frightening lack of leadership in our day: "The fathers have imparted principles to the generation ruling today, but not the capacity of the soul to let the principle-true praxis be determined by the situations." He also agreed with Hutchins that teacher and student are not equal. But every teacher who has ears and a heart will listen to the unique personal experiences of her students and help the student advance confidently from the individual experience to an organic knowledge of the world and life. Great books cannot replace such a dialogue; for no matter how high they exalt the reader they cannot offer him what the simple human meeting between teacher and pupil again and again can give: helping immediacy.

Although Hutchins also spoke of a "Civilization of the Dialogue," for him the Socratic method remained the most important method of teaching. To Buber, Socratic teaching meant dialectic but not dialogue: "I know of very few men in history to whom I stand in such a relation of both trust and veneration as Socrates." But Socrates overvalued the significance of abstract general concepts in comparison with concrete individual experiences. He "treated them as if they were more important than bones—that they are not." What is more, the questions that he posed were not real ones but merely moves in a sublime dialectical game that had as its objective revealing the person whom he questioned as one who did not really know. The real teacher, in contrast, awakens in the pupil the need to communicate of himself and at the same time learns to know ever more concretely the particular, the individual, the unique. If Hutchins should now object that there are too few good teachers, then what follows from this is that our most pressing task is to educate educators.

In 1961, Buber reaffirmed his conviction that the educator in our day has to do without any generally "valid image," which today is necessarily illusory. Closely linked with this was Buber's rejection in "Replies to My Critics" of Hugo Bergmann's expectation that a teacher should give indications as to how we should walk the way. "One shall receive direction from the teacher," responded Buber, "but not the manner in which one must apply this direction: that each must discover and acquire for himself in a work that demands of him his fullest potentiality yet also presents him with a treasure that enriches his existence." That does not mean, as Marvin Fox supposed, that Buber saw every genuine moral decision as an event "of great struggle and searching." There can be a difficult wrestling of the soul in a situation full of contradiction, but it is also possible to "catch the situation in an instant, as the good tennis player returns the ball with the proper stroke." "I know and love many such men for whom all, as it were, has already been decided, and the original decision transforms itself as from beyond the dimension of time into the current and wholly special." One does not have to link one's moral decision with God. On the contrary, said Buber, "I find it glorious when the pious man does the good with his whole soul 'without thinking of God,'" and he utterly rejected Fox's inference that in Buber's view he who confesses no belief knows no values! Nor could he accept Fox's assumption that for him there were no universally valid moral rules:

I have never doubted the absolute validity of the command, "Honor thy father and thy mother," but he who says to me that one, in fact, knows always and under all circumstances what "to honor" means and what it does not, of him I say that he does not know what he is talking about. Man must expound the eternal values, and, to be sure, [exemplify these] with his own life.

Always the doing of right involves a risk, but even in the midst of this risk, with its tension between absolute law and concrete reality, one can perform with one's whole soul was Buber's answer to a question of Ernst Simon's. Buber took for an example a political decision, which meant, for him and Simon alike, a moral one. In the midst of the conflict in which the cruel reality of both sides inflicts itself on you, you may again and again "perceive with surprise, at times positively overpoweringly, what of truth and justice can be realized in this situation," and "at just this moment . . . the forces of your soul . . . concentrate as into a crystal." Such a decision of the whole being has nothing to do with that solicitude which Emmanuel Levinas, following Heidegger, praised in his essay as the access to the otherness of the other. If one has this access already, one will have it in solicitude, Buber rejoined, "but he who does not have it . . . may clothe the naked and feed the hungry all day and it will remain difficult for him to say a true Thou." In fact, "the real ethical problem would become wholly visible for the first time" only when "all were well clothed and well nourished," for only then would the direct demand of relationship come into its own. In 1963, Levinas responded that he saw the hunger of others as the *embodiment* of the Thou, just as speaking is embodied in but goes far beyond the phonetic organs or the organs of artistic activity. In contrast to Buber, Levinas saw the I-Thou relationship as *essentially* asymmetrical.

Buber's invarying insistence on the concrete shone through in the way he again and again based his responses on actual personal observation rather than on some logical extension of his own views. To Paul Pfuetze's question why, "even at his best, man feels an inordinate tug of self-interest," Buber responded that this in no way accorded with the actual lives of persons he knew of whose inwardness he could perceive something:

> I see how they concern themselves, each in his own way, the one noisily or awkwardly, the other goodnaturedly and at times even tenderly, with their family, comrades, passers-by with open spirit for what takes place, and, not infrequently ready with participation, information, and help. . . . I sometimes watch boys playing. What really concerns the individual is just the game itself, and that means, of course, before all, his share in it; but I see such a boy, often, also really concern

himself about . . . the other's fortune and misfortune, and at times I see such a young heart, as it were, fly across to where the other stands, with the wish that he could help there where, according to the rules of the game, no help at all is possible.

Partly because of the concerns of his critics, more of Buber's replies in both volumes centered on the philosophy of religion than on any other subject. Although he rejected the separation between the I-Thou relationship with God and that with his fellowmen and refused to pose the question of which of the two meetings is "the primary one," he stated that the human person might be conceivable without the meeting with other men but not without that with God:

> On the plane of personal life-experience, the meeting with men is naturally the first; nevertheless, one only has to take seriously the insight that the genetically underivable uniqueness of every man presupposes the share played by a creative act, and the original nature of the contact between God and man is evident.

This is not, as it might appear, a theological statement. Buber could not acknowledge theology's claim for exclusiveness and therefore he could not take seriously von Balthasar's reproach that he was see-sawing between theology and philosophy of religion. "The categories themselves have fallen into see-sawing before my eyes, and they are not to be halted." "Where I may draw out of primal depths that had opened to me as he who I am, I must acknowledge it." But he had to deal with the plurality of religions in all its reality, and not merely historically or psychologically, recognizing that he was not within that reality. "I pursue no theology as theology and no philosophy of religion as philosophy of religion," he asserted. "Honor to those who can still today bind these categories with all their strength to the strong bough of a revelation; I have not been able to go their way."

What Buber could and did affirm was a vibrant connection between the moments of Thou and the presence of the eternal Thou as primarily real for the man of genuine faith. Precisely this was the meaning of *emunah* to Buber: These are the moments in which the I, present in its wholeness, speaks into the distance of all distances the Thou of the greatest nearness. Just from addressing the "eternal Thou" the I knows itself as Thou. Those moments flash up out of a darkness rich with possibility, a darkness in which we perceive nothing "and in which we nonetheless trust as the ground and meaning of our existence." That the lines of I-Thou relationships "intersect in the eternal Thou is grounded 'in the fact that the man who says Thou ultimately means his eternal Thou." The legitimately religious existence of man consists in genuinely accepting and mastering the discontinuity that is basic to human life. Remaining open to the lead of the I-Thou, "the grace that appears ever anew in earthly material," is the only way in which the existence of man can become whole, and it is to this theme that Buber dedicated his work in all spheres. In this sense of the concern for the *wholeness* of life, Buber acknowledged that his thought might be called religious but not as starting from a religion, as did Pascal, Hamaan, and Kierkegaard—three thinkers from whom Buber learned things that he could not forget while pursuing a course fundamentally different from theirs.

In answer to the German theologian Friedrich Thieberger's question in the *Interrogations* concerning a counterfeit Thou, Buber could only point to the wholeness of the soul and the unity of life: "Life in the service of an idol, however it is called, disintegrates hour by hour, success by success; life in the service of God collects itself ever again in all stillness, even in the shallows of disappointments and in the depths of failures." I asked Buber whether his words in *I and Thou* concerning that pure relation in which potential is still actual being and "the unbroken world of Thou which binds up the isolated moments of relation in a life of world solidarity" meant that we relate to the actual and present eternal Thou even when the temporal Thou has again become only past and potential. Buber in response resolutely distanced himself from the metaphysics into which an answer to my question would have drawn him:

> I perceive in this question, from words of mine which have been quoted here, that I have already come close to the limit of what is accessible to our experience. I hesitate to go a step further with words the full responsibility for which I cannot bear. *In our experience* our relation to God does *not* include our I-It relations. What is the case beyond our experience, thus, so to speak, from the side of God, no longer belongs to what can be discussed. Perhaps I have here and there, swayed by the duty of the heart that bids me point out what I have to point out, already said too much.

Totally consonant with this position was Buber's reply to Pfuetze that if there were a cogent proof of God's existence, there would no longer be any difference between belief and unbelief. "I have no metaphysics on which to establish my faith, I have created none for myself, I do not desire any, I need none, I am not capable of one."

One of the questions that had haunted me after my own experience in mystic meditation and my immersion in Buber's thought was whether God is loved only through the creature and never apart from him, as Buber seemed to imply in "The Question to the Single One." "Prayer and devotional literature of all religions," I commented, "speak tirelessly of a direct relation to God, a turning toward, and praying to, him which does not seem to come necessarily through the relation to any creature, even though it does not exclude such relation." "When I speak of the exclusion of the world from the relation to God," Buber declared in the *Interrogations,* "I do not speak of the *hour* of man, but of his *life.*"

> I regard it as unqualifiedly legitimate when a man again and again, in an hour of religious fervor, adoring and praying enters into a direct, "world-free" relation to God; and my heart understands as well the Byzantine composer of hymns who speaks as "the alone to the Alone," as also that Hasidic rabbi who, feeling himself a stranger on earth, asks God, who is also, indeed, a stranger on earth, to grant him, just for that reason his friendship. But a "life with God" erected on the rejection of the living is no life with God. Often we hear of animals who have been loved by holy hermits, but I would not be able to regard anyone as holy who in the desert ceased to love the men whom he had left.

Some of Buber's responses in the *Interrogations* were delightful on a purely personal level, as when Arthur Cohen prefaced a question by saying, "If you will excuse a direct question," and Buber replied, "I do not have to excuse direct questions, I prefer them." Or when, asked by Rollo May to what extent he was an existentialist, Buber replied: "I cannot, of couse, be particularly pleased when, instead of paying attention to what I directly have to say, a questioner furnishes me with the label of an 'ism' and then wants to know concerning it." Then there is Buber's response to William Ernest Hocking, who said that if there is an absolute good, there must also be an absolute evil: "We become acquainted day after day with all degrees of relative stupidity; shall we conclude from that there exists an absolute stupidity?"

The reality of the evil to which Hocking pointed Buber acknowledged: There are many in our time who would not have believed themselves capable of wanting to save someone like a Goebbels before themselves, said Buber. Yet he refused to reject the possibility, almost incomprehensible though it is, that we can help the man who has apparently completely succumbed to arrogant self-affirmation to find the way out. "I confess that I can hold no one to be 'absolutely' unredeemable." Even the person who says I will sin and then repent may, in a later hour, be seized, "like a heart-purifying lightning flash," by the insight that he cannot be forgiven. "What can transpire between the real God and a real man is of so paradoxical a nature that no saying, be it ever so 'true,' is equal to it." Evil radicalizes itself, but it is granted us to cooperate in its deradicalization. It is easy to pronounce me a romantic optimist because I have always clung to the messianic belief in redemption, said Buber to Pfuetze, but that charge is false because I have never and nowhere asserted that man can overcome the inner conflict of human existence through his own power and "good will." "I am a realistic meliorist," Buber claimed. Human life approaches its fulfillment and redemption in the measure that the I-Thou relationship becomes strong in it.

Buber's faith was not based on a biblical theology. Rather his insight into the Bible was based upon his experience of faith, including that threat of infinity which brought him close to suicide as a boy of fourteen. In "What Is Man?" Buber asserted that the present epoch of "homelessness" has proceeded out of the Copernican invasion of the infinite. But in *Philosophical Interrogations* he added that "this invasion has had the effect that it had only because man has merely opposed to it the Kantian antinomy of the infinity and finiteness of space and time." What Buber now pointed to as transcending this antinomy is precisely that sense of the eternal which he attained when he surmounted this crisis of his youth: So far man has not opposed to this invasion "a greater image of God than the traditional one, a greater one *and yet one that can still be addressed,* the image of a God who out of his eternity has set in being this infinite-finite, space-time world, and who embraces and rules over it with his eternity." The awful silence in the spaces between the stars that terrified Pascal and the "indefiniteness that shadows forth the heartless voids and immensities of the universe and stabs us from behind with the thought of annihilation when beholding the white depths of the Milky Way" (Melville), Buber encompassed, at the end of his life as at the beginning, with a renewed and deepened existential trust.

CHAPTER 12

The Interpretation of Hasidism:
Buber versus Scholem

BUBER'S REPLY TO Gershom Scholem's critique of his interpretation of Hasidism is a chapter in itself.

When Scholem published the English edition of his book *Major Trends in Jewish Mysticism* in 1946, at a time when he had already done a great deal of his research on the Kabbala and Sabbatianism, his final chapter on Hasidism not only contained no criticism of Buber's interpretation but agreed with it in almost every important respect. According to Scholem, Hasidism "neutralized" the messianic element in Jewish mysticism without renouncing the popular appeal of later Kabbalism, hence achieving what Buber called "the messianism of the everyday." Its heroic period during the first fifty years after the death of the Baal-Shem was characterized by a spirit of enthusiasm based on the idea of the immanence of God in all that exists. "Within a geographically small area and also within a surprisingly short period, the ghetto gave birth to a whole galaxy of saint-mystics, each of them a startling individuality." This burst of mystical energy did not produce new religious ideas or theories of mystical knowledge. The new element was rather "the spontaneity of feeling generated in sensitive minds by the encounter with the living incarnations of mysticism."

Although the continuity of Kabbalistic thought was not really interrupted, the Kabbala was used as an instrument of mystical psychology and self-knowledge rather than a penetration of the upper worlds for their own sake. In this "mysticism of the personal life" "almost all the Kabbalistic ideas are now placed in relation to values peculiar to the individual life, and those which are not remain empty and ineffective." "The originality of Hasidism lies in the fact that mystics who had attained their spiritual aim . . . turned to the people with their mystical knowledge, their 'Kabbalism become Ethos' [a quote from Buber's introduction to *The Tales of Rabbi Nachman*]." The existence of the *zaddik* was the actual proof of the possibility of living up to the ideal— "He who . . . is capable of being alone with God is the true center of the community." The life of the Hasidim centers on the personality of the *zaddik*. The opinions of the *zaddik* are less important than his character. "*Personality* takes the place of *doctrine;* what is lost in rationality by this change is gained in efficacy." "A ray of God's essence is present and perceptible everywhere and at every moment." It is the *zaddik* who helps make this palpable for the Hasid. The *zaddik* becomes the center of the new myth, and the Hasidic tale about the *zaddik* is the religious carrying forward of that myth.

> The revival of a new mythology in the world of Hasidism to which attention has been drawn occasionally, especially by Martin Buber, draws not the least part of its strength from its connection between the magical and the mystical faculties of its heroes. When all is said and done it is this myth which represents the greatest creative expression of Hasidism. In the place of the theoretical disquisition, or at least side by side with it, you get the Hasidic tale. Around the lives of the great Zaddikim, the bearers of that irrational something which their mode of life expressed, legends were spun often in their own lifetime. . . . To tell a story of the deeds of the saints has become a new religious value, and there is something of the celebration of a religious rite about it. Not a few great Zaddikim . . . have laid down the whole treasure of their ideas in such tales. Their Torah took the form of an inexhaustible fountain of story-telling. Nothing at all has remained theory, everything has become a story.

In 1948, Scholem came to the University of Chicago and spoke to one of Joachim Wach's classes. "He is the sort of historian of religion that I like," Wach said of Scholem, whom he had known as a fellow graduate student in Germany. When Scholem came to visit Wach in Switzerland, where Wach went every summer to be with his mother, Wach sensed a tension between Scholem and Buber. This tension came out in the open not many years later when Scholem began publicly criticizing Buber in his lectures in England and America. Abraham Joshua Heschel was extremely distressed by the nature of these attacks. "You know I do not like some of what Buber has done with Hasidism," Heschel said, "but whom else do we have like him?"

Both Paul Arthur Schilpp and Fritz Kaufmann wrote to Scholem urging him to contribute an essay on Buber's interpretation of Hasidism to *The Philosophy of Martin Buber,* and Fritz Kaufmann did not give up even after the first attempts met with no success. After Buber had received our list of those we hoped would contribute, he wrote in December 1956, "I am curious what Scholem, whom I appreciate very highly, will do with it. He has a somewhat ambivalent relation to the subject [of Buber's interpretation of Hasidism]. My new essay on Hasidism is in some regards an answer to his objections." The essay to which Buber was referring was "Hasidism and Modern Man," which I set at the head of the volume of Buber's Hasidic interpretations collected under this title. It was also the introduction to the second volume, *The Origin and Meaning of Hasidism;* for in it Buber looked back over his half century of work in interpreting Hasidism and bringing it to the West, distilling from this variegated labor the simple, central message which he more and more came to see as the core of Hasidic life and teaching: "Man cannot approach the divine by reaching beyond the human; he can approach Him through becoming human. To become human is what he, this individual man, has been created for."

The First World War, which brought Buber to the understanding of dialogue, also brought him to the realization that the Hasidic way of life was involved in some mysterious way in the task that had claimed him.

> I could not become a Hasid. It would have been an unpermissible masquerading had I taken on the Hasidic manner of life—I who had a wholly other relation to Jewish tradition, since I must distinguish in my innermost being between what is commanded me and what is not commanded me. It was necessary, rather, to take into my own existence as much as I actually could of what had been truly exemplified for me in Hasidism, that is to say, of the realization of that dialogue with being whose possibility my thought had shown me.

The form of the "legendary anecdote" that evolved over the years enabled Buber to portray the Hasidic life in such a way that it became visible as at once reality and teaching. Although Buber saw the kernel of Hasidic life as given over to decay and destruction, he held in "Hasidism and Modern Man" that it is still capable of working on the life of men in the present-day West because of its central concern, preserved in personal as well as in communal existence, to overcome the fundamental separation between the sacred and the profane.

Although Kierkegaard and Marx already pointed to the crisis and alienation of modern man a century ago, and the psychoanalysts did the same at the turn of the century, only now can we really understand this crisis in its true depth and take the injured wholeness of man upon us. Although modern man no longer knows the holy face to face, he knows its heir, the "spiritual," and "recognizes" it without allowing it to determine life in any way. One takes culture and ideas with grim seriousness, placing them on golden thrones to which their limbs are chained, but any claim of the spirit on personal existence is warded off through a comprehensive apparatus. "No false piety has ever attained this concentrated degree of inauthenticity." To this behavior of present-day man who has got rid of the command of hallowing, "Hasidism sets the simple truth that the wretchedness of our world is grounded in its resistance to the entrance of the holy into lived life." "A life that does not seek to realize what the living person, in the ground of his self-awareness, understands or glimpses as the right is not merely unworthy of the spirit; it is also unworthy of life." What underlay this seemingly harsh judgment was Buber's recognition that what was in question was not some separate sphere of the religious or holy, but the quality of life itself, its call to become "humanly holy" in the measure and manner of our personal existence.

Hasidism, Buber claimed, freed the myths that it took over from the Kabbala from their gnostic nature and restored them to their original condition. This mythical essence of Hasidism "has entered into the lived life of seven generations, as whose late-born interpreter I function." The impact of this interpretation on the non-Jewish world was such that it was often suggested to Buber that he should liberate Hasidism from its "confessional limitations" as part of Judaism and proclaim it as an unfettered teaching of mankind. Buber's response to this demand is one of the finest illustrations of how the life of dialogue meant for him meeting the other *and* holding one's ground in that meeting:

Taking such a "universal" path would have been for me pure arbitrariness. In order to speak to the world what I have heard, I am not bound to step into the street. I may remain standing in the door of my ancestral house: here too the word that is uttered does not go astray.

As a response to Scholem's objections, this essay was hardly effective, since Scholem had not spelled out these objections and Buber did not in any way refer to them.

In November 1957, in consenting to a plan for the two volumes of his Hasidic interpretations, Buber declared: "I have in mind to add at some place an explanation of my view about the relation between Hasidism and the Kabbala, of course in Vol. II." It is possible that he had Scholem's objections in mind here too, but the explanation was never added. In 1960 when Eugenia and I went for four months to Jerusalem, I visited Scholem and asked him personally whether he would reconsider his decision not to contribute an essay on Buber's interpretation of Hasidism to *The Philosophy of Martin Buber*. Scholem was adamant. "Don't you have something already written?" I persisted. "I do, but I wouldn't give it to *you*," he answered. "Besides I don't believe in the principle of The Library of Living Philosophers," he asserted. "Why not?" I asked. "Because," replied Scholem, "it gives the philosopher the last word." This reply, as Scholem was later to say of one of Buber's, was unforgettable. He did suggest one of his disciples, Rivka Schatz-Uffenheimer, and she agreed to write an essay on the subject. She completed a forty-page monograph by that fall, which was translated from Hebrew into German and English by Fritz Kaufmann's daughter Renate, who had recently moved to Jerusalem, where she worked as a librarian at the Hebrew University.

Rivka Schatz's essay on "Man's Relation to God and World in Buber's Rendering of the Hasidic Teaching" begins and ends with a paragraph of praise in between which are forty pages of solid Scholemite criticism. "There is no doubt that Buber has done more than any other scholar to open men's hearts for a profound understanding of Hasidism," she wrote. "And even if portions of his teachings appear to me open to question on essential points, it remains true that these questions grew on that soil which Buber had prepared and sowed." The severity of her criticism was "not meant as a verdict on the final value of Buber's teaching," Schatz added, since that "must be measured by another standard than that of historical criticism." Although Buber insisted in conversation with Rivka Schatz that he had no system in his representation of the Hasidic world, she stressed that his synthetic tapestry was woven of selected strands, and it was he who determined the hue of the cloth. Specifically, the affection with which Buber regarded reality as such led him to see Hasidism as closing the chasm between God and world, "as though Hasidism taught that there is nothing to distinguish this time from the time of the Messiah, the Zaddik from the ordinary man, the holy from the profane." Schatz portrayed Buber as full of enthusiasm for the very concrete reality that Hasidism saw as problematic, as boundlessly loving that very "world" whose whole ontic existence is set at naught in the eyes of Hasidism. "In the eyes of the Hasidim the greatness of the Zaddikim lay in their knowing how to turn . . . the divine 'being' that has fallen into the world back to its 'nothing,' which is the true being." Man's contact with creation is an ideal mission that demanded of man the nullification of creation and of the concrete as such. Life in the world was transformed into life in God because Hasidism developed an indifference to the concrete. Hasidism held that God speaks to us *also* in corporeal reality and that we must serve God in that reality by redeeming it. But it did not hold that every action is of equal worth and equally endowed with "sacramental possibility," a view which Schatz-Uffenheimer sees as originating in Buber's own antinomian relation to the Torah, whose claims set prior limitations on the extension of the holy over the profane.

Schatz-Uffenheimer did not see Buber as drawing his conclusions out of thin air. "He succumbed to the plenitude of the Hasidic world of aphorism: this plenitude sharpened to a point, in which you can find everything in the most brilliant and exaggerated form, in which every saying embodies a revolution." But like Scholem, she places Hasidism firmly within the context of the Kabbala and that means of *gnosis* and *not* of *devotio:*

> Hasidism in fact never for a moment divested itself of the gnostic mode of consciousness and never forgot that our world, in its present state, is the result of "the breaking of the vessels" of the divinity. It never, even on one page of the thousands on which its teaching is transmitted, forsook its yearning for the restoration of the world to its "primordial" condition.

Unlike Scholem, Schatz-Uffenheimer did not entirely deny the validity of Buber's interpretation of Hasidism. She said that it was one-sided, which it unquestionably is, and that is another way of saying that it is based much more on the tales than on the teachings, even though Buber was thoroughly familiar with the latter.

The chapter on Hasidism is the longest section in Buber's "Replies to My Critics." Buber used it as "a welcome occasion to clarify my thought with definitive precision." In so doing he was replying to Scholem as well as to Schatz. Agreeing with Schatz-Uffenheimer's view that his tapestry of Hasidic interpretation is woven of elective strands, Buber stated that since 1910, when he reached a basic study of the sources, his aim had not been to present a historically comprehensive picture of Hasidism but only a selective one. But the principle of selection that ruled here, as in that of his work on Judaism in general, was not a subjective one. "I have dealt with that in the life and teachings of Judaism which, according to my insight, is its proper truth and is decisive for its function in the previous and future history of the human spirit." This involves evaluation from its base up, Buber conceded, but this evaluation had its origin in the immovable central existence of values. "Since I have attained to the maturity of this insight, I have not made use of a filter; I became a filter."

Comparing Hasidism with Zen Buddhism, the Sufis, and the Franciscans, Buber pointed out that in all of them there prevailed devotion to the divine and the hallowing of life through this devotion. In Hasidism and in Hasidism alone, however, it is not the life of monks that is reported but that of spiritual leaders who are married and produce children and who stand at the head of communities composed of families. "In Hasidism the hallowing extends fundamentally to the natural and social life. Here alone the whole man, as God has created him, enters into the hallowing." Scholem rightfully designated *devekut,* the "cleaving" of the souls to God, as the central tendency of the Hasidic teaching. But Buber in his reply distinguished between two kinds of *devekut* as neither Scholem nor Schatz-Uffenheimer did:

> Among the zaddikim who sought . . . to elaborate the Kabbalistic doctrine, there predominated the view, already familiar to us from Gnosis, that one must lift oneself out of the "corporeal" reality of human life into the "nothing" of pure spirit in order to attain contact with God. . . . But opposed to them—without a contest between the two taking place—is the view that this "constant being with God" . . . is rather reached through man's dedicating to God all that is lived by him.

Devekut as a Gnostic spiritualization of existence is first found in Hasidism in its great thinker the Maggid of Mezritch. But before that, *devekut* as the hallowing of all life originated with his teacher, the Baal-Shem-Tov. Thus the teaching of *hallowing* is the original thesis of Hasidism and *not* that of spiritualization.

Asked by the author of Kabbalistic writings about the secret *kavanot,* or "intentions," that entered into Hasidism through the Kabbalistic prayer book that it took over, Rabbi Moshe of Kobryn warned:

> You must keep in mind that the word Kabbala is derived from *kabbel:* to accept; and the word kavana from *kavven:* to direct. For the final meaning of all the wisdom of the Kabbala is to take on oneself the yoke of God's will and the final meaning of all the art of kavanot is to direct one's heart to God.

Here, according to Buber, the life of devoted cleaving to God meant by the primal faith of Israel opposes itself to the hypertrophy of mystical-magical doctrine. The Baal-Shem included everything corporeal without exception in the sphere of what can be hallowed through *kavana,* or intention, *not* excluding the coupling of man and wife. "Of a 'nullification' of the concrete there is in *this* line of Hasidism—which begins with its beginning—nothing to be found." The beings and things continue to exist undiminished, and when the divine "sparks" are raised from them, this is no annihilation but rather dedication, hallowing, transformation without suspension of concreteness. When the Baal-Shem says, "In the hour when on account of sin you carry out the turning, you raise the sparks that were in it into the upper world," that is no nullification but a bridge-building. It is not "Hasidism" that was faced with the "critical problem" of "life split apart into external action and inner intention," but its spiritual coinage, and extension which won the upper hand in the school of the Maggid of Mezritch. But wherever the new mode of life became stronger than the doctrine that grew out of the Kabbalistic tradition, the acceptance of the concrete for the sake of its hallowing took place as "decision" and not as "problem." What ultimately concerned Buber was not an act for its own sake, as Schatz-Uffenheimer imagined, but "the restoration of the immediacy between God and man for the sake of overcoming the eclipse of God."

Therefore, Buber's selection "necessarily directed itself to the unjustly despised 'anecdotes'—stories of lived life—and 'aphorisms'—sayings in which life documents itself." For both expressed with great pregnancy the life of the *zaddikim.* Some *zaddikim* were predominantly teachers of future *zaddikim;* others, like Levi Yitzhak of Berdtichev, R. Zusya, and R. Moshe Leib of Sasov, are popular figures who help the broad circle of followers among the Hasidim. These latter represent the simply unique in Hasidism. The relationship of the master to the disciples has also perhaps taken exemplary shape in the writings of Zen Buddhism, but that of the master to ignorant people is no-where in the world expressed as it is here.

At another place in the "Replies" Buber addressed himself to a criticism of Hugo Bergmann's, also made by Schatz and Scholem, that his presentation of the Hasidic conception of a "messianism of all times" had weakened the messianic belief. The ever-recurring event of redemption preceding the messianic fulfillment in the ages in no way injures the devotion to the *eschaton,* the final redemption, Buber asserted:

> Just as I believe not merely in the creative act in the beginning, but also in the creation at all times, in which man has a share as "God's comrade in the work of creation," and just as I believe not merely in the great acts of revelation in the incomprehensible hours in which one "sees the voices," but also in the secret and yet revelatory coming into contact of above and below, so I believe in the redeeming act poured forth over the ages, in which man again has a share. These events do not add themselves to one another, but all together they cooperate secretly in preparing the coming redemption of the world.

In *Philosophical Interrogations* Buber explicitly asked that his in-terpretation of Hasidic teaching not be confused with his own thought. "I can by no means in my own thinking take responsibility for Hasidic ideas, although my thinking is indebted to them and bound up with them." For example, he would not say, in representing his own thought, that God *wishes* to redeem us or that everything *desires* to become a sacrament; yet the reality meant by these two statements has its place in "my more cautious thought." He also stated at another place that there was much in Hasidism that he could by no means make his own, in particular the Kabbalistic ideas of the emana-tions of God and their relationship to one another. "These are essen-tially Gnostic ideas, and I have always decisively opposed Gnosis, which presumes to know, so to speak, the inner history of God."

In his essay "Martin Buber and Mysticism" in *The Philosophy of Mar-tin Buber,* Hugo Bergmann challenged the validity of the distinction between *gnosis* and *devotio,* charging that Buber created spurious ab-stractions for polemical reasons, "tilting against an artificial construc-tion to which he applies the term gnosticism." "Actually both gnosis and devotion are ways to God and it is inadmissible to contrapose the two in this fashion and play them off against one another. . . ." "We are always assured by the modern gnostics that without religious de-votion no progress can be made in gnosis." Rather than interpreting his *own self* as the divine self, as Buber thinks, a gnostic such as Sri Aurobindo wishes to extinguish his ego completely and to serve God by the full surrender thereof. At this point, noted Bergmann, Buber's "thought remains enmeshed in a rationalistic prejudice." "He is really paying tribute here to the world view of the nineteenth century." "It is necessary to pierce through these limitations if we are to develop further Buber's own thought in the direction of that 'Great Reality' of which the mystical books of his youth give evidence."

Bergmann quoted Rudolf Steiner's statement that the "investigator of the spirit" practices devotion "toward the truth and the knowledge." "When I have talked of devotion," Buber replied, "I mean by that, exclusively, life as personal service to God." Buber respected completely faithfulness to knowledge, but what mattered to him was whether it proceeded from and is determined by unmediated devotion to God. Not all gnostics, Buber conceded, find the Absolute in the depths of their own soul, though from Simon Magus to modern times there are expressions of this sort. The turning away from one's I postulated by some gnostics, to which Bergmann alluded, Buber could not accept as conclusive evidence against his view, because it is founded upon "precisely the distinction between the surface 'I,' as that which is to be stripped away, and the true self, as that in whose depths the Godhead is to be discovered."

In July 1961, Buber wrote me that he had read in the journals about Scholem's lecture in which he criticized his approach to Hasidism. "If he publishes it I must answer, and I think to do it in a more general and comprehensive manner than I have done in my answer to Rivka Schatz. I must clarify the difference between a scientific and a religious approach to a great fact in the history of religion. (The 'religious' approach may of course involve some very precise scientific work, philological and historical). I hope you will translate this essay of mine too." Scholem did indeed publish, if not this lecture, one like it. Norman Podhoretz, the editor of *Commentary,* some time before this wrote to Michael Wyschogrod asking him to review a number of Buber books in such a way as to help combat "the Buber cult." Wyschogrod replied that if he already knew the conclusion, he should review them himself! Podhoretz then heard about Scholem's views on Buber's Hasidism and asked him for a critical essay, which Scholem gave him, thus fulfilling his own desire to have the last word rather than let the philosopher have it. This essay was published in the October 1961 issue of *Commentary* and later in Scholem's *Messianic Idea of Judaism.*

Scholem too began with words of praise. Buber "has that rare combination of a probing spirit and literary elegance which makes for a great writer":

> When an author of such stature and such subtlety set down with untiring seriousness what to him seemed the very soul of Hasidism, it was bound to make a deep impression on our age. In one sense or another we are all his disciples. In fact most of us, when we speak about Hasidism, probably think primarily in terms of the concepts that have become familiar through Buber's philosophical interpretation.

A critical analysis of Buber's interpretation of Hasidism is made exceedingly difficult, Scholem added, because "Buber, to whom no one denies possession of an exact knowledge of Hasidic literature, does not write as a scholar who gives clear references to support his contentions." Buber combines facts and quotations in order to present Hasidism as a spiritual phenomenon and in so doing does not even consider a great deal of material of great significance for the understanding of Hasidism as a historical phenomenon, such as the magical element in Hasidism and the social character of the Hasidic community. Since the creative impulse in Hasidism was what really mattered to Buber, he felt justified in almost completely ignoring its Kabbalistic or "gnostic" element, which he saw as "a kind of umbilical cord which must be severed as soon as the new spiritual creation exists in its own right." Of the two types of Hasidic literature—the teachings which embrace well over a thousand volumes and the legends that have adorned every single leading Hasidic personality—Buber based his presentation and interpretation almost exclusively on the legends, claiming that they and not the theoretical literature are our chief source of knowledge of Hasidism. But, said Scholem, the teachings were the first and most authoritative presentation of the meaning of Hasidic life, whereas the legends were not written down until nearly fifty years later. "The Hasidic authors obviously did not believe they had in any way broken with the gnostic tradition of the Kabbala and, little as Buber wants to admit it, they wrote clearly and plainly as Gnostics."

At this point the divergence between Scholem as an intellectual historian and Buber as a filter of Hasidic life and spirit becomes most evident. For Scholem identified the "real doctrines" of Sufism and Catholicism with their dogma, and he put forth the theoretical teachings of Hasidism as the primary source for what Hasidic legends and sayings "really meant." In striking contrast to his statement in *Major*

Trends, Scholem now claimed that the Baal-Shem's reinterpretation of individual Kabbalistic concepts as key words for the personal life of the pious did not deprive them of their original meaning. Scholem agreed with Buber that Hasidism teaches that man meets God in the concreteness of his dealings with the world and that Hasidism's transformation of simple and insignificant action into vehicles for the sacred was one of the most original aspects of the movement. But like Schatz, he asserted that this contact was for the sake of annihilation. The undaunted and enthusiastic joy that Hasidism demanded of its adherents is not a joy in the here and now but in what is *hidden* in the essentially irrelevant garment of the here and now. Letting the hidden life shine forth destroys the here and now instead of realizing it in its full concreteness. The concrete meeting of man with reality is a springboard to transcend reality, not to fulfill it. In fact, Buber's existential interpretation to the contrary, the classical literature of Hasidism consistently treats the individual and concrete existence or phenomenon quite disdainfully and disparagingly. "The concrete in Buber's sense does not even exist in Hasidism."

In contrast to his earlier statements about neutralizing messianism, Scholem now claimed that the mystic's actions were aimed at the *messianic* reality in which all things have been restored to their proper place in the scheme of creation and thereby deeply transformed and transfigured. Scholem granted that many Hasidim regarded the holy sparks not as metaphysical elements of divine being but as subjective feelings of joy and affirmation which are projected into the relation between man and his environment. But this popular or vulgar version, which is reflected in the world of Hasidic legends and "provides the relative justification for Buber's highly simplified view," does not derive "from the theology of the founders of Hasidism but from the mood of some of its followers."

Buber's approach to *yihud,* or "unification," as personal direction rather than magic formula is "very modern, appealing, and suggestive," concluded Scholem, but it is not acceptable. Although Buber's presentation of Hasidic legends and sayings in the mature form of the anecdote, which dominates his later writings, "will in large measure stand the test of time," the spiritual message he has read into his interpretation of Hasidism "is far too closely tied to assumptions that derive from his own philosophy of religious anarchism and existentialism and have no roots in the texts themselves." Scholem's corrective to Buber's interpretation is as one-sided as what he set out to correct: "If we want to understand the real phenomenon of Hasidism, both in its grandeur and in its decay (which are in many ways connected), we shall have to start again from the beginning."

Buber was invited by *Commentary* to write a reply to Scholem, but because of repeated illness he could not do so for almost two years. In November 1961, Buber said that he intended to use as much as possible out of the chapter on Hasidism in "Replies to My Critics" plus some paragraphs on general problems, "as for instance the religious and the scientific approach to Religion." "The article will not have the form of a rebuttal but only refer as much as necessary to Scholem's opinion." Buber's reply was held up not only by ill health but by Scholem's decision to publish his article in a somewhat changed form in German in the *Neue Zürcher Zeitung*, a form which raised different problems of a technical kind which Buber felt he had to deal with. In February 1962, Buber declared that "a kind of general weakness, together with rather enormous daily obligations, make concentrated mind-work impossible. I have decided to go in the beginning of March for about 10 days with my daughter to Tiberias and, putting all other things aside, to do my best in order to finish there the answer to Scholem. There is no other way."

A year later, after his eighty-fifth birthday, Buber announced that he had written an answer to Scholem some time ago which completed what he said in the *Responsa* on the matter, and that both would be published in the third, Hasidic volume of his *Werke*, the latter in somewhat shortened form so that the reader could understand everything without being obliged to read the article by Schatz-Uffenheimer. He spoke of combining both into one essay for *Commentary* and asked me to translate it. The essay appeared in the September 1963 issue of *Commentary* and began with a long section on the "two different ways in which a great tradition of religious faith can be rescued from the rubble of time and brought back into the light"— that of historical scholarship and that of faithfully and adequately communicating the vitality and power of this faith. The latter "approach derives from the desire to convey to our own time the force of a former life of faith and to help our age renew its ruptured bond with the Absolute." For this approach it is necessary to have an adequate knowledge of the tradition in all its spiritual and historical connections, but it is not necessary to present all of them but only a selection of those elements in which its vitalizing element was embodied, a selection based not upon objective scholarship but "upon the reliability of the person making the selection in the face of criteria; for what may appear to be mere 'subjectivity' to the detached scholar can sooner or later prove to be necessary to the process of renewal." Second, this person "should not be expected to turn away from the traditional reports concerning the life of the pious in order to give primary emphasis to the theoretical doctrine to which the founder and his disciples appealed for their authority." Even in the founding of the great world religions, what was essential was not a comprehensible doctrine but an event which was at once life and word. And when, as in Hasidism, religious life reaches back to a much earlier doctrine in order to establish its legitimacy, it is not the old teaching as such which engenders the new life of faith in a later age but rather the context of personal and community existence in which a far-reaching transformation of the earlier teachings takes place.

In reply to Scholem's objection that his interpretation rested largely upon legendary writings written down fifty years after the theoretical writings produced in the age "in which Hasidism was actually productive," Buber pointed out that the genre of writing in question, the "legendary anecdote," was fully developed only in the literatures of Sufism, Zen Buddhism, and Hasidism, and that in all three it is not theoretical works but legendary tale that stand at the center of their religious-historical development. This is true not for all kinds of religious mysticism but for the kind whose essential development can be seen most clearly in the *mode of lived realization,* in that of the *event.* It is not the theological doctrines of Al-Junaid but the stories and sayings handed down about his tenth-century contemporary Al-Hallaj which were decisive for Sufism; for their relationship to God was "so basically an existential one that no theoretical discussion can do it justice, and the only suitable vehicle for expressing this relationship is the anecdote." "When God is well-disposed to His servant, He opens the gates of deeds for him and closes the gates of discussion." This is still truer in Zen, in which the disciples experience the "enlightenment" that comes solely from the indescribable mystery of the event, which is narrated just as it happened. In Hasidism the didactic character of the legendary anecdote is developed in incomparably stronger fashion than in Sufism and Zen. In all three movements the legends were first transmitted orally and recorded only much later; whereas their theories were set down by those who originated them or by their immediate disciples.

In the history of human faith whenever there is a pressing need to transmit the *factual* character of the spoken teaching to the future generations and to save it from the danger of "objective" conceptualization, the tendency is to keep the teaching tied to the happening that bore it, to hand it down as part of the personal occurrence from which it is inseparable. Nothing can do this so well as oral transmission which is always assisted by tone and gesture.

In Hasidism this oral transmission was aided by recording, wherever possible, the names of earlier figures who relayed the legends along with the legends themselves. Eventually, to preserve them from too much corruption, the legends were written down and collected. The fact that this took place later, fifty-five years after the death of the Baal-Shem, in no way invalidates their authenticity as sources. This is a principle which Buber stated with all explicitness in the Preface to the second edition of *The Kingship of God:*

> A judgment concerning age or youth of a literary stratum by no means involves one concerning age or youth of the corresponding stratum of religious development, because it still remains to be investigated, for example, whether an early genuine tradition has reached us in a late form or transformation; . . . without the cooperation of an investigation . . . of the compilations of tradition and of the forms of bias which determine them, the criticism of sources must miscalculate and lead astray.

The fourth part of Buber's *Commentary* essay on "Interpreting Hasidism" was essentially identical with his reply to Schatz in *The Philosophy of Martin Buber.* Scholem, in *Major Trends,* had described Hasidism as a "revival movement," "but where in the world," commented Buber, "has there ever been a 'revival' with such power to inspire individual conduct and communal enthusiasm for seven generations?" Here, as earlier, Buber emphasized that the inner dialectic between transcending earthly life and hallowing it does not belong to a later development of Hasidism, but is already apparent in its earliest stages and that the teaching of hallowing the everyday was the original thesis, the doctrine of spiritualization a later accretion. What was at issue was not a spiritual matter that indirectly affects life but the conduct of life itself. What was most important to Rabbi Shlomo was "whatever he happened to be doing at the moment." The whole of one's life can be actively dedicated to God and become an altar for him. There are no words or actions that are idle in themselves; one makes them so when one talks and acts idly.

In the brief reply to Buber's essay which he appended as a postscript to his own, Scholem does not deal at all with Buber's principal response to both Schatz-Uffenheimer and himself, namely that there are *two* streams within Hasidism and that the earlier one, originating with the Baal-Shem, emphasizes the hallowing of the everyday rather than the nullifying of it. What he does do is to repeat his questioning of the legends as a reliable source for understanding Hasidism.

> There is no basis whatever in the Hasidic tradition for the attempt to construct a possible contradiction between the specifics of this group life and the concepts through which it unfolded. . . . The older and more authentic the historical and social framework within which many of these oldest legends move or are enclosed, the less do they stand in real contradiction to the theoretical writings, produced in the same milieu, at the same time or considerably earlier.

Beyond this, Scholem rejected the parallels Buber drew with Zen stories, saying that they are not really legends at all but exercises for meditations, a statement which may be true of some of the koans proper in Zen but which does not hold for the stories of master-disciple relationship that Zen also gives us.

Scholem closed his postscript with a story about Buber himself. Scholem "once asked Buber why in his writings he had suppressed the significant and unfathomable words regarding the Messianic age that were transmitted in the name of Rabbi Israel of Rizhin." One of these was that in the days of the Messiah man will no longer quarrel with his fellow but with himself; another his suggestion that the messianic world will be a world without images "in which the image and its object can no longer be related." "I shall always remember his reply," recounts Scholem. Buber said, "Because I do not understand them." To Scholem these sayings were historic evidence of the continuing power of the utopian element of messianic redemption and examples of the Kabbalists' attempts to fathom its unfathomable depths. Thus Scholem too did not understand these sayings. What Buber could not understand he would not present as a vital force of Hasidic faith.

"Both are right," Agnon said to me concerning the Scholem-Buber controversy. It should be said, rather, that both are right *and* wrong, that is, both are one-sided. Until Scholem and his disciples published what they did, Buber was looked to by the Western world as *the* interpreter of Hasidism just as D. T. Suzuki used to be looked to as *the* interpreter of Zen. Because this was so, it was indeed a scholarly lack on Buber's part that he did not indicate more clearly in his essays interpreting Hasidism that he was presenting only one of the two major streams of Hasidic tradition, as he later did say in reply to Scholem. On the other hand, Scholem's failure to recognize the stream stemming from the Baal-Shem and his total rejection of the "hallowing of the everyday" as a valid interpretation of Hasidism are even more misleading since now nearly everyone thinks of Scholem as *the* scholarly interpreter, and few recognize *his* one-sidedness.

Both Agnon and Simon felt that Scholem's essay was on a higher intellectual level than Buber's, but "The impact which Buber's stories have would never be attained by objective scholarship," Simon said, while objecting, as Scholem did not, that the sanctification of the secular attained by Hasidism depended to a very large extent on the fulfillment of the Jewish Law. "Buber would not deny that," Simon asserted, "but the stories do not carry enough of the atmosphere of Halakhic life." In a memorial address on Buber, Simon commented that Buber stuck to his original view of Hasidism despite Scholem's vigorous criticism:

> Buber saw in Hasidism the last great religious movement of the Jewish people, and one of our great contributions to the Messianic attempt to approach the Kingdom of God on this earth. Perhaps for this reason he underestimated the weight of the great theoretical writings of the early Hasidic masters, and stressed the anecdotes about their exemplary lives and teachings. He showed them in their daily give-and-take with their disciples, i. e. again in the sphere of dialogue.

The distinguished American philosopher and Jewish theologian Emil Fackenheim remarked in 1961 in a speech to the Central Conference of American Rabbis that he found most of the criticisms directed against Buber's interpretation of Hasidism unimpressive.

> The most common criticism is that Buber, instead of writing the kind of history which separates sources in painstaking analysis, has given the kind which is a creative synthesis. But the prejudices of positivistic scholarship to the contrary notwithstanding, there is always need for the latter as well as the former type of history, unless one is to be left, not with the spirit of the age or movement one seeks to understand, but merely with its dead bones. Moreover, while Buber's kind of history has great dangers of subjectivity and distortion—which incidentally, Buber himself has been the first to admit—Buber would seem to have coped with these with extraordinary success. His treatment of Hasidism shows him to be capable of practicing the emphatic openness which he preaches.

According to Fackenheim, it was the fundamental aim of Hasidism to reopen the channels clogged by Orthodox authority so that the interrupted life between God and Israel might be resumed. Its uniqueness lies in the passion with which it sought to storm the Heavens, seeking for the God of the here and now, the God of Israel. Fackenheim concluded his talk on "Two Types of Reform: Reflections Occasioned by Hasidism" with the question of whether such an effort is a concrete possibility of modern life and compatible with modern thought. As answer, he pointed to Buber's "narrow ridge" upon which we must walk ourselves, not imitating the Hasidim, which would be a misunderstanding of Hasidism itself, but walking as they walked—not in a world of others but in their own.

> Man comes to worship feeling instead of God; the symbol, not what it stands for; Jewish genius, not Him whose presence, stimulates it. There is, to be sure, an idolatrous emotionalism which, born of impatient need, mistakes projected desires for God. But there is also an idolatry of pseudo-sophistication which, denying man's actual need of the present God, treats the human as if it were divine. Between these two abysses the liberal Jew of Today must walk, in sophisticated simplicity, on a narrow ridge. . . . Those who walk on the ridge, open to the future, will find strength in the Hasidic example:

In 1966, at the annual Eranos Conference in Switzerland, Scholem broadened his attack on Buber into a full-scale polemic against Buber's treatment of Judaism. As Ernst Simon remarked in his article "Buber and Scholem," precisely that which makes Sholem a great scholar is lacking in this critique: the fruitful synthesis between empathy and historical analysis, between spiritual involvement and critical detachment. At the same time, passages in this long essay give us insight into layers of the Buber-Scholem controversy that lie deeper than questions of scholarship. The first of these reads, in fact, like a personal confession:

> No one who has known Buber could escape the strong beams that radiated from him and that made controversy with him doubly passionate. To enter into controversy with Buber meant to be thrown back and forth between admiration and rejection, between the readiness to hear his message and the disappointment over this message and the impossibility of realizing it.

Buber sought influence over Jewish youth, wrote Scholem, and it belonged to Buber's bitterest experiences that in the years of the First World War and the years just before and during Hitler's regime this meeting ended in deep estrangement. "One could equally well say that it belonged to the bitterest experiences of these youths that Buber never drew forth the expected consequences of his message."

Buber, a highly multifaceted and developed man, had called these youths to go to the land of Israel and undertake out of a creative impulse the formation of the new life that should grow there. They never forgave him that he did not go with them when the hour struck. . . . Buber, whose conversations, speeches, and summons centered around the word "realization" had himself, so it seemed to the disappointed ones, refused it . . . he had made another personal decision, chosen another medium of realization.

The pathos in this personal statement appears even stronger when we recall how hard Scholem himself worked during the years between 1926 and 1938 to help bring Buber to Israel, even if Buber's own eagerness to come during all that time belies what, to the uninformed reader, Scholem might seem to be implying by his statements.

Scholem recognized Buber's creative transformation of Judaism: "From the hour when as a twenty-year-old he attached himself to the just emerging movement of Zionism to the end of his days he tirelessly sharpened, preserved, and developed the meaning of the creative transformation in the phenomena closest to his heart. The provocative in his conception of Judaism and its history . . . was unmistakable, and Buber, to whom neither self-awareness nor courage can be denied, was ready to pay the price for this . . . new vision." When Scholem visited Buber in Germany in 1932 he said to him: "Why do you not write finally a presentation of the theology of Hasidism?" "I intend to do that," he answered, "but only after you have written a book on the Kabbala." "Is that a promise?" asked Scholem. "Perhaps," Buber replied. "I did not understand at that time that he could not have any scientific attitude toward this theme," commented Scholem. In 1943, two years after the appearance of Scholem's book on the Kabbala, he went to Buber to lay before him the fundamental criticisms of Buber's interpretation of Hasidism that Scholem had formed during long years of continual study of the texts. Buber listened with great earnestness and tension.

When I had finished, he was silent for a long time. Then he said slowly and with emphasis on every word: "If what you have said be true, dear Scholem, then I have occupied myself with Hasidism for forty years wholly in vain, for then it would indeed not at all *interest* me." It was the last conversation that I had with Buber over the factual problems of Hasidism. It closed speech for me. I understood that there was nothing more to say.*

---

*See Note in Sources for Chapter 12.

In 1963 a meeting took place in Buber's home in Talbiyeh to celebrate the completion of his almost forty-year-long project of translating the Hebrew Bible into German. Scholem, in his speech on this occasion, asked Buber for what audience this work was undertaken, since the German-Jewish community for whose sake Buber and Rosenzweig had originally started the project was no more. After the meeting was over and Buber and Simon were alone, Buber said to Simon: "I do not care what Scholem says about me. We all have disciples; some of us have produced schools; but only Scholem has created an academic field." By saying this, Simon pointed out, Buber renounced any suggestion that he himself had created a new field through his work on Hasidism. "If Scholem was Joshua, Buber was Moses," Walter Kaufmann remarked concerning the Buber-Scholem controversy in a speech at the Buber Centennial Conferences in Israel and America. The value of Scholem's scholarly contributions for the generations to come is incontestable. But if anything in this analogy could be regarded by Jew and non-Jew alike as "the Promised Land," it would not be Scholem's destruction of the Jericho walls of all previous scholarship on the Kabbala but Buber's *Tales of the Hasidism, For the Sake of Heaven,* and *The Way of Man.*

A number of years ago, a group of African students met with Abraham Joshua Heschel and Heschel's own student of twenty years before, Rabbi Arnold Jacob Wolf, Hillel chaplain at Yale University. "How should we begin the study of Hasidism?" they asked Heschel. Forgetting the Talmudic dictum that one should not speak in the presence of one's teacher, Wolf responded, "We now have Scholem in English. Read him." But Abraham Heschel, the direct descendant of a long line of distinguished *zaddikim* reaching back to the Maggid of Mezritch and a scholar whose knowledge and understanding of the theoretical teachings of Hasidism was second to none, said, "No, if you want to know Hasidism as it was, begin with Buber."

Like the relationship between Buber and Herzl and between the Yehudi and the Seer, the controversy between Buber and Scholem touches on the soil of tragedy, "the cruel antitheticalness of existence itself," where just because each is as he is, different life-stances, instead of contributing dialogue, are crystallized into fixed opposition. If "every controversy that takes place for the sake of heaven endures," as the Talmud says, then this controversy too will endure in its profound two-sidedness and not, as many people suppose today, with a decision *for* Scholem and *against* Buber.

PART IV

Dialogue as the Way to Peace

(1952–1965)

CHAPTER 13

Dag Hammarskjøld and Buber:
The Covenant of Peace

THE ADDRESS THAT Buber gave at the farewell celebration for him in
April 1952 in Carnegie Hall, New York City, was titled "Hope for
This Hour." In it he confronted the situation created by the "cold
war" between America and the Soviet Union, a war in which he refused to take sides: "The human world is today, as never before, split
into two camps, each of which regards the other as the embodiment of
falsehood and itself as the embodiment of truth. . . . Each side has
assumed monopoly of the sunlight and has plunged its antagonist into
night, and each side demands that you decide between day and
night." Not only is the opponent seen as false, as in former ages, but
as fundamentally out of order, its "ideas" mere ideologies masking
selfish interest. As a result, genuine dialogue between persons of different kinds and convictions is becoming ever more difficult and rare.
"The abysses between man and man threaten ever more pitilessly to
become unbridgeable." Buber saw this inability to carry on a genuine

dialogue from one camp to the other as the severest symptom of that existential mistrust which is the sickness of present-day man, and this in turn stemmed from the inner poisoning of the total human organism by the destruction of trust in human existence. "At its core the conflict between mistrust and trust of man conceals the conflict between the mistrust and trust of eternity."

All great civilizations have to some extent been "civilizations of dialogue," said Buber, using a phrase of Robert Hutchins's, but the demonry of basic mistrust stands in the way of such a civilization arising in our time, and this demonry is fed by the mutual unmasking and seeing-through that thinkers such as Marx, Freud, and Nietzsche have promoted. "Seeing-through and unmasking is now becoming the great sport between men," and this game only becomes complete as it becomes reciprocal and the unmasker is himself unmasked. "One may foresee in the future a degree of reciprocity in existential mistrust where speech will turn into dumbness and sense into madness." Despite this growth of universal mistrust, the human need for confirmation continues and, finding no natural satisfaction, sets out on two false paths: self-confirmation and confirmation by a collective. If the former ends in knowing oneself as being inevitably abandoned, the latter is pure fiction, since the collective accepts and employs each of its members for that person's usefulness to the collective but not in his or her own being. The only salvation is the renewal of the dialogical relation, and that means, above all, the overcoming of existential mistrust. As a beginning for this task, Buber suggested, as a leading methodological postulate of all anthropological knowledge, drawing demarcation lines for the validity of theses about newly uncovered elements to prevent precisely that reduction of man that Marxist theories of ideology and Freudian theories of rationalization have led to. "This boundless simplification has contributed decisively to the development of existential mistrust." If we wish to overcome this mistrust, said Buber, we must reach a greater and more penetrating realism.

> Man is not to be seen through, but to be perceived ever more completely in his openness and his hiddenness and in the relation of the two to each other. We wish to trust him, not blindly indeed but clearsightedly. We wish to perceive his manifoldness and his wholeness, his proper character, without any preconceptions about this or that background, and with the intention of accepting, accrediting and confirming him to the extent that this perception will allow.

Beyond this Buber called for the true representatives and spokes-men of the peoples—"independent persons with no authority save that of the spirit"—to come together to sift out of the alleged antago-nisms the real conflicts between genuine needs. Only after this was done could the consideration of the necessary and possible settle-ments between them begin. The hope for this hour depends, Buber concluded, upon those who feel most deeply the sickness of present-day man and who speak in his name the word without which no healing takes place: *I will live.* It depends upon the renewal of dialog-ical immediacy between persons. "If our mouths succeed in genuinely saying 'thou,' then, after long silence and stammering, we shall have addressed our eternal 'Thou' anew. Reconciliation leads towards rec-onciliation."

When Buber sent the German original of "Hope for This Hour" from Los Angeles in March 1952 to be translated, he wrote that "it was rather a piece of work. If you demand, as you must, the utmost from your heart, it gets tired at times." He went on to say that he had received an invitation to lecture at the Paris Exposition ("Masterpieces of the 20th Century") of the Congress for Cultural Freedom, but would refuse. "I think you will understand," he added, meaning that he could not support an organization the main purpose of which was to strengthen the American side of the cold war. After the lecture had been given, Buber asked if some American journal could be found in which to publish "Hope for This Hour" that was not, like *Commentary*, specifically Jewish, since its subject was in no way Jewish. With Buber's consent, I submitted it to my colleague William Phillips, who was an editor of *Partisan Review*. Phillips rejected it on the ground that it did not take into account "the realities of the cold war." In communicat-ing this to Buber I also mentioned that Phillips taught a good deal of Sartre. A man who likes Sartre "must either dislike or (preferably) ignore me," Buber responded in September 1952. In October he declared that Phillips's letter had inspired him to write a very short explanation on the "philosophical" and "political" treatment of the cold war which he later titled "Abstract and Concrete" and included in *Pointing the Way* directly after "Hope for This Hour."

In "Abstract and Concrete," Buber remarked that he had received comments on "Hope for This Hour" criticizing him for dealing with the cold war as an abstract philosophical question instead of a con-crete political one, "which latter treatment obviously amounts to help-ing swell the literature of invective piling up in both camps." I have appealed from the political not to the philosophical, Buber rejoined, but "to the genuine concrete, to the actual life of actual men which has become crusted over with the varnish of political fictitiousness." Although many of the reproaches hurled from one side upon the other were valid, nonetheless they had to be freed from the encrustation of catchwords if they were to be regarded *in concreto*. Enmeshed in political machinery, we cannot possibly penetrate to the factual and find means to relieve the present situation, the "natural end" of which is the technically perfect suicide of the human race. What is needed today is men in both camps capable of recognizing the impotence of mere politics and of reflecting, not theoretically but in concrete terms, on existence. If men such as these can distinguish between the exaggerated conflicts of interests of peoples and their actual differences of interest and speak with one another as partakers of human reality, "a tiny seed of change will have been sown that could lead to a transformation of the whole situation."

In "The Validity and Limitation of the Political Principle," the speech that he gave at the German universities in 1953, Buber spoke of a front that cuts across all the fronts of the hour, the front of all those engaged in the one fight for human truth. The experienced administrators of the political principle are unable to meet the problem of common human destiny which confronts mankind at this juncture. The current political jargon, fit only for declamations, can never serve as a language to understand one another. "For sheer power they are impotent, for sheer tricks they are incapable of acting decisively." In the face of this impotence those who stand on the crossfront and have the common language of faithfulness to the human truth that they cannot possess must unite "to give to man what is man's in order to rescue him from being devoured by the political principle."

"Genuine Dialogue and the Possibilities of Peace," Buber's address on the occasion of receiving the Peace Prize of the German Book Trade in September 1953, continued the concern of "Hope for This Hour" about the effect of mistrust in preventing genuine dialogue. Speaking of that "Great Peace," which has never before appeared in history, Buber resumed on a world scale his early teaching of giving direction to the passions, or the "evil urge." The human passions that flow into war "must enter into the great peace as ore into the fire that melts and transforms it." It is the crisis of man that has brought forth the total war and the unreal peace which followed. To overcome this crisis we must turn to the age-old adversary of war—the speech of genuine conversation in which persons come to a mutual understanding. But "the man in crisis will no longer entrust his cause to conversation because its presupposition—trust—is lacking."

> The debates between statesmen, which the radio conveys to us, no longer have anything in common with a human conversation: diplomats do not address one another but the faceless public. Even the congresses and conferences which convene in the name of mutual understanding lack the substance which alone can elevate the deliberations to genuine talk: candour and directness in address and answer.

All this is the concentrated expression of reciprocal mistrust. The crisis of speech is bound up with this crisis of trust in the closest possible fashion, "for I can only speak to someone in the true sense of the term if I expect him to accept my word as genuine."

Despite all this, Buber reaffirmed his belief that the peoples in this hour could enter into true dialogue with another. "In a genuine dialogue each of the partners, even when he stands in opposition to the other, heeds, affirms, and confirms his opponent as an existing other. Even though conflict cannot be eliminated from the world, through genuine dialogue it can be humanly arbitrated and led towards its overcoming." Those who carry on today, within each people, the battle against the antihuman have the task of initiating this conversation and speaking unreservedly with each other. That element that profits from the divisions between the peoples, the contrahuman which is opposed to man's will to become a true humanity, Buber called by its Hebrew name Satan, which means in the Hebrew Bible "the hinderer." "Let us not allow this Satanic element in men to hinder us from realizing man!" Buber appealed at the end of his address to the president of the Bundesrepublik and the other Germans assembled to honor him. "Let us release speech from its ban! Let us dare, despite all, to trust!" If I had to choose one sentence to summarize the whole message of Buber's life and thought it would be this: "Let us dare, despite all, to trust!"

Fritz Bartsch, who broadcast a commentary on Buber's address and its first effects on the Hessian radio in Frankfurt the following Sunday, reported that after the ceremony the West German Republic minister of justice, Dr. Thomas Dehler, sat together with his friend, Georg-August Zinn, president of the Hessian ministry, and discussed how they might reconcile their opposing views. The following week Dr. Dehler announced over the Bavarian radio a demand for real dialogue with the Russians, a new step for a minister in the Adenauer coalition. In supporting this call, Bartsch also cited Carlos Romulo, the Philippine ambassador to the United Nations, who once said: "Words and ideas are mightier than cannons in the fight for human values. The only front that can never be shattered is that of the understanding among men!" "The Jewish philosopher Buber, the Philippine ambassador to the United Nations, and the West German Republic Minister of Justice stand in a single front in the fight for the world-validation of the word," Bartsch concluded.

In April 1954, Buber told me that he had been asked by the editor of the *Pulpit Digest* to submit a message about the world situation in connection with the cobalt bomb, which was meant to be even stronger than the hydrogen bomb, according to the terrifying details that Buber was sent. The essence of the message Buber wrote is contained in its title—"Stop!" If people do not tell the politicians to stop before it is too late, there will come a time when "the war game will mean destruction of all the lands and peoples involved—till there remains nothing to be destroyed—and nobody to do the destruction."

On a more personal note, Buber wrote in July 1955 to Lambert Schneider consoling him for the death of his mother. "I, who have barely known my mother, for that very reason know perhaps in a special way what it means for a person to lose his." The following month Buber sent a touching reminiscence to Hans Lindau, a friend from his student days at Leipzig University, on the occasion of his eightieth birthday. "A minute ago, just as I arose from my window seat in order to go to my desk, I looked out on the high old cypresses in the garden. It was for me as if we sat, Thou and I, two young lads, together in August Schmarsow's evening parlor, drinking beer and studiously applying ourselves to analogical thinking. Now, at the desk, I am again as old as I 'really' am, . . . but the strange moment has made me feel somewhat stronger. Do you remember Rembrandt's Matthias? . . . Even as one's own old hand touches the breast, an eternally young one touches the shoulder." And it was just that that Buber wished this friend of his youth.

In January 1956, Buber wrote me that Professor Michael Landmann of the Free University of Berlin had informed him that he wanted to nominate Buber for the Nobel Peace Prize but that he needed more exact biographical information—which I sent him, along with a copy of *The Life of Dialogue*. When I asked Buber about this matter in May, he replied that he had not heard anything further about it: "As you know, my way is not to ask people at all about such things. I like pleasant surprises, but I do not deal with them in my heart, and their not coming is no disillusion." Some years later, when

Buber was again nominated for a Nobel Prize, he stated that if he had approached certain persons, he might perhaps have received one, but this was something he would not do.

In August 1957, Buber received a letter from the American Committee on Africa signed by Eleanor Roosevelt, Bishop James A. Pike, and Martin Luther King, appealing for his cooperation in a worldwide protest against the organized inhumanity of the government of the Union of South Africa. In the letter they referred to the policy of apartheid and to the totalitarian force brought to bear on all the "not-whites" of South Africa in almost every sphere of human life. They asked Buber to join them as a leading member of an international committee to set aside December 10, 1957, as a day of protest and of demand that the Union fulfill its obligations under the Charter of the United Nations. In October, Eleanor Roosevelt wrote to Buber personally thanking him for his splended response to their invitation and informing him that leaders from eighty-three nations were ready to take part in the day of protest. "Surely the South Africans of good will, who work on for justice and freedom, regardless of the danger to their lives, freedom and future, are thankful for your announcement of support and participation," she concluded.

In October 1957, Buber reported that Irwin Ross of the New York *Post* had cabled him from London that he would come to Israel if Buber would grant him an interview. "I have done it, because I want to say something publicly on the subject of world politics now." This article appeared in the New York *Post* in November as the second in a series of articles titled "Voice of the Sages." In the course of the interview Buber commented on the strain he observed among people in the United States during his two visits. He used to think that people were serene—for the first half hour of conversation. "Then the mask would fall—and you would see the tension, quite naked." Although Buber believed that the horror attendant upon another war would be unimaginable, he strongly doubted that the threat of mutual destruction would in itself keep the peace. The politicians who continue preparing for atomic war will come to a moment when the situation will slip out of their control and the machines will take over. Again Buber saw as the main practical problem that people were no longer really talking to one another:

> Historically, there have been three types of talk: simple, straightforward communication between a man and his neighbor; diplomatic parleying—with language as a weapon to maximize strategic advantage, but with a moment always arising when real differences are distin-

guished from apparent differences, when some common interests are discerned and opposing interests may be compromised; and, finally, there is talk as propaganda—"talking out the window," with the UN being the prime example.

Again Buber proposed a grand dialogue between the disinterested, independent spirits of East and West, bypassing the politicians, diplomats, hucksters, and journalists for "philosophers," persons who think independently about the roots of things, and about the ends as well as the means. An occasional politician of sufficient intellectual independence might be welcomed to such an experimental dialogue, which Buber said should be secret so that the members could talk unreservedly to one another, and only after the conferees had come to some meeting of minds—*if* they did—should they try to influence the politicians of their respective countries. The presidents of the high courts of justice of various lands might be one type of representative, although the best would be the real spiritual representatives of each people, if these could be determined (they would not, Buber opined, be identical with the heads of the various churches). As long as peace can be maintained, Buber saw hope for all despite the world crisis. He believed that great changes might be impending in the Soviet Union. "I often think that the Russian people are now sleeping," said Buber to Ross. "They are perhaps incubating some new forms of political life." But to wait for this we must learn patience, as we must learn patience regarding the Arab-Israeli conflict, to which Buber could see no solution until the cold war had substantially abated.

After reading my translation of *Pointing the Way,* Dag Hammarskjøld initiated communication with Martin Buber on April 15, 1958, just five days after his reinduction for a second term as secretary general of the United Nations:

> You do not know me personally, but I am afraid you have not been able to escape knowing about me. . . .
> I wish to tell you how strongly I have responded to what you write about our age of distrust and to the background of your observations which I find in your general philosophy of unity created "out of the manifold." Certainly, for me, this is a case of "parallel ways."
> Once in a while I have my way to Jerusalem. It would, indeed, give me very great pleasure if on a forthcoming visit I may call on you.

Henry P. Van Dusen, in his book on Hammarskjøld, concluded that *Pointing the Way* was Hammarskjøld's introduction to Buber's thought, since he had been three times in Jerusalem before without attempting to make contact with Buber. At Van Dusen's request I read carefully Hammarskjøld's remarkable memoirs in the posthumous book *Markings* and confirmed his impression that there was no evidence in it of influence by Buber, although there were a number of "parallel ways," such as Hammarskjøld's concern about real interhuman contact:

> The overtones are lost, and what is left are conversations which, in their poverty, cannot hide the lack of real contact. We glide past each other. But why? Why—?
>
> We reach out towards the other. In vain—because we have never dared to give ourselves.

> Without the humility and warmth which you have to develop in your relations to the few with whom you are personally involved, you will never be able to do anything for the many. . . . It is better for the health of the soul to make one man good than "to sacrifice oneself for mankind." (1956)

Real contact, for Hammarskjøld as for Buber, was not only dialogue with persons but also "a humble and spontaneous response to Life— with its endless possibilities, and its unique present which never happens twice" (1959). For Hammarskjøld, as for Buber, to live meaningfully meant to live in response to the demand of the situation. This response to demands meant for Hammarskjøld, as for Buber, a hallowing of the everyday: "In our era, the road to holiness necessarily passes through the world of action." It also meant for both men *respect for the word:* "To misuse the word is to show contempt for man. It undermines the bridges and poisons the wells." Hammarskjøld's concern for responsibility to the unique other included an approach to conflict similar to Buber's: "You can only hope to find a lasting solution to a conflict if you have learned to see the other objectively, but, at the same time, to experience his difficulties subjectively" (1955).

Hammarskjøld, too, knew dialogue with the "eternal Thou" in life and in prayer: "Prayer, crystallized in words, assigns a permanent wave length on which the dialogue has to be continued, even when our mind is occupied with other matters" (1961). Hammarskjøld, too, knew a realistic and active mysticism which does not turn away from the world but preserves the immediacy of the relation to it, guards the concreteness of the absolute, and demands the involvement of the whole being:

The "mystical experience." Always *here* and *now*—in that freedom which is one with distance, in that stillness which is born of silence. But—this is a freedom in the midst of action, a stillness in the midst of other human beings. . . . (1955)

There are, however, *differences* between *Markings* and Buber's thought, one of which is that while Buber was also decisively influenced by Meister Eckhart, Hammarskjøld seemed to remain Kierkegaardian precisely in the way that Buber did not, i.e., focusing on the I-Thou relationship with God somewhat at the expense of that with man. There was, indeed, a Kierkegaardian quality of loneliness and isolation about Hammarskjøld even in the midst of his intense activity, which Buber did not share. Hammarskjøld, too, was concerned about the tension between "being" and "seeming," but he saw no resolution of this tension in authentic interhuman contact as Buber did. What is more, in Hammarskjøld's concern for God and others there was a note of denial of the self that was very foreign to Buber.

After writing Buber in Jerusalem, Hammarskjøld discovered through the press that he was in Princeton and then warmly invited him to visit him at the United Nations on May 1. Hammarskjøld's secretaries were "under strict instructions that under no circumstances were he and his guest to be interrupted," reports Van Dusen. "Several important mesages were impatiently brushed aside as the two men continued in intense conversation for more than two hours." In a speech over the Swedish radio in 1962 Buber himself described this meeting and commented on its significance:

> When we then met in the house of the organization so remarkably named the United Nations, it proved to be the case that both of us were indeed concerned about the same thing: he who stood in the most exposed position of international responsibility, I who stand in the loneliness of a spiritual tower, which is in reality a watchtower from which all the distances and depths of the planetary crisis can be described. . . . We were both pained in the same way by the pseudo-speaking of representatives of states and groups of states who, permeated by a fundamental reciprocal mistrust, talked past one another out the windows. We both hoped, we both believed that, still in sufficient time before the catastrophe, faithful representatives of the people, faithful to their mission, would enter into a genuine dialogue, a genuine dealing with one another out of which would emerge in all clarity the fact that the common interests of the peoples were stronger still than those which kept them in opposition to one another. . . . At that time, in the house of the United Nations, sitting across from each other, we both recognized,

Dag Hammarskjøld and I, what it was essentially that bound us to each other. But I sensed, looking at and listening to him, something else that I could not explain to myself, something fateful that in some way was connected with his function in this world-hour.

In an address at Cambridge University in England on June 5, 1958, Hammarskjøld analyzed the world situation precisely in the terms of Buber's own approach to the "covenant of peace" in the concluding essays of *Pointing the Way,* and he did so explicitly quoting "Hope for This Hour":

The widening of our political horizons to embrace in a new sense the whole of the world, should have meant an approach to the ideal sung in Schiller's "Ode to Joy," but it has, paradoxically, led to new conflicts and to new difficulties to establish even simple human contact and communication. . . . The dividing line goes within ourselves, within our own peoples and also within other nations. It does not coincide with any political or geographical boundaries. The ultimate fight is one between the human and the subhuman. We are on dangerous ground if we believe that any individual, any nation or any ideology has a monopoly on rightness, liberty and human dignity.

When we fully recognize this and translate our insight into words and action, we may also be able to re-establish full human contact and communications across geographical and political boundaries, and to get out of a public debate which often seems to be inspired more by a wish to impress than by a will to understand and to be understood. . . . What then is wrong? . . . I would in this context like to quote one of the influential thinkers of our time, whose personal history and national experience have given him a vantage point of significance.

In an address in Carnegie Hall in New York, in 1952, Martin Buber had the following to say: "One no longer merely fears that the other will voluntarily dissemble, but one takes it for granted that he cannot do otherwise. . . . The other communicates to me the perspective that he has acquired on a certain subject, but I do not really take cognizance of his communication as knowledge. . . . Rather I listen for what drives the other to say what he says, for an unconscious motive. . . . Since it is the idea of the other, it is for me an 'ideology.' My main task in my intercourse with my fellow-man becomes more and more . . . to see through and unmask him. . . . It is no longer the uprightness, the honesty of the other which is in question, but the inner integrity of his existence itself. . . . This game naturally only becomes complete as it becomes reciprocal. . . . Hence one may foresee in the future a degree of reciprocity in existential mistrust where speech will turn into dumbness and sense into madness." . . . Out of the depth of his feelings Martin Buber has found expressions which it would be vain for me to try to improve.

Hammarskjøld visited Jerusalem in September 1958, after which he reported at a press conference "one out-of-the-way tourism with a strong personal accent. I had the pleasure of paying a personal call on Professor Martin Buber for whom I have a sincere admiration." In his next and last visit to Jerusalem in January 1959, Hammarskjøld and Buber had their longest and most intimate conversation over dinner in Buber's home. Speaking of this meeting at a press conference in January 1959, Hammarskjøld confirmed "that the moment I get the time for it, I would like very much to translate not the whole volume of *Pointing the Way*—I would never find time for that—but some three or four essays." Hammarskjøld reminded the press of his quotation from "Hope for This Hour" at his June speech in Cambridge and added:

> When Professor Buber talks about philosophy and politics, he implicitly, of course, refers to his own well-known views, which are very well expressed indeed in the final essays in the book *Pointing the Way*.
> On very many points I see eye to eye with him; on other points, naturally, there must be nuances. But as to the basic reaction, I think that he has made a major contribution and I would like to make that more broadly known.

Buber also spoke about this visit in his radio address in Sweden:

> In the center of our conversation stood the problem that has ever again laid claim to me in the course of my life: the failure of the spiritual man in his historical undertakings. I illustrated it by one of the highest of the examples that have become known to us: the abortive attempt of Plato to establish his just state in Sicily. I felt, and Hammarskjøld—of that I was certain—also felt as I did, we too were the recipients of that letter in which Plato tells of his failure and of his overcoming his failure.

Hammarskjøld "was not as austere as some people thought," Buber said in conversation with Aubrey Hodes. "In my talks with him I found him warm and capable of reaching a true understanding." Hammarskjøld told Buber that there were two books he kept near him and read passages from almost every day—the writings of Meister Eckhart and the Psalms. "He had a deep knowledge of the Psalms," Buber reported to Hodes, "and when I referred to Psalm 73 he quoted part of it to me. This is, as you know, my favorite among all the Psalms. And it was one of those to which Hammarskjøld too felt closest." The two men also talked briefly about Israeli-Arab relations and the problem of the Arab refugees which had brought Hammarskjøld to Jerusalem.

In June 1959, Hammarskjøld submitted to the Nobel Prize Committee in Sweden a four-page memorandum nominating Buber for a Nobel Prize. Van Dusen describes this document as "a characteristically detailed, discerning and scrupulously objective account of Buber's work and influence which reveals as much about its author as about his subject." One might also characterize it as an ambivalent document, since it spends most of its time on Buber's qualifications as candidate for a Nobel Prize in Literature yet concludes by recommending him for a Peace Prize instead! Although it could not have done Buber's hopes much good, this ambivalence undoubtedly arose from Hammarskjøld's bending over backward to be fair and probably also not to influence the Nobel Prize Committee unduly. Hammarskjøld referred to Buber "as the spokesman of humanistic internationalism, based on elements of Jewish thought." Hammarskjøld also stated that Buber's "literary work is closed to us (only a small part of it was made public)" and that "after the war he has become to an ever-growing extent an active force in the international discussion, e.g., in the Anglo-American world." Then Hammarskjøld discussed the, to him, surprising fact that, despite his great name, Buber did not occupy as important a place in Jewish thinking as an outsider would have expected. He accounted for this by Buber's position as spokesman for Israeli-Arab "friendship" as well as by Buber's religious and philosophical convictions, which he saw as alien to contemporary Jewry:

> The mysticism of personality . . . that Buber has developed, under the influence of Hasidism but also under that of the Christian-medieval mysticism, sets itself in the sharpest opposition to the rationalistic materialism which especially characterizes Ben Gurion, for example, as also to the formalistic Orthodoxy and religious intolerance which is just as often present in Israel.

Nonetheless, Hammarskjøld saw Buber as more central to the tradition than those who opposed him: "Although Buber's position within the Jewish people is thus controversial, he appears nonetheless to everyone who has plumbed his work, as an interpreter of genius of some of the most prominent and purest elements in Jewish tradition and Jewish spiritual life."

Discussing Buber's work with Hasidic legends, Hammarskjøld claimed that Buber had "endowed Western literature with something stable and rich" and characterized Buber as "an outstanding storyteller whose linguistic ability puts him in line with the greatest masters of prose of the first part of this century." Although they are "just recordings" which "technically should be classed with similar collections," Hammarskjøld considered them the "fruit of creative art" "because they were preceded by a poetic gift of humble listening, careful sifting of a rich material and a re-rendering by a sharp ear," and the whole surrounded by a spiritual atmosphere that reflects Buber's view of the human being and of life. Hammarskjøld characterized *Ich und Du* as "the work in which Buber best succeeded in giving his basic view a comprehensive and fitting expression" and its philosophy as "a most fertilizing view of life that combines features of mystic pantheism" with "the depth and dramatic nature of a dualistic God-relation" and casts "Kant's law about man as an end in new terms, endowing it with new human wealth and warmth."

> With the years Buber realized with ever-increasing concern a decrease in the ability to communicate and in the continued existence of the living and meaningful dialogue between individuals and groups. At the same time he points to the influence of "politicization" on life. He called attention to the vulgarization of language as a result of propaganda and externalized news-communication, standing under the sign of sensation. He also indicated a decline in the attitude toward poetry, diminishing its importance as a form of living communication between persons.

Hammarskjøld compared Buber with Bergson as a philosopher on a similar high level who "became one of those shapers of opinion who defended most eloquently and with the deepest roots in spiritual realities those forms of interpersonal contact which poetry too seeks." He also suggested that we are standing at the beginning of the development that Buber engendered. After concluding that "Buber could without doubt be considered as a Nobel-Prize candidate," he expressed several reservations: "he is, an eighty-year-old person, whose life-work is sealed, and his creation touches only indirectly upon the field intended by the Nobel Prize": his greatest virtue is probably his being an interpreter of such purity and intensity of an important culture, whose son he is, that already in his life he is a prominent symbol of this culture. After all this, Hammarskjøld contradicted and nullified much of his long letter in his final paragraph:

> In spite of the admiration for Buber rising from these lines, I would hesitate to see him awarded the Nobel Prize for Literature. A more natural form of appreciation would be to award him the Peace Prize.

After an interval of two years Hammarskjøld wrote Buber in August 1961 that he had been reading the essays in *Between Man and Man,* which he had not seen before, and felt the need to send Buber a greeting "after far too long a time of silence, understandable only in the light of the pressure of circumstances." What Buber wrote about "signs" in "Dialogue" and, in the essay that followed, about the responsibility of the "Single One" in the political sphere, so remarkably formulated shared experiences that they made Buber's writings themselves "very much what you would call a 'sign'" for Hammarskjøld himself. "It is strange—over a gulf of time and a gulf of differences as to background and outer experience—to find a bridge built which, in one move, eliminates the distance." Hammarskjøld reiterated his idea of translating Buber to bring him closer to his Swedish countrymen, but it was increasingly difficult to choose which work, and the nuances of Buber's German made him shy.

Buber responded at once, thanking him for his letter as "a token of true understanding—rather a rare gift in this world of ours." Buber recommended that Hammarskjøld translate *Ich und Du,* the most difficult of all his works "but the most apt to introduce the reader into the realm of dialogue," and Hammarskjøld wrote Buber in turn that he saw this as a silent summons "to try a translation of this key work, as decisive in its message as supremely beautiful in its form." "If all this works out," he added, "may I tell you how much it would mean to me also by providing me with justification for a broadened and intensified contact with you personally." Hammarskjøld got in touch with his Swedish publishers and in less than two weeks had a favorable response, and on September 12, 1961, the day he flew from New York for the Congo, Hammarskjøld informed Buber of this in what must have been the last letter he ever wrote. Aside from Thomas à Kempis's *Imitation of Christ* the only book that Hammarskjøld took with him on the plane was the new German edition of *Ich und Du* that he had just received from Buber, and en route to and during his stay in Léopoldville, where he tried to stop the fighting between Moise Tshombe's army in Katanga and the United Nations force, he translated twelve pages. Thus, on his way to his final mission as "servant of peace," Hammarskjøld worked toward the completion of a cherished dream that would bring him closer to Buber.

The book and manuscript were not with Hammarskjøld on his fatal flight to Ndola, on January 18, where he had arranged to have face-to-face talks with Tshombe about the secession of Katanga, but were found among his effects in the home of the head of the U.N. mission to the Congo in Léopoldville, of which Hammarskjøld's nephew Knut informed Buber in a letter of October 5. Two days before, George Ivan Smith, a friend of Hammarskjøld and personal assistant to him during many of his trips, wrote Buber from the United Nations in New York that Dr. Sture Linner of the Congo U.N. mission had told him at the funeral service at Uppsala "that before Dag boarded the aircraft, almost the last conversation he had with Linner concerned your work," adding that the last words he remembered Dag saying before the aircraft took off "referred to your work and to medieval mystics. 'Love, for them,' he said, 'was a surplus of power which they felt completely filled them when they began to live in self-forgetfulness.'" Smith concluded with a touching description of the last rites of this remarkable man and its unforgettable impact on him:

> I have just returned from Stockholm and Uppsala. The service in the cathedral was magnificent, but the walk through the cobbled streets of Uppsala and through the ranks of university students who lined the route to the graveyard was quite the most moving experience of all. The utter simplicity, the quiet dignity and the intense depth of feeling in the audience made the final moment at the church-yard the most memorable of my life. At the very end, when the representatives of kings and governments were dispersing, I caught sight of a man in highly colored folk dress standing under the shadow of the nearby chapel from where he had watched the service. I made my way to him and through an interpreter discovered that he was a guide from northern Lapland who had been with Dag on many northern journeys. He had made his own way south for the funeral. The sorrow expressed in that man's face is something else I shall not forget.

Buber received Hammarskjøld's last letter an hour after he had heard over the radio about the latter's death in the plane crash in the Congo. Thus the dialogue between the two men was a present reality from both sides even after Hammarskjøld's death. In Hammarskjøld, Buber saw a man of good will who tried to do something but who had been abandoned. "Doing his utmost," Buber said to Meyer Levin, "Hammarskjøld still lacked the technical means to carry out his peace mission, and so he was martyred in his death." On September 28, Buber sent me the German translation of an article from the paper *Dagens Nyheter* in Stockholm about Hammarskjøld's plan to translate *Ich und Du* and the intention of Stockholm's leading publishing house, Bonnier, to continue with plans to publish a translation of it in Hammarskjøld's honor. "In the last weeks of his life I received (after a long silence) three remarkable letters from him on this subject," Buber revealed. On October 1, the *New York Times* also carried this story.

On October 22, on the front page of the Sunday edition of the New York *Herald Tribune* there appeared an article which reported that "one of Dag Hammarskjøld's last acts before his death on September 18, was to recommend that Martin Buber, distinguished Jewish philosopher and theologian, receive the Nobel Prize for literature" and added:

> Because of the great sense of personal tragedy felt throughout Sweden at the death of the Secretary General, Mr. Hammarskjøld's final recommendation, it is believed, will carry great weight with the Academy, and will make Dr. Buber a leading contender for the award this year.

In September 1963, Buber agreed, if his health permitted, to give a Dag Hammarskjøld Memorial Lecture the following month. This lecture was to be part of an impressive series in which thirty distinguished lecturers on five continents participated, each lecturer choosing a university in his own country as his platform. Buber, of course, chose the Hebrew University. The other lecturers included Ralph Bunche, Paul Hoffman, Lady Barbara Ward Jackson, Judge Philip Jessup, Sir Zafrulla Khan, Trygve Lie, Dean Rusk, Adlai Stevenson, and U. Thant. Buber's title was to have been "Serving Spirit in the Realm of Power." His health did not permit him to give the lecture.

In 1961, the Nobel Prize Committee of the Norwegian Storting posthumously conferred the Peace Prize on Dag Hammarskjøld in recognition of his attempts to bring peace to the Congo. At the same time it conferred the 1960 Peace Prize on the African Chieftain Albert John Luthuli of South Africa for his work for human rights and brotherhood among races through peaceful means. On March 11, 1962, the NBC "Eternal Light" radio program presented a dramatization of the Buber-Hammarskjøld relationship under the title "A World Dialogue." Here, if anywhere, indeed, that "Dialogue with the World" that occupied Buber's life since he reached the maturity of *I and Thou* is fully visible.

In 1959, in a Jerusalem interview with Thilo Koch for the West German radio and television station, Buber told the story of a Chinese emperor who sought in vain for a man to put at the head of his government so that he might restore peace. Finally he heard of a man who preserved the peace in his own household and sent for him.

"Peace between peoples has its origin ultimately in peace in the individual people, in the individual group, in the individual families of this group, indeed, even in the individual souls," Buber commented. Buber spoke of how once in a time of political crisis he sat hour after hour at the radio listening to the discussions of the United Nations— and clearly heard how they talked not to each other but out the window, since their goal was not mutual understanding but propaganda. Asked about the "totalitarian claim of communism," Buber replied that this was a formula of the cold war, not a present reality with which one had to reckon. "Naturally the people who say it are convinced that it is so, but I do not believe that in our historical epoch it has the character of reality."

In December 1960, Albrecht Goes wrote to Buber that he found himself back at the place where he had written him twenty-five years before for counsel. "There seems to be no human possibility of crying 'Stop!' effectively to the cynical and willful administration in Bonn" whose judgment had been beclouded by the anonymous forces of the armament industry. Resistance by more than one person was regularly broken by the police force. Attempts at protest on Goes's part were met with silence or hostility by others in the church. Buber's own sense of the political atmosphere was no more optimistic at that time. In an unpublished address on "Fraternity" to the World Brotherhood Association in California in 1952, Buber complained that the three principles of the French Revolution have come apart in our day, with the West (the capitalist nations) emphasizing liberty and the East (the communist nations) emphasizing equality and both losing sight of fraternity, the social cement which prevents the other two from becoming empty political catchwords.* In 1961 Buber published a little poem in answer to Hans Meinke's plea to him that "in a time of confusion you pray for my people—I will pray for yours!"

> *Yes, let each pray for the people of the other,*
> *Both wandering through the dark chasm of time*
> *And know, both, and they do not know:*
> *Does the light come—come toward us now?*

This poem-prayer is closely similar in spirit to a letter that Buber wrote in 1953 to Professor Louis Massignon of the College of France, the well-known authority on Islamic mysticism:

---

*See Note 1 to Chapter 13.

Yom Kippur falls this year on September 19th. If you wish it, I shall fast with you for Israel and its adversaries since I unite the one with the other in my fasting and my prayers and since I implore the great forgiveness of our common Father for their misdeeds—I might almost dare to say: for their common misdeeds. I shall as always begin with myself, the one person whose evil I wholly know; then I shall plead for my people and further for its neighbors, who are united by a common task and a common guilt; the guilt of having misconstrued the task that was entrusted to them and of misconstruing it again. May the All-Merciful hear my prayer and yours as if they were a single prayer for the unfortunate children of Adam.

Buber's answer to a peace questionnaire from the Novosti Press Agency in Moscow about what the world will be like in twenty years was more hopeful, though only cautiously so. Even if one assumed that war will have been averted, everything depends, responded Buber, upon whether world peace signifies mere cessation of the cold war or real coexistence. The former could only lead to a new and still more dangerous cold war. But real cooperation for the mastery of the common problems of the human race is possible, Buber maintained, "despite the fundamental differences of views of social justice and individual freedom . . . if in direct, unprejudiced, and comprehensive discussion qualified, independent, and realistically thinking men from both camps succeed in recognizing the urgency of vital common interests." So far as Buber knew, his reply was never published. In December 1960, Buber noted "a Russian academician's fulminating criticism of my philosophy. It is rather instructive." On the other hand, the affinity between Buber's thought and that of the Russian dissident physicist and Nobel Peace Prize winner Andrei Dmitrivich Sakharov is so striking that an American expert on Russia was convinced in 1968 that Sakharov had based some of his *Progress, Coexistence, and Intellectual Freedom* on Buber's "Hope for This Hour." On the American side of the cold war, the black West Point graduate Cornelius Cooper became a conscientious objector in 1971 largely because of Buber's I-Thou philosophy, as both he and Dr. Roger Shinn, Reinhold Niebuhr Professor of Social Ethics at Union Theological Seminary in New York, testified at great length at his CO hearing.

During this period Albert Schweitzer and Buber cooperated several times on appeals against the spread of nuclear weapons. In October 1961, abortive demonstrations were called by the Israeli Public Committee against Nuclear Tests. The committee was formed spontaneously by a group of intellectuals including Buber and Hugo Bergmann. In November, Buber joined Pablo Casals, Albert Schweitzer, Bertrand Russell, François Mauriac, Brock Chisholm, and Max Born in appealing to President John F. Kennedy to abstain from nuclear testing.

In the fall of 1960, Buber attended the Mediterranean Colloquium in Florence sponsored by Giorgio La Pira, the mayor of Florence and professor at the University of Florence. This conference consisted of a number of well-known persons from Mediterranean countries, including Israelis and Arabs, and was thus the *only* place where the latter met face to face. Buber had been urged to go by Joseph Golan, at that time the political adviser of Nahum Goldmann, president of the Jewish World Congress. Golan told Buber that the Egyptians set great store on his coming, and Buber wrote to Simon Shereshevsky, fellow leader of Ihud, that he would be very happy to be allowed still to do something "for our cause." Buber, who was in close touch with the Israeli Committee for a Nuclear-Free Zone in the Middle East, discussed the differences between a small peace and a great peace. "After the lecture of a very gifted Egyptian," Buber reported in November, "I invited him to sit with me at the presidential table and to talk the problems over before everyone and we did it thoroughly and directly; it was a rather symbolic moment." To Meyer Levin he later said of this discussion of Arab-Israeli problems with George Henein: "It was a real talk, in which we tried to pierce the hard core of the political sphere. Yes, I say it is still, it is always possible in human terms."

Meanwhile Buber had become enormously concerned about the plight of the Soviet Jews, who were not allowed even the ordinary cultural freedom of their fellow citizens and who were increasingly the brunt of government discrimination. In August 1960, Buber wrote to Carl J. Burckhardt reporting to him the results of consultation with Nahum Goldmann, head of the Jewish Agency, and others about the advisability of calling a conference on the Soviet Jews. "I was particularly in favor of the conference," Buber declared, "because rightly conducted it might exercise a favorable influence on the internal Russian debate over the Jewish question (a statement such as Suslov's, 'It cannot be our affair to revive dead cultures!' must be understood in terms of this debate)." Simon Shereshevsky sent Buber a letter strongly urging him not to go along with the conference because of the danger that it might make matters still worse for the Soviet Jews. Buber replied that what depended on him was not whether or not there would be a conference but what he was to say in the keynote address. In that he wanted to point out that the method of determining the fate of the Jews in a country according to the usual categories—nation, religion, or ethnic group—is false because Judaism is a unique phenomenon to be understood only in terms of its particular history.

Just so, after declaring his nonalignment with either the United States or the Soviet Union in their cold war, Buber began his speech at the Conference on the Situation of the Soviet Jews held in Paris in September 1960. Stalin followed through with such consequence on the notion that the Jews had merely an "ethnic unity" and therefore deserved to be "integrated" (i.e., dissolved) into the larger national culture, that he had all the leading writers of Yiddish exterminated. Lenin saw in Hebrew the language of capitalism (sic!) and forbade the publication of the Hebrew Bible in the Soviet Union, yet he not only tolerated but furthered Yiddish writing, press, theater, and education. Neither seemed to be aware that Karl Marx, himself of Jewish descent, was only translating into modern technical language (itself in need of humanizing) the Jewish faith in, and the will to create, justice that is to be found in the Hebrew Bible. Marx mistakenly held the Jews to be the chief historical facilitator of capitalism; Lenin trusted the Jewish masses and discovered in their midst an avant-garde of fighting proletariats. Stalin at the height of his power was as mistrustful as Nero, and in the atmosphere of mistrust that he created, accusations against the Jews as cosmopolitan, individualist, and lacking in attachment to the fatherland, quickened. Buber referred, in this connection, to his discussion of reciprocal existential mistrust in "Hope for This Hour" and stressed the need to overcome it not only in the relations among states but also in that of the state with its peoples. Buber asked that the Jews be treated according to their uniqueness and that even those young Soviet Jews who had become "integrated" have a chance to form a new tie with their fathers and their forefathers. Together with the others present at this conference (which he characterized as "too official" in a letter to me), Buber signed declarations demanding that the Soviet authorities grant the Russian Jews full civil and religious liberty.*

In May 1961, the Soviet Union reinstated the death penalty for economic offenses, and a high proportion of those sentenced to death proved to be Jews. Bertrand Russell was known to be in good standing

---

*See Note 2 to Chapter 13.

in the Soviet Union and in touch with Premier Nikita Khrushchev, as a result of which Buber decided in March 1962 to write Russell and ask him to intervene on behalf of Soviet Jewry. Buber pointed out that capital punishment for economic crimes had not existed in the Soviet Union since the days of the Revolution forty years before and declared that all enemies of capital punishment must energetically protest the reinstitution of the death penalty for such crimes, as being incompatible with the role of a great and progressive nation. He also pointed out that in the majority of the cases those sentenced to death were Jews and added that, though his own attitude would not be one whit different if those sentenced were non-Jews, he saw it as a grave threat to the whole Jewish community in the Soviet Union if in the eyes of the general population Jews were regarded as figuring prominently in economic crimes. "We should do our utmost to struggle against such a danger," said Buber, undoubtedly thinking of how precisely such measures in Nazi Germany eventually led to the total dispossession and extermination of the Jews. Buber proposed that Bertrand Russell, Eleanor Roosevelt, and the distinguished French Catholic writer and Nobel Prize winner François Mauriac should telegraph to Khrushchev to commute the sentences.

Eleanor Roosevelt replied from New York that unfortunately she could not send a telegram to Khrushchev together with Lord Russell, since she did not agree with some of his views, but she would gladly write Khrushchev directly if Buber held that to be appropriate, which Buber urged her to do. Russell and Mauriac immediately assented, with one change suggested by Russell: the deletion of the word *moral* from the statement that they had "no intention to harm the moral position the Soviet Union enjoys in the world." "Governments such as the Soviet Union and the United States have no moral position in the world," Russell explained to Buber. On March 20 the following text, translated into Russian, was telegraphed to Premier Khrushchev:

> News has come to us, through the Soviet and international press, that in the Soviet Union the death penalty has been instituted for economic and other offences, for which it is not generally the custom to punish with death.
>
> The undersigned belong to those who, as a matter of principle, are opposed to the death penalty. The Soviet Union has for many years been one of the countries where the death penalty did not exist, and this aroused our sympathy. And just because of it, we are gravely concerned that as from about nine months ago increasing death sentences have been passed for economic offences and the like. We consider that this judicial custom does not agree with a great progressive and cul-

tured people, and we call on the Government of the Soviet Union to abolish this system of internal contest against economic offences. We zealously call upon you to prevent the execution of the death sentences which have already been passed by Soviet courts. We are further concerned by the fact that the majority of those sentenced to death for economic offences, and whose names were published in the Soviet press, are Jews. In view of the fact that prejudices have not yet been rooted out from the wide masses towards some minorities living among them, these causes might eventually bare the entire Jewish community to grave dangers, those, of course, being contrary to the aims of the Soviet Union itself.

We are positive that you will see in this application no intention to harm the position the Soviet Union enjoys in the world. We are driven solely by the concern for the maintenance of universal human standards, as well as for the good name of the Soviet Union, so as to render easier international understanding towards world peace.

When the Jerusalem *Post* carried the story of this appeal in April, it pointed out that sixteen of the twenty-one sentenced to death were Jews.

Hodes reports that Russell's intervention with Khrushchev on behalf of the Soviet Jews was one of the reasons the Jerusalem Municipality awarded him its first Literary Prize for Human Freedom in the spring of 1963. Ralph Schoenman, Russell's secretary, who accepted the Prize for Russell, joined Hodes, Ernst Simon, Shereshevsky, the leaders of the Israeli Committee for a Nuclear-Free Zone in the Middle East, and Simcha Flappan of *New Outlook* for an evening at Buber's home devoted to a discussion of how the danger of introducing nuclear weapons into the region might be averted. These discussions resulted in a private appeal by Russell to the heads of eleven states and later in a public declaration in *New Outlook* by ten eminent scientists and moral leaders, including Max Born, Danilo Dolci, Martin Niemoller, Linus Pauling, Eugene Rabinowitsch, Jean-Paul Sartre, and Albert Schweitzer. In connection with Buber's deft informal chairing of this meeting, Hodes writes:

> When a knotty point arose, or the discussion strayed from the main issue, it was Buber who, with a phrase that did not order or insist but suggested, proposed, hinted almost, led the group skillfully back to the main flow of the talk. . . . Buber was the perfect chairman of a committee composed of factions hostile to one another, or a delicate international conference. He had all the tact, composure, and rapier-like subtlety of a first-class statesman. If anyone could have brought Arabs and Israelis around a table to a common understanding, Buber could have—if he had been given the opportunity.

In September 1963, it was Bertrand Russell who asked Buber to sign a similar appeal, not only pointing to the majority of Jews sentenced for economic offenses but also to the fact that Jewish culture and religion were suppressed in the Soviet Union in a way that no other minority's were. Russell expressed hope that the attempt of the Soviet Union and the United States to regulate atomic weapons and the better international situation this created might further the chances of such an appeal. Buber, of course, agreed at once and himself wrote to Nahum Goldmann suggesting an appeal to the Soviet regime be made from Jerusalem, to which Goldmann agreed.

The cooperation of Martin Buber and Bertrand Russell took place despite about as great a difference in their approaches to existence as was possible for two philosophers of the same era. Russell's concerns were mathematics and logic, and even his broad-ranging interest in education and social welfare bore the imprint of a basically rationalistic and skeptical mind. What is more, Russell was much more concerned with the "political principle" than the social. In fact, Buber's 1951 essay "Society and the State," in which he set forth the essential distinction between the political and social principles, began with a quotation from Bertrand Russell's book *Power* (1938) as a typical example of the confusion between these two principles in our time, one hundred years after the rise of scientific sociology. Russell's confusion, according to Buber, lay in his defining the social purely in terms of political power. Buber's contribution to a tribute to Russell on the occasion of his ninetieth birthday was informed by a similar refusal to see the crisis of modern man as merely political:

> In a memorable sentence Bertrand Russell tells us: "The question is a simple one: Is it possible for a scientific society to continue to exist or must such a society inevitably bring itself to destruction?"
>
> The answer, so it seems to me, can be given only in a conditional form. "A scientific society" can, I think, continue to exist only if science is humanized, i.e. if in its very action it asserts the existence of man as such. The theory of modern physics has made the first step by including the obsever, man as observer, in its object of research. It is now for the practice of modern physics to make the second and decisive step: to include man as a whole, human life and death, in its reckonings. This would mean, of course, that at the sight of the nearing catastrophe the mind of man will disobey.

On the other hand, how much Buber and Russell did share in a stubborn fight for peace we can sense from the image of Russell at the center of the tribute by Isaac Deutscher:

In an age of great events and small men Bertrand Russell testifies to the enduring greatness of the human character. The image of the philosopher squatting on the pavement of Whitehall to awaken men's conscience, and leading people seventy years younger to fight—or beg?—for mankind's survival, is a moment of our contemporary history of which we may be truly proud. . . . This image of Russell will live on in the ages and move posterity.

Buber was not much given to demonstrations, but he was intensely aware of what it was that made Russell lay his body on the line in order to break through the stolidity of the compact majority. In a statement on "The Problem of the Community of Opinion," written for Robert Weltsch's sixtieth birthday, Buber defined a truly living community of opinion as one that is ever again tested and renewed in common meetings. "The 'men who hold the same views' must ever again loosen up one another's views as they threaten to become encrusted." Instead of this, people in general are concerned with nothing else than pressing oneself and others to cling to what has been laid down, suppressing in one another the strength to reflect from the depths and draw out of opinion that which is true. "Finally narrow-minded cliquism no longer leaves its adherents any free ground, only a sheepfold." At this point the bond between human beings has sunk back into the prehuman situation in which all reality is divided into the "we" in the foreground and, in the background, the threatening "they," neither with any true personal existence.

In his "Replies to My Critics" in *The Philosophy of Martin Buber,* Buber stated the claims of the "community of otherness" more positively. Rejecting Emmanuel Levinas's view that Buber saw in an *amitié toute spirituelle* the peak of the I-Thou relationship, Buber asserted:

On the contrary, this relationship seems to me to win its true greatness and powerfulness precisely there where two men without a strong spiritual ground in common, even of very different kinds of spirit, yes of opposite dispositions, still stand over against each other so that each of the two knows and means, recognizes and acknowledges, accepts and confirms the other, even in the severest conflict, as this particular person. In the common situation, even in the common situation of fighting with each other, he holds present to himself the experience-side of the other, his living through this situation. This is no friendship, this is only the comradeship of the human creature, a comradeship that has reached fulfillment. No "ether," as Levinas thinks, but the hard human earth, the common in the uncommon.

In his attitude toward civil disobedience, Buber was close to Martin

Luther King.* As King was the disciple of Gandhi on the path of nonviolent resistance, so Gandhi in his turn was deeply influenced by an American of the century before—Henry Thoreau. Writing on the centennial of Thoreau's death, Buber testified in 1962 that reading Thoreau's classic tract on "Civil Disobedience" had had a strong impact on him in his youth, but that it was only much later that he understood why.

> It was the concrete, the personal, the "here and now" in the writing that won my heart for it. Thoreau did not formulate a general principle as such; he set forth and grounded his attitude in a particular historical-biographical situation. He spoke to his reader in the realm of this situation common to them so that the reader not only learned why Thoreau at that time acted as he acted, but also—provided that this reader was only honest and unbiased—that he himself, the reader, must act, should the occasion present itself, in exactly that way if he were seriously concerned about making his human existence real.

In writing these words, Buber, like Thoreau, was not concerned merely with one of the many cases in which powerless truth struggles against a power inimical to truth. For Buber, as for Thoreau, it was "a question of the wholly concrete indication of the point at which time and again this struggle becomes the duty of man *as man*." Because Thoreau, Gandhi, King, and Buber spoke as concretely as they did from the standpoint of their historical situation, each expressed in the right way what is valid for all human history.

In 1963, Buber applied his view of civil disobedience to the international situation at that time. Civil disobedience, if it is to be legitimate, must be obedience to a higher authority than the one that we here and now obey. But there is no general way of demonstrating the legitimacy of this higher authority or of setting the limit to what we have to give to Caesar. Not at all times and places but only in the particular situation, in the here and now, can this question be answered.

In our present situation, however, it is easier to reply than ever before, Buber declared, for we are today on the point of letting the determination of our fate slip out of our hands. The universal military preparations and the bellicose surprises, one outstripping the other, on all sides in the cold war may reach such a point of automation as to transform the human cosmos "into a chaos beyond which we can no longer think." If the rulers of the hour cannot wake up before

---

*See Note 3 to Chapter 13.

it is too late, command a halt to the machinery, and learn to talk *to* instead of *past* one another, then who will come to the rescue while there is still time but the "disobedient," those who personally set their faces against the power that has gone astray? "Must not a planetary front of such civil disobedients stand ready, not for battle like other fronts, but for saving dialogue? But who are these if not those who hear the voice that addresses them from the situation—the situation of the human crisis—and obey it?"

After the Cuban missile crisis in the fall of 1962, Buber foresaw the possibility of young people forging personal relationships even in the heat of crisis, just as Kennedy and Khrushchev did, and then the leaders on both sides would not be able to order them to kill one another. This might be the beginning of a worldwide movement which on its negative side would be called civil disobedience but on its positive side a determination to live together. "Rather than take part in a suicidal 'victory,'" Hodes quotes Buber, "young people of all nations would be justified in following the way of civil disobedience as Thoreau suggested."

Two such "civil disobedients," Anthony Brooke, an exile from Sarawak and the British Commonwealth, and Michael Scott, an exile from South Africa, attempted to form a World Peace Brigade made up of unarmed volunteers sent to areas of conflict to help the refugees and wounded and endeavor to bring the combatants together through passive resistance and persuasion. They decided to hold the founding conference of the brigade in the resort town of Burmana in Lebanon at the end of December 1961 and asked Buber if he would be able to attend. Charles Malik, the former Lebanese ambassador to the United Nations, had taught a course in Buber's philosophy at the American University in Beirut for many years. (In fact, Malik and Hayim Greenberg of Israel once met at the United Nations to discuss *I and Thou*.) But no Israeli citizen had ever been openly allowed to enter by an Arab state. If Buber had gone, he would have become the first Israeli citizen to be invited to an international conference in an Arab country. In his reply, Buber made it clear to Brooke and Scott that the first meeting should be held only in a country which would admit every single one of the sponsors, without discrimination, and he was ready to demand that the conference be transferred somewhere else if Lebanon did not admit him. Although Buber was ill and his doctor had definitely declared that any more exhausting journeys abroad were out of the question, Buber hoped he might let him go if he understood how important it was to him. "What made this incident memorable for me," testifies Hodes, "was Buber's eagerness at the age of eighty-three to embark on this unpredictable trip if there was the slightest chance his presence could contribute to the beginning of an Israeli-Arab dialogue." Buber's health got worse, and the trip became out of the question. "I have not been at the Conference in Lebanon," Buber reported in January. "The doctors would not have let me go." Nor would the Lebanese have been likely to allow him in: "The Brigade People, who obviously did not know anything about the real state of things, I mean about the utter lack of communication between Israel and that country, did not really prepare anything. After the Conference some of them came to see me, and I gave them somewhat critical advice."

In 1962, Reinhold Niebuhr and I wrote secretly to a number of prominent men throughout the world supporting the nomination of Martin Buber for a Nobel Prize in Literature. The letter began with a statement by Reinhold's brother, the eminent theologian H. Richard Niebuhr, on the occasion of Buber's eightieth birthday at a celebration in America: "More than any other person in the modern world, more even than Kierkegaard, Martin Buber has been for me, and for many of my companions, the prophet of the soul and the witness to that truth which is required of the soul not as solitary but as companionable being." Unfortunately, Professor H. Richard Niebuhr died of heart failure at the very time that Reinhold's and my letter was sent to him. The responses from the others, however, were immediate and wholehearted. Of these the most astonishing and heartwarming was that from the Lebanese statesman and philosopher Charles Malik. In 1960, Buber told Eugenia and me how Malik had wandered by mistake into the Israeli pavilion at the Brussels Exposition and signed his name to the guest register. The newspapers picked this up, and Malik as a result lost his position as ambassador to the U.N. and any possibility of holding public office in Lebanon. It would not have been at all surprising if he had declined to sign the letter to the Nobel Prize Committee. Instead Malik not only signed the letter but added under his signature an eloquent statement:

> Buber is one of the important influences for my thought, especially through his "Ich und Du." I also conceived a high regard for him and the late Dr. Magnes in connection with the Palestine Question. I always felt that he and I would agree on many things, spiritual and political. The type of spirit he represents could still help in bringing about a reconciliation, in God's own time, between Arab and Israeli. If only political passion on both sides would make it possible to "meet," in

Buber's sense of the term, in an atmosphere of Christian love and forgiveness! But man is so limited and history is so tragic and the mystery of God is so unfathomable. I trust the Swedish Academy would give this matter their most serious consideration, for no living man, in my opinion, deserves the Nobel Prize for literature more worthily than Martin Buber.

In a separate letter that was not forwarded to the Academy, Malik wrote: "It gives me the greatest pleasure to join you and Dr. Niebuhr in this most worthy endeavor. I wish there was something else I could do for this noble soul. Buber is greater than even the fine eulogy you compiled for him in your draft letter."

When informed of these actions on his behalf, Buber mentioned Hammarskjøld's earlier nomination of him and that he even had an extract of his letter to the Swedish Academy. In 1961 the newspapers actually reported that Buber was favored to receive the Nobel Prize for Literature, but here too the decision went against him. Referring to this last decision, Buber said: "Some people think there are certain political motives behind it, but I have done nothing, as you will understand, to get further information." Aubrey Hodes, without citing his sources, reports that the reason Buber did not get it that year was that no citizen of an Arab state of equivalent stature to Buber could be found for a joint presentation of the Prize.

Aside from Charles Malik, Reinhold Niebuhr, and myself, the signatories to the letter to the Swedish Academy included W. H. Auden, T. S. Eliot, Emil Brunner, Albrecht Goes, Victor Gollancz (the English writer and publisher), Hermann Hesse, Gabriel Marcel, Sir Herbert Read, Ignazio Silone, and the German philosopher Wilhelm Szilasi. In his letter to me, T. S. Eliot confirmed the sense of real meeting that Buber had told me about when he and I first met in person in 1951: "I once had a conversation with Dr. Buber, . . . and I got the strong impression that I was in the company of a great man. There are only a very few men of those whom I have met in my lifetime, whose presence has given me that feeling."*

---

*See Note 4 to Chapter 13.

CHAPTER 14

Buber versus Ben-Gurion

When I was in Jerusalem in 1960, a doctor from Hadassah Hospital said to me, "We have two 'B's' in Israel—Buber and Ben-Gurion. We wish the former would stick to philosophy and the latter to politics!" In his 1930 essay on "Gandhi and Us," Buber declared that no one can be either political or apolitical on principle. Buber was, in fact, always enormously concerned with politics and, as everyone who knew him testified, surprisingly well informed about what was going on in Israel and in the world in general. Nahum Goldmann used to come to see him regularly whenever he was in Israel to brief him on local, national, and international developments, and Buber followed them with keen interest, concerned not only for their immediate effect but also as to what they might mean a generaton or two hence. Although they had known each other since the founding of *Der Jude* in 1916, Buber and Goldmann were brought particularly close together during the last ten years of Buber's life by their common attitude toward the Arab problem. Buber regarded the existence of Israel as dependent upon its integration into a federation of the Near

East. Small states cannot maintain their existence except in a larger federation. Goldmann opposed Ben-Gurion's Arab policy in much the same terms. Buber often urged Goldmann to enter the political life of Israel and take over its foreign policy.

Goldmann found Buber extraordinary in his combination of the philosopher, the person who took a detailed interest in political problems, and a man who understood the practical problems of ordinary life. "He could have been a great businessman had he not been a philosopher," Goldmann said. Once Goldmann was with Buber for two hours when they went over every clause in a contract with a publisher. He did not care about a luxurious life and he was not money-minded, reported Goldmann, but he did not want to be fooled by businessmen and he wanted them to know he was as shrewd as they were. Buber also had an uncanny memory. In his eighties he could quote from books that he had read twenty or thirty years before, and there was not a book in his library that he could not refer to, even by the page. He also organized his life so that he could work fourteen to sixteen hours a day without wasting a minute, concentrating on the important things and never committing himself to what was not his. "If admission to Paradise depends upon how one uses one's talents, you will be in the front row," Goldmann said to Buber. "God gave them to me as a loan," Buber replied. "Therefore, I must use them."

The conflict between Buber and Ben-Gurion was not based on their differing attitudes to the Arab-Jewish quesion alone. Buber was a social anarchist in the biblical sense. He was very distrustful of the state organization; whereas Ben-Gurion was *the* representative of the cult of the state and of *Realpolitik.* When Ben-Zion Dinur went to see Buber in 1952 to ask him to be head of the Ministry of Education, Buber refused, saying that the individual must be first instead of society as a whole, as far as culture is concerned. Society as a whole can come only after you have aroused in the individual a thirst for culture—a thirst to know and to think. "In this area I have tried to work," Buber said. This does not mean that Buber opposed the state as such, as does the traditional anarchist. In his American Friends of Ihud speech in 1958, Buber said:

> I have accepted as mine the State of Israel, the form of the new Jewish Community that has arisen from the war. I have nothing in common with those Jews who imagine that they may contest the factual shape which Jewish independence has taken. The command to serve the spirit is to be fulfilled by us today in this state, starting from it. But he who will truly serve the spirit must seek to make good all that was

once missed: he must seek to free once again the blocked path to an understanding with the Arab peoples.

In a 1949 interview with a French Zionist journalist, Buber said that all the groups that had favored a bi-national Palestine had, of course, given that up since the establishment of the State of Israel but they had not given up the idea of a Near East Federation nor, despite the exacerbation on both sides due to the war, the possibility of working with the Arabs. "A great part of the youth of Israel have the real wish to come to an understanding with the Arabs. Many are seriously learning Arabic. In the new settlements there are often excellent relationships between the Arabs and the Jews." The Arabic and Jewish elements could not merge, but they could cooperate and reciprocally enrich each other. In the same interview Buber was asked if he thought Jerusalem should be part of a Jewish state. "No," he replied. "I have always wanted the internationalization of Jerusalem. It should become a great center of cooperation. Not only between Jews and Arabs, but between the nations in general, something like the symbol of a beginning of real accord among human beings."

In 1954, Buber granted a similar interview to Uri Avneri, the editor in chief of a popular but politically independent Israeli weekly newsmagazine. The interview, printed in January 1955, was titled "We Need the Arabs, They Need Us!" and was billed as "the first one the famous philosopher has granted in fifteen years." On the cover page was a full-page picture of Buber with the two-line caption underneath: "Philosopher Martin Buber/Needed: Pax Semitica." Buber was criticized by some for making use of such a medium, but he pointed out that it interviewed him on "the Arab question, which has become the question of our existence," and gave it the broadest possible circulation.

In this interview Buber affirmed his belief that the time was near when it will be possible to reach an agreement resulting in cooperation between Israel and the Arab States and that a federation of the whole Middle Eastern region was the only meaningful form in which such cooperation could take place. This Buber saw as a world political matter depending not only upon the cooperation of both peoples but of the great powers: "Naturally the federation would have to be established in such a way that the majority could not exercise undue influence over the minority, or our national existence would be endangered. That is to say, the federation charter would have to be some sort of international Magna Carta." Our chief error, Buber added, was that we did not try to get the Arabs' confidence on political and economic matters when we first came here. "With the State's rebirth some of our followers deserted us. They believed the problem was solved." "I did not make any reply to the deserters because fear gripped me," Buber candidly confessed. "But in the present state of affairs everyone devoted to our cause must express himself openly."

Buber reported that three years earlier some friends and he were invited to meet one of Israel's leaders (whom he identified seven years later as Ben-Gurion). Asked by Ben-Gurion how the government might shape the spiritual and moral code of the nation, Buber replied that the government could do something that would arouse the people's conscience, such as taking the initiative and inviting the interested states to a convention to decide the problem of the Arab refugees. In a private talk he had later with Ben-Gurion, the latter said, "Don't think I don't agree with what you said. But in history the time is either too early or too late." Only a few days later, mediation talks were called and the initiative was taken out of Israel's hands. What is needed now, Buber noted, is not a new personality but a general reform. "But the man who will fearlessly do what the moment demands will be the true hero of the nation. We must all pave the way for this man who has not yet arrived on the political scene."

No one can be blamed for the thwarting of the hopes for an organic development of the Yishuv, Buber remarked; for the hordes of homeless and displaced people created a psychological pressure that Zionism was unable to withstand. The state was not built on the basis of mutual trust in the Middle Eastern area, as Buber's group had hoped. But what they could do now was to recognize that they did not yet have a living culture of high quality: "We have a great tradition and people endowed with abilities, authors, poets, artists, philosophers, scientists and research workers. We also have excellent educational and cultural institutions. But a culture whose influence is felt in all walks of the nation's life—that we do not have." A "Jewish renaissance" no longer was enough for Buber. As long as there was no decisive order of justice and truth which determined the course of life, there could be no true culture.

In August 1953, Ludwig Strauss, the German-Israeli poet and husband of Buber's daughter Eva, died. Buber was close to Strauss not only as his father-in-law but also as a friend harking back to when the younger man was twenty. During Buber's centenary year Verlag Lambert Schneider announced (but has not yet brought out) a 250-page book titled *Martin Buber and Ludwig Strauss: A Life-Testimony in*

Letters, including letters from 1912 to 1953. When Buber learned the news of Ludwig's death, he sent Eva a remarkable letter of comfort:

> My beloved Evie, since the news came yesterday afternoon I have several times had the impression that Ludwig's soul-image was near me, and just now, before I took up this piece of paper, it seemed as if he stood next to me, each time without concerning himself about me, but also without strangeness. But it was not at all the Ludwig whom I had seen when I took leave of him and have since borne in mind, nor was it an earlier Ludwig, and yet it was not shadowy and indistinct: I mean that it was the completed image, the gestalt in its completion, such as a person can achieve only through the deepest suffering. And it seems to me that the peace of his last days has to do with that completion in a manner that no survivor can understand; it seems to me that the great weakness of the dying earthly being was only the visible in it, the invisible was the presentiment of becoming complete that overcame all infirmity.
>
> God comfort you and bless you and your sons!

When Fritz Kaufmann learned of Ludwig's death in June of 1954, he wrote Buber from Buffalo that he had met Strauss only once when Salman Schocken brought them together while Strauss was doing his work in the Hölderlin Archives in Stuttgart. But "it was a contact with so noble a human being that I have never been able to forget it." From then on Strauss's poems remained very close to Fritz—not least of all in Israel, for whose wonderful colors he had prepared Kaufmann: the pulp covering the ground under the orange grove, the grazing of the sun on the walls of Jerusalem, the blue silence of the night that rises against the sallow earth. "I don't know whether it was granted to him to bear the 'image and . . . command' of his dream into reality," Kaufmann added, but he fulfilled it as a person, even in error and confusion, and allowed it to irradiate his life. In August 1955, Buber's old friend Kurt Singer wrote him from Australia that he had been moved by the news of Ludwig's death. "I have often recalled that still, circling evening when we met for the first and last time in Hamburg. He appeared to me to be made of such pure poetic material, to stride through this earth so defenseless that I almost wondered that he could endure for as long as he did."

In January 1954, the American Jewish Stephen Wise Prize was given to Buber and his old Zionist friend and comrade Joseph Sprinzak. At that time Buber wrote Sprinzak that in his view the greatest danger to the Western Continental type of democracy (such as Fránce) was in the multiplication of parties. The only thing that could avert this danger would be the influence of personalities who, despite loyalty to their own parties, stood between the parties, transcending their differences. "You are one of the few personalities who provides this model today in the democracies in general, and therein lies your historical significance." In May 1954, Buber communicated with another leading Zionist friend, Kurt Blumenfeld, saying he had guarded "soul-winning" speech in a time that had more and more turned it into mere propaganda. What bound Buber and Blumenfeld was not only a common depth of feeling but, even more, a common secret bond with a perhaps yet unborn generation that would be concerned with more than simple survival.

In January 1955, in response to Hans Blüher's expression of concern about Buber's isolation in Israel, Buber responded that he did not feel at all isolated and painted a picture of his life in Israel that showed he understood clearly his position in his adopted home:

> I have enough friends and disciples. I am unpopular, to be sure, and for a nonconformist such as I have been from my youth . . . and remain in my old age, it could not be otherwise. What the "broader circles" mostly reproach me for is that since 1917 I have expressly come out for cooperation with the Arabs—until 1947 in the form of a bi-national state and, since the victory of Israel over the seven states that attacked it, in the form of a Near-Eastern federation of peoples—and have led political actions supporting Jewish-Arab rapprochement. Secondly, that I have . . . opposed confounding the German people with the murdering insects of the gaschambers organization.

When a group of Israeli soldiers in a reprisal action killed sixty men, women, and children in the Jordanian village of Kibya in 1953, Buber and his political friends openly protested. He also attacked the Israeli rabbinate because it said not a word against the Kibya incident. A rabbinate that concerned itself only with rituals and ignored transgressions against humanity would itself be ignored, Buber felt. Buber later expressed indignation over the Kafr Kassem massacre in October 1956 when forty-seven Arabs were shot down returning from the fields because of a curfew about which they had not been informed. In his 1958 speech for the American Friends of Ihud in New York, Buber expressed his sorrow in unmistakable terms:

> It happened one day . . . that, having nothing to do with the regular conduct of the war, a band of armed Jews fell on an Arab village and destroyed it. Often, in earlier times, Arab hordes had committed outrages of this kind, and my soul bled with the sacrifice; but here it was a

matter of our own, or my own crime, of the crime of the Jews against the spirit. Even today I cannot yet think about this without feeling myself guilty. Our active faith in the spirit was too weak to prevent the outbreak and spread of the demonic false teaching.

Buber was equally opposed to the invasion of Sinai that Ben-Gurion undertook in the fall of 1956 with the cooperation of France and England. When Werner Kraft asked Buber whether he meant this opposition politically-strategically or morally, Buber responded that he did not recognize any isolated morality. He held the "right" politics to be "moral." Buber deemed Ben-Gurion's politics false and Ben-Gurion himself a "dreamer" who had not rightly estimated the powers with which he leagued himself. As a result of the Sinai invasion, America's position was totally reversed and the Russians finally brought into the closest proximity. When I wrote Buber about the Sinai invasion, he responded, in December 1956, "Of course, the situation is particularly heavy for me who cannot settle it in my mind by opposing 'principles' to it. By the way, I had sharply opposed in Ihud a more radical resolution thanking the U.N., an institution in which I cannot put any trust." The U.N. had issued a resolution condemning Israel, and Buber could not go along with that any more than with Ben-Gurion's action.

Buber's grandson Micha Strauss was drafted for the Sinai invasion but later discharged, and Buber reported with relief to his friends Ewald and Sophie Wasmuth in November 1956 that the intoxication of victory was nowhere to be noticed. Lambert Schneider wrote Buber from Heidelberg that although the world press was critical of Israel and he himself was a categorical opponent of military engagements, he recognized that there were moments in the life of a people in which an act of force is necessary. Recalling the time of Hitler and how people let things go until it was too late "and we all live now in the chaos that man created," he felt that Nasser too had to be stopped, although he doubted, realistically, whether this small field action could do it and whether Israel might not be compelled to halt its advance at some point, as did indeed happen through the joint pressure of the United States and the Soviet Union.

At the Jerusalem Ideological Conference in August 1957 the opposing positions of Ben-Gurion and Buber received almost classic expression. In his speech, "Vision and Redemption," Ben-Gurion seemed at first to be in entire accord with Buber in viewing the revival of the Jewish people as based upon a vision of the Jewish state as a

moral state. *"Anyone who does not realize that the Messianic vision of redemption is central to the uniqueness of our people, does not realize the basic
truth of Jewish history and the cornerstone of the Jewish faith."* But Ben-
Gurion's messianism was not Buber's; for he was able to see in the
State of Israel not only the *greatest* but also the *only* common asset of the
entire Jewish people, divided in values and disintegrated in structure.
"The rise of Israel . . . straightened the back of every Jew wherever he
lived" and "restored to the people living in its midst their wholeness as
Jews and human beings." "Our historic goal is a new society built on
freedom, equality, tolerance, mutual assistance and love of humanity,
in other words, a society without exploitation, discrimination, enslavement, the rule of man over man, the violation of conscience and
tyranny." But the professed liberal values that Ben-Gurion ascribed to
the state were not, in fact, being applied to the Arab minority. Nor
could the three means of deepening the consciousness of the Jewish
mission and Jewish unity that he put forward—Hebrew education,
the intensification of the personal bond with Israel, and deepening
the attachment to the messianic vision of redemption—lead to such a
goal as long as the security of the state was put foremost.

In a less formal speech on "Zionism and Pseudo-Zionism," Ben-
Gurion, addressing Buber, denied "the existence of two separate
worlds, the world of the spirit and the world of the flesh"—an astonishing misreading of Buber's position which Buber immediately rejected. "Perhaps there is no difference of opinion between us in this
respect," Ben-Gurion went on, "but I want to emphasize that at the
same time as they fervently preached righteousness, lovingkindness
and mercy, the Prophets of Israel also foretold material and political
redemption for their people," and then he repeated his denial of
separate worlds of matter and spirit! The real issue between the two
men—their difference in the estimate of the state—Ben-Gurion expressed in words again addressed entirely to Buber:

> Professor Buber says that the State is only an instrument. Of course it
> is an instrument—but it is a precious instrument without which there
> can be no freedom and independence, no possibility of free, creative
> activity, suitable to our needs, our aspirations and our values. . . . The
> miracle that has taken place in our generation is that there has been
> established an instrument for the implementation and realization of the
> vision of redemption—and the instrument is the State of Israel, in other
> words the sovereign people in Israel. For that reason, give honor to the
> State of Israel. It is not merely an instrument. . . . it is the beginning of
> the redemption, a small part of the redemption.

Ben-Gurion claimed to go beyond Buber's statement that the means sanctify or defile the goal by saying that there is no final goal, no finished achievement. "And there is another thing I want to say to Professor Buber. Man has not only values but also needs and we must also take into account his needs. . . . When they are not met, the result is suffering and injustice." In what followed, "values" and "needs" were merged by Ben-Gurion in the "vision of Messianic redemption" and that in turn became identical with the actual goals of the State: "action for the conquest of the desert, for the absorption of the immigrants, for the security of the State," which he identified in turn "with the forces that make for redemption and progress *in our time*." That the question of means did not seriously bother Ben-Gurion, as it did Buber, is implicit in his simply adding to the series of "values" that he mentioned "and also the unflinching effort to achieve a society built on liberty and peace, equality and justice among the nations." Ben-Gurion concluded by identifying the "command of the conscience" that had spurred on the best men in Israel for several generations with "as Professor Buber put it, 'subordination to the Divine.'"

Buber's own speech at the 1957 Jerusalem Ideological Conference was titled "Israel's Mission and Zion," and he placed it at the end of the 1963 revised edition of *Israel and the World* along with his 1958 American Friends of Ihud speech, "Israel and the Command of the Spirit." Just as Ben-Gurion's second speech was addressed exclusively to Buber, so Buber's speech was throughout an explicit reply to Ben-Gurion. In Buber's speech the classic opposition between king and prophet in ancient Israel is given a modern context.

> Ben Gurion is right in saying that youth in Israel is very much interested in certain parts of the Bible, especially in the stories about the conquest of the land, in the stories of the hero-kings and also in some words of the prophets. But on no account are the prophets to be regarded apart from their historic mission which sent them to those men who had seized the reins of power in order to summon them to stand in judgment before their God who had made them king provisionally.

It is not enough to set the redemption of Israel side by side with the redemption of the human race, as Ben-Gurion did. The destiny of Israel depends upon the fulfillment of the demand that Israel "make an exemplary beginning in the actual work of realization, that it be a nation which establishes justice and truth in its institutions and activities." To Buber the prophetic demand applied not only to the generations of the Bible but to all the generations since and especially to our own, which, for the first time in two millennia, "has the prerequisite for fulfilling its task, . . . the power to determine for itself in no small measure its institutions, its modes of life and its relations to other nations." The sharpness of the words that Buber now addressed to Ben-Gurion is part of that concern that led him during these same years to see the "politicization" of the relations between nations as leading to the "technically perfect suicide of mankind":

> Behind everything that Ben Gurion has said on that point, there lies, it seems to me, the will to make the political factor supreme. He is one of the proponents of that kind of secularization which cultivates its "thoughts" and "visions" so diligently that it keeps men from hearing the voice of the living God. This secularization takes the form of an exaggerated "politicization." This "politicization" of life here strikes at the very spirit itself. The spirit with all its thoughts and visions descends and becomes a function of politics.

Buber went on to point out that this phenomenon, "which is supreme in the whole world at present," has roots which reach back to the biblical times in which some kings in Israel (King Ahab for one) "employ false prophets whose prophesying was merely a function of state policy."

The quasi-Zionism, which strives to have a country only, has attained its purpose. But the true Zionism of the lovers of Zion demands, in Israel as well as abroad, "Zionists of Zion" who remain faithful to that dream that still has found no fulfillment. "What Ben Gurion has said about the present Israeli generation is no doubt true of its majority"; for after a generation which was unable to confront the catastrophe there has come one which clings to the practical execution of great ideas. "The members of this generation . . . suspect ideas as ideas and put their trust only in tangible reality as such." In his concluding words Buber answered Ben-Gurion's claim, that the messianic idea is alive and will live, with the question: "In how many hearts of this generation in our country does the Messianic idea live in a form other than the narrow nationalistic form which is restricted to the Ingathering of the Exiles?"

> A Messianic idea without the yearning for the redemption of mankind and without the desire to take part in its realization, is no longer identical with the Messianic visions of the prophets of Israel, nor can that prophetic mission be identified with a Messianic ideal emptied of belief in the coming of the kingdom of God.

For Buber's eightieth birthday in 1958 there was a celebration in the Aula of the Hebrew University. When Buber entered the auditorium, the five to six hundred persons present spontaneously rose from their seats in a great ovation. Ben-Gurion came to honor Buber on this occasion and sat in the front row next to Paula Buber, which pleased Buber greatly. Three generations of Buber's pupils spoke in his honor, recalling a memorable past to those who had felt the power of his spirit and leadership in Germany, Central Europe, and, since 1938, in Palestine and Israel. For many of the young sabras who came out of curiosity or out of pride in their university, this was the first real introduction to the man who occupied the anomalous position of being the best-known Israeli scholar and philosopher to the world at large and yet, up to that time, a man known more to the older Zionists and the European Aliyah than to the new generations. When Buber himself spoke, he told of how, as a young man, he was editor of Theodor Herzl's Zionist weekly, *Die Welt.* One day before a Zionist Congress, Herzl came to him and said, "We need a new word, Herr Buber." To this the young man of twenty-two replied after some hesitation, "What we need, Doctor, is not a new word but a new spirit."

In this same year, 1958, the conflict between Buber and Ben-Gurion broke out afresh in connection with the indictment of Aharon Cohen for meeting a Soviet agent in his kibbutz and not reporting it to the authorities. Cohen, an authority on the Arab world and on Jewish-Arab relations in Palestine, was a member of the Mapam (Labor Zionist) kibbutz, Sh'ar Ha'amakim, and was Mapam's chief representative in the League for Jewish-Arab Understanding and Cooperation. Although Aharon Cohen was a Marxist to the left of Mapam, Buber was impressed by Cohen's energy, dedication, organizational ability, voluminous knowledge about Jewish-Arab relations, and his enthusiastic belief in the possibility of improving them. Buber, in fact, wrote the preface to the third volume of Cohen's trilogy, *Israel and the Arab World,* which he described as an objective and extremely important scientific work based on an inner knowledge of the events and written with fervor and love of the cause.

Cohen's trouble arose in connection with this very trilogy, which narrated the history of the relations between Zionism and the Arabs of Palestine and neighboring lands from the late nineteenth century to the present, a book, not at all incidentally, highly critical of Ben-Gurion's attitude toward the Arabs. Unable to obtain from the Hebrew University and the National Library Russian-language periodicals on the Middle East dating back to before the Russian Revolution, Cohen got in touch with the Russian Scientific Mission in Jerusalem, and in the course of meetings with them not only expressed openly his critical views on Israel's Middle East policies but also wrote down the names of the Mapam leadership in a personal code in order to conceal the visits of the Russians from the leaders of Mapam, who preferred to conduct all talks with Russians themselves and who had criticized Cohen for his overemphasis on Marxist theory. By Israeli law anyone meeting a "foreign agent," the definition of which was unclear, could be accused of passing information if he could not satisfactorily explain the meeting, even if there were no evidence that he had in fact done so. Cohen was arrested under this law in 1958, at the very time that his book was being prepared for publication. Cohen believed this was done to stop the publication of his book, parts of which were impounded to be used at the trial, which was held in 1962, three and a half years later.

Buber took Cohen's side without a moment's hesitation and issued a statement together with Ernst Simon and Dr. Shereshevsky the very day the attorney general released Cohen's name. They asked for the maximal possible publicity under the given conditions of security for the arrest, which was not yet a matter under judicial consideration. Buber was immediately attacked by the political writer Arye Gelblum in the influential evening newspaper *Ma-ariv* for meddling in the lowlands of politics. Totally undeterred, Buber did not relax his efforts in Cohen's behalf from the day of his arrest until he was released from jail. He signed a letter drafted by the Israeli philosopher Nathan Rotenstreich, who, along with Moshe Sharett, undertook to defend Cohen within Mapam. "Ben Gurion won politically and lost morally," Rotenstreich said about Cohen's sentencing. Buber was the first to declare himself willing to testify before the Haifa District Court, and when the trial opened, the eighty-four-year-old Buber, ignoring all medical considerations, made the strenuous trip to Haifa and testified for three hours in Cohen's favor.

Appearing as the first witness for the defense, Buber testified before the crowded courtroom that he had known Cohen since 1941, when they had both been among the first members of the League for Jewish-Arab Rapprochement, along with Henrietta Szold and Judah Magnes. Buber met frequently with Cohen (who became secretary of the league at the end of 1941), particularly after Cohen's visit to Syria and Lebanon in 1942 and his testimony, together with Ernst Simon, before the Anglo-American Commission of Inquiry in 1946. Buber appeared as a character witness, and he did not hesitate to claim that he was, indeed, a judge of character who had founded his entire philosophical thinking on a study of actual human beings from the time of his youth. The prosecutor objected that Buber's remarks were abstractions irrelevant to the trial, but the judge allowed him to continue, and Buber went on to attest to Cohen's extreme sincerity as a person who basically said what he thought, one whose thoughts and speech were of a piece. When Justice S. Kassan rephrased this as, "His heart and his mouth are one," Buber agreed that this was for him the main thing. "For nearly three hours he remained there," reports Aubrey Hodes, "replying patiently to all the queries leveled at him, his voice clear and unhurried, explaining in an almost fatherly way his conviction that a man such as Cohen could not possibly have acted deceitfully in the way the prosecution claimed." In a relationship of over twenty years, Buber could not recall a single incident which would contradict his conviction that Aharon Cohen was a man who meant what he said.

Buber's words made a profound impression upon the judges, none of whom believed that Cohen had given any information to the foreign agents he had met. Nonetheless, they did not find his explanation of his contacts convincing and sentenced him to five years in prison. Ben-Gurion was pleased with the verdict and the sentence as well as with the court's arguments, praising privately the wisdom of the Israeli judiciary. He was not so pleased when the Israeli Supreme Court took a different line, one justice wanting to quash the verdict and release the prisoner immediately and the other two, including the chief justice, reducing the sentence by half, not joining their colleague only because they felt that the law, highly dubious and draconic though it was, still was binding upon them and left them no other choice. "Public opinion in Israel generally regarded this as the vindication of Aharon Cohen which Buber and his friends had demanded from the first," reports Simon. Ihud's official journal, *Ner*, in its November–December 1961 issues protested against Cohen's arrest and conviction in the strongest terms and with an impressive marshaling of arguments. On December 21, 1962, Buber, Agnon, Rotenstreich, Scholem, Simon, and Shereshevsky submitted a petition to Ben-Zvi, the president of Israel, to pardon Cohen because of the state of his health. They received in reply a curt note from the president's legal adviser that "The President has weighed all the arguments in your request . . . , but he has reached the conclusion that the material at hand did not warrant reducing the sentence," which *Ner* again protested in a long, detailed, and vigorous article.

In February 1963, on the occasion of Buber's eightieth birthday, Ben-Gurion sent him best wishes, "the wish of a friend, an admirer and opponent."

> Your deep and original philosophy, your faithful participation in the work of the rebirth of Israel from your youth to the present day, your deep ideal and existential relationship to the vision that the prophets of Israel had of national and universal redemption and a reign of righteousness, peace, and brotherhood in the world, the total agreement between your strivings and demands and the conduct of your life—for all these you are entitled to praise and fame in the history of our people and our time.

Ben-Gurion signed this letter "in love and veneration," and Buber replied that he had been made truly happy by this letter, which touched on a complicated realm of interhuman relationships—the type of opposition that does not exclude personal closeness. "I may say to you that I agree with you in this, and that, with all factual reservations, I could characterize my position toward you in words similar to the friendly ones that you have used in writing me." But Buber went on to say that he saw in this letter a sort of continuation of Ben-Gurion's previous letter to him of February 1962 in which he refused to pardon Aharon Cohen:

> Allow me on this occasion to make an observation concerning our controversy. Some time has elapsed meanwhile, and perhaps you now see a possibility, in the framework of your authority, to pardon and to release the ailing Aharon Cohen from prison. That would make me very happy.

Ben-Gurion immediately replied to this letter, once more refusing to pardon Cohen. One of the first actions of Buber's friend Zalman Shazar, when he became president of Israel, was to fulfill Buber's wish and pardon Cohen, an action which he communicated personally to Buber.

On February 24, 1958, Prime Minister Ben-Gurion received a deputation of Ihud, composed of Buber, Simon, and Shereshevsky, which submitted a memorandum calling on him to restrict the scope and jurisdiction of the military government in Israel and complaining of the "military government ideology" "which takes it for granted that part of the population of the State of Israel—the Arab minority—is deprived of the rule of civil law that applies to the rest of the population." Although in principle they were for the outright abolition of military government, they recognized the difficult security problems that this step might entail and suggested instead that military rule be lifted from all areas which were not in proximity to the frontier; that in the border areas all residents be treated equally, without discrimination; that the implementation of all matters not closely tied up with security must be entrusted to civil authorities and civilian officials. These changes would make it possible to introduce suitable elements among the educated Arabs into the ranks of officials and to abolish the travel permits to students which Ben-Gurion himself had termed "absurd." Later in 1958, Ihud contacted outstanding individuals, thinkers, and men of action with a proposed proclamation, "Against Military Government," which was later published over the signature of Markus Reiner of the Haifa Technion and Ernst Simon of Jerusalem with accompanying signatures of almost 200 prominent Israelis, including, of course, Buber. Despite the Israel Declaration of Independence which guarantees "fully equal social and political rights for all citizens irrespective of creed, race, or sex," ten years after the birth of the State 200,000 Israeli citizens "who differ from the majority in religion and nationality, are denied equal rights and suffer discrimination."

> The bulk of Israel's Arab population is subject to a military rule that denies them the basic rights of any free citizen. They have no freedom of movement of residence; they are not accepted as equal members in the trade unions, and not employed on the same basis as others in most organizations or government departments. Their entire life depends on the good graces of the military governors and their aides. . . .
>
> Ten years of discrimination have created and fostered discouragements, bitterness and despair among the Arab population, which falls prey, as a result, to all sorts of incitement that exploit this mood for party gain. Allowing this situation to go on may gravely threaten the state's internal security.
>
> On the other hand, a fundamental change in the conditions will call forth a favourable reaction among the Arab population and pave the way for the two peoples' living together on a basis of mutual respect.

In the memorandum that Buber, Simon, and Shereshevsky submitted to Ben-Gurion in February 1958 there was also a statement concerning the problem of the Arab refugees uprooted within the boundaries of the state *and* the Arab refugees in the Arab states. This statement urged the prime minister to do all he could to relieve the situation of the refugees within the country, as he had indeed promised to do, but also to take the initiative in calling an international conference to deal with the problem of the refugees in Arab lands. This meant, in effect, asking the Israeli government to abandon its position that the refugees could be dealt with only within the framework of a general political peace settlement. If all the concerned parties would pool their resources to this difficult problem, Israel should show its readiness to do its part for regional and world peace by agreeing to settle a certain number of refugees within its borders. It would thereby make it impossible for anyone to say that Israel is an aggressor that opposes any peaceful solution.

> We want to move the Arab states, which have consistently refused to sit down together with us even at world conferences on purely scientific or cultural issues, to work together with our experts in a great constructive enterprise. We want such a common international endeavor to provide the opportunity for renewed collaboration and interaction between Jews and Arabs as well as between East and West.

In September 1959 the Executive of Ihud decided to bring its position on the Arab refugees to the attention of the Israeli public through holding a press conference in Buber's home. Nearly all Israeli newspapers gave a prominent place to reports on this press conference, and many wrote special articles expressing appreciation of the meeting and of Buber, in particular, who took the central role.

Buber shook hands warmly with each of the dozen journalists who were introduced to him and, with a degree of alertness and liveliness difficult to find even among the young, directed the conversation. He began by pointing out that the refugee problem would be given more serious and realistic treatment at the forthcoming General Assembly of the United Nations and that the meeting between Eisenhower and Khrushchev in Washington might also result in a relaxation of tension in the Middle East that would make it possible to do something about this problem. The time had perhaps come, he thought, for Israel to take that initiative on the Arab refugee problem which he suggested to Ben-Gurion in his talk with him ten years before. Such an initiative Buber saw as an unconditional moral-political duty in the present situation, independent of a peace treaty with the Arab states. "I am doubtful," Buber added, "whether after the U.N. General Assembly session the matter will still remain in our hands."

In October 1961, Buber issued a statement on the Arab refugee problem for Ihud expressing "deep sorrow at the Prime Minister's statement of October 11, 1961, in which he firmly rejects 'the insidious proposal for freedom of choice for the refugees' between returning to Israel and accepting compensations and resettlement elsewhere,'" a proposal which reiterated the belief that the means could be found to have hundreds of thousands of refugees transferred to a productive life as peace-loving citizens in the Arab States and in the State of Israel. Buber called for a cooperation between Israel, the Arab States, the refugees, and the U.N., in which joint committees of experts should devise "projects for rehabilitation of the refugees and methods of carrying them out 'in a constructive spirit and with a sense of justice and realism' (Hammarskjøld), taking into account the economic, demographic, humanitarian and, particularly, security conditions involved in this operation." It would be the special task of these committees "to ensure that the choice of the refugees will really be a free one, based on objective information of the conditions prevailing in Israel and in the Arab States." Thus Ihud coupled an awareness of problems concerning security with a deep humanitarian concern over the refugees' plight.

Ben-Gurion in a long statement repeated the standard governmental position that the Arabs left under orders of the Arab leaders on the assumption that the invasion of the Arab armies would destroy the Jewish state and throw all the Jews into the sea. He also claimed that the number of Arab refugees from the area allocated to the Jewish State was not larger than the number of the Jewish refugees from the Arab countries, amounting to "an unplanned, but effective exchange of populations" and that any compensation for loss of property should go to the Jewish refugees from Arab countries just as much as for Arab refugees from Palestine. Israel absorbed the Jewish refugees. The "only one practical and fair solution" to the problem of the Arab refugees, similarly, is "to resettle them among their own people in countries having plenty of good land and water and which are in need of additional manpower." Once more he tied the whole question of any help on Israel's part to an overall peace settlement. Five years later when he was filmed for the National Educational Television film *Dialogue: Buber and Israel,* Ben-Gurion took the identical position, adding that if the Arab refugees are prevented from being settled in Arab lands, "it is because the Arab states keep the refugees as a weapon for destruction of Israel." What is striking is that, along with all the true facts Ben-Gurion marshaled, there is a total lack of recognition of the plight of the Arab refugees as a *common* problem and responsibility of Israel and the Arab states, *whatever its historical origins.*

In August 1961, Dr. Joseph E. Johnson, president of the Carnegie Endowment for International Peace, was appointed special representative of the United Nations Conciliation Commission for Palestine to undertake a visit to the Middle East to explore with the host governments and with Israel practical means of seeking progress on the Palestine Arab refugee problem in accordance with Resolution 1604 of the United Nations General Assembly. When Johnson came to Israel in 1962, the only nonofficial Israeli he met with was Buber. He spent several hours in Buber's home discussing the Ihud proposals for offering the Arab refugees a choice between staying in Arab lands and receiving compensation or returning to Israel as full citizens. Johnson worked conscientiously at his task and made detailed and realistic reports. Unfortunately, the four Arab states involved and Israel were not prepared to accept the plan that he recommended for a step-by-step approach to the problem, which he himself realized was one fraught with deep mutual mistrust and fear, and in January 1963 he resigned as special representative of the Commission to return to his work in the Carnegie Foundation.

Buber's last statement on the Arab refugee problem was published in *New Outlook,* January–February 1965, as part of a series of replies solicited by its editors to a proposal of Bashir Ben-Yahmed for a Near East federation in *Jeune Afrique* in December 1964. Buber's reply, "A Time to Try," was published first in the series, before that of Ben-Gurion. In it Buber said that this unprecedented initiative from an Arab source might acquire historical significance if it awakened an echo in the Arab nation. He also pointed to the clear need for an understanding between Israel and the Arab peoples based on a federal or, better still, confederative union with considerably larger national autonomy for every part, and compared the situation of the two peoples to that of the entire world: "The decay of mankind will be inevitable if the cold war will be replaced only by a non-war; what should come in its place must be no less than a true cooperation in dealing with the great common problems of humanity." Buber adhered to the "narrow ridge" here too by declaring that in such a confederative union no partner should be allowed to injure the national existence of the other, which meant that Jews must not criticize the national movement of the Arabs or vice versa, including the author of the article who had spoken disparagingly of Zionism. Here too Buber called for cooperation in this unprecedented task on the part of spiritual representatives of each people, persons who are independent in the full sense of the word. If a true dialogue based on mutual sincerity and recognition will come about between such persons, "its significance will spread far beyond the territory of the Near East; it may show whether in this late hour of history the spirit of man can influence his fate."

In his contribution to this inquiry, Ben-Gurion called the young African's plea merely "a voice in the wilderness" amid the mounting general hostility to Israel among the Arab masses in all countries as a result of the virulent propaganda incessantly disseminated by radio and press against Israel and Zionism. "Our neighbours are multiplying on a large scale and at a great pace; they are making progress in the material and the cultural sense; and their hatred is growing." Ernst Simon, in contrast, said that Bashir Ben-Yahmed's proposals broke up the appearance of uniformity and might for that reason be a significant step toward peace. At the same time, he too called for a confederative union with autonomy and reproved Ben-Yahmed for comparing the Arab refugee camps to the Nazi death camps. "The ghettoes of the Nazi camps were used as preparatory stages for the total annihilation of their Jewish inhabitants, and with this in view the conditions of their life were deliberately worsened from year to year and finally from day to day—until the bitter end." "The living conditions of the Arab citizens of Israel have, on the contrary, been improved gradually in various aspects of life, and this applies also to those subject to military rule," by which Simon was referring to a relaxation of the restrictions. If the difference between the Nazi death camps and the Arab refugee camps actually were one of degree and not kind, "the Arab states which, together with Israel, are responsible for the creation of the refugee problem would long ago have hastened to seek a solution within their own boundaries. I say this in spite of the fact that today, as always, I support the demand that Israel receive back some of these refugees." Simon too, like Buber, walked the "narrow ridge" and eschewed political slogans and polarizations!

Ben-Gurion made mistake after mistake, Buber remarked to Werner Kraft in 1959. There *had* been real possibilities of understanding with the Arabs. In saying this, Buber showed no trace of wishing to whitewash the Arabs. In Moshe Sharett, on the other hand, Buber saw the leader of a group of the dominant party of Mapai that was close to Ihud. In a reply in *Philosophical Interrogations* written about this time, Buber showed his continuing hope for Israel despite the dominance of Ben-Gurion's position:

But as for the State of Israel, the hour for a verdict on it has by no means arrived. He who lives here senses how in the hearts of a growing segment of the young is ever more strongly fought out the battle between the two kinds of nationalism, the opposition between which I pointed out in that speech of 1921 [at the Karlsbad Zionist Conference].

In 1959, in a statement in honor of his old Zionist friend Kurt Blumenfeld, Buber sharpened this into an opposition between two types of states: "Every attempt to replace the living idea of 'Zion' through the establishment of a state must end in failure," wrote Buber. "The state is not, as Hegel thought, the 'self-determination' of the spirit in which alone man can have a rational existence. It is at best a supporting structure that the spirit employs in its work; but it can also be a hindrance." Zion can grow out of a state that is faithful to the spirit but not out of one that forgets it unless it recollects itself and "turns." The people need the land and freedom to organize their own life in order to realize the goal of community, Buber wrote in *Israel and Palestine.* But the state as such is at best only a *means* to the goal of Zion, and it may even be an obstacle to it if the true nature of Zion as commission and task is not held uppermost.

> Zion means a destiny of mutual perfecting. It is not a calculation but a command; not an idea but a hidden figure waiting to be revealed. Israel would lose its own self if it replaced Palestine by another land and it would lose its own self if it replaced Zion by Palestine.

The next clash between Buber and Ben-Gurion came in connection with the "Lavon affair," a political thicket with roots that reached back to the formation of the state. Before the establishment of the state in 1948, many leaders of Mapai objected that the declaration of the state involved too grave a risk and wanted to wait for the decision of the United Nations. This was Ben-Gurion's finest hour. He said, "No, now is the time to act with force; we shall get no second chance." His success built up his charisma to the point where he was able to get rid of the whole summit of his party, including Moshe Sharett, Joseph Sprinzak, and David Remez, whom by degrees he put in minor positions. Lavon was younger, and he began to gather around him a group of young activists—among them Moshe Dayan and Simon Peres, whom he regarded as the future leaders. In 1953, Ben-Gurion, cornered by the old-timers in Mapai, resigned, appointing Sharett as prime minister, Lavon as minister of security, and Dayan as chief of staff, to secure his return to power. Declaring he was taking leave for a year or two, he actually conducted the state from Sde Boker, his kibbutz in the Negev, as a result of which some say that Ben-Gurion himself was responsible for the whole Lavon affair and that at any rate he knew about it before Sharett, who learned of it from the newspapers!

The affair itself started at the time that the Egyptians tried to nationalize the Suez Canal. According to rumor, Moshe Dayan's plan was to plant bombs in the American Embassy to cause an incident between the Americans and the Egyptians and win the Americans over to the Israeli side. The six Israelis involved in the plan were caught and executed, resulting in a public scandal and a concerted attempt by everyone involved to shift the blame to someone else. First they began with an Israeli lieutenant colonel, then with an Israeli civilian who was in Egypt and received the messages, after which the Israeli, the lieutenant colonel, and Dayan all shifted the blame to Lavon. As minister of defense, Lavon had previously ordered the Kibya raid without notifying Prime Minister Sharett. There were, in fact, at this time, two governments, acting independently of each other: that of Sharett in Jerusalem and that of Lavon, Dayan, and the head of intelligence in Tel Aviv, who acted in perfect concert and kept what they did secret "for security reasons." After the affair broke out in 1954, Sharett appointed a two-member secret committee to investigate the matter. They did not reach a conclusion, and both the chief of intelligence of the army and Lavon, the minister of defense, were forced to resign. This did not prevent Lavon from becoming secretary general of the powerful labor organization Histadrut, which he turned into a one-man organization and used to build up his power. When the Israeli who had been the message link in Egypt was tried on secret charges, he said that he and the chief of intelligence framed Lavon and that he was ordered to do so or otherwise be in trouble himself. He was sentenced to a ten-year term, but the news of his testimony leaked out to Lavon, who thought that his hour had come to take over the government. In 1960, as a result, Lavon asked that the case be reopened on the basis of this new evidence and demanded that Ben-Gurion exonerate him. Ben-Gurion, as a result, decided that Lavon had to go and resigned his position as prime minister in order to force him out.

In December 1960, the intellectuals issued a manifesto titled "The Danger to Democracy," specifically protesting against Ben-Gurion's intervention. This statement was signed by fifty professors and by some of the most important and prominent persons in the state, calling on the leaders to take action to clear the atmosphere' and regain the confidence of the people:

> The Israeli society is presently undergoing a crisis of confidence. Large parts of public opinion are inclined to believe that the regular functioning of the authorities subject to public control is growing more and more devious. Many citizens are shocked at the outbreak of disputes and instigations engendering feuds and regard the quarrels among politicians not as disputes for the sake of heaven or as struggle for principles, but as a struggle for positions of power.
>
> Hidden in these trends of opinion is a grave danger to the future of the State of Israel. The citizens' feeling of helplessness turns quickly into an attitude of indifference and then into scorn toward politics and its makers. . . . The greatest danger to a democratic regime and its values is from a scorn of criticism and an attitude of contempt towards the opponent. This danger is many times greater in a society which is still in the process of crystallizing its political and social regime, and in which large parts of the population lack the experience of democratic government and a sense of proportion to distinguish between the important and the subsidiary in a controversy between the parties. . . . Our project of national revival attained its achievements mainly due to the mixture of personal responsibility and free decision of the individual, on the one hand, and the readiness to bear the common destiny and lot on the other. Without this combination the staying power of our state will be damaged, no matter what its material achievements and organizational arrangements are.

Among those who signed this manifesto were Hugo Bergmann, Lea Goldberg, Zvi Verblovski, Jacob Talmon, Dov Sadan, Ernst Simon, Shai Agnon, Nathan Rotenstreich, and Gershom Scholem, with Buber's name leading the list. Ben-Gurion was furious, and he was particularly offended that Buber, for whom he had great respect, should take sides against him. Up to this point, Ben-Gurion belonged to the Mosad Bialik committee that Buber headed for the translation of the classics into Hebrew and had visited Buber in his home to discuss the translation of Spinoza, in which he was very much interested. Now Ben-Gurion publicly resigned from this committee. At the end of January 1961, Raphael Bashan published a long interview with Buber in *Ma-ariv*, with the title, "Why Did I Sign the Professors' Manifesto?" and the subtitle: " 'Not because of Lavon, whom I don't know,' declares the aged thinker, 'but I had more serious grounds and they were decisive.' "

In this interview Buber talked again about Plato's desire to make philosophers kings and kings philosophers, and Kant's more realistic view, in the second edition of his book *Toward Eternal Peace,* that philosophers should not rule but should be listened to. Buber's definition of a philosopher in this context was very close to his own conception of the biblical prophet: "A philosopher is a man who penetrates to the inmost reality of human life, who examines the changing situations, understands what brings about the concatenations of certain events, where they may lead, and tries also to find a line, a way, a cause, which will lead to an exit from the situation. One could actually say that a real philosopher sees what will happen in the future." "There are fateful hours of crisis when rulers should lend their ears to those who think of the political reality without bias, who understand which processes are actually operating, where they come from and where they might lead to." He signed the manifesto because he believed that this was precisely one of those times in which a person is obliged to raise his voice. Buber distinguished this from the philosopher accepting a definite office; for it is impossible for one who rules to be unbiased. One cannot engage in practical political affairs and at the same time remain above those affairs, to examine, inspect, and judge them properly. Nor was he even now taking sides between Ben-Gurion and Lavon, the latter of whom he knew little. When Bashan asked him exactly what danger he had in mind, Buber showed that he was absolutely conversant with everyday problems down to the last detail, that he knew the inmost intrigues of the political parties and the way an army is run. "He suddenly impressed me as a most mysterious man, pulling a hundred strings of secret information," Bashan confided. But what Buber said during that hour he asked Bashan not to publicize. Bashan concluded from this long talk that Buber believed unconditionally that the Middle East was on the eve of radical political and social changes which might bring about a sharp turn in Israel's international relations. "If renunciations are imposed upon us from without, this will be a catastrophe," Buber said. "But if we renounce willingly, this will be politics."

"I heard that the Prime Minister was hurt by my signing the professors' manifesto," Buber added and said that while he could not write to Ben-Gurion, as people suggested, if Ben-Gurion wanted to meet him, he was ready to explain everything to him. Later Ben-Gurion did in fact inquire of Buber why he was against him, and Buber wrote a sharp reply that Ben-Gurion did not make public. Ben-Gurion's declaration that he would not return to the government until Lavon was demoted had the desired effect, and in the end of January 1961, Lavon was removed from his position as secretary general of the

Histadrut. The professors drew up but did not publish a second manifesto concerning the demotion of Lavon because it amounted to crying over spilt milk, but the text of the unofficial draft resolution was published in *Ha-aretz* without any signatures. "A great injustice was committed in Israel, and we believe that it is *forbidden* to establish once again the political leadership on the basis of this injustice," read the central sentence, followed by a call to all parties and their leaders *not* to lend a hand to Ben-Gurion in his attempts to establish a new cabinet. After the elections, when Mapai lost votes and Ben-Gurion had a hard time forming a coalition, he let it be known in the Knesset that he was ready to meet with the professors. They replied that they would be glad to meet with him after he had formed a government, and Ben-Gurion, very much offended, did so, lecturing them for an hour. Buber was not among them, but Hugo Bergmann spoke for them, saying that they had not come for a lecture, and each one gave Ben-Gurion a piece of his mind, including Scholem, Jacob Katz, and Nathan Rotenstreich. Ben-Gurion was angry, and the meeting ended badly.

After Ben-Gurion retired a second time and then started attacking the new prime minister, Levi Eshkol, at a public meeting, Buber said to Rotenstreich that Ben-Gurion wanted to get back into power, and this proved to be the case. The final act of the drama began in 1964 when the Lavon affair was opened again with Eshkol in power. A committee of seven ministers was appointed, over Ben-Gurion's objections, and the committee found Lavon not guilty. Ben-Gurion had already resigned from the government in protest in 1963. Before he did so, he had authorized a journalist to search all the secret files for material to show that Lavon was guilty once for all. The journalist submitted this material secretly to Ben-Gurion after he was no longer in power, even though it included all sorts of state and security secrets. Ben-Gurion kept this silent for a year, but when he saw that Eshkol was independent and was not his puppet, he brought up these findings and demanded that the government reject publicly the findings of the seven ministers' committee and reopen the case on the basis of new evidence.

Eshkol said "No," and Ben-Gurion tried to wrest the power from him at a Mapai party meeting. At this time the professors again sent a telegram, which they read to Buber and which he signed, though he was very ill at the time. Eshkol gave a plenary speech to the party in January 1965 in which he said: "It is either I or Ben-Gurion." Moshe Sharett, who was about to die of cancer, was brought to the stage in a wheelchair, and his speech won the session for Eshkol. After the party decided for Eshkol, Ben-Gurion, unable even then to give up the power he had clung to for so long, started a dissident movement within Mapai, claiming that he was the real Mapai, Eshkol an upstart. The final result was that Ben-Gurion was expelled from Mapai, as were Moshe Dayan and Peres.

Buber's most famous conflict with Ben-Gurion concerned the trial and execution of Adolf Eichmann, an issue that reached far beyond internal Israeli affairs to postwar Germany and the modern world in general. Although by no means the person most responsible for the Holocaust, Eichmann had been entrusted with the organization and to some extent the execution of the "final solution." As a result his capture and kidnapping by Israeli secret police in Argentina in 1961 and his subsequent prosecution by Gideon Hausner before a court of Israeli judges was a sensational series of events that aroused great controversy regarding international law, war crimes, and the justice of Eichmann's being tried and executed by an Israeli court. Buber believed that Eichmann should be tried in Israel but by an international court, because he did not believe that the Jews, who were the victims of the Holocaust, should also be the judge. He understood psychologically Eichmann's kidnappers and agreed with those who felt that the Germans did not do enough to capture their war criminals. He also made it very clear, in his interview with Bashan, that he was not for any mitigation of Eichmann's sentence. He wrote me at the same time: "I am disgusted with the Eichmann process." What disgusted Buber, undoubtedly, was not only that an Israeli court was trying Eichmann but, too, the amount of sensational publicity connected with it.

At the end of his interview with Bashan on January 28, Buber invited the young people of Israel to write him. Many did, including some who questioned his stand against trying Eichmann by an Israeli court. One of these suggested that it was not only Eichmann who was on trial but mankind, which had closed its eyes and ears while Eichmann carried out his diabolic deeds. Another wrote:

> We, the youth in the Land, lack personalities such as yourself, lack pointers of the way, persons on whose forehead the word "Peace" stands written. . . . I am convinced that persons such as you can take the necessary first step to lead our public life out of the great hysteria, and the blind hatred which prevents our taking our place among the peoples of the region and out of pessimism regarding a lasting peace in the Near East.

A week after Bashan's interview, Eliezer Be'eri, Gerson's right-hand man among the Werkleute, wrote Buber from Kibbutz Hazorea that the current crisis in Israel had closed the ears of many to the voices of conscience and of reason. "And who has taught us as you have that no opposition between conscience and reason exists? It is good that you have made public your views. It seems to me that not for decades has there been a time in which so many people were ready to hear what you have to say."

In August 1961, Ernst Simon wrote Buber that as the time of the announcement of the verdict against Eichmann drew nearer he had given much thought to what their eventual action should be. The sentence of the judge certainly *must* be death, but "it must by no means be executed, on that we are agreed." But instead of asking the president for *clemency,* Simon proposed that the Knesset should pass an ad hoc law saying, "The sentence of death against Eichmann is not to be executed." Simon thought they might convince Ben-Gurion and even, perhaps, a majority, that this was the course to take. In the same month, Julius Stone, Professor of International Law and Jurisprudence at the University of Sydney and official observer of the earlier stages of the Eichmann trial for the Australian Branch and World Headquarters of the International Commission of Jurists, wrote a long article on the trial in which he pointed out "that the crimes charged burst out from the confines within which our societies, our law and our morals ordinarily move. They create limit situations for our thinking which force us to rethink our positions." He reported a long interview with Buber in which the latter rejected as fanciful Stone's notion that any sentence on Eichmann be suspended on condition that he be put on trial successively in other countries and thus kept before mankind as a prophetic mirror. Nor could Buber agree that the evil which the trial had revealed was new. It was, on the contrary, old in human history.

On December 14, 1961, the *Jerusalem Post* reported from Saarbrücken in West Germany that Buber would ask President Ben-Zvi for a stay of execution should Eichmann be sentenced to death. The head of the Saar region branch of the World Christian Federation for Reconciliation, a friend of Albert Schweitzer, had sent Buber an inquiry on this matter, to which he replied. On December 15, Eichmann was sentenced to death by the Israeli court. Buber telephoned Ben-Gurion and asked him if he could meet with him. Ben-Gurion replied, "I am younger than you. I shall come to you." The two men talked for two hours at Buber's home in Talbiyeh, where

Buber pleaded with the other to commute the sentence to life imprisonment. Ben-Gurion, who earlier had said that he was concerned about the trial and not about the sentence (in *Eichmann in Jerusalem* Hannah Arendt characterized Ben-Gurion as the "invisible stage manager of the trial"), said that he himself was not intent upon the execution. But President Ben-Zvi was determined that Eichmann be executed. In a Histadrut convention in the thirties, Ben-Zvi was the only member who did *not* want the abolition of capital punishment, which was, in fact, abolished with the foundation of the state except for high treason in wartime and for war crimes against humanity or the Jewish people. Buber also appealed directly to Ben-Zvi, but here, too, his plea was unsuccessful. "Indirectly, Ben Gurion gave a public answer to Buber," reported *Time* on March 23, 1962. "As the Israeli Supreme Court prepared to consider Eichmann's own appeal before handing down a verdict, the official government gazette published a regulation authorizing the appointment of 'a man to execute a death sentence.'" The principal reason for Buber's opposition to the execution, which was the identical position taken by Hugo Bergmann, was that the Commandment "Thou shalt not kill" applies with equal force to the state and the individual. "I do not accept the state's right to take the life of any man," Buber said. Although it is not possible to keep the Commandments in all situations, "as far as it depends on us, we should not kill, neither as individuals nor as a society." When *Time* magazine quoted Buber as quoting Rabbi Mendel of Kotsk, "What the Torah teaches us is this: none but God can command us to destroy a man," Buber wrote a letter to *Time* saying that the main point of the story was not these words but the sequel: "And if the very smallest angel comes after the command has been given and cautions us: 'Lay not thy hand upon . . .' we must obey him." Buber also stated to *Newsweek:* "The death sentence has not diminished crime—on the contrary, all this exasperates the souls of men. . . . Killing awakens killing."

The other reason for Buber's opposition to Eichmann's execution was the fear that the German youth might take Eichmann's execution for a symbolic justice that would relieve them of the burden of German guilt for the Holocaust. This seemed to be particularly so because of the enormous worldwide attention the trial had received, which raised it far beyond *any* other trial of an individual. No punishment could really expiate Eichmann's crimes, Buber declared. What he had done went far beyond any human punishment that could be devised. To oppose his execution had nothing to do with clemency or mercy. Buber had no feeling of compassion or pity for Eichmann, for whom, as Hodes recounts, "Buber felt nothing but distaste and horror."

Buber proposed instead that Eichmann should be given life imprisonment—not in a cell like an ordinary criminal but, as a symbol of the Holocaust, be put to work on the land in a kibbutz farming the soil of Israel so that, as Buber said to Hodes, Eichmann would "be made to feel that the Jewish people were not exterminated by the Nazis and that they live on here in Israel." He recognized, of course, the problems of preventing him from escaping and of protecting him from those who might seek to kill him. But he saw killing him as "too facile and commonplace a way out of this unique dilemma." When the Israeli newspapers learned of Buber's plea not to execute Eichmann, public reaction was overwhelmingly against him. According to *Newsweek* the newspapers were full of snide remarks about the "merciful professor" who intervened for Eichmann but "did not lift a finger when the British hanged Jewish terrorists in the forties." Shmuel Katz, a former officer in the Irgun Zvai Le'umi, published an attack in *Ha-aretz* asking, "Where was the shock, the outcry, the use of his famous name, when in the past, in his immediate environment, in this country, people were being judged and hanged." Katz was aware, as many others were not, that Buber had signed a petition to the British High Commission asking that the death sentences of Jewish terrorists be commuted to life imprisonment. But Katz claimed that Buber had only signed the petition, whereas in the case of Eichmann Buber was taking the initiative.

After Eichmann's hanging on May 31, 1962, Buber gave an interview to the *New York Times* in which he called the execution of Eichmann a "mistake of historical dimension." He expressed fear that the act of taking Eichmann's life might serve to expiate the guilt felt by many young persons in Germany who were beginning to feel a resurgence of humanism. Without that conscience, an obstacle will have been removed from antihuman tendencies manifesting themselves throughout the world. He pointed out that it was not a question of mitigation, and neither was it simply his opposition in principle to the death penalty. "For such crimes there is no penalty." His plea was not based on any doubts about the severity of the sentence nor on any feeling of pity. "I feel here no pity at all," Buber said. "I have pity only for those whose actions I understand in my heart." But it was pointless to seek retribution; for there can be no retribution for crimes so monstrous. Eichmann's death served none of the accepted purposes of punishment. Buber accepted the necessity of a judgment, and he agreed that Jerusalem was the proper place for the trial, even though he felt that Eichmann should have been brought before an international tribunal in Jerusalem "with a certain adequate representation of humanity to give it the right kind of horizon." "Israel's role should have been that of the accuser and not of the judge." "Once the trial began, it was conducted with utter correctness," Buber concluded.

Buber was afraid also that a second-rate figure like Eichmann might become some sort of mythical hero because of his execution. This fear proved unrealistic, Schalom Ben-Chorin points out, "Buber saw the daemonic in evil but not its banality," using the phrase of Hannah Arendt. Israel Iserles, writing in *New Outlook* in January 1962 after the trial was over, stated:

> One certainly cannot question the noble motives of humanitarians such as Lord Russell and Professor Martin Buber who are in favor of granting Eichmann his life. . . . The traditional debate over the usefulness or permissibility of the death sentence lies, in our opinion, outside the framework of crimes such as genocide. . . . The Jerusalem trial will not have its full effect unless it is brought to the absolute end with Eichmann's execution.

This was, of course, a total misunderstanding of Buber's position, which recognized fully the uniqueness of Eichmann's crimes. The equal and opposite misunderstanding was expressed by the editorial writer of the New York *Herald Tribune* who said: "We on earth administer man's justice, not God's, and by man's justice it is fitting that Eichmann, after a fair, complete, and scrupulous hearing, should be hanged like a common criminal among a people whose kin he ruthlessly persecuted and murdered." Eichmann was not a common criminal, and common criminals are not hanged in Israel! The Berlin evening newspaper *Der Abend,* on the other hand, expressed a warning close in spirit to that of Buber's:

> Germans should beware of wanting to close the chapter on "Germany and the Jews" with the execution of Eichmann. . . . This danger exists and that is why the Jewish philosopher, Martin Buber, opposed the death sentence. He did not want to have the living reminder, Adolf Eichmann, removed from the world.

In December 1977, Elie Wiesel reported at a public lecture in San Diego that in the last few years more than sixty books have come out all over the world, not claiming that the Holocaust was exaggerated, as the pro-Nazi elements in Germany did in the 1950s (these claimed only one million Jews had been killed instead of six!), but that it was a complete fabrication, that it never took place!

In July 1962, Leo Shulman of Ramat Hasharon wrote the following letter to the Hebrew University in Jerusalem:

> My condolences to Professor Martin Buber on the hanging of Adolph Eichmann. The learned professor may find some consolation in the fact that breaking the neck is one sure way of telling the culprit to go and sin no more. He definitely won't, and this applies equally well to any future misguided Nazis who might learn the wrong lesson.
>
> But it should be pointed out that misguided Nazis are not the only ones to make wrong decisions. Some screwball professors have been known to do the same thing, and they are equally obnoxious.

Hannah Arendt also attacked Buber, though on a higher level, as was to be expected. She pointed out that Itzhak Ben-Zvi received hundreds of letters and telegrams from all over the world, pleading for clemency; outstanding among the senders were the Central Conference of American Rabbis, the representative body of Reform Judaism in America, and a group of professors from the Hebrew University in Jerusalem, who had been opposed to the trial from the start. She also pointed up the ironic fact that Buber's argument echoed Eichmann's own ideas, since Eichmann wanted to hang himself in public in order to lift the burden of guilt from the shoulders of German youngsters. That such a guilt existed at all she contemptuously pooh-poohed:

> It is strange that Buber, a man not only of eminence but of very great intelligence, should not see how spurious these much publicized guilt feelings necessarily are. It is quite gratifying to feel guilty if you haven't done anything wrong: how noble! Whereas it is rather hard and certainly depressing to admit guilt and to repent. The youth of Germany is surrounded, on all sides and in all walks of life, by men in positions of authority and in public office who are very guilty indeed but who *feel* nothing of the sort. The normal reaction to this state of affairs should be indignation, but indignation would be quite risky—not a danger to life and limb but definitely a handicap in a career. Those young German men and women who every once in a while—on the occasion of all the *Diary of Anne Frank* hubbub and of the Eichmann trial—treat us to hysterical outbreaks of guilt feelings are not staggering under the burden of the past, their fathers' guilt; rather they are trying to escape from the pressure of very present and actual problems into a cheap sentimentality.

To Buber's long quotation in the *New York Times* interview from his German Peace Prize speech, including the sentence that he had "only in a formal sense a common humanity with those who took part" in the acts of the Third Reich, Arendt retorted that "the law presupposes precisely that we have a common humanity with those whom we accuse and judge and condemn." After this remarkable evasion of the heart of the problem—that no law can cover such a crime or confer a common humanity on such a criminal—she expressed *her* disappointment at Buber's "dodging, on the highest possible level, the very problem Eichmann and his deeds had posed"!

What is particularly interesting about her attack is that she once identified herself with Ihud. One of her essays was among those that I was going to edit for the Magnes Foundation, and as late as 1957 she came to one of the meetings of our Executive Committee of the American Friends of Ihud in New York. It is fitting, therefore, that the Council of Jews from Germany should have published in 1963 a book replying to Arendt's *Eichmann in Jerusalem,* which was serialized in *The New Yorker* magazine before it was published as a book. Most of the replies were concerned with her contention that the Jews in Germany simply cooperated with the Nazis and did not try to resist them, an accusation the falsity of which should be clear to any reader of *this* book. But Ernst Simon and Buber also discussed her criticism of Buber's opposition of Eichmann's execution. Fiorello LaGuardia, the former mayor of New York City, was credited with the saying, "We must have the facts before we distort them." "But Hannah Arendt often appears not to have undertaken even these preliminary efforts," wrote Simon. Thus she claimed that Buber had undertaken an action for "clemency" for Eichmann; whereas, to the contrary, he always insisted that that merciless subhuman deserved no mercy. She characterized the fifteen Israeli men and women who petitioned the President of the State as "professors" who were by no means all professors, and left out of account the reason for their petition, which was not that they were against the trial from the start, as she claimed, but that they did not want to see Eichmann compel Israel to erect a gallows for the first time. She stated, "So far as I know, Buber was the only philosopher who openly expressed himself on the question of Eichmann's execution." Yet several among the professors who petitioned the president were themselves philosophers or scholars whose fields were close to philosophy: Hugo Bergmann, Nathan Rotenstreich, Shmuel Samburski, Gerhard Scholem, and Ernst Simon. Simon also pointed out that in Hannah Arendt's book *The Origins of*

Totalitarianism she had made a statement very close in spirit to Buber's own statement for "Genuine Dialogue and the Possibilities of Peace":

> The death penalty is absurd when it has to do not with murderers who know what murder is but with politicians of populations who organize the murder of millions in such a way that all who take part in it are subjectively innocent. . . . The gas chambers of the Third Reich and the concentration camps of the Soviet Union have broken the continuity of Western history because no one took responsibility for them in earnest and one can make no one responsible for them in earnest. At the same time they threaten that solidarity of people with one another which is the presupposition of our in general being able to condemn and exonerate the actions of others.*

This last sentence, as Simon points out, is particularly close to Buber's statement, "They have so radically removed themselves from the human sphere, so transposed themselves into a sphere of monstrous inhumanity inaccessible to my conception, that not even hatred, much less an overcoming of hatred, was able to arise in me."

Buber, in his own reply, remarked that obviously Hannah Arendt knew of his position only from what she had read in an interview (June 5, 1962, *New York Times*), and he felt obliged, therefore, to supplement that meager information. Arendt had opposed Eichmann's being tried by an Israeli court and called for an international court, citing Karl Jaspers as support for this position. Buber pointed out that when Eichmann was first brought to Israel, and thus before the statement of Jaspers mentioned by Arendt, Nahum Goldmann and some other Jews, including himself, took the stand that the trial belonged not to an Israeli court but to an international one that would meet in Israel and be given worldwide publicity. When the verdict was pronounced, Buber's general opposition to capital punishment, against which he had been on record since 1928, was replaced by a more specific motive: "Do we have the right, through the execution of one of the perpetrators of the Holocaust, to participate in the *seeming* rectification of the crime of the German leadership committed against us, the greatest mass murder in world history? Shall *we* make it possible for the execution to be regarded as having 'settled the score'?" "These are the questions (along with others) that I posed in conversation with the Israeli Prime Minister David Ben Gurion." There was another question which Buber did not express: "Is it for us, Israel, again to fasten the chains of death?"

---

*See Note A in Sources for Chapter 14.

Of this question, which at that time overwhelmed my heart, Hannah Arendt could, of course, know nothing. Everything else she could have known. If she did not want to assemble the material published in the Hebrew press, she could have learned it by the simple path of directing a question to me before she wrote what she wrote—and then she could have also learned even that deepest of motives.

On January 17, 1962, Buber gave an interview to Lawrence Fellows, the same correspondent of the *New York Times* who later interviewed him about the execution of Eichmann, in which he took Ben-Gurion to task for having said that most of the Israeli Arabs, "if given the opportunity, would help destroy Israel." What the *Times* picked up was an Ihud statement signed by Buber, Simon, and Shereshevsky, replying to an interview of Ben-Gurion that appeared in the French newspaper *Le Figaro* on January 5. There Ben-Gurion was quoted as saying:

> The Arabs in Israel enjoy economic, social and educational conditions superior to those in any Arab country, yet they are discontented or hostile toward Israel.
> Not that they wish for still quicker material or social advancement, but it is a question of sentiment and solidarity—they are imbued with Arab nationalism.
> While highly appreciating the benefits they personally derive from Israel's development, most of them would prefer this country to be an Arab state and if given the opportunity would help destroy Israel.

This is the kind of expression that would make bad citizens of the Arabs, Buber said to Fellows, and is unworthy of the early ideals of the founders of the Jewish state. The Ihud statement similarly remarked:

> Mr. Ben Gurion conveniently forgets what the history and ideology of the Zionist movement taught us: that a comparatively high standard of living does not compensate for a lack of personal and national dignity.

The Ihud statement also pointed out that at the inception of the state complete equality with the Jewish citizens was promised to the Arab population, yet Israel had imbued her Arab inhabitants with the feeling that they were second-rate citizens; Ihud pointed to the military government under which most of Israel's 240,000 Arabs are ruled as a prime example of this discriminatory treatment and demanded the abolition of the military government in the Arab areas of the country, as well as all other forms of discrimination.

As the result of the publication of this article in the *New York Times*, the American Council for Judaism, the last stronghold of anti-Zionism among the Jewish community in America, because they hold Judaism to be a religion not a nation, wrote Buber asking him to write an article for its journal *Issues* on the Arab refugee problem and to propose measures that could lead to a peace between Israelis and Arabs. They were afraid that Ben-Gurion's remarks about the Arabs in Israel would increase the hostility that many American Jews already felt toward the Arabs. Buber replied that he could not fulfill their request; for this would mean in some respect identifying his standpoint regarding the great problem of Zionism with theirs. "But in reality they are far apart. Ihud's criticism of the Israeli government's Arab policies comes from within, yours from without. Our program for Jewish-Arab cooperation is not inferior to what is called official Zionism; rather it is a greater Zionism. We would like to bring the Jewish people to understand this greater Zionism and make it their own." Once again Buber walked the narrow ridge with measured certainty.

The last action that Buber engaged in for Ihud with regard to Jewish-Arab relations in Israel was no longer addressed to Ben-Gurion but to his successor, Prime Minister Levi Eshkol. After a meeting of the Ihud executive committee at his home in October 1964, Buber wrote personally to Eshkol to communicate to him their conclusions. These were connected with the expropriation of the farming land of Arab villages in order to erect the new Jewish city of Carmiel in the Galilee. Ihud welcomed the Eshkol government's plan for the development of the Galilee, but it expressed concern that this plan be sufficiently comprehensive to take into consideration the needs of Arabs as well as Jews, including fair compensation for the expropriated land and an effort to employ the displaced Arabs in the new industries that were being created. These measures would preclude any charges that Arab farmers were being driven from the soil of their fathers.

Buber added a personal word that was clearly meant as a contrast between Eshkol's regime and that of Ben-Gurion. "Since you have taken office as Prime Minister, a clear change in tone and to a certain extent also in the political lines is to be felt in important spheres, including the attitude toward the Arab citizens of Israel." Eshkol replied the following week, thanking Buber for his letter and the form in which he had expressed his criticism and encouraging him not to hesitate in the future to send him any protests and statements of position whenever he felt it necessary. Eshkol saw the conclusions of Ihud as consonant with those that he himself had put forward in the Knesset regarding the development of the Galilee. He hoped that this work would be a blessing to all the inhabitants, and he claimed that Carmiel, the newest city being developed, was already bringing blessing to its Arab inhabitants.*

Buber could not subscribe fully to any Israeli party, but neither did he abstain totally from participation in them. According to the situation, he would at times support the left-radical socialists of the Mapam or the Liberal Progressives, who consulted him as a mentor. In his 1960 autobiography, *A Life of Strife*, Max Brod expressed great admiration for Ben-Gurion's politics and said that he had often been the pathbreaker and leader of the people. "His enormous service in the founding of the State in a most difficult time and in overcoming a series of crises has a firm place in history." At the same time he expressed regret concerning Ben-Gurion's attitude toward the Arab refugees.

> But [what is] incomprehensible to me is that Ben Gurion and the representatives of the great parties have until now not considered that a man like Martin Buber belongs in the government of this young state. For such a uniquely qualified man of great wisdom, power of action, and international fame not to serve in the time of the historical transformation . . . of our people—that downright borders on mad wastefulness.

Brod had observed Buber's political activity at Zionist congresses, such as Karlsbad: Buber's breadth of vision, his spiritual presence and adroitness in action, his warmth and openness in conversations, to say nothing of his scholarship and his religious depth. "Martin Buber is, among other things, also a great politician. It should not have been allowed to happen that at critical times he stood aside. In the future, in historical retrospect, this will be adduced as our most serious error, as a sad curiosity." Brod called on the government to remedy this error, but of course that did not happen.

In February 1966, *New Outlook, The Middle East Monthly* ran as its lead article an essay by Ernst Simon published in *Ner* shortly after Buber's death and titled "Buber or Ben Gurion?" "The tragic circumstances of Israel's birth brought the Statesman to the fore and left the Philosopher in the shade," reads the summary at the top. "Israel's

---

*See Note B in Sources for Chapter 14.

future depends on a more fruitful dialogue between the two." The opening paragraph of the article, however, does not take so moderate or well balanced a position:

> It seems that these two, the thinker and the statesman, have to share the honor of being the most famous Jews of the middle of the twentieth century. Some would say that they complement each other, that each has what the other lacks; others see them as the personifications of an extreme contrast between two wholly irreconcilable attitudes. I intend to show that Buber and Ben Gurion cannot exist in one and the same spiritual and moral climate, and that we must make a deliberate choice between them.

Simon acknowledged that Ben-Gurion showed more respect for Buber than for perhaps any other figure in the world of the spirit, but he attributed this not to what Buber stood for but to Ben-Gurion's "well-developed and sure instinct for discerning power in general, and Jewish power in particular, wherever it might be located." "When the power reaches the mass consciousness . . . , Ben Gurion, the statesman, will acknowledge the actual situation and will be prepared to deal with those who command it as with his equals." But, said Simon, there was no true respect between the two, because their common ground was too narrow to provide a basis for their being willing to learn anything from each other. Simon then proceeded to demonstrate this at length by separate sections devoted to the Arab question, the Aharon Cohen case, and the endeavors to make the Middle East a nuclear-free zone. Buber helped in every way he could, including giving advice and using his home as a meeting place for consultations, from the day the Committee for Nuclear Disarmament of the Israeli-Arab Region was established, all in opposition to the expressed views and determined wishes of Ben-Gurion—who, in demanding total disarmament or nothing, made sure that nothing would be done and made impossible the first step of nuclear disarmament. Simon traced these concrete differences of policy to an essential difference in the spiritual-moral climate between Buber and Ben-Gurion. He characterized Ben-Gurion as the slogan-monger, who during his long reign did everything within his power to distort the accepted meaning of truth, justice, and peace and, by turning these values upside down, undermined the people's belief in spoken and written statements. He is, said Simon, the unilateral monologist "who regards himself as the One and Only" and "puts himself beyond and above all accepted law and custom" ("I and I alone decide whose hand I shall shake and whose I shall not," *Ha-aretz*, August 16, 1965). In contrast, Simon characterized Buber as the man of dialogue, of careful speech, of the "small, still voice." "There can be no compromise between them, and every one of us is called upon to choose."

In the final section of his article Simon modified this strict disjunction in favor of a possible future situation in which the image of the history of Israel would look as follows: "The establishment of the state was not possible otherwise than under the aegis of Ben Gurion, but the fact that it could continue to exist can only be explained by its being penetrated by Buber's spirit to the extent where [that spirit] informed its leaders and most of its people." This must happen, said Simon, if Israel is not to live forever by the sword—under the sign of Mars. "That is the hope which never left Buber, almost to his last day, and for the sake of which he kept faith with the State of Israel which is so largely the handiwork of Ben Gurion." To set the state on a better way "demands much effort and striving; a striving in which we will be guided by the spirit of our teacher who has left us." This is not, to be sure, a "balanced" view, but it is the view of Ernst Simon—a man of great moral integrity who came to Israel before 1930 and has given unstintingly of his talents and spirit for the building of the state *and* for that justice, peace, and truth which he feels that the practical politics of Ben-Gurion subverted.

The difference between the predominantly political approach of Bertrand Russell and the predominantly social one of Buber was also manifested in the area of Arab-Jewish relations. To Russell the conflict between Israel and the Arab world constituted "an intolerable danger to the peoples of these countries and the peoples of the world." In addition to the actions he took in common with Buber and others, he appealed directly to the leaders of Israel and the Arab governments to put an end to their enmity through dialogue. In this, he and Buber were quite close. But Russell had a belief in the power of political demonstrations that Buber did not have. Hodes reports a conversation between himself and Buber in which he suggested that there should be demonstrations, protests, and some kind of action rather than just talking and issuing statements. Buber's question was about the purpose of the action. Quoting the admonition of Jeremiah, "Seekest thou great things for thyself? Seek them not," Buber asked whether a demonstration was desirable because it would be noisy and exciting, attracting attention and getting in the newspapers, or because this was really the way to influence the people who have power.

"Instead of a hundred people marching along the street to the Knesset, perhaps it would be better if each of them would make contact with a single Arab family. Then there would be ties of friendship between a hundred Jewish and a hundred Arab families, and these ties would have more effect than a demonstration which would be over in two hours."

After Buber's death a fund was established "to advance Martin Buber's doctrine of peace," and on September 4–7, 1966, a "Buber Memorial Seminar on Jewish-Arab Understanding" was held at Givat Haviva, the full proceedings of which were published in the December 1966 issue of *New Outlook*. The seminar assembled an impressive array of persons informed about and committed to Jewish-Arab understanding. These included Seymour Melman, Professor of Industrial Engineering at Columbia University, Mario Primicerio, secretary of the Mediterranean Colloquiums in which Buber had taken part, Aharon Cohen, author of *Israel and the Arab World,* Amnon Rubenstein, lecturer in law at the Hebrew University, plus Arabs, kibbutznikim, journalists, scientists, students, and many other veteran workers for Jewish-Arab understanding. Although less than a year later the Six-Day War took place, which again exacerbated the whole situation in the Middle East, the Declaration of the seminar pointed in a spirit very close to Buber's own to a way in which, in the long run, peace and understanding might still come about. It called for a realistic approach to practical economic agreement between Arabs and Jews within Israel and in the region as a whole, for educational activities in Jewish and Arab schools and on mass media, and for a dialogue between the peoples, built on the readiness to understand each other's viewpoint and to recognize the measure of justice in each other's claims. "The starting point of any dialogue must be the recognition that a people's honor rests in its peaceful undertakings rather than in military prestige." It demanded that the Arab world allow Israel to integrate herself within the region and that Israel integrate her own Arab citizens, with the promised end of the military administration as a first step in returning to the Arab community its self-respect. "The dialogue has begun. For the present it is only a monologue of two," the Declaration realistically concluded, "but from this Seminar and other meetings we already hear the sounds of a true dialogue."

In Dag Hammarskjøld's 1959 letter nominating Buber for a Nobel Prize, he pointed in his contrast between Buber and Ben-Gurion to that very tension between biblical king and biblical prophet that Buber undoubtedly had in mind when he wrote his speech for the Zionist Ideological Conference in Jerusalem in 1957:

> If Ben Gurion and his predecessors have received the heritage of a fighting nationalism which characterizes the historic Israel, one can say of Buber that he makes living the essential traits of the heritage of the prophets. Perhaps one might dare to predict that this time too it will prove to be the case that the voice of the prophet will reach further into the future than that of the military leader.

Just as the Second World War enabled Buber to complete *For the Sake of Heaven,* it seems probable that it is this very opposition between himself and Ben-Gurion that enabled Buber to go back to the theme that had fascinated him as a young man and complete in 1956 his one piece of drama, *Elijah: A Mystery Play.* The way in which Buber portrayed the opposition between King Ahab and the prophet Elijah in his play is itself an essential part of the understanding of dialogue as a way to peace. Ahab is not pictured as a "wicked king," as Melville puts it in *Moby Dick,* but as someone who, even in his failure to decide, remains bound up in dialogue with God, from whom he has turned. Elijah does not see himself as Ahab's enemy, nor does Elijah's God. For this reason, too, *Elijah* is a great statement of existential trust, precisely where it departs from the Hebrew Bible with its starker story of Elijah killing the four hundred priests of Baal after they are defeated on Mount Carmel.

Elijah speaks to the people out of his own dialogue with God and into the concrete historical moment. He does not submit to a superior divine force which uses him as a mere instrument. He responds to what calls him forth from the depths of his being. And God is with him, the righteous man who suffers for the sake of redemption. But God is also with the people in the midst of their uncleanness, even with King Ahab who *falls* to Baal—the emptiness of dream wishes— rather than *decides* for Baal. It is the mystery of God's nearness in the very pit of suffering that the Voice bids Elijah impart to men when, instead of entering into the radiance of God's heaven, he asks and is allowed to be the Lord's "runner" on earth. In Jewish tradition, Elijah is this runner, and he is also the forerunner of the Messiah who is still to come.

Nothing so characterizes Buber's own life as the blessing that Elijah gives to Elisha in this mystery-play. When Elijah takes final leave of Elisha, he tells him that no one ripens into a prophet who does not learn to bear loneliness. Elisha asks for the blessing of Elijah's spirit, but Elijah replies that he has never possessed the spirit, that it has come and gone. He blesses him with obedience to the spirit *and* that he withstand the Lord. These two together—"obedient listening" and contending—make up the very heart of *Elijah,* as of Buber's philosophy of dialogue. *Elijah* not only summarizes the motifs of Buber's biblical Judaism, it speaks to us of the concerns that lay closest to Buber's heart and of the attitudes that were embodied in his life, including his own dialogue with Ben-Gurion.*

---

*See Note to Chapter 14, *Elijah.*

PART V

Last Years

(1960–1965)

CHAPTER 15

<hr>

Surfeited with Honors

<hr>

IN CONVERSATION WITH Werner Kraft during his last years, Buber described himself at one point as "surfeited with honors." Buber's eightieth birthday was celebrated at special meetings in Israel and America where Buber himself was able to be present and by Festschriften in Germany, including a small book with contributions by Theodor Heuss, Robert Weltsch, Albrecht Goes, Otto Michel, Ewald Wasmuth, and Schalom Ben-Chorin. The Israeli newspaper *Davar* printed a special interview for the occasion in which the interviewer described Buber as easy in manner, alert in his movements, full of youthful energy causing the questioner to wonder at the hidden springs from which Buber drew his power. "I work from twelve to sixteen hours a day," Buber said and then, lest it sound like bragging, added shyly, "I am no longer bothered by sleep." "His eyes are open, big, shining," the interviewer said, "as if celebrating the fact that the years could not defeat or dim them." Hermann Hesse sent Buber a particularly beautiful letter on this occasion, and Albert Schweitzer conveyed his condolences, noting that from eighty on everything becomes more difficult from year to year! The Sorbonne gave Buber an honorary doctorate, and Emmanuel Levinas and Wilhelm Szilasi wrote special evaluations of Buber's place in European culture for a series of radio programs on "The World of Martin Buber" that I conducted for the Pacifica Radio stations in New York, San Francisco, and Los Angeles.

In May 1959 the German philologist Fritz Herbster wrote Buber that reading Buber's book *Einsichten* (Insights) and also Paul Schälluck's eightieth birthday speech on Buber had helped in "the venture of reconciliation" in his own family. Herbster greeted Buber as "perhaps the most faithful viceregent of the Socratic spirit on earth at this time." In January 1959, Simon Halkin, Professor of Hebrew Liberature at the Hebrew University, nominated Buber for the Nobel Prize in Literature with the concurrence of the senate of the Hebrew University.

To the many persons who wrote him from around the world on the occasion of his eightieth birthday Buber sent an expression of thanks, "directed to each individual," in which he said that the older one becomes, so much more grows the inclination to thank—what is above for the unearned gift of life, and especially each entirely good hour, which one receives like an unexpected present, and also to thank one's fellowman "for really meeting me, seeing and hearing me and not another, and opening what I really addressed, his well-closed heart."

In November 1958, Walter Kaufmann sent Buber a long letter in which he expressed his disappointment in Buber's letter of the previous April. Buber had said that he had read a good deal of Kaufmann's *Critique of Religion and Philosophy,* to much of which he assented and with much of which he disagreed. Though deeply affected by its candor and directness, he simply lacked the time to write letters about books. Kaufmann regarded his book as summing up all his past life, and, moreover, as a question addressed to Buber. Asserting that a letter could be a more meaningful dialogue between two persons than a face-to-face seminar of twenty men and women, Kaufmann asked, "How many persons are there in my generation whom a few words from you about what they are trying to do and doing could help so much as me?" Buber's response seemed particularly paradoxical to Kaufmann, since Buber's writing dealt with the lack of and need for genuine dialogue! "When I ask you questions 'on the knees of my heart' and you reply that you lack time to answer, how can I see it as anything else than a rejection?"

"In these last years I have been forced to give up writing real letters (not only about books)," Buber replied. "They no longer have for me the character of 'contemporaneity,' the living reciprocity that they had earlier; I need the 'back and forth,' the 'on the spot,' the unique meeting of each other of speaking and listening." Since he did not know when they could next talk and since he was deeply touched by Kaufmann's reproach, Buber asked him to say which passages in his book he most wanted Buber's opinion on and he would reply as best he could. This did not satisfy Kaufmann, however, and, as Rafael Buber himself told me, Kaufmann's whole attitude toward Buber from then on (including, perhaps the *heightened* ambivalence that one finds in his centenary speech on "Buber's Triumphs and Failures"*) stems from this disappointment. Buber wrote twice to Kaufmann about his understanding of the Book of Job, including the remarkable statement that, although he had spoken of God's cruelty at the end of "The Dialogue Between Heaven and Earth," Job spoke for Buber too when he said, "I *know* that my redeemer lives." "All this and not less than this I call trust in God." In 1962–1963 Kaufmann was visiting professor at the Hebrew University in Jerusalem and was able once again to talk with Buber personally.

My own dialogue with Buber continued by correspondence. In June 1959, Buber sent me a statement that he wrote for use on the cover of the paperback edition of *Martin Buber: The Life of Dialogue*, to be published as a Harper Torchbook in 1960: "To systematize a wild-grown thought as mine is, without impairing its elementary character, seems to me a remarkable achievement. On a rather multifarious work Dr. Friedman has not imposed an artificial unity; he has disclosed the hidden one." In July, I wrote him about a dialogue which my colleague Helen Merrell Lynd and I had at Sarah Lawrence about her book *On Shame and the Search for Identity*. Lynd illuminates the existential nature of shame in that book, as nowhere else I have seen, but guilt she views as merely social. I objected that where there is real responsibility there must be real guilt. "In your controversy with Helen Lynd I am utterly on your side," Buber commented, "when you say [guilt] 'cannot be merely additive and atomistic,' but it must be clear that the single acts (and omissions) must get a full illumination."

The end of October 1959 Buber announced that, feeling somewhat better, he was immersed in the definitive translation of the Bible,

---

*See Kaufmann's essay, somewhat revised, in *Encounter*, May 1979, and my letter in response to it in *Encounter*, February 1980.

which was nearly finished. In December, he wrote Albrecht Goes that he had occupied himself for two months with nothing else than Job, the so-called Preacher, the Song of Songs, and the Lamentations. In an earlier letter Buber informed Malcolm Diamond that the weather in the last weeks had been rather unpleasant, and his health had been vacillating in a downright humorous fashion. ("One learns to treat one's body with ever more humor, despite all.") Once Buber said to me, "As you grow older, your body punishes you for every abuse in your earlier years."

I and Thou was translated into Japanese from the English in 1958 by Keisuki Nogushi under the title *The Individual and Love (I and Thou)*. The following year *Paths in Utopia* was also published in Japanese translation. In August 1959, Hiroshi Kojima, Professor of Philosophy at the Kantogakuin University in Yokohama, wrote Buber that the confusion caused by the deep conflict between traditional Oriental collectivism and the postwar individualism introduced from America made the dimension of the interhuman in Buber's philosophy a necessary corrective. He saw Buber's philosophy as neither Oriental (Chinese or Indian) or Western but entirely peculiar to itself, the original form of Hebraism before it had become Hellenized. He asked permission to translate *The Problem of Man* ("What Is Man?") and *Images of Good and Evil;* the former was published in Tokyo in his translation in 1961. In 1962, Kojima notified Buber that the interest in *The Problem of Man* was found almost exclusively in Christian circles and not in general, but he cited a number of very striking reviews and comments that showed that in *those* circles its impact was indeed great, including its critique of Heidegger, who was very popular among philosophers in Japan. In 1963, Buber received a letter from Ikuro Teshima, Professor of Political Economy at the University of Kumamoto, telling him that his works were to him an inexhaustible source of inspiration and illumination, and expressing the desire to translate *Good and Evil* into Japanese for the sake of his countrymen and particularly for the Johannine Christian group "God's Tabernacle," of which he was the leader. "We are happy that we have found the richly spiritual piety of Hasidism," he added. In 1963, Avraham Shapira wrote Buber from Kibbutz Jezreel that a group of Japanese youth had come to Israel to learn Hebrew and "the teaching of Martin Buber," including the son of Ikuro Teshima. All of them knew the Japanese book by Akira Matzumoto applying I-Thou to the philosophy of education, of which the author had sent copies to Buber and me. In November 1964, Hans Fischer-Barnicol wrote Buber that, among the surprising echoes that his essay on Buber in the German journal *Kairos* had produced, the most astonishing was that of "Asia's Heidegger," the distinguished Zen scholar and philosopher Professor Keji Nishitani, who, with a comprehensive knowledge of Western philosophy and of Christian theology, insisted that only Buber's "between" captured the mystery of the "I" of Zen, which can be spoken of only if the other dimension is opened through meeting and dialogue. Despite his personal closeness to Heidegger, with whom he studied when he was younger, he found it necessary to turn to the principle of dialogue for a Western equivalent of Zen.

In 1960 a longstanding dream of ours was fulfilled: Eugenia and I went to spend four months in Jerusalem near Buber. Before we came, Buber wrote me, "Ernst Simon who came yesterday to see me thinks it is the most important thing for you when in Israel to learn as much of Hebrew as you can, and I feel he is right,—although I understand very well your counterarguments." By the last he meant the research and writing I had to do on *Problematic Rebel*. "What I mean is not 'learning to talk' but studying the language in this atmosphere here, the atmosphere that makes you hear it even in your dreams." Buber went out of his way to help us find an apartment in which to stay in Jerusalem—no easy matter—and through the efforts of his daughter Eva and finally of his granddaughter Barbara (Rafael's daughter), who had become the factotum of his household since the death of Paula, did, in fact, find us one.*

One of the first things we did while in Jerusalem was to attend two evenings in succession for the students of the Ulpan Akiva in Natanya, Shulamit Katz-Nelson's famous "international" ulpan where there were students from at least thirty countries. During the first, former prime minister Moshe Sharett sang, charmed, and exhilarated the whole group, speaking to each person in his or her language. The second night Eugenia and I went to Buber's house in Talbiyeh, and we rode together in the taxi to the meeting of the Ulpan on Mount Herzl. Buber asked if anyone had a question for him, and a young Parisian woman, named Danièle, asked him about the "chosen people," a concept which she clearly found distasteful. In contrast to Sharett, who spoke a little to everyone, Buber addressed himself in depth for two hours to her and to her question, not lecturing at her but insisting that she speak with him too and tell him what was in her heart. To Buber Israel was "chosen" not as a privilege but for a task—

*See Note to Chapter 15.

making real the kingship of God in true community. Danièle was very pretty and intelligent, but it also seemed to Eugenia and me that she was rather hostile. On the way back to Buber's house, we reproached him for spending so much time on her. "I asked the group whom they wanted to speak for them, and she spoke," Buber replied.

For two evenings a week, Eugenia and I spent four hours with Buber in his study in a relaxed atmosphere in welcome contrast to his more pressured visits to America. We talked about everything from Israel and Jerusalem, politics, literature, and religion, to anecdotes from Buber's life as we sat together on the couch, having wine, tea, and cookies that would always be brought in by Barbara at some point in the evening. (I can still hear the way Barbara said to us, "He was always lovable," when we went to visit her in Talbiyeh in 1966 after Buber's death.) The Buber household cats were now down to three, who came in and out the window of his study as they pleased. Sometimes we talked about the difficulty of translating his works into English, and Buber remarked, "Some of these words do not even exist in German!" At other times Buber and Eugenia would read passages from the New Testament in the original koiné Greek which they both loved. Occasionally Buber would tell stories, such as the time the people in the hometown of the great Italian composer Rossini decided to build a statue in his honor. Rossini, who was himself living in near-poverty, offered to stand on the pedestal for several hours each day if they would give him the money instead! Or the little old Jew who sat in the front row of Hitler's lectures laughing until Hitler could bear it no more and asked him, "Why do you laugh?" "There was a man called Hamann, and he wanted to do in the Jewish people," the little old man replied, "and later there was another man, and now there is you!" During the evenings Buber would try to tend the big stove that kept his room warm and added light to boot, though his eyes were bad, and he could not in fact see well (he had to use a magnifying glass for most of his reading). We had the impression that he did not want us to observe too much these weaknesses of age and still more on the rare occasions when he spoke in public did he not want it noticed that he had a hard time finding his way.

Buber possessed enormous energy. He would be still going strong at midnight while Eugenia and I would be drooping. On his desk was a huge pile of unanswered mail from all over the world. "It is a terrible thing to be this thing called famous!" Buber said to me. Occasionally he expressed the wistful desire that I might be his secretary. Once he asked me to write Robert Smith, an American who had sent him an impossible list of questions about his dissertation on Buber and Jung. I wrote him from Florence that he would have to be content with Buber's written works, but then Buber, to his and my amazement, actually answered his letter point by point, even if briefly. Once Buber told me of a man who came to visit him who made him uncomfortable all during the visit, and he did not know why. As they got up to go and Buber walked with him to the door of his study, the man, himself older than Buber, said to him, "You are the Messiah!" Then Buber understood. "I cannot talk with someone from above to below," Buber said. Buber did not see himself as above others, and he resolutely rejected the title of "prophet" that people were wont to thrust on him, as much because of his beard as because of his wisdom. "I am only someone who has seen something and who goes to a window and points," he said at the eightieth birthday celebration that the American friends of the Hebrew University held for him in New York. "I am really not a saint," Buber said to Eugenia and me in Jerusalem. "During the first half of my life I had to refrain from pushing myself and other people over into evil. Only in the second half of my life did I master this tendency."

Buber was elected first president of the Israel Academy of Science, founded in 1959. "There was one blackball," Buber reported, and speculated whether it might have been Scholem. At the first general meeting of the Academy at the Hebrew University in February, Prime Minister Ben-Gurion outlined the functions of the "Centre for the Advancement of Human Culture" that accompanied it: to draw to its ranks the finest scientists living in Israel, to advance scientific activity in Israel, to advise the government in projects pertaining to research of national significance and in the scientific planning of the country's development and related enterprises, and to represent Israeli science in international bodies and conferences in coordination with the other governmental bodies. Buber and Professor Katzir were received afterward by President Itzhak Ben-Zvi.

While we were in Jerusalem we visited a lawyer who had done the first translation of Plato into Hebrew. Since he knew of and asked about my interest in Buber and I knew of his translations from Greek into Hebrew, I told him that I had recently translated an essay of Buber's on Heraclitus ("What Is Common to All"). "Buber does not know enough Greek to write on Heraclitus," he responded. Although I knew that Greek had been Buber's favorite language since he was six, I kept silent. Then the lawyer added, "It was all right for Nietzsche to distort Heraclitus, for he was a philosopher." "Is Buber then not a philosopher?" I asked him. "Why, he has lived around the corner from me for seventeen years!" he exclaimed.

In Buber's house we got to know Barbara and her husband, Zeev Goldschmidt, as well as the two children, Tamar and Gideon ("Gigi"). Buber invited us to supper with his daughter Eva, and we visited her in her home in a suburb of Jerusalem, where she gave me a copy of Ludwig Strauss's *Wintersaat*. Later she remarried (a composer) and moved to Tel Aviv, but at that time she was working with children. Barbara was an artist, but a most simple and unpretentious one with a lovely human warmth. When I saw her painting of her grandfather in the Buber room in the Martin Buber Center for Adult Education at the Hebrew University on Mount Scopus in January 1978, I was astonished by its forcefulness.

During our last meeting in Jerusalem, I went to see Buber alone at night. I asked him a question about his translation of two key passages in the Book of Job for the section on the "Biblical Image of Man" of my book *Problematic Rebel*. He showed me the original and went over the text with me. Instead of "Though he slay me, yet will I trust in him" of the King James Version and "He will slay me; I have no hope" of the Revised Standard, Buber translated the familiar passage, "He may slay me, I await it," expressing being in God's hands and yet trusting at the same time. For the other passage, instead of translating it "I know that my redeemer lives and in my flesh I shall see God," he rendered it, "I know that my redeemer lives and that when my skin has been stripped away, I shall see God." This, to Buber, meant no reference to a life after death but to the progressive deterioration of his body which Job was experiencing and expected. It was this latter passage that he expounded at length in his letter to Walter Kaufmann, of which he sent me a copy, and of which he wrote in his Introduction to the translation of the Book of Job.

Buber felt that I had done enough work on my book in writing Melville and Dostoevsky and advised me against including Kafka too. "Kafka is the man of the hour, and it will take you a whole year to do him justice. Besides," he added, "in another century Melville and Dostoevsky will remain but Kafka may not."

Our conversation also included amusing anecdotes about Buber's life. Buber once told us that when he had gone to an Israeli hotel for a rest, he made out a check with an extra zero. "An absent-minded professor!" exclaimed the desk clerk. "No," replied Buber, "present elsewhere." Actually what struck me most about Buber, and more during the four months of this visit than ever before, was that he, more than anyone I knew, was fully present at each moment and situation. Once I asked myself whether Buber was charismatic and decided, "No, it is just that he is really present when he is with you, and most of us, including myself, are not." That made his presence sometimes uncomfortable; for it demanded of you that you be present too. In the summer of 1961, I paid a visit to Frederic Spiegelberg, distinguished professor of Comparative Religions at Stanford University. Spiegelberg told me how he had traveled 7,000 miles to meet Sri Aurobindo Ghose, and was told that he would only be given four seconds to look into his eyes, since there were thousands of pilgrims who had walked thousands of miles to do the same thing. When he complained, they told him he would not be able to stand any more. "And they were right!" Spiegelberg said to me. "Looking into his eyes was looking right through to the Absolute." I asked myself how I would compare that with my experience of looking into Buber's eyes, the depth of which had always struck me. My answer was that when you looked into Buber's eyes, you did not see the Absolute; rather you knew that he really meant you. At the same time, I found Buber every time I met him not only the most *concrete* person I knew and the most insistent on the concrete, but also the most *objective*, dispassionately *interested* person I had met, and there seemed to be no limit to what interested him.

Buber was in Munich in July of 1960 to give the paper on "The Word That Is Spoken" at the Bavarian Academy of Fine Arts, where he spoke in clear, firm tones of "the fruitful ambiguity of speech and language." It was a great occasion. More than a thousand people filled the great hall of the University of Munich. Arnold Bergstraesser came from the University of Freiburg, where he had become a leading professor and had initiated the American field of political science. Romano Guardini and Albrecht Goes were present too. On this occasion Buber was also given the Culture Prize of the City of Munich, and the newspapers and journals were full of accounts of the happenings. The Prize of 15,000 marks had before then been awarded only to the physicist Werner Heisenberg and the composer Bruno Walter. "Munich has long been a city of culture, the arts, and the sciences," Professor Emil Preetorius, president of the Academy of Fine Arts, said. Its Culture Prize was established to thank not only those who have fructified it from within but also from without. Buber was the first person honored who came from without. In presenting the prize to Buber, Mayor Dr. Vogel said that it was to honor not only an outstanding writer and scholar but also the man. Buber's cultural-ethical Zionism made him the outstanding representative of the renewed relationships between the Jewish and the German peoples, Vogel added, and spoke of his wish that one day the cleft between the two peoples be healed entirely. Buber thanked him, saying that the ceremony had a special significance for him because he had close and longstanding ties with Munich, where Paula grew up and Gustav Landauer was murdered for his part in the Revolution.

Buber's speech before the academy proved to be his final contribution to his anthropology, *The Knowledge of Man* (1965). What makes designations problematic Buber said, is not that there are no single, agreed-on definitions but because they do not show a concrete context that can be controlled. Every abstraction must stand the test of being related to a concrete reality without which it has no meaning. We do not clarify designations in order to reach agreement or unanimity but in order to discuss them and relate to each other in terms of them, whether in cooperation or opposition. Useful as precision and definition are for the exact sciences, the true humanity and the very meaning of language depend upon its being brought back to the fruitful disagreement of lived speech between men whose meanings necessarily differ because of the difference of their attitudes and situations.

Buber did not follow Heidegger in seeing the truth of lived speech as the *aletheia* of the Greeks—"the sublime 'unconcealment' suitable to Being itself." Instead he saw it as "the simple conception of truth of the Hebrew Bible whose *etymon* means 'faithfulness,' the faithfulness of man or the faithfulness of God." As at the beginning of the essay he distinguished among three modes-of-being of language—its present continuance, potential possession, and actual occurrence—so at the end he distinguished three elements in the truth of the word that is genuinely spoken—faithful truth in relation to, first, the reality that was once perceived and is now expressed, second, the person addressed, whom the speaker means as such, and third, the factual existence of the speaker in all its hidden structure. "This concrete person, in the life-space allotted to him, answers with his faithfulness for the word that is spoken by him."

In December 1960, Buber was awarded the Henrietta Szold Prize for his work in education and in May 1961, he was the first Israeli to be elected to honorary membership in the American Academy of Arts and Sciences. In December 1961, Buber received the Bialik Prize of the City of Tel Aviv for his contribution to Jewish Studies. In October 1964, the Albert Schweitzer Medal for "having exemplified the spirit of reverence for life and other tenets of the philosophy of Dr. Schweitzer" was bestowed upon him. The medal had previously been given to Schweitzer himself, to Pablo Casals, the cellist, and to the Indian Gandhian philosopher Amiya Chakravarty. One of the most interesting of the many awards and honorary doctorates that Buber received was the honorary doctor of medicine conferred on him in 1962 by the University of Münster for the contribution of his philosophy of dialogue to the relationship between doctor and patient. In fact, in the award ceremony Buber was called a "doctor of souls."

In 1960, Buber told Schalom Ben-Chorin that while he had perhaps not had success in any other sphere, he could claim some success in combating the Marcionite trend within the Christian Church and in helping create a more positive attitude toward the Hebrew Bible and Judaism. Buber held that participation of Jews in the Second Ecumenical Council in Rome, such as had been suggested in America, was questionable, since creating an "Una sancta" of the Church with Israel was impossible. When Buber was in Florence in September 1960, Mayor La Pira wanted to set up an audience for him with Pope John XXIII, but Buber declined the offer, since he did not care for representative conversations at a distance and he did not believe a simple human dialogue possible with a pope, not even with such a human pope.

In November 1960, Buber declared that on his way home more than a month before he had fallen seriously ill and was recovering very slowly and could make no plans for traveling abroad. "I have got a warning and must learn to live 'economically.' This means of course not leisure but work. I have a lot of work here for next year." In March 1961, he reported that his nephritis had assumed a chronic character and that his doctors had advised caution. It was this, in fact, which led to the uremic poisoning of which he died four years later. This, of course, imposed further restrictions on his travel.

> It is even uncertain whether I shall be able this year to go to Europe, especially as my daughter has remarried (her husband is a musician and a very nice man) and will not be free to accompany me. As to Barbara, she is ready to do it, but she cannot leave her husband and children for more than three weeks. I have even been obliged to refuse to go now to Vienna, where the Government has accorded me the Grosser Staatspreis and wanted me to come to the ceremony.

In July 1962, Buber claimed that his illness had unfavorably influenced his literary work. "In order to restore my peace of mind, I have decided not to take upon myself any new writing obligations. I must become free from literary obligations altogether. To make an exception would destroy the whole thing." Several times he complained of his eyes and asked me to use darker ink in my typewritten letters to him.

In March 1961, Buber admitted that reasons of health had induced him to give up including the (yet unwritten) essay on the unconscious in the anthropology volume. "By the way," he added, "it was assuming in my mind the size of a little book by itself rather than that of one of those essays." (While at the Hebrew University in 1966, I copied more than forty pages of notes from two folders in the Martin Buber Archives on the unconscious and dreams that would, indeed, have provided the basis for a most important book.)

A good picture of Buber's day-by-day life during his last years is given us by a letter he wrote his friends Ewald and Sophie Wasmuth in November 1961:

> One does not feel oneself "really ill," but if one behaves as though one were well, dares perhaps to go out for an evening in order to hear Casals play, then the next day one must do penance. So one sits at one's desk and reads the latest pageproofs of the latest volume of the "Bible"—and in bween times one sits on the terrace and does oneself good by breathing. One has to be sure, God be thanked, one's faith on one's right, but without humor on one's left, one cannot manage. There is thinking of all kinds, also young people come ever again with questions, among them not a few from Germany. . . . And in the middle of all this one feels again and again memory weave around the forehead, and the living friends with whom one has them in common, are not anywhere else than here, in this moment wholly here.

In May 1962, Ludwig Binswanger wrote Buber that in the Foreword to the third edition of his *Grundformen und Erkenntnis menschlichen Daseins* (Basic Forms and Knowledge of Human Existence) he had again stressed Buber's decisive significance for this voluminous basic work of his. "We are very close in our emphasizing of the 'WEness' *(Wirheit)* and specifically against Heidegger." But against Buber's accusation of Heidegger as practicing "monologizing hybris" Binswanger objected that, after his reading of the second volume of Heidegger's *Nietzsche,* he knew Heidegger to be, "in fact and in truth, in a previously unsuspected *enduring* dialogue with the great philosophers of all ages." Buber replied that what Binswanger described as "enduring dialogue" could not in general be concretely understood as dialogue. "Dialogue in the sense meant by me necessarily implies the unforeseeable, and its life-element is surpise, the surprising mutuality."

In July 1962, Buber received a letter from Witold O., a Christian schoolmate from his Polish gymnasium in Lemberg to whom he had sent a copy of his "Autobiographical Fragments." In addition to his reminiscences of their schooldays, Witold O. made some touching conjectures about their present: "If I am not mistaken, the richness of youthful feelings and the 'thrust into the heights' has been neither exhausted nor extinguished in either of us. The Eternal Light burns—even if before another altar." Though their enthusiasms served different goals, he added, both ways lead to the ideal—with the difference that Buber did not have to struggle with his spiritual heritage, against which, on the other hand, Witold had had to struggle for long years before he finally found himself. "You were a great help to me in my redemption, but it finally came not from the outside but from my own soul, and it formed me anew from the ground up." "And I—when death takes me in its arms," concluded Witold, "shall I stand face to face with you?"

When Hermann Hesse learned in August 1962 that a serious illness had made doubtful Buber's seeing him, he commented: "It seems that we have both taken the same step and heard the same call at the same time." Hesse's own illness seemed harmless at first, but it led to a great weakness and loss of blood which necessitated transfusions. The doctor, a good friend of his, had forbidden his customary vacation in Engadine. So he would be staying in Mantagnola, and Buber would find him there in case, God willing, he should again be able to travel. The next letter Buber received was from Hesse's wife, Ninon, thanking him for his "comforting letter out of whose lines longing for Hermann Hesse speaks. His death came suddenly, in sleep, through apoplexy of the brain—he was spared heavy suffering, the doctor says. H. hoped so very much to see you again! He became ever weaker and more tired—still he was active until his last day."

In September 1962, Buber received a letter from the Archimandrite Symeon informing him that his holiness the ecumenical Patriarch Athenagoras had read much concerning his great personality and his spiritual work and had asked him to send Buber his greetings and his warm good wishes as well as his desire to possess some of his books, particularly *I and Thou*. The following month Buber wrote his old friend Margarete Susman on the occasion of her ninetieth birthday: "A life of the spirit, yet lived without any diminution of immediacy—that is what we think of who praise you on this day. Service or grace? Surely both in one, inseparable." She replied that life had not always been for her gentle, especially "in this dark time with its deathly accompaniments." "But on this difficult day, surrounded by much life and friendship, of which your words are the crown, it seems really gentle and blessed." The following month Buber received a touching letter from the well-known novelist Luise Rinser, former wife of the German composer Carl Orff, who told him that, asked to choose a book for the series "The Book of Your Choice," she had chosen without hesitation *The Tales of the Hasidim,* which she had read almost daily for twenty-five years, along with the Old Testament and the Gospels, and which had never failed her. Her visit with Buber in Jerusalem was a confirmation to her of a relationship that had existed for all those years.

> In Lucerne, I was very shy just because my heart had so much to say to you. But nonetheless it was beautiful. Until my death I shall never forget how you looked when you said (to my question whether you *loved* God) "Yes. With all my heart."
>
> I think of you very much. Better: I am much with you; you are always present to me; I pray for you that your way may prove to be the right one bidden for you.

In 1962, Holt, Rinehart and Winston wrote Buber that they would like to publish an English translation of *Daniel.* Buber agreed on the condition that I translate it and "write an introduction, explaining, even at some length, that this is an early book in which there is already expressed the great duality of human life, but only in its cognitive and not yet in its communicative and existential character. This book is obviously a book of transition to a new kind of thinking and must be characterized as such." The long Introductory Essay to *Daniel,* Buber found to be "a very good piece of work, particularly the—sometimes rather surprising—parallelization and comparison with other passages of my writings." *Daniel* was published in my translation in hardback in 1964 and in paperback in 1965. On the other hand, Buber rejected a proposal from Kurt Wolff of Pantheon Books to publish *Ecstatic Confessions* in an English translation. "This book may mislead many readers not knowing enough about the development of my thinking. Here an introduction would not be sufficient."

In April 1962, Buber lent his support to the establishment of a new Reform synagogue in Israel under the leadership of his friend Schalom Ben-Chorin. In October, Buber reported a German governmental grant that would make possible the publication of his works in

three large volumes, about four thousand pages in all, by Kösel Verlag in Munich and Lambert Schneider in Heidelberg. The first
volume, *On Philosophy,* appeared the following year. When asked why
the essays from *Ereignisse und Begegnungen* (Events and Meetings),
most of which had been translated for the first part of *Pointing the
Way,* did not appear in it, Buber replied that it was "because they
belong more to literature than to philosophy."

The poetess and translator Ruth Finer Mintz told of a young man
who went to see Buber and asked him whether he should marry a girl
who was not an intellectual. Buber said, "Why not?" "But what could
she teach me?" complained the young man. At this Buber's eyes
flashed and he said, "She might teach you what it is to be a woman!"
To the end of his life Buber remained a teacher. He was editor in
chief of Israel's Encyclopedia of Education and also himself wrote a
long article for it in 1961 on "The Aims of Adult Education." He was
also very much interested in the work of the journalist Alissa Leven-
berg, who was the first to really live with and teach the Oriental Jews
in the new city of Dimona in the Negev. Also through the publication
of *Am v'Olam* (People and World) in 1961, Buber's political and social
thought and his views on education became known to many sabras
who did not have access to them before. Buber felt a strong kinship
with the generation of his grandchildren that he did not feel at all
with that of his own children, and in the last few years of his life
young people came more and more to see him, vaguely dissatisfied
with those political goals that before had been all and all to them.
Buber's most important impact during the last five years of his life was
on the young people of the kibbutzim and on the active kibbutz education movement in Israel.

During the 1950s, the social experiment of the kibbutz often suffered from the political atmosphere which divided kibbutz from kibbutz and often split the members of the same kibbutz according to
party lines. In 1960, the members of the kibbutz still represented, for
many Israelis, an aristocracy of merit—those who bear the hardships
of frontier life and reclaim that life. But the very centrality of the
kibbutz made it inevitable that "society" would insinuate itself into the
attempt at a realization of "community," as Buber pointed out in one
of his replies on social philosophy in *Philosophical Interrogations:*

I have observed that here in the land of Israel, in the not unprob-
lematic development of the *kibbutzim,* and, in fact, in two manifestations: as a result of the economic principle, the growing subjection to

the market, which has as its consequence the fact that in times of crisis the *kibbutzim* could not arouse the courage and energy needed for taking the initiative in the reduction in price of the products; and, as a result of the political principle, the cleavage of unified fellowships into party groups fighting one another, which has repeatedly led to the self-destruction of communities.

In an interview with Avraham El'Hanani for *Davar,* Buber spoke of how the hopes and dreams of the kibbutzim were coming to naught in these days. Eliezer Be'eri wrote him from Kibbutz Hazorea protesting that such a statement did injustice to the great work of thousands of kibbutznikim day in and day out in agriculture, industry, and cultural life and asked Buber how he could say what he did, since, as he himself said. he did not know the kibbutz from within. Buber explained:

> Earlier I believed in the magnetic force of the movement, in the force of its influence on the state and on the whole people, and I have suffered a disappointment. Party politics got the upper hand, and the kibbutz has not been able to withstand it. That means that the element of the "group" has overpowered that of community. You ask: "How do you know that?," and I can only answer: "As long as I breathe I know the condition of the atmosphere in this Land, and I do not need to travel about to do so." If you can believe that, good; if not, I cannot change it; for it is really hard to believe. But I shall gladly come to visit you as soon as I am half-way well; for I am still weak.

Unfortunately, though Buber again and again planned to visit Kibbutz Hazorea, especially in connection with the Martin Buber Forest that was planned there, he did not succeed in doing so, and the forest was first planted in 1970.

In another explanation of his *Davar* interview in response to Jifrach Haviv, a member of Kibbutz Keshet in the Lower Galilee and a kibbutz educator and writer, Buber wrote:

> Earlier the kibbutz movement had an indirect influence on the human life together in the city and in the land settlements, and at the same time a powerful direct influence on the hearts of the youth in the Diaspora. This second influence has today become less deep while the first has entirely disappeared. I am far from making the men and women of the kibbutz responsible for this. I know well the share of politicization of our life as well as the growing dependence on the world market. Nonetheless the fact remains that earlier I sensed the might of self-realizing spirit, and today no longer. But do not believe that I despair, for I set my hope on a new type of discontent, on an inner

transformation, on a renewal of the kibbutz movement; for without such a transformation we shall become a nation like all other nations even if we attain the highest "cultural" rung.

It was precisely this discontent and the beginning of a new transformation which Buber came into contact with in his relationship to kibbutz education during the last few years of his life. In an interview in 1966 for the NET film *Dialogue: Buber and Israel* Menachem (Hermann) Gerson said that when they came to Israel, many of them thought they no longer needed Buber's concern for Jewish heritage.

> Now we are finding out by experience that this type of youth in Israel, in the kibbutz, feels itself sometimes a little bit shallow and itself puts forward the need for renewed bonds with the Jewish spiritual heritage. Things are moving. I am quite convinced that Buber may become again in this respect a leader, a spiritual leader for youth in Israel.
>
> If you are a pure individualist who regards his personal aspirations and development as the only yardstick to be used, you can't be a kibbutznik. If you believe in collectivism which does away with the individual, the kibbutz is not the right thing for you. If you adopt Buber's thought that the individual for his own growing, for the development of his own personality needs the other person, then you can become a member of a kibbutz.

Gerson himself was active at this time in kibbutz education work. But it was a much younger kibbutznik, Avraham Shapira of Kibbutz Jezreel, who spearheaded the most fruitful contacts between Buber and the kibbutz education movement.

A circle of young kibbutz men and women came together once a month from all over the country to talk about literature in the spirit of Buber, and many others were deeply impressed by reading what Buber wrote and by talking with him. A whole issue of *Alei-Siah'*, a sixty-page kibbutz educational book, was devoted to Buber's *For the Sake of Heaven* and its implications for the kibbutz, including an exposition of Buber's Hasidic chronicle-novel by Avraham Shapira and discussion by many others. Rivka Gurfine, a journalist, wrote up the discussion of *For the Sake of Heaven* in Kibbutz Jezreel in a way that captures the concrete situation:

> A simple, wooden hut, guests sitting for many hours on hard wooden chairs. Only a few of those gathered had dealt many hours in their lives with spiritual matters. Most of them were enveloped with a certain, imperceptible smell of dealing with concrete, real things—the land to be

ploughed, the cows to be milked, the food to be prepared, and a child to be brought up. These men had their faces open toward the sun and the winds, and they were fighting with the elements. All the members of the kibbutz were sitting here—fathers and children, first, second, and third generations, and all were sitting in order to study. It was already night and stars were twinkling in the sky with the darkness of the mountain slope surrounding the valley.

The aim of Buber's inner struggle is the human in its Jewish expression. His heritage knocks on every unquiet heart and enhances its disquiet. It is doubtful whether it can reach and settle in a peaceful heart. Tragic solitude is the fate, even within community, of those with sublime doctrines the transfer of which to living reality is very complex.

I was astonished to see the extent to which this secular group transcended its normal categories of thought and agreed to the symbolic mixing together of the higher worlds and the lower ones, to going beyond the region of reality to the field of mysticism and magic. It was Buber's great right, the right of a great, lonely Jew in the midst of us who blazed past, to return those reading and discussing to a great spiritual stream in Judaism—Hasidism. . . . The group in which I was sitting understood the meaning of the book to the full and adapted to it their own search for reality, as if they found there the fathers of their own spiritual life, their own quest, their own search, their struggles, their crises, and their overcoming of crises. They understood the full meaning of this struggle between strong forces, at its base ideological, and this so human quest laden with passions of desire for power, jealousy, and religious zeal. Within all this they perceived the tiny voice of the human which more than once determines the character of life.

On July 26, 1963, members of Kibbutz Afikim met with Buber, and this meeting was later published in full in the Israeli journal *Sdemot*. One young man asked Buber how a feeling of community can be created in a large kibbutz (Afikim, with more than two thousand members, is the largest kibbutz in Israel). Buber distinguished between *closeness* and *relation* and declared any kibbutz of six or seven hundred members, much less two thousand, to be a social monster that needed to be broken down into smaller, interlocking groups in which each person could feel a part of the group. He also emphasized the need for enough space for each individual to have some distance from his comrade through which alone he might enter into relation with them, and this should include the possibility of meditation and contemplation as well. Asked about religious observance, Buber said that one thing that should be in common to the kibbutz and to Hasidism is *kavana,* doing what one does wholeheartedly. "Human life deserves this name if and only if a person does everything out of *kavana*—for its own sake—but this is not necessarily a religious affair.

In my opinion in a kibbutz one could live the life of *kavana* without religious concern." He stressed the influence the kibbutz educators could have, not through their theories but through their personal lives, through the power of human example. This power is effective even when one must live contrary to the principles of one's own kibbutz. "Real influence is slow. A man lives and actualizes what he intends to teach to others. Sometimes he must devote the whole of his life to this, but such a life is worth living."

Buber told of how he read in the Bible with Eva and Rafael every day when they were children without asking them to believe anything. Later when Rafael was a soldier in the Austrian army and Buber was walking with him in the forest, Rafael said to him that he had been greatly influenced by this reading of the Bible. Although he could not believe as the people of the Bible did, the fact that they believed so completely, and strongly, and with such vehemence, influenced him, "and this influence on me grows daily." Buber denied that the lesson of the Holocaust was the need for a strong military state, saying that what would influence the course of history was the state not in abnormal situations but in the normal. In three or four generations, if the politicization which is now devouring a great part of the powers of the nations disappears, there will be a much greater, more internal usefulness of the state, Buber predicted. There will be a renewal, even a religious one, not as a continuation but as a new beginning. The hope for this is not based on education or tradition, but "on the fact that today there is a new generation of young people dealing with these problems, longing for self-renewal. Today I see these longings." Buber did not call them longings for religion, a word which young people did not want to hear and he felt himself forbidden to use by the command of the situation.

Perhaps most significant in Buber's conversation with the Afikim members was his advice as to teaching itself, not teaching of subjects but of how really to deal with young people. He advised veteran kibbutz members that they "should uncover the bitter truth which as a rule people do not want to hear; yet when it is heard some of them are influenced by it." Such influence would result in a passionate discussion on how to change the situation. When talking with the young, they should be aware of the time when such a person might despair and come to the one he or she trusts to ask about the meaning of his or her life. This is a time for real personal contact and for trust. Those who had to deal with young people from the cities or elsewhere and decide whether they should be allowed to remain in the kibbutz were counseled by Buber to reject theories that viewed education as finished by a certain age, to listen to the heart even of the boy who stole cars or the girl who became a prostitute, and to appeal to the people with experience and training in the kibbutz to participate in these difficult decisions.

During the last five years of Buber's life many leaders and educators of kibbutzim came to see him and discuss kibbutz problems with him. Many of these discussions were published and aroused echoes in other kibbutzim. "Every time Buber astonished those whom he met by the freshness of his thought and by the way he entered in as soon as it became concrete," Avraham Shapira reported in a long essay on "Meetings with Buber." By the same token he eschewed ideas and ideologies in favor of the question whether the young have a real trust in the person to whom they listen. "That and not the idea is the alpha." Shapira gave a clear picture not only of what Buber said but of the way in which he said it:

> His words were spoken in a very clear-cut fashion, emphasizing each letter and word. When he finished his short answer, he used to wait for a sign that he was understood. When he told a story, he finished it with a caesura, as if allowing a certain amount of time for his listener to absorb his words, and then he used to look down, to lean over his desk or to sit back in his chair, but without relieving himself of the tension of the conversation. Only in his last years at the end of the conversation I noticed how concentrated he had been in them and how exhausted he was by them.

Often Buber would recoil from answering specific questions, saying he could not discuss what he was unacquainted with. In the face of Shapira's enthusiasm for his work in kibbutz education, Buber emphasized the importance of limits but also that one could not know the limit until one had gone on and hit one's head on the wall. "Saying this, he gave himself a sound knock on his forehead to make the matter concrete." To comrades from Ein Gedi who expressed pessimism concerning the corruption in political life (a scandal concerning the mayor of Beer Sheva), Buber said: "He who pays attention everyday not only to bad surprises but also to good ones will soon be aware of the quality of persons and not of the quality of institutions." Our concern should be with those individuals who are responsible for those institutions.

In all these meetings Buber never consented to start the conversation. "I came only to answer the questions of the comrades." Only when questions were asked, did the conversation begin.

It was marvelous to see how young comrades who came with hesitation and awe became in one evening interlocutors of Buber. After sitting tensely in the beginning, they relaxed in their chairs. It was as if the scales of armor fell. Then people started to listen, to talk, to wonder about the thing they heard. Sometimes only the eyes were talking. Sometimes they would reply hesitatingly, sometimes argue vehemently.

To the kibbutz educator Buber emphasized uniqueness—of the person, of the relationship—but he also decried the lack of complete mutuality. The fact that in our world the relationship is that between *one* educator and *several* persons being educated should not preclude the awareness of each person as a person. Even in technical training, it is the way that the student feels in every phase, the "how" and not the "what," that counts. "The main thing is the humanization of the technique, that the real connections between people be all the stronger within the technique."

Shapira illustrated Buber's approach to education by a story he heard from a veteran kibbutz educator about a strike which took place once in the Solel-Boneh Company. A strike within the Histadrut caused a great shock in the labor movement at that time. Ben-Gurion came to the strikers, explaining and demanding from above, but was met with deaf ears. Then Berl Katz-Nelson, the labor leader, came and started talking with a group of workers in the corner of the yard. That friend-to-friend discussion continued for hours until it surpassed the expectation of the workers themselves. "And Berl himself forgot that he was supposed to talk to the workers. He talked *with* them and did not talk *to* them—[such were the] two personalities and their different ways." But Buber's approach also had its drawbacks, because Buber refused to replace life-attitudes with general principles concerning the spiritual world and social realities. Once Buber told Shapira with some show of anger of a meeting with educators from kibbutzim which ended in a *malentendu* because of their demand that Buber give them principles. "People want me to give them generalities so as to relieve them of personal decisions which they must make."

Shapira told of a friend of his who knew Buber's writings well and who had met him personally many times. When he would go to see him again, he would think to himself that he had already absorbed from him everything that could be. "But in almost every meeting I was surprised anew when realizing that he was drawing from himself more and more and that he had much which he had not been able to summarize in written form." In Buber's conversation with kibbutz members there was a thrilling though hidden suspense, which fit in with his idea of redemption taking place at every moment. Each moment has its own aim and reason; each is tangential to the secret of fulfillment; each is not an event in the soul but a tangible event in the world. The deepest contact came, of course, in Shapira's personal meetings with Buber.

> Then you were aware of all the humanity of his personality. In these conversations you were a witness to his wrestling with the problem, his efforts to work it through, to have it wholly worked out. My heart was touched when he tried to do the same thing in the days when he was ill and weak. Then I witnessed with my own eyes how he fought the limits of the unruly body and overcame them.

Buber's eighty-fifth birthday was an even greater event than his eightieth one. He was honored in Israel and throughout the world. Ernst Simon, Margarete Susman, Schalom Ben-Chorin, Siegfried Moses, Kurt Blumenfeld, Pinhas Rosenblüth, and many of Buber's other friends everywhere wrote long articles celebrating the occasion. Issues of journals were dedicated to him. The Hebrew University had a special ceremony for him and announced its intention to reprint the original 1902 pamphlet by Buber, Chaim Weizmann, and Berthold Feiwel in which the establishment of a Hebrew University was first proposed. But perhaps the most remarkable event of all and, to judge by the picture that we have of it, the most gratifying to Buber personally was a spontaneous torchlight parade of the students from Hebrew University to his home in Talbiyeh. Something of the charm of this occasion was captured by *Time:*

> Bedtime for Israel's most distinguished philosopher, Martin Buber, is 10 o'clock. But his 85th birthday was an exception. At the stroke of 11, some 400 students from the Hebrew University . . . paraded up Jerusalem's Lovers of Zion Street to the door of Buber's villa, carrying torches and singing in Hebrew "For Martin's a jolly good fellow." On the veranda, a pretty coed garlanded the white-whiskered Hasidic sage with flowers and soundly bussed his cheek. "What?" asked Buber with a merry twinkle. "Is there only one girl student here?" Then the students presented him with honorary membership in their student union. "I have a drawer full of honorary degrees, in everything from theology to medicine," said Buber, "But this is the first time I've been made an honorary student. This is a great honor for me."

Although this custom was followed in some European universities, it is the first time it had ever been done in Israel. Buber saw in this occasion the possible signing of the pact between himself and the generation of his grandchildren and their children, and was "radiantly happy," as Hodes reports. If to be a student means to be a person who naturally studies, as John Huizinga spoke of the natural playing man (*homo ludens*), "someone for whom learning and study are equally an expression of human freedom," then I am delighted to be a partner in it! Asked if he himself had taken part in such a torchlight parade as a young man, Buber said he had, but only a few times, since he had not liked most of his professors! Buber was delighted by the event, which took him back to his own student days in Germany and Austria, but the tributes he received from all over the world did not deflect him from his writing and editing.

To the many letters of congratulation that came to him, Buber again sent a special expression of thanks. This time he meditated on the meaning of the word "thank" in many languages, its link to thinking, and therefore remembering, in English and German, and to acknowledging someone in Hebrew. Acknowledging includes remembering, of course, but it is not an occurrence in the soul alone but an event in the world: the confirmation of this person in his existence.

In February 1963, Nechama Leibowitz, then Bible teacher in a seminar in Jerusalem and since 1968 professor at the University of Tel Aviv, wrote Buber of her great joy in the fact that a translation into Hebrew of his essays on the interpretation of the Bible was to appear *(Darko shel Mikra)* and urgently requested that it be provided with an index of biblical passages, which she offered to help prepare. Only if such an index were present could the teacher refer to the appropriate citation and then find something flashing within him which would help him bring the passage closer to his students. "Who knows how many hearts would be kindled at the first spark?" Buber also heard at this time of the intention of founding a Martin Buber Chair of Judaica at the University of Cologne in Germany and of the Martin Buber Forest, which a group of his well-wishers in Germany had funded in his honor, led by Romano Guardini, who composed the summons for this appeal. This is the forest that was later planted at Kibbutz Hazorea.

In January 1963, I sent Buber the Introductory Essay I had written, which became Chapter One of his anthropology, *The Knowledge of Man.* "Your introductory essay to the anthropology volume is very good," Buber acknowledged in February; "probably it is the best you have written on my thought." As usual, he sent his remarks, including his suggestions for changes. In August, he wrote that he had had a talk with Lambert Schneider, who came to see him in the sanitorium Sonnmatt in Lucerne, Switzerland, about a German volume including the essays on the knowledge of man and the introduction, in which Schneider was interested.

In January 1963, Buber received a letter from the business director of the Erasmus Prize Foundation (established in 1958 on the initiative of Prince Bernhard of Holland) announcing that he had been chosen for the 1963 award of the Prize, which had been given to the Austrian people in 1958, to the French statesman Robert Schuman and the German philosopher Karl Jaspers in 1959, to the painters Marc Chagall and Oskar Kokoschka in 1960, and to Romano Guardini in 1962. The Erasmus Prize was to be given to Buber to honor the significance of his work in furthering the spiritual life and consciousness of the peoples of Europe, above all in reference to the dissemination of his own philosophy and for the general awakening of an interest in, and an understanding of, Hasidism. Buber accepted the Prize of 100,000 Dutch guilder on the understanding that three-fourths of it would go to the Leo Baeck Foundation for a scholarly anthology on "Judaism and the European Crisis" (the Hitler period).

The Erasmus Prize was intended, in principle, as comparable to the Nobel Prize, to act as a stimulus award to individuals or institutions whose work is considered of outstanding merit for the spiritual and cultural resurgence of an integrated Europe. Unlike the Nobel Prize, it was to be partially expended in grants for cultural, social, or social-scientific projects for unifying European spirit and culture. Nineteen sixty-three was the first time the prize was awarded on Dutch soil.

On July 3, 1963, seven hundred prominent invited guests filled to capacity the hall of the Royal Institute for the Tropics in Amsterdam to watch Prince Bernhard award Martin Buber the Erasmus Prize in the presence of Queen Juliana. In granting the Prize to Buber, Prince Bernhard stated:

> He has enriched the spiritual life of Europe with his versatile gifts for more than half a century;
> he has translated the Biblia Hebraica into the German language and in doing so has endowed the Scriptures with an original and new meaning;
> he has recaptured the religious and moral treasures which lay buried in the legends of the devout Hasidim in Eastern Europe and transmitted them to the Western European of the 20th century;
> he has elucidated the religion of Israel on the basis of "the life of dialogue" in a profound exposition embodying the governing

philosophic and psychological conceptions and has thereby freed from misconception and prejudice the contact between Judaism and Christianity on the one hand and between belief in the Bible and modern culture on the other.

Professor Dr. M. A. Beek, an Old Testament scholar from Amsterdam and later a coauthor of a book on Buber, echoed the gratitude of a whole generation of scholars in his address "The Mediator and His Task":

> This man has been willing to devote his great gifts of mind and heart to the humblest service which could be asked of him: that of interpreter and mediator. To be a good interpreter one must listen respectfully to both sides and scrupulously keep asking oneself: have I understood, and do I make myself understood?
> Mediating between a religious outlook on life and the ruling philosophical and psychological views of one's own time demands staking every scrap of conviction but also, and above all, respect and love for one's fellow-men, without which no fruitful conversation is possible at all.

Prince Bernhard in his own personal remarks counted himself among those who honor Martin Buber as "the Teacher of the Dialogic Principle" and recounted two Hasidic tales on his own. He also stressed the importance of Arab-Jewish reconciliation and recalled Buber's advocacy of it as early as the Twelfth Zionist Congress in 1921. Yehudi and Hepzibah Menuhin played Ernst Bloch's *Baal-Shem* Suite. In the Erasmus Prize booklet there are charming pictures of Buber with the Menuhins, a delightful picture of Buber with Princess Beatrix, and an altogether different Buber—serious and even stern—delivering his own speech, "Believing Humanism."

The believing humanism of Erasmus meant two separate spheres in the life of the human person, neither of which limited the other and to each of which belonged special times and activities, said Buber. In contrast, Buber put forth a believing humanism in which humanity and faith penetrate each other and work together so fully "that we may say our faith has our humanity as its foundation, and our humanity has our faith as its foundation." Then, elaborating, Buber pointed to two separate answers to the modern question as to what *humanum* in its most positive sense is—that stream of German philosophy from Hegel to Heidegger that sees man as the being in whom Being attains to consciousness of itself and hence regards "reflexion," bending back on oneself, reflecting on oneself, as the preeminently human activity, and that which finds the *humanum* in the fact that "in the history of the world it is first through man that 'meeting' has become possible, as meeting of the one with the other." In the former definition humanity and faith necessarily exclude each other in our lives because we can "meet" this empty Being in all metaphysics but not in the lived life of the human person for whom faith means trust in the God that is *there*. "A genuine believing humanism can no longer grow from this soil." For the latter the true *humanum* and the experience of faith are rooted in the same soil of meeting. "Indeed, the fundamental experience of faith itself may be regarded as the highest intensification of the reality of meeting." Although very little of such a believing humanism is to be discerned in our age in which the observing and exploiting type of man predominates, nonetheless, a powerful education toward a new and genuine believing humanism has arisen in the present in the crisis which threatens the human race with extinction—leaderless technology, unlimited mastery of means without any end, voluntary enslavement of man in the service of the split atom. The growing awareness of this crisis in the still malleable generation summons the only counterforce that can again elevate great clear ends above rebellious means—the new believing humanism. "From the land of Erasmus I greet the believing humanists in all the world," Buber concluded, "—those who are already active and those who are only ripening."

The Erasmus Prize was the last high point for Buber, reports Grete Schaeder, and for his gradually waning powers it was an elixir whose effects continued through a cure in Sonnmatt in the rest of the summer. The pictures show the great earnestness of his audience, the liveliness flaming up in conversation, the concentrated spiritual force of his lecture and, always, the shining of the dark eyes. "Taken together they are a mirror of the intensive presentness that revealed itself in such high points of experience as the expression of a deep and shy piety." This was Buber's last trip to Europe.

In August 1963, Buber received a letter from Hermann Meier-Cronemeyer, the young author of works on the Jewish youth movement and the kibbutzim, saying that after reading Buber's essay "Society and the State" *(Pointing the Way)* he felt that the youth movement was not wrong when it saw itself as "apolitical." At the same time he wondered whether the politics of the "social principle" ought not really be labeled "anarchism," as the ideas of Proudhon, Kropotkin, and Landauer (all of whom Buber dealt with favorably in *Paths in Utopia*) are, in fact, labeled. Pointing out that "mutualistic" is a synonym for "anarchistic" in Proudhon and that George Woodcock had mentioned Buber in his book *Anarchism: A History of Libertarian Ideas and Movements* (1963), Meier-Cronemeyer asked Buber whether it was reluctance because of the pejorative ring of the word, or other reasons, that kept Buber from applying this term to himself. Buber replied that anarchism did not apply to him because it meant a suspension of relations of power—"and this is impossible as long as the nature of man is what it is." For this reason Buber pointed instead to a delimitation and restriction of the relations of power as far as possible. It is interesting in the light of this interchange that in 1975 the German scholar Wolf-Dieter Gudopp published a book titled *Martin Buber's Dialogical Anarchism,* much of which is devoted to Buber's critique of Marx, his concept of community, and his utopian socialism.

In August 1963, Buber received a long and remarkable letter from Jean-Bernard Lang of Geneva, who sent him, as a belated birthday present, his book *Martin Buber und das dialogische Leben* (Martin Buber and the Life of Dialogue). "You are right for us in the most cruel way," he wrote. "The removal of the Jewish element from Christianity literally means the removal of the divine demand and of concrete messianism. The soul of Europe is sick from the consciousness of not having mastered its own task. I myself feel it in my own body. Your service remains to have shown those living today the demands of our time, a humanly possible way that makes human existence possible."

Buber at this time sent me a statement on my book *Problematic Rebel,* which expressed in new form his opposition of the "eclipse of God" to the "death of God":

> *Problematic Rebel* is . . . especially important because its theme is not expounded through the discussion of concepts but through representative figures of the narrative literature of two generations—that of Melville and Dostoievsky and that of Kafka and Camus. The theme is the revolt of man against an existence emptied of meaning, the existence after the so-called "death of God." This emptying of meaning is not to be overcome through the illusionary program of a free "creation of values," as we know it in Nietzsche and Sartre. One must withstand this meaninglessness, must suffer it to the end, must do battle with it undauntedly, until out of the contradiction experienced in conflict and suffering, meaning shines forth anew.

In 1964, in a closely similar spirit Buber wrote a tribute, unpublished until "Gleanings," for his old friend the Russian Jewish existentialist Leo Shestov. Buber saw Shestov as one of the representative thinkers of our epoch precisely because he has no finished answers in his pocket, because he teaches us to ask, because he does not shy away from finding two answers that contradict each other. "Thereby he teaches us something very important for us contemporary men: that one may not overcome such contradictions prematurely—and that means seemingly." For Buber and for Shestov, metaphysics and theology both represented *seeming* overcoming of the real paradoxes of existence. Neither man was willing to subordinate God to Aristotle's logic. Once, during these last years of his life, Buber received a visit in Jerusalem from a Zen master accompanied by an American disciple. While the American talked to Buber incessantly, the Zen master sat silent on his chair. Finally the American concluded his verbal outpouring with the assertion that the essence of all religions is identical. Then Buber asked sharply: "And what is this essence?" At this point the Zen master sprang up and vigorously shook Buber's hand!

In February 1964, Buber had to have a dangerous eye operation. The operation was successful, but an inflammation of the nerves developed afterward. By July 1964, complications had developed in the eye that had been operated on, and his doctors decided that they could not allow him to go abroad that year.

In February 1964, Albrecht Goes informed Buber that he had dedicated his new novella *The Boychik,* which was to be published in the fall, "For Martin Buber, Teacher, Father, Friend." In March 1964, Heinrich Ott, who has succeeded Karl Barth as Professor of Systematic Theology at the University of Basel, notified Buber that he was writing a work on "Faith and Reality," one volume of which he wanted to dedicate to Buber's thought, and indicated his desire to come to Jerusalem in the course of the year to talk with him. In September after their meeting, Ott wrote Buber that his talk with him in Jerusalem had helped him to a clear understanding of his own problem: how we can understandably and credibly talk of God so that the reality of human existence is encountered in doing so. Just after talking with Buber he read the Postscript to *I and Thou* and was strengthened in his conviction that "we must apply your thinking and the experience out of which you think to the present situation of Christian theology." "I have long held the existential interpretation of the talk of God to be a necessary path in our thought," he went on, "but in the way that this path is mostly followed today I see the danger of an 'ideologization' of faith, i.e., the danger that the character of faith as a personal meeting will be darkened. Out of your thinking a

priceless auxiliary may grow for Christian theology." To this Ott
added a remarkable personal witness:

> What you said to me about your position toward Christianity remains
> to me unforgettable. But I must say to you that as a Christian I must
> agree with you, and that I have never been able to understand my
> Christianity otherwise than as solidarity with the whole world that is to
> be redeemed—never as merely private certainty of salvation. I believe
> that this universalist trait has existed in Christianity from the beginning,
> and that today the world hour begins in which it must wholly unfold.

One of Buber's last public statements was regarding a "mercy-
death" killing. An Israeli mother killed her child, who was a hopeless
mental defective, as well as blind, deaf, and dumb. The Mercy Killing
Public Committee pressed for a change in Israeli law, which recognized only premeditated murder and manslaughter (the charge was
reduced from the former to the latter). In response to this committee,
Buber said he did not see changing the law as an answer but rather,
exerting influence in each particular case. Everything here depends
upon motive, and this cannot be judged according to any general
rule. Considering motives might be very hard and perhaps impracti-
cal, "but we are not talking about what is practical and easy: we are
talking about what is right or wrong." Did this mother think only of
herself "or did she seek to free the sufferer from an atrocious life that
cannot be called human any more?" Was the fundamental feeling in
her heart that dominated her imagination her thought of the child
suffering for years and years and of making the other children in the
family suffer as well? "Love and mercy show her the deed of death as
the only way out." Anyone who concluded from this that Buber was
for mercy-killing would miss the whole point; for, however justifiable
a particular case might seem on the face of it, if the motives were *not*
such as he imagined, the act would be wrong.

In July 1964, Buber expressed to Lambert Schneider how happy he
was that the three volumes of the *Werke*—Philosophy, Hasidism, and
the Bible—were now completed. "One can really say now that 'the
corn is in the barn.'" In September, Hermann Levin-Goldschmidt
asked Buber from Zurich why his monumental volume of essays on
The Jew and His Jewishness was a separate volume rather than being
included with the works. "Your effort has been just to bring Judaism
into the world, to make the world conscious of it. Now it is again stuck
in the ghetto." Buber replied that he had not included *Der Jude und*

sein Judentum in the *Werke* because his writings on Judaism, Zionism, and the like did not have the character of "works" in the strict sense of the term but of occasional writings. They were, indeed, "Words to the Time."

In November 1964, Lambert Schneider communicated with Buber concerning one of the last honors Buber received, an honorary doctorate from Heidelberg, for which Schneider himself read the short reminiscence "In Heidelberg" that is published in "Gleanings." In December, Buber confided to Schneider his disappointment that the Bachem family who took over the direction of Jakob Hegner Verlag after Hegner's death did not feel in a position to cooperate with other publishers in bringing out soon a popular edition of Buber's translation of the Hebrew Bible. "Now it appears that I must give up this hope of my heart." Buber also told Schneider of how Margot Cohn and he had assembled two hundred texts, including a number unpublished, from among which they were selecting the "Gleanings" that Buber felt worthy of being preserved. In October 1964, Buber wrote concerning the new edition of *Between Man and Man* which appeared in Macmillan Paperbacks in 1965 with the addition of an Introduction by me and my translation of "The History of the Dialogical Principle." "Since this book, one of my most important works, is now already much too long a time out of the market, you would oblige me very much by using, if possible, your influence in order to accelerate the publication." In December, Buber finally received the book *Philosophical Interrogations:* "It makes an excellent impression."*

---

*See Note in Sources for Chapter 15.

CHAPTER 16

"On the World's Edge"

IN OCTOBER 1963, Paul Tillich visited Buber at his home in Talbiyeh
and they shared "a great evening of reminiscences and exchanges."
When Tillich left Buber, he asked him whether he would come again
to Europe or America. "He answered with a clear 'No,' and he looked
at me with an expression in his eyes which said unmistakably: This is a
final farewell.' It was." Not long after that Buber sent me a reprint
inscribed simply, "*Ave et Vale!*"

Two months before Tillich's visit Buber reported from the
Kurhaus in Sonnmatt near Lucerne, where he had gone after the
Erasmus Prize ceremonies: "I am feeling rather well. Our family
friend, Naemah Beer-Hofmann (younger sister of Miriam B-H), is
very helpful not only in matters of health but in work too." Naemah,
younger daughter of Buber's friend the poet and playwright Richard
Beer-Hofmann, was a gifted physiotherapist who was able to do much
for Buber during the summers of 1962 and 1963 at the sanitarium
Sonnmatt. In August 1962, she came to Israel to accompany Buber

back to Lucerne. By help in his work, Buber meant in part the Introduction that he wrote to Richard Beer-Hofmann's collected works, published in Germany in 1962. The basic motif that Buber saw running through Beer-Hofmann's poetry was that of death. Buber saw this motif as common to other German-language poets of his time and atmosphere, especially the Austrian poets, and, among these, above all the Jews, and he singled out for attention the Vienna circle of his three friends Beer-Hofmann, Arthur Schnitzler, and Hugo von Hofmannsthal, the last of whom descended from Jews on one side of his family. What is remarkable about Buber's tracing of this theme in Beer-Hofmann's writings is that it is, in each of its central manifestations, identical with Buber's own basic attitudes toward death. Thus the theme of the forebears in Beer-Hofmann's famous "Lullaby to Miriam" (his elder daughter) is identical with the motif of the vital connection with ancestors which Buber stressed in his early talks on Judaism. In Beer-Hofmann's poem "Aging" (1906) Buber found the poetizing of a great but incomplete insight of Kant's:

> *Space, like time: spun web, ghosts*
> *Which the senses have woven around you!*

And he sees Beer-Hofmann's response to this as very close to his own early response to the threat of infinity, which was also connected with Kant:

Here the presentiment of eternity is spoken of, a clear presentiment but one that removes us from all warmth of earth—the eternity of the primal ground out of which time and space arise. These two prove themselves, indeed, when we wish to take them as ultimate realities, as inconceivable to the point of absurdity, no matter whether we seek to imagine them as finite or as infinite: only as borne by a timeless and spaceless eternity are they comprehensible.

But here Buber puts them together—the vital connection with the ancestors and the presentiment of an eternity above time—in an explicit nexus that one cannot find in his writings: "Only he who knows the twofold answer to death, that which arises out of our reality and that which can only be glimpsed, this side of death, only he who knows both in one knows the answer." A third variation Buber finds in the *Count of Charolais,* in which he sees Beer-Hofmann as deeply struck by "the insight into how much there was intermixed in the 'unrest and pride' of the blood of the fathers the experience of the injuries that had been done to them in body and soul—done to them under the eyes of God." This insight leads to a great search for meaning in which the theme of the forebears is now inserted into a framework in which we encounter for the first time "the meaning-filled image of an Israel that suffers for God's sake as his witness, that becomes through this suffering the 'light of the peoples' and overcomes the death of a people," which Buber speaks of as "death in its most threatening form." Regarding this third variant of the motif, which appears poetically in Beer-Hofmann's *Jacob's Dream* as in Buber's *Prophetic Faith*, Buber also speaks of that *emunah* which was central to his own attitude toward death. "The world stands on trust," the trust which is part of a love for God "as He is, cruel and merciful," and of "the sun of love that warms throughout the world: the love of God for his creatures." We may presume that Beer-Hofmann's vision of David's way to death was also Buber's own: "from the grace of the election through sin to that higher grace which is only granted to those who have turned."

Through her warmth and friendship and almost childlike spirit of openness (to which many have touchingly testified), Naemah Beer-Hofmann helped to heal in part the great wound of Paula's death and the lifelong wound of his mother's desertion. Naemah spoke of how happy and relaxed Buber was during those summers at Sonnmatt, and some of her pictures of him there bear striking testimony to his happy frame of mind at this time.

Yet the concern with death remained with him too as an ever-present theme. Naemah told of one young nun who was shocked to discover that Buber was afraid of death. "But, Professor Buber," she remonstrated, "*you* should not be afraid of death."

Other women, to a lesser extent, did for Buber what Naemah had done during these last two or three years of his life. One was the German-Jewish psychiatrist Anna Maria Jokl, who under Buber's influence had finally come to live in Israel. When she first met Buber at a conference in Germany in the late 1950s, she startled him by her great knowledge of Hasidic tales. The first time she visited Israel she thanked Buber for his Hasidic tales, which had meant so much to her over the years, but felt that that had finished their business together. When she visited Israel for a second time, she went to see Buber only at the insistence of Hugo Bergmann, who said, "He has a right to see you." On this second visit, Buber began asking questions and advancing insights. Anna Maria Jokl was astonished. "Yes, that's true, that's very true!" she exclaimed. Then she put her hand on Buber's and said, "Now I have told Buber that he is clever!" They both laughed, he held out his arms to her, and they became close friends. Buber told her, "I had what the psychoanalysts would call a bad childhood. Yet I have no fear. How do you explain that?" "You do not fear when you belong," she said. "Fear is fear of not belonging." Buber was silent for a long while, then he said that he understood and agreed. This was not a matter of belonging to *something* but just of belonging, of relationship. Buber had written in *Good and Evil* about that fear of abandonment which is a foretaste of death—a foretaste that Buber knew from the time that his mother abandoned him. At the end, when Buber did have fear, he made a point of saying to Anna Maria that it was not psychological: It was because of physical deterioration. Even in the face of this fear Buber still retained his trust. When Buber went to sleep at night, he often prayed, "Into thy hands I commit my spirit."

Shulamit Katz-Nelson, the director of Ulpan Akiva, came to know Buber through Hugo Bergmann and went to see Buber regularly during the last ten years of his life. Both Anna Maria and Shulamit have testified, independently of each other, that in his early years Buber helped build the image people had of him and then found himself imprisoned in it. He needed someone who would reach out to him and meet him as a person and not just as a famous man or a fount of wisdom and knowledge.

Another woman who spent some time with Buber during the period before his death was the American psychologist Katherine Whiteside Taylor. "Have you ever thought of life after death?" she asked Buber. "Who has not?" he replied. "Do you believe in life after death?" she persevered. "After is the wrong word," he replied. "It is an entirely different dimension. Time and space are crystallizations out of God. At the last hour all will be revealed."

In April 1962, Buber complained to Werner Kraft about his memory: "The old things I see quite clearly, but I forget much of the new," to which Kraft replied that the same was true of him. "But you are still a young fellow!" Buber exclaimed to the sixty-six-year-old Kraft. In March 1963, Kraft noted in his journal: "The verve of this man who is becoming ever older is wonderful. He may have anxiety about death, but he is free from all melancholy. His desires are as intact as those of a young man. He lives." Kraft found in Buber an example of his own dictum that at each stage of life the person has his whole life before him. In December 1963, before Buber had his cataract operation, Schalom Ben-Chorin found him buried deep in the task of correcting proofs. "I want to bring everything into the barn before the operation," he said to Ben-Chorin, almost as if excusing himself. When Kraft went to visit Buber in January 1964, he found that he listened and spoke as always but for the first time he gave Kraft the impression of being *spiritually* tired. "He lives now in a kind of timelessness," Kraft entered in his journal, "often no longer knowing what day of the week it is." Yet a week later Kraft wrote: "He is now almost eighty-six years old. He speaks freely. His spirit affected me this evening like that of a young man." In March 1964, Kraft reported that Buber was sick again, in bed with a high fever. "The doctors have decided to know nothing about my sickness," Buber said in the five minutes Kraft was with him. "That is already a resignation close to death," Kraft commented. But Barbara said to Kraft that he was better at times and would speak of plans to travel. "This uncanny affirmation of life up to the end is of overwhelming grandeur," Kraft added. "Although the spirit is present in Buber in the highest degree, it has nothing to do with this affirmation of life." Other times Kraft found Buber lively, or tired but fresh. Kraft once left, saying Buber was perhaps tired, and Buber responded, "I am always tired." "He is still himself," Kraft commented, "but fading." In March 1965, he found Buber on the floor sitting amid a gigantic pile of papers. "What are you doing?" Kraft asked. "Don't you know what that means: to put one's house in order?" replied Buber. Isaiah said that, Kraft recalled: "Put your house in order, for you are going to die."

Another woman who played a role in Buber's life similar to that of Naemah Beer-Hofmann and Anna Maria Jokl was Grete Schaeder, who spent much time with him between 1961 and 1965. Thanks to her, we have a remarkable poem that Buber wrote in February 1964, at the very time that he had to have the dangerous cataract operation. This poem expresses with poignant immediacy the continued ascetic discipline and sacrifice that Buber had to make to renounce, for the love of the world, that mystic ecstasy that came to him so naturally:

> *A strange (loud) voice speaks:*
> *A rope is stretched across the abyss,*
> *Now set your foot on it*
> *And, before your step awakens the contradiction,*
> *Run!*
> *A rope is tightly strung across the abyss,*
> *Renounce on the way all that is here!*
> *Already there beckons to you from over there a hand:*
> *"To me!"*

> *The familiar (soft) voice speaks:*
> *Follow not the demanding call!*
> *He who created you*
> *Intended for you: "Be ready*
> *For every earthly time!"*
> *Already his hand ever holds you—*
> *Remain turned toward the world in love!*

The figure of the rope stretched across the abyss was one that Buber had already used in *The Legend of the Baal-Shem* in 1908, where he wrote of that *hitlahavut,* or ecstasy, that dropped out of sight almost entirely in his later interpretations of Hasidism, with the exception of *For the Sake of Heaven.* The sentence in the second stanza, "Already his hand ever holds you," is an unmistakable reference to a passage from Psalm 73:

> *And nevertheless I am always with you,*
> *You have taken hold of my right hand.*
> *You guide me with your counsel*
> *And afterward you take me into honor.*

It was Psalm 73 that Buber read at Franz Rosenzweig's funeral, and it was these four lines from Psalm 73 that were inscribed on Buber's tombstone at his own request. Psalm 73 thus embodies, as no other traditional literature, Buber's own deepest attitude toward death.

Happily, Buber himself left us a key to this attitude in his interpretation of Psalm 73 in his *Good and Evil.* This chapter of his existential exegesis of five psalms Buber titled "The Heart Determines," because, as the dominant key word in the Psalm shows, it is the state of the heart that determines the nearness to God of the man who is "pure in heart" and the nothingness in which the "wicked" end—those who deliberately persist in impurity of heart. What is remarkable about Psalm 73, Buber stated at the outset, is that a man tells how he reached the true meaning of his experience of life, and that this meaning borders directly on the eternal. We tend to turn the decisive experiences of our life to use without penetrating to their heart. It requires deeper experience to teach us to do this latter.

The speaker of the Psalm, like Buber himself, "is a man of Israel in Israel's bitter hour of need, and in his personal suffering the suffering of Israel has been concentrated, so that what he now has to suffer he suffers as Israel." "In the destiny of an authentic person the destiny of his people is gathered up, and only now becomes truly manifest."

Insofar as the Psalmist becomes pure in heart, he experiences God's goodness, not as some reward, but as the revelation of what he cannot know from his side of the dialogue—that he is continually with God. This is not a pious feeling, Buber cautioned. "From man's side there is no continuity of presence, only from God's side." The Psalmist cannot say "Thou art with me," like the speaker in Psalm 23—"Though I walk through the valley of the shadow of death / I shall fear no evil / For thou art with me." Rather he says, "I am continually with thee." But he does not know this from his own consciousness and feeling; for no human being is able to be continually turned to the presence of God. "He can say it only in the strength of the revelation that God is continually with him," and this revelation is expressed not as a word of God but as a gesture—the very one that Buber inserted into his poem on mystic ecstasy: that God has taken his right hand. Despite all his own personal experience of the prosperity of the wicked, of which the speaker of Psalm 73 complained, Buber compared this to the way in which in the dark a father takes his little son by the hand, only partially to lead him "but primarily in order to make present to him, in the warm touch of coursing blood, the fact that he, the father, is continually with him."

Buber took the speaker in this Psalm far too seriously to accept the notion that the guiding that he now experiences from God is some constant oracle which would exonerate him from the duty of weighing and deciding what he must do.

> The guiding counsel of God seems to me to be simply the divine Presence communicating itself directly to the pure in heart. He who is aware of this Presence acts in the changing situations of his life differently from him who does not perceive this Presence. The Presence acts as counsel: God counsels by making known that He is present. He has led his son out of darkness into the light, and now he can walk in the light. He is not relieved of taking and directing his own steps.

This revealing has not only changed the life and the meaning of life of the speaker. It has also changed his perspective on death, and we cannot doubt that what Buber now put forward, written in 1951 after his own experience of the Holocaust and of the war in Palestine, represented Buber's own deepest attitude toward death.

> For the "oppressed" man death was only the mouth towards which the sluggish stream of suffering and trouble flows. But now it has become the event in which God—the continually Present One, the One who grasps the man's hand, the Good One—"takes" a man.

The way in which Buber now "unpacked" this image of God's "taking" this man includes all those stages of attitudes toward death that he pointed to in his interpretation of the works of his friend Beer-Hofmann. The tellers of legends show the living Elijah as being taken away by God Himself to Heaven (this is not the way Buber ends *Elijah*). The Psalmist transfers this taking from the realm of the miraculous to that of the most personal expression of piety. There is nothing in Psalm 73 about being able to enter heaven after death, Buber claimed. "And, so far as I see, there is nowhere in the 'Old Testament' anything about this." The "honor" *(kavod)* into which one is afterward taken is not some glorious afterlife but, rather from man's point of view, the fulfillment of existence, and from God's the entrance into God's eternity. The Psalmist neither aspires to enter heaven after death nor to remain on earth, and he imagines no personal immortality, no continuation in time's dimension.

> It is not merely his flesh which vanishes in death, but also his heart, that inmost personal organ of the soul, which formerly "rose up" in rebellion against the human fate and which he then "purified" till he became pure in heart—this personal soul also vanishes. But He who was the true part and true fate of this person, the "rock" of his heart, God, is eternal. It is into His eternity that he who is pure in heart moves in death, and this eternity is something absolutely different from any kind of time.

In the end, therefore, the dynamic of farness and nearness from God is broken by death when it breaks the life of the person. With death there vanishes the heart, that human inwardness out of which the "pictures" of the imagination arose, the heart which rises up in defiance but can also be purified. Separation, separate souls, and time itself vanish. Only the rock in which the human heart is concealed does not vanish; for it does not stand in time. "The time of the world disappears before eternity, but existing man dies into eternity as into the perfect existence." "The Heart Determines" is Buber's fullest unfolding of that 1928 statement "After Death" that Buber put at the end of "Gleanings."

Grete Schaeder has given us a perceptive picture of Buber in the last year of his life. Buber continued, with great energy, improving his translation of the Bible. In the winter of 1964–1965, he assembled the material for "Gleanings." Meanwhile his works on philosophical anthropology, dialogical thought, Jewish and Zionist humanism, and interpretation of the Bible were brought to the attention of the younger generation of Israel for the first time through their publication in Hebrew translation. Buber's work discipline, a fixed division of each day, was admirable. Also a certain amount of time was reserved daily for answering correspondence, which continued to flow in from all countries, from persons known and unknown, consisting of letters, publications, demands. Buber fought tirelessly against the flood and took pains to give an answer to each one: a few words of thanks, of encouragement, of personal advice. Despite all efforts, not a few of these who received letters from Buber may have felt, like Walter Kaufmann, that they resembled more the old Goethe than what one expected from Martin Buber—just because in his kindness and justice he wanted to answer as many of them as possible and because his correspondents did not realize the limited capacity of a very old man for work and for entering personal relationship. Not the least because he so little wanted to admit his age and in good times, through a will to live and experience more, fought against it.

Schaeder further comments:

> But it is shattering how a man who was ever an opponent of fixed forms and a champion of spontaneous utterance at the end ever more frequently employed the same turns of speech, phrases which *sounded* as if they were unique and personal, as he got caught in the net of his own formulas. Very often he pointed out in his short letters that the problem that the other brought before him could only be clarified through conversation. Precisely his letters of old age show that the written expression was not a form of communication that was really suited to Buber, only a substitute for the conversation that was so often not possible.

In 1964, Buber wrote me, in the midst of letters that were becoming ever more infrequent and more devoid of anything really personal, "It would indeed be pleasant and useful to talk with you once more."

In personal conversation, aside from the times when he was very weak, Buber's spontaneity was preserved until the last. "It was," says Schaeder, "the enlivening element for him," bringing powerfully to mind the statement that a friend of Rabbi Moshe of Kobryn made about the rabbi after his death: "If there had been someone to whom he could have talked, he would still be alive." Buber had daily visitors, often several a day, from near and far, including an increasing number from Germany. As usual, Buber tolerated no small talk and forced the persons who came to see him to carry on a real dialogue.

What he liked best was that his guests should bring him burning problems, which enabled him to unfold the richness of his thoughts and his feelings. At these times even his memory and the presence of his knowledge were remarkable. Buber particularly liked the visit of young persons, even of whole groups who posed questions and told him of their lives. He liked persons with an original gift for narration and communicating themselves. With them, he forgot his age and felt himself alive. When they were shy, he encouraged them with turns of phrase which gradually took on a somewhat formal character. They should speak to him of what troubled them when they awoke in the gray of dawn and would not let them go to sleep again. When his carefully weighed balance of work and relaxation, fellowship and rest, was disturbed, as if often was, by pain he was helped over it by his undaunted will to live and by his humor, which he called the "milk-brother of faith." Barbara would try to limit his callers, but Buber insisted, "If they seek me out, I must see them."

In 1965, a young friend of mine went to Israel and talked with Buber two months before his death. Upon his return he indicated that he had been disappointed in his talk with Buber, but did not say why. The following year I learned the reason in Jerusalem from the woman assistant to Buber's photographer, Alfred Bernheim. She told me of the young American who had come to Israel just to see Buber and who had become part of their German-Jewish group because of his excellent command of German and his understanding of German poetry. "What will you ask Buber when you go to see him?" she had asked my young friend. "I don't need to think about that," he replied. "You are mistaken," she said. "You ought to have a question in mind." Not heeding her words, the young man went to see Buber. Buber received him at the door of his study, took his hand, looked deeply into his eyes, and asked him to sit down. "I wrote a Master's thesis on Whitman and you," the young scholar said. "Oh," said Buber, "I didn't know that." After that they sat in total silence for eight minutes until the young visitor could bear it no longer, seized Buber's hand, and left.

At first glance this seems like a repetition of that earlier mismeeting in which Buber failed to be present for Herr Méhé during the First World War because he failed to guess the questions the other did not ask—the only difference being that that was two months before Méhé's death, this two months before Buber's own. But the similarity is merely superficial, masking a deeper contrast. My friend's life-question was a *real* one, but he left it to Buber to carry on both sides of the dialogue, assuming that he would understand his question without having to ask it. The young man in "The Conversion," in contrast, did not look to Buber as the magic helper who would reach into his soul and extract his question. He did not simply *have* a question: he concentrated his whole being into *becoming* a question. It was the address of this unuttered question that Buber might have heard behind every spoken question that Herr Méhé *did* ask, if Buber had been "present in spirit"—if he had brought himself into the dialogue with the whole of his being, rather than with the intellectual and social fragments left over from his preoccupation with that morning's mystical experience. What Buber learned from this earlier mismeeting is exactly what he brought to the later one: to be wholly present but also *not* to take over for the other, not to handle *both* sides of the dialogue. In his old age Buber was no longer "an oracle who would listen to reason," but he was a person who confirmed the other by contending with him or her, as well as by accepting and affirming.

Schaeder does not agree with Kraft's judgment that Buber did not experience that lowering of spirits that comes to most persons when age and illness attacks them.

> Behind his well-guarded façade melancholy often hid, but not his mouth, only the darkness of his eyes, expressed it. Persons came and went; there was always leavetaking and often the death of those younger than he; but weariness remained and increased, which was in itself a little death. With it there overtook him a . . . reality no longer heightened by the intensity of the life-stream.

In January 1964, again after a leavetaking, Buber wrote a poem on melancholy "Besides Me," in connection with the artist Albrecht Dürer's *Melancolia:*

> *Beside me sits melancholy*
> *(Thus once the master had seen her).*
> *She does not speak to me, she never whispers.*
> *Only the hesitant stirring of her breath*
> *Carries to me, unto my innermost ear,*
> *The lament of the spirit which—when then? How?—*
> *Lost the life of the soul.*

Commenting on this poem, Grete Schaeder writes:

> The life of the soul for Buber was the power of relationship with its tensions and animations, an original spontaneity of the heart, the ele-

ment of the "between" in his world. In the poem the human background disappears. The poem meant resignation and overcoming. It
was inextricably at once creation and service of God and thereby
touched on the mystery of Buber's life.

This is one of the very few poems that Buber selected to be preserved
in his "Gleanings." Another poem that was saved for posterity in this
way is "The Fiddler," which Buber wrote in October 1964 and dedicated to Grete Schaeder, indicating, as nothing else could, how much
her relationship to him meant in these last months of his life. There is
nothing of melancholy in "The Fiddler," but it expresses with great
poignancy what it meant to Buber to live "on the world's edge" during
this final stage:

> *Here on the world's edge at this hour I have*
> *Wondrously settled my life.*
> *Behind me in a boundless circle*
> *The All is silent, only that fiddler fiddles.*
> *Dark one, already I stand in covenant with you,*
> *Ready to learn from your tones*
> *Wherein I became guilty without knowing it.*
> *Let me feel, let there be revealed*
> *To this hale soul each wound*
> *That I have incorrigibly inflicted and remained in illusion.*
> *Do not stop, holy player, before then!*

This poem contains two untranslatable puns. One is the contrast between *heilen* and *heillos* in *heilen Seele* and *ich heillos schlug. Heilen* carries
the meaning of whole, hale, untouched, innocent, uninjured, intact,
even ignorant, whereas *heillos* carries the double meaning of an incur-
able wound and of a God-forsaken, damned, or unholy infliction of
that wound. I have used "incorrigibly" in my translation because of its
ambiguity, suggesting both an incorrigible wound and that the one
who inflicts it is himself incorrigible in inflicting it. The other pun is in
the word *Schein,* which mean illusion, in the sense of being unaware
that he inflicted the wounds, but also undoubtedly refers to the contrast that Buber made between "being" and "seeming" in "Elements
of the Interhuman." The poem takes on another dimension of meaning if we keep in mind the relationship between Buber's contrast of
"being" and "seeming" *and* existential guilt. The basic temptation of
man is to allow seeming to creep into the interhuman and thus destroy the authenticity not only of the interhuman but of the human as
such. No person is entirely a "being" person and none entirely "seem-

ing." We are all a mixture of the two. As a result, we all share to some extent in the injury that "seeming" inflicts on the common order of speech-with-meaning that we build up in our relationships with one another. This injury to the common order is existential guilt in the exact sense of the term.

What is so deeply moving about "The Fiddler" is *not* that Buber composed a poem to express his philosophical anthropology, but that he really lived his philosophy and prayed before death to be given to know and to face his guilt. As Buber said at the end of his essay on Richard Beer-Hofmann, the higher grace "is only granted to those who have turned."

After reading my interpretation of "The Fiddler," Grete Schaeder sent me a quite different interpretation of "her" poem based on its connection with Buber's essay "The Heart Determines"—that very exegesis of Psalm 73 that we have already discussed at length in this chapter in connection with the poem of the rope stretched across the abyss that she preserved for us. Her interpretation (which I reproduce in full below)* turns on the same word *Schein* (seeming or illusion) which led me to "Elements of the Interhuman." This word is central to the general paragraph which Buber puts at the head of his more specific interpretation of Psalm 73:

> For the most part we understand only gradually the decisive experiences which we have in our relation with the world. First we accept what they seem to offer us, we express it, we weave it into a "view" *(Anschauung)*, and then think we are aware of our world. But we come to see that what we look on in this view is only an appearance *(Schein)*. Not that our experiences have deceived us. But we have turned them to our use, without penetrating to their heart. What is it that teaches us to penetrate to their heart? Deeper experience.

Only the person who has become pure in heart (attained a whole or hale soul) and who draws near to God and experiences that God is good to him is able to get beyond appearance, "Schein," to reality and thus become aware also of wherein he is guilty toward his fellowman.

> The state of the heart determines whether a man lives in the truth, in which God's goodness is experienced, or in the semblance *(Schein)* of truth, where the fact that it "goes ill" with him is confused with the illusion that God is not good to him.

---

*See Note A to Chapter 16.

This interpretation gives more room for the play of meaning, as Schaeder points out, and it alone explains how Buber could have spoken of himself as "this hale soul" (Diese heilen Seele). But what won me to Schaeder's interpretation even above my own (which I retain because it is valid and because the mark of a good poem, as Schaeder says, and this *is* one, is that it leaves the possibility of more than one interpretation) was when I opened the second volume of Buber's collected works, the one in fact last completed, on the Bible and read a much more personal version of the first paragraph of "The Heart Determines" than the one with which I was familiar:

> I return today once again to this psalm that I once, in accordance with Franz Rosenzweig's wishes, spoke at his graveside.
> What is it that so draws me to this poem that is pieced together out of description, report, and confession and draws me ever more strongly the older I become? I think it is this, that here a person reports how he attained to the true sense of his life experience and that this sense touches directly on the eternal.

Psalm 73 is not only Buber's "death poem," as Schaeder puts it, but also his "life poem," for it captures that trust and that remarkable intuition of the eternal that accompanied him on his way from the time of the crisis over the infinity of time and space that brought him close to suicide at the age of fourteen.

The last letter I received from Buber was dated April 14, 1965. "It is with a feeling of true sympathy I learned from your letter about the death of your father," Buber wrote. "I know well by my own experience what it means to lose a loving father. It is now just forty years since I lost mine. He was then as old as I am now." Twelve days later, on the evening of April 26, Buber broke his right leg through a fall and had to be operated on that same night. The break and the wound from the operation healed satisfactorily, and Buber insisted on coming home, since he did not want to die in the Hadassah hospital. In the next weeks Buber's chronic nephritis grew steadily worse, producing uremic poisoning.

As Buber lay dying, a shameful battle was being fought out in the Jerusalem City Hall. The mayor of Jerusalem, Mordecai Ish-Shalom (Hebrew for Friedman), fought to have Buber awarded the "Freedom of the City," an honor which before had been given to Chaim Weizmann, President Itzhak Ben-Zvi, and Shmuel Joseph Agnon, among others. Ish-Shalom was supported in the Council by the other members of Mapai and by the Mapam and liberal representatives, but he was opposed by the rightist Herut, who could not forgive Buber for opposing the execution of Eichmann, and by the Orthodox, who bitterly resented Buber's interpretation of Judaism in general and of Hasidism in particular. According to Albrecht Goes, in the face of this stalemate someone came to Buber, to ask whether he would accept the Freedom of the City in case they mustered a majority in favor of granting it to him. Buber replied: "I do not know yet, but first let them fight it out." The most beautiful thing about this story is not that the majority finally came around, comments Goes, but Buber's composure, humor, and wisdom in those all too human circumstances. Finally the resolution was adopted ten to six with two abstentions and two absences. The *Jerusalem Post* write-up of this story on May 10 says all that need be said:

> The Jerusalem Municipal Council last night noisily decided to grant the "Freedom of the City" to Professor Martin Buber. The resolution . . . had been debated behind-the-scenes for two years. . . . Mr. A. Axelrod (Herut) cried that "a minority decision" was a "disgrace" to the Municipality (of the 21 Councillors less than half were in favour).
>
> Speakers were constantly interrupted by heckling and the dropping of teaspoons.
>
> Mayor Ish-Shalom expressed his regret that he had failed to persuade leaders of the Herut and N.R.P. parties to vote in favour of the decision, in keeping with the custom to accord such honours unanimously.
>
> Dr. David Cohen stated that Herut was opposing the motion because the party did not want to be associated with Prof. Buber's view or with the man who had "fought against the fighters for the freedom of Jerusalem and the State of Israel"; who had broken the embargo on Germany by accepting a literary prize; and who asked that Eichmann be reprieved.
>
> Mr. S. Druck (Poalei Agudat Yisrael) said his party could not support a decision to grant the Freedom of the Holy City to a man who is not a believer.

Thus Martin Buber, the most famous inhabitant of Jerusalem in the world, became the fifteenth Freeman of the City! Mayor Ish-Shalom and Agnon, himself an Honorary Citizen of Jerusalem, rushed to Buber's bedside. Buber listened intently for a few minutes, but could no longer reply. Adding to the irony, no one on the Jerusalem Council had read a book of Buber's according to Shereshevsky. Two days before his death Shulamit Katz-Nelson said to Hugo Bergmann that she wanted to go to see Buber. "If you will go, I will come too," said Bergmann. When they arrived they found that

Buber had shrunk to the size of a child. Bergmann could not bear to come near, but Shulamit took Buber's hand. "You are coming straight from life," said Buber looking directly at Bergmann. "I have been for so long so far from life. Tell me something about life." Shulamit thought to herself: What would I want to hear if I were dying? That people still loved and cared for me. So she told Buber that in the latest *Pendle Hill Bulletin* there was an announcement of a course on *I and Thou* to be given by Dan Wilson, the director. "That is not life," said Buber. Then she told him that the Israeli news magazine *Davar* had announced that still another of his books would be translated into Hebrew. "That is still not life," Buber complained. Finally, she said, "My husband passed the Israel bar exam." "Shulamit, *that* is life!" said Buber. This was the nearest Buber came to dying "with a human hand in my own," as he wrote in "Books and Men." Shortly before the end Buber said to Ernst Simon, "I am not afraid of death but of dying."

On June 13, 1965, Martin Buber died. At his bedside were Eva, Rafael, Barbara and Zeev Goldschmidt, and all his great-grandchildren. Eugenia and I were living at Pendle Hill, and Dan Wilson, the director, came to see me, just as he had four months before when my father died. I had, indeed, lost a second father.* I was not able to experience my own grief in depth until one day the following spring when I came, as usual, to work at the Hebrew University and National Library in Jerusalem doing research for this book. On the second floor I found an exhibition of pictures of Buber's family and of Buber himself in childhood and youth, and this brought Buber's presence *and* his absence so vividly before me that I wept.

After Buber died the first person to come to the house in Talbiyeh was Zalman Shazar, the president of Israel. David Ben-Gurion and Shmuel Agnon came and sat by the body for five hours, telling each other stories at the expense of Buber, much to the indignation of Rafael! When Buber was buried in the ordinary Jerusalem cemetery, Teddy Kolleck, the former mayor of Jerusalem, asked Rafael why he was not buried on Mount Herzl with the other great men of Israel. "That is not for me to initiate," replied Rafael. Ben-Gurion insisted on accompanying the body to the Hadassah hospital. That evening over Kol Yisrael, Israel's national radio station, Ben-Gurion spoke of Buber's death as "a great loss to Israel's spiritual life" and of Buber

---

*See Note A in Sources for Chapter 16.

himself as "a metaphysical entity in his own class, a true man of the spirit."

Buber was given a traditional Jewish funeral, without a coffin, and Rabbi Aharon Phillip of Simon's Emet Ve-emuna congregation performed the funeral service. He was buried in the "Hill of Rest" at the place reserved for professors from the Hebrew University.

The most complete of the reports of Buber's funeral is that of Aubrey Hodes in his *Intimate Portrait.* At ten o'clock on the morning of June 14, Buber's body was brought from the Hadassah hospital covered by a *talit*—a black and white prayer shawl—and carried by President Eliahu Elath of the Hebrew University, Nathan Rotenstreich, the rector, Ernst Simon, Benyamin Mazar, Alexander Dushkin, and Zvi Werblovsky. Together with Agnon and a representative of the students they formed a guard of honor, which was changed every fifteen minutes until noon. Classes were canceled from twelve to two in Buber's honor, but from ten on hundreds of students lined up to file slowly past Buber's body along with friends, kibbutznikim, Christian monks, Arab Moslems and Christians, representatives of foreign embassies, and hundreds of others. Levi Eshkol, Prime Minister of Israel, began the eulogies:

> The passing of Mordecai Martin Buber marks the end of an era in the annals of the spiritual and territorial resurgence of the Jewish people in modern times. The Jewish people today mourns a luminary and a teacher, a man of thought and achievement, who revealed the soul of Judaism with a new philosophic daring. All mankind mourns with us one of the spiritual giants of this century. I do not know whether there is anyone else in our midst, in the sphere of spiritual life, who was so much a part of the heritage of the entire world; but he was deeply anchored—to a depth that few could reach—in his Jewishness, in the Jewish people, in the resurgence of Israel and the love of Jewry.

Overcome with emotion, Hugo Bergmann cried out the words of Elisha when he saw Elijah taken up to heaven in a whirlwind: "My father, my father, Israel's chariot and its horsemen!" Bergmann finished his speech, Hodes tells us, "with a cry from the heart, an outpouring of personal grief and loss which moved all of us": "You have done your share. We shall try to follow in your footsteps. . . . We thank you, dear Martin Buber." Rafael Buber recited the Kaddish— the traditional prayer for the dead—and the body was carried to the hearse by President Shazar, Prime Minister Eshkol, Agnon, President Elath of the Hebrew University, the Speaker of the Knesset, Yigal

Allon, Scholem, and Simon, among others. At the graveside Gershom Scholem spoke of Buber as a man of true dialogue, of advice and action, and of hope and optimism, a great speaker and listener, and a teacher who wanted his pupils to be rebels who would follow their own paths like Scholem himself. Ernst Simon spoke of Buber as an envoy and emissary to the Gentile world who had never been summoned by his people, a man who was alone when he fought, with even smaller support in times of peace than in times of crisis and disaster. Avraham Shapira spoke some words for the members of the kibbutz movement; the Independent Liberals and Mapam laid wreaths on Buber's grave; and three Arab students, representing all Arabs at the Hebrew University, placed a wreath of roses, carnations, and gladioli on the freshly turned earth.*

The Israeli Knesset had a memorial session for Buber while eulogies and messages of condolence poured in from all over the world—from the West German president and the chancellor, from former Chancellor Konrad Adenauer, from Giorgio La Pira, the former mayor of Florence, from the mayor of Vienna, from American Secretary of State Dean Rusk and the permanent U.S. ambassador to the United Nations Adlai Stevenson. Senator Abraham Ribicoff of Connecticut and Senator Jacob Javits of New York entered statements in the *Congressional Record* along with the long obituary from the *New York Times*. The editorial in the *Times* on June 14 reads in part:

> Martin Buber was the foremost Jewish religious thinker of our time and one of the world's most influential philosophers. He was a theological bridge-builder long before ecumenism achieved its present popularity. He served as a kind of patron saint for such towering Christian intellectuals as Paul Tillich, Reinhold Niebuhr, Jacques Maritain and Gabriel Marcel.
>
> If today the ancient cold war between the faiths is being replaced by dialogue and friendly personal confrontation, much of the credit must be given to Martin Buber. It was he, with his doctrine of "I-Thou" personalism, who showed the way.

Abraham Joshua Heschel, in Jerusalem but unable to get in to see Buber before his death, told the local *Newsweek* reporter:

> I know of no one with a life as rich with intellectual adventures or who so strongly responded to their challenges as Martin Buber. His

---

*See Note B to Chapter 16.

greatest contribution was himself, his very being. There was magic in his personality, richness in his soul. His sheer presence was joy. . . . He loved to listen and to talk, and our conversations sometimes lasted twelve to thirteen hours. "I am not a Jewish philosopher," he once told Heschel. "I am a universal philosopher." Buber spoke to Jews in a way that all men found relevant. There were no apologetics, no parochialism. . . . He exposed the challenges of modern society, and at the same time insisted upon loyalty to Jewish insight.

The "national universalism" that Buber saw in the prophets he too espoused. As he himself said, he did not need to leave his ancestral house of Judaism in order to speak to those outside it. The word that Martin Buber uttered standing in the doorway of that house and speaking into the street of mankind has not gone astray. It has spoken into the very life of our time, and it will continue to speak to that of the generations to come. Even more important is the image of authentic human existence that Buber has left us—that of a person whose very life was an "encounter on the narrow ridge."

Martin Buber withstood the thousandfold questioning glance of countless persons and measured hourly the depths of responsibility with the sounding lead of his presence, his decision, his words. He gave to the problematic person for whom life had become baseless "the certitude that 'there *is* a soil, there *is* an existence. . . . The world *can* be redeemed. *I* can be redeemed because there is this trust.'" "Trust, trust in the world, because this human exists"—that was Martin Buber's most precious gift to the persons of our age and the ages to come. Martin Buber was our comrade. He lived with us, won our trust through real-life relationship, and helped us to walk with him the way of the creature who *accepts* the creation. The innermost core of Buber's teaching and of his existence was the combination of this existential trust with the mystery of suffering—of our suffering for the sake of redemption and of God's suffering with us.

> Man penetrates step by step into the dark which hangs over the meaning of events, until the mystery is disclosed in the flash of light: the *zaddik*, the man justified by God, suffers for the sake of God and of His work of redemption, and God is with him in his suffering.

No one has joined trust and contending in his life and thought more clearly than Martin Buber—in his spiritual leadership of the German Jews under Hitler, in his lonely stance in relation to postwar Germany and Eichmann, in his lifelong fight for Jewish-Arab rapprochement and understanding, in his insistence that the state of Israel and the reality of Zion not be separated, in his opposition to the cold war and his call for genuine dialogue as a way to peace, in his fight for the becoming of one humanity. In an era of the "eclipse of God" Buber withstood and contended with meaninglessness, sustaining in the darkness the living substance of faith.

Notes and Sources

SOURCES FOR CHAPTER 1
Jewish-Arab Rapprochement
and Conflict

Susan Lee Hattis, *The Bi-National Idea in Palestine during Mandatory Times* (Haifa: Shikmona Pub. Co., 1970), pp. 209, 222 f., 227 f., 256–59, 263 f., 286–90, 303–05.

Buber, "They and We" (November 1939), in E. William Rollins and Harry Zohn, eds., *Men of Dialogue: Martin Buber and Albrecht Goes*, pref. Maurice Friedman (New York: Funk & Wagnalls, 1969), pp. 241f.

Buber, *Am v'Olam* (Hebrew) (Jerusalem: Sifriah Zionit, 1962), "On Our Policy" (1939, pp. 5–7; "We Establish an Organ": (1944); "Many or Majority" (1944); "A Dialogue about Biltmore" (1944), pp. 8–12, trans. for me by Uri Margolin.

Buber, *Der Jude und sein Judentum, Gesammelte Aufsätze und Reden,* intro. Robert Weltsch (Cologne: Joseph Melzer Verlag, 1963), "Sie und Wir" (November 1939), pp. 648–54; "Regeneration eines Volkstums" (1943), pp. 249–71; "Zweierlei Zionismus" (May 1948), pp. 349–52.

Buber, *Israel and the World* (New York: Schocken Books, 1963), "The Gods of the Nations and God" (1941), pp. 197–213; "Hebrew Humanism" (1942), pp. 240–52; "False Prophets" (1942), pp. 113–18; "Israel and the Command of the Spirit," trans. by Maurice Friedman, pp. 255f.

Aharon Cohen, *Israel and the Arab World,* abridged ed. (Boston: Beacon Press, 1976), pp. 141–43, 164f., 207.

Ernst Simon, "Nationalismus, Zionismus und der jüdisch-arabische Konflikt in Martin Bubers Theorie und Wirksamkeit," *Bulletin des Leo Baeck Instituts,* Vol. IX, No. 33 (Tel Aviv, 1966), pp. 73–78.

Buber, "'Defaitismus.' Zu einer Diskussion," *Mitteilungsblatt,* Vol. XI, No. 50 (December 12, 1941), p. 2.

Norman Bentwich, *For Zion's Sake: A Biography of Judah L. Magnes* (Philadelphia: The Jewish Publication Society, 1954), pp. 248f., 252f., 256–73.

Schalom Ben-Chorin, *Zwiesprache mit Martin Buber: Ein Erinnerungsbuch* (Munich: Paul List Verlag, 1966), pp. 47–49, 70, 102f., 107f.

Ernst Simon, "Buber's Political Way" (Introduction to *Am v'Olam*), trans. for me by Uri Margolin.

Martin Buber, *Briefwechsel aus sieben Jahrzehnten,* ed. and intro. Grete Schaeder in consultation with Ernst Simon and in cooperation with Rafael Buber, Margot Cohn, and Gavriel Stern, Vol. III: 1938–1965 (Heidelberg: Verlag Lambert Schneider, 1975), #63. Bruno Balscheit to MB, September 1, 1943, p. 75; #64. Gideon Freudenberg to MB, October 15, 1943, p. 77; #72. MB to Hermann Hesse, September 16, 1945, pp. 90f.; #73. Leonhard Ragaz to MB, October 8, 1945, pp. 91f.; #74. MB to Hans Trüb, October 9, 1945, pp. 92–94; #75. Robert Weltsch to MB, Nürenberg, December 5, 1945, p. 96; #76. MB to Hans Trüb, December 20, 1945, pp. 96f.; #79. Albert Einstein to MB, January 29, 1946, pp. 98–100; #80. Eduard Strauss to MB, January 30, 1946, p. 101; #84. MB to Ludwig Binswanger, June 4, 1946, p. 103; #85. Martin Buber and Mosche Smilansky to the Commander in Chief of the British Armies in Palestine (General Sir Evelyn Barker), June 16, 1946, pp. 104f.; #91. MB to Hans Trüb, August 4, 1946, pp. 113f.; #105. Hugo Bergmann to MB, April 10, 1947, pp. 128f.; #107. David Werner Senator to MB, June 15, 1947, pp. 130–32; #108. MB to Judah Leib Magnes, July 1947, pp. 133–35; #119. MB to Arnold Zweig, November 8, 1947, p. 150; #120. Arnold Zweig to MB, November 16, 1947, p. 151; #127. MB to Ernst Simon, New York, January 27, 1948, pp. 160f.; #128. Ernest Simon to MB, New York, January 30, 1948, p. 162; #131. Judah L. Magnes to MB, February 1948, pp. 165–68; #136. MB to Hugo Bergmann, March 22, 1948, p. 174; #137. MB to Nahum N. Glatzer, April 7, 1948, p. 174; #139. MB to Lambert Schneider, July 26, 1948, pp. 176f.; #141. Eduard Strauss to MB, August 29, 1948, pp. 179f.

Buber, "Zion and the Other National Concepts" (1944), *Ner. Monthly for Political and Social Problems and for Jewish-Arab Rapprochement,* Vol. XV, No. 9–10 (1965), p. 3.

Buber, "Our Reply" in Martin Buber, Judah L. Magnes, and Ernst Simon, eds., *Towards Union in Palestine: Essays on Zionism and Jewish-Arab Cooperation* (Jerusalem: Ihud Association, 1945), pp. 33–36.

Walter B. Goldstein, *Martin Buber. Gespräche, Briefe, Worte* (Jerusalem: Rubin Mass Verlag, 1967), pp. 84, 131, 136–38.

Aubrey Hodes, *Martin Buber: An Intimate Portrait* (New York: The Viking Press, 1971), pp. 96–99.

Maurice S. Friedman, "Martin Buber: Prophet and Philosopher, *Faith Today,* December 1954–January 1955, pp. 39f.

Buber, *Two Types of Faith,* trans. Norman P. Goldhawk (New York: Harper Torchbooks, 1961), p. 15.

Coversation with Mrs. Judah Magnes in Jerusalem, Summer 1966.

Conversation with Gavriel Stern in Jerusalem, Spring 1966.

Conversation with Simon Shereshevski, M.D., in Jerusalem, Spring 1966.

Werner Kraft, *Gespräche mit Martin Buber* (Munich: Kosel Verlag, 1966), pp. 19, 145.

Buber, "Let Us Make an End to Falsities!" *Freeland,* Vol. V, No. 1 (January 1949), p. 3 (trans. from *Ba'ayot,* October 1, 1948).

Buber, *A Believing Humanism: Gleanings*, trans. with intro. and explanatory notes by Maurice Friedman (New York: Simon & Schuster, 1969), "November," p. 221. For the German original, see p. 220.

Albrecht Goes, "Der älte Vater aus Jersualem. Persönliche Begegnungen mit Martin Buber," III Program, Westdeutscher Rundfunk (Köln), September 29, 1962.

Richard Massie Graves, *Experiment in Anarchy* (London: Victor Gollancz, 1949). Graves was the mayor of Jerusalem from June 1947 to April 1948. "Mayor" equals chairman of the Jerusalem Municipal Corporation, appointed by the Secretary of State for the Colonies.

Georg Munk [Paula Buber], *Am lebendigen Wasser* (Wiesbaden: Insel Verlag, 1952), 659 pp.

Buber, *A Believing Humanism: Gleanings*, "The Unconscious," pp. 153–73.

SOURCES FOR CHAPTER 2
Biblical Judaism and Hasidic Tales

• ——————————————————————— •

Biblical Judaism

Letter from Martin Buber to Ronald Gregor Smith, #35. Talbiyeh, Jerusalem, July 9, 1949, Archives of Harvard University.

Buber, *Israel and the World*, "The Spirit of Israel and the World of Today," pp. 183–92; "The Gods of the Nations and God," pp. 195–213.

Buber, *Moses. The Revelation and the Covenant* (New York: Harper Torchbooks, 1958), pp. 16–18, 52f., 57–59, 61, 75–59, 88f., 127, 130f., 136, 144, 158, 188–90, 194.

Buber, "Samuel and Agag," *Meetings*, ed. with intro. and bibliography by Maurice Friedman (La Salle, Ill.: Open Court, 1973), pp. 52–54.

Buber Briefwechsel III, #118. Eduard Strauss to MB, October 28, 1947, p. 149; #151. Max Brod to MB, February 17, 1949, p. 189; #166. Rudolf Pannwitz to MB, August 7, 1949, p. 207; #223. Ewald Wasmuth to MB, March 1, 1951, p. 273; #405. Walter Kaufmann to MB, November 23, 1958, p. 471; #406. MB to Walter Kaufmann, December 7, 1958, pp. 472f.

Walter Goldstein, *Martin Buber. Gespräche, Briefe, Worte*, p. 116.

Paul Arthur Schilpp and Maurice Friedman, eds., *The Philosophy of Martin Buber*, Vol. XII, The Library of Living Philosophers (La Salle, Ill.: The Open Court Publishing Co., 1967), Max Brod, "Judaism and Christianity in the Work of Martin Buber," p. 319; James Muilenburg, "Buber as an Interpreter of the Bible," pp. 388–92.

Buber, *The Prophetic Faith*, trans. from the Hebrew by Carlyle Witton-Davies (New York: Harper Torchbooks, 1960), pp. 44f., 94, 102–104, 115f., 129, 144, 164f., 172, 177, 183, 193, 195f., 202, 217, 229, 232–34.

J. Coert Rylaarsdam, "The Prophetic Faith," *Theology Today*, Vol. VII (October 1950), pp. 399ff.

Jewish-Christian Dialogue

Schalom Ben-Chorin, *Zwiesprache mit Martin Buber,* pp. 84f., 87–92, 98.
Schalom Ben-Chorin, *Ich lebe in Jerusalem* (Munich: Paul List, 1972), p. 125.
Conversation with Schalom Ben-Chorin, Jerusalem, Spring 1966.
Briefwechsel III, #36. MB to Schalom Ben-Chorin, October 17, 1940, pp. 39f;
#37. Schalom Ben-Chorin to MB, October 17, 1940, pp. 40f.; #55.
Schalom Ben-Chorin to MB, November 20, 1942, pp. 64f.; and note 1 to
p. 64; #61. MB to Lina Lewy, February 4, 1943, p. 72; #66. Leonhard
Ragaz to MB, November 19, 1943, p. 82; #77. MB to Lina Lewy, Decem-
ber 24, 1945, p. 97.
Maurice Friedman, *Martin Buber: The Life of Dialogue,* 3rd ed. rev. (Chicago:
The University of Chicago Press, 1976), p. 279.
Buber, "Ragaz and 'Israel'" (Address at a Memorial for Ragaz in the Syna-
gogue Emet ve-Emuna, Jerusalem), *Neue Wege* (Zurich), Vol. XLI, No. 11
(November 1947), pp. 504–09.
Buber, "God's Word and Man's Interpretation," a letter to *The Palestine Post,*
April 8, 1946, p. 3.

Philosophy and Psychology

Briefwechsel III, #122. Hugo Bergmann to MB, December 1, 1947, p. 153;
#123. MB to Hugo Bergmann, December 14, 1947, pp. 154–56; #153.
MB to Walter Kaufmann, February 27, 1949, pp. 191f.; #167. Werner
Hollman to MB, August 30, 1949, pp. 208f.; #169. MB to Werner Holl-
mann, September 16, 1949; #195. MB to Ernst Michel, March 18, 1950,
p. 241; #94. MB to Hans Trüb, August 27, 1946, pp. 117–19; #95. MB
to Hans Trüb, September 9, 1946, p. 120; #170. MB to Ernst Michel,
September 23, 1949, pp. 211–13; #176. Ernst Michel to MB, October 22,
1949, pp. 221–23.
Buber, *A Believing Humanism: Gleanings,* "On the Situation of Philosophy,"
pp. 136f.

Personal and Literary

Briefwechsel III, #104. MB to Ernst Michel, March 3, 1947, p. 127; #110. MB
to Salman Schocken, Zurich, July 17, 1947, pp. 137–39; #109. Benjamin
Joseph Morse to MB, July 13, 1947, pp. 136f.; #112. MB To Benjamin
Joseph Morse, Parpan, July 26, 1947, p. 141; #113. Benjamin Joseph
Morse to MB, July 30, 1947, p. 142; #209. MB to Benjamin Joseph
Morse, July 13, 1950, pp. 256f.; #111. Lambert Schneider to MB, July
21, 1947, pp. 139f.; #117. MB to Hugo Bergmann, October 10, 1947,
pp. 147f.; #118. Eduard Strauss to MB, October 28, 1947, pp. 148f.;
#124. Kurt Singer to MB, January 12, 1948, p. 157; #125. Nahum N.
Glatzer to MB, January 22, 1948, p. 158; #126. Hugo Bergmann to MB,
January 26, 1948, pp. 159f., #163. MB to Bernard Rang, June 27, 1949,
pp. 202f.; #164. MB to Max Brod, July 1949, pp. 203f.

Buber, "Advice to Frequenters of Libraries," *Books for Your Vacation, Branch Library Book News,* The New York Public Library, Vol. XXI, No. 5 (May 1944), pp. 81f.

Buber, *Pointing the Way: Collected Essays,* trans. with intro. by Maurice Friedman (New York: Harper & Bros., 1957), "Books and Men," pp. 3f. Also in "Autobiographical Fragments" and *Meetings.* "Books and Men" was originally printed by Tschudy Verlag, St. Gallen, Switzerland, in 1947.

Buber, *Pointing the Way,* "Books and Men," pp. 3f.

Tales of the Hasidim and *The Way of Man*

Buber, *Tales of the Hasidim. The Early Masters,* trans. Olga Marx (New York: Schocken Books, 1947, 1970), Preface, pp. 5–12, Introduction, pp. 1–34.

Buber, *Tales of the Hasidim. The Later Masters,* trans. Olga Marx (New York: Schocken Books, 1948, 1970), Introduction, pp. 7–46.

The story about Kazantzakis I heard at a lecture of Professor Arnold Band of the University of California at Los Angeles.

Buber, *Die Erzählungen der Chassidim. Manesse-Bibliothek der Weltliteratur* (Zurich: Manesse-Verlag, 1950).

Buber, *A Believing Humanism: Gleanings,* "Do You Still Know It? . . ." p. 51. See p. 50 for German original.

Hermann Hesse, *Briefe,* Vol. III of *Gesammelte Werke* (Berlin: Suhrkamp Verlag, 1951), pp. 266, 324ff.

Briefwechsel III, #180. MB to Herman Hesse, November 22, 1949, p. 225; #181. Hermann Hesse to MB, end of November 1949, p. 226; #183. Rudolf Pannwitz to MB, December 3, 1949, p. 228.

Maurice Friedman, "Tales of the Hasidim, The Early Masters and The Later Masters," *Religious Education* (November–December 1961).

Walter Kaufmann, "Martin Buber's Religious Significance," in Paul Arthur Schilpp and Maurice Friedman, eds., *The Philosophy of Martin Buber,* pp. 678–81.

Martin Buber, *The Way of Man, according to the Teachings of Hasidism* (Secaucus, N.J.: Citadel Press, 1966). Also Book IV of Buber, *Hasidism and Modern Man* (New York: Harper Torchbooks, 1966) and in Walter Kaufmann, *Religion from Tolstoy to Camus* (New York: Harper Torchbooks, 1964).

Briefwechsel III, #145. Hermann Hesse to MB, October 18, 1948, p. 184.

Schalom Ben-Chorin, *Zwiesprache mit Martin Buber,* p. 44.

Buber, *The Origin and Meaning of Hasidism,* ed. and trans. with an intro. by Maurice Friedman (New York: Horizon Press, 1972), "Author's Foreword," p. 22.

Conversation with Moshe Klebanoff, Jerusalem, Israel, 1966.

Gershom Scholem, *The Messianic Idea in Judaism. And Other Essays in Jewish Spirituality,* trans. Michael A. Meyer (New York: Schocken Books, 1971), "Martin Buber's Interpretation of Hasidism," p. 231.

SOURCES FOR CHAPTER 3
Kibbutz Socialism and Adult Education in Israel

•————————————————————————————•

Paths in Utopia and Kibbutz Socialism

Maurice Friedman, *Martin Buber: The Life of Dialogue*, Chap. 23, "Social Philosophy," pp. 208–22.

Letter from Professor S. H. Frankel, The Knoll House, Ninksey Hill, Oxford, England, to MB, March 3, 1950; letter from MB to S. H. Frankel, March 13, 1950, Martin Buber Files of the Hebrew University Archives, Jerusalem.

Heinz-Joachim Heydorn, "Martin Buber und der Sozialismus," *Gewerkschaftliche Monatshefte*, Vol. IV, No. 12 (December 1953), pp. 705–09.

Buber, *Paths in Utopia*, trans. R. F. C. Hull, Introduction by Ephraim Fischoff (Boston: Beacon Paperback, 1958), Chap. I, "In the Midst of Crisis"; Epilogue, "An Experiment That Did Not Fail."

Buber, *A Believing Humanism: Gleanings*, "Community and Environment," pp. 93–95.

Conversation with Menachem Gerson, Kibbutz Hazorea, Israel, Spring 1966.

Buber, *Am v'Olam* (Hebrew), "Ideas on National and Pioneer Training" (1940), trans. for me by Uri Margolin.

Buber, "Social Experiments in Jewish Palestine," *The New Palestine*, Vol. XXXV, No. 1 (October 13, 1944), pp. 14f.

Buber, "Character Change and Social Experiment in Israel," ed. Maurice Friedman, in Moshe Davis, *Israel, Its Role in Civilization* (New York: Seminary Israel Institute, 1956), pp. 204–13.

Buber Briefwechsel III, #62. Elasar Halivni to Paula and Martin Buber, Ramat Jochanan, May 1, 1943, pp. 73–75; #64. Gideon Freudenberg to MB, Culture Commission Nahalal, October 15, 1943, pp. 76f. and note 4, pp. 77f.; #188. MB to Lambert Schneider, January 12, 1950, p. 233.

Adult Education in Israel

"Adult Education through the Hebrew University," 8-pp. pamphlet printed in Jerusalem, Israel.

Briefwechsel III, #116. MB to David Werner Senator, September 7, 1947, pp. 145–47; #140. Nathan Rotenstreich to MB, August 2, 1948, pp. 177–79.

Buber, *Am v'Olam* (Hebrew), "Adult Education" (1950), trans. for me by Uri Margolin. See especially the last two sections of this long essay—"Adult Education in Israel" and "Beth Midrash l'Morei Am."

Buber, "The Principle of Dialogue in Education," in Kalman Yaron, ed., *Lifelong Education in Israel*. Prepared for the Third World Conference on Adult Education, Tokyo, July 1972, The Public Advisory Council on Adult Education to the Ministry of Education and Culture, The Adult Education Association of Israel, The Israel National Commission for Unesco, 1972. Copies available from The Adult Education Association of Israel, 12 Ben-Yehuda Street, Jerusalem, Israel.

Buber, "A New Venture in Adult Education," *The Hebrew University of Jerusalem,* Semi-Jubilee Volume (Jerusalem: The Hebrew University, April 1950), pp. 115–19.

Buber, "Erwachsenentbildung," *Festschrift der Nueva Communidad Israelita 5700–5710,* ed. Rabbi Hans Harf and Dr. Hardi Swarensky (Buenos Aires, 1949), pp. 77–81.

Buber, "Adult Education in Israel," ed. Maurice Friedman, *The Torch,* publication of The National Federation of Jewish Men's Clubs (Philadelphia), Vol. XI, No. 3 (Spring 1952), pp. 7–10, 59.

Conversation with Professor Gideon Freudenberg, Jerusalem, 1966.

Ernst Simon, "Martin Buber. Educator of the People" (Hebrew), Lecture at a meeting of the members of the Association for Adult Education in Israel at the Hebrew University, Jerusalem, June 7, 1966, trans. for me by Uri Margolin.

"Martin Buber Zentrum für Erwachsenentbildung," *Scopus. Zeitschrift der Gesellschaften der Freunde der Hebräischen Universität Jerusalem,* Vol. I, No. 1 (1965), pp. 18f.

Conversations with Dr. Kalman Yaron, Jerusalem, 1966 and 1978.

NOTE TO CHAPTER 4
Two Types of Faith: Jesus and Paul

If we did not know of the longstanding personal dialogue between Buber and the great Protestant Neo-Orthodox theologian Emil Brunner, we might regard Brunner's response to *Two Types of Faith* as a "lonely dialogue." In the third volume of his *Dogmatics* Brunner wrote: "Since Buber adduces his arguments in a thoroughly original, disinterested manner which is also the result of a penetrating and scholarly investigation of the Bible, one would have expected that Christian theology would have seriously taken up the challenge of his book." Brunner felt that he, at least, should meet this challenge not only because no one else had but also because through Buber's teaching about the two dimensions of I-Thou and I-It, "he has performed a tremendous service to theology, which Karl Heim was the first to appreciate as a 'Copernican Revolution.'"

Brunner devoted a long section to *Two Types of Faith* in his *Dogmatics,* presenting in expanded form what he had said in his essay in *The Philosophy of Martin Buber,* to which Buber did not even refer in his "Replies to My Critics." In neither book did Brunner himself even mention Buber's impassioned attack on his understanding of Christ as "the Mediator." But in both he went as far as he could, starting from his own ground, to meet and understand Buber's position. He perceptively outlined a threefold purpose for *Two Types of Faith,* a "relatively small book, weighty in its exegetical insight and in the author's great knowledge in the field of comparative religion." The first two—clarifying the religious message of Judaism and illuminating the message of the Jesus of history as a phenomenon belonging to this same Jewish biblical world—Buber fulfilled in such a way that "the open-minded Christian reader can only be thankful," including the readiness to acknowledge that which makes Jesus tower above his contemporaries and to concede to Jesus an undefinable uniqueness. The third purpose—"to demonstrate that the theology of the apostles, particularly that of Paul, is separate from the preceding two by an unbridgeable chasm"—is what Brunner engaged himself with at length in both books. "With this third aspect Buber succeeds in such a superbly impressive manner" that an open-minded Christian reader might find the Gnostic-Hellenistic theologies of Paul and John that Buber pieces together totally alien to the biblical personalist conception of faith.

> Although Buber, in the preface to his book, declares that both apologetics as well as polemics are entirely foreign to his intentions—and anyone who knows him will not question his word—his presentation of Pauline theology is so convincing that, without or even against the author's will, the book turns out to be a major attack on Christianity.

In his response to this "attack," Brunner reproached Buber "for the fact that, in his presentation of Jewish faith, he leaves the factor of historical revelation almost wholly out of consideration." This statement, totally incomprehensible in the context of Buber's own presentation of biblical Judaism, becomes comprehensible in the light of Brunner's own understanding of revelation in the New Testament: "To recognize the life of Jesus, and more particularly his death on the cross, as God's self-revelation and in it to know oneself as judged and as graciously pardoned—this is faith as Paul and the other apostles . . . understand it." "To believe that" is not a Hellenistic proposition for Brunner "but an aspect of an indivisible act in which man opens himself to the self-communication of God." But this is a faith, according to Brunner, which "only he who knows himself to be a sinner can understand in trust of obedience as God's self-communication."

Here, as Brunner rightly thought, is his real divergence from Buber. Recalling a conversation about sin in the home of the psychiatrist Viktor von Weizsäcker in the late 1920s, when he first met Buber in person, Brunner reported that Buber "opposed sharply the New Testament concept, above all, the Pauline concept of sin, because he saw in this a slur cast upon man's responsibility to himself and his freedom." It is hard not to see what Brunner then states as predominantly *pistis*, even if it is filled with *emunah:* "Here the decision is made, whether one can believe in Christ, accept Him and His reconciliation as the Word of God." The same is true of Brunner's contention that the suffering servant of Deutero-Isaiah cannot really be understood except through a "Christological interpretation of the Old Testament." "What the prophet only promises in the enigmatic word about the Servant of God . . . is now fulfilled." The New Covenant of forgiveness "*has* been concluded because the Servant of God has appeared who 'bears the sins of many.'" This faith Brunner sees not as a "faith that" something is the case but as an "existential happening, an identification with the Crucified in which man accepts the condemnation and gives himself over to death, giving Christ our sin and receiving from Him His righteousness, the sonship of God, as a gift bestowed upon us." In the whole of Scripture, conversion means the turning away of a man from the previous way of living of his own choosing and a turning to the will and way of God. Now the prophetic call for turning is radicalized and universalized and this means, for Brunner and other Neo-Orthodox theologians, a reworking of Buber's I-Thou relationship into a Thou-I one in which *God* always initiates and man responds *only* after receiving grace. It also means for them a choice *between* "I" and "Thou" in which the self must be given up for the sake of God.

Brunner quite rightly described this decision of faith between I or Thou as one in which "the dialogical relation at the same time comes to its fulfillment and loses its character as dialogue." "Only the man who has been set free from self-centeredness of sinful man can 'live freedom,' the man who possesses it not in his 'ego' but in the 'Thou' of God. This is a freedom which we do not choose because it is bestowed upon us by the grace of the Holy Spirit. The only real freedom . . . is freedom from self." To Brunner, indeed, this ending of the real mutuality of dialogue by daring to go out of one's self is the real meaning of biblical trust which "the Old Testament always intended but could never fully attain." Although he pointed to his own book *Wahrheit als Begegnung* (Truth as Meeting, translated as *The Divine-Human Encounter*) as carrying on the battle, of which Buber was the leader, "to differentiate the relationship with God, as one of an I-Thou relation, from every abstract, material It-relationship, and to understand . . . the necessity of responding to God's call," Brunner did not mean "meeting" in Buber's quite concrete, fully human, mutual sense of the term. In an either/or that Buber would regard as entirely false, Brunner saw the Old Testament believer as focusing on the rightness of his trust in contrast to the New Testament believer whose "total confidence depends solely upon the gracious promise of God." For Buber reality was not *in* man or *in* God but *between* them, and it is just this *betweenness* that gets lost in even the most sympathetic Neo-Orthodox version of the I-Thou relationship.

In 1962 Buber wrote to a teacher of religious philosophy that how a Christian related to *Two Types of Faith* was not his affair:

> It has not been inwardly possible for me to respond to the section that Emil Brunner devoted to my book in his *Dogmatik* and just as little to the writing of Urs von Balthasar. As basically different as their standpoints are, I still feel in all of them, even where I am actively interested, one thing, that it is not I who am here addressed, although I am obliged to follow with the greatest attention the process that has here begun.

In December 1953, Brunner wrote Buber from Tokyo thanking him for sending him *Hinweise (Pointing the Way)* and telling him that he had brought all Buber's books that he owned with him to the International Christian University, where he was spending his last years on the missionary front teaching "Christian Ethics and Philosophy" rather than theology. "The decision was not easy, but I do not doubt that it was the right one. I send you a heartfelt greeting from the other end of the continent of Asia and remain always bound to you in grateful friendship."

In *Philosophical Interrogations* the French philosopher Maurice Nédoncelle asked Buber whether he still held to his distinction between "the *emunah* of the Jews and the *pistis* of the Christians": and whether he held "that the notion

of the chosen people suffices for the obedience of the believing Israelite."
Buber responded that it was wholly alien to him to accept the notion of the
chosen people as "sufficient for the obedience of the believing Israelite": for
to him the relationship of Israel to God was only the *origin* and not the essence
of the relation of the believing Jew to God. "The great trust, as for example it
is expressed with unconditional clarity in Psalm 73, is a *personal* trust of the
person as such." That personal trust was decisive for Buber, although "it ever
again evolves out of the experience and hope of Israel."

SOURCES FOR CHAPTER 4 AND FOR NOTE TO CHAPTER 4

Two Types of Faith: Jesus and Paul

•───────────────────────────────────────•

Karl Thieme, ed., *Freiburger Rundbrief zur Förderung der Freundschaft zwischen
dem alten und dem neuen Gottesvolk—im Geiste der Beiden Testamente,* Vol. II
(1949/1950), No. 5/6 (December 1949), p. 10. "Aussprache und Echo:
Ein Briefwechsel mit Martin Buber," pp. 20–23.

Karl Thieme, "Zwei Glaubensweisen," *Freiburger Rundbrief,* Vol. III (1950/
1951), No. 10/11 (January 1951), pp. 20–23.

Willehad Paul Eckert, "Zwei Glaubensweisen. Frage und Versuch einer Ant-
wort," in W. P. Eckert and E. L. Ehrlich, eds., *Judenhass—Schuld der
Christen?! Versuch eines Gesprächs.* In Memory of Karl Thieme (Essen:
Hans Driewer Verlag, 1964), pp. 439–56.

Buber Briefwechsel III, #158. MB to Karl Thieme, March 23, 1949, p. 196;
#159. MB to Rudolph Bultmann, May 4, 1949, p. 196; #160. Hugo
Bergmann to MB, May 30, 1949, pp. 197–99; #161. MB to Karl Thieme,
June 12, 1949, p. 200 and note to p. 200; #162. MB to Karl Thieme,
June 25, 1949, pp. 201f.; #173. MB to Karl Thieme, October 10, 1949,
pp. 215f.; #175. Karl Thieme to MB, October 15, 1949, pp. 217–21;
#224. Albert Schweitzer to MB, Lambaréné, April 4, 1951, pp. 274–76;
#242. Eugen Rosenstock-Huessy to MB, December 25, 1951, pp. 298f.;
#330. MB to Karl Heinrich Rengstorf, July 7, 1955, pp. 394f.; #269.
Hermann Maas to MB, February 1953, pp. 233f., 665; #293. Emil Brun-
ner to MB, December 20, 1953, p. 356; #480. MB to Manfred Beyer,
April 4, 1962, p. 544. See also #381. MB to Hans Paeschke, January 4,
1958, p. 446.

Buber, *Two Types of Faith,* trans. Norman P. Goldhawk (New York: Harper
Torchbooks, 1961).

Werner Kraft, *Gespräche mit Martin Buber,* p. 48, and note p. 152.

Ernst Simon, "Martin Buber and Judaism" (Hebrew), *Iyyun* (1958).

Schalom Ben-Chorin, *Zwiesprache mit Martin Buber,* pp. 82, 150, 181, 201f.,
223–25.

Franz Freiherr von Hammerstein, *Das Messias Problem bei Martin Buber. Studia
Delitzschiana. Abhandlungen und Texte aus dem Institutum Delitzschianum*
(Münster), Vol. I (Stuttgart: W. Kohlhammer Verlag, 1958), pp. 58–64.

Paul Arthur Schilpp and Maurice Friedman, eds., *The Philosophy of Martin Buber,* Emil Brunner, "Judaism and Christianity in Buber," pp. 311–17; Max Brod, "Judaism and Christianity in the Work of Martin Buber," pp. 326–40; Nahum N. Glatzer, "Buber as an Interpreter of the Bible," pp. 375, 379f.; James Muilenburg, "Buber as an Interpreter of the Bible," pp. 382, 402; Buber, "Replies to My Critics," pp. 702–05.

Emil Brunner, *The Christian Doctrine of the Church, Faith and the Consummation. Dogmatics,* Vol. III (London: Lutterworth Press, 1962), pp. 159–289.

Maurice Friedman, *Martin Buber: The Life of Dialogue,* Chap. 27, "Buber and Christianity," pp. 268–80.

Sydney and Beatrice Rome, eds., *Philosophical Interrogations* (New York: Harper Torchbooks, 1970), "Martin Buber," Section, conducted and with Buber's replies trans. Maurice Friedman, pp. 108f.

Letter from Martin Buber to Maurice Friedman, February 19, 1959.

Gerard S. Sloyan, "Buber and the Significance of Jesus," in *The Bridge. A Yearbook of Judaeo-Christian Studies,* ed. John M. Oesterreicher, Vol. III (New York: Pantheon Books, 1958), pp. 209–33.

Rudolf Pannwitz, "Der Chassidismus," *Merkur* (Munich), Vol. VIII, No. 9–79 (September 1954), pp. 810–30.

Buber, *The Origin and Meaning of Hasidism,* ed. and trans. with an Introduction by Maurice Friedman (New York: Horizon Press [paperback], 1972), Chap. 9, "Supplement: Christ, Hasidism, Gnosis." For original of Buber's reply to Pannwitz, see Buber, "Christus, Chassidismus, Gnosis. Einige Bemerkungen," *Merkur,* Vol. VIII, No. 90 (October 1954).

Rudolf Pannwitz, "Mythos, Gnosis, Religion" (Pannwitz's reply to Buber's reply), *Merkur,* Vol. VIII, No. 11–81 (November 1954), pp. 1068–71.

Buber, *Between Man and Man,* "Afterword: The History of the Dialogical Principle," trans. Maurice Friedman, pp. 223f.

NOTE TO CHAPTER 5

•————————————————————————•

In my "Critical Reader," *The Worlds of Existentialism,* I published eight pages of translations from Schneeberger's *Nachlese zu Heidegger,* not to point out that Heidegger was an active Nazi, but to examine the question whether, as many claim, Heidegger's political activities have no bearing on the meaning and value of his philosophy:

> An existentialist philosopher who is concerned about authenticating his philosophy in his existence cannot fail to raise a question in our minds when he lends his life, thought, and work to such a movement as Nazism. . . . We cannot fail to be struck in reading these selections by the integral relationship between Heidegger's Nazi terminology and his existentialist philosophy, particularly that of his later thought about Being. Nor can we fail to ask how Heidegger, whose central emphasis in *Being and Time* is on one's ownmost possibilities which must be realized in opposition to all tendencies to fall into

the anonymity of the They, could have lent his thought to a totalitarianism that swallowed up and destroyed the unique individual in a way more terrible than any other in history.*

Even Abraham J. Heschel, who was the least given to defamation of any person I have known, told me in 1965 that Heidegger had recently said to a friend of Heschel that it was too bad that some of the Jewish professors had managed to escape and not been exterminated by the Nazis!

SOURCES FOR CHAPTER 5
Postwar Germany and the Peace Prize

Buber Briefwechsel III, #87. Adolf Sindler to MB, June 30, 1946, pp. 107–09; #89. MB to Adolf Sindler, July 19, 1946, pp. 109–11; #88. Ernst Michel to MB, July 15, 1946, p. 109; #98. Ernst Michel to MB, September 21, 1946, pp. 122f.; #99. MB to Josef Minn, September 23, 1946, pp. 123f.; #106. MB to Hans Trüb, Copenhagen, June 13, 1947, pp. 129f.; #139. MB to Lambert Schneider, July 26, 1948, p. 177; #194. Karl Heinrich Rengstorf to MB, March 11, 1950, p. 240; #201.MB to Alfred Döblin, April 26, 1950, p. 248; #202. MB to Alfred Döblin, April 26, 1950, pp. 248f; #204. Alfred Döblin to MB, May 4, 1950, p. 250; #206. Karl Heinrich Rengstorf to MB, May 20, 1950, pp. 252f.; #208. Karl Heinrich Rengstorf to MB, July 10, 1950, pp. 255f.; #212. MB to Karl Heinrich Rengstorf, August 20, 1950, pp. 259f.; #218. Karl Thieme to MB, January 20, 1951, p. 267; #219. Viktor von Weizsäcker to MB, January 26, 1951, p. 269; #220. Elisabeth Rotten to MB, January 26, 1951, p. 270; #222. Joachim Jeremias to MB, February 17, 1951, p. 272; #228. MB to Karl Heinrich Rengstorf, April 22, 1951, p. 278; #234. MB to Hans Carossa, July 6, 1951, pp. 286f.; #240. Bruno Snell to MB, December 7, 1951, p. 297; #241. MB to Bruno Snell, New York, December 22, 1951, p. 298; #243. Karl Heinrich Rengstorf to MB, December 30, 1951; #244. Karl Heinrich Rengstorf to MB, January 5, 1952, pp. 301f.; #248. MB to Karl Heinrich Rengstorf, January 18, 1952, p. 300; #249. David Werner Senator to MB, January 19, 1952, pp. 308f.; #250. MB to Bruno Snell, Los Angeles, January 25, 1952, p. 310; #254. Lambert Schneider to MB, March 10, 1952, p. 314; #262. MB to Romano Guardini, December 12, 1952, p. 323; #273. Bruno Snell to MB, February 13, 1953, pp. 336f.; #271. Hans Blüher to MB, February 8, 1953, p. 335; #275. MB to Hans Blüher, March 13, 1953, pp. 337–40; #307. Hans Blüher to MB, April 3, 1954, pp. 369–73; #308. MB to Hans Blüher, April 3, 1954, pp. 373–75; #323. Hans Blüher to MB, December 20, 1954, pp. 387f.; #325. MB to Hans Blüher, January 19, 1955, pp. 389f.; #279. Erich

---

*Maurice Friedman, "The Meeting-Point between Heidegger's Nazism and His Existentialism," in Part VII, "Issues and Conclusions," of *The Worlds of Existentialism*, ed. Maurice Friedman, pp. 525f.

Lüth to MB, June 3, 1953, pp. 344f.; #280. MB to Albrecht Goes, June 6, 1953, p. 345; #282. Arthur Georgi to MB, June 17, 1953, pp. 346f. and 347, note 3; #283. MB to Arthur Georgi, June 20, 1953, p. 348; #289. Albert Dann to MB, October 5, 1953, pp. 352f.; #297. MB to Albert Dann, December 27, 1953; #291. Olympia von Weizsäcker to MB, December 8, 1953, p. 355; #292. MB to Olympia von Weizsäcker, December 16, 1953, pp. 355f.; #296. MB to Lambert Schneider, December 27, 1953, p. 358; #298. Fritz Kaufmann to MB, January 2, 1954, p. 361; #300. Erich Weniger to MB, January 11, 1954, pp. 363f. and p. 364, note 2; #319. Oskar Hammeslbeck to MB, October 17, 1954, pp. 384f.; #320. MB to Albrecht Goes, October 19, 1954, p. 385; #321. Albrecht Goes to MB, November 6, 1954, p. 386 and note 1, p. 386; #322. Romano Guardini to MB, November 10, 1954, p. 387; #336. Albrecht Goes to MB, August 28, 1955, p. 399; #440. Der Geschäftsführer der Gesellschaft für christlich-jüdische Zusammenarbeit Darmstadt an MB, July 11, 1960, pp. 506f.; #442. MB to die Gesellschaft für christlich-jüdische Zusammenarbeit Darmstadt, Wenger, August 7, 1960, p. 508; #382. Theodor Heuss to MB, January 24, 1958, pp. 447–49; #386. MB to Theodor Heuss [undated], p. 453; #548. Hans A. Fischer-Barnicol to MB, November 3, 1964, pp. 623–26 and note 10, p. 626.

E. William Rollins and Harry Zohn, eds., *Men of Dialogue*, Albrecht Goes, "Martin Buber, Our Support," pp. 12–19; Albrecht Goes, "The 'Patriarch' from Jerusalem" (1962), pp. 204–14.

Buber Briefwechsel, Vol. I: 1897–1918, intro. by Ernst Simon and a biographical sketch as intro. by Grete Schaeder (Heidelberg: Verlag Lambert Schneider, 1972), Grete Schaeder, "Ein biographischer Abriss," p. 57.

Buber, *The Knowledge of Man: A Philosophy of the Interhuman*, ed. with an Introductory Essay (Chap. 1) by Maurice Friedman (London: George Allen & Unwin, 1965; New York: Harper & Row and Harper Torchbooks, 1966), "Guilt and Guilt Feelings," trans. Maurice Friedman, p. 126.

Buber, "Nachtrag zu einem Gespräch," *Die neue Zeitung*, No. 44 (February 21, 1951), p. 7.

Paul Arthur Schilpp and Maurice Friedman, eds., *The Philosophy of Martin Buber*, Buber, "Replies to My Critics," trans. Maurice Friedman, pp. 720f.

Konstantin Prinz von Bayern, *Die grossen Namen. Begegnungen mit bedeutenden Deutschen unserer Zeit* (Munich: Kindler Verlag, 1956), "Martin Buber," pp. 75–84.

Fritz Bartsch, "Kommentar über die Friedensrede Professor Bubers und ihre ersten Auswirkungen," October 3, 1953, Hessischer Rundfunk, Frankfurt am Main.

Shmuel Hugo Bergmann, "Sentinel of Mankind. One Year after the Death of Martin Buber," radio address on Kol Yisrael and in *Jerusalem Post*, June 14, 1965.

"Buber Explains Why He Accepted Prize," *Jerusalem Post*, January 1, 1952.

The Worlds of Existentialism: A Critical Reader, ed. with Introductions and a Conclusion by Maurice Friedman (Chicago: The University of Chicago Press Phoenix Books, 1973), pp. 527–35.

Nachlese zu Heidegger. Dokumente zu seinem Leben und Denken (Bern: 1962), ed. and privately printed by Dr. Guido Schneeberger, Hochfeldstrasse 88, Bern, Switzerland. $2.75 (mailing costs included).

Werner Kraft, *Gespräche mit Martin Buber,* pp. 26f., 146 note, 90, 96.

Buber, *Eclipse of God. Studies in the Relation Between Religion and Philosophy,* trans. Maurice Friedman, et al. (New York: Harper Torchbooks, 1957), "Religion and Modern Thinking," pp. 76f.

Buber, *Pointing the Way,* "Genuine Dialogue and the Possibilities of Peace" (1953), pp. 232–34.

Martin Buber; Fünf Ansprachen anlässlich der Verleihung des Friedenspreises des deutschen Buchhandels (Frankfurt a. M.: Börsenverein deutscher Verlager und Buchhändlerverbände, 1953).

"Ewige Feindschaft? Hans Klee und Martin Buber über das Verhältnis zwischen Juden und Deutschen," *Freiburger Rundbrief,* Vol. VII, 1954/1955 (September 1954, No. 25/28), 7. Rundschau 7.10), pp. 46, pp. 1–6. Taken from *Mitteilungsblatt des Irgun olej Merkas Europa* (Tel Aviv), No. 23 (June 4, 1954), pp. 46f. Title supplied by *Freiburger Rundbrief.* The quotation from Buber, "Geltung und Grenze des politischen Prinzips" is slightly different from the version I translated for *Pointing the Way,* "The Validity and Limitation of the Political Principle," p. 217, no doubt corresponding to the way Buber actually gave the lecture in Heidelberg at the time of receiving the Goethe Prize.

Buber, "Geltung und Grenze des politischen Prinzips" in *Gedenkschrift zur Verleihung des Hansischen Goethe-Preises 1951 der gemeinnützigen Stiftung F.V.S. zu Hamburg an M.B., überreicht am 24. Juni 1953.*

Friedrich Hielscher, Fünfzig Jahre unter Deutschen (Hamburg: Rowohlt Verlag, 1954), pp. 222, 231–33.

Buber, *Tales of the Hasidim. The Early Masters,* p. 276.

"Aus Erster Hand," conversation between Martin Buber and Thilo Koch, Nord- und Westdeutscher Rundfunkverband-Fernsehen-Hamburg-Lokstedt, May 25, 1959.

"Ein Nachmittag bei Martin Buber," *Deutsch-Israelische Studiengruppe an der kirchlichen Hochschule Berlin. Notiz einer Studienfahrt durch Israel.* Fall 1960.

Paul Schallück, "Moses Mendelssohn und die deutsche Aufklärung," in Thilo Koch, ed., *Porträts deutsch-jüdischer Geistesgeschichte* (Köln: Verlag M. Dumont Schauberg, 1961), p. 35f.

Heinz Kremers (Kettwig/Ruhr), "Das Verhältnis Deutschlands zu Israel," in *Kirche, Kinder, Zeit, Evangelische Kirchenzeitung* (Düsseldorf), Vol. XVI, No. 12 (December 1961), p. 461.

Paul Rohrig, "Der Bergriff der Verantwortung bei Martin Buber. Ein Versuch über die Situation des Gespräches," in Willehad Paul Eckert and E. L. Ehrlich, *Judenhass—Schuld der Christen?! Versuch eines Gesprächs* (Essen: Hans Driewer Verlag, 1964), pp. 475–77.

Hans Kohn, "Martin Buber Achtzigjährig," *Deutsche Rundschau,* Vol. LXXXIIII, No. 2 (February 1958), pp. 158–61.

Letters from Martin Buber to Maurice Friedman (all in English, in my personal possession with Xerox copies in the Martin Buber Archives of the National and Hebrew University Library, Jerusalem), Jerusalem, December 10, 1953; May 14, 1954; August 8, 1957.

Aubrey Hodes, *Martin Buber: An Intimate Portrait* (New York: The Viking Press, 1971), p. 111.

Buber, *A Believing Humanism: Gleanings,* "Greeting and Welcome" (1960), pp. 215f.

Letter from Margarete Exler to Maurice Friedman, Ludwigstrasse 16, 6148 Heppenheim/Bergstrasse, March 28, 1978.

NOTE TO CHAPTER 6

First Visit to America: *Eclipse of God*

• ——————————————————————————— •

Buber asked me for a copy of a letter from Professor Arnold Bergstraesser to me, and later told me that he had received an extraordinary letter from Bergstraesser, one which I have been unable to locate in the Buber Archives but which I believe to be concerned with Bergstraesser's own concern for his guilt in the Nazi Germany which he left almost at the same time as Buber. Once when Buber's wife Paula rode a train in Germany, some German students who belonged to the Tat-Kreis (the Action Circle) spoke to one another of Bergstraesser, their professor from whom they hoped for great things. Bergstraesser returned to Germany for the last years of his life, where he established the unknown American discipline of "Political Science" and occupied such an important place at the University of Heidelberg that he marched before Heidegger at the celebration on the university's millennium. He became active in politics but not decisively. I last saw him, two years before his death, at a reception for Buber after Buber's lecture at the University of Munich in 1960. Ten years before, when I had finished my dissertation on Buber, Bergstraesser, whom I thought of as tremendously cultured but not as religious, astonished me by asking, "Do you know Buber's secret? It is prayer." By this Bergstraesser did not mean that Buber spent so many hours a day praying, but that he brought himself every hour of his life in real openness.

SOURCES FOR CHAPTER 6

First Visit to America: *Eclipse of God*

• ——————————————————————————— •

Buber Briefwechsel III, #127. MB to Ernst Simon, January 27, 1948, p. 161; #147. MB to Louis Finkelstein, December 6, 1948, p. 186; #155. MB to Louis Finkelstein, March 8, 1949, p. 193; Maurice Friedman to MB, St. Louis, March 19, 1950, pp. 241–44 (all the correspondence between Buber and me was conducted in English but is here printed in German translation); #199. MB to Maurice Friedman, April 6, 1950, pp. 246f.; #207. MB to Ernst Szilagyi, July 2, 1950, pp. 253–55. #210. MB to Maurice Friedman, August 4, 1950, p. 258; #211. MB to Maurice Friedman, August 23, 1950, p. 260; #215. Maurice Friedman to MB, September 9, 1950, pp. 261–64; #231. MB to Maurice Friedman, May 3, 1951, pp. 281f.; #236. MB to Maurice Friedman, August 11, 1951, pp. 289–94; #237. MB to Maurice Friedman, September 17, 1951, p. 294; #252. MB to Albert Camus, p. 312; #253. Albert Camus to MB, Paris, February 22, 1952, p. 313; #255. MB to Maurice Friedman, Los Angeles, March 22, 1952, pp. 314–16; #267. MB to Kurt Singer, February 1, 1953, p. 331; #344. MB to Rudolf Kayser, January 28, 1956, p. 405; #347. Rudolf Kayser to MB, February 15, 1956, p. 407 and note 3; #322. MB to Kurt Singer, July 22, 1944, pp. 396f.

Letters from Martin Buber to Maurice Friedman (all in English, in my possession and with Xerox copies in the Martin Buber Archives in the Hebrew and National University Library, Jerusalem): April 6, 1950; August 20, 1950; August 23, 1950; October 14, 1950; Zurich, November 16, 1950; Zurich, December 22, 1950; Glasgow, Scotland, February 17, 1951; London, March 1, 1951; Rome, March 30, 1951; April 19, 1951; Heidelberg, July 23, 1951; August 8, 1951; September 7, 1951; September 10, 1951; September 17, 1951; September 20, 1951; September 25, 1951; October 5, 1951; October 14, 1951; Los Angeles, January 11, 1952; January 24, 1952; January 25, 1952; January 31, 1952; February 1, 1952; February 9, 1952; February 18, 1952; February 23, 1952; March 1, 1952; March 2, 1952; March 12, 1952; March 16, 1952; March 18, 1952; March 22, 1952; Zurich, May 5, 1952; Zurich, May 8, 1952; Munich, May 18, 1952; Munich, May 19, 1952; Zurich, June 1, 1952; Venice, June 6, 1952; Jerusalem, June 18, 1952; June 27, 1952; July 2, 1952; July 18, 1952; July 23, 1952; August 5, 1952.

Buber, *Eclipse of God. Studies in the Relation between Religion and Philosophy* (New York: Harper Torchbooks, 1952), Chap. 2, "Religion and Reality"; Chap. 3, "Religion and Philosophy," trans. Maurice Friedman, pp. 27–46; Chap. 5, "Religion and Modern Thinking," trans. Maurice Friedman, pp. 63–78; Chap. 7, "On the Suspension of the Ethical," trans. Maurice Friedman, pp. 113–20; Chap. 8, "God and the Spirit of Man," trans. Maurice Friedman, pp. 121–30; Notes to Chapter 5, pp. 141f.

Buber, *On Judaism,* ed. Nahum N. Glatzer (New York: Schocken Books, 1967), "Judaism and Civilization," pp. 191–201; "The Silent Question," pp. 202–13; "The Dialogue between Heaven and Earth," pp. 214–25.

Buber, *I and Thou,* 2d rev. ed. with a Postscript by the author added, trans. Ronald Gregor Smith (New York: Charles Scribner's Sons, 1958, 1960), Postscript, pp. 136f.

Maurice Friedman, *The Hidden Human Image* (New York: Delta Books, 1974), p. 120.

Buber, *Good and Evil. Two Interpretations* (includes *Right and Wrong* and *Images of Good and Evil*) (New York: Scribner's Paperback, 1961).

Hugo Bergmann, "Gottesfinsternis," *Neue Wege,* Vol. XLVII (1953), Septemberheft, pp. 345–49.

Buber, "Zwischen Religion und Philosophie" (reply to Hugo Bergmann), *Neue Wege,* Vol. XLVII (1953), Dezemberheft, pp. 436–39.

Maurice Friedman, *Problematic Rebel: Melville, Dostoievsky, Kafka, Camus,* 2d rev., enlarged, and radically reorganized ed. (Chicago: The University of Chicago Press, Phoenix Books, 1970) pp. 486f.

R. W. B. Lewis, *The Picaresque Saint* (Philadelphia and New York: J. B. Lippincott, 1959), p. 103. Cf. p. 302, notes 32 and 33 to Chap. 3.

Albert Salomon, "Tribute to Martin Buber," *New School Bulletin* (November 1951).

Albrecht Goes, "The Cab Driver" (1962), in E. William Rollins and Harry Zohn, eds., *Men of Dialogue*, pp. 215f.

Maurice Friedman, *Martin Buber: The Life of Dialogue*, 3d ed. rev. with Preface to the Third Edition (pp. vii–xvii) and updated bibliography of Buber's works and books about Buber (Chicago: The University of Chicago Press, Phoenix Books, 1976), Chap. 15, "The Nature of Evil," pp. 101–12.

Buber, *Werke*, Vol. I—*Schriften zur Philosophie* (Munich: Kösel-Verlag and Heidelberg: Verlag Lambert Schneider, 1962), p. 554, note 16.

Buber, *The Knowledge of Man*, "Man and His Image-Work," trans. Maurice Friedman, p. 156.

Douglas V. Steere, *On Confirming the Deepest Thing in Another*, published by the Brothers, St. Mary's College Press, pp. 2–5.

Jochanan Bloch, *Die Aporie des Du. Probleme der Dialogik Martin Bubers*, Vol. II of *Phronesis. Eine Schriftenreihe* (Heidelberg: Verlag Lambert Schneider, 1977), p. 215, note 11.

Gerald Holton, "The Roots of Complementarity," *Daedalus*, Vol. XCIX, No. 4 (Fall 1970), p. 1021.

On Buber's critique of Simone Weil in "The Silent Question" *(Buber on Judaism)* see *Buber Briefwechsel* III, #310. MB to Fritz Kaufmann, April 9, 1954, p. 377.

The Worlds of Existentialism, ed. with Introductions and a Conclusion by Maurice Friedman (Chicago: The University of Chicago Press, Phoenix Books, 1973), Martin Heidegger, "Letter on Humanism," pp. 260–63.

Martin Heidegger, *Unterwegs zur Sprache* (Pfullingen, 1959), pp. 129f., quoted in Johannes Ernst Seiffert, *Das Erzieherische in Martin Bubers chassidischen Anekdoten* (Takatsuki, Japan: Printing House Seishindo, 1963), p. 130, note 1.

Paul Arthur Schilpp and Maurice Friedman, eds., *The Philosophy of Martin Buber*, Emil L. Fackenheim, "Martin Buber's Concept of Revelation," pp. 273–96; Jean Wahl, "Martin Buber and the Philosophies of Existence," pp. 475–510; Buber, "Replies to My Critics," pp. 715f.

SOURCES FOR CHAPTER 7
Devotio versus *Gnosis:* Buber *versus* Jung

Buber, *Eclipse of God*, "Religion and Modern Thinking," trans. Maurice Friedman, pp. 78–92; "Supplement: Reply to C. G. Jung," trans. Maurice Friedman, pp. 133–37.

C. G. Jung, Reply to Buber and to Keyserling, *Merkur* (Munich)(May 1952). Jung's reply to Buber was publishd in the American Jungian annual, *Spring*, 1958, trans. Edward Whitmont.

Maurice Friedman, "Religion and Psychology: The Limits of the Psyche as Touchstone of Reality," *Quaker Religious Thought* Vol. XII, No. 1 (Winter 1970), pp. 8–24, 28. This critique of Jung is presented in condensed form in Maurice Friedman, *Touchstones of Reality: Existential Trust and the Community of Peace* (New York: Dutton Paperbacks, 1974), pp. 253–58. For a full-scale critique of Jung see Maurice Friedman, *To Deny Our Nothingness: Contemporary Images of Man*, 3rd ed., rev., with new Preface and Appendix (Chicago: The University of Chicago Press, Phoenix Books, 1978), Chap. 9, pp. 146–67.

C. G. Jung, *Letters*, sel. and ed. Gerhard Adler in collaboration with Aniela Jaffé, trans. from the German by R. F. C. Hull, Vol. II, *1951–1961*, Bollingen Series XCV: 2 (Princeton: Princeton University Press, 1975), pp. 61, 68f., 101f., 147, 367f., 370–72, 375–79, 572f.

For an excellent and penetrating discussion of the Buber-Jung controversy from the side of Jung, see Edward C. Whitmont, "Prefatory Note to Jung's Reply to Buber," *Spring. An Annual of Archetypal Psychology and Jungian Thought, 1973* (New York: Spring Publications, 1973), pp. 188–95. The translation of Jung's "A Reply to Martin Buber" is also reprinted in this volume, pp. 196–203.

Letters from Martin Buber to Maurice Friedman, Jerusalem, June 26, 1952; July 23, 1952.

Buber Briefwechsel III, #239. MB to Maurice Friedman, June 23, 1952, pp. 319f.

Leter from Martin Buber to Robert C. Smith, Wengen, Switzerland, August 29, 1960. This letter is part of a total correspondence that Dr. Smith, Professor of Philosophy at Trenton State College, Trenton, New Jersey, sent me and which he may have succeeded in getting published.

Buber, *The Origin and Meaning of Hasidism*, "The Beginnings," pp. 24f., 27–29, 34–36, 40, 42f., 50–56; "The Foundation Stone," pp. 62–66, 68–72, 77–83, 85–88; "God and the Soul," pp. 195–99; "The Place of Hasidism in the History of Religion," pp. 219–40; "Supplement: Christ, Hasidism, Gnosis," pp. 252–54.

Paul Arthur Schilpp and Maurice Friedman, *The Philosophy of Martin Buber*, Martin Buber, "Replies to My Critics," trans. Maurice Friedman, pp. 716f., 743.

Jung's "confession" of the Gnostic god Abraxas was in his 1936 work *Septem Sermones ad Mortuos* (Seven Sermons to the Dead); published as Appendix V in C. G. Jung, *Memories, Dreams, Reflections*, recorded by Aniela Jaffé, trans. Richard and Clara Winston (New York: Vintage Books, 1965), pp. 378–90.

SOURCES FOR CHAPTER 8
Dialogues with Americans

•————————————————————————•

Letters from Martin Buber to Maurice Friedman, Jerusalem, August 5, 1952; August 18, 1952; October 10, 1952; October 15, 1952; December 26, 1952; January 17, 1953, January 25, 1953 (including copy of letter of same date to Will Herberg, also in English); March 2, 1953; April 27, 1953; April 30, 1953; Heidelberg, June 27, 1953; Amsterdam, September 1, 1953; Heidelberg, September 26, 1953; Jerusalem, November 25, 1953; January 23, 1945; March 9, 1954; March 27, 1954; April 28, 1954; May 31, 1954; June 17, 1954; Zurich, July 5, 1954; Heidelberg, July 18, 1954; Tübingen, August 8, 1954; August 11, 1954; August 15, 1954; August 20, 1954; August 21, 1954; August 23, 1954; September 7, 1954; September 13, 1954; October 4, 1954; October 21, 1954; Naples, November 26, 1954; Jerusalem, December 7, 1954; December 14, 1954; January 16, 1955; March 8, 1955; May 28, 1955; June 21, 1955; September 16, 1955; September 20, 1955; October 25, 1955; November 13, 1955; December 10, 1955, December 15, 1955; December 27, 1955; January 12, 1956; January 30, 1956; February 9, 1956; March 28, 1956; Heidelberg, June 12, 1956; Zurich, July 11, 1956; Jerusalem, September 25, 1956; October 22, 1956; November 29, 1956; January 16, 1957.

Letter from Martin Buber to Mitchell Bedford, Jerusalem, December 26, 1952. In my possession and in Buber Archives.

Buber Briefwechsel III, #261. Mitchell Bedford to MB, October 6, 1952, pp. 321f.; #263. MB to Mitchell Bedford, December 26, 1952, pp. 323–25; #265. MB to Will Herberg, January 25, 1953, pp. 325–28; #276. Will Herberg to MB, March 21, 1953, pp. 340f.; #278. MB to Maurice Friedman, April 30, 1953, pp. 342–44; #305. MB to Maurice Friedman, March 27, 1954, p. 368; #316. MB to Maurice Friedman, August 15, 1954, pp. 381f.; #318. MB to Maurice Friedman, September 7, 1954, pp. 382–84; #365. MB to Emil Marmorstein, January 15, 1957, pp. 426f.; #337. MB to Maurice Friedman, November 13, 1955, p. 399; #338. MB to Maurice Friedman, December 10, 1955, p. 400; #342. MB to Maurice Friedman, January 12, 1956, pp. 402f.

Gershom Scholem, "Martin Bubers Auffassung des Judentums," in Adolf Portmann, ed., *Schöpfung und Gestaltung. Eranos-Jahrbuch 1966* (Zurich: Rhein Verlag, 1967), pp. 12, 48–51. This essay was reprinted as "Martin Buber's Conception of Judaism" in Gershom Scholem, *Jews and Judaism in Crisis* (1976).

Buber, *Pointing the Way*, "The Validity and Limitation of the Political Principle" (1953), pp. 208–19; "Prophecy, Apocalyptic, and the Historical Hour" (1954), pp. 192–207.

Conversations with Harold Stahmer, New York to Tel Aviv and Tel Aviv to New York, January 1978.

Martin Buber, *Die Legende des Baalschem*, rev. new ed., *Manesse Bibliothek der Weltliteratur* (Zurich: Manesse Verlag, 1955).

Maurice Friedman, "Martin Buber: Prophet and Philosopher," *Faith Today*, (December–January 1954/1955).

Martin Buber, *Die Geschichten des Rabbi Nachman*, rev. ed. (Frankfurt am Main and Hamburg: Fischer Bücherei, 1955).

Buber, *A Believing Humanism: Gleanings*, "A Realist of the Spirit," pp. 55f.

Letter from Martin Buber to Professor John Hutchinson, Chairman, Department of Religion, Columbia University, January 30, 1956, unpublished, in my possesssion.

Schalom Ben-Chorin, *Zwiesprache mit Martin Buber*, p. 160.

SOURCES FOR CHAPTER 9
Second Visit to America: Encounter with Psychotherapy

• ————————————————————————— •

Letters from Martin Buber to Maurice Friedman, Jerusalem, March 7, 1956; March 28, 1956; April 4, 1956; Paris, May 4, 1956; London, May 12, 1956; Jerusalem, August 4, 1956; August 22, 1956; August 23, 1956; September 8, 1956; October 9, 1956; October 27, 1956; November 1, 1956; November 13, 1956; November 29, 1956; December 7, 1956, January 8, 1957; January 16, 1957; January 18, 1957, January 24, 1957; February 2, 1957; February 5, 1957, February 19, 1957.

Buber Briefwechsel III, #345. MB to Maurice Friedman, January 30, 1956, pp. 405f.; #349. MB to Maurice Friedman, March 2, 1956, pp. 408f.; #351. Leslie H. Farber to MB, Washington, March 17, 1956, pp. 410–412; #353. MB to Leslie H. Farber, April 1, 1956; #354. Leslie H. Farber to MB, April 9, 1956, pp. 413–15; #357. MB to Leslie H. Farber, September 1, 1956, pp. 417–19; #358. Leslie H. Farber to MB, October 25, 1956, pp. 419–21; #363. Leslie H. Farber to MB, December 29, 1956, p. 425; #364. MB to Leslie H. Farber, January 9, 1957, p. 426; #366. Leslie H. Farber to MB, February 12, 1957, p. 528; #367. MB to Leslie H. Farber, February 19, 1957, p. 429; #368. Malcolm L. Diamond to MB, April 2, 1957, pp. 429f.

Buber, *The Knowledge of Man*, Chap. 1, "Introductory Essay" by Maurice Friedman, pp. 11–58; Chap. 3, "Elements of the Interhuman," trans. Ronald Gregor Smith, pp. 72–87; Chap. 4, "What Is Common to All," trans. Maurice Friedman, pp. 88–108; Chap. 6, "Guilt and Guilt Feelings," trans. Maurice Friedman, pp. 120–47.

Buber, *Pointing the Way*, "Healing through Meeting" (1951), pp. 93–97.

Note A

Buber, *A Believing Humanism: Gleanings*, "Healing through Meeting" (1951), pp. 138–43; "The Unconscious" (1957), notes taken by Maurice Friedman at the seminars at the Washington (D.C.) School of Psychiatry, pp. 153–73. No stenogram was kept of the seminars, so the only record of it is the notes which I took. When I was editing *The Knowledge of Man*, I asked Buber whether I could incorporate these notes into my long introductory essay which forms Chapter I of the book. Buber agreed only to a summary and paraphrase and not the actual interchange between participants as I had recorded it. One of Buber's last wishes before his death, however, was that my notes be translated into German for *Nachlese*, as a result of which I included the original notes in my English translation of *A Believing Humanism: Gleanings*.

Maurice Friedman, *Martin Buber: The Life of Dialogue*, Chap. 21, "Psychotherapy," pp. 191–94, 197, Supplementary Note.

Carl R. Rogers, *On Becoming a Person* (Boston: Houghton Mifflin, 1961).

Leslie H. Farber, "Introduction," to Martin Buber, "The William Alanson White Lectures, Fourth Series," *Psychiatry*, Vol. XX, No. 2 (May 1957), pp. 95f. Also quoted in Maurice Friedman, *The Hidden Human Image* (New York: Delta Books, 1974), p. 75.

The story about David Rioch's response to Buber's refusal to speak about God in the seminars at the Washington School of Psychiatry was told me by Ursula Neibuhr, wife of Reinhold, the following year when I was lecturing at Barnard College.

Note B

In the office next door to where the Columbia Seminars on Biblical Faith were being held, Buber said once to Michael Wyschogrod and me during a break, "Do you think we can get Jesus back for Judaism?"

Conversations and interchange with Harold Stahmer and Michael Wyschogrod at "The Thought of Martin Buber" Centennial Conference at the Ben Gurion University of the Negev, Beer-Sheva, Israel, January 3–6, 1978.

Speech of Leslie H. Faber at the "Humanizing Society" Buber Centenary Conference, Fordham University, New York City, February 9, 1978.

Buber, *A Believing Humanism: Gleanings,* trans. with an Introduction and Explanatory Comments by Maurice Friedman (New York: Simon & Schuster Paperbacks, 1969), "Fragments of Revelation," sec. 3, "The Exclusive Attitude of the Religions," p. 115.

SOURCES FOR CHAPTER 10

Last Visit to America and Paula's Death

•──────────────────────────────•

Letters from Martin Buber to Maurice Friedman, London, May 12, 1956; Jerusalem, August 8, 1956; August 22, 1956; May 28, 1957; August 8, 1957; August 14, 1957; August 31, 1957; September 13, 1957; October 1, 1957; October 6, 1957; November 8, 1957; November 10, 1957; November 12, 1957; November 20, 1957; November 24, 1957; November 30, 1957; December 8, 1957; January 1, 1958; January 15, 1958; February 3, 1958; February 13, 1958; February 18, 1958; March 7, 1958; Soglio, Italy, July 11, 1958; July 12, 1958; July 13, 1958; July 16, 1958; Venice, August 2, 1958; August 13, 1958; Jerusalem, September 8, 1958; September 22, 1958; October 8, 1958.

Buber, *A Believing Humanism: Gleanings,* "Hermann Hesse's Service to the Spirit" (1957), pp. 70–79; "Spirits and Men" (1961), pp. 52–54.

Buber Briefwechsel III, #379. Hermann Hesse to MB, November 1957, p. 443; #376. Mascha Kaleko to MB, New York, October 23 1957, pp. 440f.; #378. MB to Mascha Kaleko, November 5, 1957, p. 442; #395. MB to Ewald and Sophie Wasmuth, Venice, August 7, 1958, pp. 462f.; #396. MB to Ewald and Sophie Wasmuth, Venice-Lido, August 13, 1958, p. 463; #397. MB to Maurice Friedman, Jerusalem, September 8, 1958, pp. 463f.; #400. MB to Ewald Wasmuth, October 4, 1958, p. 466; #402. Hans Jonas to MB, New York, October 13, 1958, p. 467; #414. Albrecht

Goes to MB, Venice, June 12, 1959, p. 478; #418. MB to Maurice Friedman, Flims, August 15, 1959, p. 481; #469. Heinz and Susi Helmerking to MB, St. Gallen, Dreikönigstag, 1962, pp. 534f.

Fritz Kaufmann, "Baeck and Buber," trans. Maurice Friedman, *Conservative Judaism*, Vol. XII, No. 2 (Winter 1958) pp. 9–22.

Buber, *Israel and the World*, 2d enlarged ed. (1963), "Israel and the Command of the Spirit," trans. Maurice Friedman, pp. 253–57.

Buber, *Pointing the Way*, "Foreword."

Albrecht Goes, "A Solid House," in E. William Rollins and Harry Zohn, eds. *Men of Dialogue*, pp. 217–19.

Hugo Bergmann, "Paula Buber," MB *(Mitteilungsblatt)*, Vol. XXVI, No. 34 (August 22, 1958), p. 4.

Note

After the American Friends of Ihud eightieth birthday meeting I naïvely imagined that I could raise what had increasingly seemed to be a central issue (the growing predominance of anti-Zionists on the Executive Committee) by resigning as chairman. I mentioned this informally to Don Peretz, who reported it to the Executive Committee and got himself elected chairman in my place at a meeting held without me. Simon remonstrated with me, saying that he had worked for Ihud and its predecessor for over thirty years, and Buber himself said that it was an irrational act on my part. It was certainly a naïve one, but within a few months Ihud formally communicated with the American Friends of Ihud and demanded that they desist from using the name of Ihud since, after my departure, the organization became more and more openly anti-Zionist. It is not easy in America (or in Israel or anywhere else) to walk the narrow ridge!

NOTE TO CHAPTER 11
Replies to Critics

• ——————————————————— •

In the Introductory Essay to his anthology *Existentialism from Dostoevsky to Sartre,* Walter Kaufmann explained his omission of the religious existentialists, such as Berdyaev, Buber, Bultmann, Tillich, and Marcel, first, on the ground that "religion has always been existentialist" (which seems to be more a reason for *including* them); second, on the palpably false ground that "not one of the later religious existentialists has so far left a mark, like Kierkegaard, on literature or on philosophy"; and third, on the rather whimsical note that an anthology "is not a collection of flowers or a meadow on which we pick a blossom here and there" but "an attempt to tell a story and follow a path." "The religious existentialists have not played an important part in our story," he added—for the reason that he had arbitrarily shaped his story to exclude all of them but Kierkegaard.

SOURCES FOR CHAPTER 11 AND FOR NOTE TO CHAPTER 11
Replies to Critics

•————————————————————————————•

Letters from Martin Buber to Maurice Friedman, January 30, 1956; July 15, 1956; September 25, 1956; September 26, 1956; October 9, 1956; October 24, 1956; October 27, 1956; December 7, 1956; January 16, 1957; February 5, 1957; February 16, 1957; February 19, 1957; May 28, 1957; August 8, 1957; September 13, 1957; September 23, 1957; October 6, 1957; October 13, 1957; November 8, 1957; November 10, 1957; November 20, 1957; December 8, 1957; December 11, 1957; January 24, 1958; February 11, 1958; March 2, 1958; March 24, 1958; July 11, 1958; September 8, 1958; September 13, 1958; September 23, 1958; October 4, 1958; October 7, 1958; November 8, 1958; November 24, 1958; December 14, 1958; January 13, 1959; February 19, 1959; March 14, 1959; April 2, 1959; April 5, 1959; May 10, 1959; September 7, 1959; September 11, 1959; December 14, 1959; March 8, 1961; May 25, 1961; July 6, 1961; August 6, 1961; January 1, 1962; February 10, 1962; February 18, 1962; April 4, 1962; June 4, 1962; October 14, 1962; November 25, 1962; May 15, 1963; June 23, 1964; March 1, 1965.

Buber Briefwechsel III, #362. Fritz Kaufmann to MB, December 19, 1956, pp. 424f.; #371. MB to Fritz Kaufmann, August 27, 1957, p. 434; #372. Fritz Kaufmann to MB, September 8, 1957, pp. 434–36; #373. MB to Malcolm Diamond, September 19, 1957, pp. 437f. #392. MB to Maurice Friedman, Soglio, July 11, 1958, pp. 459f.; #397. MB to Maurice Friedman, Jerusalem, September 8, 1958, p. 464; #399. MB to Maurice Friedman, September 22, 1958, p. 465; #418. MB to Maurice Friedman, Flims, August 15, 1959, p. 481; #454. Hermann Hesse to MB, March 1961, p. 520; #515. Emmanuel Levinas to MB, March 11, 1963, p. 582; #522. Hans A. Fischer-Barnicol to MB, May 19, 1963, p. 591 and p. 591, note 4.

Buber, *I and Thou*, "Postscript," pp. 123–37.

Paul Arthur Schilpp and Maurice Friedman, eds., *The Philosophy of Martin Buber*, "Editor's Preface," p. xvii; Buber, "Replies to Critics," pp. 689–97, 702–06, 711–13, 717–20, 722–25, 741–44; Walter Kaufmann, "Buber's Religious Significance," p. 685.

Sydney and Beatrice Rome, eds., *Philosophical Interrogations* (New York: Harper Torchbooks, 1970), "Interrogation of Martin Buber," conducted by Maurice Friedman with Buber's replies trans. Maurice Friedman, Preface by Maurice S. Friedman, pp. 15f.; I. "The Philosophy of Dialogue," pp. 18, 28, 31–40, 44; II. "Theory of Knowledge," pp. 47–58; III. "Education," pp. 61f., 64–68; V. "Philosophy of Religion," pp. 81–86; VI. "The Bible and Biblical Judaism," pp. 99f., 104; VII. "Evil," pp. 110–12, 114–17.

Walter Kaufmann, *Existentialism from Dostoevsky to Sartre* (New York: Meridian Books, 1956), pp. 49f.

SOURCES FOR CHAPTER 12
The Interpretation of Hasidism: Buber versus Scholem

• ———————————————————————————— •

Gershom G. Scholem, *Major Trends in Jewish Mysticism,* rev. ed. (New York: Schocken Books, 1964), Ninth Lecture, "Hasidism: The Latest Phase," pp. 329f., 334–44, 348f.

Letters from Martin Buber to Maurice Friedman, December 7, 1956; November 10, 1957; November 11, 1958; August 29, 1960; July 6, 1961; November 9, 1961; January 21, 1962; February 10, 1962; February 19, 1963; March 10, 1963; May 15, 1963; June 12, 1963.

Buber Briefwechsel III, #511. MB to Maurice Friedman, February 19, 1963, p. 579.

Buber, *Hasidism and Modern Man,* ed. and trans. with Introduction by Maurice Friedman (New York: Horizon Press, 1973), Book I, "Hasidism and Modern Man," pp. 21–43.

Paul A. Schilpp and Maurice Friedman, eds., *The Philosophy of Martin Buber,* Hugo Bergmann, "Martin Buber and Mysticism," pp. 306–08; Rivka Schatz-Uffenheimer, "Man's Relation to God and World in Buber's Rendering of the Hasidic Teaching," pp. 403–34; Buber, "Replies to My Critics," pp. 714, 716A, and IX. "On Hasidism," pp. 731–41. (The last two pages of this reply I discussed in Chapter 11 in connection with *For the Sake of Heaven.*)

Sydney and Beatrice Rome, eds., *Philosophical Interrogations,* "Interrogation of Martin Buber," pp. 88–91.

Gershom Scholem, "Martin Buber's Hasidism, A Critique," *Commentary,* Vol. XXXII, No. 4 (October 1961), pp. 304–16.

Gershom Scholem, *The Messianic Idea in Judaism* (New York: Schocken Books, 1971), pp. 34f., and "Martin Buber's Interpretation of Hasidism," pp. 228–50. Although a different translation, this essay is identical with the one in *Commentary* except for the omission of Scholem's statement that "religious anarchist" is not meant to disparage Buber and his confession "I am an anarchist myself, though not one of Buber's persuasion."

Buber, "Interpreting Hasidism," ed. and trans. Maurice Friedman, *Commentary,* Vol. XXXVI, No. 3 (September 1963), pp. 218–25.

Buber, *The Kingship of God,* trans. Richard Scheimann (New York: Harper & Row, 1967), p. 43.

Conversation with Shmuel Agnon, Jerusalem, Spring 1966.

Conversation with Ernst Simon, Jerusalem, Spring 1966.

Ernst Simon, "From Dialogue to Peace. Some Consequences of Martin Buber's Philosophy," *Jerusalem Post,* June 18, 1965.

Emil L. Fackenheim, "Two Types of Reform: Reflections Occasioned by Hasidism," *Central Conference of American Rabbis,* 72nd Annual Convention, June 20–24, 1961, New York, Vol. LXXI, ed. Sidney Regner (New York: U.A.H.C., 1962).

Gershom Scholem, "Martin Bubers Auffassung des Judentums," in *Schöpfung und Gestaltung. Eranos Jahrbuch 1966,* Vol. XXXV, ed. Adolf Portmann (Zurich: Rhein-Verlag, 1967), pp. 10–13, 47–51.

Ernst Simon, "Scholem und Buber," *Neue Zürcher Zeitung,* June 11, 1967, "Literatur und Kunst."

Walter Kaufmann, "Buber's Triumphs and Failures," Centennial Conference on Martin Buber's Thought, Beer-Sheva, Israel, January 3–6, 1978. Jochanan Bloch, Haim Gordon, and Menachem Dorman, eds., *Martin Buber: A Centenary Volume* (Hebrew) (Israel: Kibbutz Meahad, 1981), pp. 21–36; Jochanan Bloch and Haim Gordon, eds., *Martin Buber: Bilanz seines Denken* (Freiburg: Herder Verlag, 1983), Walter Kaufmann, "Bubers Fehlschlage und seine Triumphe," pp. 22–39. This essay was published in revised form in *Encounter* (May 1979). Cf. Maurice Friedman, "Walter Kaufmann's Mismeeting with Martin Buber," *Judaism,* Vol. XXXI, No. 2 (Spring 1982), pp. 229–39.

Arnold Jacob Wolf, "The Social Challenge Buber Has Left Us," an address at the conference "Humanizing Society. A Celebration of the Centennial of the Birth of Martin Buber," sponsored by Fordham University and Hebrew Union College–Jewish Institute of Religion, New York City, February 9, 1978. My own paper at this conference was published in the Buber Commemorative Issue of *Thought,* Vol. LII, No. 210 (September 1978).

Note

Gershom Scholem, "Martin Bubers Auffassung des Judentums," in *Schöpfung und Gestaltung. Eranos Jahrbuch 1966,* Vol. XXXV, ed. Adolf Portmann (Zurich: Rhein-Verlag, 1967), pp. 10–13, 47–51. This essay is published in English translation under the title "Martin Buber's Conception of Judaism" in Gershom Scholem, *On Jews and Judaism in Crisis,* ed. Werner J. Dannhauser (New York: Schocken Books, 1976), pp. 126–71. In this essay Scholem makes an illuminating, if still somewhat distorted, observation on the difference between Buber's biblical and his Hasidic interpretations:

> Buber's writings on the Bible present themselves, at least in their literary structure and manner of execution, as scientific analysis. They fit into the traditional framework of scientific questioning; they are circumscribed—by precise indications of sources and—compared to his other writings—a downright strikingly rich and seemingly ostentatious discussion of scholarly literature on the subject. His exegeses are, to be sure, as I have already said, pneumatic exegeses when it comes to the crunch. But it is a pneumatic exegesis with learned notes, which cause its pneumatic character to recede a bit or even blot it out. His Hasidic writings, however, avoid all these accessories. They represent *ex cathedra* pronouncements which offer no encouragement of help or verification by their sources. [p. 165.]

NOTES TO CHAPTER 13

Dag Hammarskjøld and Buber: The Covenant of Peace

•————————————————————————————•

Note 1

In 1960 Buber wrote a poem to this effect—"The Three"—which was one of the very few of his unpublished poems that he selected for preservation in his *Gleanings:*

> *In that so tumultuous time,*
> *From which we all unwillingly stem,*
> *These three lived together, three-in-one:*
> *Freedom, equality, and brotherhood.*
> *Yet if of the three that dwell with one another,*
> *Two are hardly anything but abstractions,*
> *Only concretized through the life breath*
> *Of the third, one can quite easily disband the three,*
> *One flies easily to the West, another to the East,*
> *Yes, one has here and one has there use*
> *For the ideas—now they are near completion.*

Note 2

One of those present at this conference was the distinguished American Episcopal bishop, James Pike. In 1961, when he was showing me around Grace Cathedral in San Francisco, Pike told me that Buber had said to him in Paris, "I understand what you mean by the Trinity, but why do you still have to use a third-century philosophy to express it?" Impressed by the force of this question, Pike went on record against the *formulation* of the Trinitarian creed, and this was one of the things that led to his later heresy trial initiated by southern Episcopalian bishops!

Note 3

I wrote to Coretta King after King's assassination of the affinity between him and Buber. In my chapter "Martin Luther King" in *The Hidden Human Image,* I point, in fact, to both King and Buber as examples of "The Modern Job," and I also point to Albert Camus. The two books that King took with him to prison were Camus's *The Rebel* and Buber's *Between Man and Man.*

Note 4

In June 1963, Buber joined in an appeal to President Kennedy for clemency for Morton Sobell, convicted of conspiracy to commit espionage in 1951 and sentenced to thirty years in prison. In 1963, Buber had a significant exchange of letters with Anthony Wedgewood Benn, a British politician who the next year entered the cabinet of Prime Minister Harold Wilson. Benn raised important questions concerning the place of political analysis and activity in the fight against evil and the necessity of a new political movement arising in the atomic age on the basis of the common interests of the peoples. Could not politicians be just those "merchants of peace" for whom Buber called in an interview in *Life* magazine? Buber responded with an expression of sympathy for Benn's concerns. The questions he raised were questions of situation, Buber added, and needed to be discussed in person. He invited him to come see him during the summer of 1963 when he would be in a sanatorium in Lucerne. In 1963, Peter Benenson of Amnesty International also wrote Buber from London, in this case a long and impassioned appeal for Buber's help in protest against the mounting racial discrimination in South Africa, in connection with which he cited the activities of Nobel Prize winner Albert Luthuli and others. In May 1964, in what may have been his last action of this sort before the onset of the illness that eventually led to his death, Buber and the famous Israeli novelist Mazaz issued a joint appeal to the South African government to halt the current trials. Calling for the release of Nelson Mandeller and other leaders of the struggle against apartheid, Buber and Mazaz urged the South African government to use this "supreme opportunity of proclaiming the supremacy of sanity of understanding over ruthlessness." "All men of good-will share the accuseds' abhorrence of the idea of exclusive white supremacy and their simple desire to live as free men."

SOURCES FOR CHAPTER 13 AND FOR NOTES TO CHAPTER 13
Dag Hammarskjøld and Buber:
The Covenant of Peace

• ───────────────────────────────────── •

Buber, *Pointing the Way,* "Society and the State" (1951), p. 161; "The Validity and Limitation of the Political Principle" (1953), pp. 218f.; "Hope for This Hour" (1952), pp. 220–29; "Abstract and Concrete" (1952), pp. 230f.

Buber, *A Believing Humanism: Gleanings,* "Memories of Hammarskjøld" (1962), pp. 57–59; "In Twenty Years" (1961), p. 180; "On 'Civil Disobedience'" (1962), p. 191; "More on 'Civil Disobedience'" (1963), pp. 192f.; "Genuine Dialogue and the Possibilities of Peace" (1963), pp. 196–202; "Stop!" (1957), pp. 203f.; "On the Problem of the Community of Opinion" (1951), p. 211; "The Three" (1960), p. 219 (for the German original see p. 218).

Fritz Bartsch, "Kommentar über die Friedensrede Professor Bubers und ihre erste Auswirkungen," October 3, 1953. Hessischer Rundfunk, Frankfurt am Main (3-pp. ms., unpublished).

Letters from Martin Buber to Maurice Friedman, March 16, 1952; March 18, 1952; September 14, 1952; October 10, 1952; April 28, 1954; January 3, 1956; Paris, May 4, 1956; Jerusalem, October 6, 1957; January 8, 1958; August 26, 1959; November 11, 1960; December 10, 1960; January 5, 1961; September 28, 1961; January 21, 1962.

Buber Briefwechsel III, #287. MB to Louis Massignon, St. Märgen, September 13, 1953, p. 351; #353. MB to Lambert Schneider, July 23, 1955, p. 397; #334. MB to Hans Indau, August 6, 1955, pp. 397f.; #370. American Committee on Africa, signed Eleanor Roosevelt, James A. Pike, Martin Luther King, to MB, August 15, 1957, pp. 432f.; #375. Eleanor Roosevelt to MB, October 14, 1957, pp. 439f.; #388. Dag Hammarskjøld to MB, April 16, 1958, pp. 454f.; #433. Nahum Goldmann to MB, February 26, 1960, pp. 498f.; #434. MB to Nahum Goldmann, March 24, 1960, p. 500; #436. MB to François Mauriac, May 7, 1960, p. 502; #445. MB to Carl J. Burckhardt, Wengen, August 29, 1960, pp. 511f.; #446. MB to Simon Shereshevsky, Zurich, September 7, 1960, pp. 512f.; #447. Albrecht Goes to MB, December 24, 1960, pp. 513f.; #460. Dag Hammarskjøld to MB, August 17, 1961, pp. 524f.; #462. MB to Dag Hammarskjøld, August 23, 1961, p. 527; #463. Knut Hammarskjøld to MB, October 5, 1961, pp. 527f.; #466. MB to Novosti Press Agency, Peace Questionnaire, Moscow, November 13, 1961, pp. 530f.; #474. MB to Bertrand Russell, March 4, 1962, pp. 538f.; #475. Eleanor Roosevelt to MB, March 12, 1962, p. 539; #477. MB to François Mauriac, March 25, 1962, pp. 540f.; #498. Anthony Wedgewood Benn to MB, January 15, 1963, pp. 560–62; #512. MB to Anthony Wedgewood Benn, February 21, 1963, pp. 580f.; #528. Peter Benenson to MB, August 27,1963, pp. 605–07; #529. Bertrand Russell to MB, September 9, 1963, pp. 607f.; #531. Nahum Goldmann to MB, September 24, 1963. p. 669.

Irwin Ross, "Voice of the Sages, Article II, Martin Buber," New York *Post*, November 7, 1957, p. M2.

Henry P. Van Dusen, *Dag Hammarskjöld: The Statesman and His Faith* (New York: Harper & Row, 1967), pp. 76f., 87, 98f., 186–88, 133, and Note: "Dag Hammarskjöld and Martin Buber," pp. 215–19. This note includes excerpts from the correspondence between Hammarskjøld and Buber.

Dag Hammarskjöld, *Markings*, trans. from the Swedish by Leif Sjöberg and W. H. Auden, with a Foreword by W. H. Auden (New York: Alfred A. Knopf, 1965), pp. 40, 47, 59, 78, 82, 87, 92f., 96, 99, 106, 110, 112, 114f., 120, 122, 129, 173, 214f.

The text of Hammarskjøld's Cambridge address in which he quotes at length "Hope for This Hour" is found in Wilder Foote, ed., *Servant of Peace: A Selection of the Speeches and Statements of Dag Hammarskjöld* (New York: Harper & Row, 1963), "The Walls of Distrust," p. 186. I have abridged the actual quotation.

United Nations Press Release, Note No. 134, February 5, 1959.

Aubrey Hodes, *Martin Buber: An Intimate Portrait* (New York: The Viking Press, 1971), pp. 59–62, 103f., 143f., 147f., 150–60, 204.

Letter from Dag Hammarskjøld to the Nobel Prize Committee on Martin Buber, trans. for me from the Hebrew by Uri Margolin, *Ha-aretz* (Tel Aviv), Literary Supplement, October 22, 1965. Henry P. Van Dusen has placed a copy of this translation in the Dag Hammarskjöld Collection in the Princeton University Library.

Letter from Dag Hammarskjøld to Maurice Friedman, United Nations, New York, September 25, 1959.

Letter from George Ivan Smith to Martin Buber, United Nations, New York, October 3, 1961.

Letter from Henry P. Van Dusen to Maurice Friedman, September 24, 1966.

I have permission from Governor Bo Hammarskjøld to quote from Hammarskjøld's letters to Buber, though actually all cited here have already been published in the *Buber Briefwechsel* III and in Henry P. Van Dusen's book on Hammarskjøld.

John Molleson, "Dag's Choice—Dr. Buber for a Nobel," New York *Herald Tribune,* October 22, 1961, pp. 1, 8.

Martin Buber File, Third Folder, 1953–1963, the Hebrew University Archives, The Hebrew University, Jerusalem.

New York Times, October 1, 1961, p. 31:2; November 15, 1961, p. 18:6, June 27, 1963, p. 8:8.

The Eternal Light, Chap. 731, "A World Dialogue" by Irwin Gonshak, broadcast over NBC, March 11, 1962, prepared by Jewish Theological Seminary of America, pp. 3–12.

Meyer Levin, "Sage Who Inspired Hammarskjøld," *New York Times Magazine,* December 3, 1961.

Übersetzung aus *Dagens Nyheter* (Stockholm), September 23, 1961 (on Dag's plans to translate *Ich und Du*).

"Aus Erster Hand," A Dialogue with Prof. Dr. Martin Buber, Jerusalem: Dialogue Partner: Thilo Koch; Nord- und Westdeutscher Rundfunkverband-Fernsehen- Hamburg-Lokstedt, broadcast May 25, 1959. 11-pp. MS. unpublished, in Martin Buber Archives, Hebrew and National University Library, Jerusalem.

Castrum Peregrini, LVIII (Amsterdam), 1961.

The report of the Russian academician's attack on Buber was published in *Ha-aretz* (Tel Aviv), according to a letter from Buber to me, presumably some time in December 1960.

Jerusalem Post, October 30, 1961; April 8, 1962; May 22, 1964.

Into the Tenth Decade: Tribute to Bertrand Russell, printed by Malvern Press Ltd., London. Program for a Musical Tribute, Royal Festival Hall, May 19, 1962, statements by Martin Buber and Isaac Deutscher on p. 3.

Paul Arthur Schilpp and Maurice Friedman, eds., *The Philosophy of Martin Buber,* Buber, "Replies to My Critics," p. 723.

Maurice Friedman, *The Hidden Human Image* (New York: Delta Books, 1974), Chap. 18, "Martin Luther King: An American Gandhi and a Modern Job."

Letter from Reinhold Niebuhr and Maurice Friedman to the Nobel Academy, Sweden, July 30, 1962.

Letter from Charles Malik to Maurice Friedman, June 27, 1962.

Letter from T. S. Eliot to Maurice Friedman, June 27, 1962.

Buber, *Der Jude und sein Judentum,* "Die Sowjets und das Judentum" (1960), pp. 543–54.

Cf. Werner Kraft, *Gespräche mit Buber,* pp. 61–63, 101, 104, 116, 140.

Cf. Schalom Ben-Chorin, *Zwiesprache mit Martin Buber,* pp. 151, 178, 206f.

Andrei D. Sakharov, *Progress, Coexistence, and Intellectual Freedom,* with Introduction, Afterword, and Notes by Harrison E. Salisbury (New York:

W. W. Norton & Co., 1968, 1970). These proposals were published in full by the *New York Times* on June 22, 1968. On the basis of them, Dorothy Fosdick, daughter of Harry Emerson Fosdick and special assistant to Senator Jackson's subcommittee preparing for disarmament (SALT) talks with the Soviet Union, told Professor Donald Douglas of the University of Washington in 1970 that she believed that Sakharov was quoting "Hope for This Hour," without mentioning Buber's name. See also Andrei D. Sakharov, *Sakharov Speaks*, ed. with a Foreword by Harrison E. Salisbury (New York: Alfred A. Knopf, 1974) and Andrei D. Sakharov, *My Country and the World*, trans. Guy V. Daniels (New York: Vintage Books, 1975).

Marvin M. Karpatkin, "Professionals Protest: West Pointers Go CO," *Civil Liberties*, Publication of the American Civil Liberties Union, No. 277 (April 1971), pp. 1, 4.

SOURCES FOR CHAPTER 14
Buber versus Ben-Gurion

• ——————————————————————————— •

Interview with Dr. Nahum Goldmann, Head of the Jewish Agency, for the National Educational Television film *Dialogue: Buber and Israel*, Jerusalem, Spring 1966.

Ben-Zion Dinur, "Three Meetings with Buber," *Molad* (Hebrew), Tamuz-Av. Vol. I. No. 2 (1967).

"Interview mit Martin Buber," reprinted from *Cahiers Sioniens*, Paris, Vol. III, No. 5 (January 1, 1949), pp. 14–15, *Rundbrief zur Förderung der Freundschaft zwischen dem Alten und dem Neuen Gottesvolks—im Geiste der beiden Testamente*, Vol. II, No. 7, Folge 1949/1950 (Freiburg, April 1950), p. 7.

Buber, "We Need the Arabs, They Need Us!" Interview in *Frontpage: The Israel Weekly Newsmagazine*, Vol. II, No. 3, January 20, 1955. National Edition, pp. 10–11.

Martin Buber und Ludwig Strauss: Ein Lebenszeugnis in Briefen, ed. with an Introduction by Tuvi Rübner (Heidelberg: Verlag Lambert Schneider, 198?).

Buber Briefwechsel III, #285. MB to Eva Strauss, August 1950, pp. 349f.; #312. Fritz Kaufmann to MB, June 6, 1954, pp. 378f.; #335. Kurt Singer to MB, August 16, 1955, p. 398; #299. MB to Joseph Sprinzak, January 4, 1954, p. 363; #301. MB to Schalom Ben-Chorin, February 7, 1954, p. 365; #311. MB to Kurt Blumenfeld, May 28, 1954, p. 378; #325. MB to Hans Blüher, January 19, 1955, p. 390; #355. Yael Dayan and Joel Hofmann to MB, May 11, 1956, p. 416; #360. MB to Ewald and Sophie Wasmuth, November 12, 1956, pp. 421f.; #361. Lambert Schneider to MB, November 19, 1956, p. 422; #450. Uri Lev to MB, January 28, 1961, pp. 516f.; #451. Jehuda Schochat to MB, January 29,

1961, p. 418; #452. Eliezer Be'eri to MB, February 6, 1961, p. 518; #457. MB to Robert Weltsch, June 20, 1961, p. 523; #459. Ernst Simon to MB, August 7, 1961, p. 524; #476. MB to American Council for Judaism, March 23, 1962, p. 540; #505. David Ben-Gurion to MB, February 5, 1963, p. 572; #510. MB to David Ben-Gurion, February 19, 1963, p. 578; #546. MB to Levi Eshkol, October 26, 1964, p. 622; #549. Levi Eshkol to MB, November 4, 1964, pp. 626f.

Buber, *A Believing Humanism: Gleanings,* "Authentic Bilingualism," pp. 80–84.

Schalom Ben-Chorin, *Zwiesprache mit Martin Buber,* pp. 103f., 108, 178, 206–09.

Buber, *Israel and the World,* "Israel and the Command of the Spirit" (1958), p. 257; "Israel's Mission and Zion" (1957), pp. 258–63.

Werner Kraft, *Gespräche mit Martin Buber,* pp. 28, 30, 57, 137.

Letters from Martin Buber to Maurice Friedman, November 13, 1956; December 2, 1956; December 17, 1958; October 31, 1959; January 5, 1961.

Conversation with Nathan Rotenstreich, Jerusalem, Israel, Spring 1966.

David Ben-Gurion, "Vision and Redemption" and "Zionism and Pseudo-Zionism: in *Forum for the Problems of Zionism, World Jewry and the State of Israel,* Vol. IV—*Proceedings of the Jerusalem Ideological Conference,* World Zionist Organization, Spring 1959, ed. Nathan Rotenstreich, Shulamith Schartz Nardi, Zalman Shazar, pp. 112–22, 148–54. Buber's speech, "Israel's Mission and Zion," is printed on pp. 145–47 of the *Forum.*

Ernst Simon, "Buber or Ben-Gurion?" *New Outlook,* Vol. IX, No. 2 (77) (February 1966), pp. 9–17, trans. from the Hebrew original in *Ner,* Vol. XV, No. 3–10 (1965).

Aubrey Hodes, *Martin Buber: An Intimate Portrait,* pp. 18, 28f., 62–66, 101f., 111–16, 153, 203.

"Aharon Cohen Found Guilty of Espionage," *Ner,* Vol. XIII, No. 3–4 (November–December 1961), pp. I–II.

"No Pardon for Aharon Cohen," *Ner,* Vol. XIV, No. 4–6 (December 1962–January 1963), pp. IV–VII.

"Deputation of 'IHUD' Received by Prime Minister" and "Memorandum for the Arab Minority," *Ner,* Vol. IX, No. 5–7 (February–April 1958), pp. 55–53.

"Against Military Rule (Statement of 'Ihud'; Proclamation and Signatures)," *Ner,* Vol. IX, No. 10–12 (July–September 1958), pp. 48–53.

"The Ihud Press Conference in Jerusalem" and T. Raoul, "Martin Buber on the Refugee Problem," *Ner,* Vol. XI, No. 2–4 (November 1959–January 1960), pp. VI–IX.

"Statements on the Arab Refugees, Statement of 'IHUD,' Statement of Prime Minister Ben Gurion," *Ner,* Vol. XIII, No. 1–2 (September–October 1961), pp. II–IV.

David Ben-Gurion, Statement on Arab Refugees in *Dialogue: Martin Buber and Israel,* National Educational Television Film, 1967.

Documentation: From the Report of Dr. Joseph E. Johnson, Special Representative of the United Nations Conciliation Commission for Palestine," *Ner,* Vol. XII, No. 3–4 (November–December 1961), pp. XXXVIII–XLIII.

"Documentation: "The Resignation of Dr. J. Johnson (Exchange of Letters),"
Ner, Vol. XIV, No. 4–6 (December 1962–January 1963), pp. XXXIV–
XXXVI.

"Beginning of a Dialogue?": Bashir Ben-Yahmed, "An Israel-Arab Federation," "Readers of *Jeune Afrique* React," and "A *New Outlook* Enquiry"—
answer to *Jeune Afrique:* Martin Buber, "The Time to Try"; David Ben-
Gurion, "A Voice in the Wilderness"; Ernst Simon, "A Decisive Step?"
New Outlook, Vol. VIII, No. 1 (68) (January–February 1965), pp. 8–14,
16–19.

Sydney and Beatrice Rome, eds., *Philosophical Interrogations,* p. 78.

Buber, "Für Kurt Blumenfeld," *MB (Mitteilungsblatt),* Vol. XXVII, No. 22
(May 29, 1959).

Buber, *Israel and Palestine: The History of an Idea,* trans. Stanley Godman (London: East and West Library; New York: Farrar, Straus & Young, 1952),
pp. 142–45. (This book has been republished by Schocken Books under
the title *On Zion.*)

I am grateful to Uri Margolin of Jerusalem for his elucidation of the history
of the Lavon affair.

Conversation with Professor Jacob Katz of the Hebrew University, Jerusalem,
Spring 1966.

"The 'Danger to Democracy' Manifesto," *Ha-aretz* (Hebrew), December 30,
1960, p. 1, and sequel stories, February 4 and 7, 1961, trans. for me by
Uri Margolin.

Rafael Bashan, "The Week's Interview with Professor Martin Buber, 'Why
Did I Sign the Professors' Manifesto?'" *Ma-ariv,* January 27, 1961, trans.
for me from the Hebrew by Uri Margolin.

Julius Stone, "The Eichmann Trial: Prophetic Mirror for Mankind,"
Jerusalem Post, August 6, 1961.

Jerusalem Post, December 14, 1961, p. 2.

Hannah Arendt, *Eichmann in Jerusalem: A Study in the Banality of Evil,* rev. and
enlarged ed. (New York: The Viking Press, 1964), pp. 249–52.

Newsweek, December 25, 1961, "After the Verdict: The Dissenting Voices,"
p. 29; and *Newsweek* file, June 6, 1962.

Time, March 23, 1962, "Philosopher's Plea"; April 13, 1962, "Buber Speaks"
(Letters to the Editor); June 15, 1962, "Battle for the 'Human' Man."

Lawrence Fellows, "Philosopher Assails Ben-Gurion for Calling Israel Arabs a
Peril," *New York Times,* January 18, 1962.

Lawrence Fellows, "Buber Calls Eichmann Execution Great 'Mistake,'" *New
York Times,* June 5, 1962.

Israel Iserles, "Now That the Trial Is Over," *New Outlook,* Vol. V, No. 1 (41)
(January 1962), p. 14.

V. C., "Eichmann Is Dead but the Problem Remains," "Viewpoints," *New
Outlook,* Vol. V, No. 5 (45) (June 1962), pp. 11f.

Martin Buber Files, The Archives of the Hebrew University, Jerusalem,
Third Folder, 1953–1963, letter from Leo Shulman of Ramat Hasharon
to the Hebrew University, July 7, 1962.

Nach dem Eichmann Prozess. Zu einer Kontroverse über die Haltung der Juden,
Council of Jews from Germany. London-Jerusalem-New York (Tel Aviv,

1963), Ernst Simon, "Hannah Arendt—Eine Analyse," pp. 80–83; Martin Buber, "Nachbemerkung," pp. 99–101.

Note A

Hannah Arendt, *Elemente und Ürsprünge totaler Herrschaft* (Frankfurt a. M.: Europäische Verlagsanstalt, 1958), p. 725 quoted by Ernst Simon in *Nach dem Eichmann Prozess*. The paragraph in the text is my translation from the German, since I could find no corresponding passage in the English. Two somewhat parallel passages that I discovered are:

> Totalitarian regimes have discovered without knowing it that there are crimes which men can neither punish nor forgive. When the impossible was made possible it became the unpunishable, unforgivable absolute evil which could no longer be understood and explained by the evil motives of self-interest, greed, covetousness, resentment, lust for power, and cowardice; and which therefore anger could not revenge, love could not endure, friendship could not forgive. Just as the victims in the death factories or the holes of oblivion are no longer "human" in the eyes of their executioners, so this newest species of criminals is beyond the pale even of solidarity in human sinfulness. . . . We actually have nothing to fall back on in order to understand a phenomenon that nevertheless confronts us with its overpowering reality and breaks down all the standards we know.
>
> . . . If it is true that the link between totalitarian countries and the civilized world was broken through the monstrous crimes of totalitarian regimes, it is also true that this criminality was not due to simple aggressiveness, ruthlessness, warfare and treachery, but to a conscious break of that *consensus iuris* which, according to Cicero, constitutes a "people," and which, as international law, in modern times has constituted the civilized world insofar as it remains the foundation-stone of international relations even under the conditions of war. Both moral judgment and legal punishment presuppose this basic consent; the criminal can be judged justly only because he takes part in the *consensus iuris*. (Hannah Arendt, *The Origins of Totalitarianism*, new ed. [New York: Harcourt, Brace & World, 1966], pp. 459, 462).

Yitzhak Oded, "Israel's Arab Villagers Are Being Driven from Their Land," *Ner,* Vol. XIII, No. 11–12 (July–August 1962), pp. I–VI, reprinted from *Ha-aretz,* and "Knesset Finance Committee Hears Delegation from Villages of Deir Al-Asad and Bi'na," pp. XXVIf.

Simon Shereshevsky, "Carmiel" and related articles on the expropriation of Arab villages, *Ner,* Vol. XV, NO. 4–5 (December 1964–January 1965), pp. IX–XVII.

Public Statement of "Ihud" Association for Jewish-Arab Rapprochement, P.O.B. 451, Jerusalem, January 14, 1965, signed by Prof. E. Simon, Dr. H. Strauss, Dr. S. Shereshevsky, and on back, "Public Statement by Residents of the Villages of Deir el-Asad and el-Bi'neh," January 25, 1965, signed by twenty-six Arab residents of these Israeli villages. (Distributed with above issue of *Ner.*)

Max Brod, *Streitbares Leben* (Munich: Kindler Verlag, 1960), pp. 314f.

"Buber Memorial Fund for Jewish-Arab Understanding" (brochure), announcing the First Annual Buber Seminar on Jewish-Arab understanding, September 4–7, 1966, at the Institute for Jewish-Arab and Afro-Asian Studies, Givat Haviva. For further information, write to Buber Memorial Fund, Karl Netter 8, Tel Aviv.

"Proceedings of the Buber Memorial Seminar on Jewish-Arab Understanding," *New Outlook,* Vol. IX, No. 9 (84) (December 1966), pp. 11–79. In the following issue of *New Outlook,* No. 10 (85), reports from the committees of the seminar were published.

For a detailed and perceptive analysis of this whole period of Buber's life and activity see Jonathan Woocher, *The Politics of Dialogue: Martin Buber and Albert Camus,* Ph.D. dissertation in the Department of Religious Studies, Temple University, Philadelphia, 1973. Professor Woocher's dissertation, which he wrote under my direction, is a remarkable study which eminently deserves publication.

Note B

In December 1964, *Ner* published a long and detailed article about the situation in Carmiel, and in January, Ihud made a public statement after Simon, Shereshevsky, and Dr. H. Strauss had visited the Carmiel area at the invitation of the prime minister's office. The statement was a mild and balanced one, but it still expressed concern "that the expropriated area be cut down to the minimum and no further expropriations be made; 2) that the owners of expropriated lands and quarries be given fair and full compensation; 3) that new land be cleared for agricultural cultivation and handed over to all expropriated landowners who are prepared to accept it as compensation; 4) that residents of the villages be assured of employment in the enterprises that are being established in Carmiel." Buber by this time was far too ill to make the visit with them and therefore did not sign the report.

NOTE TO CHAPTER 14:
Elijah

•——————————————————•

Although *Elijah* was not written until 1956 and was not published in German until 1963, Buber's active interest in writing a play on Elijah dates back to 1901 and the Jewish Renaissance Movement. Two of the poems which he published on Elijah in that period seemed to Buber of sufficient lasting worth to be taken up into his *Nachlese,* or "Gleanings," prepared just before his death. The first poem, "Elijah," gives us a sense of the personal passion which racked Buber at that period and which later, given personal direction, remained with him throughout his life. If in this first poem "the voice of a thin silence," coming after storm and quake and fire, is found within the earth, within the motherly, within oneself, in the second poem, "The Word to Elijah," in which Buber speaks for the "son of man," it is found in the new becoming made possible through relationship to those who have gone before.

Elijah entered again into Buber's thought in the second period of his interpretation of Judaism: the "Three Speeches on Judaism" that he gave for the Prague Bar Kochba Union in the years 1909–1911. Hugo Bergmann, one of the leaders of that union, sought in a Hebrew-language article to introduce the Hebrew reader to the thought of the "Three Speeches." In his article Bergmann pointed out the relation between Buber's demand for unity and the words of the prophet Elijah about "hopping on two twigs" (I Kings 18:21). On September 12, 1912, Buber sent Bergmann a card from Riccione in Italy in which he said: "I have read your essay with great joy, and found therein many valuable supplements. What was most welcome to me was the citation from the Elijah story for the sake of which alone your expositions will remain unforgettable to me."

In his second of "Three Speeches on Judaism" (1916), Buber incorporated this very passage, to which Bergmann had referred, into the heart of his presentation of the struggle within the Orient and particularly within Judaism "of creative minds, of leaders and redeemers, against the aimlessness of the people's drives." The argument here is already a direct precursor of the central motif of the play *Elijah*, composed forty years later:

> The cognizance of inner duality and the immanent demand for decision—that is, of the soul's unification—divided the people into two psychologically distinct factions: one consisted of men who choose, who make decisions, who are impelled toward unconditionality and are dedicated to their goal; the other of laissez-faire men, decisionless men, men who remain indolently inert in their conditionality, and whose aim is self-aggrandizement and self-satisfaction—or, in biblical terms, men who are servants of God, and men who are servants of Baal. It should be remembered, however, that those men do not by any means decide for Baal and against God, but that, as stated by Elijah, they "hobble along on two tree-limbs" (I Kings 18:21).

It is also striking that this passage exactly anticipates Buber's later teaching of the first stage of evil as decisionlessness and the second as the crystallizing of this course of failures to decide into a refusal to allow oneself to be called to account by anything: "What I say is true because *I* say it; what I do is good because *I* do it." In the second of his second "Three Speeches on Judaism," Buber again repeated the quote from Elijah in connection with his attempt "to extricate the unique character of Jewish religiousness" from "the rubble with which rabbinism and rationalism have covered it."

The circumstances surrounding the publication of Buber's *Elijah* seem to share in something of the hiddenness that Buber found inseparable from the mystery of the "suffering servant." When Buber finally wrote the play in the spring of 1955, he showed the first draft to Ernst Simon and to Werner Kraft, a distinguished literary and dramatic critic. Both men urged him not to publish it, and Buber agreed and set the book aside. This interchange touches not only on the merits of the play as a literary work but on the question whether it was intended for production and whether it could be produced. Early in 1955 Werner Kraft wrote to Buber:

I have twice read your mystery play attentively, and I must say to you that I can say neither Yes nor No, I am simply uncertain in my judgment. You should not expect from me a judgment that would lead you to reject this piece. Rather you should regard it as an artistic attempt in a certain stage of its development. My impression is that you have given voice to a great thing— of that I have no doubt—but not great enough, and I believe that arises from the fact that where you do not adhere to the Bible, as, for example, in the conclusion, you do not let your voice speak freely enough. You want to show by an example what a prophet is, *who* that is. I would say that you have succeeded in that, but at the cost of the speech, and all poetic speech is most certainly one's *own* speech, or would you not agree? For I imagine that an ethical problem is concealed here that is important to you. There is here the possibility of setting aside the traditional language of the Bible while at the same time creating it.

A great poet who is nothing more than this, but also nothing less, would not shrink from this. You have hesitated to do this. You evidently wanted something less in the belief that this less would be more. But I can only say that such an attempt, even if I concede that it is not lacking in grandeur, in the final analysis does not have a convincing effect on me, not yet convincing. . . . A decisive objection to the action is that the Baal cult is conventionally portrayed, whether it goes back to the Bible or to other sources. When it says . . . that "Baal does not speak," that may be factually correct and profound, but one may question whether it is *dramatically* effective. If you could liberate yourself from that, then the whole problem of language would play its part with Baal speaking *majestically* and the *simple* word of the prophet refuting him. In this connection I have the impression that Ahab and especially Jezebel occasionally speak no proper kingly language just where they appear, I might say, as Shakespearian villains. For me, in general, the speech seems to project too little beyond the action in which the speakers are set. That may in any event be connected with the "less" of which I spoke.

In his answer of March 17, 1955, Buber seemed quite content to accept Kraft's judgment as the final word on the matter:

You have fulfilled my request exactly and in so doing have even descended to a depth which it has surprised me to hear out of the mouth of a fellowman. The judgment which you have reached corresponds to my own basic feeling, and to have this feeling corroborated thus is just what I needed.

Much to Kraft's surprise, however, Buber did not ultimately leave the book unpublished. When his collected works appeared in German, Buber included *Elijah* in the volume of the Bible, partly, he explained to Kraft, in order that the second volume, which was lacking in material, might be as large as the other two. But he also told Kraft that he had taken the manuscript with him to Tübingen, Germany, and read it aloud to his friends there. "And they found it good!" writes Kraft and adds, "Their judgment had finally the same weight as mine and that of Ernst Simon who had also rejected the play." Indeed, Buber not only had *Elijah* published separately as well, at the urging of his German publisher, Lambert Schneider, but began thinking in terms of a German production of it!

That Buber himself was not entirely at ease with his later decision is shown by the fact that he could not lay the matter to rest. On March 3, 1963, he wrote Kraft a long letter of further explanation:

> Just after you left I found that letter of yours and immediately reread it (complaining about my memory which has become so bad). I read it with particular interest and even not without agreement—except that I simply cannot "make it otherwise." To exemplify by your strongest objection: a "poetic" Baal could and should, to be sure, "speak majestically," but the authentic Phoenician Baal—known to us to some extent from the Ugaritic texts—did not know how to say anything other than to praise his palace and the like. He is quite simply the anti-dialogical god, the enemy of speech, the enemy of all contact that was not possession. It would be counterfeit work if I wanted to recast him into a new poetic mold in this matter. Then I should have had finally to give up writing this play (which long before I had made a rough sketch of and rejected). How it fared with me in this, however, was similar to how I finally wrote *For the Sake of Heaven.*

Kraft's comment on this letter is: "Everything that he says may be right. But in 1955 he understood what he now correctly refutes. Something has happened in between, success or possible success, and he now views differently."

Though agreeing with Kraft about the nature of Buber's language in *Elijah*, the German writer Hans Fischer-Barnicol has a radically different estimate of its value. Fischer-Barnicol explains the scant attention which *Elijah* received after its publication in Germany in 1963 partly because few readers take the biblical event seriously, but partly also because of the rare economy of the speech: "What is surprising in this work is the renunciation of all dramatic willfulness, even of all linguistic surprise. The biblical story is presented simply and without any adornment—an elemental, sacramental event that takes place without any psychological or literary devices." Fischer-Barnicol's conclusion is not, however, that Buber remained close to the Bible at the expense of being a true poet, as Kraft feels. On the contrary, "One must perhaps be a poet," he noted, "in order . . . to withstand every poetic temptation, in order to add nothing at all, in order to establish the example."

Fischer-Barnicol, while not an eminent dramatic critic like Werner Kraft, possibly understood something which the latter, with his more classical notions of the demands of drama, missed, namely, the way in which Buber found in *Elijah* the only appropriate form for what had to be said there—the very form which in forty years of earnest wrestling he found for the Hebrew Bible itself. It took Buber a lifetime, indeed, to *become* what his father, by his own testimony, *was:* "an elemental story-teller" who always reported only the simple event without any embroidery, "nothing further than the existence of human creatures and what took place between them." One may object that such elemental story telling has its place in Hasidic tales, but not in drama and the theater. Yet the very core of drama and the theater, as Buber understood them, was the dialogical event—the tension between man and man, between understanding and misunderstanding, in the concrete situation. Judging from a perspective to which neither Kraft nor Fischer-Barnicol had more than imaginative access—that of the transformation of Buber's *Elijah* from the written drama into flesh-and-blood theater—the play is indeed dramatically effective or at least has the unmistakable potentiality of being so.

Actually a reading of my translation of *Elijah* at Pendle Hill, in which I myself read the part of Elijah and Eugenia read the "Voice" (of the Lord), was in some ways more effective than a full-scale production of *Elijah* at Manhattanville College of the Sacred Heart in January 1966, even though the latter with music composed for the play and a chorus, was incomparably more of a dramatic spectacle.

In one of his last letters to me Buber said that when he had written *Elijah*, he had not intended that it be produced, yet we were all struck by the cumulative dramatic force which built up even in our readings. Buber was surprised to learn that I had translated *Elijah* for Manhattanville; shortly before his death, he read my translation and was satisfied with it. When the news of Buber's death reached me, it was *Elijah* I thought of above all, and my own personal mourning was mingled with the awesome sense of the prophet and contender with God who is also the "suffering servant" of the Lord.

According to the dictionary definition, Buber's *Elijah* is really closer to the lives of miracle-working saints and martyrs of the medieval miracle play than to the medieval mystery play developed from the liturgy and based on scenes from the life of Christ. The German dictionary, in fact, translates *Mysterium* as "miracle play." But *Elijah* is not merely a miracle play. It is also a mystery play, based on the mystery to which Buber had already pointed in "Reach for the World, Ha-Bima!": the God who dwells with us in our uncleanness, the tragic contradiction that is a part of the dramatic reality of existence, and the conviction that this tragedy can be taken up into the higher reality of the annunciation of the Shekinah without weakening or glossing over the antitheses.

Buber's mystery play, *Elijah*, contains in dramatic form all the central motifs in Buber's understanding of biblical and Jewish existence: the demand that the covenant with Israel places on the people and the king to make real the kingship of God through justice, righteousness, and loving-kindness; the task of building the covenant of peace with other nations and of building true community; the attack on all forms of dualism that relegate religion to the cultic and the "spiritual" and place no demand on everyday life; the biblical *emunah*, or unconditional trust in the relation to the imageless God who offers no security or success yet who will be with us *as* He will be with us; the summons and sending of the prophet to whom God calls but whom He does not compel; the call of the prophet for real decision in the present—the people's turning back to God with the whole of their existence—rather than the apocalyptic prediction of a fixed future; evil as the failure to make real decision; the king as the viceroy of God who is anointed to realize God's kingship but who has no "divine right" to rule in God's stead; the "suffering servant" as the messianic figure who will lead the "holy remnant" of those who remain faithful to the covenant to set the dialogue right through free and wholehearted response.

In *Elijah*, Buber has not only mixed in biblical sayings ·that were not connected with the Elijah story but also mythical and popular elements that have attached themselves to the Elijah legend down through the centuries. Thus the final speeches of the Voice in the last scene of *Elijah* recall Isaiah 40:30–31 in which those who wait for the Lord receive new strength in exchange for their exhaustion, and Malachi 4:5 with its promise: "Behold, I will send you Elijah the prophet before the great and terrible day of the Lord comes. And he will turn the hearts of fathers to their children and the hearts of children to their fathers."

What does remain of the biblical story of Elijah is what concerned Buber since the days of his early "Speeches on Judaism": the demand for decision, and it is this which lies at the heart of his anthropological understanding of good and evil. In one of his responses in *Philosophical Interrogations,* Buber himself explicitly linked Elijah's demand not to be like the bird that hops on two trees at once with his own understanding of the problem of evil:

> In "Images of Good and Evil" I have pointed out that evil proper is the affirmation and strengthening of one's own decisionlessness against the God who demands decision, hence as Yes and No at the same time. But the Yes in it is in no way a Yes of decision. One does not decide for Baal, one falls to him; in other words, one does not *decide for* the Having (Baal is the "possessor" who grants the Having) against the Being, one is *swallowed* by the Having. . . . Adolf Hitler, the Baalish man, is precisely the exemplary living being with whom a dialogue is no longer possible.

With King Ahab of Buber's *Elijah* and with Ben-Gurion, dialogue was still possible!

SOURCES FOR NOTE TO CHAPTER 14:
Elijah

Dag Hammarskjøld, "Letter to the Nobel Prize Committee, Stockholm" (see sources for Chapter 13).
Buber, *A Believing Humanism: Gleanings,* "Elijah" and "The Word to Elijah" plus the German originals, pp. 36–39.
Hugo Bergmann, "Aus frühen Briefen Martin Bubers," *M.B., Wochenzeitung des Irgun Olej Merkas Europa,* "Zu Martin Bubers 85. Geburtstag," February 8, 1963, p. 6.
Buber, *On Judaism,*"The Spirit of the Orient and Judaism," trans. Eva Jospe, pp. 73f.
Ibid., "Jewish Religiousness" [not "Religiosity" as Jospe has translated it!], p. 81.
Kraft, *Gespräche mit Martin Buber,* pp. 160f., 110, 163, 113.
Hans Fischer-Barnicol, " . . . und Poet dazu'. Die Einheit von Denken und Dichten bei Martin Buber," *Bulletin des Leo Baeck Instituts* (Tel Aviv), Vol. IX, No. 33 (1966), pp. 12f.
Martin Buber and the Theater, ed. and trans. with Three Introductory Essays by Maurice Friedman (New York: Funk & Wagnalls, 1969), Part III: *Elijah,* Chap. 7, "Martin Buber's *Elijah*" by Maurice Friedman, Chap. 8, "*Elijah—A Mystery Play,*" pp. 95–164. This is the only place where *Elijah* is published in English. *Martin Buber and the Theater* is out of print, and Rafael Buber (who thinks *Elijah* his father's "worst book") has no plans to bring it back into print.

Schalom Ben-Chorin, *Zwiesprache mit Martin Buber,* p. 251.

Sydney and Beatrice Rome, eds., *Philosophical Interrogations,* p. 105.

Buber Briefwechsel I, #187. MB to Hugo Bergmann, Riccione, September 12, 1912, pp. 312f.

Buber Briefwechsel III, #327. MB to Werner Kraft, March 12, 1955, p. 392; #328. Werner Kraft to MB, March 12, 1955, pp. 393f.; #329. MB to Werner Kraft, March 17, 1955, p. 394; #514. MB to Werner Kraft, March 3, 1963, p. 581.

NOTE TO CHAPTER 15:

Surfeited with Honors

•⸻•

After our four-month stay in Israel in 1960 I wrote this description of the city of Jerusalem, the setting in which Buber lived from 1938 until his death in 1965:

"Tel Aviv is already a cosmopolitan center of business and culture, not unlike many other cities in Europe and America; whereas Jerusalem is one of the unique cities of the world, overwhelming in its otherness and its variegated assortment of Jews from every country and culture, race, level of education, and type of background. We rode from Tel Aviv to Jerusalem over a rocky landscape with picturesque, terraced hills built by the Arabs to keep the soil from eroding, with rising mountains over roads along whose sides we still saw the ruins of armored cars and trucks from the 'War of Independence.' The steady ascent through groves of olive and cypress trees, overlooking deep wadis, or valleys, and Arab cities on the hillside, finally brought us to the breathtaking entrance to Jerusalem itself—an approach like that of few cities—and with Jerusalem the silence of the city on the hill that always came as such a great and welcome contrast to Tel Aviv. Here, unlike Tel Aviv which was eighty degrees Fahrenheit when we arrived in January, it was quite cold during January and February with a strong wind, and it seemed all the colder because all the buildings in Jerusalem are made of stone. From the end of February it was just like spring, however, with one bright clear jewel-like day after the other, brilliant sunshine and nights whose skies were startlingly black and clear and whose stars were amazingly bright.

"In May came the *hamsin*—a dryness with no wind, from the desert. The sky became gray, leaden colored—a blanket-like oppressiveness, while the air was often loaded with fine sand particles, or in the *sharav*, or sandstorm, not so fine ones. We were told that one never gets used to the *hamsin*, that it becomes harder to bear each year.

"The mixture of the old and the new in Jerusalem was vividly exemplified in the view from our balcony. Directly across from us was an old abandoned mosque and a lovely minaret, now used as a school, while next to these was the ultramodern Histadrut Building, the headquarters of Israel's powerful labor movement. Two blocks from our apartment in one direction was the center of business and traffic in Jerusalem; yet one block in another direction was the section where the Bukharin Jews lived with their native costumes and women who still carried huge bundles on their heads like Russian peasants. Two blocks in still another direction was the famous *Mea She'arim* ("100 Gates"), the quarters of the most Orthodox Hasidic Jews, many of whom still wear the long caftans, the *streimls,* or fox-fur caps, the leggings, and sandals of their native Poland, Galicia, or Ukraine. On the Sabbath, when every business establishment, movie, café had shut down and all traffic was brought to a standstill, we could see from our balcony or on our own afternoon walk the groups of the Orthodox, and in particular the Hasidim, who found in the quiet of the Sabbath the high point of joy and living in the week. In the Hasidic synagogues that we visited, the Sabbath was welcomed with fervor and ecstasy and beautiful, wordless melodies—*niggunim*—were sung. Unlike the tunes of the Yemenite synagogues, the melodies of the Hasidim are not melancholy, but happy and energetic. The men all have beards and earlocks *(payoth),* long coats of pale yellow, black, or gold, snow-white shirts and stockings. The Hasidim throng around the *Rebbe* to receive his word of wisdom or the *shrirayim,* the pieces of food that he passes out from the ceremonial meal.

"Jerusalem in 1960 was a mixture of the the old and the new, but it was also, until two years after Buber's death, a separation of the two, since the Old City of Jerusalem was held by Jordan and was divided from Israel by a barbed-wire border that cut the Israelis off from the Wailing Wall of the Second Temple and the Hebrew University buildings on Mount Scopus. Many Jerusalemites spoke to us of the siege of Jerusalem, in which the city was cut off from the supply lines of the rest of Israel and was without food and water while subject to constant shelling. Now the war remained plainly in evidence, what with the Jordanian soldiers on the roof next to us, as we looked out from the roof of Martin Buber's old house in Dir Abu Tor at the historic places from which we were excluded: the Valley of Gehinnom, where the first-born children were sacrificed to Moloch, the three-thousand-year-old tombs of the biblical Kings, the stones in the Old City wall from the time of Solomon, the famous Mosque of Omar, the Garden of Gethsemane, in the midst of which is a Russian Orthodox Church with onion-shaped cupolas, and the range of hills stretching to the Dead Sea. No wonder Buber called the new city merely a suburb and the Old City the real Jerusalem!

"Although Tel Aviv was the cultural center of Israel as far as opera, theater, and symphony are concerned, it was in Jerusalem that one found the greatest concentration of intellectual and highly cultured people. This was partly because of the presence of the Hebrew University—a new university with modern architecture and the large spaciousness that its location in the hills outside the city makes possible. The students are older than the average American college student, since all young men and women must serve in the Israeli army from the age of eighteen to twenty. As a result, they tended to be serious, single-mindedly interested in education and what it may bring them, and, since most of them lived off the campus and worked, not involved in the sort of social and extracurricular activities that mark the American university. The most popular major, I was told by the Dean of Humanities, was History; for it gave the students 'a window to the world.' The student interest in politics, music, philosophy, and any serious lecture, in fact, was high; yet the sort of intellectual atmosphere that one finds (or found!) in many American universities was lacking, to say nothing of the intellectual fads. The sabra prided himself or herself on being *pragmatic*—too concerned with building the country and making his or her contribution to it to waste too much time on theoretical questions of religion or philosophy.

"The majority of the Israelis were secular. They disliked the Orthodox and the Hasidim who keep themselves apart, refuse to join the Army, attack the State, obstruct progress, and generally strive to preserve the eighteenth century in the twentieth. Yet the Israelis tolerate the control by the Orthodox of the Sabbath, birth registration, marriage, divorce. Only after a very severe fight was the Hebrew Union College-Jewish Institute of Religion able to establish a school in Jerusalem—an event that materialized only because the mayor of Jerusalem staked his political career in going against the demands of the Orthodox rabbis. There was very little in evidence between extreme Orthodoxy and complete secularism. Most Israelis we met identified with their kibbutzim, with the State of Israel, with a Hebrew-speaking culture, or with the Jewish people rather than with covenantal Judaism. They all studied the Bible with great care, but more as a historical, archaeological, and national document than as a religious one. The major Jewish holidays were observed, but again as cultural or national holidays, like the Passover seder which we attended at Kibbutz Kinneret: in the Haggadah (or seder prayer-book) Israel's Declaration of Independence took the place of the coming of the Messiah!

"We found two quite separate cultures in Jerusalem, the one of the oriental Jews—the Jews from Yemen, Aden, Morocco, Iran, Syria, Iraq, and other Arab countries—the other of the Jews from Europe. The former we would meet in our apartment building or at the cinemas where they laughed at all the sentimental passages, smoked, talked, and all got up to go before the long Hollywood endings. The latter we met at the Bach concerts, the Philippine Dance company, Marcel Marceau, Chopin, or the performance, in Lea Goildberg's Hebrew translation, of Stravinsky's "L'Histoire du Soldat." Entertainment for this more cultured group was never the cocktail party, but rather teas with pastries or after-dinner wine and cognac. Among our more memorable teas was one with Moshe Sharett, the former Prime Minister, one at the home of Hugo Bergmann, and one that we provided ourselves when we joined Martin Buber, his children Eva and Rafael, his granddaughter Barbara, and his two great-grandchildren Tamar and Gigi on his eighty-second birthday."

SOURCES FOR CHAPTER 15
Surfeited with Honors

•————————————————————————•

Martin Buber. Reden und Aufsätze zum 80. Geburstag. Schriften des Zentralrats der Juden in Deutschland, No. 2 (Düsseldorf, 1958).

Avraham H. El'Hanani, "An Interview with Buber on his 80th Birthday," *Davar* (February 7, 1958), trans. for me from the Hebrew by Uri Margolin.

Buber Briefwechsel III, #384. Hermann Hesse to MB, pp. 450f.; #485. Albert Schweitzer to MB, March 3, 1958, pp. 451f.; #404. Ehud Avriel to MB, November 18, 1958, p. 469; #412. Fritz Herbster to MB, May 1, 1959, p. 477; #405. Walter Kaufmann to MB, November 23, 1958, p. 471; #406. MB to Walter Kaufmann, December 7, 1958, pp. 472f.; #435. MB to Walter Kaufmann, April 30, 1960, pp. 501f.; #478. MB to Walter Kaufmann, April 8, 1962, p. 542; #417. MB to Malcolm Diamond, July 15, 1959, pp. 480f.; #421. Hiroshi Kojima to MB, Tokyo, August 28, 1959, p. 486; #479. Hiroshi Kojima to MB, April 10, 1962, pp. 542f.; #509 Ikuro Teshima to MB, February 15, 1963, pp. 576f.; #524. Avraham Shapira to MB, May 27, 1953, p. 594; #423. Eliezer Be'eri to MB, September 30, 1959, pp. 487f.; #424. MB to Eliezer Be'eri, October 13, 1959, p. 489; #430. MB to Jifrach Chaviv, December 22, 1959, pp. 495f.; #500. Avraham Shapira to MB, January 25, 1963, pp. 564f.; #524. Avraham Shapira to MB, May 27, 1963, p. 594; #534. Avraham Shapira to MB, December 8, 1963, p. 611; #429. MB to Albrecht Goes, December 19, 1959, p. 494; #464. MB to Ewald and Sophie Wasmuth, November 1, 1961, p. 528; #483. Ludwig Binswanger to MB, May 8, 1962, pp. 546f.; #484. MB to Ludwig Binswanger, May 14, 1962, p. 547; #487. Witold O. to MB, July 29, 1962, pp. 551f.; #489. Hermann Hesse to MB, pp. 554f.; #490. Ninon Hesse to MB, p. 55; #491. Archimandrite Symeon to MB, September 28, 1962, p. 556; #493. MB to Margarete Susman, October 10, 1962, p. 557; #494. Margarete Susman to MB, October 24, 1962, pp. 557f.; #495. Luise Rinser to MB, November 20, 1962, p. 558; #501. Kurt Blumenfeld to MB, January 27, 1963, pp. 565f.; #504. Lambert Schneider to MB, February 4, 1963, p. 571; #506. Nechamia Leibowitz to MB, February 6, 1963, p. 573; #516. Alfred de Quervain to MB, March 23, 1963, pp. 584–86; #518. Gertrud Luckner to MB, April 3, 1963, p. 587 and note 1, p. 587; #526. Hermann Meier-Cronemeyer to MB, August 15, 1963, pp. 597f.; #530. MB to Hermann Meier-Cronemeyer, September 22, 1963; #499. Der Geschäftsführer der "Stiftung Praemium Erasmianum" to MB, Amsterdam, January 23, 1963, pp. 562–64; #527. Jean-Bernard Lang to MB, August 26, 1963, pp. 601–04; #532. MB to Jean-Bernard Lang, October 1, 1963, pp. 609f.; #535. Lambert Schneider to MB, February 5, 1964, p. 612; #536. Albrecht Goes to MB, February 12, 1964, pp. 612f.; #538. Heinrich Ott to MB, March 18, 1964, p. 615; #544. Heinrich Ott to MB, September 14, 1964, pp. 620f.; #542. MB to Lambert Schneider, July 1, 1964, p. 618; #543. Hermann Levin-Goldschmidt to MB, September 3, 1964, p. 619; #545. MB to Hermann Levin-Goldschmidt, September 22, 1964, p. 621; #550. Lambert Schneider to MB, November 30, 1964, pp. 628f.; #551. MB to Lambert Schneider, December 23, 1964, p. 629.

Letters from Martin Buber to Maurice Friedman, February 13, 1958; September 28, 1958; April 2, 1959; April 18, 1959; June 3, 1959; July 12, 1959; August 26, 1959; September 11, 1959; October 31, 1959; November 10, 1959; December 6, 1959; December 20, 1959; December 31, 1959; August 28, 1960; November 7, 1960; November 11, 1960; January 5, 1961; March 8, 1961; March 28, 1961; May 25, 1961; July 6, 1961; July 9, 1961; August 6, 1961; November 9, 1961; January 1, 1962; February

10, 1962; March 2, 1962; July 6, 1962; July 18, 1962; October 14, 1962; February 19, 1963; May 15, 1963; August 13, 1963; December 11, 1963; January 19, 1964; July 1, 1964; October 4, 1964; December 13, 1964.

Buber, *A Believing Humanism: Gleanings,* "In Heidelberg" (1964), pp. 34f.; "On Leo Shestov" (1964), p. 60; "Believing Humanism" (1963), pp. 117–22; "Expression of Thanks, 1958," p. 225; "Expression of Thanks, 1963," p. 230.

Letter from Simon Halkin to the Nobel Prize Committee, Stockholm, January 1959, Martin Buber File, Folder Three, Hebrew University Archives, Jerusalem.

Schalom Ben-Chorin, *Zwiesprache mit Martin Buber,* pp. 127, 130, 203, 216, 221, 227.

Jerusalem Post, February 29, 1960; May 2, 1961; May 11, 1961; December 17, 1961; December 19, 1961; March 3, 1963; July 4, 1963; September 18, 1963; October 16, 1964; October 28, 1964.

Maurice Friedman, "Report from Israel," *Jubilee,* January 1962.

"Ehrenpreis für Martin Buber," *Münchner Merkur,* July 14, 1960.

"Die fruchtbare Mehrdeutigkeit des Wortes. Martin Buber spricht vor der Akademie der Schönen Künste," *Die Wirtschaft* (Munich), July 13, 1960.

"Münchner Kulturpreis für Martin Buber," *Feuilleton* (Munich), July 14, 1960.

München ehrt Martin Buber (Munich: Ner-Tamid-Verlag, 1961).

"Hadassah Presents Five Szold Awards," *New York Times,* December 16, 1960, 24:1.

"Reform Synagogue in Israel," *New York Times,* April 15, 1962.

Buber, *The Knowledge of Man,* Chap. 1, "Introductory Essay," by Maurice Friedman, pp. 11–58; Chap. 5, "The Word That Is Spoken," pp. 110–120.

Harold Stahmer, *"Speak That I May See Thee!": The Religious Significance of Language* (New York: The Macmillan Company, 1968).

Aubrey Hodes, *Martin Buber: An Intimate Portrait,* pp. 10, 194–200, 209–12.

Paul Tillich, *Biblical Religion and the Search for Ultimate Reality* (Chicago: The University of Chicago Press, 1955).

Maurice Friedman, *Problematic Rebel: An Image of Modern Man* (New York: Random House, 1963). The revised, enlarged, and radically reorganized second edition was published under the subtitle *Melville, Dostoievsky, Kafka, Camus* (Chicago: The University of Chicago Press and Phoenix Books, 1970).

Buber, *Daniel. Dialogues of Realization,* trans. with an Introductory Essay by Maurice Friedman (New York: Holt, Rinehart & Winston, 1964; McGraw-Hill Paperbacks, 1965).

Buber, *Werke,* Vol. I: *Schriften zur Philosophie* (Munich: Kösel Verlag, 1962); Vol. II: *Schriften zur Bibel* (1964); Vol. III: *Schriften zum Chassidismus* (1963).

Buber, *Am v'Olam* (Hebrew) (Jerusalem: Sifriah Zionit, 1962).

Alei-Siah', #2, "Three Conversations about the Book *For the Sake of Heaven* by Mordecai Martin Buber" (in Hebrew), 1966.

"A Meeting of Members of Kibbutz Afikim with Martin Buber" (Hebrew), *Sdemot* (Winter 1966).

Avraham Shapira, "Meeting with Martin Buber" (Hebrew), *Amot* (1966).

Buber, editor in chief, *Encyclopedia Hinuchit* (Hebrew), Vol. I, ed. Ernst Simon (Jerusalem: Mossad Bialik, 1961), Martin Buber, "The Aims of Adult Education," trans. for me by Uri Margolin.

Rivka Gurfine, "A Literary Circle in a Kibbutz Reading Buber" (Hebrew), *Dvar Hapoielet*, No. 1 (January 1966).

Sydney and Beatrice Rome, eds., *Philosophical Interrogations*, p. 73.

Conversation with Ruth Finer Mintz, Jerusalem, Spring 1966.

Margarete Susman, "Zu Martin Bubers 85. Geburtstag," *Neue Wege*, Vol. LVII, No. 3 (March 1963), pp. 71f.

"Martin Buber zum 85. Geburtstag," *MB*, Vol. XXXI, No. 6 (February 8, 1963).

Schalom Ben-Chorin, "Dialogisches Leben, Martin Buber zum 85. Geburtstag," *Sonntagsblatt*, No. 6 (February 10, 1963), "Umschau und Kritik," p. 25.

Ernst Simon, "The Reality and the Deed" (Hebrew), *Davar* (February 15, 1963).

Scopus (English), Vol. XVII, No. 2 (June 1963), cover picture: "Age and youth meet as students honour Martin Buber on his 85th birthday with a torchlight procession to his home."

Time, February 22, 1963.

Henriette Boas, "Prince Tells Hassidic Legends. Dutch Royalty Honoured Prof. Martin Buber," *Jerusalem Post*, July 12, 1963.

Praemium Erasmianum MCMLXIII, Inveniemus viam aut Faciemus.

Praemium Erasmianum MCMLXIII, 3 Juli 1963.

Grete Schaeder, "Martin Buber. Ein biographischer Abriss," *Buber Briefwechsel* I, pp. 136f.

George Woodcock, *Anarchism: A History of Libertarian Ideas and Movements* (Harmondsworth: Penguin, 1963).

Wolf-Dieter Gudopp, *Martin Bubers dialogischer Anarchismus* (Bern und Frankfurt am M.: H. Lang, 1975).

Bernhard Lang, *Martin Buber und das dialogische Leben* (Bern: H. Lang, 1963).

Albrecht Goes, "The Boychik," in E. William Rollins and Harry Zohn, eds., *Men of Dialogue*, pp. 143–81.

"Thou Shalt Not Kill Controversy," *Jerusalem Post Weekly*, May 22, 1964.

Note

In the spring of 1963, I taught a course at the New School for Social Research in New York City on "The Philosophy of Dialogue," about which Buber told me he had received some enthusiastic reports. This course did give rise, with no initiative on my part, to a group of adult students who met together monthly for the next four years under my leadership, reading and discussing almost everything of Buber's that was available in English. In December 1964, Buber wrote me of how touched he was that this "Buber group" wanted to give him a present. Knowing that he had great difficulty with his eyes, they thought of sending him a tape recorder. "Please tell them not to send a tape recorder," Buber responded, "as I would have to pay here at the customs not less than 165 percent of its value."

NOTES TO CHAPTER 16:
"On the World's Edge"

•————————————————————————————————————•

Note A

In an undated letter to me of February 1983, Grete Schaeder wrote a long commentary on Buber's poem "The Fiddler." Although some of this interpretation in German of a German poem will inevitably be lost, it is of sufficient importance that I feel impelled to reproduce it here in my translation:

"It can be a good sign for a poem if it is not all too simple, if it leaves several possibilities of interpretation in suspense, if it has many meanings. I remember clearly how Buber in October 1974 handed me the poem in his study and then left the room for a few minutes in order to allow me to read it in his absence. In the first moment I did not take in anything in particular. I felt only a wave of sadness rise up in me over the fact of how close he felt himself to death—that had not been so at the beginning of the same year when, after a several month stay in Jerusalem, I departed. 'Your relation to death has changed' was the first thing I said, and then, half reflecting, half asking 'appearance' *(Schein)*. He nodded and changed the subject of the conversation.

"*Schein* is indeed the key word. You are right that with this poem every translation is at the same time an interpretation and that it is impossible to render the puns. What speaks in favor of your explanation in the sense of 'being and seeming' *(Sein und Scheinen)* after 'Elements of the Interhuman' is the fact that not only the verb *scheinen* (to seem, to appear) is present but also many times *'Schein'* ('seeming,' 'appearance'). I myself have interpreted 'my' poem otherwise. I did not speak with Buber any more about it out of shyness before the nearness to death which was expressed in it. I have explained it in connection with Buber's elucidation of Psalm 73, his death psalm. In this elucidation Buber uses the noun 'Schein' for something that is seen with a view *(Anschauung)*, that has not yet been attained on the ground of that life experience that touches on the eternal. I proceeded in my interpretation from the self-description *'heile Seele,'* from *'heil'* which undoubtedly means hale, healthy in the religious sense for Buber, 'pure in heart' in the elucidation of the psalm, in reference to the relation to God as it is finally grasped in Psalm 73. 'Heillos' would then refer not to the wounds, meaning therefore that they could not be healed, but to the one who caused the wounds, who just without his knowing was not hale or not yet hale. 'Offenbaren' (to reveal) is a strong word; therefore, I link it to the fact that in his interpretation of the psalm Buber says that a genuine revelation is needed in order to attain the state of the 'pure in heart.' Now the music of death shall reveal to him whether he unknowingly has done that which makes him guilty toward his fellowmen and was therefore *'heillos'* and *'im Schein,'* thus being in the state of having attained a preliminary and not the final view. With this exegesis the poem receives a greater room for play of meaning than in the thought context of 'Elements of the Interhuman.' I do not know whether Buber would otherwise describe himself without futher ado as *'heile Seele'* (hale soul)—in the context of Psalm 73 it is wholly natural. Also 'heillos' in connection with a wound is an unusual form of speech. Too bad that we can no longer ask Buber!"

Note B

On July 13, 1965, a month after Buber's death, a memorial meeting was held for Buber at the Park Avenue Synagogue in New York City under the auspices of the American Friends of the Hebrew University. Although there was very little publicity, more than two thousand persons jammed all available space, including the basement, where they listened through loudspeakers to the speeches given in the auditorium above. In a memorial issue of *The Reconstructionist* the German-Jewish-American sociologist Werner Cahnman commented: "This puts to rest, more effectively than words can do, the whispering campaign that had been carried on for years, that Martin Buber was an esoteric philosopher whom hardly anybody could understand and whose quality as a genuine interpreter of Jewish values was dubious." The three major speakers at this memorial meeting were myself, Professor Seymour Siegel of the Jewish Theological Seminary, and Paul Tillich in that order. I shall quote a little of my long address here, because it too is an event of that time:

> For us who came together tonight, the name Martin Buber evokes a presence, and our witness to him is a response to this presence. . . . The death of Martin Buber has brought home to us the fact that here was "one of the great figures not only of a people but of mankind, not only for this age but for the ages to come." Our grief that he is no longer with us must be tempered with gratitude for the "fullness of days" that was allotted to him and with awe before his ability "to begin anew, to be old in a young way." . . . In Martin Buber person and thinker were inseparably conjoined. He was the philosopher of dialogue only because in the first instance he lived "the life of dialogue." . . . This does not mean that Buber was a man who lived his ideals. He was not an idealist, but "a realist of the spirit." He was the most insistently and even disconcertingly concrete man I have ever known. The unity of Buber's life and thought was the unity of his person: his words and his actions were equally an expression of his courage, his responsibility, his openness, his readiness to meet the person or situation before him. . . . He was really *present*, as most of us are not, and *his* presentness encouraged and demanded *ours*. . . .
>
> In a time in which we are in danger of losing our birthright as human beings, Martin Buber has given us again an image of man. In a time in which human thought preserves the *idea* of God but destroys the reality of our relationship to him, Buber has pointed us anew to the meeting with the "eternal Thou."

Paul Tillich witnessed how Buber pierced through the armor of his conceptual façade to the deeper problem that lay beneath. Concepts like "ultimate reality" or "unconditional concern" do not appear in the three volumes of Tillich's sermons, he pointed out. "This awareness, produced by Martin Buber, enabled me, I believe, to preach at all." In all Tillich's encounters with Buber, something happened which for him transcended in importance the dialogue itself:

It was the experience of a man whose whole being was impregnated by the experience of the divine presence. He was, as one could say, "God-possessed." God never could become an object in Martin Buber's presence.... Our dialogues never were Jewish-Christian dialogues, but dialogues about the relation of God, man, and nature. They were dialogues between a Jew and a Protestant who had transcended the limits of Judaism as well as of Protestantism, while remaining a Jew the one, and a Protestant the other. This concrete universalism seems to me to be the only justifiable form of universalism.

... Buber knew that the prophetic, without the mystical element, degenerates into legalism and moralism while the mystical element alone leads to an escape from reality and from the demands of the here and now.... This gave Martin Buber his freedom from ritualism and his freedom for the secular world.... He anticipated the freedom from religion, including the institutions of religion, in the name of that to which religion points. This attitude is a reason for Martin Buber's far reaching influence on the secular world and particularly on the younger generation for which the traditional activities and assertions of churches and synagogues have become largely irrelevant. He knew that we cannot produce new symbols at will, but he also knew that we cannot use them as if nothing had happened in history. This makes him a genuine theologian.

As long as I have known Martin Buber, I felt his reality as something which transcends bodily presence or intellectual influence. He was there in the midst of the Western world, a part of it, a power in it, through his person, but also independent of him as an individual being, as a Spiritual reality impossible to be overlooked, provoking Yes or No or both. This Spiritual reality which was in the man Martin Buber will last for a long time in future history and open up for many that which is above history.

Deeply moved by his speech, I went up to Tillich afterward and thanked him for coming.

In May of 1961 I wrote Buber that if I were to write *The Life of Dialogue* again, I would add a chapter showing that existential trust was the real core of his life and thought. Buber replied: "What you say about 'existential trust' is obviously true ('the real core')." In my chapter on "The Existentialist of Dialogue" in my 1967 book *To Deny Our Nothingness* I explicitly pointed this out:

At the center of Buber's existentialism stands existential trust. This is the "holy insecurity" which is willing to go out to meet the unique present, rather than taking refuge in orientation and knowing one's way about. The man of "know how" wants to master the situation. The man of existential trust is able to accept the unique which is present in each new situation, despite all resemblances to the past.... Existential trust refuses the security of the false Either/Ors in favor of the insecurity of the "narrow ridge...." The life of dialogue realizes the unity of the contraries in meeting others *and* in holding one's ground when one meets them. This is the existential trust that "all real living is meeting," that meaning is open and accessible in the lived concrete, that transcendence addresses us in the events of everyday life, that man's true concern is not *gnosis*—unravelling the divine mysteries—but *devotio*—the way of man in partnership with creation.

Five years later in *Touchstones of Reality* I expressed this same central attitude as my own personal witness in my chapters on "Partnership of Existence" and "Existential Trust: The Courage to Address and the Courage to Respond."

SOURCES FOR CHAPTER 16:
"On the World's Edge"

• ———————————————————————————— •

Letters from Martin Buber to Maurice Friedman, May 22, 1961; August 13, 1963; October 28, 1963; April 26, 1964; April 14, 1965.

Schalom Ben-Chorin, *Zwiesprache mit Martin Buber*, pp. 49–52, 226, 233, 237–

Buber, *A Believing Humanism: Gleanings*, "On Richard Beer-Hofmann" (1962), pp. 61–69; "Beside Me" (1964), p. 227 (German original, p. 226); "The Fiddler" (1964), p. 229 (German original, p. 228), Explanatory Comment by Maurice Friedman to "The Fiddler," pp. 244f.; "After Death" (1928), p. 231.

Richard Beer-Hofmann, *Gesammelte Werke* (Berlin: Fischer Verlag, 1962).

Richard Beer-Hofman, *Jacob's Dream*, trans. Ida Benison Wynn, with an Introduction by Thornton Wilder (New York: Johannespresse, 1964).

Conversations in New York City with Naemah Beer-Hofmann and Miriam Beer-Hofmann Lens.

Conversations in Jerusalem with Anna Maria Jokl.

Conversations with Shulamit Katz-Nelson, Ulpan Akiva, Natanya, Israel.

Conversation with Katherine Whiteside Taylor, Pendle Hill, 1969.

Werner Kraft, *Gespräche mit Martin Buber*, pp. 31, 100, 113, 124–26, 133, 135f., 139.

Grete Schaeder, *Martin Buber: Hebräischer Humanismus*, p. 6. Buber's poem on ecstasy was written on February 9, 1964, and was printed for the first time in Schaeder's *Martin Buber* along with the facsimile of Buber's own handwritten version (between pp. 8 and 9), from which we may conclude that Buber gave this poem to Grete Schaeder while she was with him in Jerusalem. The translation of the poem is my own from Buber's German. For a variant translation see Grete Schaeder, *The Hebrew Humanism of Martin Buber*, trans. Noah J. Jacobs (Detroit: Wayne State University Press, 1973).

Buber, *Good and Evil. Two Interpretations* (New York: Charles Scribner's Sons, 1953), I. "Right and Wrong. An Interpretation of Some Psalms," Chap. 4, "The Heart Determines (Psalm 73)," pp. 31–50.

Buber, *Werke*, II, *Schriften zur Bibel* (Munich: Kösel Verlag; Heidelberg, Lambert Schneider, 1964), p. 973.

Buber, *Die Schriftwerke*, trans. into German from the Hebrew by Martin Buber, newly rev. ed. (Köln & Olten: Jakob Hegner Verlag, 1962), "Das Buch der Preisungen," LXXIII, pp. 109–11.

Grete Schaeder, "Martin Buber. Ein biographischer Abriss," *Buber Briefwechsel* I, pp. 137–41.

Buber, *Tales of the Hasidim. The Later Masters*, p. 172.

"NRP Objects to Step Honouring Martin Buber," *Jerusalem Post*, March 30, 1965.

"Martin Buber Accorded Freedom of Jerusalem," *Jerusalem Post,* May 10, 1965.

Albrecht Goes, "Martin Buber. geb. am 8. Februar 1878 in Wien, gest. am 13. Juni 1965 in Jerusalem," *Jahresring 1965–66* (Stuttgart: Deutsche Verlagsanstalt, 1965), pp. 344–47; also in *Der Quäker: Monatshefte der deutschen Freunde,* XXXIX, No. 9 (1965), pp. 236–39.

Buber Briefwechsel III, #55. President of the State Zalman Shazar to MB, May 10, 1965, p. 632.

Jerusalem Post, June 14, 1965, "Martin Buber, 87, Dead in Jerusalem"; "Buber: Philosopher, Author, Educator."

Jerusalem Post, June 15, 1965, "State, Academic Leaders Attend Buber's Funeral"; "Eulogies"; "Yesterday's Press: Buber's Death."

Obituary of Martin Buber in *World Jewry,* Vol. VIII, No. 4 (July/August 1965), p. 11. Quoted in Roy Oliver, *The Wanderer and the Way: The Hebrew Tradition in the Writings of Martin Buber* (Ithaca, N.Y.: Cornell University Press, 1968; London: East & West Library, 1968).

Aubrey Hodes, *Martin Buber: An Intimate Portrait,* pp. 216–29.

Newsweek File #4203950 on Buber's death, June 16, 1965; June 17, 1965 (interview with Heschel).

"'All Life Is a Meeting,'" *Time,* June 25, 1965, p. 82.

"Martin Buber—'Presence of Greatness,'" *Newsweek,* June 28, 1965, pp. 76f.

Editorial, *New York Times,* June 14, 1965.

Walter Kaufmann, "Martin Buber's Religious Significance," in Paul A. Schilpp and Maurice Friedman, eds., *The Philosophy of Martin Buber,* p. 685.

Martin Buber File, The Hebrew University Archives, Jerusalem, Fourth Folder, 1964–66, tributes to Buber from Hans-Jochen Vogel, mayor of Munich; mayor of Frankfurt; Jean Back, director, United Nations Information Centre for Greece, Israel, Turkey, and Cyprus; Hadassah from New York; The Jewish Community of Stockholm; the B'nai B'rith Lodge of Rio de Janeiro; the Zionist Federation of Chile; Federation of Jewish Communities of Yugoslavia; Argentine Association of Friends of the Hebrew University; Rektor of Johann Wolfgang Goethe-Universität, Frankfurt am Main; Central Conference of American Rabbis. Memorial Meeting co-sponsored by the Costa Rican Association of Philosophy and the Centro Israelita de Costa Rica. Plans for building The Martin Buber Centre for Adult Education and Continuing Education at the Hebrew University. Buber Memorial Fund for Jewish-Arab Understanding.

Albrecht Goes, "In Memoriam Martin Buber," In E. William Rollins and Harry Zohn, eds., *Men of Dialogue,* pp. 276f. This is only a very partial translation of the German original listed above.

Aubrey Hodes, "In Memoriam Martin Buber," editorial, *New Outlook,* Vol. VIII, No. 4 (71): (June 1965), p. 2.

Robert Mizrahi, "Le professeur Martin Buber est mort à Jerusalem. Un philosophe du dialogue," *Le Monde,* June 15, 1965, p. 5.

Max Brod, "Martin Buber in Memoriam," *Scopus. Zeitschrift der Gesellschaften der Freunde der Hebräischen Universität Jerusalem,* Vol. I, No. 1 (1965), pp. 10f.

Hugo Bergmann, "Juden und Deutsche in der Sicht Martin Bubers," *ibid.*, pp. 11f.

Werner J. Cahnman, "Martin Buber: A Reminiscence," *Reconstructionist. Martin Buber Memorial Issue*, Vol. XXXI, No. 12 (October 15, 1965), pp. 7–12.

George Dugan, "Rabbis in City Pay Homage to Buber. He Opened Hasidic World to West, Miller Says," *New York Times*, June 20, 1965, 72:1.

Shmuel Hugo Bergmann, "Sentinel of Mankind. One year after the death of Martin Buber," *Jerusalem Post*, June 14, 1966.

Werner Kraft, "Gedenkrede auf Martin Buber," *MB (Mitteilungsblatt)* (Tel Aviv), Vol. XXXIV, No. 24 (June 17, 1966), pp. 9f.

"Martin Buber / zum ersten Todestag": "Ein stern is untergegangen," by Hans Tramer, "Randbemerkungen zu Bubers 'Nachlese'" by Hugo Bergmann, *MB (Mitteilungsblatt)*, Vol. XXXIV, No. 22, June 3, 1966, pp. 3f.

Robert Weltsch, "Zur Bubers erstem Jahrzeittag," *Israelitisches Wochenblatt. Journal Israelie Suisse* (Zurich), Vol. LXVI, No. 23 (June 10, 1966), pp. 5f.

"School in Israel to Honor Truman," *New York Times*, January 20, 1966.

"Buber Street in West Berlin," *Jerusalem Post*, June 14, 1966.

"Buber Library to Truman Peace Centre," *Jerusalem Post*, June 15, 1966.

"Protokollnotizen. Besprechung am Dienstag, den 18. November 1975 in Ffm., Mittelweg 10 über die Verwendung des Martin-Buber-Hauses in Heppenheim." My chief correspondent for the Committee to Preserve Martin Buber's House was Margarete Exler, 6148 Heppenheim, Ludwigstrasse 16, Bundesrepublik Deutschland. They sent me several fine photographs of the house and the views from it.

Martin Buber 1878–1965. An Appreciation of His Life and Thought. Proceedings of the Memorial Meeting held at the Park Avenue Synagogue, New York City, July 13, 1965, under the auspices of the American Friends of the Hebrew University (11 East 69th Street, New York, N.Y. 10021). Maurice S. Friedman, pp. 1–6; Paul Tillich, pp. 10–13.

Maurice Friedman, *To Deny Our Nothingness: Contemporary Images of Man*, 3rd rev. ed. with a new Preface and an Appendix (Chicago: The University of Chicago Press and Phoenix Books, 1978), p. 288.

Maurice Friedman, *Touchstones of Reality: Existential Trust and the Community of Peace* (New York: E. P. Dutton, 1972: Dutton Paperbacks, 1974).

Buber, *Two Types of Faith*, p. 144.

Note A

I was kept on the phone for hours by the *New York Times, Time* magazine, and *Newsweek*, all of which were hastily putting together obituaries. Kenneth Woodward, the religion editor of *Newsweek*, said to me, "I was caught unprepared on this one. I don't want to be unprepared with Tillich." I knew well the time pressures under which *Time* and *Newsweek* writers work, but I also saw this as a symptom of our whole culture. I told this story at the first weekend seminar that I led for Esalen Institute at Big Sur, California, the following October—only to return to San Francisco that same night and discover, to my horror, that Paul Tillich himself had just died!

Note B

In the year that followed Buber's death there was a continual outpouring of articles on Buber, with memorial speeches and essays on the first anniversary of his death by Hugo Bergmann, Ernst Simon, Werner Kraft, Robert Weltsch, and many others. A main street in the Zehlendorf Borough of West Berlin, where Buber had lived before he resettled in Heppenheim, was officially renamed Martin Buberstrasse on the first anniversary of Buber's death.

Index

About the Author

Maurice Friedman is Professor of Religious Studies, Philosophy, and Comparative Literature at San Diego State University, where he has taught since 1973. He also belongs to the Guild of Tutors of International College. From 1967 to 1973 he was Professor of Religion at Temple University, Philadelphia, where he was the Director of both the Ph.D. Program in Religion and Literature and the Ph.D. Program in Religion and Psychology. From 1951 to 1964 he was Professor of Philosophy at Sarah Lawrence College, and from 1954 to 1966 he was on the Philosophy Faculty of the New School for Social Research. He has also taught at Pendle Hill (the Quaker Study Center), Manhattanville, Vassar, and Hebrew Union colleges, Union Theological Seminary, Columbia University, the Washington (D.C.) School of Psychiatry, the William Alanson White Institute of Psychiatry, Psychoanalysis, and Psychology, and the California School of Professional Psychology.

Professor Friedman is the author of *Martin Buber: The Life of Dialogue; Problematic Rebel: Melville, Dostoievsky, Kafka, Camus; The Worlds of Existentialism: A Critical Reader; To Deny Our Nothingness: Contemporary Images of Man; Touchstones of Reality; The Hidden Human Image; The Human Way: A Dialogical Approach to Religion and Human Experience;* and *The Confirmation of Otherness: In Family, Community, and Society.* He has contributed to forty other books, has edited, translated, and introduced a dozen of Martin Buber's works, and was the acting editor of *The Philosophy of Martin Buber* volume of Schilpp's Library of Living Philosophers.

Maurice Friedman holds an S.B. *magna cum laude* in Economics from Harvard University (1943), an A.M. in English from Ohio State University (1947), a Ph.D. in the History of Culture from the University of Chicago (1950), an honorary LL.D. from the University of Vermont (1961), and an A.M. in Psychology from International College (1983).